Managerial Uses of Accounting Information

Managerial Uses of Accounting Information

by

Joel S. Demski

Yale University
School of Organization and Management

Kluwer Academic Publishers
Boston/Dordrecht/London

Distributors for North America:
Kluwer Academic Publishers
101 Philip Drive
Assinippi Park
Norwell, Massachusetts 02061 USA

Distributors for all other countries:
Kluwer Academic Publishers Group
Distribution Centre
Post Office Box 322
3300 AH Dordrecht, THE NETHERLANDS

Library of Congress Cataloging-in-Publication Data

Demski, Joel S.
     Managerial uses of accounting information / by Joel S. Demski
     p. cm.
     Includes bibliographical references and index.
     ISBN 0-7923-9406-2
     1. Managerial accounting.   I. Title.
HF5657.4.D46 1994
658.15'll--dc20   93-34340
                                     CIP

Printed on acid-free paper.

Printed in the United States of America

to Millie

Contents

Preface

This book is an invitation to study managerial uses of accounting information. Three themes run throughout. First, the accounting system is profitably thought of as a library of financial statistics. Answers to a variety of questions are unlikely to be found in prefabricated format, but valuable information awaits those equipped to interrogate the library. Second, the information in the accounting library is most unlikely to be the only information at the manger's disposal. So knowing how to combine accounting and nonaccounting bits of information is an important, indeed indispensable, managerial skill. Finally, the role of a professional manager is emphasized. This is an individual with skill, talent, and imagination, an individual who brings professional quality skills to the task of managing.

This book also makes demands on the reader. It assumes the reader has had prior exposure to financial accounting, economics, statistics, and the economics of uncertainty (in the form of risk aversion and decision trees). A modest acquaintance with strategic, or equilibrium, modeling is also presumed, as is patience with abstract notation. The book does not make deep mathematical demands on the reader. An acquaintance with linear programming and the ability to take a simple derivative are presumed. The major prerequisite is a tolerance for (if not a predisposition toward) abstract notation.

This style and list of prerequisites are not matters of taste or author imposition. The study of accounting is serious business; it demands an ability to place accounting in a large environment, complete with uncertainty, strategic considerations, and a fuzzy demarcation between the organization and its environment. A professional quality manager has this ability, and the study of accounting at the level of serious professional encounter demands no less. This is the nature of the subject. To ask less of the reader is to denigrate the art of professional management and to limit unjustly our exploration.

Many forces have influenced the writing of this manuscript. A deep intellectual debt is owed to Chuck Horngren, Carl Nelson, Jerry Feltham, Bob Wilson, and David Kreps. Thanks are also due Rick Antle, Dan Hudnut, Eddie Rabin, and Richard Sansing for a meticulous reading of an earlier version of the manuscript. Peter Cramton, John Christensen, Rob Hermanson, David Sappington, Samuel Tung, and Amir Ziv have also provided valuable reading and suggestions. Robert Jaffee and Leah Kennedy contributed extensive and thorough copy editing services. Rosemary Kirby provided inestimable word processing and reading assistance.

The largest debt, though, is to my wife Millie, whose constant encouragement, support, and counsel have made this undertaking possible and enjoyable.

Joel S. Demski

Managerial Uses of Accounting Information

1

Introduction

This book is an invitation to study how accounting information is used in the management of an organization. It is a book that deals with accounting; yet the central feature is *using* the accounting, as opposed to *doing* the accounting. Stated differently, our study of accounting adopts a managerial perspective. It stresses use of the various accounting products, not their production. Emphasis is placed on use by a well-prepared and responsible manager.

This is code for a particular philosophy and approach to the study of accounting. Briefly, accounting is one of many information resources at the disposal of the professional manager. It is a highly useful, sophisticated, and adaptable resource. Used with skill, it can be of considerable value. Used without skill, it can lead to devastating and embarrassing errors. How to use the accounting resource is our focus. There is a temptation to think in terms of rules, recipes, and handy guidelines for this purpose. Yet this is the antithesis of the philosophy and approach expounded here.

Rules, recipes, and handy guidelines on how to use accounting are crutches for the less than well-prepared and responsible manager. Fortunately, managerial life is more interesting than that. The use made of accounting is critically dependent on the circumstance at hand. The professional quality manager recognizes this and is prepared to add professional judgment to the exercise. Our study can help prepare the manager to make these judgments, but it cannot relieve the manager of their necessity.

The purpose of this introductory chapter is to expand on this theme and provide an overview of our study. Following a brief reminder of the typical array of accounting resources, we examine alternate approaches to the study of accounting. We then discuss the essential ingredients for the exercise to capture the crucial features of the implied managerial task. Finally, we outline the stages of our study.

Accounting Resources

The organization's accounting system provides a number of important resources. It provides a language. Accounting is often called the "language of business." Liabilities, net worth, bottom line, cost of goods sold, periodic income, and fund balance are all well-used, familiar terms. We often use the language of accounting to convey various facts about a corporation, a partnership, or proprietorship, a not-for-profit entity, a public sector entity, or an entire economy. The focus, in turn, might be the entity as a whole or some part thereof. The widespread use of accounting as a language should be abundantly clear from the reader's prior study of financial accounting.[1]

Accounting also provides a model of consequences. Every organization charts its progress, in part, with its financial statements. A personal check book, GE's consolidated financial statements, and Yale's current fund balances provide ready examples.

What might happen to earnings per share? What will opening the new plant do to our balance sheet? Is the (accounting) revenue less the (accounting) cost positive for this product? We often use accounting summarizations to help assess the financial progress of an organization. By implication, then, we often project what we think, expect, or even hope a future accounting summarization might look like if specified policies are pursued. Accounting provides a model of consequences.

The other side to this is that accounting provides a portrayal of the organization that others will see and use. To illustrate, competitors will be interested in one's public financial record, as will taxation agencies. The astute homeowner will inquire about the insurance company's financial health, just as the astute professor seeking greener pastures at a competitor will look into budget matters. Similarly, the astute competitor will study the financial strengths of its main competitors.

Finally, accounting is a repository of financial data. It is a well-maintained, structured, and defended financial library. The manager will often find useful information in the accounting library; and the accounting renderings of the manager's current activities will be deposited in the library.

This library metaphor pervades our study. We do not go to the usual library without an understanding of how the library is organized, nor do we expect to find off-the-shelf ready made answers to every inquiry we bring. Similarly, we know of specialized libraries and have confronted the question of which library to query. Contrast the Law and Social Science Libraries at Yale, for example.[2] We also know

---

[1]Our study presumes familiarity with financial accounting (e.g., debits and credits and the accrual process), economics (e.g., allocation of a budget in light of tastes and market prices and the profit maximizing view of firm behavior), and statistics (e.g., probability and regression). We will also make modest use of calculus, optimization (especially linear programming), and abstract notation (in the form of sets and functions). Luddites erroneously believed manufacturing machinery should be destroyed as it led to lower employment. A variation on this erroneous theory is that human capital in the form of economics, statistics, and so on should not be used in the study of accounting. To the contrary, economics, statistics, and so on make our study of accounting more productive and (to my mind) more exciting.

[2]An important advantage of the accounting library is its reliability. Serious effort is given to defending it against error, or worse. Care is taken to record events with considerable accuracy. Of course, this means some types of information are delayed (or not admitted). Revenue is not recognized when the customer announces an intent to purchase, even though this may be a remarkable, euphoric piece of good news. Rather, revenue is recognized at a later stage, at a time when the veracity of the claim can be better or more easily verified.

it is sometimes preferred to acquire information on personal account. Typically, we read our daily newspaper at home, without retrieving the newspaper from the library.

The same holds for the accounting library. The professional manager knows how this library is organized and maintained, and how to retrieve information from it. The professional manager also knows what types of information are likely to be found in the accounting library, and how to combine that information with information from other sources, including those sources that are personally maintained.

The professional manager is, among other things, a skilled user of the accounting library. This skill is the focus of our study.[3]

Modes of Study

This brings us to the question of how best to study the art of using the accounting library. One method might be labeled the "imperative." The idea is to decree or divine how the accounting should be performed and used. This is how revenue should be measured, this is how product cost should be measured, this is how performance relative to budget for the division manager should be measured are all expressions of this philosophy.

While admittedly a red herring, it is worthwhile at the outset to dispense with the imperative theme. At one level it creeps in when financial reporting is encountered. This is a consequence of regulation. GAAP requires this or that treatment is a common theme. This subtly shades into an imperative. After all, while accounting can be confusing, we can at least rely on GAAP to give it structure. GAAP is comfortable in this regard; it implies a widely applicable, correct answer to the question of how the accounting should be done.

At another level, I, personally, have found this imperative mode endemic to accounting. My students are usually frustrated and disappointed when "good" accounting is not identified. They seem to want a correct answer, an imperative. (It is one thing to identify a correct calculation of product cost, given an announced algorithm, and quite another to pick the algorithm.) Yet they would be sadly disappointed if their economics professor advocated the best allocation of a family's budget without reference to tastes, opportunities, and prices. Family budget allocations are influenced by economic forces, and the same goes for accounting.

So it should be made clear at the start. We will treat the accounting library as one among many resources at the manager's disposal. It is an economic resource. How best to construct it and how best to use it depend in such critical fashion on the circumstance at hand that general guidelines and rules of thumb are not available.

---

[3] A corollary observation is the professional manager has a responsibility to help manage the accounting library. The acquisition policy at the public library is guided by consumer tastes, and we expect no less for the accounting library. From the manager's perspective, the accounting library is one more resource to be efficiently used and developed.

Professional judgment is required, in the same way that it is required when a new product is launched, when an R&D project is contemplated, or when an evaluative conference with a subordinate is being planned.

If not with the "imperative school," then how are we to proceed? Another alternative is the codification approach. Here we document practice, looking for commonalities. For example, municipalities tend to use recognition rules that formally record a purchase order as an expense. This is done to keep detailed track of commitments because spending limits are strictly enforced. The commercial organization uses a slower recognition rule but also keeps close track of purchases in its cash management operations. Similarly, hospitals tend to use elaborate product costing systems, while airlines do not think in terms of the cost of serving an individual customer. Of course, the hospital faces cost-based pricing[4] while the airline adopts more of a system or network view of its products.

Here we run the risk of being overwhelmed by detail, and not taking care to identify and document what forces are shaping the accounting product. We also invite a bias toward the status quo. Today's best practice is worthy of scrutiny and imitation. Yet our task extends from today to tomorrow.

The remaining interesting alternative is a conceptual approach. This emphasizes an image, a mental image, of the library and circumstance at hand. Several advantages follow. Our image must combine library and circumstance. We are therefore forced to provide a conceptual or generic description of a typical accounting library. This we will do in terms of aggregation, well chosen approximations to the organization's cost curve, and judicious use of cost allocation. We are also forced to provide a conceptual or generic description of circumstance. This we will do, in terms of other products, other activities, other sources of information and competitors in the product market, all of which impinge on the managerial activity at hand.

This approach also allows us to treat the accounting library as an economic resource. We think of it, abstractly, as producing benefits for a cost. Yet this serves more to place words on an important managerial judgment than to inform that judgment.

The conceptual approach also has its disadvantages. It forces us to mix accounting procedure and circumstance. Accounting procedure by itself could fill several books. It also forces us to think in terms of a small, parsimonious model of accounting and circumstance; otherwise we become overwhelmed with detail. It is also not easy. Studying methods of accounting is an inherently easier task. It is not open ended, and correct answers are readily verified (versus readily constructed).

---

[4]So-called DRG (diagnostic related group) categories have been used by Medicare to set reimbursement schedules. In turn, these prices are informed by product cost calculations; and negotiations with major commercial insurance carriers are informed by DRG prices and cost statistics. Hospitals did not install elaborate product costing schemes until the advent of these cost-based pricing procedures.

Our approach, then, is conceptual.[5] We do not purposely ignore practice; rather we will use selective illustrations from practice to develop and exercise our conceptual orientation.

Ingredients for an Interesting Stew

This book mixes several essential ingredients to bring out central features of the accounting landscape. A first ingredient is uncertainty. We routinely admit uncertainty. The reason is we want the accounting measurements to tell us something. This implies there is something we don't know. Not knowing something is modeled as uncertainty. Where possible we will suppress uncertainty, but only to develop our theme as efficiently as possible. For example, uncertainty will not play a major role when we study the manner in which product costs are calculated. Subsequently, when we study how one might extract data from the accounting library to estimate a product cost, uncertainty will play a central role. Otherwise, by definition, we would have nothing to estimate.

A second ingredient is other sources of information. It is important to understand and acknowledge that the accounting system does not have a monopoly on financial measurement or insight. We would not look to Homer for the answer to a mathematical question, just as we would not rely on our physician for insight into the market for satellite mapping services. Equally clear, we wouldn't look to the accounting system for something more readily available elsewhere. As humorous and as obvious as this appears, there is a deeper side. When multiple sources of information are available, they are often combined in highly unintuitive fashion. This will be particularly significant when we study performance evaluation in the light of various measures of performance.

A third ingredient is multiple products or services. A single product firm is just not a useful platform for our purpose. Literally, a single product story means the organization produced so many units of a good or service in a single time period and then closed down. The accounting is too easy. Accruals are irrelevant, as are interdependencies among products.[6]

---

[5]The conceptual orientation should be distinguished from a theoretical study. There we would begin with first principles and deduce various implications, such as the nature of a cost allocation scheme that has significant information content. Theory deals with underlying principles. It informs our study; indeed, references to the theoretical literature are provided at the end of various chapters. But our study is purposely structured to stay between the purely descriptive and the purely theoretical. The purely theoretical is too far removed from practice. The purely descriptive is too ephemeral.

[6]A personal computer manufactured in one period is a distinct economic product from the same personal computer manufactured in another period. The second exists at a different time, just as the resources used in its production were consumed at a different time. A single product firm has one product, in a single period setting. If we are worried about depreciation, for example, we have multiple time periods and therefore multiple products. This is why the economic theory of the single product firm has nothing to say about depreciation.

A fourth ingredient is an assumed model of behavior. To put some structure on the idea that a manager is using the accounting measures, we are forced to say something about how the measures are used. For this purpose we will assume the manager is an economic agent. This means the manager's behavior is so consistent it can be described as if the manager had a utility function and selected among alternatives so as to maximize that utility. Going a step further, we will assume this takes the form of expected utility maximization. This is done because the use of probabilities in the description allows us to say something about how information is used. In turn, this is critical to our venture, since we model accounting as providing information to and about the manager.

This behavior assumption, then, allows us to mix uncertainty, alternate sources of information, and the use of probabilities to govern the processing of information. This is useful and insightful. It is also costly. People are prone to systematic (and not so systematic) violations of the tenets of economic rationality, and we will invoke this at appropriate times in our study. Also, economic rationality is not too friendly to the view that one of the resources provided by accounting is a model of consequence. The economic actor comes ready equipped with a fully developed model of consequence. This schism, too, will be noted at appropriate points in our study.

On the other hand, economic rationality has its advantages. Economic forces are hardly benign. Using them adds structure to our task; and, as the reader will discover, leads to significant, counterintuitive insights into informed professional use of accounting measurements.

A final assumption, nearly too obvious to mention, is that accounting is not free.[7] If accounting is costly, we should then expect its practice to reflect this fact; we should expect it to be less than perfect. The inevitable tensions between cost and quality should be controlling. Our study will routinely make use of less than perfect accounting measurements. This is reality. Accounting can always be improved, if one is willing to pay the price. Economic forces enter to stop us short of the best that is feasible. We will not explicitly dwell on this theme. It is implicit throughout the study.

Overview

Th study begins with some important preliminary materials. In Chapter 2 we review the economic theory of the firm. This is the stepping-off point of our study.

---

[7]Literally, billions are expended each year on accounting for economic activity. Deeper, though, is the other side of the coin. Using accounting is costly. It takes skill, practice, and time. In addition, we humans are not expert at digesting large amounts of unstructured data. Predigested, codified, and summarized presentations are the norm. We should not make the mistake of presuming the best way to deal with accounting information is to collect and display as much as possible. Accounting aggregates data for a variety of reasons, one of which is our inability to process large amounts of data in an unstructured format.

Many managerial concepts have their roots in economic theory. What we mean by product cost, for example, is rooted in the economic theory of the firm. In Chapter 3 we contrast the economist's view of the firm with that of the accountant. This portends a continuing theme of less than perfect measurement of economic concepts, thanks to less than perfectly functioning markets. Chapter 4 surveys several important features of economic rationality. We will make use of these features at various points in the study and for this reason have collected them in a dedicated chapter.

Chapters 5 through 10 then present our study of the organization's financial data bank, or accounting library. Here the emphasis is on product costing. This is an important topic, and it serves as a vehicle to develop the library theme. We emphasize the typical accounting library makes judicious use of three building blocks: aggregation (as too much detail is overwhelming), cost curve approximation (as a more sophisticated cost expression is overbearing), and cost allocation. The same techniques are also used to measure cost incurred in a manager's department or division.

Chapters 11 through 16 then turn to managerial choice. Small and large decisions are examined, as are decisions in a competitive or strategic environment. Small decisions are those for which the above-mentioned cost curve approximations are sufficiently accurate. Large decisions strain these approximations. Underlying these examinations are decision framing techniques that call for various expressions of product cost and the use of statistical procedures to develop these expressions of product cost. Important clues to understanding a decision opportunity are often found in the accounting library. Extracting these clues requires an understanding of how the library's data were put together (the above mentioned building blocks) and the particular decision frame we find comfortable.

Chapters 17 through 23 take this one step further, to the evaluation of the manager making this choice. Just as important clues to a decision opportunity may be found in the accounting library, we rely on the library to record the accounting consequences of current managerial activity. In this way the accounting record provides fodder for evaluation of that manager. Here we encounter performance evaluation along with additional accounting library techniques, communication, budget setting and participation, and coordination. Chapter 24, the concluding chapter, provides a synthesis.

Summary

This book offers an opportunity to study managerial uses of accounting information. Compared with financial accounting, the topic is inward looking; it concerns managerial activities inside the organization. This is more pedagogical than descriptive, however. The organization can hardly survive without paying close attention to capital, labor, and product markets (not to mention governmental activities). The study flows from product costing to decision making to performance evaluation. This flow is designed to assemble all parts of the puzzle in orderly fashion. The risk in the flow is that the parts will be viewed more as separate entities than as building blocks to a more delicate and interacting fabric.

The study is also not separated from the realities of managerial life. We readily assume a setting where multiple goods and services are available. Uncertainty and multiple sources of information are also center pieces of our study. We also assume the professional manager, the user of the accounting information, responds to economic forces in a largely consistent fashion.

Finally, the study is not separated from financial accounting. External and internal reporting activities share the same library. Management's progress is, in part, judged by its financial reports; and governance of the accounting library is influenced by the regulatory apparatus of financial reporting.

Bibliographic Notes

It seems appropriate to begin with some historical perspective. Lucas Pacioli's *Suma de Arithmetica, Geometria, Proportione, et Proportionalita*, published in 1494, provided the first systematic description of the practice of double entry record keeping. Cost accounting is largely the product of the past century. For example, E. St. Elmo Lewis' third edition of *Efficient Cost Keeping*, published in 1914, states the "... first edition ... was issued in 1910 in response to what we believed to be a well-defined interest among businessmen in cost finding." Clark [1923] provided the first comprehensive treatment of costing. Solomons [1968] provides a delightful historical survey.

2

Classical Foundations

The purpose of this chapter is to review several important ideas in economics. The firm operates in and is disciplined by markets, so we begin with the economist's notions of a market and market value. Present value of a stream of future cash flows is interpreted as a market value in this context. Next we review the economist's portrayal of a firm as an institution that straddles factor and output markets. In this view, the firm uses market prices and its production function to decide what to produce and sell, and how to produce what it has chosen to produce. This characterization allows us to identify the firm's cost curve and to represent its output decision using the familiar (and dreaded) marginal revenue equals marginal cost calculation. We then extend this review to encompass firms that operate in imperfect markets and multiproduct firms.

This material is critical to our development. Inadequacies in the economist's view of the firm are what make our study of accounting both useful and vibrant. Our study of these inadequacies begins by making certain we understand their source. In addition, our ideas of cost, revenue, and income are rooted in the economist's view of the firm.

Perfect Markets and Present Value

A perfect market is a trade mechanism in which some fungible[1] item, such as a beverage, a transportation service, an hour of labor service, or an automobile, is tradable without restriction under known, constant terms of trade. This stylization is deceptively simple. Whatever the item, we know exactly what it is at the time of acquisition. We know the purity of the beverage, the reliability of the transportation service, the skill and motivation with which the hour of labor will be delivered, and the quality of the automobile. We also know the price of the item in question. We can purchase a fractional amount, no transaction costs of any kind are experienced, and no courts are necessary to enforce the terms of trade.

Some abstraction will drive the point home. Suppose trade is calibrated in a common currency, called dollars. Let q be the quantity of the item in question and P be the price expressed as dollars per unit. We know P; and q can be any real number. If q > 0 we pay Pq and receive q units. If q < 0, we receive -Pq (Remember, the negative of a negative is positive!) and deliver q units. Naturally, we would not arrange to purchase q > 0 units if we did not have Pq dollars with which to pay the supplier, just as we would not promise to deliver q < 0 units if we did not have

---

[1]That is, freely exchangeable in whole or in part.

(or have access to) these units.[2] Trade takes place without ambiguity or friction in a perfect market. If we have to ask what the price is, the market is not perfect. If the price per unit depends on how many units are involved, the market is not perfect. If we have to pay a broker to arrange the trade, the market is not perfect.

Let's now use this idea to describe a particular market in which dollars at different points in time are traded. Suppose we want to purchase $100 that will be delivered in three years. Let P_3 be the price we pay today for delivery of $1 in three years. We must pay $100P_3$ in current dollars to arrange for delivery of $100 three years hence. Conversely, suppose we want to borrow $100, and repay the loan in one installment three years later. How much do we pay in three years? The price is P_3 per dollar. Let F be the amount we will pay back. The market demands the following: $100 = FP_3$. Thus, the trade is $100 today in exchange for $F = 100/P_3$ returned in three years.

From here we readily imagine more complicated arrangements. Suppose we want to arrange for delivery of x_1 dollars one year hence, x_2 dollars two years hence, and x_3 dollars three years hence. Our market accommodates such trades by having a price in current dollars for one year dollars, P_1, two year dollars, P_2, and three year dollars, P_3. Purchasing the cash flow series $\langle x_1, x_2, x_3 \rangle$ will cost us $x_1P_1 + x_2P_2 + x_3P_3$ in current dollars. Similarly, suppose we wanted to trade $100 today for a payment of amount z in each of the next three years. What is the required annual payment, z? Here the market demands $100 = zP_1 + zP_2 + zP_3 = z(P_1 + P_2 + P_3)$.

More generally, imagine a dated series of payments displayed as follows.

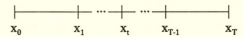

How much would we be required to pay for this series of future cash flows? To answer the question we merely sum up the required payments for each of the individual quantities. Let P_t denote the current price of $1 to be delivered at time t. Of course, the current price of $1 to be delivered at the current instant is $P_0 = 1$. The current price of the above cash flow series is therefore $x_0 + x_1P_1 + \cdots + x_TP_T$. We call this current price the *present value* of the noted cash flow series. Thus, the present value of $\langle x_0, ..., x_T \rangle$ is

$$PV = \sum_{t=0}^{T} x_tP_t.$$

In this abstract presentation, we made no assumption about whether the time intervals were in years, or were even of equal length. All we presumed was a perfect market in which we could exchange a dollar at time t for P_t current dollars.

Now assume the periods are of equal length and the ratio $P_{t+1}/P_t = (1 + r)^{-1}$, where $r > 0$, is a constant. Of course, r is an interest rate and we have $P_1 = 1/(1+r)$

---

[2] This is one of the fictions of a perfect market. People actually pay their bills.

$= (1+r)^{-1}$. With this constant price ratio assumption we also have $P_2 = (1+r)^{-2}$, and in general $P_t = (1+r)^{-t}$.

This gives our present value construction a familiar flavor:

$$PV = \sum_{t=0}^{T} x_t(1+r)^{-t}.$$

The present value of $\langle x_0, \ldots, x_t \rangle$ is the discounted value of the series, using interest rate r. One often associates the idea of discounting with the common sense notion that we would prefer having a dollar today to waiting a year to receive the dollar. We emphasize, however, that the discount rate is a market price and that the primitive idea is exchanging one series of cash flows for another in a perfect market.[3]

Output and Input Choices by the Firm

Now suppose a firm is equipped to produce some good, say, pencils. Let $q \geq 0$ denote the quantity of pencils produced and sold. The quantity produced depends on what resources or factor inputs the firm uses and what production technology it possesses. Suppose three types of factor inputs are used: labor, materials, and capital. Denote the three inputs $z_1 \geq 0$, $z_2 \geq 0$ and $z_3 \geq 0$.

How inputs can be transformed into outputs is catalogued in the firm's production function. Denote this function $q = f(z_1, z_2, z_3)$. If inputs z_1, z_2, and z_3 are supplied, an output quantity of $q = f(z_1, z_2, z_3)$ can be produced. We should think of the function $f(z_1, z_2, z_3)$ as providing a complete and reliable description of what the firm can produce.[4] We naturally assume no free lunch, in the sense that zero input produces zero output: $0 = f(0,0,0)$.

An economist often displays the production possibilities with isoquants. How many different ways can we produce q^0 units of output? The answer is to be found by locating all combinations of inputs such that $q^0 = f(z_1, z_2, z_3)$. Suppose we fix the third input at $\bar{z}_3$ and allow only the first two factors to vary. This allows us to visualize the possibilities described by $q^0 = f(z_1, z_2, \bar{z}_3)$. A familiar picture emerges when we plot isoquants for various output levels, as in Figure 2.1 below.

The isoquant curve associated with q^0 is the set of input pairs that can be combined to produce output quantity q^0. The isoquant curve for $q^1 > q^0$ is also plotted, and we see that more output requires more inputs. Also, the isoquants are

---

[3]It should be evident how we move from this point to valuing more intricate arrangements, such as trading one series of cash flows for another series of cash flows or valuing the remaining portion of a particular series at some intermediate point in the future.

[4]Being a function, $f(z_1, z_2, z_3)$ assigns exactly one output quantity q to a given input list, $z_1 \geq 0$, $z_2 \geq 0$, and $z_3 \geq 0$.

convex (bent toward the origin) and tend to flatten out as either input quantity becomes large. This implies diminishing productivity of the inputs.[5]

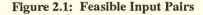

Figure 2.1: Feasible Input Pairs

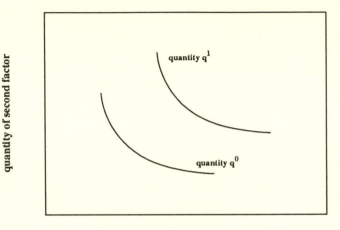

quantity q^1

quantity q^0

quantity of first factor

(quantity of second factor)

What output and inputs does the firm choose? Recall in the introduction we mentioned that the firm straddles output and input markets. So we now introduce the output and input markets in question. Let P denote the price per unit in the output market, $\hat{P}_1$ the price per unit in the first input market, $\hat{P}_2$ the price per unit in the second input market, and $\hat{P}_3$ the price per unit in the third input market. All four markets are perfect. The technical possibilities open to the firm are defined by the production function. The market prices, in turn, lead the firm to its profit maximizing choice.

Suppose the firm considers a production plan of q units of output, based on inputs of z_1, z_2, and z_3. Assume the plan is feasible, with $q = f(z_1,z_2,z_3)$. The firm will receive Pq from customers in the product market and will pay a total of $\hat{P}_1 z_1 + \hat{P}_2 z_2 + \hat{P}_3 z_3$ to suppliers in the three factor markets. Its profit, or income, will be the net of receipts and payments: $Pq - \hat{P}_1 z_1 - \hat{P}_2 z_2 - \hat{P}_3 z_3$. The firm chooses the feasible production plan with the largest profit. Symbolically, we may describe its behavior as solving the following maximization problem.[6]

---

[5]We sidestep the technical assumptions that would be placed on the function $f(z_1,z_2,z_3)$, such as strict concavity, to ensure this common sense description of the isoquants.

[6]We further presume $q \geq 0$, $z_1 \geq 0$, $z_2 \geq 0$ and $z_3 \geq 0$. Also, one might ask whether this maximization actually has a solution. The regularity conditions hinted at in the prior footnote are used to ensure problems of this nature do indeed possess a solution.

$$\underset{q, z_1, z_2, z_3}{\text{maximize}} \quad Pq - \hat{P}_1 z_1 - \hat{P}_2 z_2 - \hat{P}_3 z_3 \qquad\qquad [1]$$

$$\text{subject to:} \quad q = f(z_1, z_2, z_3)$$

Viewed in this fashion, the firm possesses some exogenously specified technology that is recorded in its production function. It then takes price signals from the input and output markets and uses these signals to select the best production plan.[7]

Two interpretive points will be important in subsequent developments. First, we have confined the exposition to three factors simply to avoid tedium. We should be thinking in terms of a *large* number of inputs, say $q = f(z_1, z_2, ..., z_m)$ where m is a large number. For example, imagine the different inputs in a modestly sized grocery store.

Second, the story we have sketched is a single period story. With more detail we would think in terms of units of output in each period, inputs of various kinds in each period, and profit defined via the present value of the resulting cash flow series. Many, many factors and a multiperiod orientation will turn out to be important elements in understanding the accountant's work.

A final point here concerns the nature of the maximization problem that we used to depict the firm's choice of output and inputs. The essential ingredients in that exercise are the production function and the market prices. We completely solved the firm's problem without any reference to cost or revenue. This is an important lesson. Much of the data in any organization's financial data bank concern the cost of various activities. It is possible to describe the firm's behavior economically with no explicit reference to cost. It is also possible to describe the firm's behavior with explicit reference to its cost. Different ways of framing a choice problem lead to different measures of cost. Cost is not a unique concept, either to the economist or the accountant.

Revenue and Cost Framing

To begin developing this theme, return to our earlier problem with one output and three inputs. Fix the output at some feasible but otherwise arbitrary quantity, say, $\hat{q}$. Now define the cost of this output quantity $\hat{q}$ to be the minimum factor payments that must be expended to produce $\hat{q}$. Call this minimum expenditure $C(\hat{q})$. We have the following construction.

$$C(\hat{q}) = \underset{z_1, z_2, z_3}{\text{minimum}} \quad \hat{P}_1 z_1 + \hat{P}_2 z_2 + \hat{P}_3 z_3$$

$$\text{subject to:} \quad \hat{q} = f(z_1, z_2, z_3)$$

---

[7]Yet another issue here is why the firm seeks to maximize profit. With perfect markets, the firm's owners unanimously prefer profit maximization. Any behavior on the part of the firm that is short of profit maximizing results in less wealth for the owners. This, in turn, resorts in tighter budget constraints for their respective consumer allocation exercises.

Repeating this process for all possible output quantities gives us a cost function, denoted $C(q)$.[8] A typical cost function might appear as follows.

Figure 2.2: Cost as a Function of Output

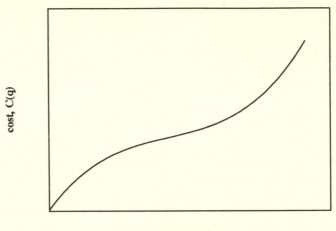

output quantity, q

Notice that $C(q) = 0$ when $q = 0$, reflecting our earlier assumption that zero input implies zero output. Beyond that, our graph depicts a situation where larger output always necessitates higher cost. Additional properties of $C(q)$ will be discussed shortly.

Now return to the original problem of locating the firm's best production plan, consisting of an output quantity and a set of inputs. It now takes a more familiar form. Let profit, as a function of output, be denoted $\pi(q)$. We have the following formulation of the firm's problem:

$$\text{maximize}_{q} \; \pi(q) = Pq - C(q). \tag{2}$$

The same decision is made as in the original formulation. All we have done is frame the analysis in revenue (i.e., Pq) and cost terms. Moreover, differentiating the profit expression provides us with the time honored marginal revenue equals marginal cost condition for optimality:[9]

---

[8]$C(\hat{q})$ clearly depends on the prevailing factor prices, $\hat{P}_1, \hat{P}_2, \hat{P}_3$.

[9]Think of $\pi(q) = Pq - C(q)$ as defining profit as a function of output, q. The first order condition for a maximum is that the first derivative with respect to q vanish, or that marginal revenue equal marginal cost. (Regularity conditions, in the form of smooth and well-behaved functions, are required to guarantee the first order condition tells the whole story.)

$$\pi'(q) = P - C'(q) = 0; \text{ or } P = C'(q),$$

where $C'(q)$ is the derivative, $dC(q)/dq$ (and $\pi'(q)$ is $d\pi(q)/dq$).

The important observation here is we have *decomposed* the firm's problem into two stages. In the first stage we solve the input question by constructing the firm's cost curve, $C(q)$. This is the minimum expenditure, or most efficient, set of inputs necessary to produce a specified output. Second, we search over the output possibilities to locate the output level with maximal profit, or maximum of revenue less cost. One way to frame the firm's problem calls for no explicit notion of product cost. We merely focus directly on inputs and outputs. This is the framing approach used in [1]. Another way to frame the firm's problem is to focus on revenue and cost of output. This calls for an explicit cost function. Here we relegate input choice to the cost function construction exercise. This is the framing approach used in [2]. The analyses in [1] and [2] are equivalent methods to locate the firm's best choice. Alternative, though equivalent, ways to frame a decision will be a recurring theme in our study.

Cost Function Terminology

Framing the firm's choice problem in revenue and cost terms is, of course, a natural, intuitive, and common way to proceed. Various derivative (no pun) notions of cost are used at this juncture.

Suppose we focus on some specific output level, say, $\hat{q}$. $C(\hat{q})$ is the *total cost* of producing output quantity $\hat{q}$. The *average cost per unit at output level $\hat{q}$*, assuming $\hat{q} > 0$, is $C(\hat{q})/\hat{q}$. Incremental cost is the change in total cost associated with some change in output quantity. The incremental cost of Δ units given output level $\hat{q}$ is $C(\hat{q}+\Delta) - C(\hat{q})$. Thus, the incremental cost of one additional unit ($\Delta = 1$) given output level $\hat{q}$ is $C(\hat{q}+1) - C(\hat{q})$.

In casual language we often refer to the incremental cost of an additional unit given output level $\hat{q}$ as the marginal cost at output level $\hat{q}$. Technically, the derivative of $C(q)$ evaluated at $\hat{q}$ is the *marginal cost at output level $\hat{q}$*. (Stated differently, marginal cost at $\hat{q}$ is the slope of the line that is tangent to the $C(q)$ curve at the point defined by $\hat{q}$.) We used this technical definition of marginal cost in making reference to the marginal revenue equals marginal cost idiom.

Consider the following example. $C(q) = 200q - 18q^2 + q^3$. For $q > 0$, average cost is $C(q)/q = 200 - 18q + q^2$. Total and average cost are listed below in Table 2.1, for selected output quantities. Total cost is also plotted in Figure 2.3, under the label long-run total cost. Now suppose $q = 9$. What is the incremental cost of one additional unit at this point? $C(10) - C(9) = 1,200 - 1,071 = 129$. Incremental cost, for $\Delta = 1$, is also listed in Table 2.1.

The average cost at $q = 9$ is 119. What is the incremental cost of $\Delta = 3$ more units, if $q = 5$? $C(5+3) - C(5) = 960 - 675 = 285$. Table 2.1 also tallies the marginal cost, computed via $C'(q) = 200 - 36q + 3q^2$. Average and marginal cost are plotted in Figure 2.4.[10]

Table 2.1: Long-run Cost Function $C(q) = 200q-18q^2+q^3$				
output q	total cost C(q)	average cost C(q)/q	marginal cost C'(q)	incremental cost of $\Delta=1$, C(q+1)-C(q)
0	0	N/A	200	183
1	183	183	167	153
5	675	135	95	93
6	768	128	92	93
7	861	123	95	99
8	960	120	104	111
9	1,071	119	119	129
10	1,200	120	140	153

Notice how average cost begins at 183 (for q = 1), declines to 119 (for q = 9), and then rises again.[11] An economist interprets this as a region of economies of scale followed by diseconomies of scale. Further notice how marginal cost declines from 200 (at q = 0) to a minimum of 92 and remains below average cost until the two are equal at q = 9. When marginal cost is below average cost, average cost is declining. Average and marginal cost are equal when average cost is a minimum. Conversely, when marginal cost is above average cost, average cost is increasing.

Now suppose the selling price is P > 119. This would imply another firm could enter the industry, produce at q = 9, and earn strictly positive profit (as its total cost at q = 9 is 1,071 = 9·119). Conversely, suppose the selling price is P < 119. This would imply our firm would earn negative profit for any q > 0 (as its minimum average cost is 119). With C(0) = 0, it would exit the industry under such circumstances. Therefore, if this product is to be produced under conditions of perfect competition, the market price will be P = 119. Our perfect markets assumption ensures viable firms in this industry will produce at the level of q = 9, where marginal revenue (119) equals marginal cost (119).

In turn, this implies our firm will earn a profit of precisely zero. The maximum in [2] occurs at q = 9, where we have Pq - C(q) = 119·9 - 1,071 = 0. This zero

---

[10]A tormented presentation would now ask you for the average incremental cost at this point!

[11]If you are handy with calculus, you will be able to convince yourself that average cost is actually a minimum when q = 9.

profit result serves as a vivid reminder of an important difference between economics and accounting.

Figure 2.3: Long-run and Short-run Total Cost

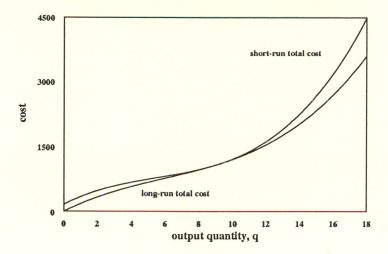

Figure 2.4: Long-run Average and Marginal Cost

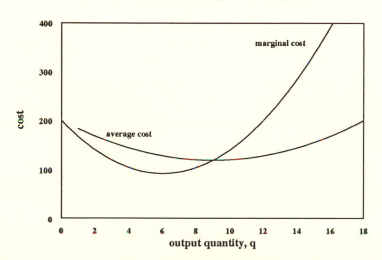

An economist's notion of cost includes payments for all factors of production. An accountant's notion of cost excludes payments to residual claimants. Recall from the study of financial accounting that net income is revenue less expenses, including interest payments but excluding any transactions with the common stockholders. If a firm had no debt whatever, its capital would be supplied entirely by the common stockholders. In such a case the economist's cost curve would include the cost of capital, while the accountant's would exclude the cost of capital.[12]

At this juncture, then, we have notions of total, average, incremental, and marginal cost. We also have a reminder that the accountant's art is not a direct application of the economist's theory. More structure and terminology enter when we distinguish short-run from long-run behavior.

Short-Run Versus Long-Run Cost

To this point we have focused on long-run behavior by our firm. The central idea in such a setting is the firm is free to vary its factor inputs at will. This is why we insisted the cost function $C(q)$ have $C(0) = 0$, or $0 = f(0,0,0)$ was one possible combination of output and inputs in the production function.

In the short-run, the firm can only vary some of its inputs. We illustrate the effect by assuming z_3 is fixed at $z_3 = \bar{z}_3$. Of course, we could envision many versions of the short-run, depending on which factors can be varied under what circumstances.

With the third input so fixed, the firm's technology is specified by the production function $q = f(z_1, z_2, \bar{z}_3)$. Proceeding as before, we define the *short-run* cost of $\hat{q}$ units as the minimum expenditure on resources that will make it possible to produce $\hat{q}$ units. This gives the following:

$$C(\hat{q};\bar{z}_3) = \underset{z_1,z_2,z_3}{\text{minimum}} \hat{P}_1 z_1 + \hat{P}_2 z_2 + \hat{P}_3 z_3$$
$$\text{subject to: } \hat{q} = f(z_1,z_2,z_3) \text{ and } z_3 = \bar{z}_3.$$

$C(\hat{q};\bar{z}_3)$ is the short-run cost of producing $\hat{q}$ units, given the third resource is fixed at level $\bar{z}_3$. Repeating this process for all q gives us the short-run cost curve, denoted $C(q;\bar{z}_3)$. Notice $C(q;\bar{z}_3)$ is constructed the same way that $C(q)$ is constructed, except we constrain $z_3 = \bar{z}_3$. This implies $C(q;\bar{z}_3) \geq C(q)$. The two cost curves are equal when (and if) q is such that the minimization solved to construct $C(q)$ selects $z_3 = \bar{z}_3$.

We can now beleaguer the reader with short-run average, short-run marginal, and short-run incremental cost. More important is the notion of fixed cost. Under $C(q)$, we assumed $C(0) = 0$. What is $C(0;\bar{z}_3)$? It is surely zero if $\bar{z}_3 = 0$. The minimum value of $C(q;\bar{z}_3)$ is $\hat{P}_3 \bar{z}_3$. This implies $C(0;\bar{z}_3) = \hat{P}_3 \bar{z}_3$. The short-run *fixed cost* is the cost the firm would incur at $q = 0$, or $C(0;\bar{z}_3) = \hat{P}_3 \bar{z}_3$. Naturally, the fixed cost depends on which factors are fixed and at what levels they are fixed.

---

[12]The gap widens in a sole proprietorship, where the accountant excludes payments for labor and capital provided by the proprietor.

We also speak of variable cost in this context. *Total variable cost at output level q* is total short-run cost less fixed cost, or $C(q;\bar{z}_3) - C(0;\bar{z}_3)$. Average variable cost may now be calculated.[13]

Return now to our earlier example where the long-run cost curve was given by $C(q) = 200q - 18q^2 + q^3$. Suppose z_3 is set in anticipation of producing $q = 9$ units, the point where long-run average cost is a minimum and the firm earns maximal profits (of zero). Further suppose the short-run cost curve is given by $C(q;\bar{z}_3) = 162 + 204.5q - 25q^2 + 1.5q^3$. Total and average short-run cost are listed in Table 2.2. Short-run total cost is plotted in Figure 2.3. Figure 2.5 provides a plot of long-run and short-run average cost. The firm's fixed cost is $C(0;\bar{z}_3) = 162$.

Table 2.2: Short-run Cost Function $C(q;\bar{z}_3) = 162 + 204.5q - 25q^2 + 1.5q^3$			
output q	total cost $C(q;\bar{z}_3)$	average cost $C(q;\bar{z}_3)/q$	marginal cost $C'(q;\bar{z}_3)$
0	162	N/A	204.5
1	343	343.0	159.0
5	747	149.4	67.0
6	813	135.5	66.5
7	883	126.1	75.0
8	966	120.8	92.5
9	1,071	119.0	119.0
10	1,207	120.7	154.5

Notice that $C(q;\bar{z}_3) > C(q)$ at all points except $q = 9$. This reflects our assumption the third, fixed factor was set in anticipation of minimum cost production at the point $q = 9$. In turn, this implies average short-run cost exceeds average long-run cost at all points, except $q = 9$ where they are equal.

A special case occurs when the short-run cost curve is linear: $C(q;\bar{z}_3) = F + vq$. In this case the fixed cost is F, the short-run marginal cost is the constant v, the average variable cost is v, and the incremental short-run cost of an additional unit (regardless of q) is v. Notice that $C(0;\bar{z}_3) = F$, $C'(q;\bar{z}_3) = v$, and $C(q+1;\bar{z}_3) - C(q;\bar{z}_3) = v$. We mention the linear case because accountants usually approximate the firm's cost curve with a linear cost function; and it is important to distinguish the economist's theory from the accountant's art.[14]

---

[13]Moreover, short-run marginal cost equals marginal variable cost, just as short-run incremental cost equals incremental variable cost.

[14]Two other points emerge here. First, a semantic qualification is in order. Common usage is to

This completes our survey of cost function terminology. Understanding the firm's cost function, or the behavior of its costs, is an important task. Specialized language has evolved to aid the manager in this task. It is important to remember, however, that a short-run cost analysis is idiosyncratic, as it depends on which specific factors are assumed unalterable. The long-run cost curve possesses no such ambiguity; all factors are alterable in the long-run. But then, how long is the long in long-run?

Figure 2.5: Long-run and Short-run Average Cost

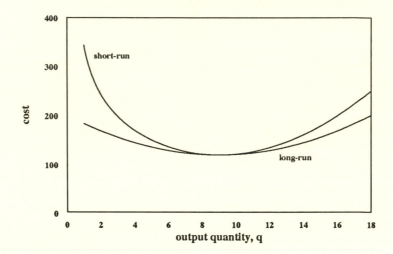

Imperfect Output Market

Most of the accounting issues we will confront arise because markets are not perfect. Imperfections may arise in many ways. Some markets may not exist. It is difficult, for example, to purchase human capital insurance. Some markets may have significant transactions costs. Housing markets are a good illustration. At this juncture we will briefly mention a specific imperfection in the output market, lack of price-taking behavior.

To begin, return to our long-run cost curve illustration where we used the cost curve $C(q) = 200q - 18q^2 + q^3$. Further suppose, just to get through this section as

---

call $C(q;\tilde{z}_3) = F + vq$ linear, though strictly speaking such a curve is linear only if $F = 0$. (Otherwise it is affine.) Second, if the short-run cost curve is linear, we have a particular problem describing the firm's behavior. If $P > v$, the firm can make arbitrarily large profit by letting q be arbitrarily large. If $P = v$, the firm is indifferent among all possible output quantities in the short run. We resolve this dilemma by putting additional restrictions on the production function, such as specifying a maximal amount of output.

quickly as possible, that all factors are variable in the short-run as well. This means we need not distinguish short-run and long-run behavior. Our firm, however, is now a monopolist. It is the only seller in the output market, and no potential competitor can enter this market.

The price per unit in the output market is given by $P(q) = 340 - 2q$, when q units are offered for sale. Total revenue, then, is $P(q) \cdot q = (340 - 2q)q$. Thus, if the firm produces $q = 4$ units, the market price will be 332, and total revenue will be $332(4) = 1,328$.

The firm's profit, as a function of quantity, will now be $\pi(q) = P(q) \cdot q - C(q) = (340 - 2q)q - 200q + 18q^2 - q^3$. Differentiating $\pi(q)$ produces

$$\pi'(q) = 340 - 4q - C'(q) = 0; \text{ or } 340 - 4q = C'(q).$$

Again we follow the marginal revenue equals marginal cost rule. The only difference is the selling price now depends on the quantity produced. Solving the equation

$$340 - 4q = C'(q) = 200 - 36q + 3q^2$$

identifies an optimal output of $q = 14$. The maximum profit is $\pi(14) = 2,352$. In this case the firm earns an *economic rent* as it is able to earn a strictly positive economic profit.[15] Notice how the firm exploits its market power. It restricts production in order to maintain a high price. Precise details depend on how price varies with quantity placed on the market and the firm's cost curve. This, in fact, is why we identified the profit maximizing output of $q = 14$ by setting marginal revenue equal to marginal cost. The point is that intimate knowledge of the demand and cost structures is relied upon to determine the firm's behavior in this setting. Further notice the firm does not now produce at its minimum average cost point.

Contrast this vignette with the case where two such firms operate in the output market. The two firms are identical and thus have identical cost curves. Their competitive encounter is highly stylized. They simultaneously produce goods for market, the market price adjusts to reflect the total quantity available for sale, and profits are earned accordingly. This is the classic case of Cournot competition. Let q_1 be the quantity produced by the first firm and q_2 be the quantity produced by the second firm. Recall that the price per unit in the output market is given by $P(q) = 340 - 2q$, when q units are offered for sale. With these output quantities, the total quantity placed on the market will be $q = q_1 + q_2$. The market price will be $P(q) = 340 - 2(q_1 + q_2)$.

The first firm's profit will be its revenue less its cost, or

$$\pi^1(q_1,q_2) = P(q)q_1 - C(q_1) = (340 - 2q_1 - 2q_2)q_1 - 200q_1 + 18q_1^2 - q_1^3;$$

[15]Put differently, economic rent arises when the firm earns more than necessary to compensate all factors of production, including capital. In a single period setting this reduces to having a strictly positive profit; in a multiperiod setting it is associated with a higher than required return on capital.

and the second firm's profit will be

$$\pi^2(q_1,q_2) = P(q)q_2 - C(q_2) = (340 - 2q_1 - 2q_2)q_2 - 200q_2 + 18q_2^2 - q_2^3.$$

Notice that each firm's profit depends on both firms' production quantities.[16]

How do the two firms behave at this point? One possibility is they collude (in violation of antitrust statutes). Here they would pick the two output quantities that maximize their total profit, $\pi^1(q_1,q_2) + \pi^2(q_1,q_2)$. It is easy to verify the solution is $q_1 = q_2 = 12.9398$ with economic profits to each firm of 1,989.09. This is the same solution a monopolist with two identical factories would provide. Intuitively, our collusive friends play the same game our earlier monopolist played, except they exploit their combined cost curve to generate greater economic rents (in total). Of course, our initial firm prefers to own the second firm; otherwise the economic rents must be split with another party.

Another behavioral possibility is the two firms operate in completely non-cooperative fashion. The idea is each will guess a behavior by the other and choose its own behavior accordingly. In equilibrium, each firm's guess will be correct. To illustrate, suppose the first firm conjectures the second will produce $q_2 = 13.4656$ units. What is its best response? Examine the profit function $\pi^1(q_1,q_2)$ when we substitute $q_2 = 13.4656$:

$$\pi^1(q_1,13.4656) = P(q)q_1 - C(q_1) = (340 - 2q_1 - 2\cdot13.4656)q_1 - C(q_1)$$

$$= (340 - 2q_1 - 2\cdot13.4656)q_1 - 200q_1 + 18q_1^2 - q_1^3.$$

The maximum occurs when $q_1 = 13.4656$. We locate the maximum by differentiating $\pi^1(q_1,13.4656)$ and setting the derivative equal to zero. Again, then, we identify the behavior by equating marginal revenue equal to marginal cost.

Perform a parallel calculation for the second firm. Suppose it conjectures the first firm will produce $q_1 = 13.4656$. Conditional on this conjecture, its best choice is to set $q_2 = 13.4656$. Respective profits are 1,982.08.

A subtle point is present here. Consider the output choices of $q_1 = q_2 = 13.4656$. This is an equilibrium if the first firm's best response to $q_2 = 13.4656$ is to set $q_1 = 13.4656$ *and* the second firm's best response to $q_1 = 13.4656$ is to set $q_2 = 13.4656$. Each firm now relies upon intimate knowledge of the demand curve, its own cost curve, and its competitor's cost curve. The analysis depends on this intimate knowledge and the mutual best response calculation.

We thus see that the firm's behavior depends on the anticipated response of its competitors. Intimate knowledge of the competitor's cost curve is used for this purpose. The web of a "mutual best response" is the glue that holds the story together. In other words, intimate knowledge of our cost curve is the end of the story in a perfectly competitive output market. But if that market is not perfectly competitive, we will want to know more about the market and about our competitors.

---

[16]The profit expressions are simplified by the fact we assume each firm faces the same cost curve.

We intend the point to be merely suggestive. The competitive encounter sketched above can be structured in many ways. It might be repeated. The players might use price instead of quantity as the competitive instrument. One player might have only partial knowledge of the other's cost structure. The cost structures might differ. One player might be able to move first, say, by irrevocably committing to a publicly observed production schedule. The list goes on and on. But the message is the same. An imperfect output market raises the specter of strategic behavior. This, in turn, creates an interest in not only knowing our own cost curve but that of our competitors.[17]

The Multiproduct Firm

A final stop on our sketch of the economist's view is the multiproduct firm. Suppose our firm uses three inputs to produce two outputs. As before, denote the input quantities z_1, z_2, and z_3. Denote the output quantities for the two products q_1 and q_2.

Here, a production plan consists of q_1 and q_2 units of the two outputs being produced using inputs of z_1, z_2 and z_3. Feasible plans are catalogued with the production function, now denoted $(q_1,q_2) = f(z_1,z_2,z_3)$.[18] Notice that the production function relates the list of outputs to the list of inputs. We do not speak of one product and its inputs, combined with the other product and its inputs. The ability to speak in separable fashion is a specialized, uncommon situation. In general, we do not expect separability.

As in our earlier setting, all markets are perfect. The input prices are denoted, recall, $\hat{P}_1$, etc. The prices in the respective output markets are denoted P_1 and P_2.

Yet again we describe the firm as straddling the input and output markets, subject to limitations imposed by its production function. Consider a feasible production plan to produce q_1 and q_2 using z_1, z_2 and z_3. The firm will receive $P_1q_1 + P_2q_2$ from customers in the product market and will pay $\hat{P}_1z_1 + \hat{P}_2z_2 + \hat{P}_3z_3$ to suppliers in the factor markets. The firm chooses the feasible production plan with the largest profit. This leads to a repetition of our earlier maximization problem:

---

[17]The story is even deeper. We will always want to know more about our competitors if they don't know we know. But if they know we know, we may want to know more or we may even be willing to pay not to know.

[18]Recall that, if $f(z_1,z_2,z_3) = f(z)$ is a function, it assigns a single output to each combination of inputs. This creates no ambiguity in the single product case but is surely ambiguous in the multi-product case. For example, $q_1 = 3$ and $q_2 = 1$ or vice versa might both be possible with the same list of inputs. Theory handles this with the idea of a production possibility set. For example, let $F(z)$ denote the set of feasible outputs when input list z is provided. Any q_1 and q_2 combination, then, must be a member of $F(z)$, and so on. This is distracting, given our purpose, so we continue with the function notation, $(q_1,q_2) = f(z)$, in the hope it creates more insight than confusion.

$$\text{maximize} \quad P_1q_1 + P_2q_2 - \hat{P}_1z_1 - \hat{P}_2z_2 - \hat{P}_3z_3 \qquad [3]$$
$$\scriptsize q_1,q_2,z_1,z_2,z_3$$
$$\text{subject to:} \quad (q_1,q_2) = f(z_1,z_2,z_3).$$

Nothing has changed, except we now think in terms of a list of products.

As before, we next divide this analysis into input and output components by constructing the firm's cost curve. The only difference is we now speak of the cost of a list of feasible outputs. Let $C(\hat{q}_1,\hat{q}_2)$ denote the cost of producing output list $(\hat{q}_1,\hat{q}_2)$. This provides a direct parallel to the development in [2]; we have the following construction.

$$C(\hat{q}_1,\hat{q}_2) \equiv \text{minimum} \quad \hat{P}_1z_1 + \hat{P}_2z_2 + \hat{P}_3z_3 \qquad [4]$$
$$\scriptsize z_1,z_2,z_3$$
$$\text{subject to:} \quad (\hat{q}_1,\hat{q}_2) = f(z_1,z_2,z_3)$$

Repeating this process for all possible output quantities gives us the firm's cost function, denoted $C(q_1,q_2)$. In turn, we are now in a position to describe the firm's behavior as though it selected the output list to maximize revenue less cost.

The Multiproduct Cost Function

Our earlier terminology extends to this setting, somewhat. As we have not constrained the inputs in any way, $C(q_1,q_2)$ is the firm's long-run cost curve. $C(q_1,q_2)$ is the total cost of producing output list (q_1,q_2). Injecting some input constraint would allow us to construct the firm's related short-run cost curve.

But what is the *total* cost of producing q_1? In general there is no answer to this question. Understanding this matter will pave the way for professional use of the accountant's product.

Suppose we can express the firm's cost curve in separable fashion:

$$C(q_1,q_2) = G(q_1) + H(q_2).$$

In such a setting we can speak unambiguously of the total cost of producing so many units of either product. $G(q_1)$, for example, is the total cost of producing q_1. This, in turn, allows us to repeat, ad nauseum, all that we said about terminology in the single product case.[19] Also, average cost is now well defined. $G(q_1)/q_1$, for example, is the average cost of producing $q_1 > 0$.

In general, though, we are unable to express the multiproduct firm's cost curve in separable fashion. One product may consume resources that are in short supply and would otherwise be used for another product. Conversely, the products may be jointly produced as when we produce steak, ribs, and hot dogs.[20]

---

[19]In the related short run case, this additivity presumes any fixed cost is separable as well. Otherwise we have $C(q_1,q_2;\bar{z}_3) = F + G(q_1;\bar{z}_3) + H(q_2;\bar{z}_3)$. Under these circumstances we could speak with conviction about the separable variable cost. But the joint or common fixed cost poses problems for our terminology.

[20]In fact, the noted separability is equivalent to the condition that $\partial^2 C(q_1,q_2)/\partial q_1 \partial q_2 \equiv 0$ for all input

This leads to some delicate terminology. First, suppose we focus on output levels $\hat{q}_1$ and $\hat{q}_2$. Further suppose we are able to vary freely the two quantities. The incremental cost of, say, 3 more units of the first product would then be $C(\hat{q}_1+3,q_2)$ - $C(\hat{q}_1,\hat{q}_2)$. The marginal cost of the first product would be the partial derivative of $C(q_1,q_2)$, with respect to the first product, evaluated at the point $(\hat{q}_1,\hat{q}_2)$. Absent our separability assumption, average cost is undefined. We know $\hat{q}_1$, but we do not know what portion of total cost $C(\hat{q}_1,\hat{q}_2)$ to associate with the first product.

For example, suppose $C(q_1,q_2) = 10q_1 + 10q_2 + 5q_1q_2$. Let $q_1 = 4$ and $q_2 = 5$. Clearly total cost is $C(4,5) = 190$. The marginal cost of the first product is $10 + 25 = 35$, and the marginal cost of the second is 30. What are their average costs? There is no answer to this question, as average cost is not defined here. How are we to apportion the $5q_1q_2 = 5(4)(5) = 100$ component between the two products? If we assign it all to the first product, respective "average" costs are 35 and 10. If we assign it all to the second they are 10 and 30. Surely this is silly.

It is also curious. Economically we do not speak of average cost in a multi-product firm, except under highly specialized conditions. In financial reporting, though, we are committed to valuing inventory at "average cost."

Even this freedom of expression is ambiguous if we admit we cannot freely vary the two quantities. The idea is that the production function, $(q_1,q_2) = f(z_1,z_2,z_3)$, is defined for a limited set of combinations of q_1 and q_2. The extreme is *fixed proportions* in which $q_1 = kq_2$ for all possible output combinations, where k is some positive constant. Here, we really have a "single" product, and must be prudent in our use of cost function terminology.[21]

Return to the case where the two quantities are freely variable. Fix the second quantity at $\hat{q}_2$. How do we interpret $C(q_1,\hat{q}_2)$? It is the total cost of producing $(q_1,\hat{q}_2)$. Similarly, $\partial C(q_1,\hat{q}_2)/\partial q_1$ is the marginal cost of the first product, at the point $(q_1,\hat{q}_2)$. We could speak of incremental cost in a similar fashion. Continuing, suppose the profit maximization problem in [3] calls for output of (q_1^*,q_2^*). Use the above trick to define $C(q_1,\hat{q}_2)$, where $\hat{q}_2 = q_2^*$. What happens when we analyze the following?

$$\underset{q_1}{\text{maximize}} \quad P_1q_1 - C(q_1,q_2^*)$$

The maximum profit must occur at $q_1 = q_1^*$. Otherwise, profit is not maximized at the point (q_1^*,q_2^*). Notice the parallel with our earlier use of a best response equilibrium. If it is optimal to produce (q_1^*,q_2^*), then it must be optimal to produce q_1^* when q_2 is fixed at q_2^*.

---

lists, (q_1,q_2). Intuitively, this means we may always express the cost of either product in a way that is independent of how many units of the other product are being produced.

[21]The accountant usually calls any nonseparable accounting cost function a setting in which joint products are produced. Fixed proportions is the extreme joint product setting. Our study will distinguish economic and accounting joint costs and joint products.

This appears arcane. But it illustrates a most important lesson in our study of managerial uses of information. We like to frame our analyses in terms of costs and benefits. We also find the firm's financial data bank contains many cost statistics. But cost is a delicate term. In this two product case, we may locate the optimal production plan with no notion of cost, with cost function $C(q_1,q_2)$, or with the pair of "conditional" cost functions $C(q_1,q_2^*)$ and $C(q_1^*,q_2)$.

Cost is not unique. By implication, when someone claims a product costs so much, we should make certain we know what the purveyor of this claim means by the term, cost.

Cost arises with particular ways of analyzing the firm's production plan. There are different, yet equivalent, ways of analyzing the firm's production plan. Moreover, there are different ways of approximating each of these formulations. Thus, there are different meanings of the phrase "cost of product." This seeming ambiguity will be encountered throughout our study.

A Two-Period Interpretation

We conclude with a highly stylized interpretation of our continuing story. For this purpose, assume q_1 denotes units of some product delivered in the first period and q_2 units of the same product delivered in the second period. This allows us to integrate present values with our review of the firm's economic cost structure.

A suggestive example will suffice. Suppose it turns out the profit maximization solution for the firm calls for one unit of each product to be produced, using one unit of each of the three inputs. Time is also a factor. The z_3 input is immediately installed. At the end of the first period, z_1 is installed, and the first output is realized. Then, at the end of the second period, z_2 is installed and the second output is realized.

The following time line summarizes our assumptions.

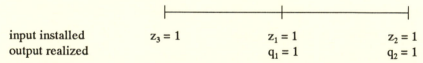

input installed	$z_3 = 1$	$z_1 = 1$	$z_2 = 1$
output realized		$q_1 = 1$	$q_2 = 1$

Further assume the *current* prices for delivery of these inputs and outputs at the above designated times are $P_1 = 190$ and $P_2 = 190$, along with $\hat{P}_1 = 90$, $\hat{P}_2 = 90$, and $\hat{P}_3 = 200$. Thus, the firm's economic profit is $190 + 190 - 90 - 90 - 200 = 0$.

Now further assume the economy is characterized by a constant interest rate of $r = 10\%$. Instead of paying $P_1 = 190$ now for delivery one period later of $q_1 = 1$, the customer could pay $190(1.1) = 209$ at the time of delivery. All other prices move in a similar manner.

If all transactions are paid at the time of delivery, the firm's cash flow would be as follows.

input installed	-200	-99	-108.9
output realized		209	229.9
net cash flow	-200	110	121

Notice that the present value of the identified cash flow series is $-200 + 110(1.1)^{-1} + 121(1.1)^{-2} = -200 + 100 + 100 = 0$. It is as if the firm invested 200, realized 110 one period hence and 121 two periods hence.

Surely, the cost in current dollars of the identified output list is 380. Conversely, it is 200 in current dollars, followed by 99 one period later, followed by 108.9 two periods later. Our constant interest rate assumption allows us to treat these two expressions as equivalent.

It remains awkward, still, to talk about the cost of either product. Remember, we have made no claim the cost function is separable. Factor z_2, for example, might be used exclusively for the second product, the first product (perhaps for post delivery service) or whatever. Even so, we do speak with some conviction about the income the firm earns. To see this, suppose we call payments from customers revenue. Then revenue in the first period is 209 and revenue in the second period is 229.9. What is the expense, or expired cost, associated with each revenue? The economist's answer is displayed below.

	period 1	period 2
revenue	209	229.9
cost of contemporaneous input	99	108.9
share of initial input	90	110
income	20	11

Notice the periodic income is calculated so the return on investment in the first period is $20/200 = 10\%$ and in the second period is $11/(200-90) = 10\%$. Also, the z_3 investment is initially valued at 200 (its cost), and at 110 at the end of the first period. 110 in fact is the present value of the remaining cash flow, as of the end of the first period: $229.9(1.1)^{-1} - 108.9(1.1)^{-1} = 209 - 99 = 110$. The investment earns 10%, not more (or less). This is what economic profit of zero means. The periodic income is such that current period income divided by beginning of period investment must be 10%. We recognize this calculation as annuity or economic depreciation from our study of financial accounting.[22]

We have stressed difficulties in speaking of the cost of a product in a multi-product setting. Yet here we continue using the economist's tools, and we speak with assurance of periodic income, or profit. One might be tempted to claim the cost

---

[22]Value is well defined in the economist's world, and economic income is simply change in value plus dividends. Economic and accounting income are contrasted in Chapter 3.

of the first product is 189, as it is sold for 209 and generates income of 20. Are we schizophrenic?

No! Income measurement takes the firm's activities and separates the flow of activity into periodic renderings. The separability that is essential for us to speak of the cost of the first product need not be present to calculate this periodic rendering. All we do is accrue the expenses in such a way as to display a constant rate of return.

If this is unclear, remember that this story began using current dollars. In that regime, our firm had a profit of zero. It paid out 380 and received 380. (No investment was made, and no cost of capital was incurred.) In that world we would not venture to speak without qualification of the cost of either product, only of the cost of both products. An equivalent telling of the story has the firm invest 200, in exchange for 110 one period later and 121 two periods later. Income of 20 in the first period and 11 in the second is a manifestation of the fact current and future prices differ by the assumed 10% time value of money. Put differently, income in this case is simply the market demanded payment for capital. Without considerable additional structure, the income of 20 has no particular usefulness in allowing us to speak of the cost of the first product.

Summary

Our review of the economist's view of the firm stresses the notion that the firm has productive opportunities, catalogued in a production function. It exploits these opportunities by straddling input and output markets, to maximize its profit. The firm is a mechanical enterprise in this view. It has no control problems, no imagination, no entrepreneurial spirit, and no professional management. It has markets and a production function.

A theory, however, is designed to focus on central features. In our case, the central feature is cost. The firm might frame its problem of selecting an optimal production plan in many ways. Various ways of framing this choice lead to various notions of cost. These notions of cost and the associated terminology will be essential in subsequent development. Total cost, incremental cost, average cost, and marginal cost are important. Also important are distinctions between long-run and various short-run expressions of total cost. In turn, a particular short-run cost curve gives rise to fixed, variable, and average variable cost as well.

Two somewhat philosophical points are also important. One is we speak of the cost of a particular product in a multiproduct setting only with considerable qualification. The qualification might take the form of assuming a separable cost function, or of fixing the other products at particular levels. The other is our interest in cost extends to an interest in our competitor's costs whenever the output market is imperfect.

Bibliographic Notes

The best place to begin a review of the economic theory of the firm is a standard economics text. More sophisticated treatments can be found in Chambers [1988], Kreps [1990], and Spulbur [1989]. Stigler [1987] is a personal favorite in the intermediate category.

Problems and Exercises

1.   The chapter stresses the idea that the firm straddles input and output markets. Explain this notion. What role does the firm's cost function play as it straddles input and output markets?

2.   Expressions [1] and [2] in the text provide equivalent descriptions of the profit maximizing firm's behavior. Why is a cost function present in expression [2] but not in expression [1]? What purpose is served by the firm's cost function?

3.   Define average, marginal, and incremental cost. Expand Table 2.1 to include all integer values of q between 0 and 20. Explain your use of these definitions as you expanded the table.

4.   Why, in general, is average cost not defined, not meaningful, in a multiproduct setting?

5.   *multiperiod firm is a multiproduct firm*
Suppose a firm produces two products. This might be two distinct products, produced in a one-period setting. It also might be the same commodity produced in two different periods. (To an economist, any good in one period is distinct from the same good in another period.) In this sense the multiperiod firm is a multiproduct firm whose activities are stretched out on the time line. Discuss.

How are we able, at the end of the chapter, to take a two-period firm and unambiguously accrue income and expense each period?

6.   *prices and present value*
Suppose the interest rate is r = 10%. What is the current price, at time t = 0, of a promise to deliver $1,000 at the end of period 3? What would the price of this promise be at the end of the first period? Explain your reasoning.

7.   *present value*
Ralph is practicing present value mechanics. For this purpose, the following cash inflows are assumed. Each cash inflow occurs at the end of the indicated year. Whatever interest rate is present is constant throughout the horizon.

end of year	amount
1	1,200
2	6,750
3	8,690
4	5,000
5	7,800
6	6,200
7	125

a] Compute the present value, as of the start of the first year, assuming a discount rate of $r = 12\%$ per year.

b] Repeat the above exercise for discount rates of 8%, 10%, 14%, and 16%.

c] Now assume a discount rate of 11%. Compute the present value, as of the start of year t of the remaining cash flows. Do this for $t = 1, 2, ..., 7$. For example, the present value at the start of year $t = 6$ will be $6200/(1.11) + 125/(1.11)^2$.

8. *construction of cost function*

Ralph must select the best combination of four factors of production, denoted z_1, z_2, z_3, and z_4, to produce q units of output. Technical requirements are defined by the following constraints:

$z_1 + z_2 \geq q$ (so the first two are perfect substitutes);

$z_3 + z_4 \geq q$ (so the last two are also perfect substitutes);

$z_1 \leq 5$;

$z_2 \leq 5$;

$z_3 \leq 6$; and

$z_4 \leq 10$.

The respective factor prices are 1, 2, 3, and 4 per unit.

Determine Ralph's cost curve, for $0 \leq q \leq 10$. Use an LP (a linear program); plot the cost curve. Also, how do you interpret the shadow prices in the LP?

9. *long-run cost function*

Ralph's firm produces a single product. Its long-run cost function is given by $C(q) = 900q - 40q^2 + q^3$.

a] Determine Ralph's total cost, average cost, marginal cost and incremental cost for each integer value of q between 0 and 30. (Let incremental cost be the cost of one additional unit.)

b] In a perfectly competitive market, what market price would you expect, and what output would you expect Ralph to produce?

10. *short-run cost function*

This is a continuation of problem 9 above. Ralph's short-run cost curve is given by $C^{SR}(q) = 1,200 + 860q - 45q^2 + 1.2q^3$.

a] Determine Ralph's fixed, total variable and average variable cost.

b] Determine Ralph's short-run total cost, average cost, marginal cost and incremental cost for each integer value of q between 0 and 30. (Again, let incremental cost be the cost of one additional unit.)

c] Plot and interpret Ralph's long-run and short-run average cost.

d] Plot and interpret Ralph's long-run and short-run marginal cost.

11. *short-run cost function*
Return to the setting of problems 9 and 10 above. The short-run cost curve depicts a case where some factors of production have been fixed at their levels at the efficient output point. Determine another short-run cost curve that could be interpreted as characterizing a case where a different set of factors of production has been fixed at the efficient point.

12. *monopolist's output*
This is a continuation of problem 9 above, where we focused on the long-run cost curve. Suppose Ralph is a monopolist. The market price, as a function of the quantity placed on the market, is $1{,}400 - 10q$, so Ralph's revenue is $(1400-10q)q$. Plot Ralph's profit as a function of output, q. Determine Ralph's optimal output and economic rent.

13. *cost in a multiproduct firm*[23]
Ralph is toying with concepts of cost. A two product firm, with quantities denoted q_1 and q_2, is being studied. Consider the three following cost functions, and note the accompanying table:

$$C^1(q_1,q_2) = 10q_1 + 5q_2;$$
$$C^2(q_1,q_2) = 6q_1 + q_1^2 + 8q_2 + q_2^2; \text{ and}$$
$$C^3(q_1,q_2) = 7q_1 + 9q_2 + q_1q_2.$$

output (q_1,q_2)	total cost	average cost of q_1	average cost of q_2	incremental cost of q_1	incremental cost of q_2
(100,50)					
(60,50)					
(40,50)					
(30,10)					
(30,50)					
(30,70)					

---

[23]Contributed by Rick Antle.

a]   As a warm-up exercise, Ralph decides you should fill in the table for each of the cost functions. (Incremental cost refers to the incremental cost of one additional unit of output.)

b]   Write a brief paragraph about your observations on this exercise.

c]   In addition, Ralph instructs you to write a brief paragraph on each of the following two questions: (i) what is the economic significance of nonlinearities in the cost functions; and (ii) what is the economic significance of interactions in a cost function (e.g., the q_1q_2 term in C^3)?

14. *periodic income in a multiperiod firm*

Return to the setting at the end of the chapter where we had periodic incomes of 20 and 11. Suppose the current prices remain the same, but the interest rate is r = 15%. Presuming all transactions are paid at the time of delivery, determine the firm's income in each of the periods. Be certain your presumed prices at the time of delivery are consistent with an interest rate of 15%. Reconcile your answer with that in the text (where r = 10% is used), and with the fact the present value of the cash flows is zero.

3

Financial Reporting Influences

Any organization generates and maintains financial records. Accounting records are an important but far from exclusive form of financial data. For example, a customer may place an order but tender no deposit or prepayment. Conventional accounting will not record such an order at the time it is received. No consideration has been received, no asset is to be recognized, and no liability is to be recognized.

Conversely, suppose the customer had accompanied the order with a down payment of 100 dollars. Conventional accounting will now record the order, to the extent of recognizing a liability for 100 dollars. In either case, yet, we would expect the organization to take notice of the customer's order.[1]

Similarly, many organizations collect market share and customer demographic information, employ forecasting services, and maintain detailed employee records. Most of this information is outside the accounting records.

This raises an important question. What can we expect to find in the organization's accounting records? We begin to answer this question in the present chapter, by reviewing financial reporting conventions.

Our review is important for several reasons. First, the organization's financial records are a data bank, or library. It behooves us, then, to be familiar with what might typically be in the library.

The accounting library is purposely restricted. What is in the accounting library must have integrity. It must pass scrutiny. We do not record speculative, unverifiable events such as alleged capital gains for a nearly unmarketable fixed asset. This information might be useful, but it would not be found in the accounting records. The accounting records are maintained with a high degree of integrity. An audit trail must be present. This influences what we place in the records.

Second, the accounting records serve many purposes. One is general purpose financial reporting. Disclosure requirements influence what the organization designs its accounting records to accomplish. For example, the arrival of cost-based reimbursement for medical services led many hospitals in the United States to adopt conventional fixed asset record-keeping procedures. Also, the FASB's proposed income tax disclosure (FAS 96) received criticism because of the cost of producing and maintaining the required records. (It was eventually superseded by FAS 109.)

---

[1]Consider a mail order merchandiser. Item X is out of stock. One customer orders X, instructing the merchandiser to charge the item to a credit card. The credit card will be charged when X is shipped. For financial reporting purposes, no record is made until X is shipped. A second customer orders X, including a check for full payment. The merchandiser immediately records cash and a liability for financial reporting purposes. In both cases, however, detailed customer records are maintained.

Third, the language used in the accounting records has an important influence on the way we frame managerial issues. This language encourages us to think in terms of accounting income, accounting cost, assets and liabilities, and so on. A financial reporting perspective lies behind this language.

Finally, a popular myth is that financial and managerial accounting are separate worlds. This myth is pedagogically useful, if one seeks to learn procedures. But it is pedagogically stifling if one seeks to learn how to use financial data. We hope the early stress we place on financial reporting will help the student visualize accounting (all accounting) as a particular data bank, complete with advantages and disadvantages.

We proceed as follows. In the first section we review the difference between cash and accrual reporting. We then look more closely at revenue recognition in the second section and matching in the third. We conclude with a review of inventory accounting.

Overview of Accrual Reporting

In Chapter 2 we discussed a stylized setting in which an organization used three inputs to produce output in each of two periods. Its production plan resulted in the following sequence of cash flows, at times t = 0, 1, and 2:

	t=0	t=1	t=2
input installed	-200	-99	-108.9
output realized		209	229.9
net cash flow	-200	110	121

How would conventional financial accounting tell this story?

To make the illustration easier to follow, we assume the following additional details. The organization was formed by the issuance of common stock for 200. This takes place just before time t = 0. At t = 0, then, the organization has a cash balance of 200. Immediately after t = 0, this 200 is spent to acquire plant and equipment. Subsequently, 209 is received from customers, 99 is paid to employees and suppliers, and so on. In addition, any cash on hand at the end of a period is paid out in dividends immediately after the books are closed for the respective period. The story continues for an additional period.

Details are summarized below. Notice the ending cash balances and the times when dividends are paid. In particular, from the investors' perspective, 200 is invested at t = 0 in exchange for dividends of 110 at t = 1 and 121 at t = 2. A gain of 110 + 121 - 200 = 31 is realized over the horizon.

	just before t=0	at t=0	at t=1	just after t=1	at t=2	just after t=2
investment by stockholders	200					
purchase of plant		-200				
receipt of revenue			209		229.9	
payment to labor and suppliers			-99		-108.9	
dividends and return of capital to shareholders				110		121
ending cash balance	200	0	110	0	121	0

the accountant's view

Financial reporting would record these various transactions in a sequence of balance sheets, income statements, and cash flow statements.

It is helpful at this point to think of accounting income in mechanical terms. Simply stated, accounting income is the change in retained earnings, exclusive of any dividends. Common stockholders invested 200 and received 110 + 121 = 231 over the life of our organization. So retained earnings exclusive of dividends must have grown by 31. Accounting income therefore totals 31 over the organization's lifetime.[2]

The more familiar approach simply tallies revenues and expenses. Our organization generated revenues of 209 + 229.9 = 438.90 during its lifetime. It also consumed resources that cost 200 + 99 + 108.9 = 407.90. Its lifetime accounting income was 438.90 - 407.90 = 31. This calculation is especially easy because we have the advantage of knowing the entire history. Advantages aside, what was the

---

[2]This 31 datum should be familiar. Assuming an interest rate of 10%, it is the total economic income over the organization's lifetime. Lifetime economic and lifetime accounting income agree in the example. Even if economic rent is zero, this will not necessarily be the case. Incorrectly measured barter transactions or unrecorded ownership perquisites are ready examples.

An emerging convention should also be acknowledged. When it is obvious the units are in dollars (or any other currency) we will forego their explicit designation.

income in each period? There are many ways to answer this question. The common theme is they all add up to 31. This is why income measurement is thought of as a question of timing. *When* do we want to recognize the 438.90 in revenue? *When* do we want to recognize the 407.90 in expense?

Cash basis accounting has a well-developed recognition rule. We recognize revenue when cash is received from customers and we recognize expenses when suppliers are paid in cash. Of course, we may have some discretion in deciding when to accept or make these payments. The recognition rule, though, is inflexible: it is keyed to consummation of cash transactions.

GAAP requires reporting of cash basis income. This is reflected in the statement of cash flows.[3] Our organization would report the following:

Cash Flow Statements

	period 1	period 2
cash received from customers	209	229.9
cash payments to suppliers	99	108.9
net cash from operations	110	121
used by investing activities,		
additions to plant	-200	
cash from financing activities		
dividends		-110
net change in cash	-90	11
beginning cash balance	200	110
ending cash balance	110	121

Cash basis income is easy to identify here. It is cash from operations plus cash used by investing activities. This amounts to -90 in period 1 and 121 in period 2, for a total of 31. More generally, debt instruments also would be present, and we would then recognize interest expense on a cash basis.[4]

Of course, GAAP also requires our organization report a balance sheet and an income statement. It is here that the recognition rules of accrual reporting have their impact. The general idea is to depict a stock (the balance sheet) and a flow (the income statement) in a way that reflects the "economic substance" of the organization's activities. If the firm acquires plant that will be used for many periods, this plant is providing services for many periods. This is an asset, just as cash on hand

---

[3]In a realistic setting we would also have the opportunity for barter. By definition, barter is a noncash transaction. These transactions will also be disclosed.

[4]Our caricature assumes a clear demarcation between debt and equity instruments. This is often far from the case, and one should remember to align the income calculation algorithm with the definition of residual claimant. Tautologically, income is change in the retained earnings associated with this ownership group, exclusive of dividends. (This assumes what accountants call a "clean surplus" procedure of linking income and retained earnings in this fashion.)

is an asset. Similarly, if the organization has manufactured but not sold some product, and if that product will be sold in a subsequent period, an asset exists.

A cash basis recognition rule takes an extremely conservative approach to asset recognition. Cash is the only asset that is recognized. This approach leads to a streamlined balance sheet, to say the least. It paints an unusual picture of the organization's financial health.

Accrual procedures recognize noncash assets. The ways in which this might be accomplished are endless. Accounting theory provides us an overview of the recording process. In general terms, we think of an *asset* as something that will render service in the future. A *liability* is an obligation to render service or transfer assets in the future. *Cost* is incurred when resources are incurred for some purpose. Revenue and expense are subdivisions of owners' equity. *Revenue* is an asset increase or liability decrease associated with serving the organization's customers. An *expense* is an asset decrease or liability increase associated with serving the organization's customers. Beyond these broad conceptions[5] considerable detail, convention, and reporting regulation are combined to produce financial reporting practice.[6]

Our immediate goal, however, is gently to remind the reader of this practice. To this end, consider the balance sheets and income statements that current practice would produce for our organization. The initial balance sheet, at the start of period 1, is easy. Nothing has yet happened.

Balance Sheet
as of start of period 1

cash	200	common stock	200
total assets	200	total equity	200

At the end of period 1 we have cash on hand of 110. What other assets are present? Presumably, the plant provides service for both periods. Let the plant asset be "valued" at 200 - d, where d is depreciation incurred during the first period. To avoid unnecessary complications we assume depreciation is expensed in period 1 as well.[7] The 99 paid to suppliers during the first period is also troublesome. Is this entire amount related to the product sold in the first period? If not, we encounter some type of prepaid expense or inventory. Let's call it inventory, and denote the

---

[5]Numerous theorists and regulatory agencies have offered more or less similar definitions of asset, liability, revenue, expense, and income.

[6]A loss is an asset decrease or liability increase not associated with serving the organization's customers.

[7]We will learn in subsequent chapters that depreciation is a component of product cost in a manufacturing setting. Thus, we may well have a case where depreciation recorded in the fixed asset accounts is different from depreciation that is actually expensed in the period.

ending inventory "value" 99 - e. Thus, e is the portion of the 99 that is expensed in the current period.

Our end-of-period 1 balance sheet takes the following form.

Balance Sheet
as of end of period 1

cash	110		
inventory	99-e	common stock	200
plant	200-d	retained earnings	209-d-e
total assets	409-d-e	total equity	409-d-e

Two points are important here. First, we rely on the accounting identity: Assets = Equities. With all other balances known, retained earnings must be 209 - d - e. Otherwise we violate the accounting identity that Assets = Equities. We know the cash and common stock amounts. Whatever inventory is, it is 99 - e. Whatever plant is, it is 200 - d. By implication, retained earnings must be the "plug" amount of 209 - d - e. Of course this is gratuitous as we have not specified d and e.

This is our second point. The accountant's art (some say black magic) produces d and e. Consider depreciation, d. If the original investment is research and development, GAAP requires d = 200. If the plant is only used in the second period, we would have d = 0. Straight line depreciation would give d = 100, and so on.

Continuing, we might have no ending inventory, implying e = 99. At the other extreme, the bulk of the labor and other factors might have been used for the product that will be sold in the second period. This would imply ending inventory of 99 - e is closer to 99 than to 0. (If this doesn't stimulate your imagination, expand the story to include many items of inventory, changing prices, and LIFO.) Naturally, or unnaturally it seems, a cash basis recognition rule is adamant. d = 200 and e = 99.

The end-of-period 2 balance sheet is not ambiguous. Cash is the only asset. It totals 121.

Balance Sheet
as of end of period 2

cash	121	common stock	200
		retained earnings	(79)
total assets	121	total equity	121

With cash totaling 121 and common stock remaining at 200, retained earnings must be (79). Notice that end-of-period 2 retained earnings plus dividends through the end of period 2 total (79) + 110 = 31.[8,9]

---

[8]At this point, capital has been returned, as we have 200 > 121. There seems little point in netting this against the common stock account for our example, so we continue with a negative retained

Finally, the respective income statements follow in straightforward fashion.

Income Statements

	period 1	period 2
revenue	209	229.9
less: depreciation	d	200-d
labor, etc.	e	207.9-e
income	209-d-e	-178+d+e
beginning retained earnings	0	209-d-e
dividends declared and paid	0	110
ending retained earnings	209-d-e	(79)

The end-of-period 2 balance sheet is unambiguous because the organization is one small step from liquidation. Cash is the only asset at that time. All recognition rules lead to the same conclusion at this point. The end-of-period 1 balance sheet, however, is ambiguous. At that time we must place an accounting value on the plant (i.e., 200 - d) and inventory (i.e., 99 - e).

This ambiguity also manifests itself in the two income statements. We know the *total* income for the two periods must be 31. This is unambiguous, since it covers the organization's entire life (save liquidation). But how much of the 31 do we accrue in period 1? The symbolic answer is 209 - d - e. A cash basis recognition rule is not ambiguous. It requires d = 200 and e = 99, the amounts paid. A noncash recognition rule, the central feature of accrual accounting, is ambiguous. Regulation, judgment, convention, and pragmatic concerns combine to specify d and e.

To recapitulate, the accounting system produces two pictures of the transactions in the life of our organization. One picture uses a cash basis recognition rule. It is available indirectly through the cash flow statement. The other picture uses an accrual recognition rule. It is available in the balance sheet and income statement. Ambiguity is absent in the former but prevalent in the latter. This ambiguity is inevitable once we depart from the economist's world of perfect markets.

Why do we dwell on this ambiguity? Suppose we look in the financial records and ask what was the cost of the product sold in period 1. We will find an answer. It is d + e, for some specific d and e. An answer will be there, with no hint of ambiguity. Now ask yourself to what question this answer is responding. d + e is the answer to the question: what was the cost *for financial reporting purposes* of the product sold in period 1?[10] Is this the question we were asking?

---

earnings balance.

[9]Notice we assume dividends are not declared until they are paid. Otherwise, an associated liability would be recognized at the end of periods 1 and 2.

[10]We will learn in later pages that some costs are expensed as part of the period in question and not related to individual products.

the economist's view

It is also possible (in a textbook) to use the economist's tools to paint a picture of our organization's life. This requires additional structure, and not surprisingly the additional structure removes any ambiguity.

The economist views the transactions as occurring in markets. Customers pay via an interaction in the product market. Labor and suppliers are paid via an interaction in the respective factor markets. Capital is paid via an interaction in the capital market. We therefore introduce market prices to complete the picture. Assume the market demands an interest rate of 10% for our organization to employ capital.

Now focus on the transactions that take place in the capital market. Initially, 200 is invested in the organization. 110 is then returned in one period, and 121 in two periods:

| | t=0 | t=1 | t=2 |
| net cash flow | -200 | 110 | 121 |

Now use the 10% interest rate to track the market value of the payments that take place in the capital market. Just after the 200 is invested, the present value of future payments is $PV_0 = 110/(1.1) + 121/(1.1)^2 = 200$. The market value at t = 0 of the identified stream of payments is 200. Just before the 110 payment is made, the present value of future payments is $PV_1 = 110 + 121/(1.1) = 220$. This is the market value at t = 1 of 110 received immediately and 121 in one period. Just before the final payment is made, the present value of future payments is $PV_2 = 121$.

Next, we use these market values to construct successive balance sheets for the organization. We do this by using a recognition rule that "values" each asset at its market value. At inception, our organization has total assets of $PV_0 = 200$. This leads to the balance sheet we constructed as of the start of period 1. Just before the final payment, the organization has total assets of $PV_2 = 121$. This leads to the balance sheet we constructed as of the end of period 2. This should come as no surprise. In both cases cash is the only asset. Conventional accounting "values" cash at its market price.

At the end of period 1, the organization has total assets of $PV_1 = 220$. The balance sheet appears as noted below. Carefully compare this with our accrual accounting balance sheet as of the end of period 1. Here we know total assets, and hence total equity. Using Assets = Equities, we know retained earnings must be 20. In the economist's world we also have markets for inventory and plant. Without belaboring the point, total market value is 220 and all markets are perfect. Therefore, d + e must total 110 + 99 + 200 - 220 = 189. So, at the end of period 1,

99 - e is the market value of the inventory and 200 - d is the market value of the plant.[11]

Balance Sheet
as of end of period 1

cash	110		
inventory	99-e	common stock	200
plant	200-d	retained earnings	20
total assets	220	total equity	220

The income statements follow immediately. Again we treat income as change in retained earnings, exclusive of dividends.

Income Statements

	period 1	period 2
revenue	209	229.9
less: depreciation		
labor, etc.	189	218.9
income	20	11
beginning retained earnings	0	20
dividends declared and paid	0	110
ending retained earnings	20	(79)

This is identical with the set of income statements we would have under accrual accounting if we set d + e = 189.

Also, the resulting income numbers have a natural, market-based interpretation. Initially, 200 is invested by the capital market. At 10%, the market demands a payment of .10(200) = 20 for use of this capital in the first year. At the end of the first year, the investors receive 110. Think of this as a 20 payment for use of the capital coupled with 90 return of capital. This means 200 - 90 = 110 of capital remains employed in the organization. The capital market demands .10(110) = 11 for use of this capital in the second year. With no economic rent (remember, markets are perfect), income computed in this fashion is simply the market mandated cost of the capital employed.[12]

Our example surely suffers from oversimplification, but it illustrates an important point. We can construct balance sheets and income statements using the

---

[11]Adding to the story would allow us to specify d and e, based on market prices for used equipment and inventory. We skip the details and work with the knowledge d + e = 189.

[12]An equivalent way to calculate and interpret economic income is to define it as change in present value of the equity position plus dividends. In period 1 we have $PV_1 - PV_0 + 0 = 220 - 200 - 0 = 20$. In period 2 we have $PV_2 - PV_1 + 110 = 121 - 220 + 110 = 11$.

economist's tools. With perfect markets, we can place a market value on each asset, each debt instrument, and each ownership instrument. This removes all ambiguity from the statements.

Of course, the economist's world exists only in textbooks. The accountant must produce balance sheets and income statements under highly different circumstances. Markets are not nearly as abundant as we assumed. This is why d and e were ambiguous in the example. It is difficult to value a trademark, unusual physical plant or real estate, employee loyalty, and so on.

The accountant also deals with an overwhelming amount of data. Recall the notation we used in Chapter 2 for a production function: $q = f(z_1,...,z_m)$. This associates output q with the list of inputs denoted z_1, ..., z_m. Think of m as a very large number. This is the accountant's world. No attempt is made to keep detailed track of every one of these inputs. They are lumped into categories: office supplies, labor of various type, materials of various types, and so on. This grouping is not perfect. Unlike items are bundled together. Detail that the economist exploits is purposely abandoned.

The accountant has neither the detail nor the market prices assumed in the economist's world. The accountant cannot replicate the economist's constructs. Yet the accountant uses the economist's language and ideas. This creates confusion. The accounting library contains many references to cost, revenue, and income. The intuitive meaning of these references is derived from economics. That intuition is inadequate. Ambiguity surrounds these references, even when we understand the particular accounting procedures that have been employed. Procedures also vary from library to library. In addition, the procedures employed are influenced by financial reporting concerns.

The professional manager understands what is in this library and how to decipher what is found to best suit the purpose at hand. The deciphering exercise is usefully thought of as identifying the revenue recognition and expense matching rules that govern the particular library.

Revenue Recognition

Financial reporting influences are varied. Fortunately we can offer a general framework that identifies an organization's financial policies. Recall that over the organization's lifetime, all approaches to accrual accounting wind up with the same totals.[13] The beginning and ending balance sheets are unambiguous, so the lifetime accounting income is unambiguous. How much of this income to record in a

---

[13]This is not a statement that in the long-run all methods of accounting accomplish the same thing. If we freeze the events, all methods of accounting will report the same cumulative income. Of course, accounting is likely to have an effect on what events take place. Were that not the case, this book would be extremely short.

particular period is the crux of the matter. (Equivalently, how to "value" the assets and equities at any point is the crux of the matter.)

Financial reporting uses a two-step process to identify the accounting income for a particular period. The first step is to identify the revenue; the second is to match expenses with the identified revenue.

The general guideline for recognizing revenue is that a substantive interaction in the product market must have occurred. Regulatory authorities call for recognition of revenue when "...(1) the earning process is complete or virtually complete and (2) an exchange transaction has taken place."[14] Stated differently, revenue is not to be recognized until the interaction between the organization and its customer is "virtually complete" and a "transaction" has occurred.[15]

This rule is easy to visualize in a fast food restaurant. A customer pays in cash as the product is delivered. Services after the product is delivered are trivial. A modest seating facility is maintained and trash is removed. Warranties are nearly nonexistent. Revenue is recognized at the point of sale. This is the time of delivery; it is also the time cash is received.

Often, revenue is recognized at the time the good or service is delivered to the customer. Complicated arrangements, however, beget complicated financial reporting practices. The customer may take delivery in exchange for a promise to pay. Estimation of bad debts then enters the calculation. Similarly, the customer may have the right to return merchandise. Department stores provide a ready example. Estimation of returns then enters the calculation.

The list continues. The sales contract may call for a price adjustment if negotiated performance standards are not met. For example, fuel consumption guarantees are often part of the sales contract between an airline and an airframe or engine manufacturer. Significant warranties may be present. Automobiles are a ready example. Tied sales arrangements may be in place. Frequent flier programs in the airline industry are a familiar example. Sale of movie rights for television broadcast (where a single price covers several showings of a movie) is another example.

Production may be time consuming. Construction is the favorite example. Unforeseen product liability also may arise. Unforeseen health hazards are the usual example.

Finally, bookkeeping and regulatory frictions may further cloud the recognition exercise. Consider an electric utility. Customer meters are read throughout the month, to even out the data gathering workload. At the end of the reporting period,

---

[14]This quotation is from APB [1970].

[15]One should not infer this dogma is crystal clear. The FASB's Concepts Statement No. 5 says revenue "...recognition involves consideration of two factors, (a) being realized or realizable and (b) being earned, with sometimes one and sometimes the other being the more important consideration" (paragraph 83).

the utility must deal with the fact some of its billing information is near or exactly on the date the books are closed, while others are almost a month old. In addition, at the time the books are closed the utility may already have an excellent idea whether the regulatory agency may force a retroactive rate roll back. Contemporary accrual reporting demands we deal with these strains of properly measuring periodic revenue.

The general idea that governs revenue recognition is straightforward. We delay recognition of revenue until the fact of a sale can be verified, until the income calculation has integrity. Idiosyncratic particulars influence the details with which this is done. Some organizations will recognize revenue sooner than others, some will employ more elaborate calculations than others, and some will display more ambiguity than others. But revenue recognition is the lead step in the financial accountant's periodic dance.[16]

Matching Expenses to the Recognized Revenue

Matching expenses is the following step. Return to our earlier fast food example. Expenses for such items as labor, material, space, and advertising will be matched with the revenue that is recognized.

Labor expense is determined by focusing on wages and salaries "earned" during the accounting period. Hourly personnel are paid as a function of hours worked during the period. Salaried personnel are paid as a function of calendar time. Payment is generally done with a lag. Accrual procedures are designed so that wage expense corresponds to hours earned rather than hours paid in such a situation. Various employment taxes, health benefits, and vacation expenses are handled in parallel fashion.

Even here, though, we see the impact of an elaborate web of recognition conventions. Suppose the organization incurs a sizable cost in hiring new employees. It might, for example, contract with an employment agency. Any such cost typically will be expensed in the period it is incurred. Likewise, suppose the organization maintains a gymnasium for its employees. The cost of the gymnasium will be expensed through time. It will not, however, show up as an explicit cost of labor.

Another example is postretirement benefits. Suppose the employees receive current payment and a pension. The pension is a form of deferred compensation. Elaborate rules govern the manner in which pension-related costs are accrued

---

[16]Remember, we are offering a sketch of the general operation of an accounting library. Pragmatic concerns lead to a focus on sale of product in most instances. Vatter [1947] is particularly eloquent on this point. "Assets are economic in nature; they are embodiments of future want satisfaction in the form of service potentials that may be transformed, exchanged, or stored against future events" (p. 17). "The concept of `matching revenue with costs´ is meaningless unless there be some act common to both revenue recognition and cost release that can be identified; this is the rendering of service, not the `making of a sale´" (p. 32).

through time. Suppose the employees are also promised postretirement health benefits. Prior to FAS 106, most corporations used a cash basis recognition rule to account for these benefits.

The restaurant also consumes various materials during the period. Trivial items are expensed when they are acquired. Miscellaneous office supplies are a ready example. Otherwise, inventory records are maintained. Consumption of materials is then determined and "valued" according to the organization's assumed inventory cost flow model: FIFO, LIFO, or average cost.[17]

Space expenses also follow a pragmatic treatment. Fixed asset items (including capital leases) will be depreciated using some standard formula such as straight line. Minor repairs will be expensed as incurred. Heat, light, property taxes, and so on also will be treated with accrual procedures. To illustrate, suppose annual property tax of 9,600 is due on July 15th. If the organization determines income on a calendar year basis, this 9,600 will be prorated across portions of two calendar years.

Finally, advertising is simply expensed in the period it is incurred. The explanation for such summary treatment is the financial data bank's emphasis on integrity. It is difficult to verify future period effects of advertising. GAAP therefore mandates a most rapid writeoff.

The view that emerges from this story is important. Some expenses are recorded as a function of time while others are geared directly to the revenue that is recognized. We use specialized terminology to warn of this distinction.

Recall that a cost is incurred when we purchase plant, employ labor, acquire materials, and so on. The cost is then converted into an expense when the resource is consumed. This "conversion" of cost to expense is recorded in one of two broad forms. One recording form focuses on product cost.

A *product cost* is an asset decrease or liability increase that flows through the organization's inventory accounts and into cost of goods sold. Costs in this category are assets until revenue from the product in question is recognized. A merchandiser would treat the price paid the supplier (and usually the shipping cost) as product cost. The product cost of a manufacturer is more complicated but follows in parallel fashion. We will learn in subsequent chapters that manufacturing product cost has direct labor, direct material, and manufacturing overhead components.

All other expenses are called period costs. A *period cost* is an asset decrease or liability increase that is matched with revenue as a function of time. This use of time in the matching process may be direct or indirect. Advertising illustrates the former. Advertising cost is expensed at the time the advertising service is rendered. General administrative cost is handled in the same manner.

Contrast this with delivery expense. A mail order merchandiser will incur substantial cost in operating the organization's warehouse. Shipping containers will be used only when a customer's order is shipped. Thus, the cost of the shipping

---

[17]In turn, the underlying records might be kept on a periodic or a perpetual basis.

containers will be expensed when these containers are used to ship products to customers. The matching with revenue is direct. Yet, shipping containers will be treated as a period cost. The reason is product cost is reserved for cost items that accumulate in the merchandise or finished goods inventory account. Shipping costs will be found on the income statement, treated as a period cost.

The recognition criteria that guide accrual accounting heavily influence *when* particular items enter the accounting library and *how* they are classified when they enter. Cash based recognition is quite different. Ambiguity and subtlety disappear. So, too, it is claimed, does common sense. Accrual reporting attempts to match effort and accomplishment in the reporting period. Cash reporting tallies cash inflows and cash outflows. It makes no effort to match effort and accomplishment.

The important point for our purpose is that the accounting library contains both summations.[18] The accounting library is rich and varied.

Inventory Accounting

A closer look at inventory procedures concludes our review. Consider a shoe store. Revenue recognition is particularly simple. Revenue is recognized when a customer purchases a pair of shoes. Expense matching, though, is not so simple.

Property taxes, insurance, energy, advertising, and labor are all treated in the fashion sketched above. Here we concentrate on cost of goods sold.

The store will have records that mirror the physical inventory. The number of pairs of shoes of various styles and sizes will be recorded in these records. When revenue is recognized, the style and size of shoes sold are noted. This information is then used to update the inventory records.

These records are also updated when additional shoes arrive from suppliers or when rejects are returned to suppliers. In this way the store maintains a record of its inventory, broken down by style and size. It can even identify sales by style, size, day, week, or month. Sales are also broken down by salesperson. It can compare its mix of sales through time with that of its competitors by using industry data.

How are these elaborate records converted into financial data? First we worry about accuracy of the records. Recording errors are bound to occur. Theft is a possibility. Auditing standards require the physical inventory be counted. So one step is to verify the records physically.[19]

---

[18]A common claim is that the accrual summation is superior to the cash based summation, as it at least attempts a proper matching. We, however, adopt the perspective of a user of the accounting library. Both summations contain information. The two together are likely to be more useful than either standing alone. Related to this is another common claim that managers succumb to the temptation of short-run behavior by trying to maximize their accounting performance. We will analyze this at length in subsequent chapters. For now notice the incongruity. Accrual procedures are designed to provide a long-run perspective, while managers are unduly tempted to maximize these measures!

[19]We often see "pre-inventory" sales. The idea is to reduce the inventory to lower the cost of

The second step is to take these verified physical records and summarize or aggregate them into a financial record. This is done by "valuing" the ending inventory at cost. Suppose the price paid to the store's suppliers never changes. Then, for any style and size of shoe in inventory, we know exactly what the supplier was paid. Price paid times quantity in stock gives us the desired inventory valuation at historical cost.

What if this price varies? For example, prices change as a matter of course. Incentives also may be present. Our store might receive a 10% reduction in the total purchase price from a supplier if its purchases exceed some base amount. The supplier also may provide short term credit or advertising credits.

As we know, changing prices is the point at which a cost flow assumption is made. The store might assume a FIFO flow, a LIFO flow, or an average cost flow.[20] It then takes wholesale price information and uses this record of prices paid its suppliers with its record of ending inventory to calculate the end-of-period accounting "value." In turn, cost of goods sold expense is calculated as total cost of purchases plus beginning accounting value of inventory less ending accounting value of inventory.

These are familiar calculations. The potential biases in the resulting financial summaries are also familiar. For example, if wholesale prices are rising, we know LIFO produces a lower end-of-period accounting "value" than does FIFO. LIFO therefore produces a higher cost of goods sold expense than does FIFO, provided wholesale prices are rising.

The picture, however, goes beyond use of a cost flow assumption. We also encounter convention in determining the historical cost of the purchased inventory. Transportation costs are usually treated as part of the cost of inventory. What about the cost incurred by searching for suppliers, by negotiating with them, by inspecting their samples, by receiving, recording, and stocking their shipments? Most of these items would be treated as a period cost in our shoe store.

What about supplier credit, volume incentives, and advertising credits? The implicit cost of trade credit is recognized in the wholesale price and treated as a product cost. Volume incentives and advertising credits are likely to be netted into cost of goods sold.

We hope this portrayal of the accountant's art has become vivid. Recall we stated earlier that cost is incurred when resources are incurred for some purpose.

---

counting the items. In addition, property taxes are often assessed on the inventory figure reported in the balance sheet. Many techniques are available for managing the inventory. Our shoe store will likely use price as such an instrument. This is illustrated by having a pre-inventory sale. It may also schedule the end of its accounting year to coincide with the time at which its inventories are naturally at a low point. A manufacturing firm has additional options. It may organize its production process so that it utilizes considerable or minimal inventory to buffer the various stages in the production process. This is just one of many tradeoffs that must be engineered.

[20]Some combination might be adopted. Variations on a theme are also possible, as in dollar LIFO.

This cost is converted to an expense when an asset decreases or liability increases in conjunction with serving the organization's customers. These general ideas guide the accountant's conversion of the organization's various activities into periodic financial summaries. Pragmatic conventions, however, temper the process. Some cost items are expensed sooner than others, and some cost items are expensed in a somewhat mechanical fashion.

Financial reporting concerns do not override all competing concerns in designing what goes into the organization's accounting library. Yet, their influence is hardly invisible.

The professional manager understands the organization's accounting library. A good way to figure out how this library is organized is to begin with financial reporting demands that are placed on it.

Summary

This chapter has reviewed the recognition rules that guide financial reporting. Our study concerns managerial uses of accounting information. The accounting side of this study begins with a review of financial reporting. One reason for this emphasis is that financial reporting is often used in the internal management of an organization. Creditors use this information to monitor the organization. Labor contracts often use this information. Executive bonus arrangements often use financial results as one of their criteria. Profit sharing plans also use financial results as a basis for contracting. In addition, large decisions, such as dropping a major product line, are usually pictured in pro forma financial statement terms. Thus, it is stifling to begin a study such as ours by denying the importance of financial accounting.

A second reason for this emphasis is that financial reporting places certain demands on what is stored in the organization's accounting library. We will soon discover other influences. But learning to use this rich resource begins with learning to diagnose what is in the library. This is why we emphasize financial reporting as an important influence.

Period versus product cost is an important distinction. The economist, recall, does not deal with this distinction. The textbook economist, equipped with perfect markets, encounters no ambiguity. Market value accounting is implemented fully.[21]

---

[21]Of course, economists directly confront market frictions when they engage in economic analysis. The American Economics Association, for example, is the largest professional organization in economics. It publishes an annual report in its journal, *The American Economic Review*. The organization attempts to implement market value accounting in its report. Marketable instruments are valued at market, unusual assets (such as old journal copies) are valued at historical cost (surprise), and an unusual hybrid procedure for recognizing earnings on the marketable instruments is employed.

Industrial organization specialists study market structure and industry performance. Here it is important to document economic rents. This means the economist must attempt estimation of economic

The period versus product cost distinction, yet, is central to the accounting process. Some cost items are associated with the product, while others are associated with the period in question. The economist stresses knowledge of the organization's cost curve. The accountant works with partial knowledge of this cost curve, and even then in highly aggregated fashion.[22]

Bibliographic Notes

Connections between accounting and economics have been explored in a variety of contexts. Paton [1923] is a classic. Whittington [1992] is an excellent introduction to accrual accounting and carries along numerous links to economics. Parker, Harcourt, and Whittington [1986] provide a collection of readings on income measurement drawn from the accounting and economics literature. Beaver [1989] emphasizes information content of the accounting measures.

Problems and Exercises

1. Define period and product costs. When is a period cost expensed? When is a product cost expensed? What does the economic theory of the firm say about the distinction between period and product costs?

2. Carefully contrast the concepts of economic income, economic rent, and accounting income.

3. *accounting versus economic valuation*
Ralph is pondering the difference between economic and accounting descriptions of financial life. Provide three explicit examples, one where a good guess is economic value exceeds accounting value, one where accounting value exceeds economic value, and one where they are about equal. In each case identify the accounting recognition rules that produce the particular bias, or lack of it, in the accounting valuation.

---

values, even when markets are less than perfect. The distinction between accounting and economic rates of return on capital is a central concern in this area. We will have more to say about this issue later in the text.

[22]An additional pressure on the product versus period cost distinction is the fact a multiproduct firm has no natural way to assign cost to products. Remember, average cost is undefined here (absent some form of extreme separability in the economic structure). Dealing with the same product at different points in time is, itself, a multiproduct story. It is no accident the economist focuses on the total cost curve and marginal cost of the various products.

4. *accounting expense versus economic cost*

Paton states "...the accountant's `expense´ for the particular business and the economist's `cost of production´ are two quite different things...[The] whole scheme of accounting is based upon the plan of showing as costs or expense only the expirations of purchased commodities and services, not the economic value of the services contributed by the business itself in furnishing capital and management" (Paton [1923], pages 493-494). Carefully comment on the difference between accounting expense and economic cost.

5. *accounting income*

We often see cases where a firm's accounting income is reported and the price of the firm's equity, traded on an organized exchange, behaves in seemingly strange fashion. Provide a coherent story in which a firm reports significantly higher income for a period and its value (as determined by traders on an organized exchange) declines.

6. *accounting versus economic valuation*

This is a continuation of problem 7 in Chapter 2. Assume an organization is formed, by issuing common stock, to purchase and manage the asset that produces the net cash flows listed in the original problem. The purchase price of the asset is 24,211.14, a familiar datum. The cash flow at the end of each year is immediately paid out in a dividend to the common stockholders.

a] Assume straight line depreciation is used, with no salvage value. Determine periodic income and end-of-period balance sheets for the organization. (Treat the noted cash flow as revenue and depreciation as the only expense.)

b] Assume r = 11% and use economic depreciation. You should treat the end-of-period value of the asset as the present value of the remaining cash flows, and depreciation as the change in value of the asset. Determine periodic income and end-of-period balance sheets for the organization.

c] Why do the two income series agree in total? Why is economic depreciation negative in one of the years?

7. *accounting versus economic history*

Ralph forms a firm by investing 1,000 dollars. This cash is immediately paid for a machine with a useful life of 3 years. The net cash inflow from this machine will be 110 at the end of the first year, 0 at the end of the second year, and 1,197.90 at the end of the third year. Net cash inflow is paid as a dividend immediately upon receipt. Also the third year net cash flow of 1,197.90 consists of 1,000 from customers and 197.90 salvage value received when the machine is retired at that time. (The firm ceases to exist after the year 3 dividend is paid.)

a] Assume Ralph's accountant uses sum of the years' digits depreciation. Tell Ralph's history with end-of-year balance sheets, periodic income statements, and periodic cash flow statements. The initial balance sheet should show an asset (call it P&E) of 1,000 and capital stock of 1,000.

b] Assume the interest rate is r = 10%. Tell Ralph's history, again with balance sheets, income statements, and cash flow statements, but in terms of economic income.

c] Construct a 3-year income statement for Ralph. Does the total of the income numbers in your answer to [a] agree with this answer? What about the total of the economic income numbers?

d] Closely examine your accounting and economic income numbers for the second year. What numbers in the overall history determine the economic income in the second period? (Hint: think in terms of change in present value plus dividends.) What numbers in the overall history determine the accounting income in the second period?

e] To what extent is it correct to say accounting income is a backward looking calculation, based on actual transactions, and economic income is a forward looking calculation, based on anticipated transactions?

8. *balance sheets and income statements under different valuation rules*
Ralph manages a two-product firm. The major events, in terms of cash flow, are as follows.
  a. Just before the start of period t = 1 the firm (a corporation) is formed by Ralph and friends investing 1,500 in cash.
  b. Just after the start of period t = 1 the firm purchases equipment, paying cash, for 1,500.
  c. At the end of period 1, 1,200 net cash flow is received:
        2,000 received from the first product's customer;
        400 wages paid;
        300 paid to suppliers of materials; and
        100 paid to miscellaneous suppliers.
  d. Dividends of 1,200 are declared and paid at the start of period 2.
  e. At the end of period 2, 720 net cash flow is received:
        1,600 received from the second product's customer;
        300 wages paid;
        500 paid to suppliers of materials; and
        80 paid to miscellaneous suppliers.
  f. Dividends of 720 are declared and paid at the start of period 3 and the firm dissolves.

a] Prepare a series of three balance sheets (for the start of period 1, the end of period 1 and the end of period 2) and associated income statements for the two periods. The statements should be based on economic valuation; assume an interest rate of 20%. (So the initial balance sheet shows cash of 1,500 and capital stock of 1,500 and the first period income is 300.)

b]   Prepare the same statements using accrual accounting. For this purpose, assume the cash outflow at the end of period 1 is expensed in period 1; similarly, the cash outflow at the end of period 2 should be expensed in period 2. Also use straight line depreciation.

c]   Repeat [a] assuming 1/4 of the cash outflow at the end of period 2 relates to the first product.

d]   Is economic income affected by the change in assumption in part [c]? Explain.

e]   Of the firm's total income of 420, how much can be assigned to each of the products? Do you see a conflict between the apparently unambiguous nature of economic income measurement and the assignment of profit or cost to each of the products?

9.   *cash versus accrual recognition*
        Ralph has designed a consumer product, and launched a manufacturing and sales organization. To keep the problem uncluttered, the organization has a life of exactly three years. The organization is incorporated at time t = 0, with Ralph acquiring all shares for 1,389.93. (No apologies are offered for this obtuse amount.) You will also notice Ralph lives in a tax-free environment.
        Subsequent to incorporation, the following cash transactions occur.

	time t = 0	end yr 1	end yr 2	end yr 3
payment for				
equipment	1,389.93			
materials		200	100	0
labor		300	400	300
sundry services		200	600	600
receipt from customers		1,400	1,600	1,500
disposal of equipment				0
dividends paid				1,800

Any cash on hand is held in a non-interest bearing account.

a]   Assume straight line depreciation. Prepare income statements and end-of-period balance sheets for each of the three years. Treat the material, labor, and administrative items as completely expensed in the year incurred. Also treat the customer receipts as revenue in the year received. (For the final year, prepare the balance sheet assuming the dividends have been paid. It may, however, be instructive to construct the balance sheet as of the end of the final year and just before the final dividend is declared and paid.)

b]   Repeat the above, using cash basis accounting. Here the focus should be on the fact the only asset recognized is the end-of-period cash balance. Do the three cash income statements, and then the balance sheets if this is not clear. (Hint: assets total 700 at the end of year 1.)

c]   Prepare a brief paragraph explaining why the total income over the 3 years is the same in the cash basis and accrual basis models.

10. *economic valuation and dividend timing*
       This is a continuation of problem 9 above.

a]   Assume Ralph's discount rate is 9%. Prepare periodic income statements and end-of-period balance sheets for Ralph using economic depreciation. (Hint: income in year 1 will be .09(1,389.93) while assets at the end of year 1 will total 1,515.02.)

b]   Prepare a short paragraph explaining why the total income calculated in [a] above is equal to the total income under cash basis or accrual basis accounting.

c]   Prepare a short paragraph explaining what will happen to your income and balance sheet calculations if Ralph builds up inventory during the early part of the story and subsequently sells it off.

d]   Suppose, instead, that any cash on hand is held in an interest bearing account that pays 9% interest. (This implies the cash balance at the end of year 2 would be 700(1.09) + 500 = 1,263.) How much would Ralph pay for this venture, assuming an interest rate of 9%, at time t = 0? Given this amount is paid, what would Ralph's economic income from the venture be in each period?

e]   Now suppose any cash on hand at the end of a period is paid out in dividends. (So dividends are 700 at the end of year 1, 500 at the end of year 2, and 600 at the end of year 3.) How much would Ralph pay for this venture? Given this amount is paid, what would Ralph's economic income from the venture be in each period? How does this relate to the story in [d]?

11. *economic valuation and disaggregation*[23]
       Ralph's firm operates in a world of complete and perfect markets. The prevailing interest rate is 10%. Ralph's firm pays out each year's cash flow in dividends.

a]   Suppose Ralph's firm consists of a single depreciable asset with a 5 year life. The asset produces end-of-year net cash flows as follows:

---

[23]Contributed by Rick Antle.

year	1	2	3	4	5
net CF	270	195	185	175	95

Construct economic balance sheets as of the beginning and end of year 1. Construct an economic income statement for year 1.

b]   Now suppose Ralph's firm consists of not one, but nine different components. The components sum to the same net cash flows for the firm as in part [a]. The cash flows from the nine components are:

year	1	2	3	4	5
components:					
1	200	200	200	200	200
2	50	40	30	20	10
3	40				
4					80
5	-35				
6	0	-60	-60	-60	-60
7					-300
8	20	20	20	20	220
9	-5	-5	-5	-5	-55
total net CF	270	195	185	175	95

Notice we have already separated items with positive cash flows from those with negative flows. This corresponds to an accountant's distinction of assets and liabilities. Prepare economic balance sheets as of the beginning and end of year 1 and the end of year 2. Try your hand at classifying items the way an accountant would: current versus long-term assets, current versus long-term liabilities, and equities. Also prepare economic income statements for years 1 and 2 with your classification. As a guideline, accounting conventions would call an increase in the value of an asset a holding gain and a decrease in value depreciation.

c]   As you do the problem, think about what assets or liabilities found in practice might have cash flow patterns similar to the 9 components of Ralph's firm. Also, think about accounting conventions of classification and aggregation in relation to economic value and economic income. Would anyone in the perfect markets setting care about the income statements and balance sheets produced in part [b]; or would they just care about the net pictured in part [a]? How would your answer change if the setting were actual practice instead of the textbook setting of perfect markets?

12. *inferring cash flow from economic measurements*
     Ralph restores financial records for organizations that have experienced disasters, such as fires, floods, and hurricanes, and lost their financial records.

Ralph's present client lost all records, except for a business plan that was prepared for the Bank of Economic Analysis. This bank insists on economic valuation as the basis for accounting. Ralph finds the following data:

initial investment:	4,000
economic earnings in year 1:	400
economic earnings in year 2:	330
economic earnings in year 3:	121

Ralph also learns that (i) a constant interest rate was used throughout the analysis; (ii) the client firm paid all available cash in dividends, so the end-of-year cash balance was always zero; and (iii) the client firm ceased to exist at the end of year 3 (after the final dividend was paid).

a]   What interest rate was used in the analysis?

b]   What dividends were paid at the end of years 1, 2, and 3?

c]   What was economic depreciation in each of the 3 years?

d]   What was the total economic income over the life of the client's firm?

e]   How much income would the firm have reported in each year if it had used accrual accounting coupled with sum of the years' digits depreciation?

13. *the accountant's task*

"Accounting...might best be defined as the art which attempts to break up the financial history of a business into specific units, a year or less in length. In other words, it is the business of the accountant to prepare valid statements of income and financial condition in terms of specific periods of time; and the propriety of a particular procedure cannot be judged fairly except in terms of its effect upon the integrity of the particular statement" (Paton [1922], page 469). Do you agree? Carefully explain your reasoning.

4

Economic Behavior Under Uncertainty

The final preliminary topic concerns managerial behavior. Our study of managerial uses of accounting information requires that we combine accounting and managerial behavior. This, in turn, demands that we adopt some image, implicit or explicit, of managerial behavior. Economic rationality is our choice.

Viewing accounting as a source of information naturally presumes information is valuable or useful. It must be able to tell us something we do not know. This implies uncertainty must be present. Economic behavior in the presence of uncertainty, then, is the center piece of our model of managerial behavior.

We begin with a brief review of economic rationality and its central idea of consistent behavior. This is then extended to a setting of explicit uncertainty, where preference is measured by expected utility. This allows us to study risk aversion, a topic that will be important later. We then extend the expected utility framework to the use of information to improve the quality of a decision. The chapter concludes with a look at consistent behavior in a strategic setting.

Economic behavior is our primary, explicit portrait of managerial behavior. This provides a parsimonious description of managerial behavior, one that emphasizes consistency in the face of economic forces. It focuses our study and leads to many important insights. It is not, however, a universal description of behavior. At appropriate junctures we will introduce the idea of systematic variations from economic rationality. This, of course, presumes we understand economic rationality in the first place.

Economic Rationality

The label of rational behavior calls to mind someone who is intelligent, wise, and enlightened. In an economic setting this colloquialism is often refined to someone who pursues self-interest and wealth with an unrelenting, even unhealthy vigor. Yet, as often happens, there is both more and less to the popular conception.

The underlying idea is straightforward. Suppose we face the problem of selecting one choice from an available set of alternatives.[1] Think of the alternatives as contained in set A. Also denote one such alternative by z. Choice is confined to some $z \in A$. This is the first half of the setup. We have an exogenously specified problem of selecting one element from set A.

The second half of the setup introduces a criterion function, or preference measure. In particular, we presume the individual's choice behavior can be

---

[1] We explore the tenets of economic rationality in terms of an individual facing a well-defined choice problem. Naturally, this holds for any economic entity, for example the behavior of a firm.

described as though some criterion function is present, say, f(z), and the best choice is the available one that produces the largest value of the criterion function. Symbolically, we have the following portrayal of the individual's choice process:

    maximize f(z)
    subject to: z∈A.

Don't pass over the subtlety. The assumption is not that the individual has or uses such a function. It is that the individual's behavior can be described *as though* such a function were present and used in the noted fashion. The assumption is that choice behavior can be described by, modeled by, represented by maximization of some function.[2]

Studying household behavior with a budget line and indifference curves is a case in point. Examine Figure 4.1, where we deal with the best feasible choice of goods x and y. The straight line depicts the budget line. Any combination on or below the line is feasible (provided $x \geq 0$ and $y \geq 0$). The curved lines are indifference curves. The individual is indifferent among all combinations of x and y on any such curve. Moving in the northeast direction is preferred. Thus, consumption of any combination on the lower indifference curve can be improved. Feasible choices that are better are available. Consumption of any combination on the highest indifference curve would be nice, but no such combination is feasible. This indifference curve is uniformly above the budget line. The middle curve is critical. It is tangent to the budget line. Anything on a lower indifference curve can be improved, while anything on a higher indifference curve is infeasible.

Nothing is said here about whether the individual walks around with these indifference curves. Rather, the story is one of describing the individual's behavior in terms of indifference curves and a budget line. The individual can identify combinations of x and y that are equivalent in terms of preference, and can identify combinations that are strictly better or worse, in terms of preference. This story is equivalent to one in which the individual's tastes are represented by a criterion function, or utility function.

Lest we doubt, let $z = (x,y)$ denote a particular choice of x and y, or consumption bundle. The story in Figure 4.1 was generated with a budget line of $x + y = 10$, and a utility function of $f(x,y) = xy$. The tangency point is located by maximizing $f(x,y) = xy$ subject to (1) $x \geq 0$; (2) $y \geq 0$; and (3) $x + y \leq 10$. The solution is $x^* = y^* = 5$. (The scaling in the diagram is not symmetric.)

The idea of economic rationality, then, is that preferences are so well defined they can be described by a criterion function, a utility function. There is no claim, no requirement, that the individual possess and use a utility function. The claim is the individual's behavior is so well defined that it can be described as though such

---

[2]The individual comes equipped with considerable skill and self insight. The fact a decision opportunity is present is known, and all of the alternatives have been identified. A is exogenously specified; and the individual behaves as though these alternatives are evaluated with the f(z) function.

a function were present. This leads to the question of what it means for behavior to be so well defined.

Figure 4.1: Budget Lines and Indifference Curves

quantity of good x

consistency

The central feature here is consistency. Suppose we must select from some set A = {a,b,c,d}. Further suppose that we rank the choices in the order of a, b, c, and d. Notice two things. Our ranking is *complete*. Take any two options from A. Either we are indifferent (e.g., a is as good as itself, a) or one is better than the other (e.g., b is better than d). Our ranking is also *transitive*. For example, a ranks above b and b ranks above c; and then a ranks above c.

Complete and transitive ranking is the hallmark of consistency. If our ranking is not complete, we are saying there are some comparisons that we find confusing; we cannot choose between them. If our rankings are intransitive, we open ourself to foolishness, or worse. Suppose we say a beats b and b beats c and c beats a. Suppose we have c. b beats c, and we pay a dollar to switch to b. But a beats b and we pay a second dollar to switch to a. Finally, c beats a and we pay a third dollar to switch to c. We are now at the beginning point of the cycle, but less $3.

It turns out that if the set A is finite, the following two statements are logically equivalent. First, we have a ranking of the elements in A that is complete and transitive. Second, there exists a function on A, say, f(z), such that for any two z,ź∈A f(z) ≥ f(ź) only when z is ranked as good as ź. In this sense we say a function on set A that represents some ranking of the elements in A exists if (and only if) that ranking is complete and transitive.[3]

This probably strikes you as well beyond anything of interest in the study of accounting. The most important feature of economic behavior, though, is consistent tastes, consistent in the sense they are complete (we know what we like) and transitive (we don't cycle). This does not say greed or self-interest. It says complete and transitive.

smoothness

You may have noticed Figure 4.1 uses an uncountable set of possible choices, while our digression on existence of a utility function used a finite set of possible choices. This leads to a second, more technical condition. If we are to have a utility function, we must have a complete and transitive ranking. But there are cases where this is not enough. These cases take the form of rankings that are not sufficiently smooth.[4] Both consistency and smoothness are required for existence of a criterion or utility function. In general terms, then, choice behavior can be described in terms of maximizing a criterion function when the underlying preferences are consistent and smooth.

Return to our initial characterization of behavior. Suppose we have identified a set of options, call it A. We then describe choice behavior in terms of the following optimization:

maximize $f(z)$
subject to: $z \in A$.

This characterization amounts to an assumption that the individual brings consistent and smooth preferences to the exercise. Consistency is the critical feature. We require the individual not cycle (i.e., be transitive) and not be confused (i.e., be

---

[3]We are being a little casual here. Let B be the set of conceivable choices and A be any nonempty subset of B. $f(z)$ is everywhere defined; it is a function on B. A particular choice problem then arises when we encounter some nonempty subset of B, the set A. We treat A and B as the same sets in our narrative, hoping to convey the central idea without burdening the discussion with details better reserved for a thorough enquiry.

[4]A lexicographic ordering is a case in point. Let $z = (x,y)$, with x and y denoting quantities of two goods. Let set A be any combination of x and y with $0 \le x \le 1$ and $0 \le y \le 1$. Suppose in comparing z and ź you always look to the first good. Take the option with the largest amount of the first good. If a tie is present, take the one with the largest amount of the second good. Notice how the second good is important only when the consumption bundles have the same amount of the first good. Though these preferences are complete and transitive, no utility function exists. The preferences are not sufficiently smooth. The technical requirement is we be able to find a subset of A that is both dense (in the sense we can use it to bracket the other elements) and countable (a trivial issue when A is finite). This is hardly intuitive, so we just invoke the requirement of smoothness.

complete). Annoying pathological cases are ruled out by the added requirement that these preferences be smooth.

Expected Utility

With this underlying idea of consistent (and smooth) choice behavior before us, we turn to a more specialized version in which the criterion function is the expected value of some random variable. The idea is the alternatives result in consequences that are uncertain at the time of choice. Each alternative is described in terms of the probabilities of various consequences. The criterion function is then the expected value of the utility of the consequences.

mechanical details

Consider a setting where we must choose between two alternatives. Call them, imaginatively, "*one*" and "*two*." So A = {*one,two*}. These alternatives are gambles, with possible dollar consequences and probabilities displayed in Table 4.1.

Table 4.1: Consequence and Probability Data			
alternative	dollar outcome or consequence		
	100	240	400
one	α	0	$1-\alpha$
two	0	1	0

Alternative *one* is a gamble over 100 and 400. It provides a 100 outcome or consequence with probability α. Alternative *two* is a degenerate gamble, it provides a 240 outcome or consequence with probability 1.

The subsequent discussion will be more compact if we think in terms of the individual's ending wealth. For this purpose, suppose our individual currently possesses wealth in the amount w. Ending wealth will then be w + 240 if *two* is selected, and w + 100 or w + 400 if *one* is selected.[5] Denote the individual's utility of wealth by $U(\hat{w}) = \hat{w}$ for wealth level $\hat{w}$.

Mechanically, then, utility of wealth is a random variable; and we measure the preferences for the alternatives by constructing the expected value of the utility of wealth. Let E[U|*one*] denote the expected utility of wealth that follows from choice of *one*. E[U|*two*] should be interpreted in parallel fashion. We now have the following criterion measures:

$$f(one) = E[U|one] = \alpha U(w+100) + (1-\alpha)U(w+400); \text{ and}$$

---

[5]For convenience we tell the story in terms of dollar wealth. The theory is based on alternatives that produce consequences described in terms of probabilities.

f(*two*) = E[U|*two*] = U(w+240).

Notice the role of the utility function, U(ŵ). It is defined on ending wealth, not on the alternatives. We construct the expected value of the utility of ending wealth (or consequences), and not the expected value of the ending wealth. The criterion function (or utility defined on alternatives), f(z), is the expected value of the utility of wealth that follows from z, E[U|z].

A decision tree display is given in Figure 4.2. Each alternative leads to an array of possible outcomes, or consequences. They are assessed in terms of their respective utility. (This is utility of ending wealth in our story.) Each branch is then "rolled back" to construct the expected value of the utilities. The rolled back calculation is the decision criterion, f(z).

Figure 4.2: Tree for Expected Utility Illustration

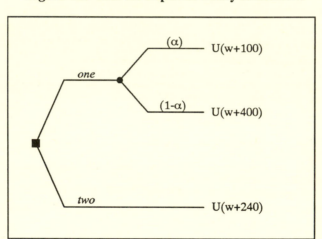

Now set α = .5. Also assume for the moment the utility function is linear, U(ŵ) = ŵ. This leads to the following evaluations:

f(*one*) = .5(w+100) + .5(w+400) = w + .5(100) + .5(400) = w + 250; and
f(*two*) = w + 240.

This is probably the format in which you first encountered expected utility analysis. The utility of the consequence is the consequence itself. Strictly speaking, this is a special case in which the utility function is linear. (It implies risk neutrality, but that is getting ahead of our story.)

Conversely, suppose U(ŵ) is the square root of ŵ. We then have the following evaluations:

$$f(one) = (.5)\sqrt{w+100} + (.5)\sqrt{w+400} \; ; \text{ and}$$
$$f(two) = \sqrt{w+240} \; .$$

Continuing, suppose initial wealth is zero, $w = 0$. We then have evaluations of $f(one) = 15 < f(two) = 15.49$ in the square root case, and $f(one) = 250 > f(two) = 240$ in the linear case.

In mechanical terms, expected utility analysis envisions a criterion function of $f(z) = E[U|z]$. The evaluation of any alternative is the expected value of the utility of the consequences associated with that alternative. The underlying assumptions are consistency and smoothness, as before, along with an independence requirement. Expected utility analysis is economic rationality of a particular form.

To provide some flavor of this additional requirement, suppose in our setting in Table 4.1 we add a third alternative (called "*three*"). This alternative consists of selecting or playing alternative *one* with probability β and alternative *two* with probability $(1-\beta)$. Under expected utility representation, its evaluation is:

$$f(three) = \beta\{\alpha U(w+100) + (1-\alpha)U(w+400)\} + (1-\beta)U(w+240)$$
$$= \beta f(one) + (1-\beta)f(two).$$

That is, the evaluation of compound or sequential gambles is the expected value of the underlying evaluations. This forces the expected value structure that is central to the story.[6]

certain equivalents

The expected value of the utility of the consequences is an awkward, long-winded expression. Restatement in terms of certain equivalents provides a useful interpretive device. Formally, alternative z's certain equivalent is that certain wealth (or consequence), CE_z, such that the individual is indifferent between z and receiving CE_z. Since CE_z is a certain amount of wealth (i.e., occurs with probability one), its evaluation is given by $U(CE_z)$. And since we are indifferent between CE_z and z we require $U(CE_z) = E[U|z] = f(z)$. Whatever alternative z entails, the individual is indifferent between it and its certain equivalent.

To illustrate, return to alternative *one* in Table 4.1 and set $w = 0$. For the linear utility case we have $U(\hat{w}) = \hat{w}$ (with $w = 0$). This implies the following certain equivalent calculation:

$$U(CE) = CE = 100\alpha + 400(1-\alpha) = f(one).$$

---

[6] It also forces a form of independence in the taste for gambles. Let z, $\acute{z}$ and g be three alternative gambles. If we prefer z to $\acute{z}$ we then prefer a compound gamble of z and g to a compound gamble of $\acute{z}$ and g (presuming z and $\acute{z}$ are both engaged with the same probability).

If $\alpha = 0$, we receive the 400 outcome for certain; and CE = 400. If $\alpha = 1$, we receive the 100 outcome for certain; and CE = 100. CE is plotted as a function of α in Figure 4.3.

Conversely, for the square root case (again with w = 0) we have

$$U(CE) = \alpha\sqrt{100} + (1-\alpha)\sqrt{400} = 10\alpha + 20(1-\alpha) = f(one).$$

Again, notice the end points are clear. $\alpha = 1$ implies CE = 100 and $\alpha = 0$ implies CE = 400. Otherwise, CE is strictly below its counterpart in the linear case (see Figure 4.3).

An alternative's certain equivalent, then, is a guaranteed or certain amount CE such that the individual is indifferent between it and the alternative in question. This provides an intuitive expression of preference. For example, when w = 0 and $\alpha = .5$, we find CE = 225 in the root utility case. (You should verify this.) In this instance, with w = 0, opting for *one* is the same as banking $225. Of course, opting for *two* is the same as banking $240.

Figure 4.3: Certain Equivalents for Linear and Root Utility Functions

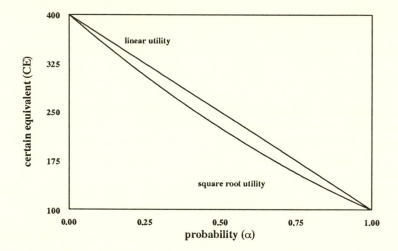

risk aversion

This provides entry to the topic of risk aversion. Suppose we are offered our choice of (1) flip a fair coin, receive 1,000 dollars if heads and nothing if tails; or (2) receive 500 dollars. Most people would jump at the second, sure amount. This is the intuitive idea of risk aversion. We would gladly trade a risky alternative for a certain amount equal to its expected value.

One more piece of notation will bring this into focus. Let $E[\hat{w}|z]$ denote the expected value of ending wealth, given choice of alternative z. We say an individual is risk averse whenever (1) $E[\hat{w}|z] \geq CE_z$ for all z; and (2) the inequality is strict whenever z has positive probability on at least two different wealth levels.[7] If wealth is at risk, the risk averse individual would gladly trade the risky prospect for a guaranteed amount equal to its expected value. Stated differently, the risk averse individual always seeks fair insurance. Risk is noxious.

If the utility function is linear, the individual always has $E[\hat{w}|z] = CE_z$. Risk is a matter of indifference. Risk neutrality is expressed by a linear utility function. On the other hand, the square root utility function displays risk aversion.

Return to alternative *one* in Table 4.1. Notice its expected value is $E[\hat{w}|one] = w + 100\alpha + 400(1-\alpha)$, given an initial wealth of w. Let $\alpha = .5$, so $E[\hat{w}|one] = w + 250$. Recall the special case of $w = 0$. There the expected value of ending wealth is 250, while the certain equivalent is 225. For an arbitrary (though positive) initial wealth, the certain equivalent is given by

$$\sqrt{CE} = .5\sqrt{w+100} + .5\sqrt{w+400}.$$

Given initial wealth, alternative *one* adds 250 to the expected ending wealth. It also adds CE - w to the certain equivalent. Relative to the starting point of w, then, we have an expected gain of 250, contrasted with a gain in certain equivalent of CE - w. Examine Figure 4.4, where we plot CE - w as a function of w, for both the linear and square root utility cases.

Naturally, for the linear case, CE - w remains constant at 250, reflecting the presumed risk neutrality. For the square root case, we have CE - w < 250, reflecting the presumed risk aversion. However, CE - w gets closer to 250 as w increases. The gamble to obtain an additional 100 or 400 becomes less daunting as initial wealth increases. Risk aversion is declining as wealth increases. (Technically, the square root function is approaching linearity in the region of the gamble as w increases.)

This is an important point. Risk aversion may depend on the status quo. It does not if the individual is risk neutral. In the square root case, risk aversion declines as initial wealth w increases. More generally, risk aversion might decline, increase, remain constant, or be some combination thereof as we vary w. A negative exponential utility function, $U(\hat{w}) = -exp\langle-r\hat{w}\rangle$, is the only one that displays risk aversion that is everywhere constant.[8]

---

[7]Alternative z's risk premium is $E[\hat{w}|z]$ - CE_z, the difference between its expected value and certain equivalent. Notice risk aversion is the same thing as positive risk premia for all alternatives with uncertain consequences. Also, the definition given is for the case of an individual who is globally (meaning everywhere) risk averse. The theory does not require risk aversion, either locally or globally. It only requires consistency, smoothness, and independence.

[8]Here r > 0. A small r connotes low risk aversion, while a larger r represents higher risk aversion.

Figure 4.4: Normalized Certain Equivalent for Alternative One

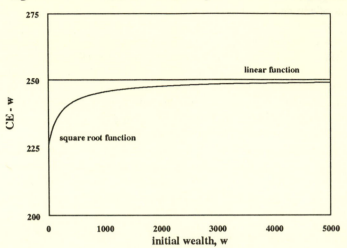

Information

We now turn to the acquisition and use of information. Expected utility representation offers an additional advantage at this point. It forces the information to be used in a particular way: systematic, consistent revision of the probabilities.

example

Return to the setting in Table 4.1, where we face choice between alternatives *one* and *two*. Let the possible outcomes under *one* be equally likely ($\alpha = .5$); and set initial wealth to zero, to avoid distraction. We will also use the square root utility specification.

Into this setting we now append the option of gathering some evidence that speaks to the risk in *one* before making the decision. In particular, this evidence will be either "good" news or "bad" news. If bad news arrives, we know the 100 outcome will materialize if *one* is selected. Good news, though, is ambiguous. This is catalogued in the joint probabilities, for good or bad news and 100 or 400 outcomes, that are displayed on the following page.

For any given r, though, risk aversion does not depend on initial wealth. To see why, suppose we add some amount of initial wealth, say k, to the status quo. We are then dealing with $-exp\langle$-r$\hat{w}$-rk$\rangle$. But this factors into $-exp\langle$-rk$\rangle exp\langle$-r$\hat{w}\rangle$, and $exp\langle$-rk$\rangle$ is some positive constant. So all we have done is multiply the utility function by a positive constant. This has no effect on the expression of preference.

The probability that good news is received and *one* produces 400 is .5. The probability *one* produces 400 is .5, the probability good news is received is .6, and so on. In turn, if bad news is received we know *one* is guaranteed to produce 100. If good news is received, *one* will produce 100 with probability 1/6 and 400 with probability 5/6.[9]

	100	400	
good	.1	.5	.6
bad	.4	0	.4
	.5	.5	

If bad news is received, we know *one* will result in 100, while *two* offers 240, an easy choice. If good news is received, *one* is the better choice, as

$$(1/6)\sqrt{100} \; + \; (5/6)\sqrt{400} \; > \; \sqrt{240} \, .$$

In short, expected utility analysis relies on tastes (encoded in the utility function) and beliefs (encoded in the probability assessments). Information alters beliefs in systematic fashion. The revised beliefs are then used to guide behavior. Good news, for example, moves α from .5 to 1/6 in our illustration; and at that point *one* is the preferred choice.

Pulling this together, the best way to use this information is to select *one* when good news is received and *two* when bad news is received. Call this the *info* option. Its expected utility is

$$.1\sqrt{100} \; + \; .5\sqrt{400} \; + \; .4\sqrt{240} \; = \; \sqrt{295.73} \; = \; 17.20.$$

The story is summarized in Table 4.2. Notice how the presence of the information allows us to construct a third, and in this case improved, alternative, *info*. Perfect information (the alternative labeled *perfect info*) is even better here. The important point is expected utility analysis leads us to think of information in terms of how it changes the odds of various outcomes or consequences and to act accordingly.

This is the sense in which information improves the quality of a decision. It allows a more informed choice of the alternatives in A; it allows us to construct a more sophisticated alternative, such as *info* in Table 4.2. Here we have f(*info*) > f(*two*) > f(*one*). Without the information, we would proceed with choice of *two*. We don't need the information, but it surely improves the quality of our decision.[10]

---

[9] Let M and N be two events, with respective probabilities p(M) > 0 and p(N) > 0. Denote their joint probability p(M and N). The conditional probability of M, given N is given by Bayes' Rule: p(M|N) = p(M and N)/p(N) = p(N|M)p(M)/p(N).

[10] In the linear utility case, we find f(*info*) > f(*one*) > f(*two*).

Information, then, enriches the opportunities. Of course, we should not blithely assume that acquiring information is a good idea. Our example has purposely assumed the information was costless, or free; and it might be too costly. This cost might be explicit. For example, we might have to pay for it, as when a consultant is hired.[11] It also may take too much time to produce or decipher the information. This book, for example, contains considerable information (at least in the author's opinion), but cannot be thoroughly studied and deciphered in a few hours. The cost might also be highly implicit. In a strategic setting, it is possible that one player's acquisition of information alters another player's behavior to such an extent the player getting the information is harmed. To illustrate, it is more difficult to sell our automobile if the would-be buyer knows we just had a mechanic thoroughly check the auto.

Table 4.2: Information Example with Root Utility				
alternative	dollar outcome or consequence 100	240	400	expected utility
one	.5	0	.5	15.00
two	0	1	0	15.49
info	.1	.4	.5	17.20
perfect info	0	.5	.5	17.75

an important aside

This leads to an important aside that reveals a great deal about the manner in which we are studying accounting. Suppose an integer between 1 and 100 is going to be picked at random. One information source will tell us whether the number is low (50 or below) or high (51 or above). Another information source will tell us whether the number is odd or even. Notice low/high tells us nothing about whether the number is odd or even, while odd/even tells us nothing about whether the number is low or high.

Suppose we have a chance to bet on the number. If the bet is odd versus even we are in great shape with the odd/even information source; and if the bet is low versus high we are in great shape with the other information source. (Of course, if the other player knows we have this information, there will be no bet.)

Here's the rub. No matter which betting game we face, knowing both odd/even and low/high is as good as knowing just one or the other, and that is as good as

---

[11]Here it is important to remember risk aversion may vary with the wealth level. Suppose we pay C for the information in the example. Then the evaluation of the information option (given we take *one* under good news) is .1U(100-C) + .5U(400-C) + .4U(240-C).

knowing nothing. (Again, the other party to the bet is unaware we have access to this information.) There is more information in knowing both than in knowing just one; and there is more information in knowing one than in knowing neither. Unfortunately, comparing odd/even and low/high is problematic. We cannot say one has more or less information than the other.

Suppose we want to identify the best information source without saying too much about the context. No difficulty arises if we know there is more information in one than the other; we would always opt for the one with more information, presuming it is costless. Yet we are not necessarily in the happy case of facing information choices that can be ranked from high to low in terms of the amount of information they offer. Odd/even versus high/low is a case in point. They tell us different things; and we cannot say which is better without knowing the context.

Now recall the underlying idea of economic rationality: consistent preferences. We are always able to decide, and we do not cycle. No measure of preference is possible without consistent preferences. Here we cannot decide between odd/even and high/low without knowing the context. This means we cannot make consistent statements about information sources in a context-free manner.

Yet in accounting we often find reference to accounting "principles." Treating accounting as a source of information, we immediately see economic forces preclude an ability to make general statements about which source of information, which accounting method, is best (odd/even versus low/high for example). The term, accounting principles, is a misnomer in the sense it conveys an ability to discern the preferred method of accounting without specifying the context. This is why we always carry context along in our discussion, and why we are reticent in making sweeping statements about the nature of good accounting practice.

Information cannot be studied without specifying the context in which it is to be used. Treating accounting as a source of information implies we cannot study accounting without specifying the context in which it is to be used.

Consistent Behavior in a Strategic Setting

The expected utility view of choice behavior, we have stressed, separates an uncertain choice problem into tastes and beliefs. These are then combined in the expected utility calculation. There is no notion in which odds are altered by the choice taken. Murphy's Law (the quintessential expression of apprehension) is inconsistent with the model, in that it assumes events such as the weather will unfold to cause the most harm given the choice taken.

The idea of reactive events can, however, be combined with the expected utility theme. These events are viewed as under the control of other individuals. At this point, the story is expanded to include a simultaneous examination of the behavior of all of the individuals involved.

A simple two player (or bimatrix) game will be sufficient for our purpose. Consider the display below. This is decoded as follows. We have two players, called Row and Column. Row must select between *up* and *down* while Column must select between *left* and *right*. In any cell, the numbers are the expected utilities of the two players, listed in the order of Row followed by Column. For example, if Row plays *down* while Column plays *right*, Row's expected utility is 6 while Column's is 1.

	left	*right*
up	1, 0	4, 5
down	2, 4	6, 1

Two assumptions are now invoked. One is that both players know this matrix. They know their alternatives as well as those of the other player, and they know the respective expected utilities. The second is that the players will engage in equilibrium behavior. Loosely this means Row will behave in a manner best for Row, given what Column is doing; Column will behave in a manner best for Column, given what Row is doing; and the two sets of behavior and expectations will be consistent.

simultaneous play

Suppose the players must make their respective choices simultaneously. Row does not see what Column does before deciding and vice versa. Does (*up, left*) make sense? Hardly; if Row plays *up* Column's best response is to play *right*. Similarly, (*up, right*) fails the self-interest test; if Column plays *right*, Row is better off playing *down*. (*down, right*) is also flawed. If Row plays *down*, Column is better off playing *left*.

(*down, left*) is another story. If Row plays *down*, Column's best response is to play *left*. Also, if Column plays *left*, Row's best response is to play *down*. (*down, left*) is an equilibrium here. *Down* is best for Row, given Column is playing *left*; and *left* is best for Column, given Row is playing *down*. Notice how Row expects Column to play *left* and plays accordingly, and Column expects Row to play *down* and plays accordingly.[12] Mutual best response is the theme. We also may recall this is the idea we invoked in Chapter 2 to identify the behavior of the two competing producers.

Games of this sort (two players, each with a finite number of choices, and simultaneous play) may have one equilibrium, as in our illustration. They may have no equilibrium, unless we allow randomized strategies. They also may have multiple equilibria.[13] When invoking equilibrium behavior, we will structure our settings

---

[12]The task of finding an equilibrium here is helped by the fact Row has a dominating choice. No matter what Column does, Row is better off playing *down*.

[13]Change Row's expected utility in the lower right cell from 6 to 1. (*down, left*) remains an

so an equilibrium exists without randomization. Also, in dealing with incentive games we will encounter multiple equilibria, but it will be clear from the context which equilibrium should be emphasized. In general, though, we should know these games are not necessarily this friendly.

sequential play

It is also important to understand the rules of the game matter. To illustrate, suppose we change our story so that Row moves first. What this means is Row decides, and that decision is observed by Column before Column's decision. Suppose Row selects *up*. Column's best response is surely to play *right*. Row's expected utility is 4. Alternatively, if Row plays *down*, Column's best response is to play *left*. Row's expected utility is 2 < 4. The equilibrium is now *up* followed by *right*.[14] Here both players prefer sequential play, with Row moving first. Alternatively, both prefer Row be able to commit to a particular choice. This removes an element of strategy from the encounter and improves both players' prospects.

Contrast this with the case where Column moves first. The equilibrium is *left* followed by *down*. Simultaneous or sequential play with Column moving first is a matter of indifference to the two players.

The important point is one of assessing uncertainties. We use probabilities to structure natural or nonstrategic uncertainties, such as technology change, demand, or cost uncertainty. We use equilibrium analysis to structure strategic uncertainties, such as competitor response uncertainty. In this way, equilibrium analysis allows us to assess strategic uncertainty in systematic fashion.

Summary

Economic behavior is the primary vehicle we will use to examine the use of accounting information for managerial purposes. This has the advantage of stressing economic forces. It allows us to be explicit about risk and risk aversion. It also allows us to be specific about how information is used. Under the expected utility story, preference is factored into taste (especially taste for risk) and belief components. Information affects beliefs, via systematic probability revision. It is also a short step to extend the story to strategic interaction.

Of course, this highly structured view of choice behavior carries a price. The individual is required to have consistent preferences. Smooth preferences are also required, though this is a technical issue that addresses pathological cases. Expected

---

equilibrium, but now (*up, right*) is also an equilibrium. The latter is better for both players, though in general there is reason to expect conflict over which equilibrium is best. Conversely, change Row's expected utility in the upper left cell from 1 to 3. Now we have no equilibrium, absent randomized strategies.

[14] So much for dominating strategies!

utility, in turn, carries this one step further, demanding an independence between tastes and beliefs.

Yet we will have occasion to depart from the highly structured regimen of expected utility representation. Framing decisions in particular ways may evoke particular cognitive patterns, for example. Also, statistical estimation is not quite consistent with having prior beliefs that are consistently revised in the light of new information. There are times when economic forces, complete with consistency and smoothness (and independence), capture the important features of the matter. Other times, a less disciplined and more cognitive view is appropriate.

Bibliographic Notes

Rationality, in the sense of preference being represented by a utility measure, is a well-studied and controversial subject, especially the expected utility variant. Machina [1987] provides a review. Demski [1980] provides an introduction to the connections with measure theory and choice among information sources. Deeper treatments are available in many places; favorites are Krantz and associates [1971] and Kreps [1988]. The world of strategic encounter and equilibrium behavior is dealt with in introductory fashion by Dixit and Nalebuff [1991] and the classic of Luce and Raiffa [1957]. Tirole [1988] provides a more technical introduction. Bazerman [1990], Dawes [1988], and Nisbett and Ross [1990] deal with the cognitive side of judgment and choice.

Problems and Exercises

1. What does it mean when we say consistency is the central feature of economic rationality? Might an individual characterized by undivided pursuit of wealth be economically rational? Might an individual characterized by undivided pursuit of social justice be economically rational?

2. How does information improve the quality of a decision? What is done in the absence of information? Continuing, a common colloquialism is that of "needed information." For example, accounting policy makers frequently describe their work as providing the information needed by investors. Is the idea of needed information consistent with economic rationality?

3. Define and contrast the terms certain equivalent and risk premium.

4. The text claims the term accounting principles is a misnomer, to the extent that it refers to an ability to design or specify the accounting method without specifying the context. Carefully explain this argument. Why is context so important in using and designing the accounting product?

5. *consistency*

Let A = {a,b,c} be a set of three alternatives. Imagine asking someone to rank the alternatives, as best they can. Give four possible responses to such a request, such that the first two display economic rationality and the second two do not.

For the first two responses, assign numerical values to the three alternatives such that the ranking of the numerical assignments agrees with the original response. Provide another set of numerical values that also agrees with the original response. Why are your numerical valuations not unique?

6. *certain equivalents*

Ralph is contemplating a lottery. A fair coin will be tossed. If the coin shows "heads," Ralph will be paid 100 dollars. If the coin shows "tails," Ralph will be paid nothing. So the expected value of this lottery is $.5(100) + .5(0) = 50$.

To think about Ralph's risk aversion, we will compare the certain equivalent for this lottery with its expected value. (Alternatively, the risk premium is the expected value less the certain equivalent.) Suppose Ralph's utility function for wealth is given by the function $U(\hat{w})$, for wealth level $\hat{w}$. Exclusive of this lottery, Ralph's current wealth is $w \geq 0$. So, recognizing initial wealth w, think of the certain equivalent for the lottery itself as that value CE for which

$$U(w+CE) = .5U(w+100) + .5U(w+0).$$

Notice the lottery is combined with the initial wealth of w. Overall, this is equivalent to a wealth of w + CE. Adding the lottery, then, is equivalent to increasing the wealth by the amount CE.

a] Suppose $U(\hat{w})$ is the square root of $\hat{w}$. Let the initial wealth be w = 0. Determine and interpret CE. In particular, why is CE < 50? Also, why is CE > 0?

b] Use the same root utility. Determine CE for $w \in \{0,5,10,25,50,100,500,1000\}$. Also construct a graph of CE as a function of w. Interpret your finding.

c] Let $U(\hat{w}) = -exp\langle-r\hat{w}\rangle$, with r = .01. Repeat the construction in [b] above. (Hint: under w = 0 you should find CE = 37.99.) Interpret your finding.

d] Let $U(\hat{w}) = -exp\langle-r\hat{w}\rangle$. Determine CE for $r \in \{.0005, .001, .01, .06, .1, 1\}$. Graph CE as a function of r. How do you interpret this finding? What happened to w in your construction?

7. *use of information*

Return to the setting of Table 4.2. The bottom two rows depict cases where choice is delayed until after an information source reveals something. Yet each is described in terms of outcomes and their probabilities. How were the probabilities in the bottom two rows derived?

8. *decision analysis*

Return to the setting of Table 4.2, but now assume the utility function is $U(\hat{w})$ = $-exp\langle-r\hat{w}\rangle$, for wealth $\hat{w}$. Set initial wealth at $w = 0$, and r at .01.

a] Suppose no information is available. Determine the best choice, its expected utility, and its certain equivalent.

b] Suppose the noted imperfect information is available. Determine the best choice if good news is received, and the best choice if bad news is received. With these choices specified, calculate the expected utility and certain equivalent.

c] Do the same for perfect information.

9. *scaling the utility function*

A seemingly awkward part of using the negative exponential utility function is the fact it is negative. Consider a utility function of $U(\hat{w}) = 10 - exp\langle-r\hat{w}\rangle$, with r = .01. Repeat parts [a] and [b] of problem 8 above. Why are the choices and certain equivalents unaffected by the addition of 10 units to the utility scale?[15]

10. *useful and useless information*

Ralph faces a choice problem in which the dollar outcome is uncertain. Ralph thinks of the uncertainty as reflecting natural and economy-wide events. For simplicity, four such events or states are possible. Denote them s_1, s_2, s_3, and s_4. The events or states are equally likely.

Ralph is risk neutral and must select from a menu of three possible choices. The outcome structure is displayed below.

	s_1	s_2	s_3	s_4
one	225	225	225	100
two	900	900	100	100
three	625	625	625	100

Thus if choice two is taken, Ralph faces 50-50 odds on an outcome of 900 or an outcome of 100.

a] Determine Ralph's best choice.

b] Now suppose Ralph can purchase information before making a choice. The information source will tell whether the actual state is s_1 or s_2 versus s_3 or s_4. You should think of this as telling Ralph whether the state will be "low" or "high" in terms of the indexing system. Put differently, the information will tell Ralph whether the outcome is confined to the two left-hand or the two right-hand columns

---

[15]In an expected utility setting, the utility function can be multiplied by an arbitrary positive constant, as well as be increased by an arbitrary constant. $U(\hat{w})$ and $\alpha + \beta U(\hat{w})$ tell the same story, as long as $\beta > 0$.

of the outcome table. How much would he pay for this information?[16] Summarize your analysis in a table patterned after Table 4.2.

c] Consider the case where the information costs 500. Ralph will not pay such a price. The information is not needed. What does Ralph substitute for the lack of information?

d] Suppose the information structure will reveal whether s_4 is true, that is, whether life is in the left three columns or the right-most column of the outcome table. How much would Ralph pay for this information?

11. *decision analysis and value of information*
Ralph is contemplating four possible choices, cleverly labeled one, two, three, and four. The outcome of any choice depends on the state of the economy. For analysis purposes, Ralph models this as four *equally likely* states, imaginatively denoted s_1, s_2, s_3, and s_4. (Think of this as various combinations of weather and consumer expectations, for example.) The net gain to Ralph, as a function of the option chosen and state of the economy, is displayed below:

	s_1	s_2	s_3	s_4
one	100	90	30	20
two	30	20	100	90
three	30	150	30	30
four	30	30	30	150

If number three is selected, for example, and state s_2 occurs, a net gain of 150 will result. Of course, the states are uncertain; number three thus offers a .25 probability of a 150 gain and a .75 probability of a 30 gain. Ralph is risk neutral in this exercise, except in part [b].

a] Draw a decision tree for Ralph; label all choices, outcomes, and probabilities.

b] Calculate the expected utility for Ralph for each of the four choices. Assume here, and only here, that Ralph is risk averse with utility measured by the square root of the gain. What is the certain equivalent for each of the choices?

c] Calculate the expected utility for Ralph for each of the four choices. Assume here and for all remaining parts of the exercise that Ralph is risk neutral.

d] Suppose before acting Ralph can learn, from an expert forecaster, whether the state of the economy will be in $\{s_1, s_3\}$ or will be in $\{s_2, s_4\}$. Notice the mnemonic of "odd" or "even." If the forecaster says odd, for example, then Ralph knows the state

---

[16]This maximum amount is called the value of the information. Under risk neutrality it is the expected value of the outcome when using the information, less the expected value of the outcome when denied the information.

will be s_1 or s_3, just not which one. What is the maximum amount Ralph would pay for this forecaster's service?

e]   Suppose instead of the "odd" or "even" story a second forecaster is able to forecast whether the state will be in $\{s_1,s_2\}$ or in $\{s_3,s_4\}$. Notice the mnemonic here of "low" or "high." What is the maximum amount Ralph would pay for this second forecaster's service? This should be answered on the assumption Ralph does not hire the first forecaster.

f]   Finally, suppose the two forecasters jointly approach Ralph and offer to combine their services. What is the maximum amount Ralph would pay for the joint forecasting service?

g]   You now have three value of information calculations: the first source, the second source, and the two sources together. Notice additivity is not present. The sum of the first two values does not equal the third. Why is additivity not present here?

12. *constant risk aversion and value of information*
    Repeat problem 11 above for the case where Ralph's utility is negative exponential, $U(\hat{w}) = -exp\langle -r\hat{w}\rangle$, where $\hat{w}$ is now interpreted as the net gain. Let $r = .001$. (Hint: when deriving the most Ralph would pay for the information it is easiest to convert the no information and information cases to certain equivalents and then take the difference. This short cut depends on constant risk aversion; see the following problem.)

13. *complications with nonconstant risk aversion*
    Return to problem 10 above. Now assume Ralph is risk averse with utility equal to the square root of the outcome. So, for example, $U(225) = 15$. What is the maximum amount Ralph would pay for the "low" versus "high" information?

14. *dominance*
    Ralph is contemplating various lotteries. The possible prizes are 100, 200, 300, or 400 dollars. Assume in what follows that more is strictly preferred to less dollars. Below are some representative lotteries:

	100	200	300	400
a	.1			.9
b	.2			.8
c	.2		.8	
d	.25	.25	.25	.25
e	.15	.35	.25	.25
f	.24	.21	.25	.30

For example, lottery *c* returns the prize of 100 with probability .2 and the prize of 300 with probability .8.

a] Consider lotteries *a*, *b*, and *c*. Which choice from among the three is best? Try an expected utility analysis with several different $U(\cdot)$ functions. Why does lottery *a* always turn out to be best?

b] Do the same thing for lotteries *d* and *f*.

c] Now consider lotteries *e* and *f*. Exhibit one $U(\cdot)$ function such that *e* is the best choice and another such that *f* is the best choice. What is the explanation?

15. *equilibrium analysis*

Locate an equilibrium in the following simultaneous move game, played between protagonists Row and Column.

	left	*right*
up	60, 10	0, 12
down	40,-40	2, 2

Now assume the rules of the game call for sequential play. Column plays first and Row sees Column's choice before acting. Locate an equilibrium. Contrast this equilibrium with that located in the simultaneous move game.

16. *risk sharing*

Ralph owns a risky lottery. With probability .5, Ralph will receive 20,000 dollars and with probability .5 Ralph will receive nothing. Ralph's utility function is given by $U(\hat{w}) = -exp\langle -r\hat{w}\rangle$, for ending wealth of $\hat{w}$. Let r = .0001.

a] Determine and interpret Ralph's certain equivalent for this lottery. (You should find 5,662.19 an interesting number.)

b] Ralph meets a second individual, one with an identical utility function. This second individual presently has no lottery, but possesses w = 7,000. Ralph, always the opportunist, offers to sell this second individual half the action for the interesting sum of 3,798.85. Thus, if the second person pays Ralph this amount, she receives 10,000 if Ralph's lottery pays off and nothing if it does not. Suppose this second individual accepts Ralph's offer. What is Ralph's certain equivalent for the modified lottery (i.e., 3,798.85 for certain plus a 50-50 chance at 10,000)? Is the offer attractive to the second person? (Hint: work out this person's certain equivalent.)

c] How do you interpret the phenomenon in part [b] above?

d] Think about this a little more. Suppose Ralph offers to pay the second individual amount b (big) if the lottery pays off and amount s (small) if it does not. So Ralph's expected utility will be

$$-.5exp\langle -.0001(20,000-b)\rangle - .5exp\langle -.0001(0-s)\rangle;$$

and the other person's expected utility will be

$-.5exp\langle-.0001(7{,}000+b)\rangle -.5exp\langle-.0001(7{,}000+s)\rangle$.

We'll make b and s as good as possible from Ralph's perspective, subject to the other person being willing to accept the offer. We solve the following problem:

maximize $\qquad -.5exp\langle-.0001(20{,}000-b)\rangle-.5exp\langle-.0001(0-s)\rangle$

subject to $\qquad -.5exp\langle-.0001(7{,}000+b)\rangle -.5exp\langle-.0001(7{,}000+s)\rangle \geq$
$\qquad\qquad -exp\langle-.0001(7{,}000)\rangle = -exp\langle-.7\rangle$.

Verify that b = 10,000 - 3,798.85 = 6,201.15 and s = - 3,798.85 is the optimal solution to this optimization problem. (To do this, use your favorite spreadsheet with a built-in nonlinear optimizer.)

e] What do you suppose makes it best for Ralph to sell the other person exactly half the action for some price?

5

Product Costing

The accounting library contains many calculations of product cost. Financial reporting requires an end-of-period accounting valuation of inventory. The accounting library also records movements of goods from one location to another within the organization. A manufacturing organization might be arranged into manufacturing and marketing divisions. The goods are transferred to various warehouses in the marketing division, once manufacturing is complete. Accounting records will show the historical cost of these transferred goods.

In addition, we usually frame managerial decisions in revenue (or benefit) and cost (or sacrifice) terms. This framing calls for estimates of the cost of various activities. These cost constructions often use data in the accounting library. They are also likely to be heavily influenced by the costing framework that the organization uses to maintain its accounting library. Thus, directly or indirectly, product costing techniques have a striking effect on the way in which costs are estimated and used.

This chapter is the first of several that deal with the question of how to estimate the cost of a product. It is best to think expansively about the setting. The product might be a service to be provided a new customer, an entire array of services, an item of merchandise, an entire department store, a new computer chassis, an educational program, a political campaign, and so on. The purpose might be financial reporting, tax reporting, managerial performance evaluation, analysis of whether to add or drop a product line, pricing, and the like. The organization might be a manufacturing, service, or merchandising entity. It might be organized as a proprietorship, corporation, or partnership; it might be a public or a nonprofit organization. The art of product costing is ubiquitous.

The purpose of this chapter is to provide an overview of the accountant's product costing art. We begin with an example. Basic building blocks of linear approximation and aggregation are then introduced. We next combine these building blocks to provide a general description of how product costs are estimated. Subsequent chapters illustrate this general description, examining a variety of costing difficulties and introducing the topic of cost allocation.

Example

Ralph, Ltd., is a management consulting organization. During its most recent year, Ralph provided service to two clients. One client, a manufacturing firm, hired Ralph to design and install a computerized accounting system. The other client, a municipality, hired Ralph to study labor turnover in the city government. Both projects were completed just as the year came to a close.

Ralph, Ltd., is legally organized as a corporation. All common stock is owned by Ralph. Besides Ralph, the firm employs three associates, several technical specialists, and several nontechnical staff.

Financial records for the year in question show the following costs were incurred.

Ralph's salary	$150,000
salary of first associate	120,000
salary of second associate	90,000
salary of third associate	80,000
salaries of technical employees	115,000
salaries of nontechnical employees	95,000
fringe benefits (insurance, employment taxes, pensions, vacations, etc.)	130,000
subcontracting	
manufacturing client	110,000
municipal client	15,000
other reimbursable costs	
manufacturing client	70,000
municipal client	35,000
advertising	15,000
supplies	48,000
transportation (other than reimbursable)	32,000
professional development	135,000
equipment	140,000
office space, heat, light, etc.	220,000
federal, state, and local taxes (exclusive of employment taxes)	95,000
interest	25,000
total	$1,720,000

Notice some costs are identified by client, i.e., subcontracting and reimbursable items. The salaries of the three associates are separately identified, while those of the others are grouped into technical and nontechnical totals. The data for our cost construction exercise arrive in aggregate form.

Professional development covers expenditures on technical materials and short courses that the employees use to maintain and increase their technical expertise. Transportation costs are due largely to leased automobiles that are used by Ralph, the three associates, and some technical employees. This is considered a routine cost of doing business and is not explicitly billed to clients. Air travel, on the other hand, is routinely billed as a reimbursable cost to specific clients.

Depreciation is included in the equipment category. Lease amortization is included in the office space and transportation categories.

Ralph and the three associates keep detailed records of how their time is spent. These records show the following.

	manufacturing client	municipal client	unbilled
Ralph	20%	30%	50%
first associate	75	0	25
second associate	0	70	30
third associate	70	30	0

Unbilled time refers to time spent by the respective employee that cannot be directly associated with any of the client projects. Time spent on professional development, searching for and bidding on new projects, training staff, and general administrative chores are all lumped into this category. Ralph expects the unbilled percentage to average about 25%.

Bonuses were also paid the various employees. The bonus pool was 250,000 dollars. It was shared among all employees in proportion to their salaries. The bonus was paid two months after the end of the year in question. Thus, it is not included in the above tally. Ralph, Ltd., also declared and paid a dividend of 120,000 at the time the bonuses were paid.

Exclusive of the bonuses and dividends, these costs total 1,720,000. What was the cost of the manufacturing client's project? What was the cost of the municipal client's project? (Do not prejudge the issue of whether the bonuses or dividends are costs.)

one among many answers

In Table 5.1 we show how a typical accounting system might answer these questions. (000) have been omitted, to avoid distractions.

The cost construction begins with the salaries of Ralph and the three associates. We know their total salaries, and the breakdown of their time across the two clients and the unbilled category. This leads to respective assignments of 176, 132, and 132. Notice we are treating the unbilled category as a third product at this point. More will be said about this choice.

Now consider the salaries of the other employees. Here we decided to assign these salaries to the three products based on the above identified salary break downs.[1] Think of the 440 total salary of Ralph and the associates as labor input that we can directly identify with the three products. We then assign the cost of the other

---

[1] We might want to use time rather than salary of Ralph and the associates here. We also might want to ask Ralph for a subjective estimate of how the other employees were used. At this juncture we are describing the basic philosophy of cost construction. Once this is well understood, we will turn our attention to the questions of how to adapt what we find in the accounting library to our purpose at hand and how to structure what is placed in the library in the first place.

labor inputs in proportion to how these directly identified inputs are used: 176/440, 132/440, and 132/440. These calculations provide us the noted total labor cost (exclusive of fringe and bonus) for the three products: 260, 195, and 195 for a total of 650.

Table 5.1: Product Cost Construction for Ralph, Ltd., (000)				
cost category	manu-facturing client	munici-pal client	un-billed	total
labor cost				
Ralph				150
.2(150)	30			
.3(150)		45		
.5(150)			75	
first associate				120
.75(120)	90			
.25(120)			30	
second associate				90
.70(90)		63		
.30(90)			27	
third associate				80
.70(80)	56			
.30(80)		24		
subtotal	176	132	132	440
technical employees				115
(176/440)(115)	46			
(132/440)(115)		34.5		
(132/440)(115)			34.5	
nontechnical employees				95
(176/440)(95)	38			
(132/440)(95)		28.5		
(132/440)(95)			28.5	
total, exclusive of fringe & bonus	260	195	195	650
fringe (130/650 = 20%)	52	39	39	130
bonus (250/650 = 38.5%)	100	75	75	250
total labor cost	412	309	309	1,030

Continued on next page.

cost category	manu-facturing client	munici-pal client	un-billed	total
Table 5.1 Continued: Product Cost Construction for Ralph, Ltd., (000)				
materials, supplies, etc.				
subcontracting	110	15		125
other directly identified items	70	35		105
supplies (48/650 = 7.4%)	19.2	14.4	14.4	48
transportation (32/650 = 4.9%)	12.8	9.6	9.6	32
subtotal	212	74	24	310
product cost (labor, materials, supplies, etc.)	624	383	333	1,340
unallocated costs				
advertising				15
development				135
equipment				140
office space				220
interest				25
taxes				95
subtotal				630
total				1,970

Next we tackle the fringe and bonus. Both are treated as a percentage of total labor cost, exclusive of fringe and bonus. We are told this is how the bonus was determined. One might take the view that the bonus is a type of periodic profit sharing and should not be assigned to individual products. This view has merit. Our construction treats it as another conduit for delivering compensation for employee services.

Fringe is likely to be a complicated affair. Younger employees have less vacation time than older employees. FICA taxes apply only up to a particular salary limit. Health insurance is a complicated package arrangement with the insurance vendor. Our construction deals with this in a nearly cavalier and common fashion. We simply average!

In this way we assign the total labor cost of 1,030 to the three products: 412, 309, and 309, respectively.

Materials, supplies, and so on are treated in a parallel manner. Subcontracting costs are identified by specific projects. We assign them accordingly. Other items are also identified by specific projects.

Supplies are not so identified. We chose to assign supplies the way we assigned fringe and bonus payments. This reflects the hunch that supplies are used with labor, and labor cost exclusive of fringe and bonus is a reasonable indicator of labor input. Transportation is treated the same way. Since transportation largely consists of automobiles supplied to various employees, it seems reasonable to assign these costs in that fashion.

The remaining costs are not assigned to specific products. We therefore wind up with a cost of 624 for the manufacturing client's project, 383 for the municipal client's project, and 333 for the "unbilled product."

What about some of our choices in this construction? Were we wise in our handling of transportation? Should we turn around and assign the unbilled product? Surely equipment and office space could be assigned to products. Feelings of uneasiness should not be suppressed. Cost construction is a matter of choice.

For example, we *decided* it was best to treat unbilled as a separate product. An important reason is that a major activity for our consulting firm is developing new clients and new skills. In this sense, one of today's products is getting ready or preparing to serve better tomorrow's clients. The current period cost of this preparation is reflected in the unbilled category.

Perhaps, then, we should have assigned all advertising (15) and all development (135) to the unbilled category. We *decided* against such an assignment because the unbilled category is in reality a murky joint product. We have lumped administrative items into this category as well. We cannot fully separate the two items. So it seemed best to adopt the construction presented. For the same reason we did not search into prior years' records to find an unbilled category to assign to the current projects.

Dividends present another dilemma. Our inclination, especially given training in financial accounting, is to keep it invisible in the cost construction. Remember, though, Ralph owns 100% of the capital stock. Is the dividend a payment to capital or a payment to labor or a return of capital?

Cost construction is a matter of choice. Our choices are catalogued in Table 5.2. We reiterate that the product costing exercise is one of constructing expressions of cost. Countless choices are involved in any such construction. We will learn that these choices depend, in subtle ways, on the circumstances at hand. For the moment, the important point is to acknowledge the presence of choices in the algorithm.

central features of the construction

Several features of our construction, and the setting in which it takes place, should be noted. Some labor and material inputs were identified directly with the products in question. Subcontracting, various materials, and time breakdowns for Ralph and the associates are of this nature. These identifications may be more or less exact. But the identification data were available, and we implicitly regarded them as sufficiently reliable to use in the construction exercise.[2] In addition, this

---

[2]Quality of source data will not be taken for granted in our study. Just to illustrate, suppose one

identification may or may not line up with payments for the inputs. Consider payments to the three associates. We identify their salaries and prorate them over the products in question. But fringe is also a part of the payment for their services. We don't have explicit prices for fringe, only the total of accrued payments. So we average.

Table 5.2: Choices in Product Cost Construction for Ralph, Ltd.,	
cost category	basis on which assigned to product
Ralph's salary	direct identification
salary of associates	direct identification
salaries of technical employees	proportional to directly identified salaries
salaries of nontechnical employees	proportional to directly identified salaries
fringe benefits	proportional to assigned salaries
employee bonuses	proportional to assigned salaries
subcontracting	direct identification
other identifiable materials, etc.	direct identification
advertising	not assigned to product
supplies	proportional to assigned salaries
transportation	proportional to assigned salaries
professional development	not assigned to product
equipment	not assigned to product
office space, heat, light, etc.	not assigned to product
federal, state, and local taxes	not assigned to product
interest	not assigned to product
dividends	not assigned to product

Contrast this with the subcontracts. There, we presume each subcontract explicitly identifies the client projects and subcontractor payments. End of story, perhaps. What if there is a long term relationship between Ralph and a subcontractor, and it is implicitly understood payments are "smoothed" through time? For example, how do we interpret the case where the auto mechanic fixes a minor item and says, "I'll catch you next time"?

Of course, many inputs are not identified by product. For some inputs this is impossible. How much of the office space is used by each product? We might

---

of the associates is new and eager to succeed. One client is "old hat." The organization has considerable experience with the client and its problems. The other client is new, and is calling on the organization to work in new and novel ways. Can we rely on our anxious associate to be consciously and subconsciously unbiased in estimating time spent on the two clients? The federal data bank on fishing stories has a similar problem.

prorate cost of office space among the products, but this space is jointly used by all the organization's productive activities.

Other inputs are not identified by product; to do so would be impractical. Supplies is an illustrative category. We don't know what is in this category, or even what each separate item costs. What we know is that a category called "everything else" is used to account for all materials that are not accounted for in more explicit fashion. Some items in this category are treated on an accrual basis, while others are treated on a cash basis. The organization does not keep track of separate items or their respective costs. Everything else, so to speak, is lumped together.

The economist, on the other hand, knows each input and the price paid for each. Jointness precludes separable cost functions, but ambiguity over input usage is never an issue. Our setting is not nearly as amicable. We know categories of inputs, more or less, and accounting cost totals (as distinct from market prices) for the various categories. We are then faced with the task of assigning categories to products in a way that will give some meaning to the notion "cost of a product."

This is why we stressed the common theme of choices in cost construction.[3] We chose not to assign some categories to products. We chose to assign other categories to products using particular assignment techniques. We chose to assign the directly identified categories to the respective products. Even this direct assignment may be ambiguous. For example, we often can associate some labor with a specific product. If the organization has a policy of full employment and we want to estimate the marginal cost of that product, it is not clear that we should assign the cost of the directly identified labor to the product.

Product costing is a well-developed art. It is an art practiced in the face of considerable ambiguity. Our immediate aim is to place some structure on this art form, as an aid to documenting the choices that lead to typical cost constructions.

The Accountant's Product Costing Art

We begin by contrasting the accountant's task with that of the economist. The economist begins with all factors, all factor prices, and the production function in full view. In this luxurious state, the cost function is derived, and various product cost measures derived. The accounting system attempts to emulate this derivation. But it begins with a handicap. Some factors are known, some market prices are known, and categories and averages of others are known. Relative to an economist, the accountant's product is by necessity delivered with ambiguity. To engage in allegory, the accountant is called upon to create nouvelle French cuisine in a high school cafeteria.[4]

---

[3]The choices are even more subtle. They extend into designing the data gathering in the first place. Which items to group together, which ancillary data to collect, and which minor items to treat on a cash basis are all matters of choice.

[4]A less apocryphal analogy arises with price indices. There we take a basket of goods and track

Return to our notation in Chapter 2. Suppose a firm produces three products, with quantities denoted q_1, q_2, and q_3. We interpret q_1 as the quantity of consulting services delivered to a manufacturing client and q_2 as the quantity of consulting services delivered to a municipal client. q_3 is interpreted as a group of development services aimed at future customers. It is akin to units of product produced to inventory rather than for immediate sale. q_3 is a self-produced set of inputs that will be used in production in a future period.

The inputs used in production are listed as z_1, z_2, ..., z_m. The production function relates inputs to outputs: $(q_1,q_2,q_3) = f(z_1,z_2,...,z_m)$. We face a particular short-run setting if some of these inputs are fixed at specified amounts. Combining this knowledge with prices in the factor markets (i.e., $\hat{P}_1$, ..., $\hat{P}_m$) we construct the firm's economic cost function. This is done by finding the least total expenditure on inputs that is consistent with producing the given level of output. In particular, suppose we are in a short-run setting with input k fixed at level $\bar{z}_k$. Then the construction leads to the short-run cost function denoted $C(q_1,q_2,q_3;\bar{z}_k)$. This is all a brief review of material developed in Chapter 2.

Next we place some suggestive structure on this cost function. Rewrite it in the following form:[5]

$$C(q_1,q_2,q_3;\bar{z}_k) = G(q_1;\bar{z}_k) + H(q_2;\bar{z}_k) + I(q_3;\bar{z}_k) + J(q_1,q_2,q_3;\bar{z}_k).$$

If the $J(\cdot)$ component is a constant, we have a very friendly cost function. The marginal cost of any product does not depend on the quantities of the other products. More generally, our intuition suggests some cost items will depend only on the quantity of the output in question, and others will depend on the quantity of all outputs.

Imagine a municipal government. Let q_1 be the amount of household garbage collected and q_2 be the amount of public education. More garbage collection will require more garbage trucks. It seems the number of trucks required to collect a given amount of garbage would not depend on the quantity of education. This suggests that the expenditure on garbage trucks would be reflected in the $G(q_1;\bar{z}_k)$ term. Similarly, more education will require more teachers. Assume the required number of teachers does not depend on the quantity of garbage collection. Presumably, the expenditure on teachers would be reflected in the $H(q_2;\bar{z}_k)$ term.

General administrative support is another matter. Personnel services and bookkeeping are likely to depend on the level of all activities. This suggests

---

the market price of that basket of goods through time. Of course, the quality of the goods may change with time, the array of substitutes may change, relative prices of other goods may change in different fashion, and so on. We use the price index to give us an overall picture, recognizing its limitations. The same holds in accounting, even when we do not use constant dollar techniques.

[5]We can always express the cost function in this form. If $G(q_1;\bar{z}_k)$, $H(q_2;\bar{z}_k)$ and $I(q_3;\bar{z}_k)$ are all identically zero, we have merely said $C(q_1,q_2,q_3;\bar{z}_k) = J(q_1,q_2,q_3;\bar{z}_k)$.

expenditures on these types of items would be reflected in the $J(q_1,q_2,q_3;\bar{z}_k)$ term.

Now take our suggestive cost function and return to Ralph, Ltd., and the cost construction in Table 5.1. Do we have $G(q_1;\bar{z}_k) = 624,000$, $H(q_2;\bar{z}_k) = 383,000$, $I(q_3;\bar{z}_k) = 333,000$, and $J(q_1,q_2,q_3;\bar{z}_k) = 630,000$? Surely we jest.

Chapters 2 and 3 are important here. Recall that accounting cost records systematically exclude capital cost. So to begin, we have items in $C(q_1,q_2,q_3;\bar{z}_k)$ that are not included in the accountant's tally of total cost for the period. This is the reason for our warning to think carefully about how to treat dividends in the Ralph, Ltd., example. Dividends might be return of capital, might be a payment to capital suppliers, or might even be a payment to Ralph for labor services.

Also recall that timing differences between economic and accounting income are likely. This implies we should anticipate timing differences on when particular cost items are recognized. Economic and accounting depreciation differ. Cash recognition procedures applied to miscellaneous supplies is another example. Various employee bonuses provide additional illustrations. In addition, the economic cost function presumes ruthless, mistake free production. Should we presume this to be the case in Ralph, Ltd.?

Finally, $C(q_1,q_2,q_3;\bar{z}_k)$ reflects an assumption that all inputs and all prices of inputs are known. The accountant, as we have discussed, does not have this knowledge. So, even if the total accounting cost agreed with $C(q_1,q_2,q_3;\bar{z}_k)$, we should expect slippage in the individual component constructions.

What, then, does the accountant do? Is there any pattern or systematic tendency that is employed in the product costing art? The answer is yes. Two building blocks are fundamental to the accountant's art: linear approximation and aggregation. These are discussed in turn. Cost allocation will be added to the recipe in a later chapter. From there we will learn to interpret the accounting data as potentially important pieces of information.

linear approximation

Consider the manner in which we assigned transportation cost to the three products in Ralph, Ltd., We took the total transportation cost of 32,000, and divided by total assigned salary cost of 650,000. Transportation cost averages 4.9% of assigned salaries. We then used the 4.9% datum to assign transportation cost to each product, as a function of their respective salary costs.

Suppose transportation cost varies with labor input. More labor input necessitates more transportation. Further suppose total assigned salaries is a good measure of labor input for this purpose. This means we should visualize transportation cost as some function of total salary cost.

What might this function look like? A typical auto lease contract calls for a monthly payment that is independent of mileage, up to a limit. The parties usually commit for several years, but monthly, weekly, and daily arrangements are also possible. In addition, mileage charges are usually imposed once mileage goes beyond the specified limit. Gasoline, insurance, tolls, parking, and so on are usually paid by the lessee.

This suggests the function would look something like that depicted in Figure 5.1. If labor input drops to zero in the short-run, the lease arrangements can likely be scaled back so only a modest payment is made.[6] If labor input jumps dramatically, the lease arrangements can likely be expanded, and on favorable grounds. The nonlinear graph in Figure 5.1, labeled the presumed cost curve, is meant to be suggestive. We gloss over details such as when to increase the fleet by another unit, and so on. The important point is we do not expect cost to be zero when labor input is zero, and we do not expect the cost to increase proportionately with labor input. For the sake of argument, our graph depicts the cost as increasing less than proportionately with labor input.

Contrast this with the manner in which we assigned the transportation cost. That assignment used the function

transportation cost = (32/650)salaries = (.049)salaries.

A salary level of 195, for example, was assigned a transportation cost of (.049)195 = 9.6. The implied cost function is also plotted in Figure 5.1. Notice we have plotted both the presumed cost function and the "linear approximation" used in our cost construction.

Figure 5.1: Presumed and Approximate Transportation Cost Curves

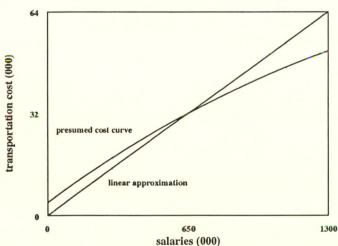

How should this be interpreted? We began our thought exercise with some presumed cost curve. For accounting purposes, we employed an assignment pro-

---

[6]Cancellation provisions are common features of automobile lease agreements.

cedure that is interpreted as an *approximation* of this presumed cost curve. The approximation may be close. Examine the graph in Figure 5.1 when salaries are close to 650. But there is no guarantee. Examine the graph when salaries are far removed from 650.

Accounting procedures invariably begin with an approximation of various components of the organization's cost curve. These approximations, in turn, are usually linear approximations. We use the phrase *local linear approximation*, or *LLA* for short, to remind ourselves of the use of this technique. The adjective *local* is carried along to remind us there is no guarantee the approximation is accurate over a wide range. The presumption is that it is sufficiently accurate over a restricted or local range.[7]

The importance of LLAs in the accountant's art is driven by three considerations. First, we simply do not know "the cost curve." We literally invented the presumed cost curve in Figure 5.1. All we really know is the single point of salaries = 650 and transportation cost = 32. Admittedly, we might collect other points from recent periods and use common sense and introspection to construct a few others.[8] Regardless, the costing exercise begins with an absence of what the economist presumes to know.

Second, even if we knew the cost curve, pragmatic considerations would lead us to use approximations. Beyond a point (no pun), there are diminishing returns to keeping track of detail. (Minutia is the operative noun.) Backing off on detail leads to an approximation. A local linear approximation turns out to be the overwhelming choice. Third, the accounting library must maintain its integrity. Verifiability is important. We must be able to verify source documents and calculations. Linear computations are easier to verify.[9]

aggregation

Imagine all the transactions that occur in a grocery story. The checkouts electronically record all the items sold. Payroll records are extremely detailed. Supplier records are also detailed. The store manager has an incomprehensible array of data. These data are aggregated for obvious reasons. The same applies to accounting records in general.

The most vivid example of this aggregation in Ralph, Ltd., is the supplies category, with a total identified cost of 48,000. Imagine what might be grouped

---

[7]This range is often called the relevant range. We will develop this terminology in subsequent chapters.

[8]Statistical procedures will be used for this purpose in Chapter 13.

[9]Pension obligations, for example, have become problematic for this reason. Elaborate, intricate calculations based on arguably subjective probability assessments are the basis on which obligations are projected.

together in this category. Miscellaneous, immaterial (pun intended) office supplies are surely included. Paper, pencils, pens, billing forms, blank time slips, and so on are all included in this manner. They are also included on a cash basis. Inventory records are not maintained for such trivial items. Computer supplies, janitorial supplies, and bulk paper are also included. The list goes on. Some individuals will use a different mix of supplies than others. One client project will entail use of a different set of supplies than another.

None of this detail is used in the cost construction exercise. Instead, we group the items together. Then we search for some expression for how the total cost of supplies varies. We search for one or more explanatory variables.[10] By its very nature this must be an approximation. We have grouped unlike items together.

Having chosen the explanatory variable (or variables), we implement this choice with an LLA. In this way we construct product cost data by working with subsets of factors, approximate expressions for how the costs of these subsets of factors vary, and by linking these building blocks to the products themselves. The linkages may be direct or second-hand. The explanatory variables used in the component of the cost function might be the products themselves or some intermediate or synthetic explanatory variable. For example, we linked the labor cost of the associates in a direct fashion, while we linked that of the technical employees in a second hand fashion.

LLA terminology

It is also useful to distinguish types of linear approximations. The general equation for a line is $y = a + bx$. Think of this as a function of x:

$$y = f(x) = a + bx.$$

By convention, we plot x on the horizontal axis and y on the vertical axis.[11]

Figure 5.2 is illustrative, where we plot $y = f(x) = 25 + 2x$. For presentation purposes, we use $0 \le x \le 20$. This implies y varies between $f(0) = 25$ and $f(20) = 65$ in the figure.

More generally, if $b = 0$, the graph is horizontal or "flat"; it has zero slope. If $b > 0$, the graph slopes upward; if $b < 0$, the graph slopes downward. The graph intercepts the y axis at $x = 0$. Stated differently, $y = a$ when $x = 0$. b is the slope[12]

---

[10]In the general estimation literature, these explanatory variables are called independent variables. Recent jargon in the accounting, marketing, and management literatures calls them cost drivers. This is a little too trendy for our taste.

[11]x is the abscissa and y is the ordinate. The function evaluated at the point $x = \hat{x}$ is denoted $f(\hat{x}) = a + b\hat{x}$. For example, $f(15) = a + 15b$.

[12]Slope is undefined if the graph is vertical, or given by the equation $x = constant$.

of the linear function y = a + bx. a is the intercept of the linear function y = a + bx. Our function in Figure 5.2 has y = 25 when x = 0, and a slope of 2.

Figure 5.2: Graph of y = 25 + 2x

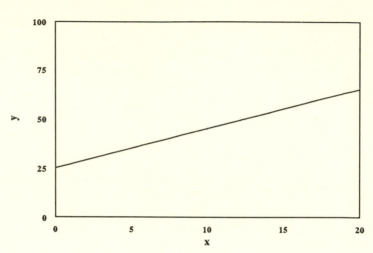

Now use these conventions to focus on a cost function, C(x) = a + bx. Cost here might be total cost, or some category of total cost. x, in turn, might be units of product or some synthetic explanatory variable. For example, we might have

y = cost of supplies = a + b(hours of assignable labor) = a + bx.

Here we would have a linear function relating cost of supplies to the synthetic explanatory variable, hours of assignable labor.

If b = 0, common usage is to say the cost of supplies is *fixed*. If a = 0, common usage is to say the cost of supplies is *strictly variable*. If a ≠ 0 and b ≠ 0, common usage is to say a is the *fixed component* of the cost of supplies and b is the *per unit variable component* of the cost of supplies.

This terminology would be precise if we were discussing an economic cost curve that was linear. Moving to an LLA requires some diligence. The algebra is the same, but the economic content is not. This leads to confusion.

Fixed and variable cost have economic meaning when we begin with the economist's cost curve. Conversely, the accountant uses a host of LLAs to construct an approximation to the economist's cost curve. Each of these LLAs relates some component of cost to some explanatory variable. This results in a function y = f(x) = a + bx. a is nothing other than the intercept of the LLA in question. b is nothing other than the slope of the LLA in question. Common usage is to call a the fixed component of the cost in question and b the per unit variable cost component of the cost in question.

It would be imprudent to deny existence of this common usage. It also would be imprudent not to dwell on the fundamental difference between (economic) fixed cost and the intercept of an LLA.

Suppose we constrain the explanatory variable to lay in some restricted range, say $x_L \leq x \leq x_U$. The interval from x_L to x_U is called the *relevant range*. It may then be the case that b is a reasonable approximation of the *marginal cost* of the cost component in question, when x is so restricted.[13] *May*, however, is a statement of possibility, not of inevitability. This is why we stress the terminology of an LLA with intercept a and slope b.

the constructive procedure

We will learn to identify and engineer specific aggregations and LLAs in our study. We close this overview of the accountant's product costing art with a paraphrase of the constructive procedure used in Ralph, Ltd.,

The cost construction begins with a classification of the identified costs of inputs. This classification is the aggregation of various cost components into a manageable number of categories. (These categories are called *cost pools*.) From our study of financial accounting, we know the costs identified for each category or pool will be some combination of actual expenditures and accrual measures of resource consumption.

For the sake of discussion, suppose we have 7 such categories along with three products:

category	description
1	directly identifiable with first product
2	directly identifiable with second product
3	directly identifiable with third product
4	indirectly identifiable with products
5	indirectly identifiable with products
6	period cost
7	period cost

Think of this as beginning with all product and period cost for the period and cataloguing these costs into 7 piles, categories, or pools. Extensive aggregation is the key. *Product costs* are costs that will be assigned to specific products; *period costs* are costs that will not be assigned to specific products, but will instead be assigned to the period.

Next we select an LLA for each product cost category. Category 1 consists of factor costs that can be directly identified with the first product. So we use an

---

[13]Recall that marginal and marginal variable cost are identical, given a particular short-run cost curve.

explanatory variable of units of the first product. Parallel choices are made for categories 2 and 3.

Subcontracting and other directly identifiable items were handled in this fashion in Ralph, Ltd., Ralph's salary and the salaries of the associates were also handled in this fashion. In effect, we placed a portion of each salary in the respective directly identifiable categories. Typically we would have many categories that can be directly identified with the various products. Our illustration simply uses one such category for each product.

Category 4 consists of factor costs that we have grouped together and will assign to the three products in some fashion. We must now select some explanatory variable that can be used to relate category 4 cost to products. To illustrate, it may be possible to identify directly the labor input of some employees with specific products. These employees are called direct labor. In turn, we may find it reasonable to view category 4 costs as well explained by the synthetic explanatory variable of x = hours or dollars of direct labor. This gives us our LLA for category 4.

Salaries of the technical and nontechnical employees were handled in this fashion in Ralph, Ltd., We used x = dollars of direct labor as the synthetic explanatory variable in our LLA for these costs. Similarly, in dealing with the fringe benefits we used x = total assigned labor cost as a synthetic explanatory variable.

Category 5 also consists of factor costs that we have grouped together and will assign to the three products. Here we might use a different explanatory variable in the LLA. Perhaps this is a manufacturing firm and we know how much manufacturing capacity, measured by hours of machine time, was used by each product. If we find it reasonable to view category 5 costs as well explained by x = machine hours, we use machine hours to assign the cost to the products. Alternative stories could be told for, say, the cost of directly identified inputs, the total of Category 1 through Category 4 costs assigned, and so on.

Finally, the Category 6 and Category 7 costs are particular aggregations of period costs. They will be assigned to the period, not the products. Of course this does not imply we are uninterested in their economic structure. It just means they are not part of the product cost calculation.

This is the general way in which product costs are constructed. We will encounter many variations on this theme. For example, we may use more than one explanatory variable for a particular cost category. We may even use a nonlinear approximation on rare occasion.[14] The extent of the aggregation will vary from situation to situation. In each case, though, the recipe is the same. We combine aggregations and approximations to mold product cost statistics. Cost allocation is also part of the recipe, but that is getting ahead of our story.

---

[14]We will refine this overview when standard costs are introduced. Aggregations and LLAs will remain. They will be further refined by use of estimated costs, as long as actual and estimate do not diverge by too large an amount.

Short-Run versus Long-Run Cost

A remaining question in this overview is whether the accountant produces product cost statistics that are more closely related to the firm's long-run or short-run cost curve. The intuitive answer is probably long-run, if we follow GAAP. But the underlying argument is too cavalier.

back to economics

To explore this question, we return to the setting of a *single* product firm. This allows us easily to draw a graph of the cost curve. More important, it allows us to speak routinely of average cost.

In Chapter 2 we explored an example in which three factors of production were used in the production of a single product. The long-run cost curve was given by $C(q) = 200q - 18q^2 + q^3$. The short-run cost curve, with the third input fixed at level $\bar{z}_3$, was given by $C(q;\bar{z}_3) = 162 + 204.5q - 25q^2 + 1.5q^3$.

Now suppose we want to construct a linear approximation to the long-run cost curve. To do this, we must specify the intercept and slope of the linear approximation. If markets are perfectly competitive, our firm will be operating at its efficient point, the point where average cost is a minimum. Let's agree, then, that we want our linear approximation to have a slope equal to the slope of $C(q)$ where average cost is a minimum.

Average long-run cost is a minimum at $q = 9$, with $C(9)/9 = 119$. Details are drawn from Chapter 2, especially Figure 2.5 and Table 2.2[15] Marginal cost is also 119 at this point. This is no accident. Average cost is a minimum at the point where average and marginal cost are equal. If average cost is above marginal cost, increasing output a small amount will decrease average cost. If average cost is below marginal cost, decreasing output a small amount will decrease average cost.

Denote our approximate cost curve by $AC(q) = a + bq$. $AC(q)$ should be interpreted as a model that relates accounting cost to output. The model is a linear function with slope b and intercept a.

We want the slope to equal $C'(9) = 119$. So we set $b = 119$. What about the intercept? Let's also agree, for the sake of illustration, that we want $C(q)$ and $AC(q)$ to coincide at the point $q = 9$, where $C(9) = 1,071$. This means, at the efficient output level, our approximate cost curve reveals both the correct total cost and the correct marginal cost.

Solve for a:

$$C(9) = 1071 = a + 9b = a + 9(119); \text{ or}$$

---

[15]We locate the minimum of the average cost curve by setting its derivative equal to zero. With average cost of $200 - 18q + q^2$, this provides $0 = -18 + 2q$, or $q = 18/2 = 9$. Figure 2.5 in Chapter 2 is instructive. Notice that average cost is "U-shaped." This means the point at which the derivative vanishes is indeed a minimum.

a = 1071 - 1071 = 0.

See Figure 5.3, where we plot the short-run and long-run cost curves, along with AC(q).

Figure 5.3: Economic Cost Curves and LLA

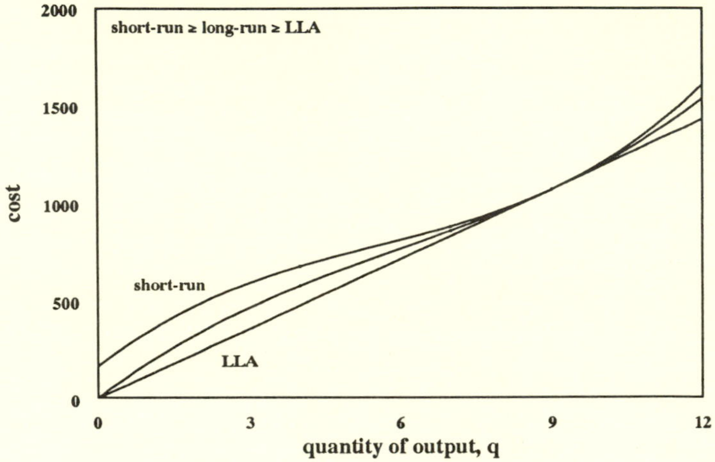

We therefore have AC(q) = 119q as our linear approximation to C(q). This was derived by dictating (1) the slope of the linear approximation equal marginal cost at the efficient output; and (2) the total approximate cost equal total cost at the efficient output.[16]

Examine Figure 5.3 more closely. In geometric terms, the LLA is located in the following manner. Take a straight line that is below C(q) and that passes through the origin. Now rotate this line about the origin, until it is just tangent to C(q). The point of tangency occurs at $q = q^*$. This is our LLA. By construction, $C(q) \geq AC(q)$. If this makes sense, you understand the economic nature of C(q).

Now consider the organization's short-run cost curve. Our example has $C(q;\bar{z}_3)$ = 162 + 204.5q - 25q² + 1.5q³. Let's do the same thing. Short-run average cost is

---

[16]Concluding a = 0 is no accident. Let C(q) be the long-run cost curve. Also let q^* be the efficient output level, the output level for which average cost is a minimum. We know average and marginal cost are equal at this point: $C(q^*)/q^* = C'(q^*)$. Now introduce the linear approximation AC(q) = a + bq. First, set $b = C'(q^*)$. Second, set a so that AC(q) = C(q) at the point $q = q^*$:

$C(q^*) = AC(q^*) = a + bq^* = a + [C'(q^*)]q^*$; or

$a = C(q^*) - [C'(q^*)]q^*$.

Substitute the fact $C'(q^*) = C(q^*)/q^*$:

$a = C(q^*) - [C(q^*)/q^*]q^* = C(q^*) - C(q^*) = 0$.

$C(q;\bar{z}_3)/q = 162/q + 204.5 - 25q + 1.5q^2$. The minimum also occurs at q = 9. In addition, $C(9;\bar{z}_3) = 1,071 = C(9)$. Thus, minimum average short-run cost is 1,071/9 = 119, a familiar number. We also have average and marginal cost equal at this point. Constructing an LLA in the same fashion produces a slope of 119 and an intercept of 0.

Is this alchemy? Not quite. A short-run cost curve arises when we freeze one or more inputs at some exogenously given level. Suppose whatever inputs we so freeze, we freeze where they would be at the efficient output level, q^*. This means short-run and long-run cost are equal at q^*. (This is why we had total long-run and short-run cost of 1,071 at q = 9 in our example.) This also means short-run marginal and long-run marginal cost are equal at q^*. If we then construct an LLA from *any* of these curves, by equating slope and total cost at q^*, we always produce an intercept of a = 0 and a slope of b = $C'(q^*)$. This is the inescapable geometry of the construction procedure we have identified.

Two critical assumptions produce the general appearance in Figure 5.3. First, we assume the short-run and long-run cost curves are equal at the long-run efficient output level of q^*. Remember, there are many ways to construct a short-run cost curve. It all depends on which inputs are fixed and at what levels they are fixed. This first assumption says no matter which inputs are fixed, they are fixed at levels that correspond to q^* on the long-run cost curve.

Second, we assume the LLA is constructed to have a slope equal to marginal cost at q^* and to identify a total cost equal to the total cost of its parent cost curve, also at q^*. Here we should remember there are countless ways to construct an LLA. We have chosen a particular one.

We began this section by asking whether the accountant's art produced an approximation to the long-run or short-run cost curve. So far the answer is "all the above." The identified LLA gives exact total, average, and marginal cost constructions, at output q = q^*, for the long-run and any related short-run cost curve.

This reassuring answer surfaces because we are asking the question in the economist's world, a world where we know C(q), where we know q^*, where we assume competitive markets force the firm to produce at q = q^*, and so on. It should come as no surprise we can invent an innocuous accounting procedure in such a setting.

back to accounting

Now return to the accountant's world. We worry about three differences. First, we remind ourselves of basic recognition differences between the economist and the accountant. At any output level, q, the total accounting cost would differ from the total economic cost. Accrual procedures contribute to this difference, as does the fact the accountant typically does not include capital cost in the tally.

Second, we remind ourselves that cost construction and geometry are different in the multiproduct setting. In that more realistic case, we should not expect a separable cost function. This implies we should be wary of attempts to construct an average cost. We also should remember marginal cost of some product will usually depend on the mix and quantity of other products in the organization's portfolio.

Third, even in the single product case, there is no presumption in the accountant's world that the firm is operating at the efficient point, $q = q^*$. Products come and go; technologies are improved; relative prices change; fads fall into disfavor; tax regulations change; population demographics change. The world is dynamic and mistakes are made. Examine Figure 5.3 again. What happens to our LLA if we ask about marginal cost at some point other than $q = q^* = 9$? This is not an idle question.

We constructed the LLA by presuming we knew C(q) and chose the efficient output level as a focal point for the approximation. In reality, we know neither C(q) nor q^*. We are more likely to know some output level q and some accounting cost associated with that output level. There is also no presumption the organization's current output level is close to q^*.

This means the accountant's LLA will not be focused on q^*. Suppose we focus on the output level at which the organization is currently operating. Further suppose we set the slope of the approximation equal to a reasonable estimate of marginal cost near the current output level. If we also want total economic cost to coincide with the LLAs cost at that point, we should not expect the intercept of the LLA to be zero.

So, is the accountant's product cost construction closer to the long-run or short-run parent? No definitive answer is possible. Consider a manufacturer. GAAP requires transfers to finished goods be recorded at "average" manufacturing cost. Suppose manufacturing cost is approximated by the cost function AC(q) = 50,000 + 20q. Further suppose q = 10,000 units are manufactured.

The typical costing system would record the transfer of manufactured goods into finished goods using a cost of 25 per unit. How is this computed? Take the total manufacturing cost of 50,000 + 20(10,000) = 250,000. Divide by the output quantity, 250/10 = 25. Suppose we ask the accounting library what the product costs. One answer in the library is 25 per unit.

There is another way to view this situation. Suppose the firm treats the intercept component of the manufacturing cost as a period cost. This means a = 50,000 will be expensed and not flow through finished goods. Now when we ask the accounting library what the product costs we will find a different answer. The library will report the product costs 20 per unit, i.e., 20(10,000)/(10,000) = 20 per unit.[17]

The 25 construction is more of an average. It is tempting to regard the 20 datum as more of a short-run cost construction and the 25 datum as more of a long-run cost construction. It is even tempting to interpret 20 as a reasonable estimate of

---

[17]Naturally, the library might contain both constructions. We will learn in subsequent chapters to recognize the 25 construction as a full or absorption cost number and the 20 construction as a variable or direct cost construction. The distinction rests on where we draw the line between product and period costs.

the short-run marginal cost and 25 as a reasonable estimate of the short-run average (and perhaps long-run marginal) cost. This temptation is best kept at bay. Cost is a contextual notion, and we must be wary of generalizations. To understand our wariness, return to the numerical example illustrated in Figure 5.3. Further suppose the firm is operating at output q = 7. Short-run economic cost is $C(7;\bar{z}_3) = 883$. Short-run marginal cost is $C'(7;\bar{z}_3) = 75$. Suppose we know q = 7, total cost of 883, and marginal cost of 75.

Now construct the LLA of AC(q) = a + bq using this information. Let the slope be b = 75. Set the intercept so AC(q) = 883, at the point q = 7. We find a = 358.[18] This provides an LLA of AC(q) = 358 + 75q. In Figure 5.4 we plot $C(q;\bar{z}_3)$ and AC(q) = 358 + 75q. Our approximation may be above or below the short-run cost function $C(q;\bar{z}_3)$. The two are, of course, equal at q = 7.

Figure 5.4: Approximation of Short-run Cost Curve

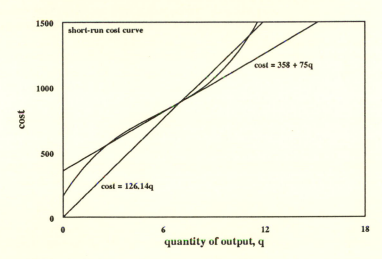

Another way to construct an LLA is to focus on output of q = 7 and total cost of 883, but force the intercept to be zero. To distinguish the two LLAs, denote this one AAC(q) = a + bq. Keeping AAC(q) = 883 at q = 7 along with a = 0 requires b = 883/7 = 126.14. See Figure 5.4.

These two LLAs are intimately related. Take the original construction of AC(q) = 358 + 75q. Then compute an average cost using AC(q), presuming q = 7. This gives us [358 + 75(7)]/7 = 883/7 = 126.14 per unit. Now treat the resulting cost per unit as the slope of a competing LLA. This boils down to an approximate cost function of AAC(q) = 0 + 126.14q. Think of this second LLA as reporting *average accounting cost* (i.e., AAC).

---

[18]That is, $AC(7) = C(7;\bar{z}_3) = 883 = a + b(7) = a + 75(7)$; or a = 883 - 525.

Begin with the first LLA of AC(q) = 358 + 75q. Following GAAP, construct an average cost off this approximation. Implicitly, this amounts to substituting one LLA for another. We substitute AAC(q) = 126.14q for AC(q) = 358 + 75q as our operative LLA. If, contrary to GAAP, we treat 358 as a period cost, we choose to stay with the original LLA. In this sense, we now have two competing LLAs:

$$AC(q) = 358 + 75q; \text{ and}$$
$$AAC(q) = 126.14q.$$

Figure 5.4 is important. We have a short-run economic cost curve and two LLAs. If q is somewhat below q = 7, the first LLA provides a closer approximation. If q is above q = 7, the second LLA provides a closer approximation. Our intuition suggests the second LLA (of 126.14) is more of an average and therefore more related to the long-run cost curve. This is simply incorrect. Both constructions are approximations. One is closer to short-run cost than the other depending on how they were constructed, the output level, and how the short-run cost curve behaves.

No doubt the same occurs when we ask which approximation is closest to the long-run cost. We skip the details.

Finally, another picture of this phenomenon is sketched in Figure 5.5. There we plot the marginal cost implied by the two LLAs alongside the short-run and long-run marginal cost curves. 126.14 is closer to either marginal cost curve for "low" or "high" output. In between, 75 is closer.

Figure 5.5: Marginal Cost Approximations

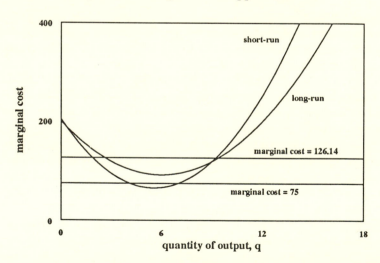

In summary, any application of the accountant's product costing art leads to a product cost statistic. Suppose we decide to treat some product cost statistic as an approximation of marginal cost. Is this best thought of as an approximation to long-run or to some short-run marginal cost? No general answer is possible. The accountant's art produces a number. This number may be close to or far removed from the portion of the long-run marginal cost curve we had in mind. Similarly, this number may be close to or far removed from the portion of some short-run marginal cost curve we had in mind.

This may appear curious or cynical. Yet it is the natural manifestation of treating accounting as a library. Various choices go into design of the library. The resulting choices may produce something that is close to what we want or not so close. We and our immediate curiosity are just one of many users of that library. How we use the library depends on how the library was constructed and on our context. Rules and recipes stand in the way of professional quality interrogation of the accounting library. Professional judgment is an essential ingredient in the use of the accounting library.

Summary

The accounting library routinely collects various product cost statistics. These cost statistics are accounting constructions. Initially, various aggregation choices are made. Costs are collected in various categories, or cost pools. Some of these categories are treated as period costs and expensed in the period in which they arise.

The remaining categories are assigned to products in some systematic, verifiable fashion. The assignment procedure for each category centers on identification of an approximation to the cost curve associated with the category in question. These category specific cost curves may use output or synthetic output variables as explanatory variables.

The cost function approximations are usually linear. Collecting the various aggregations and approximations leads to what we have termed the accounting cost curve. In linear fashion it is represented as $AC(q) = a + bq$.

More terminology enters at this point. Common usage is to refer to intercept a as fixed cost and slope b as variable cost per unit in this context. We caution the reader to understand a is the intercept and b is the slope of the local linear approximation (or LLA) denoted $AC(q) = a + bq$.

This also raises the question: Are these approximations aimed at the long-run cost curve or a specific short-run version of the long-run cost curve? Economically, we know the answer to this question, at least in the case of a single product firm. It is both, provided we construct the linear approximation to reveal the marginal cost and total cost at the firm's efficient output level.

We also know the answer to this question in the world of accounting. The answer is that it all depends. The accounting library is meant to serve a variety of purposes. When we interrogate the library we must know how the library was constructed and what we are looking for. What we find in the library may or may not be a reasonable answer to what we are looking for.

The accounting library, by nature, catalogues a wealth of information. Unfortunately, information in one circumstance is noise in another. This means we must learn to filter, to extract what is in the library. The professional manager understands the accounting library and how to extract whatever it contains that is useful to the purpose at hand.

Bibliographic Notes

The history of cost accounting is traced in Solomons [1968] and in Johnson and Kaplan [1987]. The connection between economic and accounting cost was emphasized by Clark [1923]. Demski and Feltham [1976] continue this theme, with emphasis on the idea of approximation.

Problems and Exercises

1. The cost construction illustration in Table 5.1 treats interest but not dividends as a cost. Give one set of circumstances in which dividends would not be treated as a component of economic cost and another in which they would.

2. A so-called "step cost" arises when some factor of production is acquired in specific, integer units. To illustrate, it might be possible to lease machine time at the rate of $5,000 per unit, where units are measured in thousands of hours. So any number of hours of machine time strictly above zero and below 1,000 will cost $5,000; any number between 2,000 and strictly below 3,000 will cost $10,000, and so on. Plot the implied cost curve.

In such a situation we often hear someone say "If we expand output, our fixed costs will increase." Carefully analyze this statement, in economic terms and in accounting terms.

3. Define product and period costs. How do their accounting treatments differ? Locate the product and period costs in Exhibit 5.1.

4. *product costing*
Return to the product cost construction illustration in Table 5.1. Numerous assumptions were used in the costing exercise, reflecting period versus product cost distinctions and the LLAs used to allocate product costs among the products. Now find two other sets of assumptions, one set that maximizes the product cost for the municipal client and another set that minimizes the product cost for the municipal client. Present your calculations in a format comparable to that in Table 5.1. Also, be certain to identify the LLAs in each step of each construction, and provide an adequate defense of your choices.

5. *product costing and economic cost*

What connection do you see between the exercise in problem 4 above and the economic theory of cost, as portrayed in Chapter 2?

6. *product costing*

Various nonprofit organizations report the total funds raised, the amount spent on various social services, and the amount spent on administration and fund raising. We might think of such an organization as having n products; n-1 of the products are the various social services provided by the organization and the nth is the internally consumed fund raising and administration product. What pressures might this disaggregate reporting place on the product costing apparatus?

7. *long-run versus short-run economic cost*

Suppose Ralph's long-run economic cost curve is given by
$$C(q) = 300q - 20q^2 + q^3.$$
We presume an industry characterized by perfect competition; consequently, Ralph operates at the point q = 10, where average cost is a minimum.

a] Tabulate total cost, marginal cost, incremental cost, and average cost for $q \in \{0,1,2,3,...,20\}$. Also plot average cost and marginal cost for $0 \le q \le 20$.

b] Now consider a particular short-run cost curve given by
$$C^{SR}(q) = F + 290q - 21q^2 + 1.1q^3.$$
Determine F if we are to interpret $C^{SR}(q)$ as some short-run cost curve consistent with Ralph's long-run cost curve and an efficient scale of q = 10 units.

c] Plot the resulting average and marginal short-run cost, for $0 \le q \le 20$. Contrast this with their long-run counterparts. The best way to do this is to plot all four curves on the same graph.

8. *accounting LLA*

Return to the above problem dealing with Ralph's cost curve. Now suppose Ralph's accountant approximates $C^{SR}(q)$ with an LLA: $C^{SR}(q) \approx \hat{F} + vq$. Further suppose the accountant does this by setting v equal to the marginal cost at q = 10 and $\hat{F}$ so that the total cost at q = 10 equals $C^{SR}(10)$.

Graph the LLA. What is its slope? What is its intercept? Over what range does this strike you as a reasonable approximation to the underlying short-run and long-run cost curves? Is the intercept a fixed cost?

9. *accounting LLA*

Repeat the LLA construction in problem 8 above, but with the "anchoring point" at q = 12. (So you want the LLA to agree with $C^{SR}(12)$ and v = marginal cost at q = 12.) What is its slope? What is its intercept? Over what range does this strike you as a reasonable approximation to the underlying short-run and long-run cost curves? Is the intercept a fixed cost?

10. *product costing*

Ralph's Service provides consulting expertise to not-for-profit entities. Several partners lead various consulting teams that provide the services on a contract basis. Each team consists of the aforementioned partner and a group of professional people drawn from Ralph's stable of professional labor.

Ralph employs what we will learn to call a job order costing system to document the cost of each consulting engagement. Each engagement, or client, is costed out based on (i) actual partner time, which averages $120 per hour; (ii) specific identifiable costs (such as for specialized materials); and (iii) allocated professional staff, indirect labor, and miscellaneous supplies.

During a recent month the following events occurred:

	client A	client B	client C
partner time (hours)	100	450	250
professional staff time (hours)	1,200	900	800
specific costs (dollars)	18,000	12,000	145,000

In addition, the following support costs were incurred:

professional staff labor	$55,000
indirect labor	$45,000
misc. supplies	$24,000

Determine the total cost of each of the engagements.

11. *product costing*

Ralph's Firm manufactures and sells two products, code named A and B. The manufacturing process is relatively simple, with each product passing through the same set of machines and using the same labor force. For convenience, we might think of this as a manufacturing facility with a single department. The accounting system uses three cost categories: (i) direct labor, where the cost of any labor easily identified with a specific product is recorded; (ii) direct material, where the cost of any materials readily identified with a specific product is recorded; and (iii) overhead, where all other product costs are recorded.

The accounting for direct materials uses conventional inventory accounting procedures. For convenience, we will assume the price paid suppliers for these items does not vary. In that way, we need not worry about LIFO, FIFO, or whatever in the direct material inventory accounts. (Alternatively, we could assume Ralph's Firm uses "just-in-time" inventory procedures with its suppliers.) In a similar vein, proper accrual procedures are used in recording the direct labor cost. Thus, direct labor cost in a particular period corresponds to direct labor input during that period, regardless of any lags in paying the employees. Finally, proper accrual procedures are also used in determining manufacturing overhead for any particular period. Included in this category are such things as insurance, property taxes, supervision, indirect manufacturing labor, fringe benefits for labor, miscellaneous materials, depreciation, and energy costs -- all properly concerned with manufacturing operations.

During a recent period, the following was observed (and recorded):

	product A	product B
units produced	1,200	4,800
direct material cost	$6,500	$3,500
direct labor cost	$3,000	$9,000
total manufacturing overhead	$45,000	

What is the per unit manufacturing cost of A and of B? Determine your answer by allocating total manufacturing overhead on the basis of (i) units produced; (ii) direct material cost; (iii) direct labor cost; and (iv) the total of direct material and direct labor cost.

6

Product Costing: Heterogeneous Products

The purpose of this chapter is to study how the typical accounting system constructs product cost statistics when the organization produces heterogeneous products. This material is important for two reasons. First, all costing environments are variations on this theme. Understanding issues and techniques in this environment paves the way for a broader understanding of the product costing art.

Second, the heterogeneous output setting is an important class of institutions. Consider the private sector. A tool and die manufacturing firm, a consulting firm, and a mail order merchandiser of computer equipment illustrate the genre. Alternatively, consider the not-for-profit sector. Research at a private university, CPR courses offered by the Red Cross, and religious material merchandising by a church illustrate the genre. Finally, consider the public sector. Operation of a regional exhibition hall or coliseum, law enforcement, and sale of surplus materials illustrate the genre.

This list is not random. We have covered private, not-for-profit, and public sectors. In each sector we have illustrated manufacturing, service, and merchandising operations.

We usually associate this subject with a manufacturing activity. Matching of expense and revenue requires we assign manufacturing cost to products. Overlapping periods are also possible, where the cost of partially completed products is inventoried in work-in-process inventory. Completion of the products results in a transfer from work-in-process to finished goods inventory. The assigned costs are then expensed when revenue from the respective products is recognized. The expensing thus revolves around the assignment of costs to products, or the art of product costing.

The same product cost construction exercises arise in service and merchandising organizations. The consulting firm, Ralph, Ltd., in Chapter 5 illustrates a service organization. Services, by definition, cannot be stored. So we do not associate inventory valuation difficulties with service organizations. This does not mean such an organization lacks interest in product costing. It is natural, for example, to ask how profitable various customer classes or outputs are. This requires product costing. Also, some products may not be finished at the end of an accounting period. This, too, requires some type of product costing.

A merchandising organization, on the other hand, usually has inventory ready for sale. Here we use what was paid for the goods to establish product cost. Issues of FIFO, LIFO, or weighted average, and issues of lower of cost or market arise. Treatment of transportation and stocking cost also raises important questions. Typically, though, we do not think of this as a setting where product costing art is given full expression. This is a false impression. Consider the mail order merchandiser of computer equipment. Does the cost of technical support for customers vary significantly among products? Does the cost of packaging and shipping vary significantly among products? Again, natural questions summon the product coster's services.

The product costing recipe uses aggregation and LLAs to produce product cost statistics. We begin with some additional terminology that helps us focus on the aggregation and LLAs that are typically employed here. Classification of product costs into direct and indirect categories is a central feature of the aggregation exercise. Pragmatic considerations are then introduced to simplify some assignment calculations. This entails the distinction between "actual" and "normal" costing systems. Next, we rediscover the difficulty of drawing a line between product and period cost. This leads to a distinction between "full" and "variable" costing systems. Finally, we illustrate the dramatic effect different LLA choices can have on individual product costs.

More Terminology

It will be useful to visualize an organization with heterogeneous outputs. Though perhaps not prototypical, a plumber is easy to visualize. Suppose our plumber is a sole proprietor and has no employees. Also suppose the plumbing business is incorporated, and the corporation pays the plumber an hourly wage. The plumber carries tools and miscellaneous supplies in a truck. An answering machine is used to collect messages from customers. Using this information, the plumber moves from one customer location to another. What records are kept?

The answer comes into view when we envision the plumber's invoice. It has charges for time and materials. The time charge is calculated by multiplying time on the job by the plumber's hourly *charging* (not wage) rate. The charge for materials is calculated by adding the retail price charged by the plumber for each of the identified materials. Again, we should distinguish what the plumber charges from what the item in question costs.[1] (There is also a minimum charge, and some localities also may require the plumber charge sales tax on some or all the items in the invoice.)

This suggests the plumber keeps detailed records. A time sheet, recording travel times and times at various customer locations, is maintained. Usage of various materials is recorded. Significant items taken from the truck at any particular location are noted. So many feet of 3/4 inch copper tubing used at a particular location is an example. Miscellaneous items, such as a stock faucet washer or small amount of solder, would likely not be explicitly noted.

In turn, any items purchased at the wholesale supplier for use on a particular job would be noted. A particular circulating pump is an example. Purchases to restock the truck's inventory also would be noted. Gasoline, maintenance, licensing,

---

[1]It is likely a pricing formula is used on materials, say, 200% of the wholesale price.

depreciation, parking, insurance, taxes, and general maintenance on the truck would be recorded. Tools also would be recorded. Significant items would be capitalized and depreciated. Others would be expensed in the period of purchase.

Finally, the plumber probably maintains an open account at the wholesale supplier, and perhaps at a local service station as well. A checking account and a petty cash imprest system round out the records.[2]

Several features of this story are important. First, the organization routinely collects financial (e.g., cost of supplies) and nonfinancial (e.g., time on job) data. Second, some costs can be identified directly with specific products or customers while others cannot. Gasoline for the truck cannot be so identified. Significant materials, whether off the truck or special ordered from the wholesaler, can. Third, various items are aggregated. This is best illustrated by the supplies carried on the truck. Finally, accrual techniques are at work here. The cost of materials purchased for use on a particular job is illustrative. The record keeping is careful to distinguish when that material is used from when the plumber pays the wholesaler.[3]

The pattern should be clear. Costs are collected and categorized into cost pools. Each category (other than a period cost category) is then identified with an LLA. The categorization leads to specialized terminology. *Direct labor* cost is the cost of labor inputs the organization can and finds convenient to identify with specific products. *Direct material* cost is the cost of material inputs the organization can and finds convenient to identify with specific products. All other product costs are initially classified into one or more overhead categories.

Direct labor and direct material are often called *direct* costs, and overhead is often called *indirect* cost. *Prime cost* is the total of direct labor cost and direct material cost. *Conversion cost* is the total of direct labor and overhead cost.

Pragmatic considerations are present here. Some detail is purposely clouded; some distinctions are purposely not made. For example, a large firm will employ many people just to oversee and manage purchases of materials. Where will we find the cost of these materials "overhead" items? They may be in a separate overhead cost category, they may be in a separate period cost category, or they may be commingled with other items. The direct material *cost* that is identified for some

---

[2]Tax record keeping and income measurement requirements influence the small organization's accounting library.

[3]Parenthetically, the smallness of the organization masks an important question of how reliable the initial cost categorization is likely to be. For example, is the plumber's time accurately categorized by customers? The accuracy of these categorizations should not be taken for granted. This issue falls under the topic of *source documents*. Internal control addresses the problem of ensuring the accuracy of source documents. It will be discussed in a subsequent chapter, but it should be acknowledged at the outset.

product is keyed to the historical cost of the material that was in raw materials inventory.[4]

Similarly, the direct labor *cost* that is identified for some product is keyed to payroll accounting practices. Suppose an employee's wage rate is w per hour. If time records show 12 hours were identified with some specific product, a direct labor cost of 12w will be recorded for this product. What about the employee's fringe benefits? These will almost surely be placed in some overhead category.[5]

Product Cost Construction with Actual Overhead Totals

We now focus on a specific organization and examine its product costing practices. The organization has three products. Let's call the products job 1, job 2, and job 3. These were the only products present during the accounting period in question. In addition, the total product cost identified during this period is 246,000. What is the cost of each product? We know the total is 246,000.

The data displayed in Table 6.1 have been gathered. Notice that nonfinancial data, in terms of hours of direct labor, are present. The cost of direct labor is identified for each product.[6] In addition, two types of direct material cost are identified. One category is specialty materials purchased exclusively for the jobs in question. The other category is general purpose materials that the organization routinely keeps in stock. Finally, two overhead categories have been identified.

Routine data processing, once we have designed the data gathering mechanism, gives prime cost of each product. This is 27,000 for job 1, 33,000 for job 2, and 48,000 for job 3.

We assign the overhead costs to the products by identifying approximate cost curves for each category. Suppose we tentatively decide a reasonable approximation of the overhead A cost category is $OV_A = a + b(DL\$)$, where DL\$ denotes direct labor dollars (and OV_A is shorthand for the total in the overhead A category). This

---

[4]Think of purchasing some raw material item from a supplier. The invoice amount perhaps coupled with transportation cost would be recorded as raw material inventory to begin with. When this material is used, we credit the inventory account and debit some other account. That account would be an overhead account if the material cost goes into some overhead category; it would be a work-in-process inventory account if it is treated as a direct material item.

[5]Again, it is useful to think through the underlying debits and credits. Paying the employee in a timely fashion and honoring tax withholding and payment requirements means the wages earned, at a rate of w per hour, will be routinely recorded. Fringe items are not so routine. Some, such as vacation accruals are. Others, such as periodic payments for a group health insurance plan, are not. Still others seem outside normal accrual procedures. Long-term bonuses are an example. Retiree health benefits have also traditionally been treated on a cash basis, though the FASB has recently mandated otherwise.

[6]Further notice that average direct labor cost per direct labor hour varies across the products. This is common. Wage rates are not identical, and it would be unusual to have exactly the same mix of wage rates in each product category. The organization aggregates across different wage rates.

is an LLA that uses cost of direct labor (i.e., *direct labor dollars*) as an explanatory variable.

Table 6.1: Data for Product Cost Construction Exercise				
	job 1	job 2	job 3	total
direct labor hours	900	1,800	1,300	4,000
direct labor cost	12,000	18,000	18,000	48,000
cost of specialty materials purchased expressly for product in question	10,000	5,000	15,000	30,000
cost of direct materials removed from stock for product in question	5,000	10,000	15,000	30,000
prime cost	27,000	33,000	48,000	108,000
overhead category A				96,000
overhead category B				42,000
total to assign				246,000

The data give us one point on this LLA, DL\$ = 48,000 and OV_A = 96,000. Overhead A averages 96/48 = 2 per dollar of direct labor. Job 1 consumed 12,000 of direct labor, suggesting an assignment of 2(12,000) = 24,000 of overhead A to job 1. The job 2 calculation is 2(18,000) = 36,000; and the job 3 calculation is 2(18,000) = 36,000.

Suppose we also tentatively decide a reasonable approximation of the overhead B category is OV_B = a + b(DM\$), where DM\$ denotes total direct material dollars. This LLA uses total direct material cost as an explanatory variable.

The data also give us one point on this LLA, DM\$ = 60,000 and OV_B = 42,000. Overhead B averages 42/60 = 0.7 per dollar of direct material. Job 1 consumed 15,000 of direct material, implying an overhead B assignment of .7(15,000) = 10,500. The job 2 calculation is .7(15,000) = 10,500; and the job 3 calculation is .7(30,000) = 21,000.

Table 6.2: Product Cost Construction Using OV_A = a + b(DL\$) and OV_B = a + b(DM\$)				
	job 1	job 2	job 3	total
direct labor cost	12,000	18,000	18,000	48,000
direct material cost	15,000	15,000	30,000	60,000
assigned overhead A	24,000	36,000	36,000	96,000
assigned overhead B	10,500	10,500	21,000	42,000
product cost	61,500	79,500	105,000	246,000

Our calculations are summarized in Table 6.2. Notice the total of the three product costs is 246,000.

Can you identify the LLAs we have used in the overhead assignments? Examine $OV_A = a + b(DL\$)$. Our procedure passes the LLA through the origin and through the point given by actual DL$ of 48,000 and actual OV_A of 96,000. Thus, $a = 0$ and $b = 2$. We are using an LLA of $OV_A = 2(DL\$)$. Similarly, we are using $OV_B = 0.7(DM\$)$ to assign the second overhead category.

Record Keeping Mechanics

How are these product cost constructions reflected in the organization's records? In broad terms, we have inventory procedures that "build" to an inventory valuation for each product that is equal to the above product cost statistics. We work through the mechanical details below. This is important; we must know what enters a cost pool or account if we are to interrogate the library.

Initially we would record the transactions, using the indicated aggregate categories. Consider labor cost. Some labor cost is placed in the direct cost category, some in each overhead category, and some in period cost categories. Our example focuses only on product cost, so we ignore any labor cost in the latter category. The recording entry, in highly aggregate form, would appear as follows.

[a]	direct labor cost	48,000	
	overhead A	xxx	
	overhead B	xxx	
	accrued wages payable		xxx
	withheld taxes payable		xxx

A debit entry of 48,000 to direct labor cost records the portion of labor cost that is placed in the direct cost category. Payroll records would trigger the liability for any particular payroll period. This liability encompasses payments to be made to the employees along with various tax withholdings. Additional fringe benefits are also involved, but we assume they are all placed in overhead.

Direct labor cost is an aggregate recording of all direct labor costs. Subsidiary records would record the assignments to individual jobs or products. This will become apparent.

Materials purchased for the jobs in question are easily recorded. Receipt of the materials from respective suppliers triggers the recording. We assume the materials are immediately used in the production process, rather than stored for use later.

We use a work-in-process inventory account to accumulate the costs of each product. As the name suggests, work in process is an aggregate category in which we accumulate product costs during the production process. It is also a control account, with subsidiary records maintaining individual product breakdowns. Focusing on the subsidiary records, we would have the following entries.

[b]	work in process (job 1)	10,000	
	work in process (job 2)	5,000	
	work in process (job 3)	15,000	
	accounts payable		30,000

The other materials are recorded in similar fashion. The one difference is we know these items come from the organization's inventory of materials on hand.

[c]	work in process (job 1)	5,000	
	work in process (job 2)	10,000	
	work in process (job 3)	15,000	
	raw materials inventory		30,000

Recall our original data allowed us to distinguish specialized from general purpose materials that were used in the various products. This implies that the subsidiary records maintain such a distinction.

Finally, the overhead aggregations are completed as follows. Some costs have been recorded in the above noted labor recording. Others will be drawn from raw materials inventory, for miscellaneous materials, from prepaid expenses, from accounts payable, from depreciation entries, and so on. Remember, the overhead categories contain *all* product costs except direct labor and direct material.

[d]	overhead A	xxx	
	overhead B	xxx	
	various accounts		xxx

These initial recordings give us the data with which we began our product costing exercise. The various aggregations are reflected in the formal accounting records maintained by the organization.

Direct labor and overhead accounts are temporary accounts. They are always closed at the end of the accounting cycle. So we know their opening balance was zero. Work in process is a different story. This is the inventory category for products that are partially complete.[7] Assume no products were partially complete

---

[7]The typical manufacturing organizations maintains three types of inventory accounts: raw materials, work in process, and finished goods. The raw material and finished good categories operate in familiar fashion. The cost of additions to inventory is added to the account, and the cost of items removed from inventory is subtracted. Work in process is more complicated. The cost of direct materials, direct labor, and overhead assigned to various products is recorded as additions or debits to the account. The cost of items transferred to finished goods (or expense for scrapped items) is recorded as subtractions from or credits to the account. The ending balance, then, is the cost of partially completed products. Of course, a streamlined procedure would assign the overhead costs only at the end of the accounting period. The sequence in the text is used to emphasize the product cost construction.

at the beginning of this accounting period. This implies that the opening balance of the work-in-process account was also zero. We therefore have the following balances in our product cost accounts.

direct labor cost	48,000
work-in-process control	60,000
overhead A	96,000
overhead B	42,000
	246,000

We emphasize these are the basic data at the beginning of the exercise.

Product costs total 246,000. Mechanically, we must zero out the temporary accounts and build the work-in-process inventory up to a total of 246,000. For this purpose, we take the product cost calculations in Table 6.2 and reflect them in the accounts. Necessary entries follow.

Initially, we close out the temporary direct labor cost account by moving each component of direct labor cost into the respective work-in-process category.

[e]	work in process (job 1)	12,000	
	work in process (job 2)	18,000	
	work in process (job 3)	18,000	
	direct labor cost		48,000

This might have been done in a single step, when the direct labor cost was initially recorded. We will have reason in subsequent chapters to think of these amounts as originally passing through a temporary account. So we stress the more elaborate procedure here.

Overhead assignments follow the same pattern.

[f]	work in process (job 1)	24,000	
	work in process (job 2)	36,000	
	work in process (job 3)	36,000	
	overhead A		96,000

[g]	work in process (job 1)	10,500	
	work in process (job 2)	10,500	
	work in process (job 3)	21,000	
	overhead B		42,000

At this point, work-in-process control has a balance of 246,000. The subsidiary work-in-process (job 1) account has a balance of 61,500, that of (job 2) has a balance of 79,500, and that of (job 3) has a balance of 105,000. Now suppose jobs 2 and 3 are completed. Their cost must be removed from work-in-process inventory and placed in finished goods inventory.

[h]	finished goods inventory	184,500	
	work in process (job 2)		79,500
	work in process (job 3)		105,000

The end-of-period balance in the work-in-process inventory is the partial cost of completing job 1, 61,500.

Notice that the organization maintains three types of inventory accounts, raw materials, work in process, and finished goods. Also notice that our product cost calculations determine what flows through the accounts at various times.

T accounts are helpful. We summarize the above entries in Figure 6.1 This imagery is important. Suppose we ask the accounting library what job 2 cost. The most immediate answer will be 79,500. (Check the appropriate T account in Figure 6.1.) Similarly, ask yourself how the costs flow through the accounts. We have accumulations in the various aggregate categories, followed by assignment to specific products. These assignments, in turn, are recorded in the work-in-process and finished goods accounts.

Normal Versus Actual Costing

As the number of products increases, this recording and assignment procedure becomes arduous. In addition, it relies on knowing the total accounting cost for the period. The direct labor and direct material components will likely be identified as they are incurred.[8] The overhead totals, however, are problematic. They will not be completely identified until the end of the period. This will cause delay in identifying the cost of products completed early in the accounting period. It also will force much routine record keeping to be bunched at the end of the accounting period.

Once we admit the overhead assignments are approximations, we are led to a simple and convenient modification of the procedure. We use an estimated instead of the actual overhead rate to make the overhead assignments. This allows us to assign overhead to products as they are finished and avoids bunching the record keeping at the end of the accounting period. Pragmatism has many influences.

The procedure is straightforward. Recall the way we assigned overhead A in our continuing example. We settled on an LLA of $OV_A = a + b(DL\$)$. We then took the point defined by realized direct labor dollars of 48,000 and realized overhead A of 96,000. Using that point, we constructed an LLA that passed through the origin. That is, we set intercept $a = 0$ and slope $b = 96/48 = 2$.

---

[8] There is a caveat here that we will address in Chapter 7. Suppose raw material inventory is maintained on a LIFO basis. We won't know until the end of the accounting cycle whether a LIFO layer has been depleted. Average cost poses a similar problem. As you will learn, we resolve this by estimating the cost of the materials.

Figure 6.1: T Accounts for Costing Illustration

direct labor cost			
[a]	48,000	48,000	[e]

various credits			
		48,000	[a]
		30,000	[b]
		30,000	[c]
		138,000	[a,d]

overhead A			
[a,d]	96,000	96,000	[f]

overhead B			
[a,d]	42,000	42,000	[g]

work-in-process control			
[b]	30,000	184,500	[h]
[c]	30,000		
[e]	48,000		
[f]	96,000		
[g]	42,000		

finished goods inventory			
[h2]	79,500		
[h3]	105,000		

work in process (job 1)			
[b1]	10,000		
[c1]	5,000		
[e1]	12,000		
[f1]	24,000		
[g1]	10,500		
	61,500		

work in process (job 2)			
[b2]	5,000	79,500	[h2]
[c2]	10,000		
[e2]	18,000		
[f2]	36,000		
[g2]	10,500		

work in process (job 3)			
[b3]	15,000	105,000	[h3]
[c3]	15,000		
[e3]	18,000		
[f3]	36,000		
[g3]	21,000		

legend

[a]	labor cost recording	[b]	specialty materials
[c]	stock materials	[d]	overhead recording
[e]	direct labor assignment	[f]	overhead A assignment
[g]	overhead B assignment	[h]	transfer to finished goods

We follow the same procedure, but estimate the point through which the LLA passes. For the sake of illustration, suppose our organization estimates that direct labor dollars will total about 50,000 per accounting period and overhead A will total about 105,000 per accounting period. Take this point of DL$ = 50,000 and OV_A = 105,000. Construct the LLA through the origin. We have a slope of b = 105/50 = 2.1, along with an intercept of a = 0.

Let's do the same for overhead B. Suppose our organization estimates that direct material dollars will total about 80,000 per accounting period, while overhead B will total about 48,000 per accounting period. Take this point and construct an LLA of OV_B = a + b(DM$) that passes through the origin. We have a = 0 (as usual, but be patient) and b = 48/80 = .6.

It is common practice to call the coefficient b = 2.1 in the first LLA the *burden rate* for overhead A. The burden rate for overhead A is 2.1 per direct labor dollar. The burden rate for overhead B is 0.6 per direct material dollar. We emphasize the use of separate LLAs (perhaps with multiple explanatory variables) for each overhead category.[9]

We now proceed exactly as before, except for the burden rates. We tally actual direct labor and actual direct material cost for each product. We then assign overhead to the products using the *estimated* burden rates. This product costing procedure is called *normal costing*. These estimated burden rates are often called *predetermined burden rates* to distinguish them from the *actual burden rates* used in an actual costing system.[10] Similarly, the estimated amount over which the LLA intercept is averaged is called the *normal volume*. So we are using a normal volume of DL$ = 50,000 for the A category and DM$ = 80,000 for the B category.

Normal costing tallies actual direct cost and then assigns overhead based on predetermined (i.e., estimated) burden rates. Actual costing tallies actual direct cost and then assigns overhead based on actual burden rates.

Return to our data in Table 6.1. Assignments of overhead A to the individual products is now 2.1(12,000) = 25,200 for job 1, 2.1(18,000) = 37,800 for job 2, and 2.1(18,000) = 37,800 for job 3. Assignments of overhead B to the individual products is now .6(15,000) = 9,000 for job 1, .6(15,000) = 9,000 for job 2, and .6(30,000) = 18,000 for job 3.

Product cost calculations for our normal costing procedure are detailed below in Table 6.3.

A slight complication arises. We began the exercise with 246,000 in product cost but normal costing assigns 244,800 to the products. The difference is due to the fact our burden rates did not turn out to be exact.

---

[9]We also emphasize these estimated burden rates are not developed in cavalier fashion. To the contrary, they flow from elaborate budgeting exercises. This is studied in several subsequent chapters.

[10]We will consciously refer to the predetermined burden rate at times as an estimated burden rate. It is an estimated rate, and we should think of it as an estimated rate.

Table 6.3: Product Cost Construction Using Normal Costing				
	job 1	job 2	job 3	total
direct labor cost	12,000	18,000	18,000	48,000
direct material cost	15,000	15,000	30,000	60,000
assigned overhead A	25,200	37,800	37,800	100,800
assigned overhead B	9,000	9,000	18,000	36,000
product cost	61,200	79,800	103,800	244,800

Examine the overhead accounts under this normal costing procedure. Originally, we record the actual overhead costs of 96,000 for overhead A and 42,000 for overhead B. The entries that record the assignment of overhead cost to products use the estimated burden rates:

work in process (job 1)	25,200	
work in process (job 2)	37,800	
work in process (job 3)	37,800	
overhead A		100,800

work in process (job 1)	9,000	
work in process (job 2)	9,000	
work in process (job 3)	18,000	
overhead B		36,000

Now examine the T accounts for overhead A and overhead B:

overhead A			overhead B	
96,000	25,200		42,000	9,000
	37,800			9,000
	37,800			18,000
	4,800		6,000	

Overhead A has an ending *credit* balance of 4,800 and overhead B has an ending *debit* balance of 6,000.

What shall we do with these ending balances? The answer falls under the directive of expedience. Suppose we are at the end of the accounting year. If the total of these balances is not "too large" we just close the balance to cost of goods sold. This is tidy and expedient.

What does not too large mean? We always have the option of recalculating the normal costing product costs by using the actual burden rates. At the end of the period we can convert to an actual cost system. Suppose we do. Look at the ending inventory balances. Are the ending inventory balances significantly different from what they would be under normal costing? If not, stay with normal costing. If the balances are significantly different, the estimated burden rates were not sufficiently accurate and we restate the ending inventories.[11] That is, we restate the records to show ending inventories as though they were computed using an actual cost system.

This sounds intimidating. As a practical matter, we almost never encounter this restatement problem. The typical organization has sufficient experience to estimate reasonably accurate burden rates. So, we stress the expedient procedure of closing the balance to cost of goods sold.

A word of caution, however: closing procedures are invoked at year's end. Monthly or quarterly balances typically remain in the respective overhead accounts. At the end of the accounting year we worry about closing out the temporary overhead accounts.[12]

Seasonality is another reason for not closing the overhead accounts until the end of the accounting cycle. For this chapter's pun, we don't want to burden some products with seasonal overhead, such as heating cost during the heating season. An average is sought.

To bring this to an end, suppose our data in Table 6.1 reflect product costs and activities for the year. Normal costing leaves us with the noted balances in the overhead accounts. The entries to close these accounts are straightforward. We identify the necessary debit or credit and balance the entry with an offsetting credit or debit to cost of goods sold.

| overhead A | 4,800 | |
| cost of goods sold | | 4,800 |

| cost of goods sold | 6,000 | |
| overhead B | | 6,000 |

As you might have begun to fear, this procedure has its own terminology. We say overhead A is *over-absorbed* and overhead B is *under-absorbed* here. Look at the two overhead T accounts. Overhead A has an ending credit balance of 4,800. We assigned more overhead A than we incurred. We used an estimated burden rate of 2.1 while the actual rate was 2.0 per direct labor dollar. Overhead B has an ending debit balance of 6,000. We assigned less overhead B than we incurred. We

---

[11]We enter the world of financial reporting here. Is the historical cost of the ending inventory materially misstated by our normal costing procedure? If so, we must act. Otherwise, expedience reigns.

[12]Recall that at the end of the accounting cycle we make adjusting and closing entries. The closing entries remove balances in the temporary accounts. Overhead is always a temporary account. Again, it is useful to visualize the way the organization's records are structured. When you ask the accounting library a question, it responds with answers produced by this structuring.

used an estimated burden rate of 0.6 while the actual rate was 0.7 per direct material dollar.

Variable Versus Full Product Cost

Normal costing exploits prior knowledge of the overhead cost curve to establish an estimated burden rate. This raises an interesting question of whether we know anything else about the overhead cost curve.

We introduced normal costing for overhead A by identifying the point where DL\$ = 105,000 and OV_A = 50,000 on the LLA for overhead A. Suppose it turns out we think overhead A is well estimated by the LLA of OV_A = 55,000 + 1(DL\$). This is an LLA with intercept a = 55,000 and slope b = 1.

Further suppose we expect direct labor dollars to total about 50,000. At this point, what is the average overhead A cost per direct labor dollar? The answer is [55,000 + 1(50,000)]/50,000 = 105/50 = 2.1 per direct labor dollar. Make no mistake. This is our predetermined burden rate for overhead A.

Conversely, what is the marginal cost of overhead A when we expect direct labor dollars to total about 50,000? This is the slope of the LLA, or b = 1 per direct labor dollar.

Examine Figure 6.2. One line is the equation OV_A = 55,000 + 1(DL\$). Consider the LLA's explanatory variable at DL\$ = 50,000. This implies an overhead A total of 55,000 + 50,000 = 105,000. Now pass a second line from the origin through this point of (50,000, 105,000). This is the second LLA in the figure, that is OV_A = 2.1(DL\$).

This picture is important. We began with the first LLA. Averaging produces the second LLA of OV_A = 2.1(DL\$). This second LLA is what we used to assign overhead A to products in the normal costing system.

Turn to overhead B. We originally identified a point on the overhead B LLA consisting of DM\$ = 80,000 and OV_B = 48,000. Suppose we think overhead B is well estimated by the LLA of OV_B = 32,000 + .2(DM\$). This is an LLA with intercept a = 32,000 and slope b = 0.2.

What is the average overhead B per dollar of direct material cost, if we expect direct material dollars to total about 80,000? Our predetermined burden rate for overhead B surfaces: [32,000 + .2(80,000)]/80,000 = 48/80 = .6 per direct material dollar. Similarly, the marginal cost of overhead B when we expect direct material dollars to total about 80,000 is merely the slope of the LLA, or b = 0.2 per direct material dollar.[13]

---

[13]Notice that in each case we qualified our estimate of marginal cost by expecting the explanatory variable to be near the identified point. The reason is our cost curve is an approximation. We expect the LLA to be reasonably accurate in some neighborhood or relevant range of the explanatory variable. Hence the qualification.

Figure 6.2: Overhead A Linear Approximations

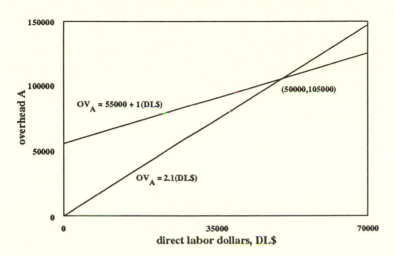

We can now construct different product cost statistics. The idea is to treat the *intercepts* of the overhead LLAs as period rather than product costs. We then assign overhead using the *slopes* of the identified LLAs as estimated burden rates. The remaining overhead is not assigned to products. It is treated as a period cost. This idea extends to the direct cost categories. It is conceivable the LLAs for direct costs might have nonzero intercepts. If so, we would assign the direct costs to products using the slopes of the respective LLAs. The intercept amounts would be expensed. For example, it may be impossible or impractical to alter the labor supply in the short-run. Simply because the organization finds it possible and convenient to identify particular labor costs with specific products does not imply that these direct costs are variable costs.

Product costing procedures of this sort are called *variable costing* systems. The earlier procedures are called *full* or *absorption costing* systems. Under a full costing regime, we begin with the distinction between period and product costs. The product costs are aggregated into various categories, and each category is described by some LLA. The LLA is used to assign the cost in the category to products.[14]

Under a variable costing regime, we begin with the same categories of product costs and the same LLAs. The single difference is we take the intercept amounts for each category's LLA and treat them, too, as period costs. As a practical matter, we often treat the direct cost category LLAs as having zero intercepts. But as we have discussed, this need not be the case.

---

[14]In a more elaborate arrangement we would have some overhead costs, in their respective categories, first assigned to other cost categories and from there to products. Energy costs being assigned to particular machine groupings and from there to products is an example.

In economic terms, the resulting variable product cost statistic is closer in appearance to a marginal cost statistic. As emphasized in Chapter 5, appearances can be deceiving. It all depends on the "real" cost curve, a curve that is not fully identified and that depends in critical ways on which factors are thought to be frozen or fixed.

We often hear variable costing explained as a costing system that expenses fixed overhead, rather than assigning it to products. This would be an apt description if (the direct costs were fully variable and) the intercepts of the overhead LLAs were fixed costs. As emphasized in Chapter 5, this would be the case only by accident. This is why we stress the language and interpretation of assigning overhead using the slope of the underlying LLA.[15]

With this preamble, we turn to constructing the variable product costs in our continuing example. We assume the direct costs are fully variable, meaning their respective LLAs have zero intercepts. Direct labor and direct material tallies, therefore, remain as before. So does the identification of overhead A of 96,000 and overhead B of 48,000. The difference is in the assignment of overhead to products.

Overhead A is assigned to products using a *variable burden rate* of 1 per direct labor dollar. Overhead B is assigned to products using a *variable burden rate* of 0.2 per direct material dollar. Details follow.[16]

Table 6.4: Product Cost Construction Using Variable Costing			
	job 1	**job 2**	**job 3**	**total**
direct labor cost	12,000	18,000	18,000	48,000
direct material cost	15,000	15,000	30,000	60,000
assigned overhead A	12,000	18,000	18,000	48,000
assigned overhead B	3,000	3,000	6,000	12,000
product cost	42,000	54,000	72,000	168,000

The overhead accounts are again closed out at the end of the accounting period. Remember the intercept amount is treated as a period cost, so it is simply expensed.

---

[15]In distinguishing full from variable product costing, it is important to remember we are talking about the intercepts of the LLAs for categories of product costs. Overhead, recall, is all product cost that is neither direct material nor direct labor. It does not include any period cost. This is why we couch the distinction in terms of where we draw the line between period and product cost.

[16]These are clearly estimated burden rates; we are dealing with a normal costing procedure. We might have numerous overhead categories, and be able to identify some of the categories as entirely "fixed" and others as entirely "variable." The former would have LLAs with a zero slope and the latter would have LLAs with a zero intercept. Keying on the LLAs, though, suggests the use of estimated burden rates; and that is why we emphasize the normal costing format.

The balance, the residual amount, is again dealt with in pragmatic fashion. Let's agree to follow our earlier routine and close it to cost of goods sold.[17]

The entries for the overhead costs are tiresome, but important. Initially, we recorded the actual overhead costs of 96,000 for overhead A and 42,000 for overhead B. The entries that record the assignment of overhead cost to products use the estimated variable burden rates:

work in process (job 1)	12,000	
work in process (job 2)	18,000	
work in process (job 3)	18,000	
overhead A		48,000

work in process (job 1)	3,000	
work in process (job 2)	3,000	
work in process (job 3)	6,000	
overhead B		12,000

Now examine the T accounts for overhead A and overhead B; just prior to closing they appear as follows:

overhead A		overhead B	
96,000	12,000	42,000	3,000
	18,000		3,000
	18,000		6,000
48,000		30,000	

At this point we expense the intercept amounts as period costs.

overhead expense	87,000	
overhead A		55,000
overhead B		32,000

The overhead accounts are now closed by moving the remaining amounts to cost of goods sold.

overhead A	7,000	
overhead B	2,000	
cost of goods sold		9,000

---

[17]A more streamlined procedure would treat the period cost component as the intercept plus the residual amount in the overhead account. We stress closing the latter to cost of goods sold in order to maintain a parallel with the earlier normal costing procedure.

Several observations should be pondered. First, the mechanical differences between full and variable costing are minor. Suppose the direct costs are fully variable. Then, under variable costing we use the slope of the underlying LLA to assign costs to products. The intercept amount is closed to overhead expense. Under full costing we use average overhead to assign overhead to products. Nothing is assigned to overhead expense. In a normal costing regime, either system will most surely end the period with a remaining balance in the overhead account. This is dealt with in pragmatic fashion by closing the remaining overhead to cost of goods sold.

Second, the economic interpretation of the two approaches is subtle and ambiguous. This was stressed in Chapter 5. Suppose we want a reasonable estimate of the incremental cost of job 1. Which costing technique gives a better estimate? There is no general answer. Each costing procedure produces a product cost statistic. Depending on the procedure, on the firm's cost curve, on which factor inputs are fixed, and on where the status quo output level is at, one or the other costing procedure might produce the more useful statistic.[18]

In a similar vein, it is common to treat direct material and direct labor as having no intercept in their respective LLAs. This, too, should be approached with caution. Suppose the labor supply cannot be altered in the short-run and some labor will be idle if a particular product is not produced. Is direct labor "fixed" here? To make matters worse, suppose the labor usually does routine maintenance when it is otherwise idle.[19] This is why we were cautious in our description of variable costing. It should be understood in terms of all product cost categories, not just the indirect ones.

Again, the economic interpretation of the accountant's product costing art is subtle and ambiguous. This art produces a general purpose cost construction that is housed in the accounting library. The astute user knows how these statistics were constructed and how to modify them for whatever purpose is at hand.

Third, one need not commit to a single approach. One common technique is to separate burden rates into "fixed" and "variable" components. This is code for identifying separately the intercept and slope components of the product cost assignments. To illustrate, it is routine to combine Tables 6.3 and 6.4. We use normal costing, but separately identify what the overhead assignments would have been under variable costing. See Table 6.5.

These calculations should be familiar. We are using LLAs of $OV_A = 55,000 + 1(DL\$)$ and $OV_B = 32,000 + .2(DM\$)$. Under variable costing we assign "variable"

---

[18]Closely related is our objection to the common phrase that variable differs from full costing in that it treats fixed overhead as a period cost. It treats the intercept of the overhead LLA as a period cost. Is this fixed cost?

[19]Continuing, suppose the only use for the direct material is for it to remain in inventory. No other uses are contemplated and the resale market is close to nil. This will be explored when we study decision framing.

overhead A using an estimated burden rate of 1 per direct labor dollar and "variable" overhead B using an estimated burden rate of 0.2 per direct material dollar.

Under normal costing, however, we used respective predetermined burden rates of 2.1 per direct labor dollar for overhead A and 0.6 per direct material dollar for overhead B. We therefore assign "fixed" overhead A at the rate of 2.1 - 1 = 1.1 per direct labor dollar and "fixed" overhead B at the rate of 0.6 - 0.2 = 0.4 per direct material dollar. All we did, in other words, was factor each normal costing, predetermined burden rate into the amount associated with the LLA's slope and the amount associated with the LLA's intercept.[20]

Table 6.5: Product Cost Construction that Displays (Normal) Full and Variable Product Cost				
	job 1	job 2	job 3	total
direct labor cost	12,000	18,000	18,000	48,000
direct material cost	15,000	15,000	30,000	60,000
assigned "variable" overhead A	12,000	18,000	18,000	48,000
assigned "variable" overhead B	3,000	3,000	6,000	12,000
variable product cost	42,000	54,000	72,000	168,000
assigned "fixed" overhead A	13,200	19,800	19,800	52,800
assigned "fixed" overhead B	6,000	6,000	12,000	24,000
full product cost	61,200	79,800	103,800	244,800

A Concluding Observation

We thus see how the building blocks of aggregation and LLA identification are used in the accountant's product costing art. It is important to understand that the aggregations and LLA identifications are matters of judgment. Also, the choices are not necessarily benign.

To see this, return to our initial attempt at constructing the actual cost of the three products, Table 6.2. What happens to our cost constructions if we begin with different LLAs? To explore this question, we focus on actual costing. This keeps the illustration uncluttered. Otherwise, we would be forced to provide the slopes and intercepts of a vast array of LLAs.

---

[20]What would show up here if we had a single product firm operating at its efficient scale?

Table 6.6 provides actual cost constructions based on various LLAs for the two overhead categories. We use direct labor dollars, direct labor hours, total direct material dollars, and cost of specialty materials in various combinations.

For example, suppose we use direct labor hours as the explanatory variable for overhead A and specialty materials acquired as the explanatory variable for overhead B. Actual costing then produces a cost construction of 62,600 for job 1, 83,200 for job 2, and 100,200 for job 3.

Table 6.6: Product Cost Constructions Using Various LLAs					
overhead A explanatory variable	overhead b explanatory variable	job 1 cost	job 2 cost	job 3 cost	total cost
direct labor dollars	direct mater- ial dollars	61,500	79,500	105,000	246,000
direct labor dollars	direct labor dollars	61,500	84,750	99,750	246,000
direct labor hours	direct labor dollars	59,100	91,950	94,950	246,000
direct labor dollars	specialty materials	65,000	76,000	105,000	246,000
direct labor hours	direct mater- ial dollars	59,100	86,700	100,200	246,000
direct labor hours	specialty materials	62,600	83,200	100,200	246,000

Notice how the product cost constructions vary. Job 1 cost varies from 59,100 to 65,000, a variation of 10%. Job 2 cost varies from 76,000 to 91,950, a variation of 21%. Job 3 cost varies from 94,950 to 105,000, a variation of 11%. Of course, these variations are not independent. We constrain the total to 246,000. If an alternative LLA drives one cost up, another cost must go down. Also, intimate knowledge of the production process would likely render some explanatory variables more plausible than others. On the other hand, the aggregations and explanatory variables are never completely obvious. They are matters of choice; and the choices can have a dramatic effect on individual product cost statistics.

Summary

We have stressed the importance of viewing the accounting library as a collection of accounting constructions. The accountant's product costing art uses various aggregations and LLAs to construct product cost statistics. Product costing in a setting of heterogeneous products is quintessential costing art. Every product cost construction is a variation on the theme developed in this chapter.

We have also emphasized the importance of choice in understanding what goes into the accounting library. Many choices are made in the product costing arena.

Initially we must select the split between period and product costs. We then must select the categories into which the product costs will be aggregated. Three broad types of categories are used for this purpose. Direct labor categories are categories of labor cost that the organization can and wants to identify directly with products. Direct material categories are categories of material cost that the organization can and wants to identify directly with products. These are the direct cost categories. All other product cost categories are indirect cost categories. Overhead is the usual name for these categories.

Once the costs have been categorized, we turn to the question of selecting LLAs that well describe each category's costs. By definition, the explanatory variable for direct categories is units of the various products. Overhead is ambiguous, again by definition. These are categories that are not direct! Some model linking cost in the category to one or more explanatory variables is selected. We have emphasized a linear construction, using a single explanatory variable for this purpose.

After the LLAs are selected, the assignment procedure is perfunctory. At least it is perfunctory in a textbook.

Pragmatic considerations now enter. Cost assignments in an actual costing system must wait until the end of the accounting period. This delays construction of some product cost statistics. More important, it bunches the accounting work at the end of the period. Enter normal costing. Under normal costing, we assign the overhead using predetermined or estimated versions of the overhead burden rates. Any "error" that remains is simply closed to cost of goods sold at the end of the accounting period.

Of course, if we have bothered to construct a predetermined overhead rate for some overhead category, we have given considerable thought to the nature of costs in that category. This raises the specter of variable costing. If we have a reasonable estimate of the slope and intercept of the underlying LLA, we can treat the intercept as a period rather than a product cost. This is the essence of variable costing.[21]

The economic interpretation of full and variable cost statistics is far from straightforward. If the LLAs have nonnegative intercepts, we know the full product cost statistic is larger than the variable product cost statistic. Which statistic is better for our purpose? This depends on our purpose and on our circumstance. All we can say of a general nature is that a costing system that catalogues both statistics (as in Table 6.5) provides more information.[22]

---

[21]We now have full or variable product costing, coupled with actual or normal overhead assignment. Our illustration of variable costing used estimated slopes and therefore was a normal costing procedure. It is possible to have an actual, variable costing procedure; but this requires any given overhead account be identified as entirely "fixed" or entirely "variable." Otherwise we have no way of knowing how much of the overhead total is to be treated as a period cost.

[22]Even this statement must be qualified. More information, even if costless, is not necessarily

The contrast between this costing exercise and that of the economist should be pondered. The accountant groups or aggregates various factors of production into categories. The cost that is accumulated in any such category may be close to or far removed from prevailing factor prices. Depreciation versus change in market value of the asset is an illustration. Another is the separation of labor cost into explicit wage payments and fringe benefits. The accountant also deals with approximate relationships between cost incidence and explanatory variables.

Finally, as seems our wont, we have identified yet additional specialized terminology. Direct labor, direct material, and overhead are the three broad categories of product cost. Movement from these categories to individual product costs may be done with an actual or with a normal costing system. Normal costing rests on estimated or predetermined burden rates. This leads to over or under-absorbed overhead. In turn, the period versus product cost distinction may be tightly drawn, in which case we are dealing with variable costing. Otherwise we are dealing with full or absorption costing.

Terminology of this nature is important. It alerts us to the nuances that may be present in any particular accounting library.

Bibliographic Notes

Where to draw the line between product and period costs remains a controversial issue. Expensing of R&D under GAAP is illustrative. Choice between full and variable costing is part of this larger issue. GAAP stresses the importance of costs that are "clearly related" to production in identifying product costs; internally, of course, the firm faces no such constraint in designing its library. A large literature debates and analyzes this issue. Green [1960], Sorter and Horngren [1962], and Fremgren [1964] provide an excellent introduction to this literature. Miller and Buckman [1987] offer a dynamic perspective.

Problems and Exercises

1. The accounting library uses aggregation and LLAs in assembling and presenting cost information. Carefully discuss the connection between these building blocks and the product cost terminology of direct labor, direct material, and overhead.

2. Consider the typical customer invoice from an automobile mechanic. The invoice is based on a posted labor rate of, say, w per hour. Does this mean the

---

desirable in a strategic setting. The difficulty in the strategic setting is the fact one player is vulnerable to what a competitor might do. Acquiring more information may, it turns out, drive the competitor to a defensive position that harms the better informed player.

average wage is w per hour? Does it mean labor costs w per hour? How should the rate of w per hour be interpreted?

3.   Suppose we have a single product firm. The firm uses normal, full costing with a normal volume equal to its efficient scale or output level (where average economic cost is a minimum). The LLA is constructed by setting the slope equal to marginal cost at the efficient output level and the intercept so the two total cost expressions agree at that point. Why is there no difference between full and variable costing in this instance?

4.   *actual, full costing*
Verify the product cost constructions in Table 6.6, using the data in Table 6.1.

5.   *normal, full costing and journal entries*
Simple Manufacturing Company manufactures and distributes a single product. It records manufacturing costs using a normal costing system with overhead applied on the basis of direct labor hours, using a normal volume of 20,000 direct labor hours. In the most recent period, Simple expected to incur $100,000 of manufacturing overhead. Any under or over-applied overhead is closed to cost of goods sold. There was no work-in-process inventory at the beginning of the period.

a]   Give the journal entries for the following events:
    issuance of $50,000 of direct materials into the factory for processing; $270,000 of direct labor cost (30,000 hours), all paid immediately; and $125,000 of manufacturing overhead, all paid in cash.

b]   Give the journal entries to allocate overhead to work in process, to transfer all work in process to finished goods and to close the overhead account. (Assume the transactions above capture all activity in manufacturing overhead.)

6.   *normal, variable costing and journal entries*
Return to the setting of Simple Manufacturing above. Suppose, now, that variable costing is used. Further suppose 40% of the overhead application rate is averaged fixed costs of manufacturing.

a]   Repeat the various journal entries required in the original problem.

b]   Assume Simple Manufacturing uses LIFO and that units sold equals units manufactured. What is the difference between variable and full cost income for the period in question?

7.   *normal, full costing and journal entries*
Return again to the Simple Manufacturing Company problem above, where normal, full costing is used. Suppose all events as described in the original problem occurred, except some of the units were unfinished at the end of the accounting

period. Suppose 80% of the direct material and 75% of the direct labor charges are associated with units that were in fact completed and transferred to finished goods. The remaining units continue to reside in work in process. Repeat the various journal entries required in the original problem.

8.   *actual versus normal costing*

Return to the setting of Ralph's Firm, problem 11 in Chapter 5. After reflection and analysis, Ralph concludes that total manufacturing overhead (OV) is best described with a linear model of the following form: $OV_t = \alpha + \beta y_t + \varepsilon_t$. α and β are constants, y_t is the total of direct labor cost plus direct material cost in period t, ε_t is a zero mean random error term in period t (arising from such things as weather, shop floor congestion, and so on), and OV_t is total manufacturing overhead in period t.

Ralph speculates that $\alpha = 20,000$ and $\beta = 1.00$. Ralph also speculates that manufacturing during the period in question will result in $y_t = 20,000$; i.e., direct labor and direct material will total $20,000. Using the output and cost data in the data in the original problem consider the following.

a]   Suppose Ralph uses this analysis and speculation to implement a normal, full costing procedure. Determine the manufacturing cost per unit for each product. Further suppose half of the current period production of A and B has been sold. Determine ending finished goods inventory and cost of goods sold.

b]   Carefully discuss how Ralph's specification of the overhead LLA removes the ambiguity encountered in the original problem.

c]   Repeat part [a], assuming Ralph uses a normal, variable costing system.

9.   *comparison of methods*

Ralph's Job deals with a small custom fabricator of display cabinets. The accounting system separately accumulates direct labor cost, direct material cost, and two overhead pools. The overhead pools are denoted, respectively, OV_A and OV_B. A recent reporting period begins with no work-in-process inventory. During the period three jobs (a, b and c) were worked on. The first two have been completed, and delivered to their customers while the third (job c) remains partially complete at the end of the period. (The data are scaled in what follows for presentation purposes.)

Various overhead and period costs incurred are as follows:

	overhead A	overhead B	period costs
hourly labor	$2,000	$1,000	$1,000
salary labor	4,000	5,000	6,000
various materials	4,000	10,000	12,000
heat and light	8,000		1,000
depreciation	6,000	2,000	2,000
misc.	9,000	5,000	3,000

Direct labor and direct material activities are summarized as follows:

	job a	job b	job c
direct labor	$2,200	$2,500	$3,500
direct material	$1,800	$5,000	$4,000

In addition, the overhead LLAs are given by $OV_A = 22,000 + 1.00DL\$$ and $OV_B = 20,000 + .50DM\$$ (where DL\$ denotes direct labor dollars and DM\$ denotes direct material dollars).

a] Suppose an actual, full cost system is used. Record these various events with journal entries. Use an account titled "misc. credits" to record the credits for wages payable, depreciation, materials, and so on. Be certain to identify the cost of each job, the ending work-in-process inventory balance, and cost of goods sold. (Notice you will use the LLAs only to identify the appropriate allocation base for each overhead pool.)

b] Repeat [a] for the case where a normal, full costing system is used. Assume respective normal volumes of DL\$ = 10,000 and DM\$ = 10,000 for the two overhead pools.

c] Repeat [a] for the case where normal, variable costing is used.

10. *normal, full costing*

Ralph's Shop manufactures custom equipment. Each customer's problem is unique, and Ralph uses job order costing to help keep track of the profitability of each job or customer. Normal, full costing is used. Overhead is applied to jobs at the rate of 110% of direct labor cost plus 18% of direct material cost.

During a recent period, Ralph's Shop had no beginning work in process. Three jobs were started, named A, B and C. Job C was partially complete at the end of period, though jobs A and B were completed and delivered to their respective customers. The accounting system recorded the following direct product costs during the period.

	job A	job B	job C
direct material	$15,000	$39,000	$18,000
direct labor	$42,000	$80,000	$65,000

In addition, manufacturing overhead totaled $216,000. Finally, the job A and job B customers were each billed $250,000; and Ralph's Shop incurred a total of $68,000 in period costs during the period.

Determine (i) the cost of job A and the cost of job B; (ii) the ending work-in-process balance; (iii) the under or over-absorbed overhead for the period; and (iv) the period's income.

11. *variable versus full costing, income effects*

Consider a single product firm with the following LLAs, where q denotes units manufactured and selling and administrative is, of course, a period cost.

direct labor $\qquad\qquad\qquad\qquad$ DL = 10q

direct material   DM = 10q
overhead   OV = 90,000 + 2DL; and
selling and administrative   SA = 120,000.

The product sells for 100 per unit. Initially no inventory is present. Production and sales quantities for five consecutive years are noted below. At no time is there any ending work-in-process inventory.

	prd. 1	prd. 2	prd. 3	prd. 4	prd. 5
production	4,500	4,500	4,500	4,500	4,500
sales	3,000	5,000	4,500	4,000	6,000

Assume the various LLAs are completely accurate. Determine the income and ending finished goods inventory for each period, using normal, full costing and using variable costing. Assume a normal volume of q = 4,500 units. How do you explain the period-by-period differences between full and variable cost income?

12. *full costing*

Ralph's Venture finds Ralph in a startup company. Ralph has prepared a business plan and a venture capitalist has agreed to provide the necessary funds. Ralph's business plan rests on the following cost and revenue structures (in summary form):

manufacturing cost $TMC = 400,000 + 80q_m$;
selling and administrative cost $S\&A = 200,000 + 20q_s$; and
total revenue $TR = 700q_s$.

q_m denotes units manufactured and q_s denotes units sold.

The business plan called for production and sale of 1,000 units in the first period, with steadily growing sales thereafter. The venture capitalist also required that Ralph present an audited financial statement at the end of each period. This statement was to be produced according to GAAP, using actual, full costing. During the first period, the estimated cost and revenue structures turned out to be exact. Ralph's Venture produced $q_m = 1,200$ units and sold $q_s = 900$ units. (So manufacturing cost totaled 496,000, S&A totaled 218,000; and revenue totaled 630,000.)

The venture capitalist now examines the financial statement prepared according to GAAP. It is much better than anticipated, and the venture capitalist turns to the telephone to call some friends and boast about Ralph's Venture.

Determine the income that was projected for the first year in Ralph's business plan and the income that was actually reported to the venture capitalist. Critically comment on the report and the venture capitalist's enthusiasm.

13. *variable versus full costing, including balance sheet effects*

Ralph's Firm manufactures and sells a single product. For convenience, only two assets are present, cash and finished goods inventory. All transactions are for cash, no dividends are paid, no interest is earned on the cash balance, and so on. Ralph uses normal, full costing coupled with FIFO. The beginning balance sheet shows

        cash   140,000
        finished goods inventory   60,000
as well as a total equity of 200,000. The beginning inventory consists of 500 units, "valued" at 89 per unit in variable cost and 31 per unit in allocated fixed manufacturing overhead. Ralph also provides the following LLAs:

direct material	$DM\$ = 16q_m$;
direct labor	$DL\$ = 48q_m$;
manufacturing overhead	$OV = 90{,}000 + .5DL\$$; and
selling and administrative	$S\&A = 50{,}000 + 2q_s$.

q_s denotes units sold and q_m units manufactured. The selling price is 200 per unit.

The following three years witnessed the events listed below; assume direct material and direct labor costs are exactly as predicted by the respective LLAs.

	year #1	year #2	year #3
production (q_m)	3,500	3,000	2,500
sales (q_s)	3,000	3,000	3,000
ending inventory (units)	1,000	1,000	500
cost (000)			
direct labor plus direct material	224	192	160
overhead	184	162	140
selling and administrative	56	56	56
revenue (000)	600	600	600
cash flow (000)	136	190	244

A normal volume of $q_m = 3{,}000$ units is used for costing purposes during the entire 3-year history.

a] Prepare full cost income statements for each of the 3 years.

b] Prepare end-of-year (full cost, FIFO) balance sheets for each of the 3 years. (Use three accounts for this purpose: cash, finished goods inventory, and total equity.)

c] Repeat parts [a] and [b] above for variable costing.

d] Reconcile the year-by-year differences between full and variable cost income and asset measures.

7

Standard Product Costs

We saw in chapter 6 how pragmatic considerations led to normal costing. There, actual direct costs are combined with indirect costs; but the indirect costs are assigned with an estimated burden rate. Use of an estimated burden rate simplifies the record keeping, with little apparent sacrifice in accuracy. We now extend this theme, by examining the product costing art in a system where all the product cost components are estimated. This is called a standard costing system.

Standard costing is a natural extension of normal costing. As usual, product costs are aggregated into various categories. For each cost category, we record actual cost incurred. We then construct the product costs using estimated quantities and prices for each factor of production. Most surely, every product cost category will have an actual amount that differs from its estimated counterpart. With a little luck, these errors will sum to a small amount. We then expense the errors, just as we expensed over or under-absorbed overhead in a normal costing system.

Why bother? There are several reasons. First, with many cost categories and products, substantial bookkeeping economy is available with a standard costing system. LIFO is easier to implement with such a system. Transfers of partially completed products from one location to another (e.g., from manufacturing to regional warehouses) are also easier to record with standard costs.

Second, the juxtaposition of actual and standard costs is often a useful exercise. This allows the manager routinely to compare actual with estimated results. Large deviations are signals that the actual or estimated costs have been compromised. Moving this juxtaposition of actual and standard into the accounting library makes these comparisons more routine. It places them within the organization's formal reporting process.

Finally, we often evaluate a manager's performance using, among other things, a comparison of results achieved with resources consumed. Resources consumed are usually measured by the cost of resources consumed. Many resources are supplied by other managerial units within the organization. For example, maintenance may be done by a maintenance group. Subcomponents may be manufactured in a separate facility. Security may be provided by a security group. One division's students may take courses in another division of the university.

In each instance an important question arises. Do we want to cost these imported services at actual or at estimated amounts per unit? The answer is subtle and varied. For example, costing imported services at their actual cost imposes supplier inefficiencies on the importing manager's evaluation. Conversely, costing them at their estimated cost shields the importing manager's evaluation from factor price changes in the supplier department.

In addition, a single organization may want to treat different managerial units differently on this score. This means we want an accounting system with the flexibility to cost these imported services as the situation demands. Standard costing is the answer.

The chapter is organized as follows. Initially we study the mechanics of standard costing. As hinted, standard costing is a simple extension of normal costing. We then take a closer look at standards, how they are aggregated into budgets and how they are estimated. The chapter then concludes with an overview of standard costing in a "large" organization where we worry about costs incurred (and revenues earned) by various managers. Nonlinear budgets are illustrated in the chapter's Appendix.

A word of reassurance is in order. We are still learning how a typical accounting library is constructed. Standard costing is an important part of the recipe. How to compare actual and standard costs in a useful way is deferred to a subsequent chapter. Similarly, how we associate particular patterns of actual and standard cost with particular managers is also deferred to subsequent chapters. Step one is to understand the library.

Mechanics of Standard Costing

The typical organization uses a host of inputs to produce its output. In the economist's terminology, we list these inputs as $z_1, ..., z_m$. The accountant, in turn, aggregates these m inputs into a set of categories, through time. The accounting cost of each category is identified. For some categories, the identified cost is expensed immediately. These are the period cost categories. For others, the identified cost is assigned to products. These are the product cost categories. Aggregation and linear approximations are the building blocks used in any such exercise.

Now imagine a normal costing system. There, we use an estimated burden rate to assign overhead to products. A standard costing system extends this blueprint to all product cost categories.

Consider direct labor. In a normal costing system, we tally actual amounts and actual cost for each product. The wage rates used in compiling these direct labor costs vary. Some workers have more seniority or are more skilled than others, and therefore receive a higher wage. Shift differentials are often paid, where a premium is paid for night work. Turnover in the organization's labor force continually alters the mix of employees. Labor contracts call for periodic changes in wage rates.[1] We

---

[1] It is also commonplace for workers to work overtime occasionally. The employees are then paid a premium, usually 150% of the wage rate, for overtime services. Weekend and holiday pay premiums are also commonplace. Premiums of this nature are usually recorded in overhead, not in the direct labor amounts. This is done to associate the "congestion" cost with all products, and not with one or two in particular.

should expect the average wage rate for any specific amount of direct labor to vary from instance to instance.

Proper wage administration demands that we keep track of every employee's earnings, so we must record the actual earnings for each employee. This does not imply we must carry this detail into the product cost records. Why not use an estimated wage rate for product costing purposes?

Having made this step, another comes into view. If we assign direct labor to products based on estimated wage rates, why not use estimated quantities of direct labor as well? We must keep track of every employee's hours, but must we maintain this level of detail in the product cost records?

A two-step procedure emerges. First we record actual direct labor cost. This is identical with the initial recording in a normal costing system. Second, we assign direct labor cost to the products based on an estimated amount multiplied by an estimated wage rate. The difference is closed to cost of goods sold, just as we did for over or under-absorbed overhead.

Direct material is treated in parallel fashion. Proper inventory accounting demands we record materials consumed in the production process. Otherwise, the inventory records are misstated.

Suppose the organization uses LIFO for financial reporting purposes. This gets awkward. LIFO valuation is a periodic computation. We value the ending inventory at the oldest recorded prices. Do we know the amount to assign to each product as it is completed? Hardly. (Of course we could make a reasonable guess.) We must wait until the end of the period to figure out the ending LIFO balance. In addition, current prices are likely to change. Why not maintain the product cost records with an estimated price for the raw materials and tidy up the LIFO valuation at the end of the accounting cycle?[2]

The same reasoning applies to FIFO or weighted average financial records. All we are doing is recognizing raw material prices vary, just as wage rates vary. These variations must be recognized but not necessarily at the product cost level.

We should foresee the next step. We use estimated raw material quantities as well. In this way we wind up assigning direct material cost based on an estimated quantity multiplied by an estimated price.

Again, a two-step procedure is used. First we record the actual consumption of direct materials. Second, we assign direct material cost to the products based on estimated amounts multiplied by estimated prices. Any difference is closed to cost of goods sold.[3]

---

[2]The true LIFO devotee is likely to ease these difficulties with the use of dollar-LIFO procedures. We don't apologize for this complication. You should also expect inventory procedures to vary within a given organization. LIFO, for example, is a U.S. phenomenon. An organization with foreign subsidiaries is likely to have a host of inventory procedures in place.

[3]This is subject to the caveat that no material misstatement results from the expensing procedure. Otherwise, recall, we must restate the product costs.

This would be the end of the story if we had no raw material inventory at the end of the accounting period. But raw material inventories are commonplace.

Standard costing is linked to the raw material inventory records in one of two ways. In one scheme we pick up the difference between estimated and actual acquisition cost at the time the material is acquired. In the other scheme we pick up the difference when the material is used. Either way, the end points of the process are the same. End-of-period raw material inventory records correspond to their financial reporting amounts, and product costs are constructed from standard costs. The difference is simply expensed.

Suppose the price variation is picked up when raw materials are used. At the end of the accounting cycle, we know the amounts of raw materials on hand. Applying the chosen inventory valuation procedure, such as LIFO, we know the ending accounting value to place on the raw material inventory balance. This gives us the total cost of raw materials placed in production. We have already assigned estimated amounts and prices to the products. The difference is closed to cost of goods sold. We thus have all the costs accounted for, product costs stated at standard, and raw material inventories properly valued for financial reporting purposes.

The other procedure recognizes the price variation when the raw materials are acquired. This is more complicated but allows for more timely identification of price variations in the juxtaposition of actual and standard cost. We will pursue this in Chapter 17.[4]

We now have direct costs assigned at standard amounts multiplied by standard prices. The remaining complication is overhead. In a normal costing system we use an estimated burden rate to assign overhead. The burden rate is expressed as an amount per unit of the explanatory variable in the overhead LLA. The explanatory variable thus functions as a pseudo quantity measure. So to maintain our parallel with direct costs, we assign the overhead to product using the estimated burden rate multiplied by an *estimated* amount of the explanatory variable.

You are probably gasping for breath or searching for a new text by now. To reiterate, these procedures are unsophisticated. The details are nearly overwhelming, but the larger picture is straightforward. Actual costs must be recorded. Product costs always pass through the records in an estimated price multiplied by estimated quantity format. Keep this larger picture of beginning with actual costs and driving toward standard in view as we turn to illustrations.

---

[4]To see how this works, remember that product cost will be assigned an estimated quantity of direct material multiplied by an estimated price per unit. Acquisitions of raw material inventory are recorded in the raw material inventory accounts at actual quantities multiplied by estimated prices. Invoices, and therefore accounts payable, use actual quantities and actual prices. The difference is accumulated and closed to cost of goods sold. At the end of the accounting period, the raw material inventory account must be engineered to display the balance required for financial reporting purposes. This is trivially accomplished.

A Numerical Illustration

Consider the running illustration in Chapter 6 (Tables 6.1 through 6.6). We now rework the mechanics to reflect standard product costs. This means we must have estimates for direct costs and the explanatory variables for the two overhead accounts.

We begin with direct labor. Suppose we estimate the direct labor wage rate at $11 per direct labor hour. Suppose we further estimate job 2 will require 1,700 direct labor hours and job 3 will require 1,600 direct labor hours. This implies an estimated direct labor cost of 11(1,700) = 18,700 for job 2 and 11(1,600) = 17,600 for job 3.

Jobs 2 and 3 were started and completed during the accounting period. Job 1 was started, but not completed. Suppose we estimate job 1 will require 2,000 direct labor hours, and that it is 50% complete with respect to direct labor input as of the end of the period. This implies an estimated direct labor quantity of .50(2,000) = 1,000 hours, and an estimated direct labor cost of 11(1,000) = 11,000. Notice we estimate the cost as a function of how complete the job is at the end of the period.

Details are summarized in Table 7.1. We have identified the estimated direct labor cost of each product. The data from Chapter 6 also give us the actual direct labor cost for each product. These, too, are noted in the table.

Now turn to direct materials. Some materials are taken from stock while others are special ordered. Suppose we estimate the latter amounts at 11,000 for job 1, 5,000 for job 2, and 14,000 for job 3. Again, the job 1 estimates reflect the fact job 1 is partially completed as of the end of the period. If all specialty materials have been placed in production, then 14,000 is the total estimated to complete the job. Otherwise, it is the estimated amount that corresponds to specialty materials actually placed in production. With a partially completed job, we simply estimate the cost of the end-of-period work-in-process items, given the actual stage of completion.

Further suppose the estimated cost of stock materials is 5,000 for job 1, 9,000 for job 2, and 17,000 for job 3. The respective actual amounts are 5,000, 10,000, and 15,000. We assume for this illustration that stock materials are placed in inventory at actual prices paid the respective suppliers.[5] In turn, the noted actual costs are simply the actual quantities used, costed at their respective actual prices. Think of the actual direct material costs as precisely what an accrual accounting procedure would recognize.[6] Details are again summarized in Table 7.1.

Overhead cost is estimated in a way that closely follows the normal costing procedure. Recall we previously assumed an LLA for the overhead A category of

---

[5]Transportation cost may also be included.

[6]Again, an alternative procedure would maintain the raw material inventories using actual quantities and estimated prices. This nuance is a distracting complication at this point, and we concentrate for the present on the more obvious procedure.

$OV_A = 55,000 + 1(DL\$)$. Under a full costing procedure we average the intercept over some estimated amount of the LLA's explanatory variable.

Table 7.1: Data for Standard Product Cost Construction Exercise				
	job 1	**job 2**	**job 3**	**total**
direct labor cost				
estimated direct labor hours	1,000	1,700	1,600	4,300
estimated direct labor cost				
(@ 11/hour)	11,000	18,700	17,600	47,300
actual direct labor hours	900	1,800	1,300	4,000
actual direct labor cost	12,000	18,000	18,000	48,000
direct material cost				
estimated cost of specialty				
materials purchased for				
product in question	11,000	5,000	14,000	30,000
actual cost of specialty				
materials purchased for				
product in question	10,000	5,000	15,000	30,000
estimated cost of direct				
materials removed from				
stock for product	5,000	9,000	17,000	31,000
actual cost of direct				
materials removed from				
stock for product	5,000	10,000	15,000	30,000
overhead cost				
estimated overhead A cost				
(@ 2.1 per *estimated* DL$)	23,100	39,270	36,960	99,330
actual overhead A cost				96,000
estimated overhead B cost				
(@ .6 per *estimated* DM$)	9,600	8,400	18,600	36,600
actual overhead B cost				42,000

For this purpose, suppose we anticipate direct labor dollars will total 50,000. This estimated amount of direct labor dollars is called the *normal volume* for overhead category A. (This is the same estimated volume we used in the normal costing illustration.)

Normal volume for an overhead cost category LLA is the estimated amount of the explanatory variable that is used to construct the predetermined burden rate. There is no reason for normal volume to equal the actual amount of the explanatory variable in question. It is common to regard normal volume as a long-term concept, as an estimate of what the explanatory variable will average over the next several

years. This is done so standard costs are not unduly influenced by short-run variations in production. In this way, standard full product cost is related vaguely to the
economist's long-run average cost.[7]

For overhead A, then, we estimate an "average overhead cost" of

$$[55,000 + 1(50,000)]/50,000 = 55/50 + 1 = 1.1 + 1 = 2.1.$$

This is our previously derived predetermined burden rate for overhead A. Of this
amount, 1 is the slope of the underlying LLA and 1.1 is the unitized intercept.

Now, in standard costing we use estimated prices and estimated quantities. The
explanatory variable in an overhead LLA is a pseudo quantity measure. We use the
estimated quantity of the pseudo quantity measure to assign overhead in a standard
costing system.

The direct labor cost for job 1 was estimated to total 11,000. Actual direct labor
dollars totaled 12,000 for job 1. We use the former to construct the assignment of
overhead A to job 1. In particular, we have an estimated price of 2.1 per direct labor
dollar, and an estimated quantity of 11,000 direct labor dollars. This gives us an
overhead A assignment to job 1 of 2.1(11,000) = 23,100.

Do not confuse this with use of a predetermined rate in a normal costing system.
There we use the actual quantity of the explanatory variable. A standard costing
system always uses *estimated* prices multiplied by *estimated* quantities.

The direct labor cost for job 2 was estimated to be 18,700, while that for job 3
was estimated to be 17,600. Respective overhead A assignments are 2.1(18,700) =
39,270 and 2.1(17,600) = 36,960.

The total overhead A cost assigned to products is 23,100 + 39,270 + 36,960 =
99,330. Actual overhead A totaled 96,000. See Table 7.1.

Overhead B is treated in parallel fashion. Recall our LLA was $OV_B = 32,000$
$+ .2(DM\$)$. This is an LLA with intercept a = 32,000 and slope b = .2. The explan-
atory variable is total direct material dollars. Suppose we assume a normal volume
of 80,000 direct material dollars. This implies a predetermined full costing burden
rate of

$$[32,000 + .2(80,000)]/80,000 = 32/80 + .2 = .4 + .2 = .6$$

Again, a familiar datum emerges. Our original predetermined burden rate for
overhead B was .6 per direct labor dollar.

We now assign overhead B using this price, multiplied by estimated quantities.
Here, estimated quantities are measured by estimated direct material dollars. Job 1
was estimated to consume specialty materials totaling 11,000 and stock materials
totaling 5,000, for a total of 16,000. Assigned overhead B is therefore .6(16,000) =
9,600. Job 2 was estimated to consume specialty materials totaling 5,000 and stock
materials totaling 9,000. Assigned overhead B is therefore .6(5,000 + 9,000) =

---

[7]We stress the adverb here. Economic average cost is undefined in a multiproduct firm.

8,400. For job 3 we have an overhead B assignment of .6(14,000 + 17,000) = 18,600.

In this way, we assign overhead B to products in the amount 9,600 + 8,400 + 18,600 = 36,600. Actual overhead B totaled 42,000.

We now rearrange the data in Table 7.1. In Table 7.2 we tally the underlying direct and indirect cost calculations to display the product standard costs. For comparison purposes, we also include the previously constructed actual and normal cost statistics.

Table 7.2: Standard Product Cost Constructions				
	job 1	job 2	job 3	total
direct labor cost	11,000	18,700	17,600	47,300
direct material cost				
specialty materials	11,000	5,000	14,000	30,000
stock materials	5,000	9,000	17,000	31,000
overhead A	23,100	39,270	36,960	99,330
overhead B	9,600	8,400	18,600	36,600
standard product cost	59,700	80,370	104,160	244,230
normal product cost				
(Table 6.3)	61,200	79,800	103,800	244,800
actual product cost				
(Table 6.2)	61,500	79,500	105,000	246,000

In Table 7.3 we separate the overhead cost assignments into "variable" and "fixed" components. Notice how it becomes nearly routine in a standard costing system to separate the variable cost construction as a subcomponent of the full cost construction. All we do is maintain separate prices for the overhead slope and intercept assignments. Any library so maintained provides immediate access to two product cost constructions.[8]

Finally, in Table 7.4 we tally the actual and standard components of each cost category. Notice that total cost exceeded standard cost, while some cost categories had totals less than their standard counterparts. In Chapter 17 we will learn to analyze these differences, often disaggregating them into price and quantity components. For now, we regard the 1,770 as closed to cost of goods sold.[9]

---

[8]Here we follow convention and treat variable product cost as prime cost plus the "variable" portion of overhead. Recall our earlier concern over linking this to the slope of the firm's approximate cost curve. For example, should we assume the direct labor LLA has a zero intercept? This is just one more illustration of why it is important to know how the accounting library is constructed and what we are trying to accomplish by interrogating the library.

[9]We will also learn to interpret the 1,770 as the difference between an actual and a budgeted cost. Any such difference is called an accounting variance. Thus, the direct labor variance is 700 while the

Table 7.3: Standard Variable and Full Product Cost Constructions				
	job 1	**job 2**	**job 3**	**total**
direct labor cost	11,000	18,700	17,600	47,300
direct material cost				
specialty materials	11,000	5,000	14,000	30,000
stock materials	5,000	9,000	17,000	31,000
"variable" overhead A				
(@ 1 per DL$)	11,000	18,700	17,600	47,300
"variable" overhead B				
(@ .2 per DM$)	3,200	2,800	6,200	12,200
standard variable cost	41,200	54,200	72,400	167,800
"fixed" overhead A				
(@ 1.1 per DL$)	12,100	20,570	19,360	52,030
"fixed" overhead B				
(@ .4 per DM$)	6,400	5,600	12,400	24,400
standard full product cost	59,700	80,370	104,160	244,230

Table 7.4: Actual versus Standard Cost Totals			
product cost category	**total actual cost**	**total standard cost**	**difference**
direct labor	48,000	47,300	700
direct material			
specialty	30,000	30,000	0
stock	30,000	31,000	(1,000)
overhead A	96,000	99,330	(3,330)
overhead B	42,000	36,600	5,400
total	246,000	244,230	1,770

Cost Flow Mechanics

Record keeping details follow in ready fashion. We invoke the normal costing motif, but insert the standard cost components at each turn. Consider labor cost. Initially we record actual labor cost, just as before. Some labor cost falls into the direct labor cost category, while the remainder falls into the overhead cost categories. Our initial entry should be familiar, though we now explicitly identify direct labor cost as a control account:

---

overhead A variance is (3,330), and so on. This terminology will be introduced in due course.

[a]	direct labor cost control	48,000	
	overhead A	xxx	
	overhead B	xxx	
	accrued wages payable		xxx
	withheld taxes payable		xxx

For later reference, we also summarize the various entries to tally the two overhead categories:

[a]	overhead A	xxx	
	overhead B	xxx	
	various accounts		xxx

We now assign the direct labor cost to products, using standard rather than actual direct labor cost. The necessary entry follows:

[b]	work in process (job 1)	11,000	
	work in process (job 2)	18,700	
	work in process (job 3)	17,600	
	direct labor cost control		47,300

Examine the direct labor cost control account after these entries have been made. It contains a debit entry of 48,000, and a credit entry of 47,300.

direct labor cost control

48,000	47,300

We have identified the actual direct labor cost; and we have assigned standard direct labor cost to the various products. What of the balance of 700? Direct labor cost is a temporary account. It will be closed at the end of the period. As advertised, it will be closed to cost of goods sold. Further notice that we would use subsidiary accounts, or records, to keep track of direct labor cost for each product. The noted direct labor account is a control account.

Direct materials are recorded in parallel fashion. We want to identify the actual cost of direct materials, and then work toward standard cost. The easiest way to do this is to open a temporary direct material cost account. We then pass actual cost into the account, and standard cost out of the account.

The actual cost of the specialty materials would be recorded as follows. (Recall, we assume these materials are acquired and immediately placed in production; otherwise they would flow through an appropriate inventory account.)

[c]	direct material cost control	30,000	
	accounts payable		30,000

The actual cost of the stock materials is recorded in similar fashion. The only difference is these items are drawn from inventory.

[d]	direct material cost control	30,000	
	raw materials inventory		30,000

We then assign direct material cost to products by transferring respective standard costs to the work-in-process accounts.

[e]	work in process (job 1)	16,000	
	work in process (job 2)	14,000	
	work in process (job 3)	31,000	
	direct material cost control		61,000

Subsidiary records would keep track of individual materials and products (such as the fact job 1 is assigned a standard cost of 11,000 for specialty and 5,000 for stock materials, along with the respective actual costs).

Overhead mechanics follow the same pattern. Actual overhead costs are recorded in the two control accounts. Product cost assignments are then made at standard:

[f]	work in process (job 1)	23,100	
	work in process (job 2)	39,270	
	work in process (job 3)	36,960	
	overhead A		99,330

[g]	work in process (job 1)	9,600	
	work in process (job 2)	8,400	
	work in process (job 3)	18,600	
	overhead B		36,600

The completion of jobs 2 and 3 is then recorded by a transfer to finished goods. Of course, we now use standard product cost. (Otherwise all our work is wasted.)

[h]	finished goods inventory	184,530	
	work in process (job 2)		80,370
	work in process (job 3)		104,160

Finally, we close the various temporary accounts, with offsetting entries posted to cost of goods sold. The difference between actual cost and (assigned) standard cost is accumulated in the direct labor cost control, direct material cost control, and overhead accounts. The necessary entries to close these accounts are calculated in the T accounts of Figure 7.1. They are also calculated in Table 7.4.

[i]	cost of goods sold	1,770	
	overhead A	3,330	
	direct material cost control	1,000	
	direct labor cost control		700
	overhead B		5,400

Carefully trace the above entry through the accounts displayed in Figure 7.1. Notice we display the work-in-process control subsidiary accounts and have not recorded any movements from finished goods to cost of goods sold. Several comments are in order. First, the general idea is to record the work-in-process and finished goods inventories at standard product cost. With many products, this technique considerably eases the bookkeeping chore. Imagine many versions of the same product, each using materials costed at slightly different amounts.

Second, there are many variations on the basic procedure. We illustrated one in which a temporary account is used for each product cost category. This is the easiest to visualize. It is possible to streamline the procedure in various ways.

Third, another variation on the theme would allow us to integrate standard variable and standard full cost into the accounts. The calculations are displayed in Table 7.3. All we would do is separate the standard overhead assignments into their slope and intercept components.

Finally, just as with normal costing, if our estimations turn out to result in materially misstated ending inventories, financial reporting would require a restatement. Otherwise, closing all the actual versus standard cost differences to cost of goods sold is the common and pragmatic procedure.

An Algebraic Illustration

For a change of pace, we turn to a different and more abstract setting. Consider a firm that produces and sells a single product. Let q_m denote the units of product manufactured during the period. Also let q_s denote the units of product sold. If q_m exceeds q_s, finished goods inventory increases by the difference. If q_s exceeds q_m, finished goods inventory decreases by the difference.[10] For simplicity, we assume no beginning or end-of-period work-in-process inventories are present.

We also assume the underlying LLAs aggregate, across direct labor, direct material and overhead, to provide an estimated manufacturing cost LLA of

$$TMC = F + vq_m.$$

The intercept is F, and the slope is v per unit manufactured. Underneath, of course, we have standard prices and quantities.

---

[10]Naturally we assume finished goods inventory cannot be negative. This implies q_s is never larger than beginning finished goods inventory plus the quantity manufactured (q_m) during the period.

Figure 7.1: T Accounts for Costing Illustration

direct labor cost control

[a]	48,000	47,300	[b]
		700	[i]

various credits

		48,000	[a]
		138,000	[a]
		30,000	[c]
		30,000	[d]

direct material cost control

[c]	30,000	61,000	[e]
[d]	30,000		
[i]	1,000		

cost of goods sold

[i]	1,770	

overhead A

[a]	96,000	99,300	[f]
[i]	3,300		

overhead B

[a]	42,000	36,600	[g]
		5,400	[i]

finished goods inventory

[h2]	80,370	
[h3]	104,160	

work in process (job 1)

[b1]	11,000	
[e1]	16,000	
[f1]	23,100	
[g1]	9,600	
	59,700	

work in process (job 2)

[b2]	18,700	80,370	[h2]
[e2]	14,000		
[f2]	39,270		
[g2]	8,400		

work in process (job 3)

[b3]	17,600	104,160	[h3]
[e3]	31,000		
[f3]	36,960		
[g3]	18,600		

legend

[a]	labor, overhead cost recording	[b]	standard direct labor
[c]	direct material recording	[d]	direct material recording
[e]	standard direct material	[f]	standard overhead A
[g]	standard overhead B	[h]	transfer to finished goods
[i]	close temporary accounts to cost of goods sold		

In parallel fashion, suppose q_m units are manufactured. Express the resulting total manufacturing cost in the following suggestive format:

$$TMC^a = F + vq_m + \varepsilon.$$

Here, ε is the difference between actual total manufacturing cost (TMC^a) and what that cost was estimated to be (TMC), given production of q_m units.[11]

full costing

Now suppose, as in the display of T accounts in Figure 7.1, the accounting library uses standard full costing. Assume the standard variable cost per unit is v. This comes right off the LLA for total manufacturing cost, and presumes the aggregate LLA is consistent with the underlying standards. A normal volume of N units is assumed for product costing purposes. This implies a "fixed cost" component of F/N per unit in the standard cost construction. The standard full product cost, then, is $F/N + v$.

Library procedures now provide the following disposition of total manufacturing cost for the period:

total manufacturing cost	$F + vq_m + \varepsilon$
transferred to finished goods	$(F/N + v)q_m$
expensed	$\varepsilon + F - (F/N)q_m$.

In turn, if q_s units are sold, the amount removed from the finished goods tally is simply $(F/N + v)q_s$. So the total product cost expensed this period is the standard cost of the goods sold together with the above noted "plug," or a total of $(F/N + v)q_s + \varepsilon + F - (F/N)q_m$.

variable costing

Conversely, under standard, variable costing the product carries a standard cost of v per unit. Library procedures provide the following:

total manufacturing cost	$F + vq_m + \varepsilon$
transferred to finished goods	vq_m
expensed	$F + \varepsilon$.

---

[11]The algebraic expressions introduced will prove useful in subsequent chapters. For example, we will use classical statistical techniques to estimate a cost category's LLA. The classical model expresses a dependent variable as a linear function of an independent variable plus an error term. This is the reason we inserted the ε term in the actual cost expressions. We will also learn how to decompose these error terms into price and quantity effects. This is the reason we stress the price times quantity construction.

Notice the split between what is inventoried versus expensed. The difference between estimated and actual total manufacturing cost, ε in our notation, is expensed in either scheme. Full costing appends F/N to each unit's variable cost, while variable costing treats intercept F as a period cost.

terminology

Before continuing, we should review and formally acknowledge some important terminology. Our illustrations portray standard cost constructions. *A standard product cost is an estimated product cost.* This estimate, in turn, is composed of a series of price times quantity calculations.

Return to Table 7.3 where we summarize the product cost constructions for our initial example. We used standard amounts of direct labor and direct materials, each costed at standard prices. Overhead was assigned using the noted LLAs and the estimated amounts of the respective explanatory variables (DL$ and DM$). In this way we speak of standard cost of a product, a set of products, and any particular category of a product's cost. *Standard cost* is a term reserved for a product level construction. It is a "per unit" cost construction. Standard costs are estimated costs expressed at the product level.

Budgeted costs are estimated costs expressed at the cost category or total cost level. *A budgeted cost is an estimate of the total cost in some cost category.* Budgeted cost can be thought of as reflecting standard costs and quantities of output. In a variable costing system, our second illustration rests on budgeted total manufacturing cost of TMC = $F + vq_m$. Similarly, our earlier illustration used overhead cost budgets for the overhead categories.

For the record, we also have what are called *fixed* and *flexible* budgets. A budget always has a quantity measure. If the quantity measure is allowed to vary, it is called a flexible budget. If not, it is called a fixed budget. Standard costing is always geared to a flexible budget. Why? The actual quantity manufactured (not what might have been anticipated or budgeted) determines what goes into finished goods.[12]

Sources of Standards

Standard costing has the virtue of streamlining costing procedures. Admittedly, this may appear to be a serious misstatement of fact. The claim is standard costing streamlines costing procedures, not that it streamlines the learning of costing procedures. Think of it as substitution of human capital for labor!

---

[12]We should anticipate profit budgets. We often treat a profit budget as fixed, and then try to sort out the reasons for actual and budgeted profit differing. The terminology of a fixed versus flexible budget is useful in such an exercise.

At a mechanical level, we simply estimate product costs and then as quickly as possible purge any difference between actual and budget from the inventory records. Naturally, this difference must be recognized. We simply expense it, assuming no material distortions arise in the financial records.

The key, of course, is beginning with an accurate standard cost. If we can estimate standard costs with a reasonable degree of accuracy, our procedure will not cause any significant distortions in the accounting library. Otherwise, we must restate the calculations, and in the process the total bookkeeping work will be increased. This raises the question of how we develop the estimates on which the standard costs are based. More generally, it raises the question of how we develop budgets.

The sources of these estimates, and the procedures for developing them, are varied. At one extreme, some individual in the organization may ponder over recent financial results and subjectively estimate the standards and budgets for the coming period. At the other extreme, many individuals may be involved, using a host of sophisticated techniques.

To illustrate, the production process may be thoroughly engineered. Industrial engineers, using time and motion studies and synthetic time standards, may have developed quantity standards for direct labor and direct material for each product. Procedures used in this process may be covered by the prevailing labor contract. The standards themselves may even be negotiated. The labor and supplier contracts provide the standard prices.

Overhead categories may be well studied, and overhead budgets developed using a combination of statistical techniques and economic introspection.

Along with these activities, budgets for various support personnel, for expansion, for new products, for product phase outs, for new investment, and so on, may be developed by a central staff. In such a case, it is likely that various managers will participate in the budget setting exercise. It is also likely that knowledge of competitors will be used in the exercise. Considerable work and skill may be devoted to the estimation exercise.

Just as sources of and procedures for developing these estimates differ, so does their attainability. The standards may be set so "tight" that only an aggressive, diligent work force coupled with favorable luck will produce an actual cost below budget. Alternatively, they may be set so "loose" that actual cost below budget is almost guaranteed. Why the variation in practice?

Consider a weather forecast. We want the forecast to be accurate, to tell us exactly what tomorrow's weather will be. Sometimes the forecast is correct, other times it is not. On average, it is probably correct. If so, we call the forecast unbiased. An unbiased forecast does not tend to over or understate weather quality, on average.

Is this a good analogy for our cost estimation exercise? Yes and no. First, there is no compelling reason for our standard costs to be unbiased estimates of actual costs. This may appear odd but standards and budgets are also used for control purposes. They become performance norms. Performance norms, as we know, may be "easy" or "difficult" to attain.

Cost overruns are legendary if not infamous in "cost plus" contracting.[13] Does this sound like a downward biased cost estimate? Any dean I have ever worked for was only pleased when course evaluations were off the scale. Does this sound like an upward biased estimate? The organization may work with upward biased, unbiased, or downward biased standards.[14] For example, the domestic airline industry recently began publishing on-time arrival statistics. The initial foray into this disclosure game was to extend scheduled arrival times. The standard was loosened. United Parcel Service, on the other hand, is well known to hold its drivers to strict schedules. More will be said about this in subsequent chapters.

Another shortcoming of our weather forecast analogy is the nature of the actual event. (Did you notice the pun?) Weather is exogenous. Many aspects of organizational performance are endogenous. We worry about whether the weather forecaster exercises due care or sufficient diligence in forecasting the weather. We worry about similar matters in setting the standard or budget. We also worry about whether actual cost was the result of due care or sufficient diligence. Both sides of the equation come into play. Was the estimate well prepared? Was the actual cost the result of diligent, efficient behavior by the organization?

Finally, dynamics are also important here. Suppose actual cost is below standard cost. What is likely to happen to the standard for the next period? This is called ratcheting. It is a caricature of a broader problem: the pattern of standards and budgets through time.

For now our study is focused on standard costing procedures. The idea is to streamline the costing exercise, to rely on estimated costs. One should not infer, however, that these estimated costs are easy to come by or are lacking in subtlety. Some organizations invest heavily in the construction of standard costs and budgets. Some organizations use "tight" budgets, tight in the sense that it takes unusual diligence and luck to beat the budget. Others use "loose" budgets. Still others use combinations. This is part of the product costing art.[15]

---

[13]A cost plus contract is one in which the supplier is paid actual cost plus a fee. The fee may be fixed, or may depend on how well the product performs and on how close actual was to estimated cost.

[14]This should not imply a lack of structure. If the standards are unrealistic, the standard costs will not be useful, and we will have defeated the original purpose. On the other hand, there are shades of gray.

[15]Two additional features of the budget scene should be mentioned. A division manager may have superior information when it comes to setting the division's budget. This may result in a slack or padded budget. We will study this issue at length when we introduce control problems. Budgets and incentives are not separable issues. One can only be understood in conjunction with the other. That is why we defer the subject, and for the moment concentrate on library procedures. Also, authorization aspects are often part of the budget process. The division's budget may call for spending some amount on R&D or new product development. The budget may also be the organization's formal authorization

Different organizations use different splits between product and period costs, different product cost categorizations, and different LLAs. Different organizations also use different procedures and styles in their cost estimation practices.

Responsibility Accounting

A concluding component of this introduction to standard costs and budgets is their use in a setting of multiple managers. The general idea is we use revenues, costs, and expenses for a variety of purposes: to aid in analysis of production plans, to measure periodic income, to monitor investments, and to evaluate the performance of various managers. Serving a variety of uses means the library is maintained in a fashion that allows the accounting products to be tailored to the purpose at hand.

Responsibility accounting is the generic phrase for the way the accounting products are tailored for purposes of evaluating various managers. The idea is straightforward. Managers are evaluated using a variety of observables, including accounting measures. Total manufacturing cost might be used in the production manager's evaluation, total marketing cost might be used in the marketing manager's evaluation, departmental cost might be used in the department manager's evaluation, and so on.

This can be visualized with a simple trick. Assign a set of indices to each cost (also to each revenue and expense) category. The indices identify the managers whose evaluation uses the category in question.

To illustrate, suppose the organization has 12 managers and 900 cost categories in its accounting library. Each category has a set of indices. Cost category 5 might have the set of indices {2,5,11}. Cost category 5, in other words, is used in the evaluation of managers 2, 5, and 11. Stated differently, manager 2 is held responsible for cost category 5, as are managers 5 and 11. Hence the term, *responsibility accounting*.

Two interrelated questions arise. How many cost categories do we want for this purpose; and which of these categories do we want to use in the evaluation of any particular manager? We will examine these questions at length in subsequent chapters. For now we will be content to sketch the customary answer, and its tie to standards and budgets.

How many categories to use in the library is often thought of in terms of homogeneity. Imagine using many more categories, in the limit one for each factor of production. If two of these more detailed categories are sufficiently similar, we group them together. Continue the grouping, or aggregation, until too much detail is lost. Tempered homogeneity is the key. Total disaggregation is simply overwhelming. Too much aggregation destroys the usefulness of the library. An intermediate solution is sought. We discussed this point in our earlier analysis of

---

for such spending. Alternatively, authorization may be a separate act. This authorization aspect is evident in public sector budgeting procedures.

product costing. It applies with equal force to the larger context of multiple uses of the accounting library.

Whether to use a particular category in the evaluation of a particular manager is often thought of in terms of *controllability*. Can the manager exert influence over the cost (revenue or expense) category in question? If so, that category should be used in the evaluation of that manager.

This approach leads to a hierarchical picture. Imagine a division in a large organization. The division is divided into production and marketing groups. The production group is subdivided into two production departments and a maintenance department. We imagine 6 managers in this thumbnail sketch. The maintenance, production 1 and production 2 managers are concerned with their respective departments and report to the production group manager. The production group manager and marketing group manager each report to the division manager. We'll stop at this point, but it is easy to imagine subordinate managers in the marketing group, other divisions with detailed organization structures, a central administrator to whom division managers report, and so on.

Now consider manufacturing cost that is incurred in this division. Suppose each manufacturing cost category arises in one of the two production departments, or in the maintenance department. Each of the lower level managers controls the cost categories that arise in their respective departments. Initially, then, each manufacturing cost category is the responsibility of one of the production 1, production 2, or maintenance managers.

Continuing, the production group manager is responsible for all manufacturing costs identified with the subordinate production 1, production 2, and maintenance managers. The group manager is also responsible for other cost categories that arise in the production group. Administrative costs are a ready illustration.

The picture that emerges is one of hierarchical tracing. Each category is initially the responsibility of some manager. That manager reports to another, one who is higher in the hierarchy. Each identified category then becomes the responsibility of the second manager to whom the first reports. In the limit, we reach the chief executive, who has responsibility for all cost (revenue and expense) categories.

Our sketch is necessarily brief. We want to introduce the idea that we purposely select some categories to evaluate a particular manager. Precisely how to do this is left open until later chapters.

The tie to standard costs and budgets is twofold. First, it is often useful to frame the evaluation in terms of performance relative to a norm. The budget becomes the norm. For example, in evaluating the production 1 manager we are likely to compare actual costs used in the evaluation with their budgeted counterparts. The budget provides a norm, a goal for performance assessment. In turn, standard costs are the building blocks on which the budget is constructed.

Second, we often introduce subtle details in drawing the line between what is and what is not included in a particular manager's evaluation. Suppose the production 1 manager is responsible for a process that uses raw materials. Further suppose these materials are purchased on long-term contracts from various suppliers. The contracts, in turn, are negotiated and monitored by the group manager, not the production 1 manager. We might then decide to hold the production 1 manager responsible for actual material used, but not for any price variations. The mechanics are trivial under standard costing. We cost the production 1 manager's use of raw materials at their standard price. A cost category reflecting the difference between actual and standard price of the materials is the responsibility of the group manager, but not the production 1 manager.

For another example, the maintenance department does maintenance for two production departments. We may want to hold the production 1 manager responsible for the cost of maintenance in the first department. One way to do this is to assign maintenance cost to the two production departments, based on the standard cost per unit of maintenance. In this way, the production departments are responsible for the quantity of maintenance used. The maintenance manager is responsible for the efficiency with which this maintenance was delivered. Again, if this is how we choose to evaluate the managers, standard costing techniques provide a simple, coherent way to make these distinctions.

Summary

Standard costing is a natural extension or evolution of normal costing. We always record actual costs. In a standard costing system, though, we convert the product cost records to standard costs as quickly as possible. Mechanical aspects are straightforward. We introduce temporary accounts for each cost category. Actual costs flow in, standard costs flow out. The remainder is expensed, most obviously to cost of goods sold.

These techniques are important for three reasons. They simplify bookkeeping; they introduce flexibility into the accounting library; and they formalize the comparison of actual with estimated results.

Additional terminology enters our study at this point. A standard product cost is an estimated product cost. Standards are "per unit" estimates. Budgets are cost category or "total" estimates. A budgeted cost is an estimated cost for the cost category in question.

Standards and budgets are intimately linked. Imagine an LLA for some cost category. This might serve as the budget for the cost category. In turn, the product cost implications of this LLA would then serve as the product cost standards that are associated with this cost category.

Standard, full cost requires some volume estimate to use in averaging LLA intercepts. These volume estimates are called normal volumes. Usually we set the normal volume to reflect anticipated activity over a horizon of several periods. That way product cost statistics are not unduly affected by short-run fluctuations in volume.

A budget expresses an estimated cost for a cost category, as a function of some explanatory variable. Examples are direct labor as a function of units produced or overhead as a function of materials used. Nonlinear budgets are encountered when we want the budget to extend beyond the range in which any particular LLA would be sufficiently accurate. This is explored in the Appendix.

Finally, responsibility accounting is the term we use to describe the selection of various cost, revenue, and expense categories that are used to evaluate a particular manager. Holding a manager responsible for some cost category is code for the organization using that cost category as an item on which that manager's performance evaluation is based. It is a short step to recognize budgets as performance norms, and performance evaluation as focusing on actual performance relative to the budgeted norm.

Appendix: Nonlinear Budgets

Standard costing procedures are designed to streamline the accounting library. Budgets expand on this view, offering an estimated cost as a function of the appropriate explanatory variables. The underlying cost category aggregations and LLAs thus resurface in budget expressions.

It is important to remember an LLA is a *local* linear approximation. Allowing the explanatory variable to vary beyond some tentative amount, or outside the intended relevant range, is an invitation to alter the underlying LLA. We caution the reader on this point by briefly discussing nonlinear budgets at this juncture.

Recall the single product illustration earlier in the chapter. Combining the various standards, we estimated a manufacturing cost budget of $TMC = F + vq_m$. Do we regard this as a useful budget, despite how large or how small q_m is? Certainly not. Though we did not discuss it at the time, implicit in all we did was the assumption q_m would fall within some relevant range. Outside the relevant range, we estimate new LLAs and repeat the procedure. In one relevant range, then, we would have one intercept, slope specification; and in another we would have a different intercept, slope specification. Putting these together on the same graph would create a nonlinear function, or a nonlinear budget.

Below we give two explicit examples. One is a so-called step cost. The other is based on a learning curve.

a step cost illustration

Imagine an organization that uses several factories to manufacture its product. If demand is low, only one factory will be in operation. As demand increases, it will eventually become economic to open a second factory. Then a third might be opened, and so on. Just to illustrate, suppose it costs 1 million dollars to open one factory. This covers such items as security, maintenance, energy, and supervision. If one factory is open, 1 million in "factory support cost" will be incurred. If two factories are open, 2 million in factory support cost will be incurred, and so on until we have exhausted the supply of idle factories.

Further suppose each factory has a capacity of 100,000 units. It is the policy of the organization to open an additional factory each time the operating units reach this capacity.

What does the budget for factory support cost look like? Let q_m denote units of output. If the relevant range is $0 \leq q_m \leq 100,000$, one factory will be open. The budget then is described by an LLA with an intercept of a = 1 million and a slope of b = 0. If the relevant range is $100,000 < q_m \leq 200,000$, two factories will be open. The budget is now described by an LLA with an intercept of a = 2 million and a slope of b = 0.

Examine Figure 7.2. This is a plot of budgeted factory support cost. The explanatory variable is units of output, q_m. The relevant range for the budget is $0 \leq q_m \leq 300,000$. This is outside the relevant range of any single LLA; so we combine the various LLAs. This gives the noted nonlinear budget. The function is often called a step cost function, because of the way it "steps" to higher and higher amounts.

Figure 7.2: Step Cost Function

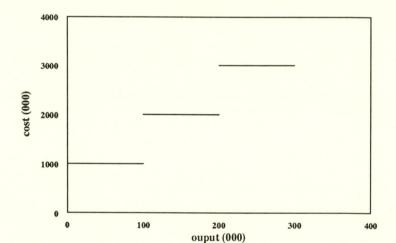

We rationalized this portrayal with a story of identical factories that are put on line as needed. The same picture emerges whenever we think of inputs that come in minimally sized amounts. A labor contract may require at least 4 hours of work if someone is asked to work overtime. A second shift requires a second set of supervisory personnel. We pay the landing fee at the airport, despite how many passengers are on the airplane. A second concert requires a second set of security services.

More broadly, we should remember the accounting library uses LLAs at every twist and turn. Combining these details into a larger picture may call for a nonlinear budget. A step cost, as illustrated in Figure 7.2, is but one illustration.

What happens as the "step size" becomes smaller and smaller? Alternatively, what happens as the relevant range for each LLA becomes smaller and smaller? In the limit, the step pattern is replaced by a smooth, though distinctly nonlinear curve. This is illustrated by a learning curve.

a learning illustration

Return, yet again, to our earlier single product illustration. Total manufacturing cost (under a variable costing system) was budgeted at $TMC = F + vq_m$. We now trace this story through time. The underlying standard prices and quantities remain constant, except the direct labor quantity standard. The estimated labor quantity per unit declines with time, as the work force becomes more experienced. This is called learning.

Suppose our organization is formed in period 1, and in the following periods produces the quantities displayed in Table 7.5. Here q_t denotes quantity produced in period t, and DLH_t denotes direct labor hours used in that production. You might want to interpret the data as production quantity and direct labor hours in units of a thousand. We suppress (000) in what follows, to avoid distraction.

\multicolumn{7}{c}{Table 7.5: Data for Learning Curve Illustration}
t	q_t	DLH_t	DLH_t/q_t	Q_t	H_t	H_t/Q_t
1	10	67.0	6.70	10	67.0	6.70
2	20	69.8	3.49	30	136.8	4.56
3	30	77.9	2.60	60	214.7	3.58
4	40	84.6	2.11	100	299.3	2.99
5	50	90.2	1.80	150	389.5	2.60
6	50	80.1	1.60	200	469.6	2.35
7	30	44.7	1.49	230	514.3	2.24

Examine the data in column 4 of Table 7.5. Direct labor hours per unit of output (i.e., DLH_t/q_t) fall from $67/10 = 6.70$ in the first period to $44.7/30 = 1.49$ hours per unit in the last period.

This type of phenomenon is often modeled with an exponential function, relating average number of hours to *cumulative* production. The cumulative output or production through period t is the quantity $Q_t = q_1 + q_2 + \cdots + q_t$. Similarly, the cumulative direct labor hours used through period t is the quantity $H_t = DLH_1 + DLH_2 + \cdots + DLH_t$.

As of period t, the average number of direct labor hours per unit produced is H_t/Q_t. Do not confuse this with the average computed using only output and direct labor use in any given period (e.g., DLH_3/q_3 in column 4). H_t/Q_t is computed in the last column of Table 7.5.

We now assume the following functional form:

$$H_t/Q_t = h_0[Q_t]^{-f}$$

where $h_0 > 0$ and $0 < f < 1$ are constants. This is called a *learning curve* for direct labor hours. The data in Table 7.5, for example, were generated by such a function with $h_0 = 15$ and $f = 0.35$; or $H_t/Q_t = 15[Q_t]^{-.35}$.

How are we to interpret this model? Suppose we manufacture one unit, implying $Q_t = 1$. Then $H_t/1 = H_t = h_0[1]^{-.35} = h_0$. In other words, h_0 is the number of direct labor hours required for the first unit of output.

Now examine Figure 7.3, where we plot the function $H_t/Q_t = 15[Q_t]^{-.35}$. Notice the average number of direct labor hours declines as cumulative output increases. This is no accident. Examine the derivative of our learning curve:

$$\frac{d(H_t/Q_t)}{dQ_t} = \frac{d(h_0 Q_t^{-f})}{dQ_t} = -f h_0 Q_t^{-f-1}.$$

The derivative is uniformly negative. This implies average direct labor hours decline with cumulative production. Of course, the model was chosen to exhibit exactly this characteristic. The unusual feature is this simple model seems to characterize learning across a variety of learning situations.

Figure 7.3: Average Direct Labor Hours

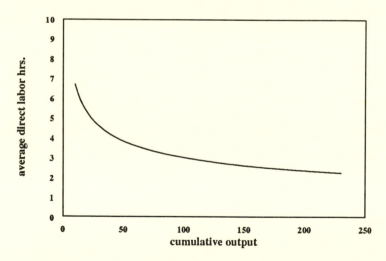

It is also possible to give an intuitive interpretation of the exponent f. If f is larger, the curve declines more steeply. This suggests that a larger f corresponds to faster learning. Following up on this, what happens when we double output? For any Q_t, the average labor hours is $h_0[Q_t]^{-f}$. Doubling cumulative output implies an average of $h_0[2Q_t]^{-f}$. Divide the new average by the original:

$$h_0[2Q_t]^{-f}/h_0[Q_t]^{-f} = 2^{-f}.$$

If we double cumulative output, the average direct labor hours declines by 2^{-f}. It declines to $100[2^{-f}]$ per cent of the original average. Using the Table 7.5 model, with $f = .35$, we have $2^{-.35} = .7846$. If we double output, average direct labor hours declines to 78% of the original average. This is called the *learning rate*. The learning rate of the learning curve is 2^{-f}.

Again return to the data in Table 7.5. Contrast $Q_t = 60$ with $Q_t = 30$. We have doubled cumulative output. The average direct labor hours declines: $3.58/4.56 = .79$. Similarly, contrast $Q_t = 200$ and $Q_t = 100$. Cumulative output is doubled, and we have $2.35/2.99 = .79$. (Rounding the data in Table 7.5 precludes a ratio that exactly agrees with the learning rate of 78%, or .7846.)

Another view of the learning curve arises when we focus on total as opposed to average hours. Multiplying the learning curve expression by Q_t, we obtain the expression for total direct labor hours:

$$Q_t(H_t/Q_t) = H_t = Q_t(h_0[Q_t]^{-f}) = h_0[Q_t]^{1-f}.$$

We plot the total hours expression for our continuing example in Figure 7.4; $H_t = 15[Q_t]^{.65}$. Total hours increases with cumulative output, but at a decreasing rate. Notice that f approaching 0 implies trivial learning. In the limit total hours are a linear function of output, and average hours per unit is a constant.

Figure 7.4: Total Direct Labor Hours

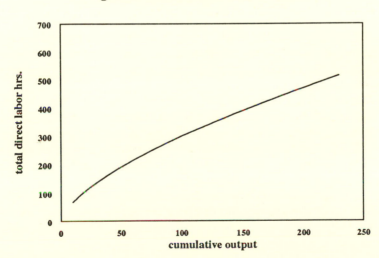

This is beginning to meander. It is important to understand that budgets are based on LLAs. We regard the LLA as sufficiently accurate while our explanatory variable is within the relevant range. Otherwise, adjustments are called for. The limit is a budget with no linear region. The above learning-based expression is designed to illustrate this point.

additional comments on the learning model

The learning curve raises many issues. We illustrated learning by focusing on direct labor hours. We might have learning in various materials, in selected indirect factors, or whatever. By convention, an expression of learning in terms of some factor of production (e.g., direct labor hours) is called a learning curve. An expression in cost terms is usually called an experience curve. (Average cost declines as experience builds.)

The economic side of learning is subtle. Suppose, just to illustrate, that learning across all factors combines to provide an average cost expression of $TC/Q_t = C_0[Q_t]^{-f}$. TC is total cost over the t period horizon. C_0 is the cost of the first unit.

To keep things simple, suppose this is a one period model, so we can drop the reference to period t. Express the average cost experience curve in terms of total cost:

$$TC = C_0[Q]^{1-f}.$$

Differentiating gives us a marginal cost of $TC' = (1-f)C_0[Q]^{-f}$. Marginal cost declines with production.

This raises some interesting questions. Can the firm exploit this fact in the marketplace? Could learning deter entry, thereby giving the large producer a competitive advantage in the product market? Are some product pricing policies more sensible than others when we worry about competitor response? Should we, for example, price close to the eventual marginal cost or might we want systematically to lower price as learning occurs?[16] Could an aggressive price signal learning to our competitors?

Also notice that learning is not necessarily exogenous. The organization might invest in cost reduction programs. Just-in-time inventory strategies are a ready example. On the surface, a just-in-time inventory policy is one in which factors of production arrive just as they are needed to maintain the production pace. No unnecessary investment in inventories occurs. Below the surface, though, programmed learning is sought. The procedure for minimizing inventories is to highlight and keep working on bottlenecks in the production process. Any success in lessening the bottlenecks manifests itself as learning.

---

[16]We only mention pricing issues at this point. There is no easy answer. The proper strategy depends in important ways on such things as market structure in the product market, technology change possibilities, and the organization's reputation.

Learning also comes in various forms. One is a so-called shared experience. As we move through different products, the learning accumulates. A shared experience connecting military and domestic airframe manufacture is a ready example. Another is a so-called spill over. If one producer learns, does this learning spill over to a competitor?

Finally, estimating a learning (or experience) curve opens up an additional set of questions. Just as an LLA is a pragmatic building block, the learning curve is a pragmatic expression for learning. So we always worry about the limitations of our simple model, just as we do for the aggregation and LLA simplifications that abound in the accounting library.

On the other hand, estimating a learning curve seems straightforward. We only need two parameters, h_0 and f in the direct labor example. Transforming with logarithms even linearizes the expression. If $H_t/Q_t = h_0[Q_t]^{-f}$, taking logarithms provides

$$log\{H_t/Q_t\} = log\{h_0[Q_t]^{-f}\} = log\{h_0\} - f \cdot log\{Q_t\}.$$

This is a linear expression with intercept $log\{h_0\}$ and slope -f. The explanatory variable is $log\{Q_t\}$.

So all we need is the intercept and slope, a familiar problem. We will study estimation problems more generally in Chapter 13. For the moment notice there is one important difference in this setting. Usually the explanatory variable is units produced during the period in question or some pseudo quantity measure referring to quantity during the period in question. Here we focus on Q_t. This is cumulative quantity, not quantity during the period in question. The simple learning model relies on cumulative quantity. In this sense, it presumes we know when learning began.[17]

Learning curves are an intuitive and prevalent example of nonlinear budgets. Learning curves also seem to illustrate the old adage of no free example. It is easy to illustrate and visualize how significant learning would lead to a nonlinear budget. The darker side is significant learning raises perplexing issues of how to estimate learning, how to accelerate it with clever engineering, and how to exploit it strategically .

Bibliographic Notes

Standard costing is not new. Solomons [1968] provides linkages to the 19th century. It certainly has a close association with the "scientific management" school (e.g., F. W. Taylor). Issues of attainability or tightness of the standards arise, as does the question of participation in setting the standards. Becker and Green [1962] provide a good entry to these themes. Our approach at this stage is, we emphasize, more modest. We are merely using the LLAs to simplify record keeping. The

---

[17]This is why we were explicit in the example to identify when production began.

learning phenomenon is also not new, though its documentation and management were popularized in the 1970s. Yelle [1979] is a good introduction. Oster [1990] and Tirole [1988] examine the strategic side of learning.

Problems and Exercises

1.   Actual, normal, and standard costing all use the basic building blocks of aggregation and linear approximation. Discuss how linear approximation is used in each of these basic approaches to product costing.

2.   Consider a firm with a manufacturing and a marketing group. The marketing group receives manufactured products from the manufacturing group, and sells them to a variety of customers. The marketing group is evaluated in terms of revenue, less marketing costs, less the manufacturing cost of the items sold. What difference does it make to the marketing group if the firm employs standard costing or normal costing? What difference does it make if full or variable costing is employed?

3.   *standard, full costing*
      Return to the setting of Table 7.1, but assume that the following actual costs have been incurred.

	job 1	job 2	job 3	total
actual direct labor hours	1,100	1,600	1,700	4,400
actual direct labor cost	14,000	20,000	19,000	53,000
actual cost of specialty materials purchased for product in question	9,000	6,000	17,000	32,000
actual cost of direct materials removed from stock for product	12,000	10,000	16,000	38,000
actual overhead A cost				99,000
actual overhead B cost				48,000

Using the same LLAs and standard costs as in the original illustration, provide all journal entries to record the underlying events. Then summarize your work in a table that parallels Table 7.4.

4.   *conversion to actual cost*
      Suppose it turns out the standards in the above exercise are deemed to be too inaccurate and ending inventory calculations, both finished goods and work in process, must be restated to reflect actual cost.
      Determine the appropriate cost for each job.

5. *standard variable cost, journal entries*

Return to the setting of Table 7.1, but now assume standard, variable costing is used. Provide all journal entries to record the underlying events. Then summarize your work in a table that parallels Table 7.4. Remember to expense the intercept of the overhead LLAs and to show this in your table.

6. *normal versus standing cost, journal entries*

This is a continuation of the Simple Manufacturing Company, problem 5 in Chapter 6. Simple now employs standard, full costing. Suppose the following LLAs are estimated:

direct labor: DL$ = 24q;
direct material: DM$ = 6q; and
overhead: OV = 40,000 + 3DLH.

The direct labor LLA reflects an underlying labor standard of 3 hours per unit. Normal volume is q = 6,667 (which implies DLH = 20,000). Production totaled q = 10,000 units, and actual costs are as noted in the original problem.

Give journal entries to record the actual costs, allocation of overhead to work in process, transfer of the completed units from work in process to finished goods, and the closing of all temporary accounts, reflecting the difference between actual and standard costs, to cost of goods sold.

7. *standard full and variable cost, journal entries*

This is a continuation of the Ralph's Job story in Chapter 6, problem 9. Here we tell the story in terms of standard costs. The overhead LLAs were specified in the original problem. Underlying standards for the direct labor and direct material costs are as follows:

	job a	job b	job c
direct labor hours	100	110	300
direct material units	175	450	490

Recall there was no beginning work-in-process inventory, and only jobs a and b were completed during the period. At the end of the period, job c is 50% complete as to labor, and 100% complete as to material. (So at this time its standard cost will be based on 150 direct labor hours and 490 material units.)

Though various skill levels are present, each with a slightly different wage rate, Ralph uses an "average" wage rate of $21 per direct labor hour for costing purposes. Similarly, an "average" material price of $10 per unit of direct material is used. All other details remain as specified in the original problem.

a]   Suppose a standard, full costing system is used. Direct labor and direct material standard costs are specified above. The two overhead LLAs are as specified in the original problem. The normal volumes for the two overhead categories are, respectively, DL$ = 10,000 and DM$ = 10,000. Record these various events with journal entries. Use an account titled "misc. credits" to record the credits for wages payable, depreciation, materials, and so on. Be certain to identify the cost of each job, the ending work-in-process inventory balance, the "plug" to cost of goods sold that closes the various temporary product cost accounts, and the total in the cost of goods sold account.

b] Repeat [a] for the case where standard, variable costing is used.

8. *normal versus standard cost, with balance sheet*
Sweet Products (SP) manufactures several types of somewhat customized recreation products, partly to order and partly for stock. Job order costing is employed. SP's balance sheet as of 8/31/yr1 is as follows:

Balance Sheet, as of 8/31/yr1

cash	$ 23,000	accounts payable	$ 21,000
accounts receivable	12,000	wages payable	14,000
raw material inventory	8,000		
work-in-process inventory	11,000	capital stock	5,000
plant and equipment (net)	47,000	retained earnings	61,000
	$101,000		$101,000

The work-in-process inventory consists entirely of job #112, which is roughly half completed.

For product costing purposes, SP uses normal, full costing with a predetermined overhead rate of 150% of direct labor cost. Any end-of-month over or under-absorbed overhead is closed to the income statement, as a separate line item. During the month 9/1/yr1 to 9/30/yr1, the following transactions took place.
(1) Purchased raw material on account for 35,000.
(2) Issued materials from inventory as follows:

direct materials: job #112	4,300
direct materials: job #113	9,500
direct materials: job #114	8,800
indirect materials:	13,500

(3) Accrued wages and salaries as follows:

direct labor: job #112	9,000
direct labor: job #113	17,500
direct labor: job #114	12,500

indirect labor and factory supervision: 24,500
general office salaries: 42,000
(4) Other manufacturing costs (all credited to accounts payable): 22,000
(5) Equipment depreciation:

plant:	3,000
office:	1,000

(6) Miscellaneous period costs: 3,000 (again credit accounts payable)
(7) Jobs finished during month: #112 and #113
(8) Sales during month (all on account):

#112	45,000
#113	115,000

(9) Cash received (from customers): 130,000
(10) Cash paid:

accounts payable:	45,000
wages:	100,000

Notice that payroll withholding, various fringe benefits, and taxes are omitted, all to keep the exercise within a reasonable time frame.

a] Prepare an ending balance sheet and an income statement for the period 9/1/yr1 to 9/30/yr1.

b] Prepare beginning and ending balance sheets and an income statement using a standard, full cost system. For this purpose, you should assume the following: (i) raw material inventory is maintained at actual price (for convenience); (ii) the standard cost of the beginning work-in-process inventory is 10,000; (iii) the factory overhead budget is OV = 50,000 + .5(direct labor dollars), with a normal volume of 50,000 direct labor dollars; and (iv) the standard direct costs of work accomplished during the month in question are:

	job #112	job #113	job #114
direct labor	10,000	18,000	14,000
direct material	4,000	9,000	12,000

c] Prepare beginning and ending balance sheets and an income statement using a standard, variable cost system. Here you should assume the beginning work in process (job #112) under the standard, *full* cost system consists of 5,000 direct material, 2,000 direct labor, and applied overhead.

9. *variable versus full costing, income effects*

Return to problem 11, Chapter 6. Standard costing is now used, based on the LLAs noted in the original problem. Production and sales remain as before. Selling and administrative totals 120,000 in each period. Manufacturing cost, though, totals as follows:

period 1: 272,500;
period 2: 267,600;
period 3: 264,800;
period 4: 275,600; and
period 5: 260,600.

Determine the income and ending finished goods inventory for each period, using standard, full costing and using standard, variable costing. How do you explain the period by period differences between full and variable cost income?

10. *variable versus full costing, information content*

Consider a single product firm. The known constant selling price for its product is 100 per unit. The firm's known cost curve is given by $TC = 100,000 + 15q + \varepsilon$.

Here, q denotes the total quantity produced in some particular period and ε is, tautologically, an error term. Think about this in the following way: we estimate the cost curve as consisting of fixed cost equal to 100,000 per period and variable cost equal to 15 per unit produced. Things may not go exactly as planned, so we add a fudge term of ε. In addition, to keep things simple, we assume that TC is paid in cash each and every period.

The firm uses standard costing. Under standard, full costing it assumes a normal volume of q = 2,000 and thus works with a standard product cost of 65 per unit. Conversely, under standard, variable costing it works with a standard product cost of 15 per unit.

a] Suppose the following data are observed.

	prd 1	prd 2	prd 3
beginning inventory (at 65 per unit)	0	32,500	19,500
cash inflow (revenue)	150,000	120,000	210,000
cash outflow (TC)	150,000	109,000	120,000
ending inventory (at 65 per unit)	32,500	19,500	13,000
revenue	150,000	120,000	210,000
expense (standard, full costing)	117,500	122,000	126,500
net income	32,500	(2,000)	83,500

Observe that all of these data would be available from the financials. The inventory balances are available on the balance sheet, the cash flow data are available on the funds statement, and so on. Given that we also know the way the measurement system works, in terms of the 65 inventory valuation datum and how expense is measured, we know a great deal here. In fact the only things we do not know are the production quantity, sales quantity, and error term in each of the three periods. But we can figure these out. Determine, using the above data, the production quantity, sales quantity, and error term for each of the three periods.

b] Now let's do the same thing with a variable cost income measurement system. The data available would now be as follows:

	prd 1	prd 2	prd 3
beginning inventory (at 15 per unit)	0	7,500	4,500
cash inflow (revenue)	150,000	120,000	210,000
cash outflow (TC)	150,000	109,000	120,000
ending inventory (at 15 per unit)	7,500	4,500	3,000
revenue	150,000	120,000	210,000
expense (standard, variable costing)	142,500	112,000	121,500
net income	7,500	8,000	88,500

Determine, using only the data in this second panel, the production quantity, sales quantity, and error term for each of the three periods.

c] Finally, reflect back on this exercise. First, why do the periodic income measures differ between the two systems? Second, why are you able with either system to discern exactly the same thing? Third, which measurement scheme is superior?

11. *nonlinear budget*[18]

Ralph's manufacturing cost (TMC) is estimated as follows, where q denotes units manufactured:

$$TMC = 8,000 + 6q, \text{ if } 0 \le q \le 2,000;$$
$$TMC = 10,000 + 5q \text{ if } 2,000 \le q \le 4,000; \text{ and}$$
$$TMC = -2,000 + 8q \text{ if } 4,000 \le q.$$

Plot Ralph's manufacturing cost. Determine the incremental cost of 50 additional units if (i) Ralph is currently manufacturing 1,800 units, or (ii) Ralph is currently manufacturing 1,990 units.

12. *learning*

Given an estimated time of 500 labor hours to build the initial unit of a new product, and a presumed learning rate of 72%, determine the firm's learning curve for labor hours. Construct a table, similar to Table 7.5, that displays period, total, and average labor hours assuming the output schedule noted in Table 7.5. Also plot your learning curve, as in Figure 7.3.

13. *cost calculations in the presence of learning*

Ralph is contemplating introduction of a new product. Various materials will cost 200 per unit; labor will cost 37 per hour. The overhead LLA is $OV = F + .3DM\$ + 42DLH$, where DM\$ denotes direct material dollars and DLH direct labor hours. The consulting engineer predicts a direct labor learning rate of 83%. (Direct materials will not exhibit any learning.) Ralph also predicts the first unit will require 140 direct labor hours. (Hint: $2^{-.2688} = .8300$.)

a] Suppose Ralph anticipates producing and selling 125 units. What is the minimum selling price per unit if this is to be a profitable product? (Assume F is zero for this calculation.)

b] Suppose Ralph proceeds with manufacturing. 220 units have been manufactured. What is the incremental cost of 15 more units?

c] What happens to the marginal cost of producing this product if Ralph manufactures the extra units in [b] above?

---

[18]Suggested by Richard Sansing.

Joint Costs and Cost Allocation

In this chapter we extend our study of the product costing art to joint costs and cost allocation. Joint costs arise when an organization produces multiple products and its cost function is not fully separable. Some costs, then, "jointly" produce the products. Cost allocation is the phrase used to describe the procedures by which product costs are constructed in the face of joint costs.

To illustrate, many aircraft use an airport's runway. It is common practice to set the landing fees to recover the cost of building, maintaining and operating the runways. Different aircraft impose different costs (e.g., large commercial versus small private aircraft). Various activities also take place at an airport (e.g., parking, ticket sales, and food sales). What, then, is the cost of a particular class of landings? Enter the art of cost allocation.

An intermediate effect of cost allocation is the assignment of costs to various responsibility centers. To illustrate, a large, divisionalized organization incurs many costs at headquarters. Information processing, finance, and general administrative are examples. It is common practice to assign at least some of these costs to the divisions. In turn, some costs assigned to the divisions may be assigned to individual products in the divisions. Alternatively, they may be treated as a period cost associated with that division's products. Either way, we ask which costs belong with which divisions. Enter the art of cost allocation.

We have already encountered joint costs in our study of product costing. The intercept of the LLA for manufacturing overhead in a job order costing environment is an example. We supply an entire chapter on the subject of joint costs for several reasons. First, important departures from economic cost arise here. Average cost is not defined in a multiproduct firm, unless the cost function is fully separable. Yet we routinely find product cost statistics that look like, and even encourage the language of, average costs. Also, cost allocation is not part of the economic cost story; it is an accounting phenomenon. Second, cost allocation practice is highly varied, and regularly deals with more complex settings than we have yet portrayed. This suggests we examine the phenomenon in more general terms. Finally, cost allocation will be important in our subsequent study of decision making and control. This, too, suggests that we take a deeper look at cost allocation.

We begin by returning to the economist's setting. This provides an opportunity to review cost concepts in the multiproduct firm, and to define economic joint costs. We then overlay the accountant's art. Joint accounting costs need not reflect economic joint costs; and economic joint costs may be present though accounting joint costs are absent. These are direct implications of the accountant's use of aggregation and LLAs in producing product cost statistics. Finally, we will see the important role played by a cost category's LLA in guiding the cost allocation art.

Specialized terminology also surfaces here. Cost allocation is an accounting, not an economic construct. We will carefully define it in terms of accounting procedures. The fact that cost allocation does not arise in the economic theory of cost should be kept in mind as we proceed.

Economic Joint Costs

Suppose our organization produces two products. Denote their respective quantities by q_1 and q_2. Also, as in Chapter 2, denote the organization's *economic* cost function by $C(q_1,q_2)$.

Now express the economic cost function in the following suggestive format:

$$C(q_1,q_2) = G(q_1) + H(q_2) + J(q_1,q_2).$$

Think of $G(q_1)$ as the portion of the economic cost curve that depends only on the first product, $H(q_2)$ as the portion that depends only on the second product, and $J(q_1,q_2)$ as the portion that depends on both products. $G(q_1)$ is the separable cost of the first product, and $H(q_2)$ is the separable cost of the second product. $J(q_1,q_2)$ is the nonseparable or *joint* economic cost of the two products.[1]

Suppose the joint cost term, $J(q_1,q_2)$, is zero for all output combinations. This implies we can write the cost function as

$$C(q_1,q_2) = G(q_1) + H(q_2).$$

It is fully separable. It is as if we combined two single product organizations by simply adding them together. Everything we said about the single product firm's cost curve applies here, on a product-by-product basis. The total cost of the first product is $G(q_1)$. Most important, each product's average cost is well-defined. Each separable product cost divided by the respective production quantity gives us unambiguous average costs: $G(q_1)/q_1$ and $H(q_2)/q_2$.

What if we cannot write the firm's cost curve so the joint cost term is everywhere zero? This means average cost is not well defined. It also means the marginal cost of one product depends on the quantity of the other product that is being produced, unless $J(q_1,q_2)$ is a constant. Separability is absent.

Examples abound. Suppose a shared capacity is fixed in the short-run. Use of the capacity to produce one product will lead to congestion and interfere with production of another. Two products, such as two automobile models, might be developed by the same design and engineering teams. The city bus carries many

---

[1]This language is not entirely casual. The marginal cost of the first product is the partial derivative of $C(q_1,q_2)$ with respect to q_1. Suppose this marginal cost does not depend on q_2 for any (q_1,q_2) combination. Similarly, suppose the marginal cost of the second product does not depend on q_1 for any (q_1,q_2) combination. Finally, suppose $C(0,0) = 0$. Then $J(q_1,q_2)$ is superfluous and the cost function is separable, or consists only of the separable costs. Otherwise, the cost function is not separable, and jointness is present. Joint costs are often called common costs.

passengers, the public school offers education to many students, the delivery truck carries many products. The list seems endless. In each case it is not multiple products that signal joint cost; it is multiple products and our suspicion that the marginal cost of one product depends on the set of products and their quantities being produced. If it is easier simultaneously to design and engineer two automobile models, to deliver multiple products with the same truck, to group school children in the same building, and so on we have joint costs.

In general terms, the essence of joint cost is lack of cost function separability. Marginal cost is well defined, it just happens to depend (generally) on the quantities of the other products. For example, the marginal cost of delivering a unit of output to some customer will depend on whether a delivery of another product is being made at a neighboring location.

Average cost is not well defined in the face of joint costs. Suppose we are producing $\hat{q}_1$ units of the first and $\hat{q}_2$ units of the second product. Total economic cost is given by the expression

$$C(\hat{q}_1, \hat{q}_2) = G(\hat{q}_1) + H(\hat{q}_2) + J(\hat{q}_1, \hat{q}_2).$$

To compute average cost, we must divide the cost between the two products and then average each portion over the respective output quantity.

Surely we assign the separable costs to the respective products. What of the joint cost term? We must assign some fraction, say α, of the joint cost to the first product and the remaining fraction, $1 - \alpha$, to the second product. (Presumably we also have $0 \le \alpha \le 1$.) The alleged average costs for the two products will be:

$$[G(\hat{q}_1) + \alpha J(\hat{q}_1, \hat{q}_2)]/\hat{q}_1; \text{ and}$$

$$[H(\hat{q}_2) + (1-\alpha)J(\hat{q}_1, \hat{q}_2)]/\hat{q}_2.$$

If we want the first product's average cost to be as low as possible, we set $\alpha = 0$. If we want the second product's average cost to be as low as possible, we set $\alpha = 1$. This is not meant to be a cynical statement. The cost function does not separate, average cost is not defined, and any attempt to force an average cost style construction is subject to a claim of arbitrariness.

This is why there is no economic notion of average cost in a multiproduct firm whose cost function is not fully separable.

unit costs

Average cost is simply not a meaningful construction in a multiproduct firm, given joint costs. The economist dismisses the notion. The accountant is not so fortunate. For inventory valuation purposes, the economist typically has a market arrangement at hand. Spot or futures prices are available. The accountant's world is not so accommodating. We know the accountant must value inventories, must do so on a cost basis, and must include all product costs in the calculation.

The accountant does not attempt to value inventory at some approximation to economic marginal cost. Economic average cost is not defined in most practical circumstances. So we cannot say the accountant attempts to value inventory at some reasonable approximation to economic average cost. We will call the accountant's product cost statistics *unit costs*.

Unit costs are product cost statistics with the property the sum of the unit costs multiplied by the respective product quantities equals the total product cost in question. Unit costs are constructed by accumulating, assigning, and averaging.[2] This means a degree of arbitrariness is present. Convention, though, surfaces to aid our understanding. A particular accounting library always adopts particular conventions for calculating unit costs. The arbitrariness, so to speak, is administered in conventional ways. This does not mean convention is fully cleansing.

an example

Consider an example in which the first product's separable cost is $G(q_1) = 10q_1$ and the second's is $H(q_2) = 1q_2$. Suppose the production plan is $\hat{q}_1 = 3,000$ units and $\hat{q}_2 = 1,000$ units, and joint cost totals $J(\hat{q}_1, \hat{q}_2) = 50,000$. What are the unit costs?

One way to compute them is to assign the joint cost based on the separable costs. The first product's separable cost is $G(3,000) = 30,000$ and the second's is $H(1,000) = 1,000$. Total separable cost is $30,000 + 1,000 = 31,000$. So we assign 30/31 or 96.77% of the joint cost to the first product. This gives us the following respective unit costs:

$$[30,000 + .9677(50,000)]/3,000 = 26.13; \text{ and}$$

$$[1,000 + .0323(50,000)]/1,000 = 2.61.$$

Another way to compute the unit costs is to assign the joint cost based on the number of units produced. With a total of $3,000 + 1,000 = 4,000$ units produced, we assign $3/(3 + 1)$ or 75% of the joint cost to the first product. This gives us the following respective unit costs:

$$[30,000 + .75(50,000)]/3,000 = 22.50; \text{ and}$$

$$[1,000 + .25(50,000)]/1,000 = 13.50.$$

Now consider a different production plan, one of $\hat{q}_1 = 2,500$ units and $\hat{q}_2 = 2,500$ units. Also suppose the joint cost is $J(\hat{q}_1, \hat{q}_2) = 55,000$. Respective separable costs are $G(2,500) = 25,000$ and $H(2,500) = 2,500$.

Using the separable costs to assign the joint costs gives us the following unit cost calculations:

---

[2]Unit costs may be constructed for actual products, or for some pseudo measure of output. For example, when we compute a predetermined burden rate we are engaging in unit costing.

[25,000 + .9091(55,000)]/2,500 = 30.00; and

[2,500 + .0909(55,000)]/2,500 = 3.00.

Conversely, using the number of units produced to assign the joint costs gives the following calculations:

[25,000 + .50(55,000)]/2,500 = 21.00; and

[2,500 + .50(55,000)]/2,500 = 12.00.

The calculations are summarized in Table 8.1.

Table 8.1: Unit Costs for Joint Cost Example				
	output	unit cost	output	unit cost
joint cost assignment based on separable costs				
product 1	3,000	26.13	2,500	30.00
product 2	1,000	2.61	2,500	3.00
joint cost assignment based on units of output				
product 1	3,000	22.50	2,500	21.00
product 2	1,000	13.50	2,500	12.00

Notice what has happened. If we compute the unit costs one way, both increase as we move from the first to the second production plan. If we compute them the other way, both decrease as we move from the first to the second production plan.[3] We cannot have two sets of average costs, one that says each average went up and the other that says each average went down! Unit costs follow from an attempt to *force* a separable cost function and then compute average costs.[4]

Accounting Joint Costs

With this lengthy preamble in place, we now turn to a closer look at how the accountant deals with joint costs. Initially we must recognize there is an important

---

[3]The same phenomenon occurs if the joint costs are constant, say, J(3000,1000) = J(2500,2500) = 50,000.

[4]The phenomenon illustrated in the example is called Simpson's Reversal Paradox. In general terms, consider conditional probabilities and various events. It is possible to have probabilities $P(A \mid B) > P(A \mid B')$, yet also have $P(A \mid B \text{ and } D) < P(A \mid B' \text{ and } D)$ and $P(A \mid B \text{ and } D') < P(A \mid B' \text{ and } D')$, where the primes denote complements. What happens in probabilistic terms is the conditioning events combine in unintuitive yet logically possible ways. What happens in the unit cost illustration is the production quantities combine in unintuitive yet logically possible ways as they are passed through the unit cost calculation. It is the lack of meaningfulness of average cost in a multiproduct setting that allows us to construct this example. Sunder [1983] is an important reference.

distinction between an economic joint cost and an accounting cost that will have the appearance of a joint cost. This leads us to focus on the accountant's allocation of accounting costs, more precisely allocation of accounting joint costs. Accounting, not economic, costs are allocated across periods, between product and period costs, across cost categories, and to products.[5]

Suppose several products are produced using the same physical capacity. The manufacturing overhead will be a joint cost. Here the economic and accounting costs both reflect a joint cost structure.

On the other hand, separate lubricants might be used in the manufacture of each product. Suppose the accounting records aggregate the cost of these lubricants into a single category. The accounting records now exhibit a joint cost structure that is not apparent in the economic structure.

Finally, suppose shared learning occurs across the products. As more of one product is produced, the work force becomes more efficient at producing all the products. The accounting system, though, might maintain separate direct labor categories that ignore the learning. In this case we would have the economic structure exhibiting a joint cost that is suppressed in the accounting records.

The accounting records, then, may or may not reflect a joint cost phenomenon, regardless of the underlying economic story. This compels us to offer a definition of an accounting joint cost. Consider a cost category whose costs are separable, are associated with a single product. This might be manufacturing cost in a dedicated facility; or it might be warranty cost for some product. Whatever, it is a separable cost. The cost depends on the one product in question. Whether treated as a product or period cost, this is not a joint accounting cost.

Manufacturing overhead in a job shop setting illustrates a joint accounting cost. Separability is not present. The LLA for this cost category might use direct labor hours as an explanatory variable. It likely has a nonzero intercept as well. This is a joint accounting cost.

Next consider a raw material item that is used in two separate products. The material is supplied by various vendors. Each acquisition is recorded in the raw material inventory records. As units of either product are manufactured, we record a transfer from the raw material inventory account into each product's work-in-process account. Is the raw material cost category a joint accounting cost? No. There is no ambiguity in moving the costs in the category to their next destination.

---

[5]Keep in mind the economist never allocates cost. The economist knows the cost curve; the accountant uses cost allocation to attempt to say something about a point on the unknown cost curve. On the other hand, the economist often worries about sharing the cost of a common facility, say, neighbors jointly sharing the cost of a neighborhood improvement. The economist uses the language of allocating the cost of the common facility among the individuals. This is a misnomer. Sharing the cost in this context is a euphemism for making payments in a way that the common facility is paid for. Do not confuse actual payments with the accountant's cost allocations. The latter always take place in the accounting library. They may be descriptive of resource transfers, but they are not resource transfers. They are calculations in a data bank.

The LLA for costs entering the cost category is units of inventory multiplied by price per unit. The LLA for costs exiting the cost category is units of inventory placed in production multiplied by price per unit.[6] Both sets of entries follow the same price times quantity calculation format.

Finally, consider a cost category that is not separable. Also suppose all the costs in the category are transferred to a single destination cost category. If this destination category is an expense, this is a joint accounting cost. It is not separable, and it will not be combined with other cost categories. We cannot deny its jointness merely by treating it as a period cost!

Conversely, suppose the destination category is not an expense. Then we will not (yet) refer to the cost as a joint accounting cost. The reason is we have not yet had to face the task of relating it to products, periods, or anything. Suppose we accumulate factory maintenance cost in a separate cost category. Further suppose this cost is then transferred to a single manufacturing overhead category. The maintenance cost *category* is not a joint cost in the strict sense. The reason is we are not done processing the costs in this category. They have yet to be related to products or expensed. Calling them joint is premature.

Combining these reflections we are ready to define joint cost in the accounting domain. We label a cost category an accounting joint cost if it provides difficulty in the product costing exercise. *A joint accounting cost is a cost category with the following three properties: (1) it is not separable, in the sense of having an LLA with a single product as its explanatory variable; (2) its LLA does not use all products as explanatory variables and have a zero intercept; and (3) it is not routinely closed into a single nonexpense category.*

Used in this manner, accounting joint cost is an accounting concept. It refers to accounting cost. It is directed at a cost category from which we have difficulty deriving product costs. The cost category's LLA does not exhibit separability; nor does it use all products as explanatory variables and a zero intercept. It is also not a holding category, awaiting assignment to a subsequent cost category.

Cost Allocation

Cost allocation now enters as the procedure by which the accountant deals with accounting joint costs. Consider any cost category that is an accounting joint cost. If the costs in the category are expensed without further separation, no allocation occurs. The costs are simply expensed. Selling and administrative costs that are not assigned to various products or divisions provide a ready example. Alternatively, if the costs in the category are not expensed, they must be transferred to or apportioned among two or more other categories. (This is one of the requirements for us to call the category an accounting joint cost.) This process of apportionment is cost

---

[6]LIFO, FIFO, or weighted average calculations might complicate the story, but we still lack the degree of ambiguity that is associated with a joint accounting cost.

allocation. Manufacturing overhead is a ready example. In a multiproduct setting, we apportion the overhead among the products and period using a cost allocation procedure.[7,8] The usual treatment of a long lived depreciable asset provides another illustration. Cost allocation is the process by which we assign the asset's cost to periods, and eventually to products if it is product cost.

Cost allocation is a specialized form of unit costing that links a joint cost category to other cost categories in the accounting library. *Cost allocation is a procedure by which the cost in a joint accounting cost category is assigned to two or more other categories, using a unit costing procedure.* Notice this procedure is a unit costing procedure. It has the property that all costs are assigned, that the sum of the unit costs multiplied by the respective quantities equals the total product cost in question.

Reflect on the theme. Unit costs are product costs that portray or carry the total cost in question. An accounting joint cost is a cost category in which unit costing is particularly difficult. Cost allocation is a procedure used in such a case. Of course we want a broad view of what constitutes a product here, as we routinely encounter situations where costs are assigned to completed units, incomplete units, intermediate units or service units, and to the period itself. Make no mistake. Unit costs, joint accounting cost and cost allocation are specialized terms we use to force a distinction between the accounting and the economic picture. Were accounting perfectly reflective of the underlying economic setting we would have no use for this terminology.

cost allocation mechanics

The mechanics of cost allocation are easy to spot. We begin with a joint cost category. (Some call this the "pool" of costs to be allocated.) We then identify the categories into which these costs will be transferred. (These same people call the destination categories the "objects" of the allocation exercise.) Finally, we link the two with a unit costing procedure. (The pool and object people call this an allocation base.) In this unit costing procedure, the cost in the joint cost category is treated as the "total product cost" and the destination categories are treated as the "products."

The important point to keep in mind is the joint cost category's LLA is almost surely not going to be in the format of a unit costing procedure. The unit costing

---

[7]This is true even if we are running a variable costing system. Suppose the manufacturing overhead LLA is $F + v$(direct labor hours). We expense the intercept (already an allocation) and we apportion the variable component without directly (pun) using the output quantities as the explanatory variables in the LLA.

[8]A single product setting is slightly different. Under normal or standard costing, we apportion the overhead among units of output and the period. This is cost allocation. In an actual costing system, though, no allocation takes place. (All the indirect costs are transferred to the work-in-process category; and this is a separable category in a single product setting.)

procedure requires the category's cost equal the sum of the "unit costs" multiplied by the respective quantities. It would be fortuitous if the category's LLA arrived in just this format. This creates an interesting picture. Costs arrive in the joint cost category according to one LLA, but depart according to another. This is the nature of cost allocation.

To illustrate, suppose a cost category's LLA is given by cost $= F + v_1q_1 + v_2q_2$. Under a normal or standard full costing procedure we assign each product some unitized portion of the intercept. Say we assign f_1 to the first product and f_2 to the second. This means the respective product costs are $f_1 + v_1$ and $f_2 + v_2$.

Now visualize how costs appear to enter and exit this accounting joint cost category. They enter according to the relationship

$$cost = F + v_1q_1 + v_2q_2.$$

They leave according to the relationship

$$cost' = (f_1 + v_1)q_1 + (f_2 + v_2)q_2.$$

The difference, *cost - cost'*, is expensed.

Are the product costs, $f_1 + v_1$ and $f_2 + v_2$, unit costs here? There is no guarantee that $(f_1 + v_1)q_1 + (f_2 + v_2)q_2 = F + v_1q_1 + v_2q_2$. In a narrow sense, the product costs are unit costs with respect to *cost'*. In a larger sense, notice that *cost - cost'* becomes a period cost, and we always have $cost - cost' + (f_1 + v_1)q_1 + (f_2 + v_2)q_2 = F + v_1q_1 + v_2q_2$. This is a unit costing procedure in which "the period" is treated as one of the products.

Treatment of manufacturing overhead in a full costing system is a ready illustration. The costs arrive, say, according to an LLA of $F + v$(direct labor hours), but are assigned to products based on some constant amount per direct labor hour. Assignment takes place according to an LLA of $0 + f$(direct labor hours) for some constant f.

a familiar illustration

The job order costing example that was explored in Chapters 6 and 7 provides a ready illustration of cost allocation. The essence of the story was three products, each with direct labor and direct materials identified, and two manufacturing overhead cost categories. The LLAs for the two overhead categories were (1) 55,000 + 1DL\$; and (2) 32,000 + .2DM\$.

Neither overhead category is separable. Neither comes with an LLA that uses the three products as explanatory variables (with a zero intercept). Neither is closed to a single nonexpense category. Instead, each overhead category is closed to work-in-process accounts for each product (and often an expense category). These overhead costs are accounting joint cost categories.

In each costing procedure illustrated with this running example, we used DL\$ to allocate the first overhead category's cost and DM\$ to allocate the second overhead category's cost to the three products (and periods). Do not overlook the fact that the variable costing procedures rely on allocating the overhead. There, part of the overhead is assigned to the period and the remainder is assigned to the products. The destination categories are three work-in-process categories and a period expense category.[9]

Additional Illustrations

We now sketch two additional illustrations of cost allocation. In each we focus on the economic structure and how the accounting library responds.

responsibility centers and service departments

A canonical example of cost allocation arises when we have responsibility centers that receive intermediate factors such as subcomponents or services from another responsibility center. An engineering group might provide engineering services to a variety of production departments. An advertising group might provide services to various departments in the department store. A data processing group might provide record keeping for medical and financial purposes to each department in a hospital.

Consider an organization that produces and distributes two products. The production quantities are denoted q_1 and q_2. Three departments, or responsibility centers, are present in the manufacturing facility. Department 1 manufactures the first product. Its costs are estimated by the following LLAs:

direct labor	$DL_1 = 50q_1$;
direct material	$DM_1 = 30q_1$; and
overhead	$OV_1 = 300{,}000 + 1.6DL_1$.

Notice the implied aggregate (and separable) cost structure in department 1 is

$$cost_1 = 300{,}000 + [50 + 30 + 1.6(50)]q_1 = 300{,}000 + 160q_1.$$

Department 2 manufactures the second product. Its costs are estimated by the following LLAs:

direct labor	$DL_2 = 20q_2$;
direct material	$DM_2 = 100q_2$; and
overhead	$OV_2 = 200{,}000 + 1DM_2$.

---

[9]A caveat occurs here when we are able to separate the overhead into "fixed" and "variable" categories under variable costing. Suppose the overhead in one category is regarded as "fixed" and is expensed. Further suppose the LLA for the overhead in the second category has no intercept and uses the various product quantities as explanatory variables. Now no allocation occurs. Conversely, if the second category had no intercept, but used some pseudo quantity measure as an explanatory variable, allocation would be taking place. Why?

The implied aggregate (and separable) cost structure is

$$cost_2 = 200,000 + [20 + 100 + 1(100)]q_2 = 200,000 + 220q_2.$$

This gives us two separable cost categories.[10] The third department provides us with an accounting joint cost category. This department provides services that are used by departments 1 and 2 in their respective manufacturing operations. Think of this, broadly, as a department that provides various manufacturing support services such as maintenance, material handling, and inventory control.

This service department's cost structure is estimated by the following LLA:

$$cost_3 = 200,000 + .5(DL_1 + DL_2).$$

The explanatory variable is the total direct labor cost in the first two departments.

Finally, suppose the production plan calls for $q_1 = 900$ and $q_2 = 1,800$ units. This implies departmental cost totals of

$$cost_1 = 300,000 + 144,000 = 444,000;$$
$$cost_2 = 200,000 + 396,000 = 596,000; and$$
$$cost_3 = 200,000 + \ \ 40,500 = 240,500.$$

Details are summarized in Table 8.2.

product cost calculations

The question before us is how to allocate the service department costs. The unusual feature is these joint costs arise in one department and must be combined with costs in the other departments.[11]

Since the $cost_3$ LLA uses direct labor cost as an explanatory variable, we will focus on direct labor cost in the allocation procedure. With $q_1 = 900$ and $q_2 = 1,800$, direct labor costs total $50(900) = 45,000$ in department 1 and $20(1,800) = 36,000$ in department 2. This suggests the following allocations:

$$240,500[45/(45 + 36)] = 240,500(.556) = 133,600$$

to department 1 and

---

[10]The economic story here is one in which the two manufacturing operations are housed in separate departments and give rise to separable costs. This allows us to sketch the story in terms of a department 1 cost structure that depends on q_1 and a department 2 cost structure that depends on q_2. An alternative story would have both products passing through each of these departments. One department might, for example, perform machining operations and the second assembly operations. This would give us joint cost categories for departments 1 and 2.

[11]We will focus on aggregate costs in each department as we work through the illustration. Keep in mind that direct and indirect cost categories are maintained for the two production departments. Also notice that direct labor is a small percentage of total cost in this setting. This is descriptive of highly automated, capital intensive manufacturing processes.

$$240{,}500[36/(45 + 36)] = 240{,}500(.444) = 106{,}900$$

to department 2.[12]

Table 8.2: Data for Service Department Illustration
presumed cost structure:
LLAs for department 1:
direct labor: $DL_1 = 50q_1$;
direct material: $DM_1 = 30q_1$; and
overhead: $OV_1 = 300{,}000 + 1.6DL_1$.
$cost_1 = 300{,}000 + [50 + 30 + 1.6(50)]q_1 = 300{,}000 + 160q_1$
LLAs for department 2:
direct labor: $DL_2 = 20q_2$;
direct material: $DM_2 = 100q_2$; and
overhead: $OV_2 = 200{,}000 + 1DM_2$.
$cost_2 = 200{,}000 + [20 + 100 + 1(100)]q_2 = 200{,}000 + 220q_2$
LLA for department 3:
$cost_3 = 200{,}000 + .5(DL_1 + DL_2)$
cost incurred under $q_1 = 900$ and $q_2 = 1{,}800$:
department 1:
$DL_1 = 50(900) = 45{,}000$
$DM_1 = 30(900) = 27{,}000$
$OV_1 = 300{,}000 + 1.6(45{,}000) = 372{,}000$
$cost_1 = 300{,}000 + 160(900) = 444{,}000$
department 2:
$DL_2 = 20(1{,}800) = 36{,}000$
$DM_2 = 100(1{,}800) = 180{,}000$
$OV_2 = 200{,}000 + 1(180{,}000) = 380{,}000$
$cost_2 = 200{,}000 + 220(1{,}800) = 596{,}000$
department 3:
$cost_3 = 200{,}000 + .5(45{,}000 + 36{,}000) = 240{,}500$
total cost $= 444{,}000 + 596{,}000 + 240{,}500 = 1{,}280{,}500$

Examine the procedure. We treat 240,500 as the joint cost in question, and the total of $45{,}000 + 36{,}000 = 81{,}000$ dollars of direct labor cost in the first two departments as "units." The "cost per unit" is $240.5/81 = 2.97$. We then assign $2.97(45{,}000) = 133{,}600$ of the joint cost to department 1 and $2.97(36{,}000) = 106{,}900$ to department 2.[13]

---

[12]Here and throughout the example we will round the allocation amounts to the nearest hundred.

[13]Notice how the production plan leads to a normal volume for the service department.

Cost allocation begins with a joint cost category (department 3's cost here). Recipient cost categories are identified (departments 1 and 2 here). And a unit costing procedure is invoked (based on total direct labor cost in departments 1 and 2 here).

We now combine the separable and allocated costs to produce the product cost statistics.

	product 1	product 2
separable costs, from respective departments	444,000	596,000
allocated department 3 costs	133,600	106,900
total product cost	577,600	702,900

Respective unit costs are $577.6/.9 = 641.78$ and $702.9/1.8 = 390.50$. Further observe that $641.78(900) + 390.50(1,800) = 1,280,500 = cost_1 + cost_2 + cost_3$.

Besides the procedures and their interpretation, what about our choice of allocation procedure? Why did we allocate department 3 cost using total direct labor cost in the first two departments? We assumed direct labor cost was the explanatory variable in the LLA for department 3 and merely acted on that assumption. This may appear to be an inadequate explanation, or a somewhat arbitrary allocation of joint costs. If so, we are succeeding. Cost allocation must, by its very nature, engender these concerns. We are taking accounting joint costs and painting a picture that would emerge were there no such joint costs.[14]

For the record, try allocating the joint costs on the basis of direct cost or total cost in the two production departments.

recording procedures

It is also important to recognize the cost flow in this setting. Initially we record the costs in various cost categories. This gives us the costs that are initially associated with each department. Next, we combine these various costs to assemble the product cost statistics. This allows us to group costs by responsibility and then to identify the desired product costs.

We first collect the costs in various cost categories in each department. In aggregate terms, we have something like the following:[15]

---

[14]To reinforce this point, we are not constructing average costs. Total costs are "spread" across products, and we coin the phrase "unit costs" to remind ourselves of this fact. Ambiguity sets in here because we are doing this without a prescribed purpose. We will hint in the next section that unit costs may be engineered to suit a particular purpose and will explore this theme in subsequent chapters. For now it is important to understand the accounting library stores unit costs, and to use these unit costs it is essential we know how they were constructed.

[15]Remember, separate direct and indirect categories are present here. We are presenting a streamlined, aggregate description of the record keeping.

department 1 work in process	444,000	
department 2 work in process	596,000	
department 3 cost	240,500	
various accounts		1,280,500

Next, we record the joint cost allocations. These would likely be transferred from the department 3 cost account into overhead accounts in the first two departments, and then to work in process. To spare us unnecessary detail, we streamline the procedure:

department 1 work in process	133,600	
department 2 work in process	106,900	
department 3 cost		240,500

Do not overlook the subtlety here. Suppose we have a manager in each department. We accumulate costs incurred by each department and use these to evaluate the managers. The manager in department 3 provides services to the other departments. The recording procedure tallies the cost of providing these services in department 3's records. In turn, managers in the first two departments use these services. Besides the directly accumulated costs in the first two departments, we also transfer in the allocated costs of the services. The total cost incurred by department 1 is not 444,000; it is 444,000 + 133,600 = 577,600![16]

Naturally, this would be more complicated if both products passed through departments 1 and 2. But the essential point remains. Accumulating the costs for product costing purposes is usually integrated with the process of accumulating costs for managerial evaluation purposes. Stated differently, product costing and responsibility accounting are highly integrated in the accounting library. Costs are accumulated by responsibility center, and then allocated to assemble product costs as well as more refined performance statistics. Further notice that the scheme we illustrated allocates all the service department cost to the first two departments. A variation on this theme is possible under standard costing.

Suppose the department 3 manager is unusually efficient. This means the costs in that department are unusually low. Transferring these costs to the first two departments places the performance of these two departments in a more favorable light. Conversely, suppose the department 3 manager is inefficient. Department 3 experiences a cost overrun. Allocating all the department's costs to the first two departments places their performance in a less favorable light.

---

[16]We do not have an explicit measure of the services used by the two departments. This is why we use cost allocation to reflect each consuming department's cost of services used. If we had an explicit measure, we would account for the services used in terms of quantity used multiplied by cost per unit of service. This is called a transfer pricing procedure. It is studied in Chapter 23.

So, we often find standard costs at work here. A common pattern is to allocate the service department costs using standard rates. This removes any service department efficiencies or inefficiencies from the first two departments' evaluations. The difference between actual and allocated cost in the service departments is then expensed.[17]

variable costing

The accounting library procedures under variable costing would proceed in similar fashion. We have identified the service department's LLA. Product cost will contain the variable portion of the service department's cost. (Remember, we are now speaking of variable accounting cost, not variable economic cost.)

Mimicking our earlier allocation, we now allocate the variable costs in department 3 as follows:

$$40,500[45/(45 + 36)] = 40,500(.556) = 22,500$$

to department 1 and

$$40,500[36/(45 + 36)] = 40,500(.444) = 18,000$$

to department 2.

In turn, the variable product costs are readily computed:

	product 1	product 2
separable variable costs, from respective departments	144,000	396,000
allocated department 3 variable costs	22,500	18,000
total variable product cost	166,500	414,000

This gives us respective product costs of $166.5/.9 = 185$ and $414/1.8 = 230$.

What about the recording procedures? The intercept terms in the two departments will be expensed. The intercept term in the service department will also be expensed, but will it pass through the production department accounts?

It may or may not. A common procedure is to treat the "fixed" cost in department 3 as a capacity cost and assign or allocate it to the two production departments. For the sake of argument, let's say this cost is allocated 50% to each of the first two departments. The aggregate entries would appear as follows:

---

[17]A prevalent view is that it is fair to neutralize the allocations in this fashion, to base them on standard as opposed to actual rates. (It also simplifies the bookkeeping.) We will see, however, that whether to use actual or standard rates in such a setting is far from easy to decide.

department 1 work in process	22,500	
department 2 work in process	18,000	
department 3 cost		40,500

department 1 "fixed" overhead	100,000	
department 2 "fixed" overhead	100,000	
department 3 cost		200,000

The first entry records the allocation of the variable cost of the services. This is assigned to product cost and thus goes (perhaps through a departmental overhead account) into the respective work-in-process accounts. The second entry records the allocation of the "fixed" overhead. This will be expensed and is not assigned to work in process.

product profitability assessment

Another common setting in which cost allocation issues arise is in determining the profitability of various products. This subject will be dealt with at length in a subsequent chapter, so we provide a glimpse that is sufficient to tie into our present exploration of cost allocation.

Consider a merchandiser who stocks and sells many goods or products. Focus on a specific product and ask whether it is profitable. Presumably, this means we ask whether revenue exceeds cost. Remember in Chapter 2 how we framed the firm's problem in various ways. Here we frame it to focus on this specific product. Define revenue as the selling price. This implies the cost term must carry the burden (pun) of linking the analysis into the larger picture. For example, if the product takes up space that could be devoted to other products, this should be included in the analysis. Similarly, if the product's presence encourages (or discourages) customers from arriving, that, too, should be included.

Let's agree that none of these issues arises. Let's also agree that this is a short-run question, and the marginal cost of stocking the item, dealing with customers, and so on is close to zero. Now we are down to the question of whether we can sell it for more than we pay our supplier (including transportation).[18] This gets us to a simple price versus cost comparison. Also assume transportation is close to trivial. Cost is now what we pay the supplier. The accounting library is also going to be helpful. It records the acquisition of the merchandise at cost, with cost defined to be what we paid the supplier. Further assume the price has not changed.

Here we have a case where the cost number we are looking for is in the accounting library. It also contains no cost allocations. In a merchandising setting,

---

[18]Let's also assume it does not sit on the shelf very long, leading us to worry about the cost of funds tied up in inventory.

we treat the cost of such things as sales people, space, displays, and advertising as period costs. These are accounting joint costs, but they are typically not allocated to specific products. (Many period costs may be allocated to groups of products, but the product costs themselves do not receive any of these allocations.)

By way of contrast, return to the two product, three department example discussed above. Suppose our profitability analysis focuses on the first product and takes a highly specialized form. It is possible to sell one extra unit at a price of 250 dollars. Is this sale profitable? Naturally the answer depends on whether the cost of producing one more unit is below 250.

Examine the LLAs in Table 8.2. Combining them, we estimate the cost curve for this organization to be total manufacturing cost = $cost_1 + cost_2 + cost_3 = 700,000 + 160q_1 + 220q_2 + .5(50q_1 + 20q_2) = 700,000 + 185q_1 + 230q_2$. This implies a marginal cost for the first product of 185 < 250. If our approximations are not too inaccurate and if we have not left any cost out of the analysis (e.g., delivery or corruption of future demand) we conclude the additional sale is profitable.

Can we find the data for this conclusion in the accounting library? Return to our variable costing construction. There we derived respective product costs of 185 and 230 per unit. 185 is precisely the cost datum we had in mind; and we have constructed it using an allocation procedure! The reason is to be found in the way the library recording process meshes with the economic structure. Costs are initially tallied in each of the three departments, yet two products are present. The cost structure, assuming our LLAs are accurate, is separable; at least it is separable for small variations from the current production plan. But the record keeping does not fully separate the costs. The service department costs are aggregated, creating a joint cost category. The allocation compensates for the lack of separability in the records.[19]

Cost Allocation Criteria

We see, then, how accounting joint costs give rise to cost allocation procedures in the quest to produce unit costs for the accounting library. There are a variety of allocation procedures that might be employed, and what we find in the accounting library may be close to or far removed from whatever it is we had in mind. This reflects a utilitarian view. What we are trying to do dictates the costing procedure

---

[19]Two additional observations are important here. First, we have assumed no costs such as delivery costs were left out of the analysis. This means we need not worry about product versus period distinctions. In other cases we would. Second, there are many ways to allocate the service department's cost. We exploited intimate knowledge of the setting in the profitability assessment exercise. Taxation authorities often rely on profitability data, and this creates considerable interest in finding tax-advantaged allocation procedures. In turn, general purpose allocation procedures are often used to combat such games. Stock depreciation schedules or the so-called three factor formula for allocating costs (which uses an explanatory variable based on the average of assets, payroll, and sales or volume) are ready illustrations.

that is appropriate at that time and place. In turn, this dictates how the data in the accounting library are to be engineered for whatever circumstance is at hand. Circumstance determines procedure in this view.

A more friendly view is based on "cost allocation criteria." The idea is to invoke general purpose desiderata in designing allocation procedures. We might, for example, look for procedures that assign a "fair" share of joint cost to each product, or that reflect "cause and effect" relationships in the underlying economic cost structure, or that at least reflect the "cost drivers" in the system.

This appeal to general purpose criteria removes circumstance from being the primary determinant of how to engineer the cost statistics. It is an attempt to substitute criteria for circumstance.

Cost allocation is far more subtle than looking for a fair or just way to share the accounting joint costs among the responsibility centers and products at hand.

Summary

Economic joint costs arise when the economic cost curve is not separable, when we cannot unambiguously speak of the cost of each product. Economic costs are not recorded in the accounting records. Accounting costs are. Joint accounting costs are a cousin to economic costs. They arise when we cannot unambiguously speak of the accounting cost of each product.

More precisely, accounting joint costs arise when we encounter a cost category with the following three properties: (1) it is not separable, in the sense of having an LLA with a single product as its explanatory variable; (2) its LLA does not use all products as explanatory variables and have a zero intercept; and (3) it is not routinely closed into a single nonexpense category. Cost allocation now enters as the generic technique for dealing with joint accounting costs in the accounting library.

In broadest terms, cost allocation is a procedure by which the cost in a joint accounting cost category is assigned to two or more other categories, using a unit costing procedure. In turn, a unit costing procedure is some scheme that assigns all the cost in question.

In this sense, the idea of unit costs does double duty. We use the phrase unit cost to describe the accountant's product cost statistics in a multiproduct setting, a setting where average costs are not well defined except in exceptional circumstances. We also use the phrase to describe the mechanics of moving costs to be allocated to the cost categories that are to receive the allocations. In each case, we account for the total cost involved by spreading it over the products involved.

We have now expanded the accounting recipe. Aggregation and LLAs, we see, are combined with cost allocation to construct the product costs statistics we find in the accounting library.

At one level, the study of cost allocation is disconcerting. We can find too many ways to do it, and too few defenses for any particular method. This is as it should be. We are creating the appearance of separability when cost function separability is not necessarily present. At another level, and as we shall see in subsequent chapters, we can decompose choice problems in many ways. Most require some notion of product cost. Given a choice problem and given a particular method of attack on that problem, the proper method of cost allocation comes into view.

It is this tension between wanting a clean, intuitive approach to building the accounting library and the demands of specialized product cost statistics for various uses that creates the ambiguity that surrounds cost allocation. We leave the discussion with this tension intact, and defer to later chapters the study of how cost allocation links parts of the organization's economic structure in interesting and useful ways. Remember, though, cost allocation is an accounting phenomenon. It has no reference point in the economic theory of cost; it is an accounting procedure that deals with joint accounting costs.

Appendix: Simultaneous Allocations

In this Appendix we illustrate various allocation procedures in an unusually interactive setting. For this purpose, retain everything in the Table 8.2 example, except the services. Here we make some changes.

First, we introduce a second service department. This new department provides information services to the other departments, including department 3. Its LLA uses total variable cost in the other departments as an explanatory variable. Total variable cost in the other departments is measured by $cost_1 + cost_2 + cost_3 - 700,000$. (This is the variable cost in the other departments, as defined by the assumed LLAs.) The presumed LLA for department 4 is

$$cost_4 = 100,000 + .2(cost_1 + cost_2 + cost_3 - 700,000).$$

We also alter the LLA for department 3 to reflect the fact it provides services to department 4. The following structure is assumed:

$$cost_3 = 200,000 + .5(DL_1 + DL_2 + cost_4 - 100,000).$$

Here it is assumed variable cost in department 4 (i.e., $cost_4 - 100,000$) provides a pseudo quantity measure for services of department 3 that are required by department 4. As promised, we have an interactive setting. Department 3 provides services to department 4 and vice versa.

The production plan remains at $q_1 = 900$ and $q_2 = 1,800$. The costs in the various departments will now be

$$cost_1 = 300,000 + 144,000 = 444,000;$$
$$cost_2 = 200,000 + 396,000 = 596,000;$$
$$cost_3 = 200,000 + 105,000 = 305,000; \text{ and}$$
$$cost_4 = 100,000 + 129,000 = 229,000.$$

Notice that $105,000 = .5(45,000 + 36,000 + 129,000)$ and $129,000 = .2(144,000 + 396,000 + 105,000)$. Details are summarized in Table 8.3. Be certain to verify the mutual consistency of these costs and output quantities before proceeding.

Table 8.3: Data for Interactive Service Department Illustration
presumed cost structure:
LLAs for department 1:
direct labor: $DL_1 = 50q_1$;
direct material: $DM_1 = 30q_1$; and
overhead: $OV_1 = 300,000 + 1.6DL_1$.
$cost_1 = 300,000 + [50 + 30 + 1.6(50)]q_1 = 300,000 + 160q_1$
LLAs for department 2:
direct labor: $DL_2 = 20q_2$;
direct material: $DM_2 = 100q_2$; and
overhead: $OV_2 = 200,000 + 1DM_2$.
$cost_2 = 200,000 + [20 + 100 + 1(100)]q_2 = 200,000 + 220q_2$
LLA for department 3:
$cost_3 = 200,000 + .5(DL_1 + DL_2 + cost_4 - 100,000)$
LLA for department 4:
$cost_4 = 100,000 + .2(cost_1 + cost_2 + cost_3 - 700,000)$
Cost incurred under $q_1 = 900$ and $q_2 = 1,800$:
department 1:
$DL_1 = 50(900) = 45,000$
$DM_1 = 30(900) = 27,000$
$OV_1 = 300,000 + 1.6(45,000) = 372,000$
$cost_1 = 300,000 + 160(900) = 444,000$
department 2:
$DL_2 = 20(1,800) = 36,000$
$DM_2 = 100(1,800) = 180,000$
$OV_2 = 200,000 + 1(180,000) = 380,000$
$cost_2 = 200,000 + 220(1,800) = 596,000$
department 3:
$cost_3 = 200,000 + .5(45,000 + 36,000 + 229,000 - 100,000) = 305,000$
department 4:
$cost_4 = 100,000 + .2(444,000 + 596,000 + 305,000 - 700,000) = 229,000$
total cost = 1,574,000
total variable cost = 774,000

full or variable costing

The burning question is how we reflect these reciprocal service arrangements in our cost allocation procedures. One alternative is to ignore them altogether. This could be done in two ways. One is to group the two service departments into a single cost category, and allocate the resulting cost to the two production departments. (In fact, we might go one step further and group these categories with the department 1 and 2 overhead categories into a firm-wide overhead category.) There is a presumption that grouping procedures of this nature are inaccurate because they aggregate over many specific relationships.[20]

Another approach is partially to recognize the interdependence. We might allocate department 4's cost to the other departments, and then allocate department 3's cost to the two production departments. Finally, we might engage in a simultaneous procedure.

In turn, these approaches might be coupled with a full or with a variable costing procedure. The exploration from this point on will be easier to understand in a variable costing setting. The reason is we will refer to the above stylized profitability question of whether to sell one more unit of the first product. It will turn out (with enough assumptions) that variable costing will provide the estimator of marginal cost that we seek. This is why we concentrate on the construction of variable product cost statistics in what follows. Of course, we might just as well have told a story where full costing procedures provide a better estimator of the marginal cost.

With this in mind, assume the intercept components have been expensed. This leaves us with respective departmental variable cost totals of

$$cost_1 - 300,000 = 144,000;$$
$$cost_2 - 200,000 = 396,000;$$
$$cost_3 - 200,000 = 105,000; \text{ and}$$
$$cost_4 - 100,000 = 129,000.$$

service department pooling

The most straightforward allocation procedure at this point is to pool the interactive departments. Variable service costs total $105,000 + 129,000 = 234,000$. So we merely take this amount, and assign it to the first two departments.

There are several ways to do this. For the sake of illustration, we use variable cost in the first two departments. This gives us an assignment of

$$234,000[144/(144 + 396)] = 234,000(.267) = 62,400$$

to department 1 and

$$234,000[396/(144 + 396)] = 234,000(.733) = 171,600$$

---

[20]It is not clear this presumption is well based, however. We cannot express a preference without knowing the intended use of the product cost statistics. Recall our earlier illustration in Chapter 5 where full or variable cost produced a better estimate of short-run marginal cost, depending on the circumstance. The same point holds in this setting.

to department 2. Respective variable product costs are $(144 + 62.4)/.9 = 229.33$ and $(396 + 171.6)/1.8 = 315.33$.

step-down procedure

An intermediate approach is to recognize some interrelationships. The basic idea is to begin with the most interactive cost category and assign its costs to the other categories. Then take the next most interactive and assign its cost to the *remaining* categories, and so on. This is called a step-down procedure. Its name is descriptive. We never cycle back to a category whose costs have been allocated.

It is unclear what "most interactive" means. Let's agree that department 4 is more interactive than department 3. Initially, then, we assign the department 4 cost to the other departments. Variable cost in the first three departments is the obvious basis. This gives the following allocation:

$$129,000[144/(144 + 396 + 105)] = 129,000(.223) = 28,800$$

to department 1;

$$129,000[396/(144 + 396 + 105)] = 129,000(.614) = 79,200$$

to department 2; and

$$129,000[105/(144 + 396 + 105)] = 129,000(.163) = 21,000$$

to department 3.

Department 3's variable costs now consist of the original amount plus the allocated share of department 4's cost: $105,000 + 21,000 = 126,000$. These costs are assigned to departments 1 and 2 based on direct labor cost. Again, we take our cue from the cost category's LLA, and remind ourselves there are other ways to proceed (e.g., base the allocation on direct cost). We have the following assignments:

$$126,000[45/(45 + 36)] = 126,000(.556) = 70,000$$

to department 1; and

$$126,000[36/(45 + 36)] = 126,000(.444) = 56,000$$

to department 2.

The total of variable costs incurred and allocated to department 1 is now $144,000 + 28,800 + 70,000 = 242,800$. This provides a product variable cost of $242.8/.9 = 269.78$. Similarly, in department 2 we have total variable cost of $396,000 + 79,200 + 56,000 = 531,200$. From here we readily determine a product variable cost of $531.2/1.8 = 295.11$

simultaneous equations

Finally, we might want to recognize the interactions fully. We do this with simultaneous equations. Examine the LLAs for departments 3 and 4:

$$\text{cost}_3 = 200{,}000 + .5(\text{DL}_1 + \text{DL}_2 + \text{cost}_4 - 100{,}000); \text{ and}$$
$$\text{cost}_4 = 100{,}000 + .2(\text{cost}_1 + \text{cost}_2 + \text{cost}_3 - 700{,}000).$$

Department 3 imposes costs on department 4 and vice versa. So we might ask what the cost is of either department's activities, once we consider the imposition in the other department. We continue to focus on the variable costs.

This leads to the following two equations, where c_3 is the incremental cost per dollar of service provided by department 3 and c_4 is the incremental cost per dollar of service provided by department 4:

$$c_3 = 1 + .2c_4; \text{ and}$$
$$c_4 = 1 + .5c_3.$$

The idea is one dollar of service performed by department 3, say, carries an immediate cost of one dollar, but in addition causes a .2 dollar demand for service by department 4. This .2 demand, of course, costs $.2c_4$, not simply $.2(1)$.

Now solve for the two cost variables. Substituting the second expression into the first gives us

$$c_3 = 1 + .2c_4 = 1 + .2(1 + .5c_3) = 1.2 + .1c_3; \text{ or}$$
$$c_3 - .1c_3 = .9c_3 = 1.2.$$

So $c_3 = 12/9 = 4/3$. Substituting $c_3 = 4/3$ into the second equation gives us

$$c_4 = 1 + .5c_3 = 1 + .5(4/3) = 1 + 2/3 = 5/3.$$

Implicitly, then, a unit of service costs 4/3 in department 3 and 5/3 in department 4.

We next use these revised service costs to construct the variable product costs. One unit of the first product requires services from department 3 with an immediate cost of $.5(50) = 25$, and services from department 4 with an immediate cost of $.2(160) = 32$. Costing these service demands with the c_3 and c_4 costs gives us a service cost for the first product of

$$c_3(25) + c_4(32) = (4/3)(25) + (5/3)(32) = 260/3 = 86.67.$$

This implies a variable product cost for the first product of $160 + 86.67 = 246.67$. Similarly, one unit of the second product requires services from department 3 with an immediate cost of $.5(20) = 10$, and services from department 4 with an immediate cost of $.2(220) = 44$. The service cost for a unit of the second product therefore is

$$c_3(10) + c_4(44) = (4/3)(10) + (5/3)(44) = 260/3 = 86.67.$$

This implies the second product's variable cost per unit is $220 + 86.67 = 306.67$.[21]

One question to ask is whether this is cost allocation. The answer is yes. Each dollar of service demanded of department 3 is assigned to the demanding department at a cost of 4/3 per dollar. The assignment rate for department 4 services is 5/3. Under the production plan of $q_1 = 900$ and $q_2 = 1,800$, the service demands will be as follows:

	demanded of department 3	demanded of department 4
demanded by department 1	.5(50)900	.2(160)900
demanded by department 2	.5(20)1,800	.2(220)1,800
demanded by department 3		.2(105,000)
demanded by department 4	.5(129,000)	
total	105,000	129,000

Now work through the entries to record the costs incurred and assigned. Initially, we record the variable costs incurred by each department.

department 1 work in process	144,000	
department 2 work in process	396,000	
department 3 cost	105,000	
department 4 cost	129,000	
various accounts		774,000

These are the costs that will eventually be assigned to just the first two departments. Next we assign department 3's costs, using $c_3 = 4/3$.

department 1 work in process	30,000	
department 2 work in process	24,000	
department 4 cost	86,000	
department 3 cost		140,000

For example, $30,000 = (4/3)[.5(50)900]$. Be certain to verify the other calculations.

A parallel set of calculations gives us the assignments for department 4, using the noted cost of $c_4 = 5/3$.

department 1 work in process	48,000	
department 2 work in process	132,000	
department 3 cost	35,000	
department 4 cost		215,000

---

[21]The devoted Machiavellian will see that pooling and using physical units of output to allocate the service costs will produce the identical product cost statistics in this case.

For example, $(5/3)[.2(160)900] = 48,000$.

Notice the product cost statistics that emerge. Total cost accumulated in department 1 is now $144,000 + 30,000 + 48,000 = 222,000$. This implies a product cost of $222/.9 = 246.67$. Similarly, total cost accumulated in department 2 is now $396,000 + 24,000 + 132,000 = 552,000$. This implies a product cost of $552/1.8 = 306.67$. Further observe we have assigned all the variable cost to the products, i.e., $774,000 = 222,000 + 552,000 = 246.67(900) + 306.67(1,800)$.

Figure 8.1 collects these entries in T accounts. Notice how each service department is "charged" for the cost it imposes on the other service department. Pooling or step-down procedures are not as sanguine on this score.

Figure 8.1: T Account Entries for Interactive Allocation Illustration
(Variable Cost Only)

department 1 work in process			various credits	
[a]	144,000		744,000	[a]
[b]	30,000			
[c]	48,000			
	222,000		744,000	

department 2 work in process			department 3 cost		
[a]	396,000		[a] 105,000	140,000	[b]
[b]	24,000		[c] 35,000		
[c]	132,000				
	542,000				

department 4 cost			Legend
[a]	129,000	215,000 [c]	[a] initial recording
[b]	86,000		[b] department 3 allocation
			[c] department 4 allocation

rationalization

To understand this simultaneous allocation procedure, consider the following simple linear program. We seek to minimize total cost subject to being able to produce $q_1 = 900$ and $q_2 = 1,800$:

$$\text{minimize cost}_1 + \text{cost}_2 + \text{cost}_3 + \text{cost}_4$$

subject to: $cost_1 \geq 300{,}000 + 160q_1;$
$\quad\quad\quad cost_2 \geq 200{,}000 + 220q_2;$
$\quad\quad\quad cost_3 \geq 200{,}000 + .5(50q_1 + 20q_2 + cost_4 - 100{,}000);$
$\quad\quad\quad cost_4 \geq 100{,}000 + .2(cost_1 + cost_2 + cost_3 - 700{,}000);$
$\quad\quad\quad q_1 \geq 900;$ and
$\quad\quad\quad q_2 \geq 1{,}800.$

Each department must incur costs that are sufficient to support the production schedule. Total cost incurred in the first department, for example, must be at least that prescribed by the assumed LLA of $cost_1 = 300{,}000 + 160q_1$.

The solution to this linear program is presented in Table 8.4. We also present solutions for two other cases of (1) $q_1 = 901$, $q_2 = 1{,}800$; and (2) $q_1 = 900$, $q_2 = 1{,}801$.

Table 8.4: Total Cost Constructions via Linear Program							
q_1	q_2	$cost_1$	$cost_2$	$cost_3$	$cost_4$	total
900	1,800	444,000	596,000	305,000.00	229,000.00	1,574,000.00
901	1,800	444,160	596,000	305,045.56	229,041.11	1,574,246.67
900	1,801	444,000	596,220	305,035.56	229,051.11	1,574,306.67

Notice the status quo (of $q_1 = 900$ and $q_2 = 1{,}800$) implies $cost_1 = 444{,}000$. The variable portion is 144,000, a datum we can locate in Figure 8.1. Parallel comments apply to the other cost totals.

Now examine what happens when we hold $q_2 = 1{,}800$ but increase q_1 from 900 to 901. Total cost increases by 246.67. $Cost_1$ increases by 160, $cost_3$ increases by 45.56, and $cost_4$ increases by 41.11. Service department costs, in total, increase by $45.56 + 41.11 = 86.67$. Our allocation procedure produces a product cost of 246.67. It also reassigns the service department costs to reflect each department's use of the other's services. $Cost_3$ and $cost_4$ totals, that is, are explicit costs, exclusive of any imposition one department might have on the other. Further notice what happens when we hold q_1 constant, but increase q_2 by one unit. Total cost increases by 306.67.

Is it an accident our simultaneous equations procedures is so successful in identifying the marginal cost of production (subject to accuracy of our LLAs)? Suppose we are wondering whether to produce and sell one more unit of the first product. One way to analyze this question is to solve directly for total cost at the status quo point and compare it with total cost when the output of the first unit is increased by one unit. This is exactly what our linear program does. No cost allocation is involved. A "large" focus is used, without an attempt to concentrate on one more unit of the first product.

Another way to analyze this question is to ask ourselves what the cost is of a unit of the first product, more precisely what the marginal cost is. Here we must address the question of interdependence between the service departments. Doing so creates our $c_3 = 4/3$ and $c_4 = 5/3$ variables. Cost allocation is involved here. It enters to carry the service department costs and their interactions into the profitability analysis.

Now it stands to reason the two schemes must do the same thing. They do. $4/3$ is the shadow price on the third constraint and $5/3$ is the shadow price on the fourth constraint in our linear program. Note well. We can solve the linear program directly, and not deal with any cost allocation. Alternatively, we can construct the marginal cost of the first product. Solving for the c_3 and c_4 variables in that exercise amounts to solving for the shadow prices in the linear program.[22]

Departments 3 and 4 incur costs in this setting. In deciding, say, whether to produce and sell another unit, we will be remiss if we ignore the cost in these two departments. We might treat the cost explicitly, as in the linear program. Alternatively, we might frame the question in terms of costs and benefits of the product in question. We must then implicitly deal with these costs. They are accounting joint costs. Allocation is the procedure employed.[23]

This does not imply there is a universally correct way to allocate costs, nor does it imply that variable costing is superior. We worked very hard to create a story where a particular variable cost allocation procedure produced the cost statistic we had in mind. For the record we summarize the fruits of our allocation labors in Table 8.5. This linking of cost allocation to decision making will be developed in Chapters 11 and 12.

---

[22]Can you guess the shadow prices on the last two constraints in the linear program?

[23]The allocation procedure that gives the correct marginal cost datum implicitly solves the linear program. The economics are fairly intuitive. The shadow price gives us the "marginal cost" of the service department's output; and these are the costs we want to construct the product's marginal cost. A more brute force approach to the same conclusion is as follows. Let $\hat{C}_3$ denote the variable portion of department 3's cost (i.e., $cost_3 - 200,000$). Also let $\hat{C}_4$ denote the variable portion of department 4's cost. Substituting the expressions for direct labor and total variable cost, we have the following two equations:

$$\hat{C}_3 = .5[50q_1 + 20q_2 + \hat{C}_4] \text{ and}$$
$$\hat{C}_4 = .2[160q_1 + 220q_2 + \hat{C}_3].$$

Notice we have simply taken the last two constraints from the original LP formulation and dropped the "fixed" costs.

Now solve for the two departmental cost terms. We obtain

$$\hat{C}_3 = [41q_1 + 32q_2]/.9 = 45.56q_1 + 35.56q_2; \text{ and}$$
$$\hat{C}_4 = [37q_1 + 46q_2]/.9 = 41.11q_1 + 51.11q_2.$$

This gives us expressions for the two service department variable costs, solely as functions of output. From here we readily conclude $\hat{C}_3 = 105,000$ and $\hat{C}_4 = 129,000$ when $q_1 = 900$ and $q_2 = 1,800$. Also, $\hat{C}_3$ and $\hat{C}_4$ are consistent with our departmental cost findings in Table 8.4. For example, increasing the output of the first product one unit causes $cost_3$ to increase 45.56 and $cost_4$ to increase 41.11.

Next we combine the streamlined service department cost expressions with the "variable" costs in the first two departments. This gives us a total variable cost expression of

$$160q_1 + 220q_2 + 45.56q_1 + 35.56q_2 + 41.11q_1 + 51.11q_2 = 246.67q_1 + 306.67q_2$$

This implies respective product "variable" costs of 246.67 and 306.67.

Table 8.5: Variable Product Cost Statistics		
allocation procedure	product 1	product 2
pooling of service department costs	229.33	315.33
step-down procedure	269.78	295.11
simultaneous equations	246.67	306.67

Bibliographic Notes

Cost allocation has been explored in a variety of contexts, too numerous to explore here. Decision making connections are examined in, say, Demski and Feltham [1976] and Zimmerman [1979]. Kaplan [1973] and Baker and Taylor [1979] examine the duality connection. Demski [1981] and Verrecchia [1982] explore cost allocation criteria.

Problems and Exercises

1. Can we have economic joint cost in a short-run setting in a single product firm? Can we have accounting joint cost in such a setting? Carefully explain.

2. Suppose we have a firm that produces and sells widgets in each of two periods. Economically, then, we have a multiproduct firm, as widgets in two different periods are different economic products. The most efficient arrangement is to invest in physical capital that lasts two periods, so the cost function is not separable. Yet, under perfect market conditions, we can speak unequivocally about the firm's economic income in each of the two periods. How is this possible?

3. Give four examples: one where economic and accounting joint costs are present, one where economic but not accounting joint cost is present, one where accounting but not economic joint cost is present, and one where neither is present.

4. The difficulty with the material in Chapter 8 is that joint economic costs are fairly obvious when we know the economic cost curve; yet life goes forward with accounting estimates and we must be careful not to infer too much structure from the way the accounting library is organized. This is why the terms "unit costs," "joint accounting cost," and "cost allocation" were put forward. They serve to remind us the gap (pun) between the accounting library and economic cost may be large.

Return to the setting of job order costing, where we have direct labor, direct material, and one or more overhead accounts. Where did you use unit costs and cost allocation? Be specific, and contrast actual, normal, and standard costing procedures.

5. *unit costs*

Ralph manufactures two products. The manufacturing cost curve is given by $TMC = 40,000 + 10q_1 + 5q_2$, where q_i denotes units of product i and TMC denotes total manufacturing cost.

a] Plan #1 calls for $q_1 = 2,500$ units and $q_2 = 2,500$, while plan #2 calls for $q_1 = 3,500$ and $q_2 = 1,400$ units. Determine total manufacturing cost for each plan.

b] Suppose Ralph employs a unit costing procedure in which the "fixed" cost is allocated to the products on the basis of total physical units. Determine the unit cost for each product under both plans.

c] Suppose Ralph employs a unit costing procedure in which the "fixed" cost is allocated to the products on the basis of relative separable cost incurred. Determine the unit cost for each product under both plans.

d] Repeat the above, for the cases where plan #1 uses $q_1 = 3,000$ and $q_2 = 1,000$ while plan #2 uses $q_1 = 1,000$ and $q_2 = 3,000$.

e] Carefully explain your unit cost results. Is this cost allocation?

6. *unit costs*

Verify the claim in footnote 3.

7. *unit costs*

Suppose the firm's cost curve is given by the expression $C(q_1,q_2) = G(q_1) + H(q_2) + J(q_1,q_2)$, where each product's marginal cost is strictly positive. Verify that holding q_1 constant, and with $J(q_1,q_2)$ a nonzero constant, the unit cost of the first varies with output of the second if we use units of output or relative separable cost to allocate the joint cost.

8. *cost allocation and product costs*

Return to the three department example in Table 8.2. Normal, full costing is used; also, normal volume is defined by output of $q_1 = 900$ and $q_2 = 1,800$ units. Further suppose the costing procedure allocates the department 3 cost to the other two departments, and this allocated portion is treated as an item of overhead in the first two departments. What is the full cost charging rate for department 3 services?

Continuing, suppose the first department has an opportunity to expand production. Using the LLAs in Table 8.2, determine the incremental cost to the firm as a whole of producing one more unit of the first product. Contrast this with the incremental accounting cost that will show up in department 1's cost accounts if it produces one more unit.

Finally, suppose the firm produces and sells $q_1 = 901$ and $q_2 = 1,800$ units. What will cost of goods sold total, and how does this compare with the total cost reported in Table 8.2? How do you reconcile this cost of goods sold total with your answers above?

9.   *interdepartmental cost allocation*

Return to the three department example in Table 8.2. Suppose the LLAs are perfectly accurate and output is given by $q_1 = 1{,}000$ and $q_2 = 2{,}000$ units. Also suppose department 3's cost is allocated to the other two departments.

a]   Determine the unit cost for each product assuming variable costing and also assuming normal, full costing (with normal volume defined by the noted output of $q_1 = 1{,}000$ and $q_2 = 2{,}000$ units).

b]   Record the events in the respective departmental cost accounts. Normal, full costing is used, and departments 1 and 2 each use two overhead accounts, one for locally incurred overhead and one for allocations from department 3.

c]   Repeat part [b], but on the assumption the cost incurred in department 3 is $cost_3$ = 275,000.

10.   *interdepartmental cost allocation*

Repeat part [b] of problem 9 on the assumption that variable costing is used.

11.   *decision making*

Consider a three product firm facing a constrained linear technology. The firm is organized into two departments, machining and assembly. Machine hours are constraining in the first department and labor hours are constraining in the second department. The required machine and labor times for each product are listed below:

	product 1	product 2	product 3
hours of machine time in department #1	1	2	3
hours of direct labor in department #2	2	4	5

Thus, each unit of product #1 requires 1 machine hour in department #1 and 2 direct labor hours in department #2, and so on. Total capacity is 12,000 machine hours in department #1 and 15,000 direct labor hours in department #2.

Total manufacturing cost, for any feasible production plan $q = (q_1, q_2, q_3)$, is given by TMC = $200{,}000 + 18q_1 + 24q_2 + 45q_3$. Respective selling prices are 130, 145, and 185 per unit.

The only period cost is specialized shipping "foam" that protects each of the products. This "foam" is purchased from a local supplier at a cost of 100 per pound. Each unit of product 1 requires .3 pounds of foam, each unit of product 2 requires .5 pounds of foam, and each unit of product 3 requires .7 pounds of foam.

a]   Formulate a linear program to maximize the firm's profit. Use four decision variables in your formulation, q_1, q_2, q_3, and F (the total quantity of foam purchased). Your LP should have three capacity constraints, dealing with total machine hours in department #1, total direct labor hours in department #2, and total foam consumed.

b]   Without solving the LP, what is the shadow price on the foam constraint? Carefully explain your reasoning. Then solve your LP and verify your conjecture.

c]   Formulate a linear program to maximize the firm's profit using three decision variables, q_1, q_2, and q_3. Carefully explain the relationship between your two LPs. Is cost allocation involved?

12. *decision making and cost allocation*

Return to problem 11. Now suppose indirect labor is also required, in the ratio of .5 dollars of indirect labor to every dollar of direct labor. Further assume the direct labor costs, as included in the original TMC specification, are 9, 12 and 15 dollars per unit respectively. Formulate and solve an LP to determine the optimal production schedule. Your LP should use three decision variables, q_1, q_2 and q_3. Carefully identify and rationalize your use of cost allocation in this analysis.

13. *reciprocal services*

Ralph is wrestling with reciprocal services in a manufacturing setting. Let q denote the units of product produced. It turns out that two intermediate "products" or services are utilized in the production process, say, A and B. Careful study has revealed the following production relationships:

A = q + αB; and
B = q + ßA.

Thus, each unit of output requires one unit of A and one unit of B; in addition, each unit of A requires ß units of B and each unit of B requires α units of A.

Ralph has also estimated cost curves for the production of A, the production of B, and final assembly. We denote these, respectively, as follows:

$TC_A = F_A + v_A A$,
$TC_B = F_B + v_B B$, and
$TCA = F + v \cdot q$,

where each curve is subject to the usual interpretation. Notice that the independent variable for assembly is q, while that for the other two categories is units of service, A and B. Ralph also knows $v_A = 15.60$, $v_B = 44.32$, and $v = 100$.

a]   Suppose α = ß = 0. What is the marginal cost of a unit of final output?

b]   Suppose α = 0 but ß = 1/10. What is the marginal cost of a unit of final output?

c]   Suppose α = 1/4 and ß = 1/10. What is the marginal cost of a unit of final output?

14. *decision making with reciprocal allocation*

Ralph is now managing a firm with interdependent service centers. Two such centers are involved, say, power and maintenance. For each such center, 80% of total output goes to manufacturing and 20% goes to the other service center. The variable cost of power is 10 per unit while the variable cost of maintenance is 15 per unit. Production requires 800 units of each service. Hence, 1,000 (gross) units of each are produced at a total variable cost of 25,000.

Ralph is considering an opportunity to purchase power (all or some) from an outside vendor, and the following questions are to be answered with this in mind.

a] What is the cost per unit of power? (Hint: use the simultaneous equation method of allocation.)

b] Now formulate and solve a linear program to determine the minimum cost activity levels for power and maintenance in order to provide manufacturing with at least 800 units of each service. You can infer from the noted production plan that each unit of power requires .2 units of maintenance and vice versa. So the technical constraints in your LP should be $P - .2M \geq 800$ and $M - .2P \geq 800$, where P denotes units of power and M denotes units of maintenance.

c] Compare your cost per unit of power in [a] above with the shadow price on the power constraint in [b] above. Carefully explain why they differ, if the differ, or why they are the same if they are the same. (13.5417 should be a familiar number.)

d] Suppose the outside source will sell power at 12 per unit. Should this offer be accepted? If so, determine the total saving.

e] Finally, formulate and solve an LP related to that in [b] above but with a third variable, x, units of power purchased from the outside source at 12 per unit.

f] In part [d] above you used a cost of internal power of 13.5417 to answer the sourcing question, but in the LP in [e] you used a cost of internal power of 10.00 per unit to answer the sourcing question. Carefully explain.

15. *pooling procedures*
    Verify the claim in footnote 21.

9

Alternative Costing Environments

In this chapter we extend our study of product costing procedures to alternative, more specialized production settings. This extension is important for two reasons. First, the accounting library is always fine-tuned to its environment or setting. This chapter will allow us to demonstrate that theme and to explore particular important settings. Second, whatever the setting, the library building blocks of cost aggregation and linear approximation, interlinked with cost allocation, remain.

We begin with a brief sketch of alternative production settings. These range from manufacturing to merchandising, from highly automated to labor intensive settings. We then examine joint products. Here, two or more products are concurrently produced with a common set of inputs. As we might suspect, this "ultimate joint cost" raises unusual product costing travail. We next examine a continuous flow production setting. This allows us to explore so-called process costing techniques. Finally, we explore a setting where heterogeneous products are produced in nearly continuous fashion. Questions of cost aggregation and multivariate cost assignment procedures arise. Here the techniques are called activity costing.

As we work through the settings, concentrate on how the production environment and costing procedure are aligned. Also, do not lose sight of the fact that in each instance we encounter the same product costing recipe. The only new feature is the way the recipe is varied to fine-tune the costing to the environment.

Costing Environments

Production is the generic term for converting or transforming a set of resources in one form, location, and time into another. Wheat might be planted, harvested, milled into flour, combined with other ingredients, baked, and delivered to a grocery store. Coal might be used to produce steam that, in turn, is used to generate electricity. Textbooks, chalk, the student's patience, and the teacher's human capital might be used to increase the student's human capital. Water, hoses, pumps, fire retardant chemicals, and the firefighter's skills might be used to put out a fire. The physician's skill, medicine, and the patient's rest might produce health. The list goes on. Production is ubiquitous.

In broad terms, we often classify production into manufacturing and service activities. Services, by definition, cannot be stored. We can store some factors of production but not the output. We cannot store the surgeon's procedures, though we can keep the surgeon on duty. The on-duty surgeon cannot produce by-pass procedures in advance of demand. In contrast, whole blood, automobiles, soup, and books can be produced and stored in advance of demand.

Services come in many forms. Our auto mechanic and plumber offer professional service. The management consultant offers professional service. The department store or shopping mall offers merchandising services.

The production of services and manufactured goods also comes in many forms. A job shop, where custom products are produced on demand, is one form. A tool and die shop, a portrait painter, or a custom building contractor are illustrative. So are the plumber, auto mechanic, and tax preparer specialized in unusual tax problems. Here, heterogeneity is the key feature. Each unit of output has unique features.

The opposite case is a "flow" story, where homogeneous products are produced in a more or less continuous fashion. Petroleum refining, auto assembly, and brewing are illustrative. The flow might be nearly continuous. An example is a coal mine located next to an electrical generating facility. The mining is organized to provide a continuous flow of coal. Another is a preparer of routine tax returns during busy season.

Alternatively, the flow might come in batches. A brewer will produce one brand, then switch to another, and so on. (An interesting question here is how large to set each batch.) Similarly, the high school teacher produces instruction in one subject, then switches to another.

Hybrids are also possible. The fast food purveyor will "continuously" produce sandwiches during the peak demand hours. In slack hours, batches of sandwiches will be produced as demand dictates. Similarly, the job shop may group similar jobs together, into quasi-batches. Surgery is a familiar example.

In each instance, factors of production are combined to produce some output. There may be many units of a single product, one unit of many products, or somewhere between. The output may be a manufactured good or a service. It may be produced by a proprietor, a partnership, a corporation, a not-for-profit organization, or a government agency.

Direct labor may be the largest portion of the product cost, the smallest portion of the product cost, or somewhere between. The LLA for some cost category may have a trivial slope or it may have a trivial intercept. In economic terms, a particular short-run cost curve might exhibit low or high marginal cost at some activity level.

The various products might be intimately related to one another in the production process. We don't produce lumber without producing sawdust, for example. Or they might bear only the slightest connection to one another. Valet parking and housekeeping in a luxury hotel are an example. Here, demand considerations dictate that the two services be produced at the same location. The hotel operator may, in turn, find it advantageous to produce both or to rely on a separate entrepreneur for production of parking services.

Production, as we said, is everywhere. We have studied the accountant's product costing art in job shop or heterogeneous output environments. We now extend our study to alternative production environments. Naturally enough, as the environment becomes more complex, so does the costing art. This, in turn, enhances our interest in standard costing.

Joint Products

Joint costs occur when the cost function is not separable. Joint products occur when the feasible set of production possibilities is not separable. Transportation and pollution are joint products. We cannot drive the personal automobile without producing pollution. The extreme form of joint products occurs when one product cannot be produced without inexorably producing some of another product. In such a case we cannot vary output of one product without varying the output of the others.

In general terms, joint products arise when the feasible amount of one product depends on the quantities of the other products that are being produced. For example, if we fix the amount of pollution we are willing to tolerate, we have limited the amount of driving that is feasible. Similarly, if we insist on producing 200 pounds of steak, we have said a great deal about the amount of other cuts of meat that will be produced.

Examples of joint production are numerous. Lumber, wood chips, and sawdust are joint products. As noted earlier, we can't produce lumber without producing wood chips and sawdust. Various petroleum distillates are jointly produced at the refinery. A single aircraft and flight crew jointly serve many customers and carry freight. We can't schedule a flight for passenger service without creating the possibility of carrying freight. Steak, roast, ribs, sausage, hot dogs, and leather are joint products.

Joint products may be produced in fixed or variable proportions. To a degree, we can vary the mix of steak and sausage, just as to a degree we can vary the mix of fuel oil and gasoline. It is more difficult to vary the mix of coal and environmental degradation in strip mining. Similarly, the joint production may be economically or technologically driven. We could, and do at the margin, separate passenger and freight transportation in the airline industry. We do not separate steak and rib production in the meat packing industry. Regardless, joint production places unusual demands on the accountant's product costing art.[1]

Joint products imply joint costs, so the specter of cost allocation surfaces. But the story is deeper. Under joint products the production of one product implies something about the ability to produce the other products. This interaction might be small, or it might be large. Fixed proportions is the limit point.[2]

---

[1]This should not imply dealing with joint products ends at the accountant's desk either. A rate regulator must deal with commercial and residential customers, just as the postal system must deal with various mail classifications.

[2]Of course we might take the view that a well-constructed cost function will signal joint products by having an unbounded cost for any infeasible combination of products. Conventional accounting, we shall see, offers a more subtle treatment.

Suppose we have two joint products. Denote their respective quantities q_1 and q_2. Under fixed proportions, we can only produce combinations of the two products such that $q_1 = kq_2$, for some constant $k > 0$. What is the marginal cost of the first product? Literally, we have one product here; it just comes in the form $q = q_1 = kq_2$. We can envision altering q, but not altering q_1.[3]

Here's another example. Suppose the cost curve is given by $C(q_1,q_2) = F + v_1q_1 + v_2q_2$. The only catch is that feasible production is limited by the constraint $0 \le q_1 + q_2 \le 100$. Here we can vary q_1, but only up to a maximum of $100 - q_2$.

A word of caution is in order. Accountants tend to reserve the term *joint products* for the cases of fixed and "nearly fixed" proportions. In such a setting, an accounting joint cost category will arise; and we will be faced with the task of allocating the joint cost. For this reason we will call a group of products *accounting joint products* if there exists an associated joint cost category whose LLA uses some measure of the group of products as its explanatory variable.[4]

Put differently, we encounter accounting joint products when we have a joint cost category coupled with an inability, directly or indirectly, to discern an influence on the joint cost of any particular single product. It is the group of products, taken together, that influence the joint cost. The products arise, more or less, as a group.

Suppose we have manufacturing overhead with an LLA of F + v(direct labor hours). This is a joint cost (provided F is not zero). It is not a joint products story because direct labor hours is itself a function of the various output quantities.

Conversely, suppose we have two products produced in fixed proportions. This means whatever quantities we are talking about, they always come in the form $q_1 = kq_2$. Steak and ribs, for example, always come together. If we produce one we must produce the other. In the extreme, if we produce q_2 units of steak, we must produce kq_2 units of ribs.

Accumulate the direct labor, direct material, and overhead costs into some work-in-process account for steak and ribs. What might the explanatory variable for

---

[3]Remember that what we mean by cost depends on how we frame our picture of the economic structure. Suppose the second product is always sold at a price of P per unit. What if we define revenue as revenue from the first product and cost as production cost less revenue from the second product? Under fixed proportions, we now have a frame that depends only on q_1. Let C(q) be the cost of the joint production. Remember, $q = q_1 = kq_2$. How do we interpret the expression C(q) - kPq = $C(q_1) - kPq_1$? All we have done is net the sales revenue of kq_1 against the cost!

[4]Recall from Chapter 8 that a joint accounting cost is a cost category with the following three properties: (1) it is not separable, in the sense of having an LLA with a single product as its explanatory variable; (2) its LLA does not use all products as explanatory variables and have a zero intercept; and (3) it is not routinely closed into a single nonexpense category. The accounting joint product case is now a setting where all of these properties hold and in addition the LLA uses some measure of the group of products (e.g., number of batches or physical units of the primary material) as its explanatory variable.

this LLA be? We really have a single product here. The explanatory variable would be something like units of beef, not q_1 units of ribs and q_2 units of steak. These are accounting joint products.

It is important to understand that some joint products are singled out for unusual accounting treatment or identification. Others are not. We often encounter joint products yet the accounting library records them in separable fashion. Our second illustration above, the one with $C(q_1,q_2) = F + v_1 q_1 + v_2 q_2$ and $q_1 + q_2 \leq 100$, is a case in point. Further suppose all the costs are product costs. Then the accounting library, under variable costing, would identify v_1 as the cost of the first product and v_2 as the cost of the second. This is a case of joint products, but no unusual cost allocation takes place. We would have to look beyond the accounting library to discern the presence of joint products.[5]

Costing Techniques for Accounting Joint Products

How, then, does the accountant construct product costs in the face of accounting joint products? Several techniques are used. The most common is to apportion the total cost in the joint cost category among the products in proportion to their value.

Suppose we have three joint products, imaginatively called A, B, and C. Respective quantities are 300, 600, and 100 units. Further suppose the value of the first is 15 dollars per unit, the value of the second is 20 per unit, and the value of the third is 35 per unit. The total value of the three outputs is $15(300) + 20(600) + 35(100) = 4,500 + 12,000 + 3,500 = 20,000$.

The first product contributes 4.5/20, or 22.5% of the value. It is therefore assigned 22.5% of the joint cost. The second contributes 12/20 or 60% of the value. It is assigned 60% of the joint cost. The third is assigned 17.5% of the joint cost.

Table 9.1: Data for Joint Costing Illustration				
product	units at split-off	total market value at split-off	cost of processing beyond split-off	total market value of processed product
A	300	4,500	5,000	15,000
B	600	12,000	19,000	36,000
C	100	3,500	1,000	4,000

[5]To anticipate future developments, suppose $q_1 = 80$ and $q_2 = 20$. We are producing at capacity. What is the cost of another unit of the first product? The only way to produce one more of the first is to reduce production of the second. In one sense, then, the cost of this additional unit is $v_1 - v_2$ plus the revenue foregone by reducing the output of the second product. Yet the accounting library will tell us the cost is v_1 here.

To complete the story, suppose the joint cost totals 10,000. We assign 22.5% or 2,250 to the first product, 60% or 6,000 to the second, and 17.5% or 1,750 to the third. These data are summarized in the first three columns of Table 9.1. The joint cost assignments are summarized in Table 9.2.

The accounting library records these calculations. At this stage of production, the first product will have a product cost of 2,250/300 = 7.50 per unit. The second will have a product cost of 6,000/600 = 10 per unit. The third will have a product cost of 1,750/100 = 17.50 per unit. Naturally, these are unit costs. See the last column of Table 9.2.

Table 9.2: Joint Cost Assignment Based on Relative Value at Split-off			
product	value at split	joint cost allocation	joint cost per unit
A	4,500	10,000(4.5/20) = 2,250	7.50
B	12,000	10,000(12/20) = 6,000	10.00
C	3,500	10,000(3.5/20) = 1,750	17.50
	20,000		

Before proceeding, we should note the fact the procedure uses relative value of the products. Value is measured in terms of price per unit multiplied by number of units. It is value of the output, not of a unit of output.

But where do we obtain the necessary estimates of value? Answering this requires some care, and some additional terminology. Recall that we defined accounting joint products as arising when we have a joint cost category whose LLA does not use each product's quantity as an explanatory variable (even implicitly). This means we have a cost category from which separate products emerge, though the category's LLA uses an aggregate, pseudo quantity measure. We call the point at which the separate products emerge the split-off point. *Accounting joint products reach the split-off point when separate products are identified in the accounting library.* Before split-off we do not face the problem of providing a product cost for each unit. This problem arises, by definition, at the point of split-off. (In Table 9.1 we identify separate market prices at split-off of 15, 20, and 35 per unit; these prices imply the noted market values at split-off.)

The products might be sold immediately at split-off, might be placed in finished goods inventory, or might be processed further. If they are processed further, the additional processing costs are accumulated in separate cost categories.

Examine the data in Table 9.1. Initially, 300 units of the first product (product A), 600 of the second (product B), and 100 of the third (product C) are jointly produced. Before split-off, a total joint cost of 10,000 is accumulated. Suppose we sell product A immediately. No additional cost is incurred. Suppose we process product B beyond the split-off point. The additional processing cost will be accumulated in a separate cost category. Its LLA will use units of product B as the explanatory variable. Notice in Table 9.1 we estimate that processing all 600 units of product B in this fashion will incur an additional processing cost of 19,000. Similarly, suppose we process product C beyond the split-off point. Additional costs of this processing (estimated to be 1,000 in the table) will be accumulated in another cost category. The LLA for this category will use units of product C as an explanatory variable.[6]

We now answer the valuation question. Suppose markets exist such that each product can be sold at split-off. One way to define value per unit at split-off is to use the market price at which the respective products can be sold at split-off. This is called the relative sales value method. *The relative sales value method assigns joint costs to joint products based on observable market values at split-off.*

Return to Table 9.1. Suppose the market prices at split-off for the three products are 15, 20, and 35 per unit respectively. Under the relative sales value method, we use these prices to define value of the joint products. The joint cost is assigned using these valuations, despite any further processing associated with any of the products. See Table 9.2, where we use these prices to define value at the split-off point.

There is one complication with the relative sales value method. It assumes the market for the products at split-off exists. What do we do if one or more markets does not exist, if we cannot identify a price for one or more of the products at split-off? In this case we estimate the total revenue that will be realized from the product's eventual sale, and then deduct the anticipated additional processing cost. This is called the net realizable value method. *The net realizable value method assigns joint costs to joint products based on estimated revenues less estimated additional processing costs.*

Again return to Table 9.1. Suppose none of the markets at split-off exists. This means the firm must process each product beyond split-off. Additional processing of product A will cost 5,000. The processed units will then be sold for an estimated price of 50 per unit, implying an estimated revenue of 50(300) = 15,000. The estimated additional cost is 5,000. The estimated net realizable value is the difference, 15,000 - 5,000 = 10,000. For product B we have an estimated selling price of 60 per unit, and total additional processing cost of 19,000. Product B's estimated net realizable value is 60(600) - 19,000 = 36,000 - 19,000 = 17,000. Product C's estimated net realizable value is 3,000.

This gives us a total estimated value of 10,000 + 17,000 + 3,000 = 30,000. Product A contributes 10/30 or 33.33% of this total, product B contributes 17/30 or

---

[6]We are providing a brief sketch. If the additional processing is elaborate, we would imagine various direct labor, direct material, and overhead cost categories for each product that is processed further. The aggregate picture of these various accounts would have an LLA whose explanatory variable was units of the product in question. Also notice that additional joint production is possible. Though we do not illustrate it in our example, we might combine products A and B, process them jointly, then separately, and so on.

56.67% of this value, and product C contributes 3/30 = 10%. Details are summarized in Table 9.3.[7]

These calculations assume all three products are processed further. Having no market at split-off guarantees this will be the case. What if the market at split-off exists? If we process product A further we expect revenue of 15,000 and additional cost of 5,000, for a net realizable value of 10,000. Alternatively, we might sell product A at split-off for a total of 4,500. Processing further is a winner.

Table 9.3: Joint Cost Assignment Based on Net Realizable Value (assuming no additional processing)				
product	value after processing	incremen- tal cost	net realiz- able value	joint cost allocation	joint cost per unit
A	15,000	5,000	10,000	10,000(10/30) = 3,333	11.11
B	36,000	19,000	17,000	10,000(17/30) = 5,667	9.45
C	4,000	1,000	3,000	10,000(3/30) = 1,000	10.00
			30,000		

If we process product B further, we expect the revenue to be 36,000 and the additional processing cost to be 19,000; the net realizable value is 17,000. Alternatively, selling B at split-off provides 12,000. Again, processing further is a winner.

If we process C further, we expect the revenue to be 4,000 and the additional processing cost to be 1,000. The net realizable value is 3,000. Alternatively, selling C at split-off provides 3,500. Immediate sale of C is a winner.

Table 9.4: Joint Cost Assignment Based on Net Realizable Value (assuming markets at split-off and optimal processing)				
product	sales value	incremen- tal cost	net realiz- able value	joint cost allocation	joint cost per unit
A	15,000	5,000	10,000	10,000(10/30.5) = 3,279	10.93
B	36,000	19,000	17,000	10,000(17/30.5) = 5,574	9.29
C	3,500	0	3,500	10,000(3.5/30.5) = 1,147	11.47
			30,500		

To summarize, suppose all three markets at split-off exist. We would then choose to process A and B further, but sell C at split-off. For this production plan, joint cost would total 10,000. Respective separable costs for the three products

---

[7]Rounding becomes an issue. We will round to the nearest dollar in a manner such that the total assigned equals the total to be assigned. In turn, the resulting unit costs will be displayed to the nearest cent, but it is understood we keep the totals correct.

would total 5,000, 19,000, and 0. The net realizable value calculations must reflect the processing decision and these joint and separable costs. The cost allocation details are presented in Table 9.4.

Record Keeping Details

The major, or more commonly used, joint product costing techniques are the relative sales value method and the net realizable value method. The sales value method requires a market at split-off for each product; and it ignores whether any of the products are processed beyond split-off. The net realizable value method looks to the intended processing and computes net realizable value for each product based on the intended processing.

If the product is sold at split-off, the product cost per unit that flows through finished goods (and into cost of goods sold) will be the assigned joint cost divided by the number of units of the product in question. If the product is processed further, the work-in-process inventory valuation that *enters* the subsequent processing stage will be the assigned joint cost divided by the number of units of the product in question. These per unit joint costs are then combined with the separable costs to provide the product cost statistic that flows through finished goods.

It is important to visualize the flow of cost statistics in this type of setting. Concentrate on the case in Table 9.4, where product C is not processed further and we use the net realizable value method. Initially, we record the joint costs.

work in process, joint	10,000	
various credits		10,000

Next, we invoke the joint product costing procedure, and allocate these joint costs to specific product cost categories, at split-off. Products A and B receive further processing, so their costs are transferred to respective work-in-process categories. Product C is ready for sale, and its cost is therefore transferred to a finished goods category.

work in process, A	3,279	
work in process, B	5,574	
finished goods, C	1,147	
work in process, joint		10,000

Here we should notice the unit costs that show up in the library. Product A, for example, carries an inventory value of 10.93 per unit at this point.

Following this, we record the separable processing costs for the first two products. In aggregate fashion, we have the following entry.

work in process, A	5,000	
work in process, B	19,000	
various credits		24,000

Finally, we record the transfers to finished goods.

finished goods, A	8,279	
work in process, A		8,279

finished goods, B	24,574	
work in process, B		24,574

At this point, the accounting library contains respective unit costs of 8,279/300 = 27.60, 24,575/600 = 40.96, and 1,147/100 = 11.47. See Table 9.5.

Table 9.5: Product Cost Statistics Implied by Table 9.4 Story				
product	assigned joint cost	incremental cost	assigned joint cost per unit	product cost
A	3,279	5,000	10.93	27.60
B	5,574	19,000	9.29	40.96
C	1,147	0	11.47	11.47

Other Methods

Convention calls for use of the relative sales value or net realizable value method. Other methods are available, and practice is varied.[8] We briefly note the extremes. One uses physical measures and pays no attention to market prices or additional processing. (In our running example, product A accounts for 300/1,000 or 30% of the units produced and therefore receives 30% of the joint cost, and so on.) This is regarded as acceptable as long as it does not deviate materially from what the relative sales value and net realizable value methods would produce. (It is used in coal mining, for example.)

The other merely values the inventory at split-off at its net realizable value. This means revenue is recognized at split-off, and the joint cost is expensed at split-off. (Meat packing is an example.) This has the virtue of avoiding black magic, but places considerable faith in our ability accurately to recognize revenue in advance of a sale.

By-Products

A final stop in our study of joint product costing conventions is the topic of by-products. Products in a joint product setting are called by-products if they are

---

[8]We do not imply a given organization constantly varies its approach. Consistent application of a particular approach is the norm.

"small" and considered to be of minor or "nuisance" value. Expediency then steps in, and we remove the by-products from view in unobtrusive fashion.

There are two easy ways to do this. One is to record their net realizable value as a reduction in the joint cost. The remaining joint cost is then assigned to the remaining joint products, in the usual fashion. This has the effect of treating the net realizable value of the by-products as a negative cost, or of assigning them joint cost equal to their net realizable value. The other is to treat the net realizable value of the by-products as miscellaneous income. Here no joint cost would be assigned to the by-products.

We illustrate the two methods with our example in Table 9.4. Suppose we treat product C as a by-product. Further suppose product C can be sold at split-off, though this is not necessary to treat C as a by-product. With the market open at split-off, product C will be sold at that point.

The idea of treating product C as a by-product is to remove it from the picture as soon as possible. The earliest this can be done is at split-off. Under the first method, the entry at split-off would reduce the joint cost by the net realizable value of the by-product.[9]

by-product inventory	3,500	
work in process, joint		3,500

From here, we have a joint cost totaling 10,000 - 3,500 = 6,500 that is allocated to products A and B. If product C is sold without delay, the debit half of the entry would be to cash or accounts receivable. No revenue is recognized, as net realizable value is treated as a negative cost.

Under the second method, we merely treat the credit half of the recognition entry as miscellaneous income.

by-product inventory	3,500	
miscellaneous income		3,500

From here, we have a joint cost totaling 10,000 that is allocated to the two remaining products, A and B.[10]

Either method may appear to be a case of early recognition of revenue, but remember these are small, incidental amounts in the larger picture. Expediency is

---

[9]This is easy in this case, as we are selling C at split off and know the market value is 3,500. If C were to be processed further, we would make the same type of entry, but would estimate C's net realizable value.

[10]Staying with the story in Table 9.4, treating C as a by-product and netting its net realizable value against the joint cost implies product costs of 24.69 and 38.49 for the other products. Alternatively, treating C's net realizable value as miscellaneous income implies product costs of 29.01 and 42.16 for the other products.

sought. (On this score, the actual entries may not be made until the by-product is sold. The overall picture is more clear, though, if we envision an inventory record being established at split-off for the by-product.)

Scrap is a potentially novel type of by-product. This is a form of output that, in an ideal world, would presumably not occur. Metal shavings in a tool and die factory and malfunctioning chips in a micro chip process are examples. This sounds like a by-product.

Scrap is usually monitored, as the amount of scrap is often an important indicator of performance. Scrap is generally disposed of; for example, the metal shavings might be sold to a scrap dealer. Novelty enters when the firm must pay to have the scrap disposed of. Routine garbage is an example. Here, the by-product's net realizable value is negative. Disposal cost becomes part of the joint cost!

A Caution for the Zealous Consumer

It is important to understand inventory valuation requirements produce the product costing art we see in the world of accounting joint products. The resulting product cost statistics will be found in the library. (Yes, Table 9.5 is important.) They are, however, a remarkably strange phenomenon.

Return to our example, say the Table 9.4 version where only products A and B are processed further and product C is not treated as a by-product. Suppose all the products are completed and sold. What might the income statement look like? Ignoring any other expenses or revenues, the costing technique implies something like the following:

	product A	product B	product C	total
revenue	15,000	36,000	3,500	54,500
product cost				
assigned joint cost	3,279	5,574	1,147	10,000
separable cost	5,000	19,000	0	24,000
gross margin	6,721	11,426	2,353	20,500

Notice these margins could be computed using the product cost statistics. Product A sells for 50 per unit, and carries a product cost of 27.60 per unit. 300 units were sold, implying a gross margin of $300(50 - 27.60) = 6,721$.[11]

This is a mindless exercise. We began the story by estimating a joint cost LLA in a setting of accounting joint products. By definition we do not use, or imply, individual product quantities as explanatory variables. The LLA for the cost category was viewed as not separable. We cannot vary one product's quantity without varying that of the others. Yet we recast the data to construct separable product costs, and then extract these from the library to construct separable gross margins for the products.

---

[11]Don't forget our rounding conventions.

A more sensible format does not press the separability issue. Consider the following presentation, where we identify revenue and separable cost, but refrain from any further product specific portrayal. This has the virtue of not forcing an appearance of separability.[12]

	product A	product B	product C	total
revenue	15,000	36,000	3,500	54,500
separable cost	5,000	19,000	0	24,000
net realizable value	10,000	17,000	3,500	30,500
joint cost				10,000
total gross margin				20,500

Of course, we do not have this formatting option if only some products are sold. For example, what would the income statement look like if only products A and C were sold during the current period? The cost of product B would remain in finished goods.

It is important to understand the accountant must provide inventory valuations (i.e., unit costs) for accounting joint products. This creates a wide gap between economic and accounting pictures of the production setting.[13] The message is straightforward: know the circumstance and the library. Do not extract cost statistics without understanding both the purpose and the recipe from which the library's statistics were produced.

Process Costing

Another setting in which specialized accounting techniques emerge is when the production process is continuous, or nearly continuous. This might entail several products, such as various paints or automobile models. It might entail a single product, such as a dedicated wheel rim facility or chemical process. We might have accounting joint products, continuously produced. We will, with this caution, illustrate the continuous production setting with a single product.

The idea here is to focus on the entire output during the accounting period, and then compute unit costs. This avoids recording direct product costs. It would not be possible to identify direct labor cost for each gallon of molasses in a sugar refining process. On the other hand, suppose we were constructing 50 miles of a

---

[12]Look more closely at the two formats. $6,721/10,000 = 11,426/17,000 = 2,353/3,500 = .67$. The net realizable value procedure equalizes margin as a percent of net realizable value. Is this a virtue? Certainly not in economic terms. It is an artifact produced by this particular method. Joint products remain, regardless of the accounting picture.

[13]To push the warning further, suppose one more customer arrives and offers $13 for one unit of product C. Is this an interesting offer? Presumably, we cannot manufacture one more unit of C without altering the quantities of the other products. We must look at the setting in its entirety, not focus myopically on the accounting library's unit cost here.

new highway. We might call each mile a product and invoke job order costing on a mile-by-mile basis. Alternatively, we might accumulate costs for all 50 miles, without attempting to identify direct costs on a mile-by-mile basis.

Process costing is the name given to the costing technique that shuns accumulation of costs on a product-by-product basis and focuses instead on the process. In a sense, the process becomes a single job in a job order costing system. Yet, complications arise.

Consider a setting where a single product is manufactured in a continuous process. Four manufacturing cost categories are used by the accounting library: two for different types of materials, one for labor, and one for overhead. In essence, the organization finds it worthwhile to separately identify the uses of two types of materials and labor. All other manufacturing costs are aggregated into the overhead category. For later reference, let's call the costs accumulated in these categories, respectively, M_1, M_2, L, and OV.

Further suppose 25,000 units were manufactured. Costs were accumulated as follows:

first material category	$M_1 =$	500,000
second material category	$M_2 =$	250,000
labor category	$L =$	375,000
overhead category	$OV =$	1,725,000
total manufacturing cost		2,850,000

This implies a unit cost of 2,850/25 = 114 per unit.

We also might compute a variable product cost statistic. This requires we identify the LLAs and expense the intercepts as period costs. The LLAs are displayed in Table 9.6.

Table 9.6: LLAs for Process Costing Illustration	
cost category	assumed LLA
first material	$M_1 = 20q$;
second material	$M_2 = 10q$;
labor	$L = 15q$; and
overhead	$OV = 750{,}000 + 1.8L + 0.4(M_1 + M_2)$

Under variable costing, we would expense 750,000 as a period cost. This gives us a total product cost of 2,850,000 - 750,000 = 2,100,000 and a variable product cost of 2,100/25 = 84 per unit. This is easy.

a modest complication

Now suppose we have ending work-in-process inventory. For a first pass at the resulting quagmire, suppose manufacturing began on 30,000 units during the accounting period, and 25,000 units were completed. The remaining 5,000 units are partially manufactured at the end of the period. No beginning work-in-process inventory was present.

Costs accumulated in the four categories were as follows:

$$
\begin{array}{rl}
M_1 = & 600,000 \\
M_2 = & 250,000 \\
L = & 405,000 \\
OV = & \underline{1,819,000} \\
& 3,074,000
\end{array}
$$

Of this total, how much is transferred to finished goods and how much remains in work in process? Stated differently, what is the cost of the completed units?

We answer this by working with each cost category, taking special care to identify its LLA. To begin, assume the LLA in the first material category uses units placed into manufacturing as an explanatory variable. (This might be the major materials that are combined in the initial manufacturing step.) This means M_1 refers to 30,000 units and implies a unit cost of 600/30 = 20 per unit of product *begun*. For later reference, notice the units in ending work-in-process inventory will be assigned a portion of the M_1 cost.

Now turn to the second material category. Here we assume the LLA uses units completed as an explanatory variable. (This might be interpreted as packaging or another material that is added in the final manufacturing step.) This means M_2 refers to 25,000 units, and implies a unit cost of 250/25 = 10 per unit of product *completed*. The units in ending work-in-process inventory will not be assigned any of the M_2 cost. These materials are added at a later stage in the production process.

Now turn to the labor category. The 25,000 completed units were also begun this period, since we had no beginning inventory. So 25,000 units received 100% or the necessary labor input. The remaining 5,000 units were begun but not completed. We will assume these unfinished units are 40% complete as to labor input. We therefore have 25,000(1.00) + 5,000(.40) = 27,000 equivalent units of labor. For costing purposes, it is as if 27,000 units received labor inputs. It so happens 25,000 of these have moved on to finished goods, and 2,000 remain in ending work-in-process inventory. Pulling this together, L refers to 27,000 equivalent units. This gives us a labor unit cost of 405/27 = 15 per unit of labor.

Overhead now follows in mechanical fashion. Under a variable costing system, we expense 750,000 as a period cost. Allocations based on 180% of labor cost and 40% of material cost follow in obvious fashion. Details are presented in Table 9.7. (The overhead allocation works out exactly because the illustration assumes actual cost is perfectly predicted by the LLAs. This keeps the illustration uncluttered.)

Observe how we began with total cost accumulated in the four categories of 3,074,000. 750,000 was expensed in our variable costing format. This leaves us with product cost totaling 2,324,000. Of this amount, 224,000 is allocated to ending work-in-process inventory, and 2,100,000 is allocated to completed units. The unit cost of product transferred to finished goods is 2,100/25 = 84 per unit. Under full costing, the 750,000 intercept is also treated as a product cost.[14]

Table 9.7: Calculations for Process Costing Illustration			
	(5,000) ending work in process	**(25,000) completed**	**total**
M_1 @ 20 per unit begun	100,000	500,000	600,000
M_2 @ 10 per unit completed	0	250,000	250,000
L @ 15 per equivalent unit	30,000	375,000	405,000
OV @ 1.8L +.4(M_1+M_2)	94,000	975,000	1,069,000
	224,000	2,100,000	2,324,000

Several comments are in order. First, the general idea is to treat each category as if it were a separate product. Unit cost is computed in the usual fashion for each category. Ending inventory allocations are then determined by combining the cost category unit costs in appropriate fashion. Complications arise in figuring out the appropriate amount of the explanatory variable.

Second, we call the appropriate amount of the explanatory variable for a cost category the equivalent units of output for that category. This was easy to establish for our two material categories. We assumed the first was based on units begun, and the second on units completed.[15] This was not so easy for the labor cost. There we assumed an exogenous estimate that units in process were 40% complete as to labor (to go with being 100% complete as to the first material and 0% as to the second).

Finally, the variable cost per unit of finished product turns out to be 84. This is the number we had in our first illustration. The reason is we used the same LLAs in both cases, and assumed the costs turned out to be exactly as predicted by the LLAs. This should suggest standard costs. Suppose the cost category totals were slightly different from their budgeted counterparts, based on the above LLAs. Under standard costing, we would record the ending inventories at their standard costs per unit and close any difference in the cost categories to expense. This should strike us as old hat and remind us of the importance of a pragmatic approach to the product costing art.

---

[14]Suppose we allocate the fixed overhead as a percentage of variable overhead. Assume a normal volume of 25,000 units. This implies fixed overhead will be applied to the products at the rate of 30/39 per dollar of variable overhead. (At this volume variable overhead totals 25,000[1.8(15)+.4(30)] = 975,000; and 750/975 = 30/39.) We wind up with an ending work-in-process total of 296,308, a transfer to finished goods of 2,850,000 and an over-absorbed overhead of 72,308.

[15]We might use a linearity assumption here, as we did for labor, we might assume material is used when 50% of the labor processing is complete, and so on. It all depends on the production process.

further complications

Now extend our example one more period. Suppose in this next period we begin 25,000 units, and complete 28,000. Acknowledging the 5,000 units in beginning work in process, we have 2,000 units in ending work in process. Let's also assume these latter units are 50% complete as to labor.

Costs incurred, exclusive of any beginning work-in-process amounts, are as follows:

$$
\begin{array}{rr}
M_1 = & 550,000 \\
M_2 = & 270,000 \\
L = & 432,000 \\
OV = & \underline{1,888,000} \\
& 3,140,000
\end{array}
$$

We proceed as before (continuing to assume a variable costing system). Consider the first material category. This period's beginning work in process had an opening balance of 100,000, and we have added 550,000 to this amount. In deciding how much of the 650,000 total remains in work in process, we must confront the age old inventory flow question. Did we have LIFO, FIFO, weighted average, or something else in mind?

Under weighted average, we have 650,000 cost, and 5,000 beginning plus 25,000 additional units, for a unit cost of 650/30 = 21.67. The ending work-in-process balance would be 21.67(2,000) = 43,333. (Remember, equivalent units in this category are measured as of the start of production.)

Under FIFO, the 5,000 original units are transferred out. The new units carry a unit cost of 550/25 = 22.00 per unit. This implies an ending work-in-process balance of 22(2,000) = 44,000. Under LIFO the category's ending work-in-process balance would be 20(2,000) = 40,000.

Continuing in this manner, we would construct the ending work-in-process and finished goods allocation. This is, of course, an advertisement for standard costs. If process costing techniques are employed, and if various stages and inventory complications are present, standard costing will almost surely be used. The reason is it avoids a long list of inventory calculations.[16]

Activity Costing in Complex Production Environments

The concluding stop on our tour of more specialized costing environments examines sophisticated production settings where various products are produced in nearly continuous fashion. Examples are numerous electronic components or auto-

---

[16]To bring this to an end, suppose the LLAs in Table 9.6 provide standard product cost. We then have a beginning work in process of 224,000, and ending work in process of 98,000, a transfer to finished goods of 2,352,000, an expensed fixed cost of 750,000, and a net difference between actual and applied cost of 164,000.

mobile models manufactured in the same facility. Sometimes the efficient technology allows the firm to produce various products, but in a fashion that approximates continuous production of a single product. Moreover, this nearly continuous process might exist at the firm as a whole or only in selected departments.

This conjunction of heterogeneity and continuity raises various questions and opportunities for the accounting library. For example, this technology is often combined with a policy that minimizes inventory. Materials and subassemblies arrive just as needed. Buffer stocks between work stations are small or zero. Further suppose the cycle time is short. We then have a setting where work in process at any given time is small.[17]

Library procedures can be designed to exploit this fact. Costs can be accumulated in the usual fashion, in various categories. Assignment to work-in-process categories can be essentially skipped, however. Imagine a standard costing system where we move from the accumulation categories to finished goods, with periodic expensing of the differences between actual and assigned cost. In turn, a straightforward adjusting entry would allow us to record any work-in-process inventory at the end of the accounting period. This can eliminate a considerable amount of record keeping.[18] (Recall how easy process costing was without beginning or ending work-in-process inventories.)

Another example of how costing procedures are designed to match this environment is the choice of categories in which to accumulate the initial recordings of product cost. In a job shop setting, we maintained various direct labor, direct material, and overhead categories. In a process costing setting we maintained various labor, material, and overhead categories, but all at the process level. Direct costs are absent, as no identification with individual products was made. Here we often see a mixture of the two approaches.

Direct materials of various sorts are usually identified. Direct labor may or may not. Even when it is, it often turns out to be a small percentage of total product cost. Direct labor may be less than 5% of total product cost. Naturally, if the production process and recording procedures lead to a significant decline in the relative amount of direct labor cost, the relative amounts of other costs will increase. Overhead is the likely candidate. This is the inherent nature of the production process.[19]

---

[17]Notice the information advantage in such a setting. Inventory between the work stations cannot readily hide quality difficulties. This means any difficulty that becomes apparent at the next work station will surface immediately, as the offending output cannot languish undetected in inventory.

[18]If work-in-process records are minimal, we need not worry about keeping track of each unit at each stage of the production process. Record keeping declines, since each work station is relieved of documenting the arrival and departure of each unit.

[19]For this reason, conversion cost, defined as the total of direct labor and overhead cost, becomes an important collection of cost categories in this type of setting.

Now suppose we maintain various overhead cost categories. Examples might be for purchasing, inventory control, production control, payroll taxes, overtime, building, equipment, engineering, and information processing. In turn, we might group these categories for cost allocation purposes. One group's LLA might use direct material dollars as an explanatory variable.[20] Another group's LLA might use direct labor dollars or hours.

The question now arises whether this approach is too aggregate, whether we should seek a less aggregate method of allocating the various overhead costs to products. The products vary along various dimensions, and it may be desirable to reflect more of this variability in the library.[21]

If so, we then aggregate less and use a variety of explanatory variables to construct the product costs. Less aggregation does not imply more accurate product costs. If we confine the library to direct costs and one overhead category, we have a good chance of correctly classifying the milieu of costs in the correct categories. Expanding the number of indirect categories increases the chance we encounter misclassification. On the other hand, if a number of different categories are best modeled with different explanatory variables, we may lean toward less aggregation. As with all accounting dilemmas, a balance will be struck.[22]

The resulting costing procedures are called activity based costing. This highlights the importance of focusing on a particular "activity" and costing a product in relation to its demands for services provided by that activity. (Of course, some activities may also service other activities.) The net result is a mixture of job order and process costing, since costing at the activity level is a process costing story while movement from activity to product cost is a job order costing story.

an extended illustration

We now provide an extended illustration of the aggregation and allocation issues that arise in such a setting. Our firm produces three products, with respective quantities of q_1, q_2, and q_3. You should imagine many products as we work through the illustration.

Direct labor cost is approximated by DL\$ = $20(2q_1 + 5q_2 + 12q_3)$. This reflects a standard price of 20 per hour, and respective standard quantities of 2, 5, and 12 hours per unit.

---

[20]Many call the explanatory variables in this setting "cost drivers."

[21]Recall, overhead has grown as a percent of total manufacturing cost. This raises concern over how best to mix our building blocks of aggregation and LLAs in the overhead area.

[22]The split between product and period cost also enters here. Product engineering costs are an example. It is unclear whether to allocate these costs to products or treat them as a period cost. In a similar vein, marketing costs are treated as period costs, yet serious analysis of marketing costs will raise precisely the same dilemma.

Direct material cost is approximated by DM\$ = $18q_1 + 250q_2 + 480q_3$. It is helpful to imagine a number of different materials, all aggregated to produce the respective standard direct material costs of 18, 250, and 480.

In addition, four overhead cost categories are recognized. The first uses direct labor cost as an explanatory variable. Its LLA is given by $OV_1 = 750,000 + 0.4DL\$$. This category includes the various direct labor-related costs, such as fringe benefits and supervision. Space related costs are also included here.[23]

The second overhead category contains various direct-material related costs, including items such as purchasing, receiving, inventory control, and material handling. The explanatory variables are direct material cost and an index of the number of material transactions. Let T be the number of transactions. It is modeled with T = $12q_1 + 5q_2 + 20q_3$. The first product, though having a low direct material cost requires many separate material inventory transactions (12 in particular). The second product requires 5 such transactions, and the third, 20. The LLA for this overhead category is given by $OV_2 = 200,000 + 0.2DM\$ + 1.5T$.

The third overhead cost category contains various product and process engineering costs. The LLA has only an intercept term: $OV_3 = 750,000$. This cost category may be treated as a product or a period cost in what follows. When treated as a product cost, it will be allocated to the three products in proportion to their "complexity." The idea is that more complex products demand more engineering. For this purpose, the third product is viewed as twice as complex as the first two.[24] Let U denote the number of complexity units. We model this with U = $q_1 + q_2 + 2q_3$.

The fourth overhead cost category collects setup costs. A cost is incurred each time the production process switches from one product to another. Setup costs average 1,500 per setup. The LLA is $OV_4 = 1,500$(number of setups). The number of setups is determined by how many units of each product are to be produced. The firm's policy is to produce the first product in batch sizes of 500, the second in batch sizes of 500, and the third in batch sizes of 400. Thus, a production plan of (q_1, q_2, q_3) will require $q_1/500 + q_2/500 + q_3/400$ setups (ignoring fractional solutions).

These numbing details are consolidated in Table 9.8. It is important to envision a much larger set of details and activities.

Now suppose we produce $q_1 = 2,500$, $q_2 = 2,500$, and $q_3 = 2,400$ units. What are the implied product costs? The answer is relatively straightforward under

---

[23]Equipment costs are also included in this category. If, say, equipment time were an important explanatory variable for some of the overhead costs and if direct labor cost were not a good proxy for equipment time, we would identify another overhead cost category.

[24]Complexity is meant to reflect differential demands on the engineering group. Subjective assessment, the number of assembly operations, or random sampling of engineering records are possible sources of complexity assessments. In the end, the ability to determine a reliable explanatory variable will influence the choice between treating this category as a product or a period cost. That is why we present two sets of cost statistics here, one where the category is treated as a period cost and the other where it is treated as a product cost.

variable costing, provided we are confident about the LLAs. In a very short-run story, complexity and inventory transactions, for example, are not going to be very costly. Lengthening the horizon, though, leads to more concern over these issues. So we pursue a full costing format at this juncture. More specifically, then, treating this production schedule as defining normal volume, what are the standard full costs for each product? The answer depends on how we allocate the overhead.

The production plan (of $q_1 = 2,500$, $q_2 = 2,500$, and $q_3 = 2,400$) and our assumed LLAs give the following cost category totals.

DL\$= $20[2(2,500) + 5(2,500) + 12(2,400)] = 926,000$;
DM\$ = $18(2,500) + 250(2,500) + 480(2,400) = 1,822,000$;
$OV_1 = 750,000 + 0.4(926,000) = 1,120,400$;
$OV_2 = 200,000 + 0.2(1,822,000) + 1.5[12(2,500)+5(2,500)+20(2,400)]$
$\quad = 700,150$;
$OV_3 = 750,000$; and
$OV_4 = 1,500(2,500/500 + 2,500/500 + 2,400/400) = 24,000$.

Total manufacturing cost is $5,342,550$.[25]

Table 9.8: Various Assumptions for Activity Costing Illustration	
direct labor	DL\$ = $20(2q_1 + 5q_2 + 12q_3)$
direct material	DM\$ = $18q_1 + 250q_2 + 480q_3$
number of setups	S = $q_1/500 + q_2/500 + q_3/400$
number of complexity units	U = $q_1 + q_2 + 2q_3$
number of inventory transactions	T = $12q_1 + 5q_2 + 20q_3$
first overhead category	$OV_1 = 750,000 + 0.4$DL\$
second overhead category	$OV_2 = 200,000 + 0.2$DM\$ + 1.5T
third overhead category	$OV_3 = 750,000 + 0.0$U
fourth overhead category	$OV_4 = 1,500$S

Unit costs depend on how we allocate the overhead costs. The total of the four overhead cost categories is $1,120,400 + 700,150 + 750,000 + 24,000 = 2,594,550$. One approach is to combine these into a single category for allocation purposes. Suppose we do this, and use direct material cost (DM\$) as an explanatory variable. This implies an allocation rate of $2,594.55/1,822 = 1.4240$ per dollar of direct material. The unit cost for the first product is now apparent.

---

[25]Why do we bother with this many significant digits, or with such a small OV_4 total? The answer to the first question is that carrying along the details helps link the calculations to the assumed LLAs. The answer to the second will become apparent in the problem materials. For now, ask what happens if we alter the quantities, the batch sizes, and the setup cost? The OV_4 category will become more or less important, depending on what we assume.

direct labor, 2(20)	40.00
direct material	18.00
overhead, 1.424(18)	25.63
	83.63

Calculations for the other two products follow in routine fashion. See the last column in Table 9.9.

Alternatively, we might retain the identity of the four overhead cost categories and allocate each with its respective explanatory variable. The first overhead category uses direct labor cost (DL$) as an explanatory variable. The implied allocation rate is 1,120.4/926 = 1.2099 per dollar of direct labor. Each unit of the first product receives an allocation of 1.2099(40) = 48.40.

Table 9.9: Full Costs Under Various Allocation Procedures			
output	separate pools	single pool using DL$	single pool using DM$
q_1 = 2,500	216.17	170.08	83.63
q_2 = 2,500	631.02	630.19	706.00
q_3 = 2,400	1,343.58	1,392.45	1,403.53
q_1 = 2,500	247.29	189.88	90.59
q_2 = 500	679.82	679.69	802.64
q_3 = 2,400	1,451.42	1,511.26	1,589.07
q_1 = 5,000	171.25	141.50	78.76
q_2 = 500	562.26	558.76	638.38
q_3 = 5,200	1,192.07	1,221.01	1,273.68
q_1 = 2,500	778.60	778.60	778.60
q_2 = 0			
q_3 = 0			

The second overhead category uses direct material cost and the number of inventory transactions as explanatory variables. Let's allocate the intercept of 200,000 in proportion to the "variable costs" in the category. Under the assumed production plan, "variable" cost in the second overhead category will total 0.2(1,822,000) + 1.5[12(2,500) + 5(2,500) + 20(2,400)] = 500,150. So we have an allocation rate for the intercept of 200/500.15 = .3999 per dollar of variable category 2 overhead. This implies an allocation to each unit of the first product of .2(18) + 1.5(12) + .3999[.2(18) + 1.5(12)] = 30.24.

The third overhead category is thought to be explained by product complexity. The third product, in turn, is thought to be twice as complex as the first two. The production plan gives us 1(2,500) + 1(2,500) = 2(2,400) = 9,800 "complexity units."

The implied allocation rate is 750/9.8 = 76.5306 per complexity unit. Each unit of the first product receives an allocation of 76.53.

Finally, the fourth overhead category uses number of setups as an explanatory variable. The production plan requires a total of 2,500/500 + 2,500/500 + 2,400/400 = 16 setups. The implied allocation rate is 24,000/16 = 1,500 per setup. (This is apparent from the LLA.) As 5 of these setups are for the first product, it receives an allocation of 5(1,500) = 7,500. This gives a setup cost per unit of 75/25 = 3.00. Alternatively, a batch size of 500 implies a setup cost per unit of 1,500/500 = 3.00.

Collecting the various calculations, we have the following unit cost for the first product:

direct labor, 2(20)	40.00
direct material	18.00
first overhead category	48.40
second overhead category	30.24
third overhead category	76.53
fourth overhead category	3.00
	216.17

Calculations for the other two products follow in parallel fashion. They are reported in Table 9.9. For comparison purposes, Table 9.9 also reports the unit costs when we allocate all the overhead using direct labor cost as an explanatory variable.

The unit costs clearly depend on the costing procedure. The effect, though, is subtle. The costing procedure interacts with the volume and mix of products. We illustrate this in Table 9.9 by repeating the unit cost calculations for a variety of production plans.

Dwell on the resulting patterns of unit cost statistics. If we increase production, all the unit costs decline because we are averaging the various intercept terms over more units. Naturally, the opposite occurs when we decrease production, even if we decrease production of just one product. Normal volume is assumed to vary with the production plan here.

Compare the two single pool schemes. The first product's unit cost noticeably varies. This product uses *relatively* less direct material and more direct labor. If we combine the overhead categories and use DL$ as the combined allocation base, we increase its unit cost. Similarly, if we combine the overhead categories and use DM$ as an allocation base, we decrease its unit cost.

Using separate allocation bases for each category produces less obvious results. The complexity assumption loads more of the third overhead onto the third product. Relatively more of the second overhead category is loaded onto the first product because it causes many inventory transactions.

Even so, the unit costs of the latter two products are not heavily affected by our choice of allocation procedure. This, however, reflects the fact they each use large amounts of direct labor and variable overhead, and are being produced in roughly the same amounts as the first product. A production plan that skews the resource consumption to the first product, say, $q_1 = 5,000$, $q_2 = 500$, and $q_3 = 400$ will dramatically alter this observation.

Of course, none of this makes any difference if we are producing only one of the products. In that case, all product costs are assigned to the only product being produced.[26]

Beyond this, we should remember the unit costs are affected by where we draw the line between product and period costs. To illustrate this effect, we repeat Table 9.9's calculations, in Table 9.10, for the case where the third overhead category is expensed. Recall, these costs were thought to be explained by complexity, with the third product being allocated a disproportionate share of OV_3.[27]

Table 9.10: Full Costs Under Various Allocation Procedures when OV_3 is Expensed			
output	separate pools	single pool using DL$	single pool using DM$
$q_1 = 2,500$	139.63	137.68	76.22
$q_2 = 2,500$	554.49	549.20	603.09
$q_3 = 2,400$	1190.52	1198.07	1205.94
$q_1 = 2,500$	151.14	148.55	80.38
$q_2 = 500$	583.66	576.38	660.81
$q_3 = 2,400$	1259.11	1263.32	1316.75
$q_1 = 5,000$	124.08	121.48	73.78
$q_2 = 500$	515.09	508.69	569.21
$q_3 = 5,200$	1097.73	1100.85	1140.89
$q_1 = 2,500$	478.60	478.60	478.60
$q_2 = 0$			
$q_3 = 0$			

an additional warning for the zealous consumer

Activity costing procedures are a combination of job order and process costing techniques. Some product costs are directly identified with the products, but most

[26]This does not imply we should naively take comfort in the unit cost statistic when only one product is being produced. Would we then continue to produce in batches? Would the underlying cost structure remain if we moved toward continuous production of a single product?

[27]Contrasting the two tables also drives home the imperative of understanding which costs are fixed in the circumstance at hand. We might regard the unit costs in either table as more or less accurate indicators of marginal cost, depending on the circumstance.

are identified at the process level. This, in turn, raises important questions about which allocation procedure to use in calculating unit cost statistics.

The extreme cases are not bothersome. If we have a single product, the jump from cost categories to product cost is easy. Recall the $q_2 = q_3 = 0$ case in Table 9.9. Likewise, if the overhead category LLAs use the same explanatory variable, the allocation procedure to move from cost categories to product costs is straightforward. It is the intermediate case that is troublesome.

Two facts are apparent. First, different allocation procedures can give dramatically different unit costs. Second, the gap between any given unit cost and the cost statistic appropriate for the circumstance at hand may or may not be large.

These facts are not new in our study of the accounting library. We learned in Chapter 2 that a single product firm producing at its efficient scale will exhibit identical short-run and long-run average and marginal costs. We learned in Chapter 5 that economic and accounting costs differ; and that in any particular circumstance full or variable unit cost may be a better estimator of, say, marginal cost. We also learned in Chapters 2 and 8 that average cost in a multiproduct firm is not a meaningful concept, absent separability of the cost function. This is why we stress the terminology of unit costs. Further, we learned in Chapter 6 that choice of allocation method has the potential to affect product cost statistics in a heterogeneous product setting. In short, unit costs can be affected by the allocation procedure at hand, and they must be tailored by the professional manager to the circumstance at hand.

To reinforce this observation, it is tempting to think that use of variable costing would resolve much of the difficulty and concern in this setting. It might. But ask what the cost is of another unit of, say, the first product.[28] The answer depends in part on the accuracy of the LLAs. This in turn depends on the volume and mix of products presently under production. It also depends on whether a batch size can be expanded.

We also have a shared facility. If we increase production of the first unit, do we affect our ability to produce the others? These are economic joint products; they are produced in the same facility. At some point, production of one product will interfere with the ability to produce the others. Yet variable or full costing in this setting treats the products as though they are not joint products. The aggregation and LLAs at work in the accounting library can portray a deceiving degree of independence.

We should not conclude one costing procedure is demonstrably superior to another. Circumstance is important. Instead, we should understand the procedures used in the library and the circumstances we face. This gives the keys to interpreting and engineering the unit cost statistics.

---

[28]Alternatively, what is the marginal cost? In general, the partial derivative of the total cost function will depend on the production plan at which the derivative is evaluated. Marginal cost depends on circumstance.

Summary

This chapter has provided a glimpse into how product costing procedures and the accounting library are fine-tuned to the production environment. We expect a social science library to differ from a physical science library; and we should expect the accounting library in an auto assembly factory to differ from the accounting library in a public high school.

We focused on three costing procedures: joint product costing, process costing, and activity costing. In each instance, peculiar features of the production environment lead to specialized accounting concerns and procedures. The building blocks of aggregation and LLAs for various cost categories, interlinked by cost allocation, remain the basic ingredients. Only the recipe is varied to accommodate the prevailing environment.

Joint product costing is unusual because inventory procedures demand unit costs that strain one's sense of suitability to any imaginable task. Yet it is important to know when these unit costs are in the library. It is also important to know when joint products are present, in the sense of the ability to produce one product depending on the production of the other products. This fundamental interaction among the firm's products may or may not receive recognition in the accounting library. This is why we carefully distinguish joint products from accounting joint products.

The latter arise when we have a joint cost category whose LLA does not use units of each product's output (implicitly or explicitly) as explanatory variables. The products are joint; and the cost category's LLA treats them as joint. Here we encounter the relative sales value and net realizable value methods for allocating joint cost to joint products. By-product costing is a variation on the theme, designed to focus the allocation procedure on the "important" products.

Process costing procedures arise when the production process is nearly continuous and produces essentially the same product or set of products. With so much homogeneity, individual product costing is silly; it consumes resources with no apparent benefit. Process costing enters, as a type of job costing where we treat the entire output as a single job. Even so, actual costing procedures become burdensome in this environment. The reason is we have many cost categories, with varying unit costs. Interperiod inventory calculations become ghastly; and standard costing surfaces as the obvious solution.

Finally, activity costing procedures arise in a hybrid setting where heterogeneous products are produced in nearly continuous fashion or batches. Here, a mixture of job order and process costing surfaces, in conjunction with thoughtful aggregation choices. Each activity is viewed in terms of a process, and we construct the individual product unit costs by focusing on the demands the product places on the various activities.

Bibliographic Notes

The linkage between the production environment and the accounting library's procedures is well-explored. Weil [1968] examines the relationship between economic structure and accounting joint products. Johnson and Kaplan [1987] emphasize the theme of connecting accounting procedures to the production environment, while Cooper and Kaplan [1991] provide an extensive examination of activity based costing. *Management Accounting*, a professional journal, is a continuing source of current illustrations of product costing art.

Problems and Exercises

1. Are joint accounting products economic joint products? Carefully explain your conclusion.

2. Consider an auto repair shop, a group of welfare case workers who oversee entitlements for a set of clients, and a capital intensive manufacturing setting where direct labor is not recorded and just-in-time inventory procedures are used. Speculate on how product costing might be done in each instance and how this relates to the production environment.

3. *accounting joint products*
Ralph produces three products, in fixed proportions. Call them A, B, and C. Relevant data follow.

	A	B	C
units produced	500	750	400
selling price per unit at split-off	200	300	10

The cost in the joint production facility totaled 300,000. Think of this as 500 units of "joint work" in which the three products are produced in the proportions of 1:1.5:.8. Each such unit of joint work costs 600. So 500 units of joint work entails joint cost of 300,000, and produces 500 of A, 750 of B and 400 of C.

Product B can be processed further, after the split-off point. Such processing costs 50 per unit and any product processed in this fashion sells for 375 per unit.

a] Determine Ralph's profit, initially assuming product B is not processed further and then assuming it is processed further.

b] Determine the profitability of each of Ralph's products, assuming product B is processed further. Do this six different ways: treating product C as a by-product or a joint product, and using (i) physical units; (ii) relative sales value at split-off; and (iii) net realizable value to allocate the joint cost. (In the by-product mode, treat the sales value of C as a net against the joint cost).

4. *library procedures*

This is a continuation of problem 3, part [b] above. Suppose 250 units of A, 400 units of B, and all of C are sold. The remaining units are in finished goods inventory. Assume all three products are treated as joint products, and the joint cost is allocated on the basis of net realizable value. Determine Ralph's gross margin for the period in question. Describe these events with debits and credits, using work-in-process and finished goods accounts as appropriate.

5. *more library procedures*

Repeat problem 4, but for the case product C is treated as a by-product, with its net sales value netted against the joint cost. Assume the remaining joint cost is allocated on the basis of net realizable value.

6. *links to economic analysis*

Return to the setting of problem 3 above. Suppose two extra customers arrive. One, conveniently, wants 1 unit of product A and the second, conveniently, wants 1.5 units of the processed further version of product B. (Any additional production of C can still be sold for 10 per unit; however, no additional units of A or B can be sold at the earlier noted prices.) The first customer offers 180 for the unit of A and the second offers 500 in total for the 1.5 units of (further processed) B. What is Ralph's incremental profit if these offers are accepted?

Now return to part [b] of the original problem and pick one of your costing methods, say where C is a by-product and the net joint cost is allocated on the basis of relative sales value at split-off. Using the apparent unit cost from the part [b] calculation, what is Ralph's incremental profit if these offers are accepted?

How do you reconcile the two sets of calculations? What happens here if we admit some of the joint costs are best viewed as fixed costs?

7. *an LP formulation*

This is a further continuation of problem 3 above. Now formulate an LP, using decision variables of A (units of product A), B (units of product B that are not processed further), BB (units of product B that are processed further), C (units of product C), and X ("units" of joint production). The objective function should be $200A + 300B + (375-50)BB + 10C - 600X$. The constraints should be as follows: $A \le X$; $B + BB \le 1.5X$; $C \le .8X$; and $X \le 500$. Solve the LP, and notice the original production plan has materialized.

Using the shadow prices in your LP, calculate the incremental profit of processing one additional unit of joint production (i.e., increasing X from 500 to 501 units). Carefully explain the relationship between this calculation and the one you performed in problem 6 above.

8.   *process costing*
Verify the calculations in footnote 16, where standard variable costing is used.

9.   *process costing, using full standard costing*
Verify the calculations in footnote 14. Then assume the LLAs in Table 9.6 determine the product's standard cost. Also assume the overhead intercept of 750,000 is allocated on the basis of standard variable overhead, based on a normal volume of q = 25,000 units. Determine the product's full standard cost.

Now move to the setting of footnote 16, and determine the beginning and ending work-in-process inventory, the transfer to finished goods, and the net difference between actual and applied cost.

10. *full versus variable costing*
This is a continuation of problem 9 above. Suppose 21,000 units are sold during the period. How much higher or lower is the entity's income this period if it uses standard variable costing compared with standard full costing?

11. *activity based costing*
Return to the activity based costing example in Table 9.8 of the text. The idea here, in simplified fashion, is the production operations are served by a number of support activities. These activities have been aggregated into four cost categories, described by the noted overhead categories. (A more serious illustration would have activities serving activities, and so on.)

Take the LLAs from this illustration and determine the variable product cost for each of the products. Notice the difficulty with setup costs. It is easy to identify the incremental cost of an additional batch of each product; but working at the product level forces you to deal with the setup cost.

Now suppose the entity allocates all variable overhead on the basis of direct labor dollars. Assume a normal volume of $q_1 = q_2 = 2,500$ and $q_3 = 2,400$. Determine the variable product cost for each of the products. Why must we specify a normal volume in this latter case? What has happened to your earlier difficulty with the setup costs? How do you reconcile your product costs here with their counterparts in Table 9.9?

12. *more activity based costing*
Return to the example in Table 9.8 where full costing is used. Construct a spreadsheet model that will calculate the product costs in three ways: using the four pool procedure in the text, using a single pool based on DL$, and using a single pool based on DM$. Be certain to verify that your model replicates the (full cost) numbers reported in Table 9.9. As a second check, examine the product costs when output is very large, say, 10^{13} for each product.

a]   Let the production schedule be $q_1 = 50,000$, $q_2 = 50,000$, and $q_3 = 50,000$. Interpret the results.

b]   Let the production schedule be $q_1 = 500$, $q_2 = 50,000$ and $q_3 = 50,000$. Interpret the results. Be certain you contrast the unit costs with those determined in part [a].

c]   Let the production schedule be $q_1 = 500$, $q_2 = 500$ and $q_3 = 0$. Interpret the results.

d]   Suppose the first product uses a batch size of 50 instead of 500 units. Let the production schedule be $q_1 = 50,000$, $q_2 = 50,000$ and $q_3 = 50,000$. Also try $q_1 = 2,500$, $q_2 = 2,500$ and $q_3 = 2,400$. Interpret the results.

e]   Repeat [d] for the case where the first product uses a batch size of 2,500 units.

f]   Why is the cost of the third product minimized when the separate pool procedure is used, despite the fact this product is the most complex of the three, in nearly all of these cases?

13. *even more activity based costing*

Return to problem 12 above but now assume variable costing is used. Using the same allocation procedures as before, but adapted to the variable costing format, determine the product costs for the following output schedules: (i) $q_1 = q_2 = q_3 = 50,000$; (ii) $q_1 = 500$ and $q_2 = q_3 = 50,000$; (iii) $q_2 = 500$ and $q_1 = q_3 = 50,000$; and (iv) $q_1 = q_2 = 50,000$ and $q_3 = 400$. Comment on your results.

10

Library Integrity: Internal Control

The purpose of this chapter is to introduce the subject of internal control. We have stressed the fact the accounting library is a specialized library. It emphasizes financial records that have a high degree of integrity. It is purposely designed to have a low error rate and to be difficult to manipulate.

Several design features support this emphasis on integrity. The records themselves are kept in a way that makes detection of errors easy and manipulation difficult. The records are usually audited. By implication, the records are also in a form that can be audited.

Internal control is the name given to the techniques that are used to ensure integrity of the accounting library. Studying internal control is important for two reasons. First, it is costly to maintain the integrity of the accounting library. This means resources are consumed while maintaining integrity of the financial records. It also means the financial records will be designed with an eye toward maintaining their integrity. Some data will be excluded, simply because it is too costly to maintain their integrity. The accounting library reflects a compromise between costly safeguards and procedures and information content.

For example, we typically do not value inventories at current cost. These data are costly to obtain and difficult to audit (unless we adopt mechanical price level adjustments). We stress one cost of maintaining the library's integrity is to restrict what goes into the library.

Second, studying internal control gives us our first glimpse into control problems. How does the organization ensure its policies are carried out? For example, how does the organization ensure its financial records are accurate? We will study control techniques in subsequent chapters. At this point we pose the question of how is the accounting library defended against inaccuracy and manipulation? Many techniques will be discussed. Their place in a broader perspective of dealing with control problems in general will be deferred.

The chapter is organized as follows. Initially we provide an overview of internal controls. Various interpretations will then be offered. Finally, we return to the theme that high integrity is both the strength and the weakness of the accounting library.

Basic Ingredients

Suppose we take our automobile to a small garage where the proprietor is on site. Once the automobile is repaired, the proprietor gives us an invoice, listing labor and parts charges, and accepts our payment. Most likely the proprietor has prepared the invoice and perhaps even done the repair work. If any specialized parts were acquired, it is also likely the proprietor handled the transaction with a parts supplier.[1]

Contrast this with the case where we take our automobile to a large garage, say, one associated with a franchised dealership. Once the automobile is repaired, a cashier presents an invoice and accepts our payment. Again, the invoice lists labor and parts charges. The parts charges are based on transaction records from the parts department. The labor charges are based on transaction records from the repair department. (Direct material and direct labor records should come to mind.) The parts manager never accepts payment, and never pays any of the dealership's suppliers. Cash transactions are executed by separate individuals in the organization.

Should we interpret the first story as efficiency and the second as an out of control bureaucracy? Hardly. The proprietor must suffer the consequences of the record keeping procedure in place. There is no reason to worry about proper trade-offs not being made. The same person who makes the tradeoffs incurs the costs and receives the benefits. So to speak, no unusual concerns arise because returns to record keeping are fully internalized by the proprietor.

Of course, even this story has its limit. The tax auditor has a different view! So does the banker to whom the proprietor is indebted. For managerial purposes, though, the manager and the record keeper are the same individual. Tradeoffs are internalized, in the narrow sense.

The large, franchised dealership is a different story. Here the scale of operations precludes a localization of costs and benefits associated with record keeping falling on a single individual. This being the case, how do we proceed?

Several techniques are used. First, some redundancy is designed into the system. The parts department has records for parts that are acquired and for parts that are used in the various repair jobs. Couple these records with a periodic physical inventory and we have a reasonable chance of knowing whether any material errors (no pun) are present.[2]

Redundant record keeping is also used in documenting the arrival of new parts into inventory. Shipments to the parts department are accompanied by shipping documents that identify the newly arrived items. The parts department must verify receipt of the ordered parts. A separate invoice is transmitted by the supplier to the individual in the dealership who pays the supplier. Consistency between the invoice and shipping materials (as verified by the parts department) is a prerequisite to paying the supplier. This separation makes it more difficult to pay a supplier for parts not received or to remove parts from inventory without assigning them to

---

[1]We also will likely have the option of inspecting the parts that were replaced.

[2]Our proprietor is also likely to use redundancy. Reconciling the check register with the bank's statement is illustrative. Redundancy is all around us. Parity checks in computer memory systems, multiple hydraulic systems in airplanes, and inventory safety stocks are familiar examples.

particular customer jobs or general shop use. (It is also likely a separate individual signs the check or executes an electronic funds transfer.)

We also should notice how double entry record keeping supports redundant procedures. We tend to think of recording new parts with a debit to parts inventory and a credit to accounts payable. Yet this hides the control apparatus from view. Separate source documents are used for the debit and credit half of the entry.

A second internal control technique concentrates on tempering various temptations. The parts department may find it tedious to keep writing or typing part numbers (especially long ones). Electronic data capture is likely used. This makes some record keeping perfunctory. Scanners in the food store checkout process are another illustration. Physical access to the parts department is also limited. This makes pilferage more difficult.[3]

A third category of internal control techniques is to separate various activities in the redundant record keeping chain. What happens when we purchase a part from the franchised dealer? The procedure is tedious. We go to the parts department, where we are given a sales slip, showing the item and its retail price. Next we go to the cashier. Payment is made. Payment is noted on the sales slip. The sales slip is then returned to the parts department. We then receive our part.[4] One individual issues the part and another accepts the payment.

These anecdotes provide a glimpse of the elaborate, sophisticated set of techniques that are used to ensure the accounting library's integrity. But they convey only part of the story.

internal control procedures

Auditors review, test, and evaluate the organization's internal controls.[5] The procedures are grouped into categories, providing a type of "checklist for internal controls:"[6]

> proper authorization;
> segregation of duties;

---

[3]This illustrates the importance of architecture in the design of control systems. Prisons are designed with surveillance in mind; observation structures are built into gambling casinos; and so on. These techniques are not new, either. Moats and limited access were used to combat work force pilferage during the Renaissance.

[4]If visual proximity is present, you may receive the part and the sales slip, and then go to the cashier.

[5]The Foreign Corrupt Practices Act of 1977 prohibits U.S. companies from bribing foreign political officials. It also requires public companies to maintain adequate (in a cost benefit sense) internal controls. Civil and criminal penalties, under federal securities laws, are possible actions when internal controls are inadequate.

[6]Taken from Hermanson, Strawser, and Strawser [1989].

adequate documentation;
safeguards over assets; and
independent check.

The above parts department story illustrates these categories. The parts supplier will not be paid until the invoice submitted agrees with the parts department's verification of items received. Similarly, a part will not be released to a customer until payment has been noted on the sales slip. Proper authorization is required to release the part to the customer, or to release cash to the supplier. Likewise, a large insurance company will protect its data bank by requiring an authorization code to extract data and another authorization code to alter the data in the data bank.

Physical access to the parts, physical access to the dealership's cash, and bookkeeping are separate activities in our story. Duties are segregated so as to hinder an individual from removing assets and then altering the underlying records. Seeking a second opinion before surgery further illustrates the technique. In one sense the second opinion provides additional information. In another, it separates the surgery decision from the surgeon. Authorization and implementation are often separated in sophisticated control systems.

Adequate documentation is illustrated by matching the supplier's invoice with the parts department's verification of parts received. This has two purposes. It introduces safeguards into the process of entering data into the dealership's accounting library. Absent the documentation, entries are forbidden. This helps ensure accurate records. It also provides an audit trail. The auditor cannot test the records without access to underlying source documents. Adequate documentation provides for auditability.

Adequate safeguards over assets are illustrated by limited access to the parts department. The customer cannot enter the storeroom, neither can the shop mechanic. Similarly, the parts manager cannot use the cash register or write checks. Students cannot alter the university's records of their accomplishments.[7] A faculty member can submit a grade change request (as distinct from changing the grade) only if proper, detailed, burdensome procedures (such as verifying a grading error) are documented.

Finally, independent check is illustrated by comparing a periodic physical inventory of the parts department with what the records show should be present.[8] Auditing the records by an independent auditor is another example. The bank's customers reconciling their bank balances is yet another.[9]

---

[7]Remember, these are relative statements. Computer hackers have accessed records, despite sophisticated safeguards.

[8]Generally Accepted Auditing Standards (GAAS) require verification of the audit client's inventory.

[9]The accounting library is typically audited. Internal and external auditors typically perform the audit. Notice how the work of the routine procedures and the two sets of auditors sets up an elaborate

Internal control is serious business. Our sole proprietor fails on just about every dimension. Of course, there is no one to segregate the duties, to protect the assets from, to perform an independent check, or to worry about internal controls. A nontrivial organization invests in these procedures. Yet a proper economic balance is sought. The controls will not be perfect, neither will they be perfunctory. The accounting library design balances tradeoffs.

auditability

Balancing tradeoffs implies absolute integrity is not sought. This would be too costly. On the other hand, the library lacks comparative advantage without integrity. So we should expect to see considerable resources devoted to maintaining the library's integrity.

Resources are used, for example, in carrying out the procedures that are designed to lower the error rate in recording the many, many transactions that occur. Resources are also used in making certain the records can be audited. Implicitly, resources are also consumed by the recognition rules. We are often slow to recognize revenue and quick to recognize expense. This recognition policy eases the auditing burden but lowers the library's information content.

Consider an organization that is larger than our auto dealership example. The process of acquiring raw materials (or merchandise) and maintaining the inventory records is much more elaborate than we have sketched above. Initially some department requests a particular set of materials. This request is sent to a purchasing department. The purchasing department is specialized in designing and managing contracting arrangements with vendors. It selects a vendor and issues a purchase order, formally soliciting the materials from the particular vendor.[10] Copies of the purchase order go to the requesting department (to verify the purchasing department's work), to the receiving department, and to the accounts payable department.

When the materials are received, the receiving department prepares a receiving report and reconciles this report with the purchase order. Copies of this report are sent to the requesting department, the purchasing department, and the accounts payable department. This source document also triggers entry into the inventory records.

The vendor transmits a sales invoice. This is routed to accounts payable. Consistency among the purchase order, receiving report, and invoice then triggers a payment authorization. Payment, of course, is made by yet another department.

---

mutual control mechanism. In addition, the external auditor works within a complex organization, with detailed work papers routinely reviewed. Thus, in a larger system the milieu even speaks to the question of auditing the auditor.

[10]The selection itself may be elaborate (e.g., competitive bidding) or perfunctory (e.g., a long-standing relationship with a local vendor).

For sure, we have an abundance of proper authorization, segregation of duties, documentation, and independent checks. This, in turn, allows the auditor to verify a sample of transactions. Source documents, whether electronic or paper, can be traced through the requisition, acquisition, payment process. In addition, ending accounts payable balances can be verified with vendors. This provides an independent check of the trade liabilities. The auditor also can wait beyond year end to see if any trade liabilities have been missed.

Now move on to inventories. The ending inventory will be physically verified. Its value in the library will be verified by reconciling with the source documents. The above procedure ensures that the source documents are in place. Notice how problematic the valuation verification would be if current cost or subjective value were used instead of historical cost.

Our story is getting a little out of hand. Two concluding points should be noted. We have only scratched the surface of describing the many and subtle ways the library is defended. The underlying principles extend to control systems in general.

Interpretations

What are these principles? Three ideas are present. One idea is to restrict the action possibilities. Safeguards over assets and proper authorization are examples. Another idea is to provide redundancy so a performance check of some sort is possible. Segregation of duties (which also restricts action possibilities), adequate documentation, and independent check are examples of techniques that produce redundancy. The third idea is to introduce incentives. Record keeping contests and licensing are examples.

restricted action possibilities

Restricting action possibilities is a familiar, visible control technique. Fences, limited access highways, turnstiles, and door locks are illustrative. Access codes to an organization's data bank, the combination to the vault, and ID verification to enter the university's library are also familiar examples.

The restrictions might be administrative. The parts manager in the auto dealership might be able to purchase parts from a prespecified list of approved vendors. The division manager might be able to authorize capital investments up to $2 million, without turning to central management for authorization. Each sales person might be assigned an exclusive territory or customer list. The plant manager might be allowed to decide overtime requirements, but have the production schedule (including batch sizes and sequences) set by central administration. The work sharing between internal and external auditors might have to be approved by the audit committee of the board of directors.

The point is simple. Restricting options open to individuals is an important control technique. These restrictions might be physical or administrative. Compliance might be more or less complete. Auto theft, rebel priests, computer hackers, insider trading, professional malfeasance, audit failure, and managerial impropriety are hardly unknown phenomena. Yet restricting options is an important, ubiquitous control principle.[11]

We observed this principle at work in our brief survey of internal control techniques. Proper authorization and segregation of duties assign specific elements of the action and recording chain to specific individuals. This helps provide redundancy in the records, and it places obstacles in the path of opportunism. Fraud, for example, is possible; it just requires more people.

Two additional applications of this principle should be noted. One is to substitute capital for labor. Currency counting machines and bar code readers come to mind. Automated parking facilities are another example. The other is to rotate the individuals. A records clerk must take a vacation. Auditors must rotate assignments. The dealer in a casino must take breaks. Is this altruism? Forced rotation inhibits continuity. It is a dynamic version of restricting action possibilities.[12] Similarly, managerial promotion has, as a side advantage, a rotation of duties dimension. Consultants also provide such an opportunity.

redundancy

Redundancy is also a familiar control technique. A lending officer in a large bank oversees a portfolio of loans. Larger loans in this portfolio are examined by a supervisor and perhaps a loan committee. The entire portfolio is also subject to review by the bank's hierarchy. Similarly, a surgeon's work is routinely examined by a surgery committee.

We return the students' examinations to provide feedback. A secondary purpose is to provide a check on the grading. It is common practice to write the amount on a check twice. One "entry" is numeric and the other "entry" is verbal.[13]

General and special ledgers are commonplace. Accounts receivable tallies are kept in aggregate, also at the individual customer level. The auditor prepares extensive work papers. In turn, the work papers are examined by the auditor's supervisor and the partner in charge of the audit.

Redundancy might be direct or indirect. In the direct version, the task is simply repeated in some form. Additions to inventory are recorded in receiving documents and in vendor invoices. Payrolls are recorded in aggregate and at the individual employee level. A trial balance compares total debits with total credits. When we

---

[11]For example, we will learn in subsequent chapters that task assignment interacts with ability to monitor.

[12]A well-publicized bank fraud was discovered when the perpetrator was on vacation and forgot to enter additional computer instructions to keep interbranch float in line to cover the fraud.

[13]The check itself is therefore an alphanumeric instrument.

instruct our personal computer to erase a set of files, it responds by asking whether we meant to give such an instruction.

Redundancy in the indirect version is more subtle. Quality inspection, supervision, and relative performance evaluation are examples. The quality inspector examines the fabricated item. The supervisor monitors the group's activities. Under relative performance evaluation, the group's performance is compared with that of a peer group. (An example is comparison of sales people.) In each instance, some type of performance check, repetition, or redundancy is added to the process.

Independent check in our checklist for internal controls is an example of redundancy in a control system.

incentives

Incentives are another familiar control technique. The young manager faces an array of financial, nonfinancial, promotion, and peer approval possibilities. A licensed physician might lose the necessary license. The plumber might get a reputation for inadequate service. The inventor might produce a valuable patent. The scientist might win a Nobel Prize. The bank teller who cannot count will be discovered. The parents who neglect their children run the risk of family fracture.

In a casual sense, one way to make certain the records are fairly accurate is to design in redundancy. Any error must then occur at each processing stage if it is to survive and enter the library. Another way is to design in unusual diligence in the record keeping process. We then check a small random sample. With luck, hardly any discrepancies will be discovered. Incentives enter at this point to make the necessary luck endogenous.

We want diligent record keeping. Diligence is difficult to observe, so we don't just go to the labor market and purchase so many units of diligence. Instead, we foster diligence. We stress its importance. We seek diligent employees. We randomly check some records (a form of redundancy). We then use the error rate observed in the sample as an indirect measure of the diligence supplied. A low error rate might be accompanied by supervisory approval, financial reward, promotion, self-satisfaction, and so on. A high error rate might be accompanied by supervisory disapproval, lack of self-satisfaction, loss of employment, and so on.[14] This means the record keeper's "compensation" varies with the observed error rate.

Notice the tradeoffs. Complete redundancy provides assurance the error rate is likely to be low. In the limit, this means doing everything twice (or more than twice). Less redundancy increases the risk of material errors in the records. Suppose we also introduce incentives to supply unusual diligence in the record keeping process. Redundancy decreases, as random checking is substituted for complete redundancy. Coupling this with incentives to supply unusual diligence provides

---

[14]When auditors speak of having reliable personnel they are speaking in terms of incentives. Unreliable personnel cannot be trusted with the accounting library.

assurance the necessary diligence is being applied. We balance error possibilities, redundancy costs, and incentive costs.[15]

There is also a more delicate side to the incentives story. An important internal control issue is making certain the source documents are reliable. Otherwise, the record keeping begins with errors. This is why we see consistency checks, for example, among purchase orders, receiving reports, and vendor invoices. It is important, however, not to put too much pressure on source documents. Otherwise, they may be compromised. The incentive consequences, so to speak, cannot be too severe if we are to have reliable documents.

Suppose division managers are always harassed when their budgets do not show a sizable increase in profitability. This invites, at the margin, distorted budget forecasts.[16] Similarly, suppose a special tools fabrication department has two jobs. One is unusual. The other is similar to several previous jobs. The department must self-report labor hours spent on each job. If heavy cost control effort is directed toward the familiar job (because experience suggests what it should cost), we invite less than reliable source documents. The department is tempted to assign any unusual labor usage to the unfamiliar job.[17]

a decision tree caricature

A useful caricature of these techniques and principles is provided by thinking in terms of *designing* an agent's decision tree. We want an agent, say, an employee, to provide some service. Supplying the desired service is not automatic. The agent has a choice to make. The agent might supply every ounce of insight in suggesting a marketing strategy; alternatively, a flippant response might be offered, while the agent silently makes plans for a forthcoming vacation.

Now visualize this setting in terms of the agent facing a decision tree. The organization has an important role to play in designing this decision tree. The consequences that fall to the agent at the end of any branch in the tree can be influenced by the organization; this is the topic of incentives. The choices available to the agent are also subject to design; this is the topic of restricted action possibilities. In turn, additional information may be brought to bear, for example by monitoring or by designing in redundancy. We will employ this idea of designing the agent's decision tree in our study of controls.

---

[15]A similar balancing act will characterize our approach to control problems in subsequent chapters. For the moment, we provide an intuitive though casual description of a control problem and the balancing of tradeoffs that describes its resolution.

[16]The U.S. federal government currently faces such an issue. The Gramm Rudman Act requires a balanced budget. Estimates are routinely engineered to balance the budget.

[17]The Allies in World War II consistently over estimated Axis aircraft losses. The source documents were pilot self-reports, produced in the heat of battle. See Parker [1990].

Library Content

Tradeoffs are always present. Our controls are never perfect. We trade off more extensive controls for a limited risk of control failure. We also trade off what we are trying to do, for something that is easier to control. Crime and police protection is a ready illustration.[18] Regulated financial institutions face restricted investment opportunities. Production facilities are designed with an eye toward control. Moonlighting is usually restricted; personnel are rotated. Some assignments are placed in a course to determine more easily whether the students have done the homework. As we have stressed, the same holds for the accounting library. We want the library's integrity to be maintained. At the margin, we trade off cost of maintaining integrity for what is placed in the library.

an old friend

We will illustrate this important theme by returning to the running example of job order costing that was used in Chapters 6 and 7. The organization recognizes five aggregate manufacturing cost categories: direct labor, stock direct materials, custom direct materials, overhead A, and overhead B.

When standard costing was introduced into this setting in Chapter 7, we assumed respective overhead LLAs of $OV_A = 55,000 + 1DL\$$ and $OV_B = 32,000 + .2DM\$$. We also assumed the standard price for direct labor was $11 per hour. Finally normal volumes of $DL\$ = 50,000$ and $DM\$ = 80,000$ were used to construct standard burden rates. These rates were 2.1 per direct labor dollar for overhead A and .6 per direct material dollar for overhead B.[19]

We now embellish this story in several important ways. First, assume the standard costs and underlying LLAs are reasonably accurate approximations to the economic cost curve. By implication, it will be reasonable to use these LLAs in contemplating various production possibilities. This is an important assumption. It keeps our exploration uncluttered. Costing and economic analysis assumptions need not be so closely aligned.

Second, we assume all production is to custom order. The organization cannot produce in anticipation of demand. This implies that one issue in dealing with a new customer is to anticipate additional demands that have yet to occur. Accepting a customer's order reduces the capacity available to service other customers that might arise during the period. Idle capacity has option value; and committing some capacity to a customer lessens the option value.

Third, we further assume we are just into the reporting period in question. The organization has one product that is under production, and no other customers have

---

[18]Failure of the Prohibition movement is an example. Debate over maximum speed limits is another.

[19]$[55,000 + 1(50,000)]/50,000 = 105/50 = 2.1$; and $[32,000 + .2(80,000)]/80,000 = 48/80 = 0.6$.

yet arrived. This product is job 1 in our earlier illustrations in Chapters 6 and 7. (Table 7.1 in Chapter 7 will refresh our memory.)

Now suppose a second customer arrives. This product is job 2 in our earlier illustration. It is predicted to require the following inputs:

direct labor	1,700 hours,
stock direct materials	$9,000, and
custom direct materials	$5,000.

Product market considerations dictate the customer will source the product with our organization only if the selling price is P (or less). The product market, so to speak, offers the job to our organization for a price of P. If this offer is accepted, the product must be produced and delivered this period. No adverse future demand effects are anticipated if the offer is rejected.[20]

Initially we trace through the organization's analysis of this new prospect. Now, the only product on order (and in production) is job 1. This product is predicted to require the following inputs:

direct labor	2,000 hours,
stock direct materials	$5,000, and
custom direct materials	$11,000.

The customer will pay 250,000 upon receipt of the completed order.

If the second customer's offer is rejected and no other customers arrive, our firm faces revenue of 250,000 for the period. Its manufacturing cost will consist of direct labor, direct material, overhead A, and overhead B costs. We total these as follows, using the noted LLAs:

direct labor: 11(2,000)	22,000
stock direct materials	5,000
custom direct materials	11,000
overhead A: 55,000 + 1(22,000)	77,000
overhead B: 32,000 + .2(16,000)	35,200
projected manufacturing cost	150,200

Let's also assume shipping costs will total 5,000 and general and administrative expense will total 90,000. This gives us a projected income of 4,800.

Before proceeding, we should recall some accounting skill. Shipping and G&A are period costs. They will not be found in product cost computations that find their way into the accounting library. (They will, of course, be found in the period costs!) The income statement follows:

---

[20]Do not assume the product market is necessarily this benign. Formal bidding may be involved, a sales force may manage long-term relationships with various customers, complicated negotiation may be present, and so on. Our present exploration is facilitated by assuming P is exogenous.

revenue	250,000
cost of goods sold	150,200
shipping	5,000
G&A	90,000
projected net income	4,800

Suppose the accounting library uses full costing. Then the product cost recorded in finished goods, and therefore transferred to cost of goods sold, will be computed as follows:

direct labor	22,000
direct material	16,000
overhead A: 2.1(22,000)	46,200
overhead B: .6(16,000)	9,600
job 1 full product cost	93,800

Since no other products are being produced, large under-absorbed overhead amounts also will appear. Presuming these amounts are closed to cost of goods sold, we have a total cost of goods sold figure of 93,800 + 56,400 = 150,200.[21]

Another way to see this is to remember we are assuming the LLAs are accurate. Under the assumed production plan of only job 1 being produced, manufacturing cost will total 150,200. In turn, a standard costing system would record the same total cost, but would flow some through finished goods (the standard product cost), and the difference between actual and standard cost through cost of goods sold. Assuming the LLAs are exact, this means the only difference will be due to under-absorbed overhead here.

Now return to the story and suppose the second customer is also accepted. This means production will consist of two products, jobs 1 and 2. Total manufacturing cost is computed as follows:

direct labor: 11(2,000 + 1,700)	40,700
stock direct materials: 5,000 + 9,000	14,000
custom direct materials: 11,000 + 5,000	16,000
overhead A: 55,000 + 1(40,700)	95,700
overhead B: 32,000 + .2(30,000)	38,000
projected manufacturing cost	204,400

---

[21]We should verify this calculation. 2.1 per direct labor dollar and .6 per direct material dollar are the respective full cost allocation rates for the two overhead categories. Their respective normal volumes are 50,000 direct labor dollars and 80,000 direct material dollars. Also recall the slopes of their respective LLAs are 1.0 and 0.2. This implies respective under-absorbed amounts of 55,000 - (2.1-1.0)(22,000) = 55,000 - 24,200 = 30,800 and 32,000 - (.6-.2)(16,000) = 32,000 - 6,400 = 25,600.

You might notice that our standard product cost of 93,800 differs from that reported in the Chapter 7 calculations. The reason is those calculations presumed job 1 was started but not completed during the period in question. This mystery will be resolved shortly.

Let's further assume shipping costs will total 6,000 for the second product. Also, if both products are produced, G&A expense is projected to remain constant at 90,000. This gives us a projected net income of P - 55,400:

revenue	P+250,000
cost of goods sold	204,400
shipping	11,000
G&A	90,000
projected net income	P - 55,400

Before proceeding, we should dwell on the question of which elements in this calculation would find their way into the accounting library if both products were produced. Be careful to distinguish period and product costs. Also notice the standard, full product cost is 93,800 for job 1 and 80,370 for job 2.[22]

Anyway, should the second customer be accepted? For now, assume no other customers will arrive this period. This means the organization faces a projected income of 4,800 if the offer is rejected and P - 55,400 if it is accepted. Acceptance weakly increases income if[23]

$$P - 55,400 \geq 4,800; \text{ or}$$
$$P \geq 55,400 + 4,800 = 60,200.$$

Table 10.1 provides an alternate construction of the 60,200 datum. If the new customer is accepted, total revenue will go up by P and total expense will go up by 60,200. Income will go up by P - 60,200. Now frame this in terms of the incremental revenue and cost associated with the proposed product. *Incremental* revenue is P, *incremental* cost is 60,200, and *incremental* income is P - 60,200. Further notice the incremental cost has 54,200 incremental cost of goods sold and 6,000 incremental shipping cost. (Incremental G&A is zero.)[24]

This constructive procedure has the disadvantage of forcing us to track properly under or over-absorbed overhead, as we are assuming full costing. Suppose we repeat the analysis using variable costing. Since no beginning or ending work in process is contemplated, we know the income calculations must be 4,800 without the

---

[22]We should verify this implies an under-absorbed overhead of 30,230.

[23]Here we assume the organization is interested in the new customer if its short-run income would be increased. We have already assumed no substantive difference between the economic cost curve and the LLAs on which the standard costs are based. This explains our focus on the two projected net income figures. As we shall see, it does not necessarily follow a "profit seeking organization" would or should seek to maximize its accounting income. It also does not follow risk considerations can be ignored. Here, though, we presume any such concerns are "second order" in nature. More will be said about this in subsequent chapters.

[24]The incremental expense consists of the incremental cost of goods sold plus the incremental period cost.

second job and P - 55,400 with both jobs. The product cost statistics are more revealing.

Table 10.1: Incremental Income Calculation Assuming Full Costing			
	job 1 only	**job 1 and 2**	**difference**
revenue	250,000	P+250,000	P
cost of good sold	150,200	204,400	54,200
shipping	5,000	11,000	6,000
G&A	90,000	90,000	0
projected net income	4,800	P-55,400	P-60,200

Initially we calculate the standard variable cost of job 1. This consists of direct labor, direct materials, and the "variable" portion of the overhead:

direct labor: 11(2,000)	22,000
stock direct materials	5,000
custom direct materials	11,000
overhead A: 1(22,000)	22,000
overhead B: .2(16,000)	3,200
job 1 projected variable product cost	63,200

A parallel calculation for the proposed product reveals the following:

direct labor: 11(1,700)	18,700
stock direct materials	9,000
custom direct materials	5,000
overhead A: 1(18,700)	18,700
overhead B: .2(14,000)	2,800
job 1 projected variable product cost	54,200

These calculations are now readily combined to construct projected income statements based on variable costing. Fixed manufacturing costs consist of the intercepts of the two overhead LLAs, or $55,000 + 32,000 = 87,000$. Contribution margin is calculated as revenue less variable product cost less variable period cost. The latter consists of the shipping cost in our setting. Details are summarized in Table 10.2.

Now recall our conclusion that acceptance of this customer rests on whether P $\geq 54,200 + 6,000$. 54,200 is the variable manufacturing cost of the product in question, and 6,000 is the shipping cost. Also, 54,200 is the incremental manufacturing cost (based on a status quo of manufacturing job 1); and 6,000 is the incremental shipping cost. If we accept this offer, and if the accounting library uses variable costing, we have a close affinity between our analysis and the library.

Table 10.2: Incremental Income Calculation Assuming Variable Costing			
	job 1 only	**jobs 1 and 2**	**difference**
revenue	250,000	P+250,000	P
variable cost of			
goods sold	63,200	117,400	54,200
variable shipping	5,000	11,000	6,000
contribution margin	181,800	P+121,600	P-60,200
fixed manufacturing	87,000	87,000	0
fixed G&A	90,000	90,000	0
projected net income	4,800	P - 55,400	P-60,200

This affinity is important[25] but we also should remember the example was constructed with this in mind. We assumed the LLAs on which the standard product costs were based were accurate. This rules out a case where full product cost might be a more accurate indicator of incremental cost than variable product cost. We also assumed no other customers were in sight. This rules out any concern for how the proposed product might interact with future products. For example, the supply of labor might be limited in the short-run. Using the limited supply on this job might preclude its being available for another potentially more attractive product.

an expanding mosaic

What surfaces is the potential for conflict between the recognition rules that govern the accounting library and the temporal circumstances that govern whether this product should be taken on. We explore this important theme by introducing a third product. This is job 3 of the original illustration in Chapters 6 and 7.

Required inputs are anticipated as follows:

direct labor	1,600 hours,
stock direct materials	$17,000, and
custom direct materials	$14,000.

This implies a standard variable product cost of 72,400, and a standard full product cost of 104,160.[26] It is also anticipated that shipping costs will total 12,000.

Now suppose job 1 is under production, and job 2 above has been proposed at a price of P. Job 3 *might* appear. For discussion purposes, assume the organization

---

[25]The same holds under full costing provided we are careful to track through the under or over-applied overhead calculation.

[26]The calculations should be familiar. $11(1,600) + (17,000 + 14,000) + 1[11(1,600)] + .2[17,000 + 14,000] = 72,400$, and so on.

has promised to manufacture and deliver job 3 if the customer desires. If job 3 is ordered, the customer will pay 100,000 upon delivery. The organization is waiting to hear from the job 3 customer.[27] This customer is presently unsure whether job 3 will be ordered. If ordered, the organization is committed to delivering it this period. It is uneconomic to begin production of job 3 without a firm order. The organization must immediately decide whether to accept the job 2 customer.

Suppose the LLAs remain accurate across any combination of jobs 1, 2 and 3. The implied linearity can then be used to advantage. Regardless of whether job 3 appears, the incremental cost of job 2 will be 60,200.

To see this, consider the case where job 3 does not appear. Here our earlier analysis shows an incremental cost of 60,200 and an incremental profit of P - 60,200. Now consider the case where job 3 does appear. Having rejected job 2 implies jobs 1 and 3 will be produced; and having accepted job 2 implies jobs 1, 2, and 3 will be produced. This implies we want to compare income under jobs 1 and 3 with income under jobs 1, 2, and 3. Table 10.3 presents the calculations for the more transparent variable costing case.[28]

Table 10.3: Incremental Income Calculation Assuming Variable Costing in the Presence of Job 3			
	jobs 1 and 3	jobs 1, 2 and 3	difference
revenue	350,000	P+350,000	P
variable cost of goods sold	135,600	189,800	54,200
variable shipping	17,000	23,000	6,000
contribution margin	197,400	P+137,200	P-60,200
fixed manufacturing	87,000	87,000	0
fixed G&A	90,000	90,000	0
projected net income	20,400	P - 39,800	P-60,200

The decision is straightforward. If job 3 does not appear, job 2 increases income only if $P \geq 60,200$. If job 3 does appear, job 2 increases income only if $P \geq 60,200$. Regardless of the job 3 prospects, job 2's incremental cost is 60,200 and

---

[27]The job 3 customer has an option. A useful interpretation is that this is a long-term customer, and the sales force offered the option as part of the implicit long-term relationship between the organization and this particular customer. A deeper, more complicated story would have a host of potential products, some of which might materialize.

[28]Here we use the LLAs to tally the various costs. If all three jobs are produced, 2,000 + 1,700 + 1,600 = 5,300 direct labor hours will be required, along with total direct material costs of 61,000. This implies total variable manufacturing cost of $11(5,300) + 61,000 + 1[11(5,300)] + .2[61,000] = 189,800$. The related full cost calculations are left to the reader.

income is increased by accepting job 2 if P ≥ 60,200. In addition, variable product costing ensures that the accounting library and this analysis are remarkably close in appearance.

This analysis exploits the presumed accuracy of the LLAs. It assumes away, for example, any interactions among the three products. To illustrate, suppose the organization has a policy of full employment for its skilled workers in the direct labor category. In the current period, it is committed to 3,000 hours of direct labor regardless of which products are produced. This alters our analysis, since it implies that the first 3,000 direct labor hours cause a fixed cost.

If jobs 1 and 2 are produced, 2,000 + 1,700 = 3,700 direct labor hours will be required. If only job 1 is produced, 3,000 direct labor hours will be present. This implies job 2 will necessitate acquisition of an *additional* 700 hours if job 2 is accepted and job 3 does not appear. (The extra 700 = 3,700 - 3,000 will be acquired in the spot market.) Conversely, if job 3 appears, jobs 1 and 3 will require 2,000 + 1,600 = 3,600 > 3,000 direct labor hours. Jobs 1, 2 and 3 together will require 2,000 + 1,700 + 1,600 = 5,300 hours. This implies job 2 will necessitate acquisition of an *additional* 1,700 = 5,300 - 3,600 direct labor hours if job 2 is accepted and job 3 does appear.

Alternatively notice that direct labor hours must be at least 3,000 hours. If only job 1 is present, this constraint is binding. Otherwise, the direct labor requirements exceed 3,000 hours. If job 2 is accepted in the absence of job 3, direct labor hours increase 700, as opposed to our original presumption of 1,700. Conversely, if job 2 is accepted in the presence of job 3, direct labor hours increase by 1,700. *This means the incremental cost of producing job 2 depends on whether job 3 is present.*

The incremental cost of job 2 is 60,200 if job 3 is present. It is 38,200 if job 3 is absent. Recall the 60,200 datum was calculated assuming an additional 1,700 direct labor hours would be required. The story changes if only 700 additional hours are required. In that case we would have the following calculation of job 2's incremental cost.

additional direct labor: 11(700)	7,700
additional stock direct materials	9,000
additional custom direct materials	5,000
additional overhead A: 1(7,700)	7,700
additional overhead B: .2(14,000)	2,800
additional shipping	6,000
job 1 projected variable product cost	38,200

An equivalent calculation is displayed in Table 10.4. There we follow the dictates of variable costing. Variable cost of goods sold is calculated exactly as before. Under the job 1 circumstance, though, we have 3,000 - 2,000 = 1,000 idle hours of direct labor. This is expensed as a supplementary fixed cost of 11,000 plus the associated overhead.[29] More will be said about this format shortly.

Table 10.4: Incremental Income Calculation Assuming Variable Costing and Minimum Direct Labor Hours of 3,000			
	job 1 only	**jobs 1 and 2**	**difference**
revenue	250,000	P+250,000	P
variable cost of			
goods sold	63,200	117,400	54,200
variable shipping	5,000	11,000	6,000
contribution margin	181,800	P+121,600	P-60,200
idle direct labor			
11(3,000 - 2,000)	11,000	0	-11,000
1 (11,000)	11,000	0	-11,000
fixed manufacturing	87,000	87,000	0
fixed G&A	90,000	90,000	0
projected net income	-17,200	P-55,400	P-38,200

Where are we? If job 3 does not appear, the incremental cost of job 2 is 38,200. If job 3 does appear, the incremental cost of job 2 is 60,200. Of course, it seems strange to speak of the incremental cost conditional on some event (the appearance of job 3) *after* we must decide whether the benefits of accepting the job 2 customer outweigh the costs.

We correct this by placing the job 2 cost calculation at the time of the job 2 acceptance decision. For this purpose, suppose the only uncertainty is whether job 3 will appear. Let α denote the probability job 3 appears. Further suppose the organization will accept the job 2 customer if its expected profit is higher under acceptance than under rejection of the customer.

Acceptance of the customer implies jobs 1, 2, and 3 will be produced with probability α, and jobs 1 and 2 will be produced with probability $1 - \alpha$. Respective incomes are P - 39,800 (Table 10.3) and P - 55,400 (Table 10.4). The expected income is:

$$\alpha(P - 39,800) + (1 - \alpha)(P - 55,400) = P - 55,400 + 15,600\alpha.$$

Rejection of the customer implies jobs 1 and 3 will be produced with probability α, and job 1 will be produced with probability $1 - \alpha$. Respective incomes are 20,400 (Table 10.3) and -17,200 (Table 10.4). This gives the following expected income calculation:

---

[29] We assume overhead A varies with direct labor dollars in total, not with direct labor dollars leveled for any idle hours.

$\alpha(20,400) + (1 - \alpha)(-17,200) = -17,200 + 37,600\alpha.$

Now subtract the second from the first expected income:

$P - 55,400 + 15,600\alpha - (-17,200 + 37,600\alpha) = P - 38,200 - 22,000\alpha.$

The job 2 customer is acceptable if

$P - 38,200 - 22,000\alpha \geq 0.$

This is equivalent to the condition

$P \geq 38,200 + 22,000\alpha.$

Can you interpret the right hand side of the last inequality? If $\alpha = 1$, the condition simplifies to $P \geq 60,200$. If $\alpha = 0$, it simplifies to $P \geq 38,200$. P is the incremental revenue from accepting the customer and $38,200 + 22,000\alpha$ is the expected incremental cost.

Another way to see this is to observe that

$\alpha(60,200) + (1 - \alpha)(38,200) = 38,200 + 22,000\alpha.$

The expected incremental cost of accepting job 2 is α multiplied by the incremental cost of producing job 2 if job 3 appears plus $(1 - \alpha)$ multiplied by the incremental cost of producing job 2 if job 3 does not appear.

We are now in a position where the job 2 cost expression we want is $38,200 + 22,000\alpha$. If we reject the job 2 customer, the accounting library will not report any product cost for job 2. The library is confined to actual products.[30] If we accept the job 2 customer, a variable costing library will report a variable product cost of 54,200, regardless of whether job 3 appears. (Period cost records also will note a 6,000 shipping cost.) Alternatively, suppose the identical product was produced last period, and the standards have not changed. A variable costing library will contain a variable product cost of 54,200 for this product.

The variable costing library focuses on the 54,200 datum, while our analysis focuses on $38,200 + 22,000\alpha$. Being careful to account for the shipping cost, our analysis and the library are aligned when $\alpha = 1$; otherwise they are not.[31]

Suppose $\alpha = .60$. This implies our expected incremental cost is $38,200 + .6(22,000) = 51,400$. $P = 53,000$, say, implies the customer should be accepted. At this stage and in this analysis, the cost of job 2 is 51,400. Yet this cost statistic will not be found or recorded in the accounting library.

---

[30] Imagine the difficulty in auditing or otherwise ensuring the integrity of reports concerning unexperienced events!

[31] Of course, the corresponding full product cost is 80,370. Being careful to account for shipping cost and over or under-absorbed overhead, the full costing library and analysis will also be aligned in the case of $\alpha = 1$.

The reason is the library's emphasis on integrity. The cost statistics placed in the library must be reliable; they must be auditable. Our calculation, though, is auditable only with considerable difficulty. Where does $\alpha = .60$ come from? Where does the minimum hours constraint of 3,000 come from? The former depends on managerial judgment, buttressed by an understanding of the job 3 customer's circumstances. The 3,000 construction comes from an understanding of work force requirements, anticipated vacation schedules, the ability to manage vacation schedules, anticipated absenteeism, and so on. These are important judgments that depend on local circumstances. They vary from time to time, making routine capture in the accounting library impractical. They are also difficult to audit. Their integrity cannot be defended. They are therefore excluded from the accounting library.

We warned that library integrity is an important idea. When the library reports a variable product cost of 54,200, we can be reasonably assured this has been calculated in conformance with the library's procedures. It is a starting point for calculating the 51,400 datum.[32] Library integrity influences what we place in the library.

an additional illustration

We conclude with a more complicated illustration. Suppose, as above, job 1 is in place, the job 2 customer has arrived, and one or more additional customers might arrive. Capacity is now constrained. In the short-run, only a limited amount of labor is present and large amounts of materials may be difficult to obtain.

These considerations are weighed and the job 2 customer is accepted. Eventually a third product, job 3, is taken on. At this point, difficulties emerge and the organization is unable to complete job 1, as promised. In addition, the LLAs used in the estimation process turn out to be inaccurate. What will the accounting library record?

Examine Tables 10.5 and 10.6. Table 10.5 presents the actual costs, along with standard full and variable cost constructions. For this purpose, we use the actual and standard costs from the original example. Table 10.5 is a compilation of Tables 7.1 through 7.4 in Chapter 7. Table 10.6 provides a breakdown of the actual costs, identifying ending work-in-process and expense totals. Nothing remains in finished goods, as we assume any completed job is shipped immediately.

Consider a variable costing library. Jobs 2 and 3 were started and completed; job 1 was started and partially completed. The standard cost for job 1 reflects its stage of completion (estimated to be 50% with respect to direct labor and 100% with respect to direct materials). Actual manufacturing costs are tallied, in the amount of 246,000. The difference between actual and standard is 246,000 - 254,800 = (8,800). This difference is closed to cost of goods sold. The standard costs of jobs 2 (54,200) and 3 (72,400) pass from work in process to finished goods to cost of

---

[32]Parallel comments apply to beginning the cost analysis with the full product cost statistic.

goods sold. The "fixed" manufacturing cost $(87,000 = 55,000 + 32,000)$ is also expensed.

Table 10.5: LLAs and Product Cost Statistics				
	job 1	job 2	job 3	total
estimated manufacturing cost				
estimated direct labor cost	11,000*	18,700	17,600	47,300
estimated direct material cost				
stock materials	5,000*	9,000	17,000	31,000
custom materials	11,000*	5,000	14,000	30,000
estimated overhead LLAs				
A: 55,000 + 1DL$				
B: 32,000 + .2DM$				
actual manufacturing cost				
actual direct labor cost				48,000
actual direct material cost				
stock materials				30,000
custom materials				30,000
actual overhead A				96,000
actual overhead B				42,000
total manufacturing cost				246,000
standard product cost				
direct labor	11,000*	18,700	17,600	
direct material	16,000*	14,000	31,000	
variable overhead A	11,000*	18,700	17,600	
variable overhead B	3,200*	2,800	6,200	
variable product cost	41,200*	54,200	72,400	167,800
standard fixed overhead A				
(@ 1.1 per direct labor dollar)	12,100*	20,570	19,360	
standard fixed overhead B				
(@ .4 per direct material				
dollar)	6,400*	5,600	12,400	
full product cost	59,700*	80,370	104,160	244,230
*partially completed				

Here we should notice the 246,000 datum is a compilation of manufacturing costs that reflects conventional recognition rules, such as the distinction between period and product costs. It also reflects manufacturing accomplished. Job 1 is costed as a partially completed product, with actual and standard cost compared on that basis. The fact job 1 has not been delivered to the customer in timely fashion is not explicitly recognized. We might change the story to one in which job 1 is due the following period. Nothing in these reports would change.

Table 10.6: Product Cost Statistics in Accounting Library		
	variable cost library	full cost library
total manufacturing cost incurred	246,000	246,000
budgeted manufacturing cost, standard		
cost of manufacturing accomplished	254,800	244,230
actual less budget	(8,800)	1,770
manufacturing cost expensed		
job 2 standard product cost	54,200	80,370
job 3 standard product cost	72,400	104,160
actual less budget	(8,800)	1,770
fixed overhead	87,000	N/A
total	204,800	186,300
ending work in process (job 1)	41,200	59,700
total cost expensed plus inventoried	246,000	246,000

The variable cost analysis shows actual cost below budgeted cost, hinting at a cost saving or unanticipated efficiency. This hides a darker aspect of the story. It is routine practice in this organization to have the work force work overtime when necessary. In turn, the pay premiums associated with overtime work are included in overhead A; and the overhead A LLA reflects a typical amount of overtime. Jobs 1, 2, and 3 collectively put a strain on the organization's capacity. Overtime was called for to complete the products in timely fashion. The work force, though, was unable to provide overtime services during this period.[33] Thus, job 1 is late and the accounting library reports a cost saving![34]

The accounting library is designed to record actual and standard costs, subject to established recognition conventions. It is not designed to reflect period-by-period idiosyncrasies in the environment. To do so would strain its ability to maintain integrity. For example, our earlier analysis where job 3 might appear with probability $\alpha = .6$ led to an incremental cost of job 2 of 51,400 (including shipping cost). This calculation is not reflected in the library.

---

[33]For example, the labor contract might provide a cap on annual overtime demands. Once the cap is reached, overtime work can be refused. In this interpretation, we are dealing with monthly reports. The cap was reached in the prior month, and overtime work was declined this month.

[34]Actual and standard labor hours are close in this case. The standard, however, is for the productive work accomplished. Completing job 1 would have required additional hours, which would have been supplied in overtime.

To dramatize further this important point, suppose the contract with the job 1 customer calls for a payment of 250,000 if the product is delivered this period, but only 200,000 if it is delivered next period. By not delivering the product on time, our organization has lost 50,000. Yet revenue recognition occurs on delivery. Alterations in the *anticipated* sales price are not recognized in the accounting library.

The implication is we do not blindly use the accounting library. We consume its contents with knowledge of how it works and what particular circumstances are present. Reflecting on the cost report, we know work in process remains at the end of the period. We know this is job 1. We know actual versus standard cost for the work accomplished. We know the shipping costs are recorded in period cost accounts rather than as product costs, and so on.

Tables 10.5 and 10.6 also present a full costing picture of these events. The rendering is identical, except the assignment of "fixed" manufacturing cost to products. In turn, this leads to under-absorbed overhead also being closed to cost of goods sold. Return to Table 10.6. Notice that ending work in process is larger under the full costing picture. Also notice actual cost exceeds budget in the full costing picture. This is because the budget reflects actual activity, and actual activity was below the normal volumes used in setting up the overhead allocation rates.[35]

Finally, glance back at the seemingly awkward calculation in Table 10.4. The accounting library focuses its product costing archives on actual and standard product costs. It will not reflect specific, subtle calculations that are appropriate at each and every turn. Appending these circumstances allows us to modify the library's picture to the task at hand. This is why the format of Table 10.4 begins with standard product cost and then tailors it to the circumstance at hand.

Summary

Internal control is concerned with maintaining the accounting library's integrity. In broad terms, we worry about sloppiness, inadvertent random error, and nefarious behavior compromising the library's contents. The compromise might take the form of not recording some event, such as not recording the use of miscellaneous materials in the production process. It might take the form of incorrectly recording some event, such as crediting the wrong customer's account. It might take the form of recording an event at the wrong time, such as recording a sale at the end of the reporting period when the product remains in the shipping department. Naturally, questions of internal control subtly merge into questions of what should go into the

---

[35]We should verify the differences. For ending work in process we have 59,700 - 41,200 = 18,500 = 1.1(11,000) + .4(16,000). For the difference between the respective actual less budget calculations, we have 1,770 - (-8,800) = 10,570 = 1.1(50,000 - 47,300) + .4(80,000 - 61,000). This is simply the under-absorbed fixed overhead. In a subsequent chapter we will learn to label this difference a volume variance.

library, when it should be recorded, and even what the organization is trying to accomplish.[36]

In turn, the accounting library is defended with two broad classes of instruments. Record keeping procedures that emphasize proper authorization, segregation of duties, adequate documentation, safeguards over assets, and independent check are one line of defense. Recognition rules are the other line of defense.

Some library entries are easier to defend than others. At the margin, the accounting library will trade off library content for ease in ensuring the content's integrity. The organization's decision making will be dynamic, with choices unfolding as a function of circumstances that occur. The accounting library will reflect a more rigid view of these circumstances. Product cost statistics will reflect somewhat static, easier to audit standard costs. Some actual costs will be quickly expensed (e.g., advertising, investment in work force learning, and maintenance). Revenue will not be recognized until late in the earning process.

In more philosophical terms, trading off content for integrity is an illustration of the point that we mix instruments. Extreme solutions are rare. We generally seek a mixture, one that balances tradeoffs. Control systems are not perfect; they balance costs and benefits. The accounting library is also not perfect. Its design balances costs and benefits, including costs of control.

Bibliographic Notes

In its broadest sense, internal control extends to ensuring that the organization's policies are followed. Fama and Jensen [1983] is illustrative. More narrowly, Antle [1982] focuses on the simultaneous problem of ensuring well-maintained financial records and the incentives of the auditor to audit properly and thoroughly. These two sides of the issue are not separable; for example, we use speeding citations to punish offenders and to monitor traffic enforcement personnel. This, in turn, leads to concern over coalitions, which are usually at the heart of major financial frauds. Tirole [1986] introduces coalition concerns into the design of control systems. We will see more of this in subsequent chapters.

Problems and Exercises

1.   Would internal control issues arise in perfect and complete markets? Explain.

---

[36]In this broader sense, one of the concerns is whether a manager, or management in general, pays unusual attention to the time series pattern of accounting income (or cost). For example, if hard times have fallen on the organization, maintenance might be delayed, customers might be pressed to accept early shipments, and so on. Conversely, if unusually good times have fallen, miscellaneous materials might be more quickly released to production (and expensed), work force expansion might be accelerated (with concomitant expensing of training costs), and so on. Accounting academics refer to this judicious use of timing instruments as "income smoothing." The instruments might be real (e.g., rescheduling maintenance) or accounting (e.g., lengthening depreciation lives).

2. A central theme in maintaining library integrity is restricting what goes into the library. Income is not recognized, no matter how optimistic the setting, for products in the design stage. Carefully discuss the importance of auditability in limiting what goes into the library.

3. *internal control checklist*
Examine the checkout process at your local supermarket. Using the checklist for internal controls, identify the ways in which the integrity of the process and attendant financial records are maintained.

4. *internal control techniques*
Examine the tasks of a typical bank teller. Where do you see the broad themes of restricted action possibilities, redundancy, and incentives at work?

5. Verify the claim in footnote 22.

6. *restricted recognition*
The example in Table 10.4 leads to a straightforward question of accepting or rejecting a specified offer. Yet rejection will not be recorded in the accounting library, and acceptance will result in a recording that bears little resemblance to our analysis of the offer's revenue and cost. Why is the accounting library's rendering so far removed from the analysis of whether to accept the offer?

7. *shifting LLAs*
Return to the setting of Table 10.4. Now assume 40% of variable overhead A will be incurred if direct labor is idle, while 100% of the variable amount will be incurred if direct labor is productive. Other details remain as before. Determine the minimum acceptable price, P, for the offer to be attractive.

8. *shifting income*
A textbook publisher's central management team labors under an incentive arrangement that pays a sizable bonus if income exceeds budgeted income for the year. Near the end of a recent year, management quickly "ran the numbers" and concluded it would make its bonus. It then ordered the shipping department to hold up all remaining shipments until the start of the new fiscal year. Has the accounting library's integrity been affected by this behavior? Has management behaved wisely and appropriately?

9. *shifting expenses*
A municipality typically uses encumbrance accounting. The annual budget establishes a spending ceiling for each category. Expenses are then recorded as quickly as possible. For example, in the case of major supplies, the supplies account is debited when a purchase order is placed; minor supplies, where no purchase order

is required, are recorded as soon as a supplier invoice arrives. This aggressive recognition is designed to ensure an authorization limit is not exceeded.

In a recent fraud, a municipal department instructed a supplier to post date invoices so they would signal acquisitions in the succeeding as opposed to current year. Which items on the internal controls checklist are violated here?

10. *hypothesis testing and internal control*
Sampling from a Normal population provides a caricature of quality control. Suppose a machine is operating according to tolerances, is "in control" or is "out of control." If it is out of control, it is necessary to intervene and correct whatever problem has surfaced. Suppose an in control machine produces items with a critical dimension that follows a Normal distribution with a mean of 4.5 inches and a standard deviation of .1 inch. A random sample of 10 units is selected. The sample average dimension is 4.438 inches. What is the probability of observing this or a lower sample average, assuming the machine is in control?

Suppose we expand the above story. It costs so much to inspect a unit of output, it costs so much to readjust the machine, and faulty units eventually cost so much in subsequent failure and repair cost. Building on these specifications, we design an optimal quality inspection program for the machine in question. Carefully discuss how this quality control analogy applies and does not apply to internal control.

11. *reliability engineering*
Ralph works in the back room of a commercial credit house. One of the problems under study is designing redundancy into data capture equipment, in order to minimize data processing errors economically. After thinking about this for a while, and shortly before a computer consultant makes a presentation, Ralph goes through the following thought exercise.

a] Suppose the failure rate on a particular process is given by the parameter f. If three processes are linked in series, a failure will occur only if each of the processes fails. Suppose the failure rate, or failure probability, is f = .02. What is the overall failure rate if two processes are linked in series? What is it if three processes are linked in series? Assume independence across the individual stages.

b] The consultant's literature claims a failure rate of f = .02. But Ralph knows this is a guess. Suppose, with equal probability, the failure rate is .01 or .03. Determine the overall failure rate when three or two processes are linked together, assuming independence among failure rates and processes.

c] This last exercise troubles Ralph. Does it make sense to treat the uncertainty surrounding f itself as independent? If Ralph guesses f = .01 and f = .03 obtains, each process encounters an f of .03. If this is the case, determine the overall failure rate when three or two processes are linked together.

d] Carefully explain the difference in your answers in [b] and [c] above. What does this tell you about assuming independence when you are assessing probabilities?

12. *option value of capacity*

Ralph's Custom Products (RCP) is a custom manufacturer of material handling equipment. Various just-in-time manufacturing systems require parts from suppliers that arrive in containers that are specialized to accommodate transportation and handling in the receiving facility. RCP designs and manufactures these containers.

A new customer has arrived, seeking a bid on a particular set of containers. The RCP engineer provides the following estimates:

	dept. #1	dept. #2
machine hours required	150	200
direct labor hours required	120	350
cost per hour of direct labor	$18	$24

Notice RCP uses two manufacturing departments. The direct labor rates include 20% fringe (covering various taxes, vacations, and so on). Overheads in the two departments are budgeted with the following LLAs:

$$OV_1 = 150,000 + 14 \cdot MH \text{ and}$$
$$OV_2 = 200,000 + 45 \cdot DLH,$$

where MH refers to machine hours in department #1 and DLH refers to direct labor hours in department #2. (Respective normal volumes are MH = 7,500 and DLH = 5,000.) In addition, the engineer estimates total direct material cost will be 12,000 and shipping costs will total 4,000.

a] What are the full cost overhead application rates in the two departments?

b] What is the minimum price RCP should consider in negotiating with this new customer?

c] How does the cost datum derived in [b] above relate to the cost that would be reported in the accounting library? More precisely, what product cost would be recorded in the typical accounting library?

d] Now suppose a capacity problem might exist. One of RCP's usual customers might require some modification of containers in use. If so, taking on the new customer will use up slack in department #2's schedule that should be devoted to the existing customer base; and if this happens, RCP will be forced to subcontract 200 direct labor hours, at a rate of 150 per hour. The sales force estimates the existing customer will require this modification with probability α. If RCP is risk neutral, what now is the minimum price it should consider in negotiating with this new customer?

13. *option value of capacity*

Ralph's Option finds Ralph the manager of a consulting company. At present, business is slow and Ralph has 1,200 hours of consultant's time that are not committed to one job or another. Ralph's policy is to keep the consultants on the payroll (at a rate of 30 per hour) when times are slack. It is understood that, in good times, the consultants will work overtime and not receive additional compensation. Ralph usually bills the consultants at 75 per hour to customers. Variable overhead averages about 15 per hour of consultant. Other, generally fixed, costs average about 22 per hour of consultant's time. Any additional direct costs, such as travel, subcontracting of highly technical expertise and software purchases, are directly billed to the customer.

An astute customer has just asked Ralph for help in selecting and developing a new warehouse site. This job will take about 1,000 hours of consultants' time. The customer insists he will pay no more than 35 per hour for the consulting team.

a] Determine whether Ralph should accept this offer; be certain to include an analysis of the costs and revenues.

b] Suppose accepting this offer will not allow the consulting firm to take on any new business for the remainder of the period; and any such new business cannot be deferred to a subsequent period; it is simply lost, with no ill will. Let p be the probability a customer will arrive and pay 75 per hour for the full 1,200 hours; determine the maximum value of p such that Ralph would find the 35 per hour offer attractive.

c] Determine a value of p such that insisting on a price at least equal to full product cost would be a reasonable pricing strategy.

d] Briefly discuss how the option value of idle capacity is reported in the typical accounting library.

11

Framing Decisions

The purpose of this chapter is to introduce the subject of decision making and its relationship to various cost constructions. We have referred to this topic at various points, but have deferred a systematic treatment until our study of the accounting library was complete.

Our immediate focus is the managerial art of framing decisions. Framing refers to the description of a decision problem that we construct. It is a description or representation. It is also personal. We construct it. The framing exercise is also an application of managerial art. The gifted manager can balance detail and abstraction, the quantitative and the qualitative, inclusion and exclusion in describing or framing a decision problem.

Framing is important for a variety of reasons, We will see, for example, that various frames or descriptions call for various measures of cost and benefit. This is why cost is an ambiguous notion. Its meaning depends on the context. What we mean by the cost of something depends on what the decision problem is and how we have framed that decision problem. Many find this awkward and unintuitive (if not outright false). Yet cost is the very glue that connects the explicit and the implicit consumption of resources in a decision frame. Drawing the line between what is explicit and implicit at different places leaves us with different measures of cost.

Initially we review several framing exercises that were introduced in earlier chapters. We then present and examine three principles of consistent framing. In the following chapter we relate these framing principles to various cost constructs. This provides an intimate connection between accounting and decision making.

Keep in mind that this is an introductory chapter. Important questions of framing uncertainty and strategic considerations, and of framing in a way that control considerations are included are all deferred for the moment.

Examples of Consistent Framing

Whenever we describe a decision problem, implicitly or explicitly, a framing exercise has been engaged. Whether to introduce a new product, whether to study this chapter seriously, what to eat for dinner, how to boost the morale of our work group all imply some framing of a decision problem.

We have provided several extended framing exercises in previous chapters. The most recent was the Chapter 10 question of whether job 2 was a worthwhile product. We framed this question by projecting the period's income under the assumption job 2 was produced and comparing this with its counterpart under the assumption job 2 was not produced. We compared income (or expected income) with and without job 2. We also framed the choice in incremental terms by comparing expected *incremental* revenue with expected *incremental* cost. A total income (or profit) frame was used; and an incremental income (or profit) frame was used.

The earliest illustration of framing was the discussion of revenue and cost framing in Chapter 2. There we initially focused on the profit maximizing behavior of a single product firm. The choice problem was what inputs to use to produce what output level. One frame focused on technology and market prices for the output and inputs. Another frame collapsed the technology and input portions of the exercise into a cost function. This led to a revenue less cost of output frame of the firm's problem. Short-run and long-run frames were also explored.

We also examined a two product firm in Chapter 2. One frame focused on input and output prices, and technology. Another focused on output prices (or revenue) and cost. The cost function, $C(q_1,q_2)$ was central in this latter frame. That frame highlighted the revenue and cost of both products. We also provided a frame that focused on the first product, using cost function $C(q_1,q_2^*)$, where q_2^* is the optimal output of the second product.[1]

Our study of cost allocation in Chapter 8 also produced some framing examples. The most prominent was the illustration in the Appendix of interactive service departments. One way to frame the question of whether to expand output (by a single unit) of a product was to compare incremental revenue with incremental cost. The latter might be constructed by comparing total cost with and without the additional unit of output. This was the frame that exhibited a linear program. Another approach was to focus directly on the product's cost. This was the frame that exhibited the simultaneous cost allocation exercise.[2]

A Well-Defined Choice Problem

Each of these exercises uses some combination of three framing principles. These principles are readily developed in the context of a given, though abstract, optimization problem. For this purpose, suppose we want to find the maximum value of the function $f(z)$, subject to the constraint that z be in some set A, that $z \in A$.

We symbolize the task in the following way:

maximize $f(z)$
subject to: $z \in A$.

We want to find the item in set A that makes the function take on its largest value.

---

[1]Pegging this function at q_2^* is somewhat gratuitous, as we are seeking the optimal output quantities for both products. A variation on this theme that does locate the optimal output quantities for both products will arise later in the chapter.

[2]Also recall our exploration of joint products in Chapter 9. There we analyzed the question of whether to sell or process further each of the joint products by using a frame that focused on incremental revenue and incremental cost.

We should interpret this as a decision problem. Choices are evaluated or scored by the criterion function f(z). We want a choice with the highest possible score. The available choices are listed in the set A. One and only one member of this list is to be chosen. We want to find a member of A that solves the stated maximization problem. The choice is confined to $z \in A$.

Suppose z^* is a solution to this problem. This means z^* is feasible; it is among the listed alternatives. $z^* \in A$. This also means $f(z^*) \geq f(z)$ for every $z \in A$. z^* is optimal.[3]

Consistent framing is now easily introduced. It refers to ways to transform this optimization problem, but always so a solution (z^*) is identified. This is why we speak of consistent framing. These are ways to describe or transform the optimization problem, without losing our ability to locate a solution. They are consistent in the sense they lead to an optimal choice.

Irrelevance of Increasing Transformations

The first principle of consistent framing addresses the ability to transform the criterion function, f(z). What is the best choice of z for the following?

> maximize $f(z) = z$
> subject to: $0 \leq z \leq 1$

Trivially, the answer is $z^* = 1$.[4] We can do no better than set z = 1. In contrast, what is the solution to:

> maximize $\hat{f}(z) = z + 50$
> subject to: $0 \leq z \leq 1$.

Surely the answer is also $z^* = 1$. The former achieves a maximum of $f(z^*) = z^* = 1$, while the latter achieves a maximum of $\hat{f}(z^*) = z^* + 50 = 51$. But the choice of z remains the same. Adding the constant, 50, to f(z) does not affect the choice of $z \in A$.

---

[3]The solution need not be unique. We may have more than one element of A that produces the maximal value of f(z). This is why we used the phrase of "a solution" rather than "the solution." Also, there is no guarantee a solution even exists. For example, what is the solution to: maximize f(z) = z, subject to $0 \leq z < 1$. If you claim some feasible z is optimal, we can always retort by suggesting that you try $\hat{z} = z + (1 - z)/2$. $\hat{z} > z$, and $\hat{z} < 1$! The point is not profound. Care should be exercised in making certain an optimization problem actually has a solution. Our discussion always presumes a solution exists. In turn, when presenting concrete optimization problems we are careful to make certain they are sufficiently well crafted to have a solution.

Further notice we are presuming choice behavior can be modeled as an optimization problem (such as maximize profit or minimize cost). This requires consistent choice behavior. In turn, what consistent means in this context was explored in Chapter 4.

[4]Is there a conflict with what was said in the prior footnote? $0 \leq z < 1$ and $0 \leq z \leq 1$ are different intervals. The former allows us to get arbitrarily close to z = 1, but never achieve z = 1. The latter allows us to achieve z = 1. Further observe that we have a unique solution in this case.

It simply shifts the criterion function by a constant amount, keeping every choice of z in the same relative position.

Suppose α is an arbitrary constant. Does it matter whether we maximize $f(z)$ or $f(z) + \alpha$? Suppose $\beta > 0$ is an arbitrary though strictly positive constant. Does it matter whether we maximize $f(z)$ or $\beta \cdot f(z)$? Surely not. Given set A, maximizing $f(z)$ and maximizing $\alpha + \beta \cdot f(z)$ will identify the same $z^* \in A$, for any α (whether positive or negative) and any $\beta > 0$. We use this simple idea so often its use usually goes unnoticed.

Examine Figure 11.1. Four functions are plotted over the range $3 \le z \le 7$. The maximum occurs in each case at the point $z^* = 5$. Irrespective of the given function used to evaluate our choice of z (respecting $3 \le z \le 7$), we always locate $z^* = 5$. Is this an accident?

Figure 11.1: Increasing Transformations

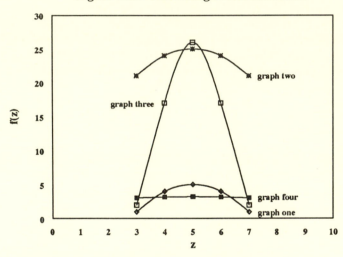

The four functions were constructed as follows:

graph one: $f_1(z) = 10z - z^2 - 20$;
graph two: $f_2(z) = f_1(z) + 20 = 10z - z^2$;
graph three: $f_3(z) = 1 + [f_1(z)]^2 = 1 + [10z - z^2 - 20]^2$; and
graph four: $f_4(z) = ln\,[f_1(z) + 20] = ln\,[f_2(z)]$.

Representative points are also displayed in Table 11.1.

Graphs two, three, and four are all judiciously chosen transformations of $f_1(z)$. Each transformation is chosen in a way that leaves the point at which the function reaches a maximum undisturbed.[5]

---

[5]Notice that the derivative of each function passes through zero at the same point, z = 5:

z	$f_1(z)$	$f_2(z)$	$f_3z)$	$f_4(z)$
	Table 11.1: Various Functions Defined On $3 \leq z \leq 7$			
3	1	21	2	3.0445
4	4	24	17	3.1781
5	5	25	26	3.2189
6	4	24	17	3.1781
7	1	21	2	3.0445

The explanation is somewhat technical but we should not attribute it to magic. The key is what is called an increasing transformation. An increasing transformation always preserves order. If one item is larger than another before transformation, it remains larger after transformation. For example, a > b if and only if $a^3 > b^3$. Similarly, a > b if and only if 2.45a - 20 > 2.45b - 20. Also, if a ≥ 0 and b ≥ 0, a > b if and only if $\sqrt{a} > \sqrt{b}$.

In general terms, we say the function T is an increasing transformation of the function f(z) when $f(z) > f(\hat{z})$ if and only if $T[f(z)] > T[f(\hat{z})]$ for every z and $\hat{z}$ in the domain of the original function.[6] Return to Figure 11.1 and consider z = 4 and z = 5.5. For the first graph we find

$$f_1(4) = 10(4) - (4)^2 - 20 = 4 < f_1(5.5) = 10(5.5) - (5.5)^2 - 20 = 4.75.$$

For the second we have

$$f_2(4) = 20 + 4 = 24 < f_2(5.5) = 20 + 4.75 = 24.75.$$

For the third we find

$$f_3(4) = 1 + (4)^2 = 17 < f_3(5.5) = 1 + (4.75)^2 = 23.5625.$$

Finally, for the fourth function we have

$$f_4(4) = ln(24) = 3.1781 < f_4(5.5) = ln(24.75) = 3.2088.$$

In each instance we find $f_i(4) < f_i(5.5)$. Continuing, for any feasible choices of $3 \leq z \leq 7$ and $3 \leq \hat{z} \leq 7$, $f_1(z) < f_1(\hat{z})$ is logically equivalent to $f_i(z) < f_i(\hat{z})$ for any of the noted transformations. This is apparent in Figure 11.1. One of the functions increases from one point to another if and only if all the other functions do as well.

$f_1'(z) = 10 - 2z;$
$f_2'(z) = 10 - 2z;$
$f_3'(z) = [2f_1(z)][10 - 2z];$ and
$f_4'(z) = [10 - 2z]/[f_2(z)].$

[6]The domain of f(z) is the set of points over which the function is defined. In our example in Figure 11.1, the domain of the function is $3 \leq z \leq 7$. This is apparent from looking at the horizontal axis in the figure.

The following fact emerges. Let z^* maximize $f(z)$ subject to $z \in A$. Also let T be an increasing transformation. Then z^* also maximizes $T[f(z)]$ subject to $z \in A$.[7]

This fact is useful. Judicious use of increasing transformations may simplify what we are looking at. Add the constant 20 to $f_1(z) = 10z - z^2 - 20$. This is surely an increasing transformation. It simply removes an irrelevant constant from view. We do this every time we ignore fixed cost in a short-run maximization problem.

Of course, some art is involved here as well. Multiplying $f(z)$ by .2 does no harm, but it doesn't appear particularly useful. Cubing $f(z)$ does no harm, but it certainly appears noxious. Graphs three and four in Figure 11.1 do no harm. Graph two gives the most streamlined function. Graph three provides a more apparent picture. Graph four clouds the picture.

Can you recall seeing judicious transformation in our earlier framing illustrations? Comparing incremental revenue and incremental cost is a vivid example. Is another unit worthwhile? Incremental profit is profit with one more unit less profit without the additional unit. It is the difference in profit, attributed to adding the additional unit of output. So, saying incremental profit is positive is the same as saying total profit is higher with the additional output.

When we focus on the difference in profit we subtract the status quo profit. This is an increasing transformation. Similarly, ignoring fixed cost in a short-run setting amounts to transforming the profit function by adding a constant equal to the fixed cost. This is illustrated by $f_2(z)$ (i.e., graph two) in Figure 11.1.

The first principle of consistent framing is that optimization problems are unaffected by increasing transformations. Simple transformations, adding a constant or multiplying by a strictly positive constant, often give a more friendly appearance. More deeply, these are but particular classes of increasing transformations.[8]

Local Searches are Possible

The second principle of consistent framing addresses our ability to search in smaller regions of set A for the maximizer of $f(z)$. The classic example is where a search committee sorts among numerous dean candidates and then submits the best three to the university president. This amounts to selecting the candidate from a pre-

---

[7]Suppose z^* maximizes $f(z)$ subject to $z \in A$. Let T be an increasing transformation. Suppose z^* does not maximize $T[f(z)]$ subject to $z \in A$. We then have some $\hat{z} \in A$ such that $T[f(\hat{z})] > T[f(z^*)]$. Since T is an increasing transformation, this means $f(\hat{z}) > f(z^*)$. And this implies z^* cannot be a maximizer of $f(z)$ subject to $z \in A$. Contradiction.

[8]It is important to remember, though, we are transforming $f(z)$, and not its individual components. This admonition will become apparent when we introduce uncertainty. There we will discover transforming a choice problem is a fairly difficult problem. You should also notice the transformation applies to the domain of $f(z)$, to the set A. In Figure 11.1, for example, we are unconcerned with any z outside of $3 \leq z \leq 7$.

screened set of alternatives. Naturally, the trick is to make certain we have not erred in the pre-screening.

Return to the exercise in Figure 11.1. We want to maximize $f_2(z) = 10z - z^2$ subject to $3 \le z \le 7$. (Notice how we have dropped the irrelevant constant!) This calls for us to search over z values between 3 and 7. Suppose instead we search over a smaller domain, say, by maximizing $f_2(z)$ subject to $4 \le z \le 7$. Consulting Figure 11.1 should convince us that the maximum occurs at $z^* = 5$, and our limited search has done no harm.

In a sense we have analyzed a smaller problem here. Our search was confined to the smaller region of $4 \le z \le 7$. We nevertheless located an optimal solution to the original, "larger" problem. No harm was done. But how do we convince ourselves no harm was done?

The answer is simple. Take the best of what we ignored, and test it against what we found. We ignored the alternatives in $3 \le z \le 4$. What is the best choice from among the alternatives we want to ignore? What is the maximum of $f_2(z) = 10z - z^2$ subject to $3 \le z \le 4$? As is obvious from Figure 11.1, the maximum over this limited range occurs at $z = 4$, and provides $f_2(4) = 24$.[9]

Our search over $4 \le z \le 7$ located $z^* = 5$, with $f_2(5) = 25$. In locating $z^* = 5$ we did *not* search all the alternatives. None of the choices we did not explicitly examine is better than $z = 4$, with $f_2(4) = 24$. Clearly, the best choice overall is $z^* = 5$. It's the best we found, and it beats everything in the subset we did not examine.

This illustrates the second principle of consistent framing. Suppose we tentatively select the best choice from a reduced set of alternatives. This tentative choice is best overall if it is better than the best of those not considered.

Suppose we must select a z value between 3 and 7. Further suppose we tentatively select the best choice between 4 and 7. This tentative choice is best overall if it is better than the best of those not considered. It is best overall if it is better than the best among the z values between 3 and 4.

The terminology of opportunity cost is used to convey this principle. Suppose we face the problem of selecting the best action from some set of available actions. As usual, we portray this task as maximizing $f(z)$ subject to $z \in A$.

Now take this set of available actions and divide it into two parts. Call the two parts A_1 and A_2. For example, divide the interval $3 \le z \le 7$ into (1) $3 \le z \le 4$ and (2) $4 \le z \le 7$.[10] Also, denote the best choice from set A_1 by z_1^*. Similarly, denote the

---

[9]The point $z = 4$ is contained in both regions. This was done to avoid dealing with a problem formulated as maximize $f_2(z)$ subject to $3 \le z < 4$. See the following note.

[10]Thus, the combination of the two intervals returns us to the original specification of $3 \le z \le 7$. In set terminology, we have $A_1 \cup A_2 = A$. It also might seem logical to make these two subsets disjoint. For example, why not use (1) $3 \le z < 4$; and (2) $4 \le z \le 7$? The answer is it is now awkward to talk about the maximum of $f_2(z)$ over the first region. Of course, we might avoid this by cleverly using (1) $3 \le z \le 4$; and (2) $4 < z \le 7$. It seems easier just to allow $z = 4$ to be included in both subsets in this instance.

best choice from set A_2 by z_2^*. Put differently, let z_1^* be a solution to maximize $f(z)$ subject to $z \in A_1$. Also let z_2^* be a solution to maximize $f(z)$ subject to $z \in A_2$.

The opportunity cost of confining our search to A_1 is the best we could do by selecting from among those alternatives in set A_2. z_1^* is optimal overall if $f(z_1^*) \geq f(z_2^*)$. So we call $f(z_2^*)$ the opportunity cost of confining our search to A_1. z_1^* is best overall if $f(z_1^*)$ is larger or equal to its opportunity cost.[11]

Our second principle of consistent framing is now easily rephrased. The best choice from set A_1 is best overall if its evaluation exceeds its opportunity cost. z_1^* is the best choice from set A_1. z_2^* is the best choice from set A_2. z_1^* is best overall if $f(z_1^*) \geq f(z_2^*)$. *Opportunity cost is the best alternative foregone from among those alternatives not explicitly searched.* It is the best alternative in the set A_2. Also notice the opportunity cost of confining the search to A_1 is $f(z_2^*)$, not z_2^* per se. Opportunity cost is stated in units of the criterion function, $f(z)$.

example

Opportunity cost is important and subtle. Suppose we have five alternatives. Describe them by set $A = \{a,b,c,d,e\}$. Further suppose the evaluation function is: $f(a) = 1$, $f(b) = 2$, $f(c) = 3$, $f(d) = 4$, and $f(e) = 5$.

Some possible ways to define the pre-screened or "included" set A_1 are noted in Table 11.2. Set A_2, the "excluded" set, contains all elements not in set A_1. In each instance, the opportunity cost of the best choice from A_1 is the evaluation of the best choice among those options excluded. Opportunity cost is used to control for those options not considered. If all options are in A_1, there is no opportunity cost. Be certain to verify the $f(z_2^*)$ constructions in Table 11.2.

It is also important to understand opportunity cost depends on what is excluded from primary, explicit consideration. To dramatize, suppose we include option e in set A_1. Then we always have $z_1^* = e$. What is the opportunity cost of searching in set A_1? Symbolically, it is $f(z_2^*)$. But $f(z_2^*)$ might be 1, 2, 3, or 4. It all depends on what is excluded from A_1.

shadow prices in a linear program

This formal notion of opportunity cost often seems awkward at first blush. Yet we have probably used the phrase in this manner when we studied linear programming. Consider the following linear program.

The definition of opportunity cost requires A_1 and A_2 to be subsets of A, and to have their union equal A: $A_1 \subseteq A$, $A_2 \subseteq A$, and $A_1 \cup A_2 = A$.

[11]If $f(z_1^*) > f(z_2^*)$, z_1^* is a best choice overall. If $f(z_1^*) < f(z_2^*)$, z_2^* is a best choice overall. If $f(z_1^*) = f(z_2^*)$, both z_1^* and z_2^* are best choices overall.

$$\text{maximize} \quad f(x,y) = 10x + 12y$$
$$x,y$$
$$\text{subject to:} \quad x + y \le 8;$$
$$x + 2y \le 12; \text{ and}$$
$$x, y \ge 0.$$

The optimal solution, as reported by a typical software package, is $x^* = 4$, $y^* = 4$, $f(x^*,y^*) = 88$, and respective *shadow prices* for the two constraints of 8 and 2.

Table 11.2: Opportunity Cost Calculations with $f(a) = 1$, $f(b) = 2$, $f(c) = 3$, $f(d) = 4$ and $f(e) = 5$					
included set A_1	excluded set A_2	best in set A_1 z_1^*	best in set A_2 z_2^*	$f(z_1^*)$	$f(z_2^*)$
{a,b,c}	{d,e}	c	e	3	5
{a,d,e}	{b,c}	e	c	5	3
{d,e}	{a,b,c}	e	c	5	3
{a,c,e}	{b,d}	e	d	5	4
{c,d,e}	{a,b}	e	b	5	2
{b,c,d,e}	{a}	e	a	5	1
{a,b,c,d,e}	null	e	N/A	5	N/A
{a}	{b,c,d,e}	a	e	1	5
{b}	{a,c,d,e}	b	e	2	5
{c}	{a,b,d,e}	c	e	3	5
{d}	{a,b,c,e}	d	e	4	5
{e}	{a,b,c,d}	e	d	5	4

In turn, the shadow prices report the *rate* at which the optimal objective function will change if we alter the constraint in question. For example, what will the solution be if we change the first constraint from $x + y \le 8$ to $x + y \le 9$. The answer is $x^* = 6$, $y^* = 3$, and $f(x^*,y^*) = 96$. Notice that 96 - 88 = 8. The increase in the objective function from 88 to 96 is no accident. It is the change in the constraint multiplied by the constraint's shadow price of 8.[12]

The shadow price is a stylized opportunity cost. Where have we searched for our optimal solution? Within the noted constraints. What does the shadow price tell us? It tells us how the optimal objective function will change as we change the constraint. If we increase the constraint parameter, we add to the list of options. The shadow price speaks to the *change* in the objective function associated with expanding the options allowed. It provides an indication of returns that are available with options that were excluded from the analysis.[13]

---

[12] The shadow prices remain valid as long as the optimal basis does not change. We use an illustration in which a unit change in the constraint leaves the shadow prices unaffected.

[13] To complete the story, suppose it is possible to alter the constraint from $x + y \le 8$ to $x + y \le 9$,

A large shadow price tells us it may be worthwhile to alter the constraint in question, if possible. For example, the x + y ≤ 8 constraint might refer to units of capacity in a manufacturing department. The shadow price of 8 raises the question of expanding this capacity. Suppose equipment can be leased on a short term basis for less than the shadow price. This tells us we have not yet found the optimal solution. The opportunity cost of confining ourselves to the stated constraints is "too large." Some interesting options remain unexplored.

Opportunity cost refers to the best among those choices not considered. The shadow prices in our LP report how the maximal objective function value will change as we change the respective constraints. This informs us about the potential returns to altering our formulation of the problem. Altering the formulation means looking beyond the alternatives allowed by the constraints, as formulated. It means looking outside set A_1.

a special case

Contrast this with a common colloquialism that opportunity cost refers to "what could have been achieved had a particular decision not been taken." Under this usage, opportunity cost refers to the best alternative foregone. This is because the phrase implies a highly specific choice of set A_1.

To see this, return to the example in Table 11.2. Suppose the included set A_1 contains a single option. As usual, A_2 contains everything else. Let A_1 contain only the first option, a. What is the opportunity cost of searching only in A_1? It is the evaluation of the best among those in A_2. Clearly this is choice e; the opportunity cost is f(e) = 5.

In this sense, the colloquialism is proper. If A_1 is a single choice, the opportunity cost refers to the best alternative foregone. This is because opportunity cost refers to the best alternative not considered. If only one option is considered, all others are not. The best of all others, the best alternative foregone, then gives us the opportunity cost. Opportunity cost arises to control for opportunities that have not entered the formal analysis.[14]

---

at a cost of C. Then the best choice among the alternatives excluded from our initial formulation is x˙ = 6 and y˙ = 3. The associated objective function evaluation is 10(6) + 12(3) - C = 96 - C. In our language, 96 - C is the opportunity cost of searching within the confines of the original constraint. In turn, 96 - 88 = 8(1) is the shadow price multiplied by the change in the constraint. The incremental gain from expanding the constraint is 8 - C. Shadow prices are opportunity costs stated in incremental terms (exclusive of the cost of changing the constraint). Also, we should not lose sight of the fact the shadow prices are local measures of rates of change. They will not remain constant as we move further away from the original formulation.

[14]Suppose A_1 contains a single option. A_2 then contains all others. Now reverse the two sets. This is equivalent to selecting among all but the one option, and then comparing the tentative selection with the single one excluded. If we search by placing a single element in A_1, the best choice -- when it is the single element in A_1 -- will be the one with the minimum opportunity cost. This is what Coase

Opportunity cost is a useful, familiar framing device. A good manager will, among other things, be good at specifying set A_1. Intuition and experience are important inputs to this pre-screening or identification exercise. In the end, though, we always ask whether something intriguing was left out of the analysis. This, in a formal sense, is the concept of opportunity cost. It naturally depends on the problem we face and on how we divide the available choices for purposes of analysis. It is also measured in terms of the criterion function we are trying to optimize.

Thus, the second principle of consistent framing allows us to confine our search for the best choice to a reduced set of alternatives. Local searches are possible. We control for the remaining options by comparing the tentative choice with its opportunity cost. In turn, this process of "divide and conquer" should be thought of as an application of managerial art. Knowing which options to consider seriously serves to pre-screen the task. Judgment is essential. In a technical sense, we envision the manager as subjectively assessing the opportunity cost and proceeding with the analysis.[15]

Component Searches are Possible

The third principle of consistent framing concerns the ability to reduce the explicit dimensionality of a decision problem. This exploits the idea that it is often easier to work on a problem in sequential format. Suppose we want to find the maximum of function $f(x,y)$, subject to the constraints of $x \in X$ and $y \in Y$. We might write this abstract problem as:

$$\underset{x \in X, \, y \in Y}{\text{maximize}} \; f(x,y).$$

The imperative is to search over combinations of $x \in X$ and $y \in Y$ to find the choices that give the maximum feasible value of $f(x,y)$.

Now rewrite the formulation in slightly different fashion:

$$\underset{x \in X}{\text{maximize}} \; \{ \underset{y \in Y}{\text{maximum}} \; f(x,y) \}.$$

Concentrate on the portion included in brackets. For any tentative choice of x, this is a one variable problem. Suppose we tentatively specify $\hat{x} \in X$. The portion in brackets now directs us to find the value of $y \in Y$ that maximizes $f(\hat{x},y)$. Denote the choice of y in this circumstance by $y = g(\hat{x})$.

[1968, page 118] means when he says, "To cover costs and to maximize profits are essentially two ways of expressing the same phenomenon." This citation draws from a reprint of some of Coase's writings on cost measurement, originally published in 1938.

[15]Another interpretation, based on bounded rationality, is satisficing. If the search over A_1 yields a sufficiently attractive alternative, the search stops. Otherwise, we look further.

In our growing list of notational embellishments, we have the following story when we specify $x = \hat{x}$:

$$\underset{y \in Y}{\text{maximum}} \, f(\hat{x},y) = f(\hat{x},g(\hat{x})).$$

That is, $g(\hat{x})$ is the choice of y that makes $f(\hat{x},y)$ as large as possible.

Now repeat this procedure for every possible $\hat{x} \in X$. In this way we construct the function $y = g(x)$. That is, function $g(x)$ gives a best choice of y to match with each possible choice of x.

From here we make use of the $g(x)$ function:

$$\underset{x \in X}{\text{maximum}} \, \{ \underset{y \in Y}{\text{maximum}} \, f(x,y)\} = \underset{x \in X}{\text{maximum}} \, f(x,g(x)).$$

In short, we have reexpressed the problem as one of selecting the value of $x \in X$ that makes the function $f(x,g(x))$ as large as possible. Our task has taken on the appearance of a single variable problem. We are searching over $x \in X$; and $f(x,g(x))$ depends only on x.

Of course, this is not uninvolved. (A double negative seems appropriate.) We had to do the work to solve the inner maximization. The point, however, is valid. It is possible to reduce the apparent dimensionality of a choice problem by "maximizing out" some choices.[16]

a modest example

A transparent example will provide some needed relief. Suppose $f(x,y)$ is given by $f(x,y) = 10x + 12y$. Let X be specified by the interval $0 \le x \le 5$ and Y by the interval $0 \le y \le 3$. Surely the optimal solution is $x^* = 5$ and $y^* = 3$, with $f(x^*,y^*) = f(5,3) = 86$. (How do we know this?)

Now ask, what is the best choice of y for any possible choice of x? Given any value of x, our function $f(x,y)$ is increasing in y. We want y as large as possible. The answer is surely to select $y = g(x) = 3$, for any feasible choice of x.

Insert this half of the solution into the original problem. We have the following expression:

$$\underset{x}{\text{maximize}} \quad f(x,g(x)) = f(x,3) = 10x + 12(3)$$

subject to: $0 \le x \le 5$.

---

[16]This is not a sleight of hand exercise. Assume the choice problem is well formulated, so the maximization problem has a solution. Also assume the inner maximization problem has a solution for every possible $x \in X$. Let x^* and y^* denote a solution to the problem as originally stated. Suppose our rewritten problem identifies $x^{**} \in X$ and $y^{**} \in Y$. What if $f(x^{**},y^{**}) > f(x^*,y^*)$? This means we didn't have the correct solution in the first place, and is a contradiction. What if $f(x^{**},y^{**}) < f(x^*,y^*)$? This means, using $y = g(x)$, $f(x^{**},g(x^{**})) < f(x^*,y^*)$. But x^* is feasible, and $f(x^*,g(x^*)) = f(x^*,y^*)$. Otherwise, we did the inner maximization incorrectly. This implies the point x^{**} and y^{**} is not a solution to the rewritten problem and is a contradiction. Thus, the only possibility is $f(x^{**},y^{**}) = f(x^*,y^*)$.

The solution is $x^* = 5$, with $f(5,3) = 86$.

All we have done is divide the problem into components. Making certain the components articulate gives us a choice problem whose apparent dimensionality has been reduced. This was done by "maximizing out" the choice of $y \in Y$.

cost functions

This idea is not new. Perhaps the most vivid illustration is construction of a cost curve. Rather than frame the firm's question in terms of simultaneously selecting inputs and outputs, we break it into stages. Input choices are first formalized in the cost curve. Output is then chosen by juxtaposing revenue and cost, with cost effectively surrogating for the myriad input choices.

We explored this strategy in Chapter 2 where we examined a one product firm with three inputs. The output quantity was denoted q and the respective input quantities were denoted z_1, z_2, z_3. Output was related to input by the production function denoted $q = f(z_1, z_2, z_3)$. The market price of output was P, while the market price of the first input was $\hat{P}_1$, and so on.

One way to frame the problem of locating the profit maximizing production plan is to focus simultaneously on output and input quantities. Repeating our earlier notation, this frame appeared as follows:[17]

$$\text{maximize}_{q, z_1, z_2, z_3} \quad Pq - \hat{P}_1 z_1 - \hat{P}_2 z_2 - \hat{P}_3 z_3$$
$$\text{subject to: } q = f(z_1, z_2, z_3).$$

Another way to frame this problem is to solve first for the most efficient combination of inputs, for each possible output level; and then solve for the profit maximizing output level. This frame initially solves the input portion of the problem and subsequently solves the output portion of the problem.

Let $\hat{q}$ denote an arbitrary output quantity. We constructed a point on the cost function, $C(\hat{q})$, by locating the minimum factor payments that must be expended to produce quantity $\hat{q}$:

$$C(\hat{q}) = \text{minimum}_{z_1, z_2, z_3} \hat{P}_1 z_1 + \hat{P}_2 z_2 + \hat{P}_3 z_3$$
$$\text{subject to: } \hat{q} = f(z_1, z_2, z_3)$$

Repeating this process for all possible output quantities gives us the cost function $C(q)$.

Finally, we then locate the optimal output with the familiar exercise of maximizing revenue less cost:

$$\text{maximize}_{q} Pq - C(q).$$

---

[17]Recall we also presume $q \geq 0$, $z_1 \geq 0$, $z_2 \geq 0$ and $z_3 \geq 0$.

A frame that calls for construction of a cost function simply divides the problem into output and input components.

We can solve for inputs and outputs in one fell swoop or we can approach the problem in stages. Product cost, in the guise of $C(q)$, carries all the factor input choices when we use a revenue less cost frame.

interactions

To this point we have focused on the case where the feasible sets do not interact. In reducing the apparent dimensionality of $f(x,y)$ we have assumed the feasible sets, X and Y, do not interact. If we think of x and y as products, this would be the case of no joint products.[18] Interactions also can be dealt with in this fashion, provided we are careful in solving the inner maximization.

Our earlier LP example is illustrative. There the two products compete for scarce capacity. As originally stated, the problem was:

$$\text{maximize} \quad f(x,y) = 10x + 12y$$
$$\text{x,y}$$
$$\text{subject to:} \quad x + y \leq 8;$$
$$x + 2y \leq 12; \text{ and}$$
$$x, y \geq 0.$$

Now ask, for any tentative value of x (between 0 and 8, of course), what is the best choice of y? The answer is simple. Each unit of y increases the objective function by 12 units, so we want y to be as large as possible. The first constraint tells us that $y \leq 8 - x$. If x = 3, this constraint limits us to $y \leq 8 - 3 = 5$. The second constraint tells us that $2y \leq 12 - x$, or $y \leq .5(12 - x)$. If x = 3, this constraint limits us to $y \leq .5(12 - 3) = 4.5$

Thus, if x = 3 the first constraint limits y to a maximum of 5 units. The second constraint limits y to a maximum of 4.5. We want y as large as possible, but must honor both constraints. So the best choice of y in this circumstance is the minimum of the two: y = minimum {5; 4.5} = 4.5. For any such x, then, our best choice of y is given by

$$y = g(x) = \text{minimum } \{8 - x; .5(12 - x)\}.$$

Examine this function more closely. Notice that for small x, the second constraint is binding while the converse is true for larger x. Also notice the constraints intersect at x = 4:

$$8 - x = .5(12 - x) = 6 - .5x; \text{ or}$$
$$2 = .5x; \text{ or } x = 4.$$

---

[18]Recall our definition of joint products: Joint products occur when the feasible set of production possibilities is not separable. In this case of no joint products the possible choices of y do not depend on the choice of x, and vice versa.

Hence, for $0 \leq x \leq 4$, we set the choice of y at $g(x) = .5(12 - x)$; otherwise we set it at $g(x) = 8 - x$. This construction can be verified by glancing at Figure 11.2. There we plot the two constraints. $g(x)$ is defined by the lower of the two lines.[19]

Figure 11.2: Constraints on Choice of y

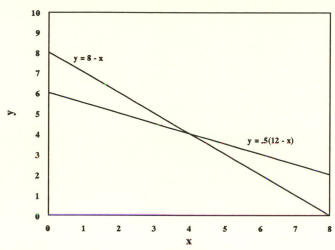

Now substitute these tentative y choices into the original objective function.

$$f(x,g(x)) = 10x + 12y = 10x + 12 \cdot \text{minimum} \{8 - x; .5(12 - x)\}$$

$$= \begin{cases} 10x + 6(12 - x) = 72 + 4x, \text{ if } 0 \leq x \leq 4; \text{ and} \\ 10x + 12(8 - x) = 96 - 2x, \text{ if } 4 \leq x \leq 8. \end{cases}$$

We now have an objective function that depends only on x. What is the maximum? The maximum occurs at $x = 4$. The slope is positive if $x \leq 4$; beyond $x = 4$ it is negative. We can do no better than set $x = 4$. See Figure 11.3.

We typically expect, as occurs in this case, that the best choice of y will depend on x. Stated differently, changing x carries with it an implied change in y. We can frame the choice problem so both effects are explicit. This is the problem of maximizing the function $f(x,y)$. Alternatively, we can frame the choice problem so x is explicitly chosen, and the effect on y is treated in implicit fashion. $Pq - C(q)$ is profit as a function of output. Inputs are implicitly framed with the cost function $C(q)$. Similarly, the $f(x,g(x))$ construction implicitly frames the choice of y.

This is the third principle of consistent framing. It is possible to frame portions of a decision problem in implicit fashion, provided we are careful to make certain

---

[19]The essence of Figure 11.2 is we cannot write the constraints in separable fashion, as $x \in X$ and $y \in Y$. They take the form $(x,y) \in \{(x,y) \mid x + y \leq 8, x + 2y \leq 12, x \geq 0, \text{ and } y \geq 0\}$.

the explicit and implicit parts of our frame articulate. Consistent framing allows us to reduce the apparent dimensionality of a choice problem.

Figure 11.3: Decomposed Maximization Example

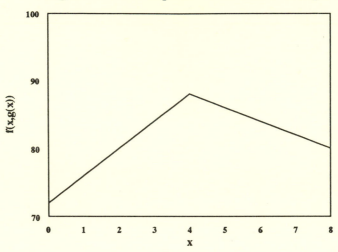

a question of interpretation

This brings us to a pithy observation. Our LP illustration began with the objective function $f(x,y) = 10x + 12y$. Substituting $y = g(x)$, we then moved on to $f(x,g(x)) = 10x + 12 \cdot \text{minimum} \{8 - x; .5(12 - x)\}$. This simplified, recall, into $10x + 6(12 - x)$ for $0 \leq x \leq 4$; and $10x + 12(8 - x)$ for $4 \leq x \leq 8$. The question now is what are these extra terms?

Suppose, for the sake of discussion, this is a short-run maximization problem. Capacity is defined by the two constraints. In the original formulation, where x and y are explicitly treated, each unit of x increases profit by 10. In the altered formulation, where y is implicitly treated, we append the additional term of $6(12 - x)$, or $12(8 - x)$. This appendage is simply $12[g(x)]$.

In the first region, $g(x) = .5(12 - x)$. Increasing x by one unit decreases y by .5. An additional unit of x directly increases the objective function by 10, but indirectly reduces it by $.5(12) = 6$. It is natural to call this indirect effect a cost of the first product.

Is it an opportunity cost? Technically, the answer is no. We are working with a frame in which $A_1 = A$. We are not limiting our search. We are only doing it in stages. The term is a type of externality cost.

This should give a hint of things to come. Altering the way we frame a choice problem often leads to an alteration in what we regard as the cost of some activity or product. In turn, this leads to a decision frame in which the cost in question is far removed from some expenditure. Cost, that is, becomes more and more distant from expenditure.

Consistent Framing

We have referred to these framing exercises as consistent framing. The consistent adjective is code for an important assumption. We assume we enter the exercise with a well defined optimization problem. Generically, it takes the form of maximizing f(z) subject to z∈A. This is given. It is exogenous. Our exploration begins with the choice problem in place.

Given this beginning, we may transform the objective function, search in limited domains, or reduce the apparent dimensionality of the problem. With care, these techniques, mixed in various ways, will lead us to identify an optimal solution.

These principles are based on optimization, on locating the maximum of some function over some defined region. In this sense, and to this degree, they are grounded in theory. Which frame is best is outside the theory. Also, where the problem statement comes from in the first place is outside the theory.

For that matter, we also might entertain some specification of the problem that is easier to analyze, even if this leads us to analyze a misspecified though easier to analyze problem. These latter concerns take us beyond our theory. This is where the theory of managerial action ends and the art begins.

Summary

Decision framing is a mixture of art and theory. The theory side of the recipe uses three ingredients: the ability to transform an objective function, to engage in local searches, and to reduce the apparent dimensionality of a decision problem. Consistently done, nothing is lost by using these ingredients.

The local search idea relies on opportunity cost as the countervailing force. We stress opportunity cost is the evaluation measure's score of the best alternative not explicitly searched. The dimensionality reduction idea relies on "maximizing out" some choices. The economist's classical cost function is the reigning example. We stress that continued use of this idea creates a notion of cost that removes us further and further from expenditures on associated factors of production. This is explored in the next chapter, where we use these framing principles to examine various costing techniques.

Bibliographic Notes

The economic theory of cost provides a stunning example of how a framing approach can lead to insight. For the technically inclined, a favorite reference is Chambers [1988]. A familiar example of transforming an objective function is when we substitute the expected value of a random variable. Reiter [1957] is an important reference in taking this idea to more substantive settings. Buchanan [1969] provides an extensive discussion of opportunity cost, linking it to the preferences that govern a decision problem. Finally, Demski and Feltham [1976] link various transformations of a decision problem, based on the principles of consistent framing, to concepts of cost.

Problems and Exercises

1.   The three principles of consistent framing were presented in terms of locating an element in a given set, say, $z \in A$, that make a given criterion function, $f(z)$, as large as possible. Carefully discuss the role of economic rationality in identifying and using these principles.

2.   *increasing transformations*
   Suppose we want to maximize $f(z) = 12z - z^2$, over $0 \le z \le 8$. Why does the first principle of consistent framing apply to transforming the entire function and not its individual components? Hint: what is the maximum of $[12z - z^2]^3$, subject to the noted constraint? Contrast this with the maximum of $[12z]^3 - [z^2]^3$, subject to the noted constraint.

3.   *substituting an expected value for a random variable*
   Suppose we want to maximize the expected value of $f(z) = \theta z - z^2$, over $z \ge 0$, where θ is a random variable. We now reframe this by substituting the random variable's expected value for the random variable. Let $\hat{\theta}$ denote the expected value of θ. Maximizing $\hat{f}(z) = \hat{\theta} z - z^2$, over $z \ge 0$, will of course locate the solution to the original problem. Discuss the principle of consistent framing that is being employed. What happens to the transparent substitution when risk aversion is present?

4.   *incremental analysis*
   Suppose a firm seeks to maximize its profit. It is presently producing and selling $\hat{q}$ units. It has an opportunity to produce and sell $\hat{q} + 1$ units. Carefully explain the use of the first principle of consistent framing when we analyze this in terms of the incremental revenue and incremental cost of the additional unit.

5.   *incremental analysis*
   Return to the special offer problem developed in Table 10.4, where we concluded the job 2 customer was acceptable if $P - 38{,}200 - 22{,}000\alpha \ge 0$. Carefully document how the three principles of consistent framing were used in that exercise.

6.   *rates of return*
   Ralph is contemplating loaning a cousin $10,000. The loan would be due in one year, with interest at 18%. Ralph figures the probability the cousin will pay back the loan (plus interest) is .80; with probability .10 only the principal will be paid back; and with probability .10 nothing will be paid by the cousin. Ralph's next

best use of the $10,000 is to invest it at the risk free rate of 4%. Ralph is risk neutral and analyzes this in the following fashion. The expected return from the cousin is $10,000(1.18)(.8) + 10,000(.1) + 0(.1) = 10,440$. So the funds can be invested at 4% or at 4.4%. The latter is a winner.

Carefully discuss how Ralph has used the principles of consistent framing in reducing this to a comparison of interest rates. As a starting point, assume Ralph's preferences are measured by the present value of expected wealth, and Ralph has a variety of investments in place.

7. *opportunity cost*

Suppose you are going to the movie. The choices are a mystery, a high adventure story, a musical, or a documentary. Further suppose you absolutely cannot stand musicals. Use the concept of opportunity cost to frame the choice by pre-screening (pun) the musical.

8. *shadow prices*

We find Ralph studying cost, and how cost depends on the way a choice problem is framed. Ralph now produces two products. Let x and y, respectively, denote the quantities of the two products that are produced and sold. Any nonnegative quantities satisfying the following constraints can be produced:

$x + y \leq 400$; and

$x + 2y \leq 500$.

Ralph estimates the contribution margin to be $10 per unit for the first product and $12 per unit for the second. This is based on respective selling prices of 40 and 42 per unit, along with respective variable costs of 30 and 30 per unit.

a] Determine an optimal solution.

b] In what sense are the shadow prices on the two constraints opportunity costs?

9. *component searches and product cost*

Return to problem 8 above. Now suppose Ralph likes to think in terms of how many units of the first product, x, to produce and sell. Clearly we require $0 \leq x \leq 400$. Within this range, it should also be clear Ralph would produce as many units of the second product as possible. This implies, for any such x, the corresponding choice of y would be $y = g(x) = \min \{400 - x; .5(500 - x)\}$. This implies a total contribution margin of $10x + 12g(x) = 10x + 12[\min \{400 - x; .5(500 - x)\}]$.

a] Plot this expression, for $0 \leq x \leq 400$. Determine the optimal choice of x.

b] Next, observe this function simplifies to $10x + 3,000 - 6x$ if $0 \leq x \leq 300$ and $10x + 4,800 - 12x$ if $300 \leq x \leq 400$. Concentrate on the first range. What is the incremental or marginal cost of the first product in this range? Carefully explain your answer, in light of the fact this product's contribution margin was previously calculated as revenue of 40 less variable cost of 30.

c]   Why does the cost of the product depend on the decision frame?

10. *combinations of the framing principles*
Suppose we want to maximize $f(x,y) = 12x - x^2 + 18y - 3y^2 - 10$, subject to x + y ≤ 8. x ≥ 0 and y ≥ 0. You should verify the solution has x = 5.25 and y = 2.75. Now consider the following. (i) Initially drop the constant of - 10. (ii) Notice that if the constraint were not present, we would never set x above 6 or y above 3. Doing so lowers the objective function. Similarly, we would never set x below 6 or y below 3. A slight increase whenever the variables are below the noted targets will increase the objective function. (iii) This insight implies, with the constraint present, we would never set x below 5 (because y would never be set above 3). (iv) Together, then, we can locate the best choice of x by maximizing $12x - x^2 + 18(8 - x) - 3(8 - x)^2$, subject to the constraint 5 ≤ x ≤ 6. Try it.
Carefully document the use of the three principles of consistent framing in this exercise.

11. *framing and LLAs*
This problem works through a sequence of framing exercises.

a]   Ralph produces a single product, with quantity denoted x. Profit is given by the expression x(10 - .5x), and capacity is constrained so 0 ≤ x ≤ 10. Determine Ralph's optimal output.

b]   A new customer arrives on the scene. Let y denote the quantity of output Ralph produces for this second customer. This customer is a mirror image of the first, so Ralph's problem is now to select quantities x and y to maximize profit of x(10 - .5x) + y(10 - .5y), subject to a capacity constraint of 0 ≤ x + y ≤ 10. Determine Ralph's optimal output of each product, i.e., x and y. You should find x = y = 5.

c]   Ralph likes to keep things simple, and enjoys working with single product decision frames. It turns out that the optimal x can be located in this case by maximizing any of the following functions:
$$x(10 - .5x) + [50 - .5x^2];$$
$$x(10 - .5x) + [-.5x^2]; \text{ or}$$
$$x(10 - .5x) + [-5x].$$
Verify this claim. Then carefully explain why each function allows us to identify the optimal choice of y. Can you relate this to cost allocation?

d]   Now suppose Ralph must immediately decide on the quantity of the first product (x); after this decision has been implemented, Ralph will learn whether demand for the second product materializes. If it does, and if Ralph supplies y units of the second product, total profit will be x(10 - .5x) + y(10 - .5y). Naturally, we still require x + y ≤ 10. Let α denote the probability demand for the second product materializes. So Ralph's problem is now to maximize expected profit of x(10 - .5x) + αy(10 - .5y), subject to a capacity constraint of 0 ≤ x + y ≤ 10. The solution is x

= 10/(1 + α) and y = 10 - x. (x now denotes the immediate choice of first product quantity, and y the choice of second product quantity provided demand materializes.) How do you interpret this solution?

e] Finally, go back to Ralph's penchant for keeping things simple. It turns out the optimal x can be located here by maximizing any of the following functions:

$$x(10 - .5x) + α[50 - .5x^2];$$
$$x(10 - .5x) + α[-.5x^2]; \text{ or}$$
$$x(10 - .5x) + [-10αx/(1 + α)].$$

Verify this claim. Then carefully relate each function to its counterpart in the initial story (where α = 1).

12. *inconsistent framing attempt*

Ralph manages a two product enterprise. Product x sells for 400 dollars per unit and product y sells for 600 per unit. Estimated manufacturing costs are as follows:

direct material	100	150
direct labor	80	120
overhead	160	240

Overhead is applied to each product on the basis of direct labor dollars (at a rate of 200%). At the firm-wide level, overhead is in fact budgeted via the following linear approximation:

overhead = 54,000 + .5DL$

where DL$ denotes direct labor dollars. In addition, marketing costs (all variable) average 30 per unit of x and 90 per unit of y.

The firm employs two production departments. The first has a capacity of 400 direct labor hours and the second has a capacity of 500 direct labor hours. Product x uses one hour in each department, while product y uses one hour in the first department and two hours in the second department;

x + y ≤ 400 and
x + 2y ≤ 500

therefore describe the capacity restrictions.

a] Determine an optimal output schedule for Ralph.

b] Ralph is worried about the overhead function in the above problem. To think some more about this, assume actual overhead is one of the following two models, with equal probability:

overhead = 63,000 + .25DL$; or
overhead = 45,000 + .75DL$.

Absent any additional information, Ralph will implement the schedule determined in part [a] above. How much would Ralph pay for a cost study that will perfectly reveal which of the two overhead models is in fact correct?

c] Ralph now tries another exercise. Instead of worrying about the overhead estimate, the estimates of available capacity in the two departments are called into question. Suppose department two's estimate is correct, but the estimate for department one is ambiguous. With equal probability, it will be either 350 or 450 hours. I want to ask you how much Ralph would pay to learn the actual capacity. But this cannot be answered without additional specification. Why can we not answer this question?

12

Applications of the Framing Principles

This chapter continues our exploration of decision framing. The ability to transform an objective function, engage in local searches, and emphasize component searches are critical techniques in constructing a decision analysis.

These techniques are often used in conjunction with approximated cost expressions, or LLAs. We begin with an extended exploration of framing considerations in the presence of LLAs. We then turn to an exploration of the intimate links between framing and the importance of cost in decision making. Useful notions of cost, such as relevant and sunk cost, arise. Finally, we raise the question of whether judgments that lead to choice of a particular decision frame are, themselves, likely to be consistent.

LLA Based Applications of Consistent Framing

Consider an organization that produces two products using three inputs. Denote the output quantities of the two products by q_1 and q_2. Similarly denote the variable input quantities by z_1, z_2, and z_3.

The production technology is simple. First we face output constraints. Capacity was acquired in an earlier period. This limits output according to the following two constraints:

$$q_1 + q_2 \leq 8,000; \text{ and}$$
$$q_1 + 2q_2 \leq 12,000.$$

We might interpret the first constraint as arising from space limitations or machine capacity. The total number of units produced cannot exceed 8,000. The second constraint might be interpreted as arising from skilled labor capacity. Each unit of the first product requires one hour of skilled labor. Each unit of the second requires two hours of skilled labor. A maximum of 12,000 hours of skilled labor is available. These constraints should be familiar, especially when expressed in thousands of units.

Second, the production technology is itself linear. The per unit input requirements are listed below:

	product 1	product 2
required units of first input per unit of output	1	2
required units of second input per unit of output	3	4
required units of third input per unit of output	2	4

This implies the inputs must be provided in quantities such that the following three constraints are satisfied:

$z_1 \geq q_1 + 2q_2;$
$z_2 \geq 3q_1 + 4q_2;$ and
$z_3 \geq 2q_1 + 4q_2.$

We interpret the first input as direct labor, the second as direct material, and the third as a composite of miscellaneous inputs.

Notice the required units of the third input grow in direct proportion to those of the first, or direct labor. This hints at calling this category overhead and using direct labor as the explanatory variable in the overhead LLA.

Finally, this is (by virtue of explicit capacity constraints) a short-run decision problem. The capacities stated in the first two constraints are given. They cannot be altered in the short-run. The cost associated with these fixed inputs is assumed to be 50,000.[1]

Profit, now, is revenue less payments for the various inputs, those acquired in the short-run and those previously acquired.

To keep things simple, we further assume that outputs are sold in perfectly competitive markets. Respective output prices are 90 per unit and 152 per unit. Respective short-run input prices are 20, 10, and 15 per unit. Recall, though, the available supply of skilled labor is limited to 12,000 hours.

an obvious frame

Collecting these various assumptions, the short-run profit maximization problem is stated as the following maximization exercise.[2]

maximize $90q_1 + 152q_2 - 20z_1 - 10z_2 - 15z_3 - 50,000$
subject to: $q_1 + q_2 \leq 8,000;$
$q_1 + 2q_1 \leq 12,000;$
$z_1 \geq q_1 + 2q_2;$
$z_2 \geq 3q_1 + 4q_2;$ and
$z_3 \geq 2q_1 + 4q_2.$

Now invoke the first principle of consistent framing and add a constant of $\alpha = 50,000$ to this objective function. We then have a standard appearing linear program, with five variables and five constraints.

Also scale each output and input so they denote units of a thousand. Our LP now appears as follows:

maximize $90q_1 + 152q_2 - 20z_1 - 10z_2 - 15z_3$ [I]

---

[1] $q_1 + 2q_1 \leq 12,000$ is a capacity constraint. Up to a maximum of 12,000 hours of skilled labor can be acquired and used. This might reflect labor supply conditions, space limitations or whatever. $z_3 \geq 2q_1 + 4q_2$ says the hours of skilled labor acquired in the market must be at least the amount required to produce the identified output quantities.

[2] The maximization is done over nonnegative choices of $q_1, q_2, z_1, z_2,$ and z_3.

$$\text{subject to: } q_1 + q_2 \leq 8;$$
$$q_1 + 2q_1 \leq 12;$$
$$z_1 \geq q_1 + 2q_2;$$
$$z_2 \geq 3q_1 + 4q_2; \text{ and}$$
$$z_3 \geq 2q_1 + 4q_2.$$

The solution is $q_1^* = 4$, $q_2^* = 4$, $z_1^* = 12$, $z_2^* = 28$ and $z_3^* = 24$. Respective shadow prices are 8, 2, -20, -10, and -15.[3] This gives us total revenue of $90(4) + 152(4) = 968$ and total expenditure on short-run inputs of $20(12) + 10(28) + 15(24) = 880$, for a net of $968 - 880 = 88$.[4]

two competing frames

With this preamble, we now invoke the framing principles to recast this choice problem in various frames. Initially we maximize out the input choices. This will give us a problem in two variables and an objective function expressed in terms of revenue less *product* cost.

Consider any combination of q_1 and q_2 that satisfies the first two constraints. What are the best choices of z_1, z_2, and z_3? The objective function decreases for each unit of each input. This implies we want to use as few units of each input as possible. So the latter three constraints will hold as equalities. Any amount above the bare minimum is wasteful; any amount below is infeasible. Our input choices therefore are:

$$z_1 = q_2 + 2q_2;$$
$$z_2 = 3q_1 + 4q_2; \text{ and}$$
$$z_3 = 2q_1 + 4q_2.$$

Now substitute these choices into the objective function. This is the step of replacing $f(x,y)$ with $f(x,g(x))$.

$$90q_1 + 152q_2 - 20z_1 - 10z_2 - 15z_3 =$$
$$90q_1 + 152q_2 - 20(q_1 + 2q_2) - 10(3q_1 + 4q_2) - 15(2q_1 + 4q_2) =$$
$$[90 - 20 - 30 - 30]q_1 + [152 - 40 - 40 - 60]q_2 = [90 - 80]q_1 + [152 - 140]q_2.$$

We now face the following LP:

---

maximize $10q_1 + 12q_2$ [II]
subject to: $q_1 + q_2 \le 8$; and
              $q_1 + 2q_1 \le 12$.

The solution is an old friend: $q_1^* = 4$ and $q_2^* = 4$, with respective shadow prices of 8 and 2.

Next, we invoke the second principle of consistent framing yet again. This is done to provide a frame that explicitly treats only the first product. For this purpose, consider any feasible choice of q_1. What is the best choice of q_2 to mate with this choice of q_1? As each unit of the second product increases the objective function, we know we want q_2 to be as large as possible. Our earlier work gives us the answer:

$$q_2 = g(q_1) = \text{minimum } \{8 - q_1;\ .5(12 - q_1)\}.$$

Substituting this choice of q_2 into the objective function gives us the following frame:

maximize $10q_1 + 12 \cdot \text{minimum } \{8 - q_1;\ .5(12 - q_1)\}$ [III]

$$= \begin{cases} 10q_1 + 6(12 - q_1) = 72 + 4q_1, \text{ if } 0 \le q_1 \le 4; \text{ and} \\ 10q_1 + 12(8 - q_1) = 96 - 2q_1, \text{ if } 4 \le q_1 \le 8. \end{cases}$$

We will spare the pain of now searching over the first region, and using opportunity cost to control for the limited search!

Frame I focuses explicitly on all products and inputs. The objective function reflects revenue from the product sales and expenditures for the three factors in their respective factor markets. We might call these latter items the cost of the factors. Notice that cost of factors and expenditure for the factors are coextensive in this frame. Also notice we have no expression of *product* cost in frame I, only *factor* cost.

Frame II focuses explicitly on both products and implicitly on the inputs. The objective function in this frame is $[90 - 80]q_1 + [152 - 140]q_2$. We know 90 is the selling price of the first product and 152 is the selling price of the second. It seems natural, then, to call 80 the cost of the first product and 140 the cost of the second product.

This terminology is readily rationalized in two equivalent ways. First, let's maximize out the choice of factor inputs for any feasible output schedule. This is what we did in constructing frame II. We know the best combination of inputs is:

$z_1 = q_1 + 2q_2$;
$z_2 = 3q_1 + 4q_2$; and
$z_3 = 2q_1 + 4q_2$.

The organization's cost curve, exclusive of the 50,000 fixed cost, turns out to be

$$C(q_1, q_2) = 20(q_1 + 2q_2) + 10(3q_1 + 4q_2) + 15(2q_1 + 4q_2) = 80q_1 + 140q_2.$$

We emphasize this cost curve has been constructed using the second principle of consistent framing.[5]

Equivalently, we might think in terms of components. We have interpreted the first factor, recall, as direct labor. Each unit of the first product requires one hour, and each unit of the second requires two hours. At 20 per hour, we have a direct labor cost of $DL = 20q_1 + 40q_2$.

The second factor was interpreted as direct material. We have a direct material cost of $DM = 30q_1 + 40q_2$.

The third factor was interpreted as a composite of miscellaneous inputs. It varies in proportion to direct labor cost. Remembering the fixed cost, we have an overhead cost of $OV = 50,000 + 1.5DL$.[6]

In other words, we have the following LLAs for our setting: $DL = 20q_1 + 40q_2$, $DM = 30q_1 + 40q_2$, and $OV = 50,000 + 1.5DL$. This allows us to construct variable product costs of

	product 1	product 2
direct labor	20	40
direct material	30	40
variable overhead	30	60
variable product cost	80	140

Also, our modest story lacks selling and administrative items. All the inputs are tallied in these product cost calculations. The products, then, have respective contribution margins of 90 - 80 = 10 and 152 - 140 = 12 per unit. Our LP in frame II is designed to maximize the total contribution margin.

The contribution margin format is a frame in which we rely on a cost curve construction to solve the factor input portion of the larger problem. The presumed linear structure is exploited for this purpose.

Two additional points should be noted. First, we have actually engaged in an allocation exercise to construct these product costs. The direct labor and direct material categories, by definition, are readily identified with the respective products. The variable overhead category, though, is not. By calling it overhead, we chose not to identify individual z_3 inputs with each of the products. Allocation arises here as part of the constructive procedure by which we estimate the product costs.

This is an important lesson. It is incorrect to say that cost allocation is the antithesis of reasoned choice. Cost allocation *may* arise as part of a consistent framing exercise. It arises in our modest example when (1) we use product costs to

---

[5] Notice the inputs are priced at their market prices here, or at their respective shadow prices from the first LP.

[6] Variable overhead is 150% of direct labor cost. $15(2q_1 + 4q_2) = 30q_1 + 60q_2 = 1.5(20q_1 + 40q_2) = 1.5DL$.

reflect input choices implicitly and (2) we construct the product costs by focusing on the underlying input cost categories.

This is our second point. This latter, constructive procedure that relies on knowledge of the LLAs does not in any way avoid the part of the decision that calls for specification of the inputs. We have not somehow sidestepped the z_i choices. Rather, we have pursued them with a different terminology. Our LLAs can only be up to the framing task if they reflect the best choices that arise from maximizing the z_i decisions out of the frame.

Thumb back to frame I, where we identified respective shadow prices of 8, 2, -20, -10, and -15. The latter three speak to the question of altering the factor input requirements. Each unit of the first product requires one unit of the first input (direct labor), three of the second (direct material), and two of the third (overhead). What is the cost of these inputs if we base the calculations on the shadow prices? We have $20(1) + 10(3) + 15(2) = 80$. A parallel calculation arises for the second product.

What is going on? In frame I we explicitly considered all outputs and inputs. In frame II, we replaced explicit consideration of the inputs with product costs. The product costs reflect the optimal input choices. We have merely solved the problem in stages. The linearity allows us to do this "by inspection." Implicitly, though, we have solved half the problem and plugged this into the cost constructions. This is why we have an intimate connection between the shadow prices in frame I and the product costs in frame II. They represent precisely the same phenomena.

A linear world also helps. When $C(q_1,q_2)$ is linear, we have $C(q_1,q_2) = F + v_1 q_1 + v_2 q_2$. We naturally call v_i the variable cost of product i in this instance. Each product's cost is unambiguous. In this way we arrive at a decision frame based on contribution margin; and product cost is a significant feature of the frame.

It also turns out in frame II that the product costs are the respective factor requirements costed at their market prices, which equal their shadow prices. We only purchase the inputs that are required, no more and no less. In frame II there is an intimate connection between product cost and factor input expenditure. Yet this reassuring conclusion is dependent on the frame.

Frame III has an objective function that depends only on q_1: $10q_1 + 12$ minimum $\{8 - q_1; .5(12 - q_1)\}$. 10 is the contribution margin per unit of the first product. The remaining item is a construction designed to reflect the impact of the q_1 choice not on factor inputs per se but on the output of the second product. The second region, where $.5(12 - q_1)$ is controlling, is the interesting case.

Here the frame III objective function simplifies to $10q_1 - 6q_1 + 72 = 4q_1 + 72$. We have already decided to call 90 the revenue per unit of the first product. Variable cost of the first product is 80. An additional cost term is present, reflecting the fact more of the first product forces us to produce less of the second. Frames I and II explicitly reflect this in the modeling, since both outputs are explicitly chosen. Frame III forces us to load this effect onto the product 1 construction.

Thus, in frame III the objective function (when $0 \le q_1 \le 4$) is $(90 - 80 - 6)q_1 + 72 = (90 - 86)q_1 + 72$. Here we have a divergence between cost and expenditure.

The product cost in frame III must expand to reflect input choices as well as q_2 choices.

We warned that it is incorrect to say cost allocation is the antithesis of reasoned choice. We now expand the warning. It is incorrect to say cost measurement that departs from expenditure is the antithesis of reasoned choice. What we mean by cost depends in intimate and subtle ways on the way our decision problem has been framed. See Table 12.1.

Table 12.1: Product Cost for Various Decision Frames			
frame	explicit choices	implicit choices	marginal cost of first product
I	q_1,q_2,z_1,z_2,z_3	N/A	N/A
II	q_1,q_2	z_1,z_2,z_3	80
III	q_1	z_1,z_2,z_3,q_2	86 or 92

another warning

Consistent framing merges inexorably into questions of proper cost measurement for decision making. In turn, the measurements are often constructed using procedures that are employed in the accounting library.[7] Yet we must remember that the circumstances and frame at hand determine what proper cost measurement is. No iron-clad rule of thumb exists. For example, it does not necessarily follow variable product cost is what we want in a frame that resembles frame II above.

To see this, we change our story in a slight but important way. Initially, we change the selling price of the second product from 152 to 149 per unit. Plugging this change into frame I provides a solution of $q_1^* = 8$, $q_2^* = 0$, $z_1^* = 8$, $z_2^* = 24$, and $z_3^* = 16$. Respective shadow prices are 10, 0, -20, -10, and -15.

We have lowered the price of the second product just enough to make it an unattractive alternative. With this price change, the cost constructions in frame II remain as before. The cost curve is

$$C(q_1,q_2) = 80q_1 + 140q_2.$$

The revenue, though, has been altered; and with this cost curve the organization's best choice is to devote its capacity to the production and sale of the first product.

Now make another change. Suppose the organization is committed to paying the skilled labor, regardless of whether all the available 12,000 hours are used. This removes any choice of z_1 from the decision. z_1 is fixed at $z_1 = 12,000$. We continue

---

[7]Indeed, we often begin the cost construction exercise with what is in the library, and subsequently modify that preliminary calculation to fit the task at hand.

to assume the other two factors will be acquired as needed. The fixed cost has increased from 50,000 to 50,000 + 20(12,000) = 290,000.

Frame I now takes the following form, where we suppress the fixed cost term:

maximize $90q_1 + 149q_2 - 10z_2 - 15z_3$ [I']
subject to: $q_1 + q_2 \le 8$;
$q_1 + 2q_1 \le 12$;
$z_2 \ge 3q_1 + 4q_2$; and
$z_3 \ge 2q_1 + 4q_2$.

The solution is $q_1^* = 4$, $q_2^* = 4$, $z_2^* = 28$, and $z_3^* = 24$. Respective shadow prices are 11, 19, - 20, and -15. Here the best choice is to produce a combination of the products.

Frame II suppresses the two factor choices. We know from our earlier work that the optimal input choices will be $z_2 = 3q_1 + 4q_2$ and $z_3 = 2q_1 + 4q_2$. Substituting these into the objective function provides:

$90q_1 + 149q_2 - 10z_2 - 15z_3 =$
$90q_1 + 149q_2 - 10(3q_1 + 4q_2) - 15(2q_1 + 4q_2) =$
$[90 - 30 - 30]q_1 + [149 - 40 - 60]q_2 = [90 - 60]q_1 + [149 - 100]q_2$.

We arrive at the following LP:

maximize $30q_1 + 49q_2$ [II']
subject to: $q_1 + q_2 \le 8$; and
$q_1 + 2q_1 \le 12$.

The solution, as we should anticipate, is $q_1^* = 4$ and $q_2^* = 4$, with respective shadow prices of 11 and 19.

The short-run cost curve, exclusive of the fixed cost, has become

$C(q_1,q_2) = 60q_1 + 100q_2$.

Now recall we began with LLAs of $DL = 20q_1 + 40q_2$, $DM = 30q_1 + 40q_2$, and $OV = 50,000 + 1.5DL$. These imply respective variable product costs of 80 and 140 per unit. The frame II' construction, however, is based on the following product cost calculations:

	product 1	product 2
direct labor	0	0
direct material	30	40
variable overhead	30	60
variable product cost	60	100

How is it, then, that we have a variable cost, direct labor here, not entering the frame II' analysis? Variable cost is defined with respect to a given set of LLAs. There is no reason to suspect a given set of LLAs is precisely what is appropriate for the decision circumstance and frame at hand. We should not expect a perfect fit. Here, direct labor is fixed, despite the presumed LLA. LLAs are important ingredients in constructing the accounting library. That library has many uses. The astute manager recognizes and acts on differences between library procedures and the decision circumstance and frame at hand.

The maxim is simple yet uncomfortable. What we mean by cost depends on the decision circumstance and frame at hand. A popular cliche maintains that cost exists independent of circumstance and frame. After all, it is routine and natural to speak of the cost of education, the cost of travel, the cost of an election, and so on.

A sloppy colloquialism is hardly the fodder of insight. In our original circumstance, the cost of the first product would be nonexistent, 80, 86, or perhaps 92 depending on our frame (and level of output). In the second circumstance, the first two frames call for a nonexistent or 60 per unit product cost measure.

Cost depends on circumstance and frame. Managerial art cannot be reduced to a formula or to a cost measurement algorithm.[8]

Decision Costing Terminology

Cost measurement is often aided by particular cost concepts, or constructs. These are useful to the extent they provide clues to the circumstance we encounter and the frame we find comfortable. The trick is to visualize a given decision opportunity in terms of benefits and costs. Judiciously invoking the framing principles then exhibits particular notions of cost. In turn, some of these notions are related to what we typically find in the accounting library.

benefit and cost expressions of f(z)

Suppose we find ourselves facing the (yes, abstract) decision problem of maximizing $f(z)$ among the available options in A. Set A and function $f(z)$ are given. We may have used the three consistent framing principles to express this decision problem in some particular frame. Whatever, we begin with $f(z)$ and A.

Now take the objective function $f(z)$ and express it as the net of a *benefit* or *revenue* component less a *cost* component:

$$f(z) = B(z) - C(z).$$

$B(z)$ is the benefit measure if option $z \in A$ is taken, and $C(z)$ is the corresponding cost measure.

For example, in frame II above, z consisted of the output quantities, q_1 and q_2, with $B(z) = 90q_1 + 152q_2$ and $C(z) = 80q_1 + 140q_2$. The important point is that we begin by separating $f(z)$ into benefit and cost components. This is always possible.[9] We also should keep in mind that the separation is often far from unique. Is a

---

[8]Clark [1923] coined the phrase "different costs for different purposes." Three-quarters of a century has taught us that purpose consists of circumstance and frame.

[9]Consider $B(z) = 0$ and $C(z) = -f(z)$!

projected bad debt a revenue reduction or cost increase? Are the net proceeds from sale of a by-product best viewed as a benefit or a cost reduction? The story begins with f(z) reexpressed as B(z) - C(z).

relevant cost

Next, ask which option gives minimum possible cost? Let ź be the option that produces minimum cost:

$$C(\acute{z}) = \underset{z \in A}{\text{minimum}} \ C(z).$$

Put differently, for any option we have $C(z) \geq C(\acute{z})$.

Using the first principle of consistent framing, add the constant $\alpha = C(\acute{z})$ to our objective function:

$$f(z) + C(\acute{z}) = B(z) - C(z) + C(\acute{z}) = B(z) - [C(z) - C(\acute{z})].$$

The quantity in brackets, $[C(z) - C(\acute{z})]$, is called the relevant cost of option z. *Relevant cost is simply that portion of the objective function's cost expression that varies with the available options.*[10]

The idea of relevant cost is to frame a decision with the least specification. If some portion of the identified cost function does not vary among the choices at hand, it is surely irrelevant to the analysis of locating the best choice. $[C(z) - C(\acute{z})]$ may be easier to specify than $C(z)$.

To illustrate, suppose one question in identifying $C(z)$ is the cost of labor inputs. Workers are paid wages and various fringe benefits. The latter include health insurance, parking, education options, a subsidized cafeteria, telephone privileges, and so on. Workers also have retirement benefits, centering on pensions and retiree health benefits. These retirement benefits depend on how long the individual works for the organization, as well as prevailing benefits at the time of the worker's retirement, and perhaps beyond. They also may depend on future changes in social health insurance arrangements. The retirement benefits are significant and implicitly defined.

Suppose the options in A do not alter the labor inputs. They might, for example, concern choice between two product designs that have essentially the same labor requirements. This suggests the quantity $[C(z) - C(\acute{z})]$ contains no such labor cost term. In this happy circumstance, there is no interest in estimating the cost of labor. The labor cost terms do not vary across $z \in A$. Labor cost is difficult to discern, and constant across the options under consideration. We can frame the decision to take advantage of the irrelevance of labor cost.[11]

---

[10]An equivalent development is to write the cost function in the suggestive format of $C(z) = k + h(z)$. Here k is the portion of $C(z)$ that does not vary with z; h(z) is confined to underlying elements that do vary with z. This implies $h(\acute{z}) = 0$, and $C(z) - C(\acute{z}) = h(z)$.

[11]Frame II' gives a setting where direct labor is irrelevant, because it is fixed (despite the LLA in

The idea, then, is to frame the decision in a way that eases the task of estimating the objective function, estimating the benefits and costs. Relevant cost stresses a parsimonious frame. We also could extend this to "relevant benefit," but will spare the details.

an important caveat

Relevance is a compelling filter. It highlights precisely those details of the circumstance that are important, or relevant, to the analysis. Needless details, by definition, are ignored. The logic appears irrefutable. By now, though, we should know nothing is this easy. So what is the catch?

Review the argument. We began, as usual, with the problem of maximizing $f(z)$ subject to $z \in A$. We then rewrote $f(z)$ as $B(z) - C(z)$. We then reframed the latter as $[C(z) - C(\acute{z})]$. The last step is a straightforward application of the first principle of consistent framing. The first is where everything we said in Chapter 11 began. It must be the middle step!

In that step we simply rewrote $f(z) = B(z) - C(z)$. The difficulty arises when we begin to interpret what $C(z)$ might be.

Some additional notation will help. The key is to distinguish between a decision's outcome and the valuation of that outcome. For discussion purposes, suppose wealth is the central focus in the decision. Let ending wealth $\hat{w}$ consist of initial wealth w plus profit π. Profit depends on our decision. In this setup, then, profit is the outcome of a decision.

Further suppose, as seems natural, we think of profit as revenue (or benefit) less cost. If decision z is taken, let the revenue *outcome* be $r(z)$ and the cost *outcome* be $c(z)$. Profit is $\pi(z) = r(z) - c(z)$ and wealth is $\hat{w} = w + \pi(z)$. Any decision results in some revenue outcome, some cost outcome, and some corresponding wealth outcome. (Yes, cost might be an outcome or an evaluation of an outcome.)

Profit is also likely to be uncertain. This means $r(z)$ and $c(z)$ are random variables. To deal with this we revert to the material in Chapter 4. Under uncertainty, we suppose the objective function takes the form of the expected value of the utility of wealth. Let $U(\hat{w})$ be our utility function. Also let $E[\cdot]$ denote the expected value of whatever is contained within the brackets. This means we write the objective function as

$$f(z) = E[U(\hat{w})] = E[U(w + r(z) - c(z))].$$

Here, $r(z)$ and $c(z)$ are outcomes, and $E[U(\cdot)]$ is the "valuation operator."

Now ask what happens to our relevant cost story as we move from certainty, to uncertainty with risk neutrality, to uncertainty with risk aversion?

---

use). In the present case, labor is not necessarily fixed. The options simply use the same amount of labor in total. So the LLAs might be 100% accurate, yet a variable cost would be irrelevant.

subjective certainty

We naturally assume more wealth is preferred to less wealth. If certainty is present, choice of z will produce a profit outcome of $\pi(z) = r(z) - c(z)$, and a wealth outcome of $w + \pi(z)$. Maximizing utility of wealth is the same as maximizing wealth here; and w is a constant. So we frame the decision in terms of maximizing profit. This means, under certainty, we can treat $f(z) = r(z) - c(z)$ as the objective function. In other words, outcome and decision valuation become the same.

The relevant cost formulation follows immediately. We merely set $B(z) = r(z)$ and $C(z) = c(z)$. In turn, this leads to

$$C(\acute{z}) = \underset{z \in A}{\text{minimum}}\ c(z).$$

The transformed evaluation measure is simply $B(z) - [C(z) - C(\acute{z})]$.

This is simple, because we have backed into a setting where the *objective function* naturally assumes a benefit less cost formulation. Frame II' in our earlier LP odyssey illustrates the use of relevant cost in such a circumstance.

This is also a source of confusion. Under certainty the step between wealth outcomes and their valuation becomes blurred. This invites confusion between the separable evaluation measure of $f(z) = B(z) - C(z)$ and the separable outcome calculation of $w + \pi(z) = w + r(z) - c(z)$.

risk neutrality

Now admit profit is uncertain, but assume risk neutrality. Then, the utility function is linear. We may write it as $U(\hat{w}) = \hat{w} = w + \pi(z)$.

With a linear utility function, the expected utility becomes[12]

$$f(z) = w + E[r(z) - c(z)] = w + E[r(z)] - E[c(z)].$$

Note well: the decision valuation becomes the expected value of the outcome. Valuation and outcome remain unusually close.

We want to write f(z) as some benefit measure less some cost measure. This is easy: simply drop the constant, w, set $B(z) = E[r(z)]$, and set $C(z) = E[c(z)]$.

Maximizing expected utility here is the same as maximizing $B(z) - [C(z) - C(\acute{z})]$. Relevant cost reemerges, albeit in a somewhat different form. We simply work from a base of

$$C(\acute{z}) = \underset{z \in A}{\text{minimum}}\ E[c(z)].$$

---

[12]Recall, the expectation of the sum of two random variables is the sum of their respective expectations.

In this instance relevant cost is the expected value of the outcome cost that varies with the circumstance at hand.

Notice how the valuation operator forges a wedge between $c(z)$ and $C(z)$ here. The cost outcomes are evaluated by their expected value. Relevant cost surfaces in expected value format, not in outcome format.

risk aversion

Strict risk aversion magnifies this schism. Here, the utility function is concave; it exhibits diminishing marginal utility. For example, assume for nonnegative $\hat{w}$ we have $U(\hat{w}) = \sqrt{\hat{w}}$. Also set $w = 0$. This implies

$$f(z) = E\sqrt{\pi(z)} = E\sqrt{r(z) - c(z)} \neq E\sqrt{r(z)} - E\sqrt{c(z)}.$$

Here, even with $w = 0$, there is no natural way to separate $f(z)$ into benefit and cost components.

This means the importance of risk in the cost domain, $c(z)$, depends on risk in the benefit domain, $r(z)$, and vice versa. Put differently, the valuation of the decision cannot be decomposed into separate valuations of the benefit and cost portions of the outcome. The valuation of the $c(z)$ risk depends on the level of $r(z)$, and vice versa. This precludes expressing $f(z)$ in a neat benefit less cost term. The risk valuations interact, so to speak.

In addition, the benefit and cost outcomes may interact. They may be positively correlated, they may be negatively correlated, or they may be uncorrelated. When correlated, we also worry about portfolio effects. The combined risk is not necessarily the summation of the individual risks.

The net result is that, in general, the entire profit spectrum is relevant at this point. We are handicapped in our search for a more parsimonious frame.[13]

example

A numerical illustration will be helpful in reinforcing this point. Suppose we must select between two options. Call them "one" and "two." The profit outcome of option one is certain: it will produce revenue of 175,000 and cost of 80,000 for a profit of $\pi(\text{one}) = 175,000 - 80,000 = 95,000$. Initial wealth is $w = 0$.

The profit outcome of option two is uncertain. With probability .5 it will produce revenue of 125,000 and cost of 75,000, implying a profit of $\pi(\text{two}) = 125,000 - 75,000 = 50,000$. Also with probability .5 it will produce revenue of

---

[13]An exception arises when we have independence between the benefit and cost streams (no portfolio effects) and constant absolute risk aversion (no wealth effects). In this case, separability is always present. It obtains because we have neutralized the two types of interactions that preclude it. Thus, risk neutrality or a negative exponential utility function coupled with independence between the benefit and cost outcomes guarantees a parsimonious frame.

300,000 and cost of 150,000. This implies a profit of π(two) = 300,000 - 150,000 = 150,000.

Thus, our story begins with a specification of options (A = {one, two}) and the profit outcomes each might produce. In turn, the profit outcomes are expressed as revenue less cost, $\pi(z) = r(z) - c(z)$.

Table 12.2 summarizes the specification. Notice the cost and revenue outcomes are perfectly correlated. This is done to keep the example uncluttered.

Table 12.2: Data for Nonseparability Illustration		
option one outcomes		
revenue		175,000
cost		80,000
profit = revenue - cost		95,000
probability		1
option two outcomes		
revenue	125,000	300,000
cost	75,000	150,000
profit = revenue - cost	50,000	150,000
probability	.5	.5
expected values	**option one**	**option two**
$E[r(z)]$	175,000	212,500
$E[c(z)]$	80,000	112,500
$E[\pi(z)]$	95,000	100,000
relevant expected values	**option one**	**option two**
$E[r(z)]$	175,000	212,500
$E[c(z)]$ - 80,000	0	32,500
$E[\hat{\pi}(z)]$	175,000	180,000

Now suppose we are risk neutral. This implies we value the profit outcomes by their expected values. For option one we have:

$$E[\pi(\text{one})] = E[r(\text{one}) - c(\text{one})] = 175,000 - 80,000 = 95,000.$$

For option two we have:

$$\begin{aligned} E[\pi(\text{two})] &= E[r(\text{two}) - c(\text{two})] \\ &= .5(125,000 - 75,000) + .5(300,000 - 150,000) \\ &= .5(50,000) + .5(150,000) = 100,000. \end{aligned}$$

Under the risk neutrality criterion, we prefer option two.

These calculations are reexpressed in Table 12.2, with a focus on expected revenue less expected cost. Notice how the profit outcome is naturally expressed as revenue less cost. In turn, the risk neutral valuation operator gives us a derivative valuation expression of *expected* revenue less *expected* cost. This provides $B(z) = E[r(z)]$ and $C(z) = E[c(z)]$.

A frame based on relevant cost readily surfaces. We have respective expected costs of $E[c(one)] = 80,000$ and $E[c(two)] = 112,500$. The minimum is $C(\acute{z}) = 80,000$. Now calculate $B(z) - [C(z) - C(\acute{z})]$ for each option.

$$B(one) - [C(one) - 80,000] = 175,000 - 0 = 175,000; \text{ and}$$
$$B(two) - [C(two) - 80,000] = 212,500 - [112,500 - 80,000]$$
$$= 212,500 - 32,500 = 180,000.$$

Notice the valuation of option two exceeds that of option one by 5,000, whether we use the original or the relevant cost frame. Further notice the relevant cost calculation is based on $C(z)$, not $c(z)$. Do not confuse the two cost expressions. We distinguish outcomes and their valuations. Relevant cost arises when we (1) express the valuation of the outcomes in benefit less cost terms and (2) focus the analysis on those elements of the valuation cost, $C(z)$, that vary with the options at hand.

The relevant cost of option one is 0, while the relevant cost of option two is 32,500. These cost measures are based on the elements of $E[c(z)]$ that vary with the choices at hand. They have, so to speak, been passed through the valuation operator.

Now try the same thing, but under an assumption of risk aversion. This implies that we will evaluate the options via the expected utility of their respective wealth outcomes. For this purpose, and with $w = 0$, we use $U(w + \pi) = \sqrt{\pi}$.

We have the following:

$$E\sqrt{\pi(one)} = \sqrt{95,000} = 308.221; \text{ and}$$
$$E\sqrt{\pi(two)} = .5\sqrt{50,000} + .5\sqrt{150,000} = 305.453.$$

Under this criterion (i.e., $f(z)$) we prefer one to two. Option two offers a higher expected value, but is risky. The risk is not worth the gain in expected value.[14]

What about relevant cost? This is problematic. We cannot write our evaluation measure $E\sqrt{\pi}$ as $B(z) - C(z)$, other than by setting $C(z) = 0$ or by setting $B(z) = 0$. The entire spectrum of profit outcomes is used by the utility measure to evaluate the decision. Separability is absent. The notion of relevant cost is inapplicable, since we are unable to begin with a separable $f(z)$ function.

Consider what happens when we forge ahead and attempt to prune our decision problem of any irrelevant cost, yet acknowledge risk aversion. Examine Table 12.2 again. Under risk neutrality, we identified $C(\acute{z}) = 80,000$. Why not remove this amount from the analysis? That is, why not use the revenue less relevant cost outcomes in our analysis?

Naively, we have the following expected utility calculations, that show a preference for the second option:

---

[14] In this case we would gladly trade option two (if we were saddled with it) for about 93,301.

$$E\sqrt{\pi(\text{one})} \;=\; \sqrt{95,000 + 80,000} \;=\; 418.330; \text{ and}$$

$$E\sqrt{\pi(\text{two})} \;=\; .5\sqrt{50,000 + 80,000} \;+\; .5\sqrt{150,000 + 80,000} \;=\; 420.069.$$

Our error is in not understanding changing attitudes toward risk. Removing 80,000 from each cost outcome increases each profit outcome by 80,000. This means each utility evaluation is done for a larger profit. But the $\sqrt{\pi}$ function is a particular type of utility measure. As π becomes larger it becomes less concave. It exhibits decreasing risk aversion. So by naively adding 80,000 to each apparent profit, by converting to a relevant cost story, we have treated the inherent risk and return tradeoff with a less noxious view of risk. Here we wind up with a decision reversal.

This is why we stress risk aversion requires the entire spectrum of profit outcomes to assess the desirability of the various options. The objective function of expected utility does not separate in this case.[15] This implies all costs and revenues are relevant under risk aversion, except in special circumstances.[16]

Should we conclude relevant cost is a useless idea? Of course not. Many choices are safely analyzed without extensive treatment of interactions. The professional manager routinely trades off streamlined analyses for more inclusive yet more complex ones. These tradeoffs, in turn, are not haphazard. They are informed by experience and circumstance. The inability of relevant cost to accommodate changing attitudes toward risk or possible dependence between revenue and cost uncertainties is one factor that bears on this tradeoff.

sunk cost

Relevant cost and accounting library procedures often intersect, giving rise to a phenomenon of sunk cost. To set the stage, suppose we are working under risk

---

[15]To be pithy, we should have evaluated these profit outcomes based on relevant cost using a utility measure with a domain of $\pi - 80,000$ and not simply the relevant cost adjusted profit. Of course, this is just another way of saying the utility measure does not separate.

It is also unclear what we mean by relevant cost when profit is uncertain and risk aversion is present. We worked the erroneous calculation using the 80,000 datum derived in the risk neutral setting. One might also focus on $c(z)$ rather than $C(z)$ for this purpose, and conclude the relevant cost of one is 5,000 and the relevant cost of two is 0 or 75,000. Try this in problem 11 at the end of the chapter.

[16]Again, special cases arise. Constant absolute risk aversion arises when the attitude toward risk is everywhere constant. Here $U(\hat{w}) = -exp(-r\hat{w})$. So adding 80,000 to each profit figure in such a case would have no effect on the analysis, as $-exp(-r\hat{w}+k) = -exp(k)exp(-r\hat{w}) = \beta U(\hat{w})$ for any constant k. Likewise, if all of the outcomes could be ranked by first order stochastic dominance, our choice of utility measure would be irrelevant (as long as we preferred more to less). We should also acknowledge more subtle aspects of risk aversion that are associated with taxes. Progressive taxes and risk neutrality are equivalent to risk aversion in pretax dollars. The reason is the progressive tax schedule acts like decreasing marginal utility.

neutrality or certainty conditions. The objective function has been separated, so we correctly speak of $f(z) = B(z) - C(z)$. Further suppose we have converted this to a relevant cost frame of $B(z) - [C(z) - C(ź)]$.

A useful place to look to specify the relevant cost term, $[C(z) - C(ź)]$, is the accounting library. What costs have been reported for similar projects in the past? Which of these are relevant in the present case?

Now the distinctions stressed in Chapters 2 and 3 should be remembered. The accounting library is based on particular recognition rules and accrual procedures. The resulting portrayals depart in important ways from those we would use for decision making purposes. Most obviously, when we encounter a decision problem we are thinking about revenues and costs that *will* or might occur. The accounting library contains accounting revenues and accounting costs that *have* occurred.

Suppose we have purchased our manufacturing equipment. Straight line depreciation is used, amounting to 10,000 per month. At present, we are not using all our manufacturing equipment. The idle equipment cannot be sold or leased to others in the short-run. We either use it ourselves or it will be idle. In contemplating our short-run options, the manufacturing capacity is a fixed resource.

It is common practice to call the monthly depreciation charge a sunk cost in this case. Somewhat casually, a sunk cost is a cost that arises from a previous decision that is irrelevant to a present decision. In this case, the equipment decision occurred at a prior time. This decision causes a pattern of equipment costs through time. Later, the equipment cost may be irrelevant. This is a sunk cost, at that later time.

This notion of a cost being somehow "sunk" is associated with its apparent inevitability. We cannot undo the prior decision; its future consequences are irrelevant to future choices.

Sunk costs are potentially useful clues while constructing a relevant cost frame of a decision. We begin with a decision opportunity. We frame the decision in terms of revenue and relevant costs. Some terms in $C(ź)$, the "irrelevant cost," may be associated with sunk costs.[17]

Why the guarded expression "associated with sunk costs?" In a relevant cost frame $[C(z) - C(ź)]$ is used to evaluate options; it is a component of our objective function. $r(z)$ and $c(z)$ are revenue and cost outcomes, as opposed to their evaluation. Important clues to future outcomes reside in the pattern of past outcomes. Past outcomes are recorded in the accounting library. A sunk cost is a label placed on a cost datum that has or will arise in the accounting library. We must move from the library, to the cost outcome, to the decision evaluation to tightly forge the link between sunk cost and relevant cost.[18]

---

[17]Sunk costs also may carry reputation effects. Cutting our losses may, for example, suggest to others that we made an error in judgment in the first place. Likewise, a commitment to make a series of payments may affect our attitude toward risk in subsequent decisions.

[18]We should now find a review of incremental cost perfunctory. Let $f(z) = B(z) - C(z)$. Select

Framing Consistencies

Our exploration has now taken on a different flavor. We began by reframing a decision problem. This problem was presented as maximizing $f(z)$ subject to $z \in A$. A and $f(z)$ were given. Gradually, though, we have merged into the reverse process of engineering the decision analysis. This is evident in the sunk cost story, where we described a process that moved from the accounting library to an eventual specification of the decision's objective function, $f(z)$. Theory has given way to art.

Two related issues now arise. One centers on tradeoffs of accuracy for ease of specification in defining the decision opportunity. Uncertainty is more difficult to deal with than presumed certainty. Risk neutrality is more friendly than risk aversion. (Recall the difficulty we encountered with the relevant cost notion!) A slightly inaccurate description may ease the burden of analysis.

Do we make such trade offs? Certainly. Deciding whether to put two or three ice cubes in a glass of water is treated in perfunctory fashion. Deciding whether to relocate at the opposite end of the country is often treated with extreme care. In the latter case we also struggle with questions of what is important in the choice and what risks we might encounter.

Some decisions are made in such routine fashion we hardly recognize the process. Others are treated to excruciating structuring, thought, and dissonance. Yet others are in between.

The second issue centers on identifying the decision opportunity. Where do the set A and objective $f(z)$ come from? A good manager, we have stressed, recognizes opportunities and knows where to concentrate the search for a good resolution. (This is set A_1 in our opportunity cost paradigm.) The process ranges from highly cognitive to highly formalized, almost ritualistic.

Planning for next year's production of a seasonal consumer product has an air of ritual. The planning task arises periodically, the organization attacks the task with a routine procedure, some measures are always constructed (such as market share and contribution margin), and some imponderables remain in view if not in the formal analysis (such as competitive developments). In contrast, a new product opportunity might arise at random. Assessing market conditions and production cost might lack the benefit of related experiences. Forging a decision team that includes marketing and manufacturing experts might be called for. Questions of trading off short-run and long-run performance might arise.

Regardless, recognizing an opportunity to act, settling on an objective function, and engaging the "appropriate" analysis are judgment tasks. Stated differently, the

---

some $z^0 \in A$. Express the objective function in incremental format: $f(z) - f(z^0)$. What is $B(z) - B(z^0)$? What is $C(z) - C(z^0)$? Why have we been careful to do this with the objective function, not the outcomes?

Incremental benefit and cost expressions arise when we subtract $[B(z^0) - C(z^0)]$ from the objective function.

decisions must be recognized and framed. This opens up the study of cognition and behavior. Here we encounter a formidable array of empirical work consistent with the claim individuals are not always reliable inferential machines. Individuals, for example, often fall prey to the use of readily *available* experiences in interpreting various situations. An urban dweller might assess the magnitude of some social ill based on local observations, forgetting that society is stratified.

Likewise, a manager might judge the costliness of a new product relying on the accounting library's product cost statistics for similar products. After all, these are the available data. With sufficient similarity, this probably leads to an informed judgment. Yet, as we have cautioned, circumstance and frame of the decision and accounting procedures in place will be important factors in judging the appropriateness of the inference. Readily available experiences, that is, may cloud or sharpen our insight.

Similarly, individuals often interpret events in light of a *representative* model of what the situation should look like. The so-called gambler's fallacy is an example. Suppose a fair coin has been flipped 10 times, resulting in 8 "heads." What is the probability of a "tail" on the next flip? Presuming independence and fairness of the coin, it must be .5. Yet people often say it is above .5, reasoning that in the long-run it must be .5 so we now need more "tails" to even out the pattern.

Our manager might be called on to judge the performance of several new hires. Suppose they are in somewhat similar situations, yet have varying experience. Further suppose it has been uncommon to bring in experienced people. Simply comparing their short-run performance, then, runs the risk of biasing the assessments against the inexperienced.

Individuals are not consistent processors.[19] At the same time, we should recognize institutions (such as periodic planning rituals), team projects, professional development, and the very mix of cognitive activities are important contributors to managerial behavior.[20]

Summary

Decisions may be framed in a wide variety of formats. We are able to move among various frames using three techniques: transforming the objective function,

---

[19]The two tendencies in the above narratives are called the availability and representativeness heuristics.

[20]Thus, a particular accounting library may have a positive or a negative effect on managerial behavior, once it is integrated with the milieu of activities, sources of information, and so on. We also should not conclude the various compensating devices are completely reliable. Nisbett and Ross [1990, page 252] observe as follows: "Between the Age of Enlightenment and the middle of the nineteenth century, thousands and perhaps millions of people died at the hands of physicians whose opportunities to witness empirical covariations between treatments and outcomes did not destroy their confidence in the therapeutic effects of such practices as blood-letting."

engaging in local searches, and reducing the apparent dimensionality by focusing on component searches. Consistently done, one frame is as good as another.

Mixing these three techniques alters the appearance of the reframed decision's objective function. Thinking about this objective function as a benefit less cost expression, we thereby arrive at altered appearances of the benefits and costs. This is why we stress the fundamental point that what we mean by cost depends on circumstance and frame. This is a consequence of our ability to frame a decision analysis in various ways.

Stepping into the art side of the recipe, we encounter the task of recognizing and framing a decision. Here particular cost concepts, such as relevant cost and sunk cost, have proven to be useful. Links to the accounting library now arise, as we browse the library as part of the framing process.

Finally, we recognize the importance of professional skill in the process. We know unaided judgment can fall prey to particular bias patterns. We also know expertise and institutions may compensate for or attenuate these bias patterns.

The professional manager mixes art and theory. Cost assessment for decision making is no exception.

Bibliographic Notes

Clark [1923] and Coase [1968] are major influences in our understanding of cost. Interactions among products and decisions is an important issue here. The option value of capacity explored in Chapter 10 is but one illustration. Banker, Datar, and Kekre [1988] focus on this theme, with an emphasis on relevant cost. Amershi, Demski, and Fellingham [1985] study the question of separating one decision from a sequence of decisions, thereby implying a lack of interaction among the decisions. Kanodia, Bushman, and Dickhaut [1989] examine the so-called sunk cost fallacy, but in a setting where the manager's reputation is affected by the sequence of decisions. Fellingham and Wolfson [1985] explore the connection between progressive taxes and risk aversion in pretax outcomes. For the erudite, axiomatic foundations of separable utility measures are explored in Krantz and associates [1971].

Machina [1987] provides an extensive review of rationality in the face of uncertainty, a topic intimately related to our stress on framing. Excellent introductions are available in Dawes [1988] and Nisbett and Ross [1990]. Also see Bell, Raiffa, and Tversky [1988] and Libby [1981].

Problems and Exercises

1.   How does cost allocation arise when we use consistent framing to focus on product revenues and product costs?

2. Sunk costs refer to expenditures or expenditure commitments made in the past that cannot be altered. The sunk cost fallacy refers to someone allowing a sunk cost to influence irrationally a future course of action. Stated differently, a standard admonition is that sunk costs should not affect a decision. What principle of consistent framing supports this conclusion?

3. There is no necessary connection between relevant cost and a product's variable cost in the accounting library. Carefully explain.

4. *framing and shadow prices*

Return to the setting of Table 12.1. Frames [I] and [II] provide shadow prices, indeed the same shadow prices, for the capacity constraints while frame [III] offers no such measure. Carefully explain.

5. *framing and marginal cost*

Return to the setting summarized in Table 12.1. Change the selling price of the second product from 152 to 153 per unit. Determine the marginal cost of the first product in each of the three frames. Why, in frame III and only in frame III, does the marginal cost of the first product depend on the selling price of the second product?

6. *framing and marginal cost*

Return to the setting of frames [I'] and [II'] in the text where factor z_1 was fixed at 12,000. Suppose this implies factor z_3 is "80% fixed" in the sense z_3 is fixed at $.8(2)(12,000) = 19,200$ and additional acquisition of this factor must satisfy a lower bound of $.2(2q_1 + 4q_2)$ if production of q_1 and q_2 is to be feasible. (Think of this as some of the z_3 consumption varies with z_1, and the remainder with output.) So the last constraint in [I'] should read $z_3 \geq .2(2q_1 + 4q_2)$ instead of $z_3 \geq 2q_1 + 4q_2$. Locate an optimal production plan, using each of the three frames. Summarize your cost calculations in a table similar to Table 12.1.

7. *framing inconsistencies in incremental analysis*

Central Hospital,[21] managed by Ralph, is contemplating the sale of its renal dialysis unit to a group of physicians who have offered to maintain the current level of service and to employ the present dialysis staff, while moving the facility to an adjacent location. Patients would be unaffected. Ralph's cost analysis reveals the following annual cost structure:

salaries and wages in dialysis unit	525,000;
other direct costs	390,000; and

---

[21]Inspired by a Yale School of Nursing case, "The Dialysis Unit of Brother Ellis Hospital," written by J. Hays and D. Diers.

indirect costs   810,000.

8,000 treatments are being performed; and the hospital is reimbursed at the rate of 140 per treatment. Ralph figures the hospital is losing quite a bit here (605,000 per year) and is anxious to see the unit taken over by the group of physicians.

The indirect costs reflect a variety of items, allocated in customary fashion. Typical items are building depreciation (square feet), employee benefits (hours), housekeeping (square feet), laundry (pounds of laundry), dietary (meals served), and nursing administration (specific identification).

What principle or principles of consistent framing has Ralph violated in analyzing the physician group's buyout offer?

8. *framing and cost allocation*

Return to Chapter 8, problem 11. Carefully document the use of consistent framing in that setting.

9. *framing and simultaneous cost allocation*

Return to Chapter 8, problem 14, part [f]. Carefully document the use of consistent framing in that setting.

10. *attributable cost*

Ralph produces and distributes two products. The various LLAs combine to imply a cost curve of $F + v_1q_1 + v_2q_2$. A perplexing problem is how to allocate the "fixed" costs to the period and products. Shillinglaw [1963] proposes the notion of attributable cost. The idea is to base unit costs on what costs would be avoided if a product were discontinued "without changing the supporting organization structure." How does this relate to sunk cost, to relevant cost, and to incremental cost?

11. *certain equivalents and relevant cost*

Return to the setting of Table 12.2, but now assume the utility measure, defined over wealth $\hat{w}$, is given by $U(\hat{w}) = -exp(-r\hat{w})$, with r = .00001.

a]   Evaluate the two options and determine their certain equivalents.

b]   Now reexpress the two options in terms of revenue less relevant cost. Evaluate them using the same utility measure. (Why is this an acceptable frame?) Determine their certain equivalents and relate them to those you determined in [a] above.

12. *certain equivalents and relevant cost*

This is a continuation of the above problem. Retain the noted exponential utility measure, but now assume the revenue and cost events in Table 12.2, for option two, are independent and equally likely events. This gives four equally likely events. Repeat your analysis in part [a] of the above problem.

13. *interactions among decisions*

Consider a setting in which Ralph is risk averse with utility function for total cash of U(total cash) = [total cash]$^{\frac{1}{2}}$. At present Ralph has 1,000 cash in hand, so we have U(x) = [1,000 + x]$^{\frac{1}{2}}$, where x denotes cash flow from whatever decision must be made.

a] First, consider an option to pay 1,000 up front in exchange for something we will call lottery L. The holder of lottery L will receive 3,000 with probability .5 and 0 with probability .5. Verify that Ralph is not too interested in such a gamble, given its price of 1,000.

b] Second, suppose Ralph already owns (actually, inherits without having to pay the 1,000 for) such a lottery and is contemplating the purchase of a second. Thus, if the additional lottery is not acquired, Ralph's cash will total 1,000 + x = 1,000 + 3,000 if good luck prevails and 1,000 + 0 otherwise. Verify that Ralph is not too interested in purchasing the second L lottery if its outcomes are independent of those of the original lottery, but is very interested if its outcomes are perfectly negatively correlated with those of the original lottery. (In the latter case the total cash will be 1,000 + x = 1,000 + 3,000 - 1,000.)

c] Finally, what does this tell you about the importance of Ralph's current stock of lotteries in evaluating yet another lottery?

14. *interactions and cost benefit framing*

Return to part [b] of the above problem. Frame the question of whether to purchase lottery L in incremental terms, by focusing on Ralph's certain equivalent. Consider the case where the existing and new lottery outcomes are independent. If the additional lottery is not acquired, Ralph's certain equivalent is 2,250; if it is acquired, the certain equivalent drops to 2,185.66. The incremental certain equivalent is -64.34.

In turn, this can be thought of as an expected benefit of .5(3,000) + .5(0) = 1,500, an acquisition cost of 1,000 and a "risk cost" of 564.34. So the net gain is 1,500 - 1,000 - 564.34.

a] Repeat the above calculation for the case of perfect negative correlation between the lottery outcomes.

b] Why does the "risk cost" component of the calculation depend on the correlation between the existing and proposed lottery outcomes?

15. *interactions and stochastic dominance*

One of the concerns in framing decisions is interactions across decisions. Ralph is trying to secure an essential service from one of three possible subcontractors. The total acquisition cost is uncertain. The cost possibilities and probabilities are summarized below.

	100	600	900
first source	.10	.20	.70
second source	.20	.20	.60
third source	.30	.00	.70

Any randomness with the acquisition cost is independent of any other randomness in the setting. Let R denote the net revenue to Ralph exclusive of acquisition cost. Also let x denote the net wealth associated with all other activities in Ralph's domain. So Ralph's utility evaluation is denoted U(x+R-C), where C is the above noted acquisition cost.

a] Suppose we know nothing about R or x and nothing about Ralph's utility function except more is preferred to less. It then turns out we can immediately dismiss the first source. To see this, look at the difference between Ralph's expected utility using the first versus the second source, for any x and R combination:

$$(.10-.20)U(x+R-100) + (.20-.20)U(x+R-600) + (.70-.60)U(x+R-900).$$

Notice the first source uncertainty puts more weight on the bad outcome (a cost of 900). The second source can be viewed as taking the first source's cost uncertainty and moving some probability weight from a bad to a good outcome. This is called first order stochastic dominance.

Now suppose we know x is rather large, but constant and R is 900. Also suppose U(·) is a square root function. With x so large Ralph is effectively risk neutral in the sourcing decision. What, under risk neutrality, is the best choice? Contrast this with the case where x is zero.

b] Why is it, then, interactions with other decisions are irrelevant in comparing the first and second sources here, but not in comparing the second and third sources?

16. *sunk cost*

Suppose you sign a one-year apartment lease; the lease cannot be broken and you cannot sublet the apartment. You must, and intend to, pay the rent. Two days after moving in, you are offered a job in a different city. A common reaction at this point is "I find the new job very interesting, but cannot break my lease." Does this reflect the sunk cost fallacy?

17. *sunk cost and interactions*

Ralph purchased 200 units of a special catalyst. The market for this catalyst has since collapsed, and it cannot be sold; it can be disposed of for zero incremental cost. Ralph paid 1,000 per unit for the catalyst.

a] The catalyst can be used to produce any feasible combination of two products. Denote their respective quantities $x \geq 0$ and $y \geq 0$. A unit of either product requires a unit of the catalyst, so the overall constraint is $x + y \leq 200$. The net gain, exclusive of any catalyst cost, from a feasible x and y combination is $240x - x^2 + 200y - y^2$.

Determine Ralph's optimal use of the 200 units. Is the 1,000 per unit acquisition cost a sunk cost?

b]   Now frame the analysis to focus explicitly on units of x. Let the incremental profit be measured by $240x - x^2 - cx$, where c should be interpreted as the cost of a unit of the catalyst. Find a value of c, a cost per unit of catalyst, such that maximizing this incremental profit measure will lead Ralph to the optimal choice.

c]   Carefully explain how a material whose cost is sunk turns out to have a strictly positive cost in part [b].

18. *sunk cost*
    Ralph has a reputation for timing, for knowing when to plunge into a new market, when to rebalance an investment portfolio, and when to engage in a product promotion. Ralph has just invested 100,000 dollars in a computer network and, upon installation, has discovered a work station product that completely dominates the new system. The dominance is so complete the new network should be replaced immediately. Ralph hesitates, on grounds the cherished reputation will be tarnished when word leaks out that 100,000 was wasted. Is Ralph's hesitation an encounter with the sunk cost fallacy?

19. *learning by doing*
    Ralph faces a choice problem with three equally likely states. You might think of these as reflecting the state of the economy or the product market's acceptance of a new product design. Four possible acts are available, with the following cash outcome possibilities:

	state 1	state 2	state 3
act 1	0	0	0
2	0	0	100
3	-9,000	-9,000	900
4	100	100	100

The catch is Ralph must (i) pick one of the four acts, (ii) observe the cash outcome, and (iii) pick from among the four acts again. Whatever state obtains is constant across the choices. Thus, if act 2 is picked and an outcome of 100 materializes, Ralph knows state 3 is present in the subsequent choice.

a]   Assume Ralph is risk neutral and seeks to maximize the sum of the expected cash flow. Determine Ralph's optimal behavior.

b]   How does Ralph use the initial outcome in your solution? Is it merely a pile of cash or does it convey information as well?

13

Extraction from the Accounting Library

In this chapter we integrate the themes of decision making and the accounting library. We concentrate on extracting cost estimates from the accounting library that are useful for decision making. More specifically, we concentrate on estimating an LLA for a particular cost category. As our study expands in later chapters to include control problems, we will see this theme also embraces cost estimates that are useful in the design and operation of a control system.

Our study naturally assumes we have identified and framed a decision in a format that calls for estimation of benefit and cost outcomes. It also assumes we have an accounting library that can speak to the estimation task at hand.

We begin by posing the classical statistics question of estimating a linear model. Regression techniques will then be used to convert a set of data into estimates of the coefficients of the linear model. Estimating an LLA should come to mind. With this background, we turn to a number of issues in using data in the accounting library to estimate LLAs. A central concern is whether the accounting treatment manifest in the accounting library should be considered in the estimation exercise.

It is also important to recognize our exploration is pragmatic. We will rely on prior exposure to statistical methods. We also will not apologize for injecting a non-Bayesian procedure to convert data in the accounting library into an estimate of cost behavior.[1] Our purpose is to deepen understanding of the accounting library. Classical estimation of a cost function using data from the accounting library is the vehicle we use. An ancillary purpose, of course, is to explore the use of classical statistics in cost estimation.

Classical Estimation of Linear Models

To fix intuition, suppose we want to develop an LLA for some overhead category. We want to relate the overhead cost in question to some explanatory variable or variables. We also want to acknowledge some randomness in the setting. This randomness might arise from measurement error, from some misspecification of the exact relationship, or from some inherently chance events that affect the overhead cost.

---

[1]Recall the Bayesian modeling of information in Chapter 4. We specify priors and a likelihood function. We then pour data into Bayes' Theorem and out pops our updated opinions. A Bayesian finds great difficulty with classical statistics; they "make sense" only when one begins with a totally diffuse prior. Of course, the serious Bayesian has access to Bayesian statistical procedures. We will be more modest. The important point is we continually encounter the question of factoring accounting treatment into our estimation procedure. Whether we are casual, subjective, highly classical, Bayesian, or some mixture we will have to confront this issue.

For the sake of discussion, suppose we will use two explanatory variables. We write our generic model as follows:

$$y_t = \beta_0 + \beta_1 x_{1t} + \beta_2 x_{2t} + \varepsilon_t. \qquad [m]$$

Think of t as denoting period t and y_t as denoting overhead in period t.[2] x_{1t} is the level of the first explanatory variable in period t, say direct labor dollars. x_{2t} is the level of the second explanatory variable in period t, say machine hours. ε_t is some random disturbance term. β_0, β_1, and β_2 are *constants* that we want to estimate. β_0 is the intercept and β_1 and β_2 are the slopes of the LLA we seek to estimate or construct.

Specialized terminology arises here. We call y_t the dependent variable and x_{1t} and x_{2t} the independent variables. y_t, so to speak, depends on the independent variables, as characterized by the model [m].

Next, suppose we have some observations of (y_t, x_{1t}, x_{2t}) for t = 1, 2, ..., n periods. Think of this as a sample of size n from the process that generates overhead. Examine Table 13.1. We have n = 16 observations of (y_t, x_{1t}, x_{2t}). The task is to convert these observations into a specific version of model [m].

Now, if the random disturbance terms were always zero, we would only need three observations to estimate the model. We have three unknowns, the intercept and the two slopes. Writing the model down with three data points, i.e., three (y_t, x_{1t}, x_{2t}) triples, is all we require to figure out the intercepts and slopes.[3]

For example, suppose we assume $\varepsilon_t = 0$ and use the first three observations in Table 13.1. This gives us the following three equations in three unknowns:

$$868,743 = \beta_0 + 9,069\beta_1 + 1,131\beta_2,$$
$$758,425 = \beta_0 + 8,413\beta_1 + 1,057\beta_2, \text{ and}$$
$$831,269 = \beta_0 + 9,773\beta_1 + 879\beta_2.$$

The solution is $\beta_0 \approx -707,149$, $\beta_1 \approx 115$, and $\beta_2 \approx 470$. In this happy case the LLA would be $OV_t \approx -700,000 + 115x_{1t} + 470x_{2t}$.

Of course, a nontrivial ε_t term presents an embarrassing difficulty. We must confront the question of how "reliable" our estimates are, given they are surely affected to some unobservable degree by the ε_t realizations. Selecting a different set of observations can lead to dramatically different estimates of the LLA. For

---

[2] Data come in time series format, cross section format, or some combination thereof. Time series data are observations on the same process through time. Cross section data are observations on distinct processes at the same point in time. An example might be overhead versus direct labor cost observations at various branch operations, all drawn from the same time period. Our discussion will emphasize time series data.

[3] This assumes the observations give us three linearly independent equations. This issue will come up shortly.

example, using the last three data points in Table 13.1 gives us an LLA of $OV_t \approx$ $-125{,}000 + 90x_{1t} + 140x_{2t}.$[4]

Table 13.1: Data for Initial Estimation Exercises			
observation t	y_t	x_{1t}	x_{2t}
1	868,743	9,069	1,131
2	758,425	8,413	1,057
3	831,269	9,773	879
4	810,850	8,935	851
5	924,473	10,654	1,227
6	933,346	11,889	1,319
7	853,018	10,706	905
8	875,034	11,047	849
9	878,518	9,065	1,164
10	885,175	9,324	1,019
11	844,283	8,595	1,131
12	857,703	10,260	921
13	889,871	9,908	1,208
14	790,301	8,841	1,067
15	918,588	10,467	972
16	859,402	9,505	1,149

Why not expand the sample size beyond n = 3, and use formal statistical procedures to estimate the intercept and slopes? To do this we must say something about the random disturbance term. For this purpose we will assume it is drawn from a Normal distribution, with zero mean and constant variance, σ^2. We also will assume the error terms are independent. In short, we assume the error terms are independent, identically distributed (or *iid*) random variables, with $\varepsilon_t \sim N(0;\sigma^2)$. (This latter, handy notation is read: random variable ε_t follows a Normal distribution, with mean 0 and variance σ^2.)

Notice our estimation task has now expanded. We have four parameters to estimate: intercept β_0, slopes β_1 and β_2, and variance σ^2. Classical statistics approaches this task with a set of assumptions and a set of data. The assumptions

---

[4]More precisely, we would find $\beta_0 \approx -126{,}329.$, $\beta_1 \approx 87$, and $\beta_2 \approx 138$. This theme of assuming $\varepsilon_t = 0$ is the central feature of the so-called "hi-lo" approach to LLA estimation. Suppose we are trying to fit a model with a single independent variable. This means we want to estimate an intercept and one slope. Two equations in two unknowns are what we need. Given a set of data, pick one point with the largest value of the independent variable and the other with the smallest value of the independent variable. Set up the two equations with two unknowns and solve them. The "hi-lo" algorithm selects the two data points to use.

are that the data are drawn from the model in [m] above, along with the proviso the error terms are *iid* with $\varepsilon_t \sim N(0;\sigma^2)$. The process that generates the data is assumed to be as modeled, with constant though unknown parameters of β_0, β_1, β_2, and σ^2. Do not lose sight of the fact we assume model [m], with constant though unknown parameters, holds throughout the estimation exercise.

the easiest case

The easiest case is when we know some parameters. To set the stage and ground our intuition, suppose we know $\beta_1 = \beta_2 = 0$. x_{1t} and x_{2t} are superfluous. Our model collapses to $y_t = \beta_0 + \varepsilon_t$.

The import of assuming the error terms are *iid* with $\varepsilon_t \sim N(0;\sigma^2)$ should be apparent. This implies y_t follows a Normal distribution with mean β_0 and variance σ^2. Estimation in such a setting is a routine exercise. We estimate β_0 with the sample mean. In turn, the sampling distribution for this estimator follows a Normal distribution if we know the variance.[5] Alternatively, if we must estimate σ^2 with the sample data as well, it follows a *t* distribution (with n - 1 degrees of freedom). Knowing the sampling distribution opens the door to hypothesis tests and confidence interval statements.

It will be useful later to recast this estimation procedure in a slightly arcane way. Let the estimate of β_0 be denoted a. Suppose we find a by minimizing the sum of the squared errors:

$$\min_a SS(a) = SS(a^*) = \min_a \Sigma_t [y_t - a]^2.$$

Differentiation provides a first order condition of $-2\Sigma_t [y_t - a] = 0$. This implies Σy_t - na = 0, or

$$a^* = (1/n)\Sigma_t y_t = \bar{y}.$$

In other words, the minimum squared error criterion provides the sample mean, $\bar{y} = \Sigma y_t/n$, is our best estimate of the unknown parameter β_0.

confidence intervals

Suppose we have the n = 16 observations of y_t listed in Table 13.1. Solving the above minimum squared error problem gives us $a^* = \bar{y} = 861,200$. This is our answer to minimizing the sum of the squared errors in the given data set.

Now assume the observations in Table 13.1 are a random sample from some population. Each observation comes from the model $y_t = \beta_0 + \varepsilon_t$. The ε_t are *iid*, each drawn from some distribution with mean zero. In other words, we have a random sample from some population with unknown mean β_0.

---

[5]In this case we have $\bar{y} \sim N(\beta_0;\sigma^2/n)$.

It now turns out our best estimator of β_0 is the sample mean, $\bar{y} = 861,200$. This estimate is best in the sense the sample mean is an unbiased and efficient estimator of the population mean. Take repeated independent samples of size n from the population. Compute the mean for each such sample. The mean is called the "test statistic" of the experiment. The mean of the sampling distribution of this test statistic is β_0. Therefore, we call $\bar{y}$ an unbiased estimator of β_0. In addition, among all unbiased estimators, the variance of the $\bar{y}$ sampling distribution is the smallest. So we call $\bar{y}$ an efficient estimator of β_0.[6] Now invoke our assumption that $\varepsilon_t \sim N(0;\sigma^2)$. (This is equivalent to the assumption the random variable $y_t \sim N(\beta_0;\sigma^2)$.) This allows us to make probabilistic statements about our estimate of β_0. Suppose we know σ^2. Then a $(1 - \alpha)\%$ confidence interval estimate of β_0 is given by

$$\bar{y} \pm z_{\alpha/2}\sigma/\sqrt{n}$$

where $z_{\alpha/2}$ is the value of the standardized normal variate that leaves probability $\alpha/2$ in each tail.[7]

This is readily illustrated with the data in Table 13.1. Suppose we know $\sigma = 56,844$.[8] With $\bar{y} = 861,200$, we have a 95% confidence interval estimate of

$$861,200 \pm 1.96(56,844)/\sqrt{16} \approx 861,200 \pm 27,900.$$

Conversely, what if we do not know σ? We then use the sample to estimate both β_0 and σ. Here, however, our test statistic is no longer Normally distributed, and we invoke the *t* distribution. Let S be the sample standard deviation:

$$S = \left[\sum_t [y_t - \bar{y}]^2/(n-1) \right]^{\frac{1}{2}}.$$

Also let $t_{\alpha/2;n-1}$ be the *t* variate with n - 1 degrees of freedom that leaves $\alpha/2$ probability weight in each tail. Our confidence interval for β_0 is now computed as

$$\bar{y} \pm t_{\alpha/2;n-1}S/\sqrt{n}$$

Using the data in Table 13.1, we find S = 47,490. A 95% confidence interval (where $t_{.025;15} = 2.131$) is

$$861,200 \pm 2.131(47,490)/4 \approx 861,200 \pm 25,300.$$

---

[6]Notice we are trying to estimate β_0 without specifying what we want to do with that estimate. This means we must import exogenous criteria to sort among alternate estimates. Classical statistics uses such notions as unbiased and efficient for this purpose.

[7]Thus, $z_t \sim N(0;1)$ and $z_{\alpha/2}$ is such that the probability of $|z| \geq z_{\alpha/2} = \alpha$. For a 95% confidence interval, we have $z_{.05/2} = 1.96$. Also recall the basic idea of a confidence interval. If we repeat the estimation procedure many, many times, $(1 - \alpha)\%$ of the resulting confidence intervals will contain β_0.

[8]This strange specification will be rationalized in due course.

Notice this latter confidence interval is tighter. If $\sigma = 56{,}844$, our estimate of S in the latter procedure is too low (due to sampling error). In fact, it is sufficiently lower that, when combined with $t_{\alpha/2;n-1} = 2.131 > 1.960$, we produce the observed tighter interval.

It would, of course, be unusual to know σ. For this reason, the t test is usually associated with estimation and hypothesis testing of the mean of a population. For larger sample sizes, though, we approximate the t distribution with the Normal. For example, $t_{.069/2;15} = t_{.059/2;30} = t_{.056/2;45} = 1.96$.

This brief summary of one sample estimation has its purpose. In particular, notice how assumptions are used to say more about the estimator. Invoke model [m], with the proviso $\beta_1 = \beta_2 = 0$. We then begin by minimizing the sum of the squared errors. At this level we are safe in calling $\bar{y}$ the estimate of β_0 that minimizes the sum of the squared errors in the sample.

Next we further suppose the error terms are *iid*, drawn from some zero mean distribution. This amounts to an assumption we have drawn a random sample from some given, fixed population. β_0 is not changing, and the randomness in each observation comes from the same distribution. We can then say $\bar{y}$ is an unbiased, efficient estimator of the unknown parameter β_0.

Finally, also assume $\varepsilon_t \sim N(0;\sigma^2)$. Not only are the error terms *iid*, they are Normal, with mean 0 and variance σ^2. This allows us to make inferential statements as well. As we said, more assumptions allow us to say more about the quality of our estimator.

specification concerns

This theme of buying insights with assumptions should be familiar. The assumptions, though, should not be taken as benign. Nor should they be taken as automatic. The informed user of statistics always asks what assumptions were employed in the exercise, and what happens to the tentative conclusions if these assumptions are violated.

This extended exercise of worrying about the assumptions goes under the name of *specification analysis*. We always ask and worry about how well the environment of the test matches the assumptions of the test. Is the world really as friendly as a Normal population and *iid* errors?

Surely the variations about the mean need not be Normal. They also need not be independent. For example, an accounting system might place some elements in the wrong period. Miscellaneous materials might be expensed as acquired. This implies too much material cost is recorded in the period of acquisition and too little in the subsequent period. Independent errors are no longer present.

Specification analysis focuses on testing the assumptions of the statistical procedure. These tests might be casual or sophisticated. On the casual side, we should always plot our data. No excuses. For the record, we plot $y_t - \bar{y}$ in Figure 13.1. Notice their seemingly random nature.[9]

Figure 13.1: Residuals from First Estimation Exercise

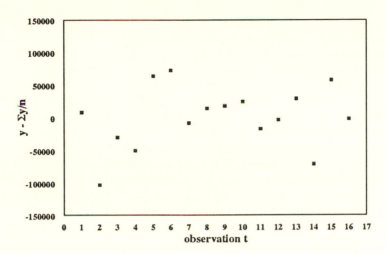

More sophisticated exercises begin by assuming some alternative set of assumptions. Consider normality. If the population is not Normal, what is it? Here we often worry about symmetry and peakedness. The Normal curve is symmetric, and is "peaked" to a particular degree. Common measures of symmetry and peakedness are called, respectively, skewness and kurtosis.

Define the ith moment, in our sample of size n, by

$$M_i = \Sigma_t [y_t - \bar{y}]^i / n$$

for i = 2, 3, 4, and so on. (Deviations about the mean are raised to the ith power for the ith moment.) The coefficient of skewness is defined to be $M_3 / (M_2)^{1.5}$. The intuitive idea is the third moment should be zero if we have a symmetric distribution. Dividing by $(M_2)^{1.5}$ is a normalization convention. The Normal distribution has a coefficient of skewness equal to zero.

Kurtosis is usually measured by $M_4 / (M_2)^2$. The Normal curve has a kurtosis measure of 3. A distribution more peaked than the Normal has a measure in excess of 3, while one less peaked (such as the *t* distribution) has a measure less than 3. Typical software packages report these skewness and kurtosis measures.[10]

---

[9]The typical software package will provide a visual Normality test based on order statistics. The resulting rankit plot should be linear if the assumption of Normality is met.

[10]The sample in Table 13.1 has a coefficient of skewness of -.47 and a kurtosis measure of 2.78.

What happens if we use the above classical procedure to estimate β_0, when our population suffers from skewness or kurtosis?[11] Stated differently, what happens when we incorrectly specify our statistical procedure by assuming normality when it is not present? It turns out, not too much. $\bar{y}$ remains an unbiased estimator of β_0. Difficulties arise with our confidence interval because it assumes a Normal population. But the central limit theorem comes to the rescue. As we increase sample size, the kurtosis effect tends to disappear rapidly, and the skewness effect disappears nearly as quickly.[12] The first piece of folk wisdom, then, is that non-normality does not appear to be too costly in the one sample confidence interval estimation game.[13]

Lack of independence is another story. To dramatize the problem, suppose we take the data in Table 13.1 and merely use each observation twice. This gives an apparent sample size of n = 32. The mean, of course, remains at $\bar{y}$ = 861,200. The sample standard deviation drops slightly, from 47,490 to 46,720.[14] The confidence interval, however, visibly tightens: $\bar{y} \pm t_{\alpha/2;n-1}S/\sqrt{n} \approx 861,200 \pm 16,800$. Of course, this is bogus. We have the original sample of size n = 16, and the correctly calculated confidence interval of 861,200 ± 25,300. We cannot simply write each observation down twice, and pretend we have more information.

This gives the insight to understand lack of independence. Suppose successive error terms are positively correlated. The sample is then not random. Our estimates of the variability of the test statistic's sampling distribution will be understated. We will consequently overstate the reliability of our conclusions. Positive correlation in the ε_t terms will cause us to overstate the confidence of our estimator.

Conversely, what happens when successive error terms are negatively correlated. This has the opposite effect. To take an extreme case, suppose successive errors are perfectly negatively correlated. This implies $\varepsilon_t + \varepsilon_{t+1} = 0$. A sample of size n = 2 will be very informative![15]

Nothing alarming arises. The data are consistent with a claim of normality. This is most apparent with the previously mentioned rankit plot.

[11]For the linguists, a kurtosis measure above 3 is called leptokurtic and one below 3 is called platykurtic.

[12]Miller [1986] suggests n = 10 is usually sufficient.

[13]Whether the confidence interval is too broad or too narrow depends on the precise disease we encounter. For example, if the population is more peaked, it will have less weight in the tails than the Normal distribution. This implies our erroneous confidence intervals are too broad. Pulling all of this together, we conclude the *t* test is not too bad in these cases. That does not mean it is efficient. You also should dwell on the fact these glimpses into skewness and kurtosis are statements about the shape of the ε_t distribution. We continue to assume the mean of the ε_t distribution is zero.

[14]We double the original $\Sigma(y_t - \bar{y})^2$, but divide by 31 instead of by 15.

[15]Define $e_t = y_t - \bar{y}$ to be the difference between the actual and estimated observation. This is called

In short, the professional manager knows and uses statistics. This entails knowing which assumptions buy which insights, and what happens to these insights when the assumptions are violated in particular ways.

simple regression

Now return to model [m] and suppose we know $\beta_2 = 0$. Let $y_t = a + bx_{1t}$ be our estimate of $y_t = \beta_0 + \beta_1 x_{1t}$. This invites the following minimum squared error exercise:

$$\min_{a,b} SS(a,b) = SS(a^*,b^*) = \min_{a,b} \Sigma_t \, [y_t - a - bx_{1t}]^2.$$

Differentiation provides first order conditions of (1) $-2\Sigma_t \, [y_t - a - bx_{1t}] = 0$; and (2) $-2\Sigma_t \, x_{1t}[y_t - a - bx_{1t}] = 0$. Statistical packages perform the calculations. Our data in Table 13.1 provide $a^* = 525,110$ and $b^* = 34.37$.[16] This solution suggests an LLA of $OV_t \approx 525,000 + 34.4x_{1t}$.

A natural question to ask is how useful is the independent variable in this minimization exercise? The answer comes in the form of the proverbial r^2. Our first attempt was to ignore the independent variable and minimize $SS(a)$, resulting in $SS(a^*) = \Sigma_t \, [y_t - \bar{y}]^2$. r^2 reports the fractional reduction in this quantity:

$$r^2 = \frac{SS(a^*) - SS(a^*,b^*)}{SS(a^*)} = \frac{\Sigma_t \, [y_1 - \bar{y}]^2 - SS(a^*,b^*)}{\Sigma_t \, [y_1 - \bar{y}]^2}.$$

$0 \leq r^2 \leq 1$. The worst case is no improvement, or $SS(a^*,b^*) = \Sigma[y_t - \bar{y}]^2$. This implies $r^2 = 0$. The best case is $SS(a^*,b^*) = 0$; this implies $r^2 = 1$.

some familiar assumptions

We now embark on a familiar path. Processing a set of data, such as presented in Table 13.1, with the minimum squared error criterion provides a slope and intercept that, literally, minimize $SS(a,b)$ in the given data set. r^2, in turn, provides a

---

an error term. If the ε_t are independent, we expect the correlation between e_t and e_{t-1} to be trivial. This is the case for the data in Table 13.1. The story is different when we engage in our erroneous exercise of writing each observation down twice. Suppose we repeat the data in the table, so $y_t = y_{t+16}$ for t = 1, ..., 16. If you now check the correlation between e_t and e_{t+1} you will discover it is trivial. If you check the correlation between e_t and e_{t+16} you will discover it is far from trivial, as $e_t = e_{t+16}$. This is an important message. To detect correlation among the error terms you must know where to look. We could arrange the data in our bogus exercise so the alarming correlation shows up with a lag of 1, a lag of 16, or some combination.

[16]All we do here is solve two equations in two unknowns. This creates no difficulty if the two equations are independent, which occurs if $\Sigma[x_{1t} - \bar{x}_1]^2 \neq 0$. (Cramer's rule helps to see this.) Intuitively, we must have some variation in the independent variable. Otherwise, it is a constant and we return to the case where we might as well treat β_1 as trivial.

popular summary measure of the usefulness of the independent variable in the minimization exercise.

Now assume the data are drawn from the model in [m], with $\beta_2 = 0$. Further suppose the error terms are zero mean, *iid* random variables. We then know a^* and b^* are unbiased and efficient estimators of, respectively, β_0 and β_1. If we further assume $\varepsilon_t \sim N(0;\sigma^2)$ we can make inferential statements about our estimates of the unknown parameters, or about the value of the dependent variable for some specific value of the independent variable.[17]

To illustrate, a typical summarization of an estimation exercise using the data in Table 13.1 would be

$$y_t = 525,110 + 34.37x_{1t}$$
$$(88,740) \quad (9.03)$$
$$r^2 = .51; \ r_a^2 = .47.$$

The numbers in parentheses are the estimated standard errors of the respective sampling distributions. The sampling distribution of the slope estimator, of b^*, is estimated to have a mean of 34.37 and a standard deviation of 9.03 (given $n = 16$). Also, the estimator follows a t distribution with $n - 2$ degrees of freedom. A 95% confidence interval estimate of β_1 is given by

$$34.37 \pm t_{.05/2;14}(9.03) = 34.37 \pm 2.145(9.03) \approx 34.37 \pm 19.37.$$

Also, an adjusted r^2 is usually reported. Intuitively, we can never worsen the minimum sum of the squared errors by adding additional independent variables. But each such addition requires we estimate another slope parameter. It uses up degrees of freedom. The adjusted measure, r_a^2, compensates for this phenomenon.[18]

specification analysis

Inferential statements of this sort rely on assumptions. Presuming the model [m] is a correct description of the process, we want *iid* error terms with $\varepsilon_t \sim N(0;\sigma^2)$ to bring the full inferential apparatus to bear. Nonnormality results in a story similar to that discussed above.[19] Otherwise, we have special names and special concerns.

---

[17]Hypothesis tests and confidence interval estimates for the parameters are available. Prediction interval estimates for the dependent variable, given some specification of the independent variable, are also available.

[18]Precisely, $r_a^2 = (1 - k)/(n - k) + (n - 1)r^2/(n - k)$, where k is the number of parameters being estimated in the linear expression (1 plus the number of independent variables).

[19]An exception is estimation of the population correlation coefficient. In this case the confidence interval estimate may be sensitive to the presence of nonnormality. A rankit plot of the residuals in our example is consistent with the error terms following a Normal distribution.

The error terms might not be *iid*. σ^2 might vary in some fashion. If so, we say *heteroscedasticity* is present. The error terms might not be independent. If so, we say *autocorrelation* is present.

Autocorrelation and heteroscedasticity are good news, bad news stories. On the positive side, the regression coefficients remain unbiased estimators of the population intercept and slope parameters. Unfortunately, they are not efficient estimators, and the standard errors associated with these estimates become unreliable.

The cardinal rule is always to plot the data. Figure 13.2 summarizes our regression of y on x_1. Notice we have plotted $y_t = 525,110 + 34.37x_{1t}$, for $8,000 \le x_1 \le 12,000$. This encompasses the range of the independent variable in our data set. We interrupt the plot at $x_1 = 8,000$ to remind ourselves we do not have any observations below this point. A parallel comment applies to $x_1 = 12,000$. Further notice the apparent random pattern of the actual (x_{1t}, y_t) points about the regression line.

Figure 13.2: Regression of y on x_1

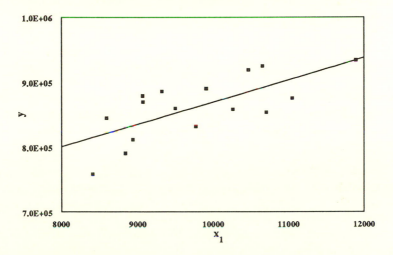

Figure 13.3 plots the residuals, $e_t = y_t - a^* - b^*x_{1t}$, as a function of t. Again notice the lack of any visually apparent pattern. Suppose σ^2 were increasing (or decreasing) with t. The "spread" in Figure 13.3 would then be increasing (or decreasing).[20] Conversely, suppose the error terms were positively correlated. We should then see more clustering of the residuals than is apparent in Figure 13.3.

---

[20]Similarly, a plot of e_t against x_{1t} should be used to question whether σ^2 shows signs of varying with the independent variable.

A common test for autocorrelation is the Durbin Watson test. This test computes a DW statistic of DW $\approx 2 - 2r_{t,t-1}$, where $r_{t,t-1}$ is the simple correlation between e_t and e_{t-1} (for t = 2, ..., n). DW near 2 is good news. DW near 0 is consistent with positive first order autocorrelation. DW near 4 is consistent with negative first order autocorrelation. Our regression has DW = 2.01; this is consistent with a claim of no first order autocorrelation. (Degrees of freedom are important in assessing significance of the DW statistic; so we do not give a rule of thumb to interpret DW. Appropriate tables should be consulted.) Further notice the null hypothesis in the DW test is no first order correlation.

Figure 13.3: Residuals from y = 525,100 + 34.37x$_1$

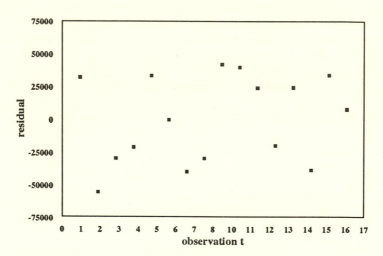

Suppose we invoke regression procedures in the presence of positive autocorrelation. Our slope and intercept estimators will be unbiased (though not efficient). The troublesome part is we will underestimate the sampling error in these estimates. This will result in confidence intervals that are too tight, similar to our earlier discussion of lack of independence. Conversely, suppose we invoke these procedures in the presence of heteroscedasticity. Our slope and intercept estimates remain unbiased, but their standard errors do not. They may be too large or too small, depending on the manner in which σ^2 varies.

The general message is professional responsibility. Assumptions buy us insights, and the professional manager knows the importance of the assumptions, and how their violation should temper the insights.

multiple regression

Now return to the data in Table 13.1, but drop the assumption $\beta_2 = 0$. Regressing y on both independent variables provides the following:

$$y_t = 408,480 + 33.26x_{1t} + 121.06x_{2t}$$
$$(93,820) \quad (7.97) \quad (53.88)$$

$$r^2 = .65; \ r_a^2 = .59.$$

This gives us an LLA of $OV_t \approx 410,000 + 33.3x_{1t} + 121.1x_{2t}$. Interpretation of these results should be a familiar drill.

At the most primitive level, we regard the coefficients in the linear expression as the solution to

$$\min_{a,b_1,b_2} SS(a,b_1,b_2) = \min_{a,b_1,b_2} \Sigma_t [y_t - a - b_1x_{1t} - b_2x_{2t}]^2$$

using the data in Table 13.1. In turn, suppose we assume the model in [m] is a correct description of the process that generated these data and that the error terms are zero mean, *iid* random variables. We then know $a^* = 408,480$, $b_1^* = 33.26$, and $b_2^* = 121.06$ are unbiased and efficient estimators of β_0, β_1, and β_2. Finally, if we further assume $\varepsilon_t \sim N(0;\sigma^2)$, we can make inferential statements about the estimators.

For example, a 95% confidence interval estimate of β_1 is now given by

$$33.26 \pm t_{.05/2;13}(7.97) = 33.26 \pm 2.160(7.97) \approx 33.26 \pm 17.22.$$

This interval is tighter than its counterpart in the simple regression. This occurs because the second independent variable is also useful in explaining the variation in y_t. The net result is the standard error of our β_1 estimator has declined. Notice that degrees of freedom have been adjusted to reflect the fact we are now using the data set to estimate an additional parameter.

Also notice both independent variables are important in the estimated model. To see this, test the hypothesis that $\beta_i = 0$. At $\alpha = 5\%$, we reject both hypotheses in favor of the alternative that $\beta_i \neq 0$.

Again, we use assumptions to buy insights. Assume [m] is the correct model; further assume the error term obeys the classical specification. Then the data are consistent with the claim $\beta_1 > 0$ and $\beta_2 > 0$.

Specification analysis follows our earlier path. We worry about nonnormality, autocorrelation, and heteroscedasticity. Again, there is no substitute for plotting the residuals. Plotting them against time, x_1, x_2, and against the predicted value of the dependent variable reveals no apparent concern with misspecification.[21] A representative plot is provided in Figure 13.4.

An additional specification consideration goes under the name multicollinearity. Suppose there is a mechanical link between the two independent variables, say $x_{2t} = kx_{1t}$ for some nonzero constant k. This means every observation of the second independent variable is simply k times the corresponding observation of the first independent variable. Any attempt to solve for three unknowns in such a case results

---

[21]A rankit plot of the residuals is consistent with a claim of normality. Also, the Durbin-Watson statistic is 2.14, which is consistent with a claim of no first order autocorrelation in the residuals.

in an ill-defined minimum squared error exercise.[22]   We have two, not three, unknowns.

Figure 13.4: Residuals from y = 408,480 + 33.26x$_1$ + 121.06x$_2$

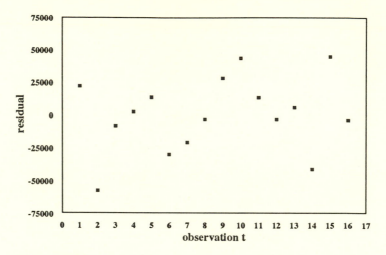

Now suppose x_{1t} and x_{2t} are imperfectly correlated. This is called *multicollinearity*. If the correlation is large, we are close to the above story. Our estimates of the coefficients remain unbiased, but the standard errors of the estimates increase.

The correlation matrix for the data in Table 13.1 is as follows:

	y	x$_1$	x$_2$
y	1.0000		
x$_1$	0.7130	1.0000	
x$_2$	0.4143	0.0620	1.0000

where, for example, 0.7130 is the correlation between y and x_1. (Recall, the unadjusted r^2 in the regression of y on x_1 was .51 = $(.713)^2$.) The correlation between x_1 and x_2 is .06, and indicates no multicollinearity in our regression.[23] There is no statistical relationship between our two independent variables.

---

[22]Differentiating SS(a,b$_1$,b$_2$) with respect to each of the three coefficients gives us a system of three equations in three unknowns: (1) $-2\Sigma[y_t - a - b_1x_{1t} - b_2x_{2t}] = 0$; (2) $-2\Sigma x_{1t}[y_t - a - b_1x_{1t} - b_2x_{2t}] = 0$; and (3) $-2\Sigma x_{2t}[y_t - a - b_1x_{1t} - b_2x_{2t}] = 0$. However, if $x_{2t} = kx_t$ the last two expressions are linearly dependent. A solution exists, but it is not unique. b_2 is essentially arbitrary. See note 16 above.

[23]Here we test for multicollinearity by examining the correlation matrix. While a useful first step, this approach is limited when more than two independent variables are present. In that case we should examine the relationship between each independent variable and all of the other independent variables.

postscript

To conclude our review of classical estimation, we reveal the source of the data in Table 13.1. This data set was generated from a model of $y_t = 500,000 + 25x_{1t} + 100x_{2t} + \varepsilon_t$. This is model [m], with $\beta_0 = 500,000$, $\beta_1 = 25$, and $\beta_2 = 100$. The error terms and independent variables were independently drawn from $\varepsilon_t \sim N(0;50,000^2)$, $x_{1t} \sim N(1,0000;900^2)$, and $x_{2t} \sim N(1,00;150^2)$.

The correct model to estimate, then, uses x_1 and x_2 as independent variables. Our regression identifies $y = 408,480 + 33.26x_1 + 121.06x_2$, as opposed to $y = 500,000 + 25x_1 + 100x_2$. These estimates are well within the realm of sampling error.[24]

Our initial regression assumed $\beta_2 = 0$. This implies we were estimating $y = \beta_0 + \beta_1 x_{1t} + [\beta_2 x_{2t} + \varepsilon_t]$. The error term in this case is the sum of the two terms in brackets. It has an expected value of $100(1,000) = 100,000$, as $x_{2t} \sim N(1,000;150^2)$ and $\varepsilon_t \sim N(0;50,000^2)$. Thus, our regression should identify $y = 500,000 + 25x_1 + 100,000 = 600,000 + 25x_1$. It actually identified $y = 525,110 + 34.37x_1$. Again, these estimates are well within the realm of sampling error.[25] Notice how omitting the second variable from the estimated regression forces us to "load" its effect on the other variables. $100x_2$ is not correlated with x_1, but it does have a nonzero mean. Thus, we expect our regression to have an intercept of β_0 plus the mean of $100x_2$.

Stated differently, regressing y on x_1 here amounts to estimating a misspecified regression. The error term is not a zero mean random variable. The two independent variables are not multicollinear. This implies $b^{\bullet}$ will be an unbiased (though inefficient) estimator of β_1. $a^{\bullet}$, however, is a biased estimator of β_0. (This issue will be explored further in the following section.)

Finally, we began our foray by assuming $\beta_1 = \beta_2 = 0$. This implies we were estimating $y_t = \beta_0 + [\beta_1 x_{1t} + \beta_2 x_{2t} + \varepsilon_t]$. The error term here has an expected value of $25(10,000) + 100(1,000) = 350,000$. This implies our population mean is $\beta_0 + 350,000 = 500,000 + 350,000 = 850,000$.[26] $\bar{y}$, then, is a biased estimator of β_0 in this case. Omitting the two independent variables precludes a clean estimate of β_0. Our sample mean is not now an unbiased estimator of β_0. It is, however, an unbiased estimator of $\beta_0 + \beta_1 E(x_{1t}) + \beta_2 E(x_{2t})$.

This is not an idle exercise. We want to impart the thought that what we expect our estimation to convey is a glimpse of the correct model, tempered by sampling

---

[24]In particular, test the hypothesis that each coefficient is the given, correct value. Also notice our estimate of σ is 30,400 in this case.

[25]Hypothesis tests parallel to those outlined in the prior note are appropriate. Also, our estimate of the standard deviation of the (combined) error term in this case is 34,500.

[26]Is our estimate of the population mean in this case consistent with the null hypothesis of 850,000? Also, it is now possible to explain our earlier assumption that this population has a standard deviation of 56,844. y_t is the sum of three random variables, $25x_{1t} + 100x_{2t} + \varepsilon_t$. Since the random variables are independent, the variance of their sum is: $[25(900)]^2 + [100(150)]^2 + [50,000]^2 = [56,844]^2$.

error and by whatever we have left out. If we omit one or two independent variables, we are estimating the model stripped of those variables.

Omitted Variables

Omitting a variable is a matter of luck and judgment. We might not know the correct model, and simply fail to include an important independent variable. Alternatively, we usually seek a parsimonious model. Too many independent variables leads to a cumbersome model.[27] We seek a balance.

To strengthen our intuition, suppose [m] is the correct model. Further suppose the two independent variables are linked by

$$x_{2t} = kx_{1t} + \gamma_t$$

where γ_t is a zero mean *iid* error term. (Notice how a nonzero k implies the independent variables are correlated.) What happens if we regress y on x_t?

The model with x_2 omitted is

$$y_t = \beta_0 + \beta_1 x_{1t} + \beta_2 x_{2t} + \varepsilon_t = \beta_0 + \beta_1 x_{1t} + \beta_2 [kx_{1t} + \gamma_t] + \varepsilon_t$$
$$= \beta_0 + [\beta_1 + \beta_2 k]x_{1t} + [\beta_2 \gamma_t + \varepsilon_t].$$

The error term now consists of $\beta_2 \gamma_t + \varepsilon_t$; and the coefficient on the independent variable is $\beta_1 + \beta_2 k$.

If k = 0, our misspecification results in a needlessly large error term, $\beta_2 \gamma_t + \varepsilon_t$ as opposed to ε_t. The additional error term is $\beta_2 \gamma_t$, which has a mean of zero, as $E(\gamma_t) = 0$, but a nontrivial variance. Hence, we increase the error term, resulting in a less efficient estimation exercise.

Contrast this with the case where we omit x_{2t} in the setting of Table 13.1. There we had $x_{2t} \sim N(1,000;150^2)$, but independent of x_{1t}. This implies $x_{2t} = kx_{1t} + \gamma_t$, with k = 0; *but* $\gamma_t \sim N(1,900;150^2)$. Here γ_t is not a zero mean random variable. This implies $E[\beta_2 \gamma_t + \varepsilon_t] \neq 0$. Therefore, we have an inefficient estimation exercise and produce a biased estimate of β_0 when we omit x_2 from the regression.

Now suppose $k \neq 0$ and we omit the second independent variable. The slope from our regression is now a biased estimator of β_1. It estimates $\beta_1 + \beta_2 k$! Presuming γ_t is a zero mean random variable, however, the misspecification does not bias the estimate of β_0.

The data in Table 13.2 are illustrative. These data were generated in the same manner as those in Table 13.1, with one exception. We used $x_{2t} = .1x_{1t} + \gamma_t$, where $\gamma_t \sim N(0;150^2)$ (and *iid*). Thus, we have $\beta_0 = 500,000$, $\beta_1 = 25$, $\beta_2 = 100$, $\varepsilon_t \sim N(0;50,000^2)$, and k = .1.

---

[27]To add a touch of cynicism, a large number of independent variables also invites the happy conjunction of chance and available measures in explaining the dependent variable's variability in a particular sample.

Table 13.2: Data for Multicollinearity Estimation Exercise			
t	y_t	x_{1t}	x_{2t}
1	917,916	10,838	1,071
2	830,113	10,280	1,180
3	755,895	8,493	808
4	905,262	11,363	1,159
5	1,007,387	10,682	1,478
6	859,451	10,592	1,190
7	886,093	9,817	1,137
8	842,893	9,764	1,072
9	875,284	11,876	1,150
10	784,444	10,257	989
11	866,420	9,075	1,035
12	814,430	9,209	857
13	893,786	10,382	1,003
14	994,695	10,790	1,307
15	794,667	10,002	922
16	779,092	8,795	956

Regressing y on x_1 produces the following:

$$y_t = 381,580 + 47.48x_{1t}$$
$$(168,310)\ (16.54)$$
$$r^2 = .37;\ r_a^2 = .33.$$

If no sampling error were present, the intercept would be $\beta_0 + \beta_2 E(\gamma_2) = 500,000 + 100(0) = 500,000$, as $\gamma_t \sim N(0;150^2)$. Similarly, the slope would be $\beta_1 + \beta_2 k = 25 + 100(.1) = 35$. In this instance we have an unbiased estimator of β_0, but a biased estimator of β_1.

In turn, the correctly specified regression provides:

$$y_t = 413,160 + 9.06x_{1t} + 330.82x_{2t}$$
$$(115,100)\ (14.62)\qquad (80.07)$$
$$r^2 = .73;\ r_a^2 = .69.$$

This is dreadful. The regression "looks nice" if we erroneously drop x_{2t}. Yet estimating the correct model does not even identify a significant coefficient for the first independent variable.

The correlation matrix displayed on the next page provides the key to understanding these results.

	y	x_1	x_2
y	1.0000		
x_1	0.6088	1.0000	
x_2	0.8485	0.6360	1.0000

The two independent variables are highly correlated. If we omit, say, the second from our regression, we bias the estimator of β_1. Conversely, if we include both variables in the regression, we must deal with increased standard errors. The choice is a biased estimator or a multicollinear estimation exercise.

This case is dramatic, since the estimators from the correctly specified regression are far removed from the correct amounts; and the first is not significant. (The estimate of β_2 is also nearly 3 standard errors away from $\beta_2 = 100$.)

For the record, regressing y on x_2 produces the following:

$$y_t = 470{,}860 + 362.37 x_{2t}$$
$$(66{,}110) \quad (60.41)$$
$$r^2 = .72; \ r_a^2 = .70.$$

This is subject to a parallel interpretation, which we leave to the reader.[28]

As we said, omitting a variable is a matter of luck and judgment. With luck, whatever we omit does little harm. With judgment, we pare down the model to a useful though not overly complex specification. Iron clad rules are not applicable here; professional judgment reigns.

Dependent Variables Drawn from the Accounting Library

Now concentrate on the accounting library. We face some decision problem and are seeking an estimate of some cost component of the decision frame. The dependent variable is drawn from the accounting library. We also have access to several independent variables that might be used in the estimation exercise. The question is how our knowledge of the accounting library might affect the way we approach the estimation exercise.

cost of goods sold

Consider cost of goods sold. Suppose we have a single product firm that uses standard costing. Manufacturing cost contains direct labor, direct material, and overhead components. In aggregate format we envision a version of model [m], linking total manufacturing cost, TMC, to output, q_m:[29]

---

[28]Plots of these data and residuals from the noted regressions reveal nothing out of the ordinary.

[29]We naturally think of this as reflecting a budget with β reflecting standard prices multiplied by

$$TMC_t = F + \beta q_{mt} + \varepsilon_t.$$

Now suppose we collect some recent data and regress TMC on q_m. If the model is correctly specified and if the error term is well behaved, we have access to the full array of statistical techniques. Suppose, instead, we are interested in a competitor's costs. Further suppose we have access to the competitor's recent financial statements but not internal accounting records. We can discern cost of goods sold, CGS_t, and quantity sold, q_{st}, for this competitor.

Also assume the competitor's manufacturing cost is accurately modeled by $TMC_t = F + \beta q_{mt} + \varepsilon_t$. We just don't know F and ß. What can we learn about the manufacturing cost function by regressing CGS on q_s?

Financial reporting uses full costing, so we know CGS_t is computed on a full costing basis. In contrast, TMC_t is the total of direct labor, direct material, and overhead. It is cost, not expense, incurred during the period. There is also the question of how q_m and q_s differ.

Further assume our competitor uses a standard costing system. In algebraic terms, we know CGS_t consists of standard product cost multiplied by the number of units sold, plus the difference between actual and standard manufacturing cost. Let N be the competitor's normal volume. Standard product cost, then, is $F/N + \beta$. Actual manufacturing cost is TMC_t. The accounting system transfers $(F/N + \beta)q_{mt}$ to finished goods. The difference is $TMC_t - (F/N + \beta)q_{mt}$. So cost of goods sold turns out to be the sum of (1) standard product cost multiplied by quantity sold and (2) the difference between actual and standard manufacturing cost:

$$CGS_t = (F/N + \beta)q_{st} + TMC_t - (F/N + \beta)q_{mt}$$

$$= (F/N + \beta)q_{st} + F + \beta q_{mt} + \varepsilon_t - (F/N + \beta)q_{mt}$$

$$= F + (F/N + \beta)q_{st} + \varepsilon_t - (F/N)q_{mt}.$$

Now what happens when we regress CGS on q_s? Quantity manufactured, q_m, is an omitted variable. Suppose q_{st} and q_{mt} are not correlated. Further suppose normal volume is equal to expected output, $N = E(q_{mt})$. Our misspecification does not bias the slope coefficient; in particular the regression estimated slope is an unbiased estimator of full cost. But the mean of the extra term turns out to be $-(F/N)E(q_{mt}) = -(F/N)N = -F$. Our regression of CGS on q_s then provides estimates of $\beta_0 = F - F = 0$, and $\beta_1 = (F/N + \beta)$. The regression estimates full product cost, or average cost in our single product setting.

Conversely, suppose q_{st} and q_{mt} are highly correlated. The misspecification now biases the estimate of the slope coefficient. Here, regression of CGS on q_s provides estimates of $\beta_0 = F$ and $\beta_1 = \beta$! In this case, production and sales are virtually the

standard quantities. The classical linear model is one of constant coefficients plus an additive error term. Maintaining the additive error term imposes structure on what is random in the underlying price times quantity constructions.

same, so full and variable cost are virtually the same. In the language of a correlated, omitted variable the resulting bias converts the full cost to a variable cost estimation setting.[30]

Two lessons emerge. First, our knowledge of the accounting library is indispensable in extracting information from that library. What we learn from regressing CGS on q_s in this setting might be an estimate of full cost, an estimate of variable cost, or something between. This follows from an understanding of how full, standard cost procedures expense manufacturing cost.

Second, the union of the accounting library and classical linear estimation is a delicate art. Model [m] assumes $ß_0$, $ß_1$, and $ß_2$ are constants. Can we reasonably assume the cost structure we are trying to estimate has constant coefficients? What if prices change, or quantities change? What if new employees arrive at periodic intervals? What if miscellaneous items are expensed rather than accrued? What if learning is present? What if the product line changes?

price changes

For a second illustration of the importance of understanding accounting library procedures, consider the data in Table 13.3. Here we want to estimate an overhead LLA using direct labor hours as an independent variable. Regressing OV on DLH provides the following:

$$OV_t = 415,940 + 79.90DLH_t$$
$$(501,810) \quad (24.54)$$
$$r^2 = .57; \ r_a^2 = .52.$$

The residuals are plotted in Figure 13.5. We appear to have positive autocorrelation. (The Durbin-Watson statistic is 1.01, which is consistent with a claim of positive first order autocorrelation.) Also, the variance of the disturbance term appears to be increasing with time.

Now add time as a second independent variable. We have:

$$OV_t = 903,810 + 44.17DLH_t + 43,670t$$
$$(154,420) \quad (8.07) \quad (4,649)$$
$$r^2 = .97; \ r_a^2 = .96.$$

This is interesting. Overhead cost increases with time. The fit is certainly respectable. The autocorrelation has disappeared. (DW = 2.17.) The residuals, though, appear to display an increasing variance. See Figure 13.6.

As the subheading suggests, we might want to think about price changes. Let ROV_t denote the overhead category cost in period t measured in constant or real dollars. Further suppose the correct model is

---

[30]If the competitor separately reported finished goods inventory, we would be able to infer q_m from the change in finished goods inventory and sales (q_s).

$$ROV_t = \beta_0 + \beta_1 DLH_t + \varepsilon_t.$$

What happens if we regress overhead measured in nominal dollars on DLH, as in our initial regression of OV on DLH?

	Table 13.3: Data for Estimation Exercise with Price Level Changes		
t	OV_t	DLH_t	ROV_t
1	1,830,054	19,873	1,830,054
2	1,840,744	18,721	1,804,651
3	1,939,565	19,943	1,864,250
4	1,977,534	21,018	1,863,474
5	1,876,832	17,782	1,733,903
6	2,149,168	21,934	1,946,567
7	1,998,320	18,529	1,774,451
8	2,245,671	23,483	1,954,992
9	2,287,760	21,071	1,952,581
10	2,295,845	21,429	1,921,061

Figure 13.5: Residuals from OV = 415,940 + 79.70DLH

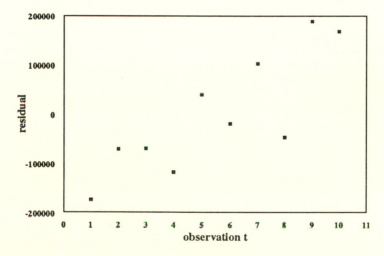

The answer depends on how we think real and nominal measures vary. Suppose we have a constant inflation rate of 2%. This implies

$$OV_t = ROV_t(1.02)^{t-1},$$

where we have chosen to normalize the measures to time t = 1 constant dollars. Under these circumstances, regressing OV on DLH is a misspecified estimation exercise:

$$OV_t = ROV_t(1.02)^{t-1} = (\beta_0 + \beta_1 DLH_t + \varepsilon_t)(1.02)^{t-1}$$

$$= \beta_0(1.02)^{t-1} + \beta_1(1.02)^{t-1}DLH_t + (1.02)^{t-1}\varepsilon_t.$$

Figure 13.6: Residuals from OV = 903,810 + 44.17DLH + 43,670t

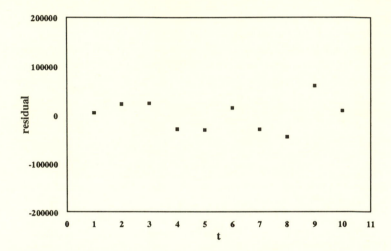

In particular, the slope and intercept are now functions of t, and the variance of the error term is also a function of t. Time is influencing what the model presumes is a set of constant coefficients. This is reflected in the correlation matrix:

	t	OV_t	DLH_t	ROV_t
t	1.0000			
OV_t	0.9127	1.0000		
DLH_t	0.4715	0.7549	1.0000	
ROV_t	0.5252	0.8263	0.9304	1.0000

For the record, the data in Table 13.3 were generated assuming $ROV_t = \beta_0 + \beta_1 DLH_t + \varepsilon_t$ with $\beta_0 = 750,000$ and $\beta_1 = 55$. Also, $\varepsilon_t \sim N(0;50,000^2)$. We then generated $OV_t = ROV_t(1.02)^{t-1}$. The correctly specified regression provides:

$$ROV_t = 1,008,900 + 41.99DLH_t$$
$$(119,560) \quad (5.85)$$
$$r^2 = .87; \ r_a^2 = .85.$$

No misspecification is apparent in the residuals.[31]

Notice how knowledge of the accounting library is important in the exercise. We began by assuming the correct specification was in real dollars. The accounting library gives us nominal dollars. Understanding the link between nominal and real overhead dollars is important in successfully concluding the estimation task.

A deeper lesson also emerges. It would be unusual for the inflation rate to be a constant 2%. This was used merely to keep the example uncluttered. Any overhead category, by definition, contains various costs that we do not find possible or convenient to relate directly to product. Some heterogeneity is to be expected. Prices of the various items are unlikely to move at the same rate; in addition, various accruals are likely to mix nominal dollars of various vintages.

Managerial judgment again enters. How much strain can we put on the fiction of a constant coefficient, linear model? It depends on the economic and accounting circumstances at hand. Judgment is required.

aggregation

Source document accuracy and aggregation of cost categories provide a final illustration of interaction between the accounting library and cost estimation. Suppose we have two overhead categories, say, OV_1 and OV_2. The LLA for the first uses direct labor hours as an independent variable, DLH, and the second uses number of setups, Z. We have

$$OV_{1t} = \beta_{10} + \beta_{11}DLH_t + \varepsilon_{1t};\text{ and}$$

$$OV_{2t} = \beta_{20} + \beta_{21}Z_t + \varepsilon_{2t}.$$

The library contains recent overhead realizations for each category, along with the values of their respective independent variables. Next step is our handy regression package.

Or is it? What if the overhead costs are not accurately measured? Suppose we can identify total manufacturing cost. Direct costs are also well identified. By implication, the *total* of the overhead costs is well identified. It is the disaggregation of the overhead costs into individual categories that raises concern.

Here we rely on source documents. Consider what happens when miscellaneous materials are removed from inventory for production purposes. This is surely overhead. How much belongs to each category? Similarly, suppose various personnel assist in setups and in support activities. They assign their time to the two overhead categories.

---

[31]The adjusted r^2 is lower here than in the case where we regress OV on DLH and t. r^2 in a misspecified regression can hardly be considered interesting. Besides, we never compare r^2s across regressions with different independent variables. They are noncomparable, since each is based on respective minimum squared errors, normalized by the squared errors about their respective means.

We can model this story in the following fashion. Let OV_{it} be the correct overhead total in category i, for period t. We observe this amount with error, however. Let O_{it} denote our observation. Set

$$O_{it} = OV_{it} + \gamma_{it}$$

where γ_{it} is the total of the classification errors for category i.

We assume total overhead is correctly measured. Therefore, $OV_{1t} + OV_{2t} = O_{1t} + O_{2t}$. γ_{1t} and γ_{2t} are perfectly negatively correlated.[32] In short, we know the total overhead incurred, but measure its disaggregation into the two categories with error.

Recognizing that we observe O_{it} instead of OV_{it}, we think of our regression models as follows:

$$O_{1t} = OV_{1t} + \gamma_{1t} = \beta_{10} + \beta_{11}DLH_t + \varepsilon_{1t} + \gamma_{1t}; \text{ and}$$

$$O_{2t} = OV_{2t} + \gamma_{2t} = \beta_{20} + \beta_{21}Z_t + \varepsilon_{2t} + \gamma_{2t}.$$

Should we separately estimate these two models, or should we estimate the combined model of

$$O_{1t} + O_{2t} = OV_{1t} + OV_{2t} = \beta_{10} + \beta_{20} + \beta_{11}DLH_t + \beta_{21}Z_t + \varepsilon_{1t} + \varepsilon_{2t}?$$

Notice that $\gamma_{1t} + \gamma_{2t} = 0$, and the classification errors therefore disappear in the combined model.

The answer relies on managerial judgment. Suppose errors carried forward from source document errors are trivial. This is an argument for separate estimation, since γ_{1t} and γ_{2t} are trivial. Suppose we cannot be so cavalier about the source document errors. γ_{1t} and γ_{2t} are not trivial. If DLH and Z are not correlated, this is an argument for combined estimation. If they are multicollinear, though, we again become interested in separate estimation. This is because of the added difficulty in obtaining accurate estimates of β_{11} and β_{21} in a model with multicollinearity.

This point should not be glossed over. The accounting library gives us disaggregate amounts in this case. It does not necessarily follow, though, that our best use of the library is to work with the disaggregate amounts. The economic situation may not call for disaggregation. Or classification errors may swamp the importance of the disaggregation.

In short, the aggregate regression removes the source document errors from the exercise, but combines the intercept terms and the ε_{it} random variables. Separate estimation avoids this but subjects each individual estimation to the γ_{it} source document errors. Their negative correlation, in term, induces negative correlation in the sampling errors of the respective estimators.

---

[32]A less extreme story would have a large negative correlation. The important point is we have difficulty classifying the total overhead cost into individual categories. This gives us measurement error. Whenever the classification is random relative to identification of the total, we introduce negatively correlated errors.

No clear choice is possible. No recipe is present. Judgment is an important force in resolving questions of this sort. As we have stated, the professional manager knows the environment and knows the accounting library. These are essential backdrops for professionally responsible use of the accounting library.

Summary

We have provided a summary of familiar estimation techniques. Linearity, independence, and normality are the key ingredients in the classical estimation theory. In turn, we recognize the world is hardly this friendly. Specification analysis is essential to understanding how our conclusions might be influenced by the environment at hand.

This summary and extension into specification concerns focused on the question of estimating an LLA. At one level, our study stresses the requirement that the informed user of statistics must always ask what assumptions were employed in the exercise and what happens to the tentative conclusions if these assumptions are violated. At a deeper level, our study has been a review of accounting techniques. The informed user of the accounting library asks what assumptions were employed in constructing the library and what happens to the tentative conclusions arrived at by delving into the library if these assumptions are violated by the setting of the task at hand.

Professional judgment is of central importance in extracting these estimates; it is well informed by a thorough knowledge of the accounting library and competing sources of information.

Bibliographic Notes

A statistics text is the best place to begin a review of classical estimation. Kaplan and Atkinson [1989] provide an extensive discussion of cost curve estimation. Beyond this, more sophisticated sources are available. Personal favorites are Miller [1986] and Hanushek and Jackson [1977]. From here we turn to sophisticated econometrics.

Problems and Exercises

1. What advantages and disadvantages do you see in using formal statistical procedures to estimate an LLA?

2. Our review of classical estimation used the data in Table 13.1, first to estimate a population mean, then a one variable linear model and then a two variable linear model. In each case the population was characterized by an underlying Normal distribution. Further recall the data were generated from model [m], using $y_t = 500,000 + 25x_{1t} + 100x_{2t} + \varepsilon_t$. The error terms and independent variables were independently drawn from $\varepsilon_t \sim N(0;50,000^2)$, $x_{1t} \sim N(10,000;900^2)$, and $x_{2t} \sim N(1,000;150^2)$. Determine the variance of the underlying population for the first case, and of the error term in the two regressions. Compare these variances with the estimates that were produced using the sample data.

3.   *Exercise with known population*
    Consider a linear model of the form $y_t = 100,000 + 100x_{1t} + 50x_{2t} + \varepsilon_t$. Also assume the error terms and independent variables are independently drawn from $\varepsilon_t \sim N(0;800^2)$, $x_{1t} \sim N(1,000;200^2)$, and $x_{2t} \sim N(500;150^2)$. A random sample of size 15 is listed below.

observation t	y_t	x_{1t}	x_{2t}
1	230,487	1,077	434
2	207,894	831	529
3	210,231	921	367
4	229,039	996	580
5	223,874	1,048	382
6	180,250	583	423
7	217,359	936	458
8	239,155	1,161	483
9	220,072	983	445
10	187,771	705	387
11	259,680	1,339	507
12	216,520	878	579
13	218,899	960	467
14	263,649	1,251	742
15	210,586	800	610

a]   Suppose you ignore the two independent variables. What is your best statistical estimate (using the above data) of the population mean from which variable y_t is drawn? Given you know the underlying population, what are its exact mean and variance? Test the hypothesis that the true mean is 225,000.

b]   Suppose you ignore the second independent variable. What is your best statistical estimate of the slope and intercept of the underlying population? What is your estimate of the variance of the population error term? How does this compare to the known variance of the error term in this misspecified regression? Test the hypothesis that the slope is 100.

c]   Now use both independent variables in your regression. Test the hypothesis that β_1 is 100 and that β_2 is 50. How does your best estimate of the variance of the population error term compare with the known variance of ε_t?

4. *ad hoc procedures*

This is a continuation of the above problem 3 where we examine ad hoc procedures for estimating the population parameters. For simplicity, we concentrate on the case where the second independent variable is ignored.

a]   Take the first two sample observations (t = 1,2). Set up two equations in two unknowns and solve for the slope and intercept. Compare this with your regression in part [b] of the earlier problem.

b]   Now select two sample observations by taking those with the largest and the smallest realization of the dependent variable (y_t). Use these two observations to determine the slope and intercept. You might enjoy footnote 4.

c]   Finally, now select two sample observations by taking those with the largest and the smallest realizations of the independent variable (x_{1t}). Use these to determine the slope and intercept.

d]   Comment on your various quick and dirty procedures for estimating the slope and intercept of a linear model.

5. *omitted variable with known population*

Return to problem 3. In part [b] you estimated a model with an omitted variable. Carefully explain how this influenced your estimation exercise and whether it led to biased estimators of β_0 and β_1.

6. *source documents*

Ralph manages a consulting company and is presently looking over the time sheets for the last 12 engagements, wondering how much staff time is involved in a typical engagement. Ralph decides to think of this as a population that is Normally distributed with unknown mean μ and unknown variance σ^2. So if x_j is the total staff time required on engagement j, Ralph regards x_j as a draw from a Normal distribution with mean μ and variance σ^2. Using the noted data and a handy statistics package, Ralph estimates the mean (142 hours) and standard deviation (29 hours). A confidence interval estimate of the mean is also provided, relying on the fact a random sample from a Normal population leads to a Student t distribution.

The times on the time sheets are reported by the staff themselves. Ralph also knows that, if the firm is particularly busy, the staff will work overtime to complete their assignments and will not report the extra hours.

a]   Is Ralph's sample mean a biased estimator of the population mean? Carefully but thoroughly explain your answer.

b]   Is Ralph's estimate of the population variance (or standard deviation) a biased estimator? Again, carefully but thoroughly explain your answer.

c]   What additional statistical exploration might Ralph engage to confirm or allay these fears?

d]   What principle of internal control is violated by this story?

7.   *standard costing procedures*
    Ralph is studying labor cost for the State of Connecticut. One of the employers in a random sample faces the following situation. Workers are paid $14 per hour. Total labor hours multiplied by 14 is the total wage bill for the period in question. State and federal employment taxes are assessed at the rate of 13.8% of the total wage bill. In addition, various benefits (medical and dental care, child care, vacations, and so on) cost the employer $7,600 per employee per year. (Retirement provisions are also an issue here, but this firm funds these items separately, with a considerable lag. So we will not worry about this issue here.)
    The employer uses standard costing. Employees work 2,000 hours per year. The standard wage rate is $1.138(14) + 7,600/2,000 = 19.732$ per hour.

a]   What is the marginal cost of an hour of labor?

b]   The employer supplies Ralph with labor cost breakouts for its monthly production over the past 18 months. When Ralph regresses labor cost on labor hours, the regression shows an insignificant intercept and a highly significant slope of 19.61. Carefully explain Ralph's statistical conclusion. (There is nothing unusual in the specification; everything is clean.)

8.   *overtime and overhead*
    Ralph now works for a manufacturing firm that produces chassis components for the automobile industry. A debate has broken out about the direct labor cost of overtime production. The industrial engineering group contends that overtime production costs about $20 extra per direct labor hour. This datum is based on an analysis of wage rates, overtime pay differentials, and so on. The accounting group has verified the above calculation but has also decided to look at the past 14 months (during which wage rates were constant). They collect the data displayed below.

a]   Suppose, exclusive of overtime premiums, the correct overhead generating model is given by $OV = F + v \cdot DLH + \varepsilon$. Overtime premiums, though, are debited to overhead. When you regress overhead on total direct labor hours, have you produced a misspecified regression? (Try it.) Explain.

b]   We now drop the assumption that the correct overhead generating model is given by $OV = F + v \cdot DLH + \varepsilon$. Regress overhead on total direct labor hours and overtime hours. Interpret your results. Is this a misspecified regression? Explain.

c]   This exercise, in turn, leads to suspicion, since a common pattern is for a worker who is forced to work overtime to have a high absentee rate in the following period. When this happens, the firm must hire temporary workers. The accounting group notes that payments to temporary workers are debited to overhead. Are the data consistent with this claim?

period	total direct labor hours	overtime hours	total overhead	lagged over-time hours
1	4,796	368	498,870	1,110
2	19,673	2,880	1,093,640	368
3	15,562	2,135	1,038,994	2,880
4	4,911	253	509,793	2,135
5	19,264	673	1,032,375	253
6	3,413	447	412,095	673
7	9,941	276	669,471	447
8	4,774	304	443,112	276
9	19,385	2,369	1,100,108	304
10	10,251	201	823,709	2,369
11	11,208	641	663,897	201
12	9,322	1,238	670,675	641
13	19,897	1,599	1,097,504	1,238
14	14,881	1,497	871,746	1,599

d] Now consider a regression of overhead on total direct labor hours, overtime hours, and lagged overtime hours. Is this consistent with the claimed story?

e] What is the cost of overtime? You don't have enough information to give a reliable numerical answer, but you do know enough to state what information you would gather.

9. *accruals*

Ralph's Firm has a linear cost curve. There are no period costs. Production costs (which equal the total of all product costs) are described by the following linear model: $TMC_t = F + vq_t + \varepsilon_t$, where $F > 0$ and $v > 0$ are constants, $\varepsilon_t \sim N(0;\sigma^2)$, i.e., is an *iid* zero mean Normal error term, and q_t is production in period t. The one catch is that production in period t must be aged, and is not sold until period t + 1. Thus, sales in period t + 1 always equals q_t, production in period t; and cost incurred in period t is given by $F + vq_t + \varepsilon_t$.

a] Suppose Ralph's Firm uses actual, full costing. What product cost will be expensed in period t?

b] Suppose Ralph's Firm uses standard, variable costing (with budgeted cost of F + vq_t in period t). What product cost will be expensed in period t?

c] Suppose Ralph's Firm uses standard, full costing (with a standard product cost of F/N + v). What product cost will be expensed in period t?

d] Suppose Ralph's Firm uses standard, variable costing, as in [b] above. Further suppose we see the Firm's income statements for periods t = 2, ..., n and regress total expense on quantity sold. Do we wind up with biased estimators of F and v? Carefully explain your answer.

10. *allocations and unit costs*

Ralph manufactures a proprietary personal computer chassis that dramatically increases the memory and speed of existing products. The firm is "under-capitalized" and operates by modifying a chassis supplied by the customer. This way inventory is minimized. Equipment and space are rented, supplies and materials are minimal, and the modification is performed by a well-trained, loyal work force. Each employee receives a guaranteed salary. At the end of the year, the employees also receive 42% of the period's accounting profit, split equally among the individuals.

For marketing reasons, the customers are categorized as private (q_1) or public (q_2) sector. Each segment is regarded as a product line, with a separate marketing manager. In turn, separate income calculations are performed for each segment, basically consisting of revenue less cost of goods sold for each segment (cgs_1 and cgs_2). Actual, full costing is employed. The following data are collected.

t	q_1	q_2	cgs_1	cgs_2
1	125,608	138,063	955,595	1,050,349
2	180,796	86,244	1,343,469	640,866
3	194,446	64,703	1,500,240	499,213
4	181,553	58,144	1,521,907	487,404
5	166,254	186,339	950,446	1,065,269
6	150,874	97,006	1,221,384	785,301
7	195,122	28,203	1,741,744	251,752
8	24,197	84,019	443,924	1,541,435
9	34,552	117,284	455,284	1,545,428
10	16,060	63,068	405,543	1,592,598
11	159,338	16,706	1,819,206	190,737
12	166,979	107	1,975,995	1,266

a] Estimate the marginal cost of a unit by regressing cgs_1 on q_1.

b] Estimate the marginal cost of a unit by regressing cgs_2 on q_2. Are your estimates consistent?

c] Now combine the data, and regress $cgs_1 + cgs_2 = cgs$ on $q_1 + q_2 = q$. Carefully explain the relationship among your regressions.

11. *multiple and hybrid independent variables in overhead model*

Ralph is studying an overhead cost category that includes a variety of production support activities: minor supplies, minor maintenance, material handling, technical supervision, and so on. Ralph feels the costs aggregated in this category vary with direct material dollars (DM$), complexity of the products (scored with a complexity index and added to give an index called complexity units) and direct labor hours (DLH). Ralph collects the following data from the last 15 months.

t	cost	DM$	complexity	DLH
1	3,775,238	2,629,042	33,411	188,111
2	3,968,754	2,781,816	49,381	204,240
3	3,685,869	2,570,599	36,844	184,435
4	3,733,128	2,771,243	34,235	200,086
5	4,101,229	2,833,266	44,215	205,445
6	3,858,395	2,740,097	33,694	200,229
7	3,887,992	2,710,630	42,619	193,254
8	3,803,625	2,687,639	35,489	196,453
9	4,067,572	2,864,410	39,095	210,573
10	3,990,740	2,713,780	34,498	197,222
11	3,844,263	2,735,144	38,005	198,575
12	3,573,820	2,560,468	37,398	186,031
13	3,820,491	2,664,075	35,734	192,437
14	3,944,296	2,746,627	40,617	199,606
15	3,775,659	2,700,240	35,705	196,983

The accountant assures Ralph the accruals have been properly done, so there is no issue of hours being recorded on a lagged basis or anything of that nature.

a]   Are the data consistent with Ralph's conjecture?

b]   Suppose Ralph's conjecture has merit, but collinearity stands in the way of statistical identification. Ralph decides to use the relationship between overhead cost and direct material dollars for library purposes. Is the regression estimate of the slope in this LLA an unbiased estimator of the correct slope?

12. *changing price level*

Cybernetics is a family held manufacturing firm. Being family held, it does not respect GAAP in its financial reporting practices. In fact, it uses cash basis accounting. The factory accounting keeps track of direct labor, direct material, and overhead cost, all on a cash basis. It is a known fact that overhead cost on a cash basis is given by the following equation

$$ROV_t = 40,000 + 10DLH_t + \varepsilon_t$$

where (i) ROV_t is overhead in period t (on a cash basis) stated in real or constant dollar terms, (ii) DLH_t is direct labor hours used in period t, and (iii) ε_t is a Normally distributed error term with a zero mean and a 6,000 standard deviation. The above equation is expressed in period 1 dollars. (See below).

During the most recent eight quarters the inflation rate has been 6 percent per quarter. Using period $t = 1$ as the base period (as we did in the above equation), this 6 percent inflation assumption means the recorded overhead in period t is

$$OV_t = ROV_t(1.06)^{t-1}.$$

Actual data are displayed below. Actual overhead denotes the overhead recorded in period t, in period t dollars. Deflated overhead is this amount converted to period 1 dollars, or ROV_t in the above expression. Naturally, DL\$ is direct labor dollars recorded in period t and therefore measured in period t dollars.

period	actual overhead	DLH	DL\$	deflated overhead
1	108,154	5,500	55,000	108,154
2	97,226	5,500	58,300	91,694
3	90,100	4,000	44,800	80,482
4	95,090	4,700	55,930	79,903
5	123,166	5,300	66,780	97,743
6	125,818	5,700	76,380	93,857
7	125,893	5,400	76,680	88,699
8	156,241	5,900	88,500	103,927

Remember, Cybernetics uses cash basis accounting. The direct labor dollars in period t (DL\$) represent dollar payments for hours worked during the respective period. Workers are always paid at the end of the month for all work done during the month. Thus, there would be no accrued wages payable at the end of any quarter if Cybernetics used accrual accounting.

A new management assistant takes the above data and contemplates running the following regressions: (i) actual overhead on DLH; (ii) actual overhead on DLH and time; (iii) actual overhead on DL\$; and (iv) deflated overhead on DLH. Run these regressions and perform whatever specification analysis you feel is warranted. You should also examine the correlation matrix.

a]   Which data used in the exercise would be found in the firm's financial records?

b]   Which of the estimated models would you regard as best portraying the overhead process at Cybernetics?

c]   Should your answer above depend on the reported r^2?

d]   Does model (i) provide a biased estimator of the DLH coefficient? Carefully explain.

e]   What happens to regression (iv) if you use period 8 rather than period 1 dollars in the conversion to constant dollars?

f]   As you step back from this specific story, what general concerns do you see in using historical data to estimate an overhead LLA when prices are changing?

13. *relevant range*

Ralph is studying a particular warranty cost account, in which all repair costs for a particular (rather expensive) industrial monitoring product are accumulated. As a first step, Ralph collects the following data concerning number of warranty claims (x_t) and cost ($cost_t$).

t	x_t	$cost_t$
1	554	968,000
2	639	1,730,000
3	598	1,403,000
4	385	303,000
5	466	587,000
6	371	267,000
7	633	1,722,000
8	467	592,000
9	667	2,009,000
10	341	210,000
11	443	513,000
12	480	678,000

Carefully analyze Ralph's data.

14. *reciprocal services*

Return to problem 13, Chapter 8 where cost was aggregated into category A (TC_A), category B (TC_B), and assembly (TCA). Further suppose we know, for output q, that the reciprocal relationship is given by $A = q + B/4$ and $B = X + A/10$.

a]   Suppose Ralph knows only this structure and the data set from 15 recent periods listed on the following page. What is Ralph's best estimate (in a statistical sense) of the marginal cost of output?

b]   What happens to your answer in [a] above if you admit that the physical relationships among units of A, B, and q in the above two equations should also have error terms attached?

t	q	TCA	TC_A	TC_B
1	2,621	304,339	52,857	134,299
2	2,770	331,979	66,358	132,751
3	2,614	311,771	59,415	139,778
4	1,756	232,231	37,820	90,595
5	2,327	286,545	48,138	119,170
6	1,606	204,749	59,360	68,659
7	1,762	232,087	43,396	88,734
8	1,232	179,371	30,648	75,338
9	2,695	306,645	73,855	152,051
10	2,439	295,026	62,632	113,754
11	2,554	296,982	57,841	135,604
12	2,007	249,453	56,190	110,152
13	1,886	238,449	51,135	109,894
14	1,813	239,089	49,366	94,832
15	1,961	242,504	41,220	101,240

Large Versus Small Decisions: Short-Run

We now begin the task of combining our study of decision framing (Chapters 11 and 12) and use of the accounting library to estimate various costs (Chapter 13). The present chapter focuses on short-run decisions, and the succeeding focuses on long-run decisions.

Two concerns should be kept in mind as we proceed. The first is signaled by the chapter's title. "Small" decisions can be treated as variations on the status quo, variations where we have reason to think that our LLAs are reasonably accurate and interactions with other decisions are inconsequential. "Large" decisions contemplate movements sufficiently beyond the status quo that our LLAs come into question, and we suspect interactions with other activities may be consequential.

Knowing when to ignore an interaction or abandon an LLA is a matter of judgment. The tension of choosing between a readily available or custom made cost construction is ever present. Short-run decisions are not necessarily small, just as long-run decisions are not necessarily large.

The second concern is the firm's objective. Following earlier treatments, we will usually focus on profit maximization, or expected profit maximization. This has its awkward moments. What do we say about a municipality, a closely held firm, a family firm, or a hospital? The theory of the firm does not provide much guidance on this score. Fortunately, the principles we explore are robust to whatever the organization's goals happen to be. Unfortunately, we cannot convey these principles with the language of a single goal that all organizations pursue.

With these concerns in mind, we initially study two preliminary topics. First, we consolidate the mechanical aspects of dealing with LLAs to make marginal or small decisions. Second, we review framing considerations with special emphasis on the short-run cost of materials held in inventory. We then explore various prototypical choices: make or buy, product evaluation, customer evaluation, and work force scheduling. Finally, formal uncertainty is explored, focusing on the implicit cost of risk and the implicit benefit of flexibility. These are often important concerns but are hidden from view when uncertainty is not formally acknowledged.

Preliminaries

We begin with a review of topics introduced in our earlier studies of product costing and decision framing. Just as judicious use of LLAs is central to the accountant's product costing art, they find their way into short-run decision analysis. In turn, departure from the LLAs found in the accounting library may be called for, depending on the circumstance and decision frame.

break-even analysis

Consider a single product firm. It expects its output and sales to be somewhere between 250 and 400 units. Let q denote quantity produced and sold. In this region, of $250 \leq q \leq 400$, the firm estimates its total revenue via

$$TR = 600q;$$

and its total cost via

$$TC = 150,000 + 100q.$$

We have two LLAs, one for revenue and one for cost. We might combine them into an estimate of profit:

$$TR - TC = 600q - 150,000 - 100q = [600 - 100]q - 150,000.$$

The quantity in brackets, 600 - 100, is the product's contribution margin. In earlier chapters we constructed the contribution margin by focusing on variable manufacturing costs and variable period costs. Given LLAs for total cost and total revenue, contribution margin is just the slope of the latter less the slope of the former.

We graph TR and TC in Figure 14.1. Notice we have interrupted the graphs at q = 250 and at q = 400, to remind ourselves $250 \leq q \leq 400$ is presumed. It should be understood that any such portrayal is confined to the region in which the LLA is reasonably accurate.[1]

At this level of abstraction, two questions might be asked. One is the effect of a marginal customer. Suppose we are producing (and selling) at some level, $\hat{q}$ (where $250 \leq \hat{q} < 400$). What is the effect of another customer arriving? Profit increases from (1) $[600 - 100]\hat{q} - 150,000$ to (2) $[600 - 100](\hat{q} + 1) - 150,000$. The difference is [600 - 100], the contribution margin. This should come as no surprise. Contribution margin is our estimate of the effect of another unit on revenue less cost.

Naturally, we could extend the calculation to the effect of several more units, always presuming we stay within the relevant range of the LLAs.

The other question we might ask is where the two graphs intersect. They intersect when TR = TC, or when profit is precisely zero. This is called the break-even point. The algebra is straightforward. Setting TR = TC, we have

$$600q = 150,000 + 100q; \text{ or}$$

$$[600 - 100]q = 150,000; \text{ or}$$

$$q_{BE} = 150,000/[600 - 100] = 150,000/500 = 300 \text{ units.}$$

---

[1]Recall that in Chapter 5 we were careful to overlay the LLAs on the underlying economic curves. Keep in mind that the LLA is always an approximation, a local linear approximation.

The break-even point occurs at the TC intercept divided by the product's contribution margin. See Figure 14.1.[2] (Of course there is no guarantee q_{BE} occurs within the relevant range, though that is the case for our illustration.)

Figure 14.1: Break-even Graph

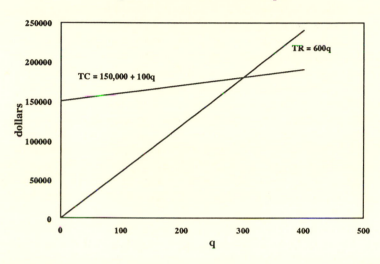

The economic interpretation is less straightforward. Of what significance is q_{BE}? The answer depends on what we have left out of the analysis.

Suppose this really is a single product firm. Further suppose its only short-run options are to shut down for the period, or to produce and sell whatever the market will bear. Let F_0 denote its best estimate of total cost when $q = 0$. Further suppose it anticipates that demand will fall within the relevant range of $250 \le q \le 400$. Also suppose no other effects are associated with temporary shutdown this period.

Shutdown provides a loss of F_0. Continuation provides a profit (or loss) of $500q - 150,000$. The worst possibility, since we assume q is in the relevant range, is $500(250) - 150,000 = 125,000 - 150,000 = -25,000$. If $F_0 \ge 25,000$ our problem is clear. Continuation is preferred, since the worst that can happen beats shutdown.

Suppose, however, that shutdown would open the door to short-run leasing the production facility. The lessee would pay F_0 plus 10,000. This means shutdown offers a guaranteed profit of 10,000, as opposed to the continuation profit of $500q - 150,000$.

---

[2]We naturally assume the contribution margin is positive. Also, a variation on this theme is to ask what output level is necessary to produce an exogenously supplied profit amount. To illustrate, what q is necessary to produce a profit of 50,000? Here we set 50,000 = TR - TC. Solving for q provides $q = (50,000 + 150,000)/500 = 400$ units.

Other stories could be told. Notice two things. We had to move beyond the LLAs to think about the shutdown option. Nowhere did q_{BE} enter our analysis. The reason is we were seeking an alternative (continue or shutdown) that leads to the best profit prospects. The break-even point is of no interest per se in the analysis.

Now change the story somewhat. The net dead weight cost of shutdown is F_0. (We have no lease option.) In addition, we do not know what demand will be. We do, however, know it will exceed q_{BE}. Now our options take the form of a guaranteed loss (shutdown) or a guaranteed though uncertain positive profit (continue). Here knowledge that $q > q_{BE}$ considerably simplifies the analysis.

Product market entry vignettes lead to a similar use of the break-even point. Suppose our firm produces many products. It is contemplating production of a new product. This new product will only be produced this period. Its production and sales are totally separate from all other activities. The firm estimates actual demand will be somewhere between 250 and 400 units. Its *incremental* revenue and *incremental* cost estimates are given by TR and TC, respectively.[3]

Is this short-run opportunity of any interest? It is if we know $q \geq q_{BE}$. And it is not if we know $q \leq q_{BE}$. Otherwise, our choice will rest on what we think is a good characterization of the probabilistic structure of demand, not to mention our attitude toward risk.

To wrap this up, we began with LLAs for revenue and cost, and therefore profit. We might use these LLAs as the basis for making marginal decisions, thereby emphasizing the product's contribution margin. We also might be engaging in larger decisions. If so, the break-even point might provide a shortcut in our analysis. Or it might not.[4]

framing subtleties

Our second preliminary excursion is a review of the costing subtleties that may arise when we adopt a decomposed decision frame. For this purpose, consider a firm that manufactures and sells (or simply merchandises) a product in each of two periods. Production and sale are contemporaneous, as the finished product cannot be stored. For simplicity, no interactions with other activities last beyond two periods. So we drop these activities from the story.

---

[3]Not engaging the new product is the status quo point. The firm's total cost will go up by 150,000 + 100q if the new product is placed in production.

[4]Variations on this theme are possible. We might have several products and worry about alterations in output holding their mix constant. This amounts to a disguised single product analysis. We also might admit nonlinear cost or revenue expressions. We might characterize demand with a probability density and compute such things as the probability of break-even, and so on.

Selling price less all variable cost *except* direct material is 100 per unit in the first period and 110 in the second. Capacity is limited to 100 units per period. Let q_t denote units produced and sold in period t.

At present, the firm has I units of direct material on hand. Let A_t denote units of material *acquired* at the start of period t, and S_t denote units of material *sold* at the start of period t.

The following constraints circumscribe our firm's alternatives:

$q_1 \leq 100$;   [capacity in period t = 1]
$q_2 \leq 100$;   [capacity in period t = 2]
$q_1 \leq I + A_1 - S_1$;   [supply of material in period t = 1]
$q_2 \leq I + A_1 - S_1 - q_1 + A_2 - S_2$;   [supply of material in period t = 2]
$q_1, q_2, A_1, A_2, S_1, S_2 \geq 0$.   [nonnegativity]

Capacity is limited to a maximum of 100 units per period. In addition, production cannot exceed the supply of material in each period. The one twist in understanding the material inventory balance is that we allow the firm to use material in production or to sell it in the material market. Therefore, material available for production in the first period is $I + A_1 - S_1$. Similarly, that available for production in the second period is $I + A_1 - S_1 - q_1 + A_2 - S_2$.

At present, the firm can purchase material at a cost of 10 per unit and sell it for a net price of 8 per unit. Let P^+ denote the acquisition cost of material in the second period, and P^- the corresponding net sale price. These are prices less transactions costs in the second period spot markets and are therefore stated in period t = 2 currency.

We assume all transactions occur in cash. The interest rate is 10%. The present value of any feasible production and sales plan is

$$\pi = 100q_1 - 10A_1 + 8S_1 + (1.10)^{-1}[110q_2 - P^+A_2 + P^-S_2].$$

Combining the present value calculation and the above constraints gives us the following LP:

maximize $\pi = 100q_1 - 10A_1 + 8S_1 + (1.10)^{-1}[110q_2 - P^+A_2 + P^-S_2]$

subject to: $q_1 \leq 100$;
$q_2 \leq 100$;
$q_1 \leq I + A_1 - S_1$;
$q_2 \leq I + A_1 - S_1 - q_1 + A_2 - S_2$; and
$q_1, q_2, A_1, A_2, S_1, S_2 \geq 0$.

Table 14.1 displays the solution for various combinations of beginning inventory and second period material prices. (The noted shadow price refers to the beginning inventory.) In all cases, we produce at capacity, with $q_1^* = q_2^* = 100$. The only variations are in how the material inventory is managed.

Dwell on these six cases. When the beginning inventory balance is I = 5, we must acquire 195 units to satisfy production requirements. The prices are such that this is best delayed as much as possible in case 1 and completely done in the first period in case 2. The same pattern emerges in cases 3 and 4, where we have I = 105. 95 units must be acquired. It is best to do this late in case 3 and early in case 4. Finally, in the last two cases, we have excess inventory. Disposal is best planned early in case 5 and late in case 6.

Table 14.1: Solutions for Two Period LP Illustration						
case	I	P^+	P^-	π^*	shadow price	A_1/S_1 A_2/S_2
1	5	10	8.00	18,140.91	10.00	95	100
2	5	15	8.00	18,050.00	10.00	195	0
3	105	10	8.00	19,136.36	9.09	0	95
4	105	15	8.00	19,050.00	10.00	95	0
5	205	10	8.00	20,040.00	8.00	-5	0
6	205	10	9.95	20,045.23	9.05	0	-5

Now ask, what is the shadow price on the beginning inventory? In the first two cases, we always buy at least enough inventory in the first period to satisfy first period production requirements. As these acquisitions cost us 10 per unit, the shadow price is 10. In cases 3 and 4 we must buy inventory to satisfy the second period's requirements, so timing is an issue. In case 3 we purchase late, implying a shadow price of $P^+/1.1 = 10/1.1 \approx 9.09$. In case 4 we purchase early. Finally, in the last two cases we dispose of extra inventory. In case 5 we dispose immediately, implying a shadow price of 8. In case 6 we dispose late, implying a shadow price of $P^-/1.1 = 9.95/1.1 \approx 9.05$.

Naturally, the beginning inventory would be recorded in the accounting library. Recognition rules are binding, however. We should expect to see it valued in the library at some variation of historical cost.[5]

With this lengthy setup, we are ready to grapple with our advertised framing subtleties. Suppose it is possible for the firm to manufacture and sell a second product in the first period. Only one unit can be sold, so the choice is between "yes" and "no." Choice of no is neutral. Present and future costs and demands are unaffected. Choice of yes will require one unit of material, and will net the firm P

---

[5]Our concern for properly ascertaining material cost in this case disappears if we assume the markets are complete and perfect. We would then be able to buy and sell at the same price; and transactions could be consummated in present or future dollars. The market structure would then fully separate the material management question from the remaining decisions. For that matter, it would be difficult to understand why inventory would be on hand; but if it were, historical and market price would presumably be aligned.

dollars, exclusive of the material cost. This additional product also will be produced outside of the firm's constrained capacity, so $q_1 = 100$ remains feasible, regardless.[6]

Let's frame this decision in terms of incremental benefits less incremental costs. The firm should select yes if P less the cost of the material is positive. What is the cost of the material? It is 10, 9.09, 8, or 9.05 depending on which of the 6 cases is present.

Using a unit of inventoried material for this product displaces that unit of material from its otherwise intended use. This use might be to forestall purchase this period or next or to be sold this period or next period.

We also should reflect on the substance of this decision frame. The original LP, with optimal present value π^*, provides our best choice for the case where we do not pursue the extra product. The following LP gives us the optimal present value, $\hat{\pi}^*$, for the case where we do pursue this product:

$$\text{maximize } \hat{\pi} = P + 100q_1 - 10A_1 + 8S_1 + (1.10)^{-1}[110q_2 - P^+A_2 + P^-S_2]$$

subject to:
$$q_1 \leq 100;$$
$$q_2 \leq 100;$$
$$q_1 \leq I + A_1 - S_1 - 1;$$
$$q_2 \leq I + A_1 - S_1 - q_1 - 1 + A_2 - S_2; \text{ and}$$
$$q_1, q_2, A_1, A_2, S_1, S_2 \geq 0.$$

Details are summarized in Table 14.2.

case	incremental π	$\hat{A}_1^*$	A_1^*	$\hat{A}_2^*$	A_2^*	$\hat{S}_1^*$	S_1^*	$\hat{S}_2^*$	S_2^*
	Table 14.2: Solutions for Extended Two Period Illustration								
1	P - 10	96	95	100	100	0	0	0	0
2	P - 10	196	195	0	0	0	0	0	0
3	P - 9.09	0	0	96	95	0	0	0	0
4	P - 10	96	95	0	0	0	0	0	0
5	P - 8	0	0	0	0	4	5	0	0
6	P - 9.05	0	0	0	0	0	0	4	5

The extra product is profitable whenever $\hat{\pi}^* - \pi^* \geq 0$. This is our incremental profit:

$$\hat{\pi}^* - \pi^* = P - 10(\hat{A}_1^* - A_1^*) + 8(\hat{S}_1^* - S_1^*) + (1.10)^{-1}[-P^+(\hat{A}_2^* - A_2^*) + P^-(\hat{S}_2^* - S_2^*)].$$

P is the incremental benefit. The negative of the remaining terms is the incremental cost of the material.

---

[6]This may not be the best economic portrayal, but it keeps the exploration as simple as possible.

The cost might be the current acquisition price, the current sale price, the present value of the future acquisition price, or the present value of the future sale price. A short-run decision problem does not necessarily reside entirely in the short-run. Similarly, the market price to place on a factor of production in some decomposed decision analysis may be far from obvious.[7] Framing is a subtle art.[8]

Make or Buy

We now examine a "make or buy" question. The generic issue in a make or buy analysis is whether to produce some intermediate product or service inside the organization or acquire it from an outside source. Examples are refuse collection in a municipality, the split between internal and external auditing, chips or keyboards in the personal computer industry, permanent or temporary faculty, overtime or temporary labor services in a period of peak demand, and so on.

In turn, the issues involved may be straightforward or involved. The risk of being dependent on an outsider, concern for quality, managing technology change, and comparative advantage may be important. The outside supplier has similar concerns. For example, considerable investment may be required of the source; and this may place the source at risk.[9] Dual sourcing, in which the item is acquired from two sources (perhaps internal and external) may be advantageous. This provides partial insurance against source failure, and it also may inject discipline into the control problem. It also may be needlessly costly.

A "small," short-run version of this theme is somewhat unambiguous. Will the firm's short-run profit be higher with inside or outside sourcing? Questions of risk, long-run effects, quality, and technology change are absent (or of second order importance). Rather, the intermediate product or service is available in the spot market. Economic forces may have led to excess capacity in this sector, and the firm suddenly finds itself in a position where an unanticipated short-run opportunity may be attractive. A downturn in the construction industry may make outside sourcing of some short-run maintenance attractive.

---

[7]To complete the tale, consider whether we are estimating the opportunity cost of the material in this exercise. Have any options not been analyzed in the comparison of π^* and π^*? When we focus on $\hat{\pi}^*$ and π^*, we are engaging in component searches, by maximizing out the other products and material supply choices. Conversely, if we begin with the first LP (and π^*), we have left one set of choices outside the analysis. The opportunity cost of proceeding with the choice implied by the first LP is P less the shadow price of I.

[8]Coase [1968] is the inspiration for this section. Coase remains particularly insightful and eloquent.

[9]A smoothly functioning just-in-time inventory relationship with an outside supplier illustrates these various risks. The purchaser requires high quality components, arriving at precisely timed intervals. Similarly, the supplier must invest in considerable infrastructure to ensure these arrangements are successful and well-maintained.

a two product illustration

Consider a firm that manufactures and sells two consumer appliance products. Numerous parts are purchased from suppliers, including partially assembled components. The manufacturing process entails further assembly of some components, in a subassembly department, and final assembly of the two products, in an assembly department.

Denote the respective quantities that are produced and sold by q_1 and q_2. Capacity is constrained in the two departments:

subassembly: $q_1 + q_2 \le 6,000$; and
assembly: $q_1 + 2q_2 \le 10,000$.

These constraints are exogenous, and unalterable. (This is a short-run setting.)

Direct labor (DL) and direct material (DM) costs in the subassembly department are described by the following LLAs:

$DL_S = 10q_1 + 10q_2$; and
$DM_S = 110q_1 + 200q_2$.

Their counterparts in the assembly department are:

$DL_A = 40q_1 + 80q_2$; and
$DM_A = 12q_1 + 15q_2$.

Overhead is estimated by $OV = 2,000,000 + 3.5(DL_S + DL_A)$. Here, a plant-wide overhead LLA is used, with direct labor dollars as the explanatory variable.

Let P_i denote the selling price of product i. Further suppose no other costs (e.g., selling and administrative) are involved. For any feasible production plan, total revenue is $P_1q_1 + P_2q_2$. Total cost is the summation of the above direct labor, direct material, and overhead costs. This gives us a short-run total contribution margin of

$$\pi(q_1,q_2) = P_1q_1 + P_2q_2 - [10q_1 + 10q_2 + 110q_1 + 200q_2 + 40q_1 + 80q_2 + 12q_1 + 15q_2 + 3.5(10q_1 + 10q_2 + 40q_1 + 80q_2)]$$

$$= [P_1 - 347]q_1 + [P_2 - 620]q_2.$$

We should recognize the expressions in brackets as the respective product contribution margins:

price	P_1	P_2
direct labor	50	90
direct material	122	215
variable overhead at 3.5(direct labor)	175	315
contribution margins	P_1-347	P_2-620

From here we identify the following LP:

maximize $\pi(q_1,q_2) = [P_1 - 347]q_1 + [P_2 - 620]q_2$

subject to: $q_1 + q_2 \leq 6{,}000$;
                     $q_1 + 2q_2 \leq 10{,}000$; and
                     $q_1, q_1 \geq 0$.

Suppose $P_1 = 600$ and $P_2 = 1{,}100$. The solution to the LP has $q_1^{\cdot} = 2{,}000$ and $q_2^{\cdot}$ $= 4{,}000$; with $\pi^{\cdot} = 2{,}426{,}000$. In addition, the shadow prices on the constraints are 26 and 227, respectively.

an unusual offer

At this juncture, a neighboring manufacturer offers to supply up to 500 units of the components for the second product that are assembled in the subassembly department. The offered price is P per unit. Any component purchased in this manner will not pass through the subassembly department but will enter directly into the assembly phase of the production process.

Let $\hat{q}_2$ denote units of the second product produced in this fashion. With this added opportunity, the direct cost LLAs become:

$DL_S = 10q_1 + 10q_2$;
$DM_S = 110q_1 + 200q_2$;
$DL_A = 40q_1 + 80q_2 + 80\hat{q}_2$; and
$DM_A = 12q_1 + 15q_2 + 15\hat{q}_2$.

Notice how the cost structure is affected. Since units manufactured with out-sourced components skip the subassembly department, DL_S and DM_S are unaffected by $\hat{q}_2$. Also, since assembly takes place in the same fashion, regardless of component source, $\hat{q}_2$ affects DL_A and DM_A in the indicated way. Of course, we also must pay the supplier. (To keep things simple, we further assume no incremental overhead is associated with the out-sourcing process.)

The contribution margin for this variation on the second product is:

price	P_2
direct labor in assembly	80
direct material in assembly	15
variable overhead at 3.5(direct labor)	280
component purchase price	P
contribution margin	$P_2 - 375 - P$

We expand the LP as follows to accommodate this new possibility:

maximize $\pi(q_1, q_2, \hat{q}_2) = [P_1 - 347]q_1 + [P_2 - 620]q_2 + [P_2 - 375 - P]\hat{q}_2$

subject to: $q_1 + q_2 \leq 6{,}000$;
                     $q_1 + 2q_2 + 2\hat{q}_2 \leq 10{,}000$;
                     $\hat{q}_2 \leq 500$; and $q_1, q_2, \hat{q}_2 \geq 0$.

Notice how $\hat{q}_2$ enters the capacity constraint for assembly operations, but not for subassembly. The idea is to subcontract the first operation to the neighboring firm. Also notice, in light of the offer, we limit this opportunity to a maximum of 500 units.

Now for some fun. Suppose, instead of $P_1 = 600$ and $P_2 = 1,100$, we have $P_1 = 600$ and $P_2 = 1,150$. This implies the second product is more profitable than in the original case. The increase is sufficient to emphasize the second product in the optimal production plan. In particular, the solution to the original LP (where $\hat{q}_2 = 0$) is now $q_1^* = 0$ and $q_2^* = 5,000$; with $\pi^* = 2,650,000$. The shadow prices on the two constraints are 0 and 265, respectively. Only the constraint in the assembly department is binding.

Let's also assume the out-sourcing offer has a price of $P = 250$. Solving the expanded LP gives us a solution of $q_1^* = 0$, $q_2^* = 5,000$ and $\hat{q}_2^* = 0$; with $\pi^* = 2,650,000$. The offer is rejected. It is more profitable to "make" than "buy" the component.

Does this make sense? Concentrate on the incremental cost of out-sourcing *one* subassembly. Using the noted LLAs, we readily construct the following:

	make	buy	difference
direct labor in subassembly	10	0	-10
direct material in subassembly	200	0	-200
variable overhead, at 3.5DL	35	0	-35
outside price	0	250	250
total	245	250	5

This is straightforward. Out-sourcing saves labor, material, and overhead *in the subassembly department*. Here, though, the savings are less than the offered price. The incremental cost of out-sourcing is $250 - 245 = 5$ per unit.

Now return to the original setting where we assumed $P_1 = 600$ and $P_2 = 1,100$. Is the offer of $P = 250$ interesting? Only the selling price of the second product has changed. The cost structure has not changed. The temptation is to claim that the would-be supplier's offer remains unattractive.

Let's be more careful. We know the solution when out-sourcing is not available has $q_1^* = 2,000$ and $q_2^* = 4,000$, with $\pi^* = 2,426,000$. Shadow prices on the two constraints are 26 and 227, recall. In contrast, when out-sourcing is available we solve the expanded LP. This gives a solution of $q_1^* = 3,000$, $q_2^* = 3,000$ and $\hat{q}_2^* = 500$. It also has $\pi^* = 2,436,500 > 2,426,000$.

Notice how the choice of q_1 varies as we introduce the out-sourcing alternative. Here, the first constraint of $q_1 + q_2 \leq 6,000$ is binding. Out-sourcing not only saves direct cost and overhead in this department; it also reduces demand on the tight capacity. This must be considered when we frame the choice in incremental terms.

Let's repeat our earlier construction of the incremental cost of out-sourcing one component, but with an important addition (pun):

	make	buy	difference
direct labor in subassembly	10	0	-10
direct material in subassembly	200	0	-200
variable overhead, at 3.5DL	35	0	-35
capacity cost	26	0	-26
outside price	0	250	250
total	271	250	-21

We have added a capacity cost of 26, which is the shadow price on the first constraint. This has the effect of changing the incremental cost of out-sourcing from + 5 to - 21. Here it is now cheaper, less costly, more profitable to out-source the component. The incremental cost of out-sourcing is negative.

To appreciate the framing exercise, let's pause and work through more of the details. Suppose we out-source one such component. This means $\hat{q}_2 = 1$. Now what are the best q_1 and q_2 choices? The answer is $q_1 = 2,002$ and $q_2 = 3,998$. (We can figure this out by solving the larger LP, but with the constraint $\hat{q}_1 = 1$.) This means our largest total contribution margin when we out-source one such component is

$$\pi(2002,3998,1) = 2,426,021.$$

Similarly, our largest total contribution margin when we do no out-sourcing is

$$\pi(2000,4000,0) = 2,426,000.$$

The difference is $\pi(2002,3998,1) - \pi(2000,4000,0) = 21$. The incremental profit from out-sourcing one component is 21. Ha!

Now, if we want to frame this analysis in terms of the incremental cost of out-sourcing, we require the cost construction to carry the net impact of the change in production plan on all other costs and revenues. This is what the capacity cost datum does in our construction.

This make or buy decision can be structured as an LP that simultaneously selects the best output schedule and source of components. Alternatively, the make or buy portion of this decision can be more tightly framed in terms of incremental cost. Then, however, we must be careful to reflect any implicit production plan variations in the cost calculation as well.

As we have said, framing is a subtle art.

statistical estimation of the overhead LLAs

Our analysis, though, remains grounded on the identified LLAs. Suppose we now question the overhead LLA of $OV = 2,000,000 + 3.5(DL_S + DL_A)$. The accounting library gives the data displayed in Table 14.3 (where OV_A denotes overhead in the assembly department and OV_S overhead in the subassembly department.)

Notice the firm's library records overhead and direct cost statistics in each department, while a firm-wide overhead LLA is used.

t	OV_A	OV_S	DL_A	DL_S	DM_A	DM_S
1	1,428	1,596	256	76	24	612
2	1,811	2,228	446	106	49	985
3	1,775	2,306	428	78	61	986
4	1,005	2,239	205	25	86	1,003
5	1,687	1,701	404	54	113	676
6	1,568	2,502	365	15	130	1,028
7	1,299	2,256	262	82	37	1,066
8	1,625	2,268	366	26	79	1,016
9	1,570	2,405	385	45	122	1,069
10	1,411	1,656	234	98	42	679

Table 14.3: Data for Make or Buy Exercise (000 omitted)

One concern is whether the slope of this LLA is consistent with the data. To examine this, we regress total overhead on total direct labor cost. This yields the following:

$$OV = 2,425,200 + 3.1DL$$
$$(481,000) \quad (1.2)$$
$$r^2 = .45; \ r_a^2 = .39$$

where $OV = OV_A + OV_S$ and $DL = DL_A + DL_S$. Figure 14.2 plots the data and regression line. No statistical concerns are present here.

Using this overhead LLA, we now estimate the contribution margins of the products as follows. Notice the third product is the product with the out-sourced component ($\hat{q}_2$ in the expanded LP):

price	P_1	P_2	P_2
direct labor	50	90	80
direct material	122	215	15
variable overhead at			
3.1(direct labor)	155	279	248
component purchase price			P
contribution margins	P_1-327	P_2-584	P_2-343-P

This implies an objective function in the expanded LP of

$$\pi(q_1, q_2, \hat{q}_2) = [P_1 - 327]q_1 + [P_2 - 584]q_2 + [P_2 - 343 - P]\hat{q}_2.$$

We continue to assume $P_1 = 600$ and $P_2 = 1,100$. Solving the expanded LP with this objective function provides a solution of $q_1^* = 3,000$, $q_2^* = 3,000$ and $\hat{q}_2^* = 500$. It also has $\pi^* = 2,620,500$. The solution remains as before, though the total contribution margin has changed to reflect the altered overhead LLA.

Figure 14.2: Total Overhead versus Total Direct Labor

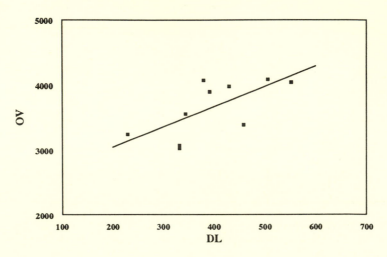

The issue of whether a firm-wide overhead LLA is sufficiently accurate remains. Suppose further exploration suggests overhead in the subassembly department is best related to direct material (DM_S), while overhead in the assembly department is best related to direct labor (DL_A).[10] The data in Table 14.3 provide the following regressions:

$$OV_S = 483,500 + 1.8DM_S$$
$$(147,400) \quad (.2)$$
$$r^2 = .94; \; r_a^2 = .93$$

and

$$OV_A = 659,700 + 2.6DL_A$$
$$(129,000) \quad (.4)$$
$$r^2 = .85; \; r_a^2 = .84.$$

A plot of the data and residuals indicates no specification concerns are present.

Using this pair of overhead LLAs, we now estimate the contribution margins as follows:

---

[10]These suggestions for appropriate independent variables come from intimate knowledge of the production process and its associated economic structure. Notice how the subassembly department appears to be "material intensive" while the assembly department appears to be "labor intensive." This is reassuring, but it is important to remember choice of independent variable is more subtle than this.

price	P_1	P_2	P_2
direct labor in assembly	40	80	80
direct labor in subassembly	10	10	0
direct material in assembly	12	15	15
direct material in subassembly	110	200	0
2.6 (assembly direct labor)	104	208	208
1.8 (subassembly direct material)	198	360	0
component purchase price			P
contribution margin	P_1-474	P_2-873	P_2-303-P

The objective function in our short-run planning exercise becomes

$$\pi(q_1, q_2, \hat{q}_2) = [P_1 - 474]q_1 + [P_2 - 873]q_2 + [P_2 - 303 - P]\hat{q}_2.$$

Solving the expanded LP with this objective function gives $q_1^* = 3,000$, $q_2^* = 3,000$ and $\hat{q}_2^* = 500$, with $\pi^* = 1,332,500$.

Dwell on the odyssey. We have called the presumed overhead LLA into question. In one stage we merely estimated the stated structure with a set of recent data. In another, we questioned the stated structure, and estimated separate LLAs for each department. For each set of LLAs, our short-run decision is unaltered. Our response to the out-sourcing option is also unaltered.

The contribution margins vary as we move among the competing LLAs. The decision, though, does not. For the present purpose, we cannot distinguish among the LLAs. Alternatively, if we subscribe to the presumption the separate models provide a superior estimate, we are left with the fact the firm-wide approximation is sufficiently accurate for this purpose. Of course, this insensitivity of the decision to the LLA would change if we changed the structure of the problem.[11]

In broader terms, we see how a make or buy type of decision naturally arises in a short-run planning context. We also see how costing concerns lead, in equally natural fashion, to use of the accounting library to shed some light on these concerns.

Product Evaluation

A parallel situation arises when we examine the profitability of a product or set of products in a short-run, small setting. The above story that centered on whether to make or buy a component also addressed the question of which combination of the two final products was best. This is an example of product evaluation.

---

[11]For example, if $P_2 = 1,150$ the choice of production plan will depend on the choice of LLA. We then must be more careful about specifying what we think is a good model of the two overhead processes.

We further illustrate the theme by introducing another potential product into the story. For this purpose we forget the make or buy question, and return to the setting in the first LP. This is done to minimize distraction. Make or buy and product profitability questions will surely interact in many instances.

Let's also agree to use the departmental overhead LLAs of $OV_S = 483,500 + 1.8DM_S$ and $OV_A = 659,700 + 2.6DL_A$. This implies respective product contribution margins of $P_1 - 474$ and $P_2 - 873$. We also continue to assume $P_1 = 600$ and $P_2 = 1,100$.

Now further suppose short-run market conditions limit each product to a maximum of 2,000 units. Our short-run maximization exercise now takes the following form:

$$\text{maximize } \pi(q_1, q_2) = [P_1 - 474]q_1 + [P_2 - 873]q_2$$

$$\begin{aligned}
\text{subject to:} \quad & q_1 + q_2 \leq 6,000; \\
& q_1 + 2q_2 \leq 10,000; \\
& q_1 \leq 2,000; \\
& q_2 \leq 2,000; \text{ and} \\
& q_1, q_2, \geq 0.
\end{aligned}$$

The obvious solution is $q_1^* = 2,000$ and $q_2^* = 2,000$, with $\pi^* = 706,000$. Also, the shadow prices on the first two constraints are zero. Our enterprise has excess capacity: $6,000 - q_1^* - q_2^* = 2,000$ in the subassembly department and $10,000 - q_1^* - 2q_2^* = 4,000$ in the assembly department. (This is the reason for introducing the additional constraints.[12])

At this point, an unanticipated customer arrives. This customer requests a bid on a special product. Capacity is available. No interactions with present or future products are anticipated. The new customer is "small" in every respect.

We might interpret this as a large retailer seeking one time production of a particular consumer product, under their brand name and according to their specifications. We also assume no interplay between sales of our existing products and this potential new one. Otherwise, demand interdependencies would have to enter the analysis.[13]

Further assume each unit of this potential product will consume one unit of the scarce resource in the subassembly and assembly departments. Let q_3 denote units of this new product. Our capacity constraints now become:

$$\begin{aligned}
\text{subassembly:} \quad & q_1 + q_2 + q_3 \leq 6,000; \text{ and} \\
\text{assembly:} \quad & q_1 + 2q_2 + q_3 \leq 10,000.
\end{aligned}$$

---

[12]Can you guess the shadow prices on the latter two constraints? The first is $600 - 474 = 126$ and the second is $1,100 - 873 = 227$. Why are these the respective contribution margins?

[13]For example, this product might be close to one of ours; and if it becomes known we are the large retailer's supplier, some customers may shift from our product to theirs.

It is further determined that manufacturing the new product will incur direct labor cost in subassembly of 10 per unit, direct material cost in subassembly of 150 per unit, direct labor cost in assembly of 50 per unit, and direct material cost in assembly of 10 per unit. This implies we have the following LLAs, where of course the subscripts denote subassembly and assembly:

$$DL_S = 10q_1 + 10q_2 + 10q_3;$$
$$DM_S = 110q_1 + 200q_2 + 150q_3;$$
$$DL_A = 40q_1 + 80q_2 + 50q_3; \text{ and}$$
$$DM_A = 12q_1 + 15q_2 + 10q_3.$$

Note well, this is assumed to be a "small" decision. Our LLAs extend in ready fashion to accommodate the new alternatives. This is an important assumption.

Let P denote the selling price per unit. We have, using the estimated departmental overhead LLAs, a contribution margin of P - 620 per unit:

price	P
direct labor in subassembly	10
direct material in subassembly	150
direct labor in assembly	50
direct material in assembly	10
1.8 (subassembly direct material)	270
2.6 (assembly direct labor)	130
contribution margin	P-620

It also turns out special tooling will be required if this new product is manufactured. This tooling will cost 15,000. Thus, if q_3 units are manufactured, and if output of the first two products remains constant, then the *incremental* profit will be $[P - 620]q_3 - 15,000$.[14]

We are now prepared to answer various questions. Suppose the price is P = 1,000. How many units must be manufactured and sold if this is to be a profitable venture? This is a break-even question. Setting incremental profit equal to zero and solving for q_3 gives

$$q_3 = 15,000/[1,000 - 620] \approx 40 \text{ units.}$$

Similarly, suppose $q_3 = 800$ units. (Notice we have the excess capacity for this many units.) What is the minimum price if this is to be an interesting product? Setting incremental profit equal to zero and solving for P (given $q_3 = 800$) gives

$$P = 620 + 15,000/800 = 620 + 18.75 = 638.75.$$

---

[14]This tooling cost is a type of setup cost. Here the story takes the form of purchasing special tools from an outside supplier. Another version arises when we shut down a group of machines in order to adjust settings, perhaps change dies, and so on. Specialized personnel are often required at this point; and highly automated techniques may be in place (as in so-called flexible manufacturing operations).

More generally, this is a classic short-run optimization exercise. Is this short-run opportunity profitable? We estimate the incremental cost of the first unit to be $15,000 + 620 = 15,620$. We estimate the incremental cost of additional units at 620. The 620 datum is constant, within the relevant range of our LLAs. Moreover, no interactions with other products are envisioned. Thus, we speak unambiguously of the product's incremental (or marginal) cost.

Rendering this picture is greatly aided by the fact we have excess capacity in the two departments. Otherwise, production of the new product interacts with the existing products.

Customer Evaluation

A parallel exercise arises when we think in terms of adding or dropping a particular customer. Again presume a short-run setting, with "small" effects. If the customer in question purchases a single specialized product, this is just a repetition of the earlier discussion. If the customer purchases a variety of products, we would repeat the earlier discussion but would focus on the particular set of products purchased.

Interesting issues arise here. For example, the customer may place unusual service demands on us. Alternatively, the customer may provide unusual feedback on product quality or insights into new product proposals.

Continuing along this line, we will eventually reach the conclusion this is not really a "small" problem. Taking on the new customer, or dropping an existing customer, is likely to have effects that interact with other activities, that last well beyond the current period, and that are not well-approximated by the existing set of LLAs.

Work Force Scheduling

This ubiquitous strain of identifying when a decision is "small" or "large" can be further explored in a work force scheduling context. Here we face a specific type of make or buy decision: whether to acquire additional labor services from the existing (permanent) work force, from a temporary work force, or from an expanded permanent work force.

Suppose demand has increased, and we are operating near capacity. Yet more customers arrive. This is good news, except we must service the customers. To make the story more specific, suppose this is a wholesaler business that sells to many retailers. The products are selling, retailers are buying, and we are getting behind in our paperwork.

Several options are present and may be pursued in combination. We might ask some of the work force to work overtime. This increases the wage per hour, but avoids the cost of searching for and training new employees. It also removes future flexibility. Too much overtime may lessen the work force's willingness to work overtime in a future period.

Temporary services might be engaged. This has the advantage of no long-term commitment; and employee benefits are typically unimportant in such an arrangement. The arrangement is clean and temporary. Of course, this also precludes learning effects. Any job-specific human capital the temporary employees acquire will be lost when their temporary stay ends.[15]

We also might expand the permanent work force. This has the advantage of better integration and a longer term relationship than the temporary option. It also raises the specter of a long-term relationship and its economic ramifications. How should we cost out benefits such as pensions, vacations, sick leave, health insurance, job training, workman's compensation, and so on?

The transactions costs are likely to vary across the options. A broker will likely provide the temporary work force. Training will be an issue. More substantive search, screening, and training will be involved in seeking new permanent employees. The use of overtime and temporary services may be governed by existing work force contracts, either explicit or implicit.

Uncertainty

The final stop on our overview of small decisions is the question of uncertainty. Surely uncertainty is present. The question is when and how to give it formal standing in a decision analysis.[16] We might ignore it. We might give it implicit standing, for example, by acknowledging our cost estimates are uncertain and then attempting to buttress them with statistical digestion of the accounting library. Or we might formally introduce risk.

The seasoned professional manager makes these judgments. Here we explore some dimensions spanned by that judgment. For this purpose, return to the special customer theme. To lighten up the details, suppose we have identified a short-run opportunity. The profit possibilities are particularly simple. The selling price is 100,000 dollars. The estimated incremental cost is 95,000. No interactions are present. All looks promising.

Further suppose the cost is uncertain. With probability .5, the incremental cost will be 70,000; and with probability .5 it will be 120,000. This gives an *expected* incremental cost of

$$.5(70,000) + .5(120,000) = 95,000.$$

---

[15]An option at this point is to turn the temporary into a permanent employee.

[16]In subsequent chapters we will not have this flexibility. Control problems only arise when uncertainty is present. Our conceptual thinking at that time must then recognize uncertainty. It is too important to gloss over in that arena.

This cost uncertainty also implies incremental profit is uncertain. It will be 100,000 - 70,000 = 30,000 with probability .5; and 100,000 - 120,000 = - 20,000 with probability .5. Is this uncertainty important?[17]

Suppose the organization is nearly (or precisely) risk neutral for decisions of this nature.[18] It is well diversified; incremental gains and losses of this magnitude carry close to nil risk premia. Then, we may safely ignore the uncertainty and focus on the expected incremental income. Conversely, suppose the organization regards risk as noxious. As in Chapter 4, let's think in terms of ending wealth, $\hat{w}$. Let the utility for wealth $\hat{w}$ be the square root of $\hat{w}$. (The root function is used merely for convenience in exposition.)

Now we must admit the decision is not entirely small. Let w denote the wealth implications of all but this particular activity. Below we consider, in turn, the cases where the status quo is riskless and risky.

riskless status quo

If we reject this opportunity, total wealth will be w. If we accept it, wealth will total w + 30,000 with probability .5 and w - 20,000 with probability .5. For example, suppose w = 25,000. Then the utility measure for the status quo is U(w) = 158.11; and for the proposed product it is:

$$.5\sqrt{25,000 + 30,000} + .5\sqrt{25,000 - 20,000} = .5(234.52) + .5(70.71) = 152.62.$$

In this case, the new product opportunity is rejected, as 152.62 < 158.11; it is too risky.

To explore this further, recall that a lottery's certain equivalent is the certain amount that is equivalent to the lottery. By definition, the decision maker is indifferent between the lottery and its certain equivalent. Here we have

$$\sqrt{CE} = .5\sqrt{w+30,000} + .5\sqrt{w-20,000}.$$

Given w = 25,000, the certain equivalent is 23,293.[19] The organization is worse off with the new product, as 23,293 < 25,000.

Next express CE as the expected value of wealth less the risk premium:

---

[17] If the selling price were at least 120,000 we could readily dismiss the uncertainty on grounds of first order stochastic dominance. The worst that might happen is no gain!

[18] Recall it is somewhat awkward to speak of the organization's utility function or preference measure. The theory of the firm, we have noted, is unsettled in important areas, including what the firm's goals might be in a setting more friction laden than perfect and complete markets. This does not negate the importance of uncertainty. It merely makes it more difficult to understand.

[19] We round the calculations to the nearest dollar.

$$CE = .5(w + 30,000) + .5(w - 20,000) - RP = w + 5,000 - RP,$$

where RP denotes the risk premium. Therefore, the new product proposal is a winner if

$$CE = w + 5,000 - RP > w; \text{ or}$$
$$5,000 - RP > 0.$$

This is important. Initially we assumed risk neutrality and evaluated the proposal in terms of the expected incremental profit. This was positive; the proposal was viewed as attractive. Here we evaluate it in terms of expected incremental profit *less the risk premium*. When w = 25,000, we have a risk premium of w + 5,000 - CE = 25,000 + 5,000 - 23,293 = 6,707. Alternatively, we have an evaluation of 5,000 - RP = 5,000 - 6,707 = - 1,707.

This may appear to be setting a record for convoluted recalculation. But an important point is emerging. Our story began with a comparison of expected incremental revenue and expected incremental cost. This is a profit oriented calculation, one with natural ties to the accounting library. (If the chapter were not getting too long, we would drive this home by engaging in a regression exercise to help estimate the incremental profit.)

We then level this expected incremental profit with a risk premium. This is an additional cost component, one that we might label the "cost of risk". This has no natural tie to the accounting library. Cost of risk is not recorded in the accounting library.[20]

Finally, we have stressed interactions between decisions. Here, the risk premium, the cost of risk, interacts with the existing activities, summarized in initial wealth w. The cost of risk depends on the other activities or decisions.

Examine Figure 14.3. There we plot RP as a function of the status quo wealth, w. Notice we must have w ≥ 20,000, otherwise we cannot take the root of w - 20,000.[21] When w = 20,000, we find RP = 12,500. RP declines as w increases, reflecting the fact that the root utility function exhibits decreasing absolute risk aversion. For example, when w = 100,000 we find RP = 1,510. Can you locate the point of indifference? (Try w = 31,250.)

Viewed in this manner, RP is a cost of risk. Figure 14.3 plots the cost of risk as a function of the status quo, w. The cost of risk enters when we frame the analysis in terms of certain equivalents and measure the certain equivalent as expected value

---

[20]Our earlier example in Chapter 10, where we worried about the possible arrival of another customer, is related. Flexibility has value and in a dynamic setting we reduce flexibility when we commit capacity to particular activities. One way to frame such an analysis relies on a cost of using the capacity, or of reducing flexibility.

[21]We mentioned earlier that the root utility function was a matter of expositional convenience. One disadvantage is it rules out negative profit. If life were only so simple.

less a risk premium. Framing the analysis directly with expected utilities would subsume the cost of risk notion.

Figure 14.3: Risk Premium for Special Customer Illustration

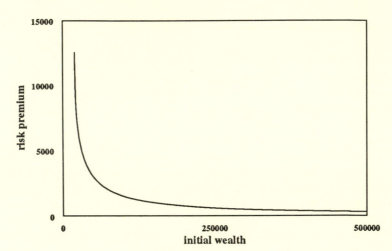

To bring this to a close, we are examining a short-run product opportunity. It is risky, but the organization's status quo has a certain wealth of w. We evaluate this type of decision in terms of its potential return and risk. Expected incremental profit less cost of risk is a particularly vivid expression. If the organization's risk aversion is constant, is independent of the status quo, we have no interaction between this decision and the status quo point. If its attitude toward risk varies with w, we have an interaction. Our particular illustration, we stress, was one in which there was an interaction caused by decreasing absolute risk aversion. If w is large enough, the product is interesting.

risky status quo

When w is certain, the only risk in sight in our continuing example is the cost uncertainty. This makes a risk-return analysis straightforward, because the risk is so well defined. Matters change if w itself is uncertain.

Suppose the organization's status quo is one in which wealth will be 70,000 with probability .5 and 20,000 with probability .5. Using the root utility function, the status quo certain equivalent is 41,208:

$$\sqrt{41,208} = .5\sqrt{70,000} + .5\sqrt{20,000}.$$

When we now introduce the special customer proposal we have to worry about the probabilistic relationship between the two sources of uncertainty. One extreme is perfectly negative correlation. If the status quo turns out well, the new product does not, and vice versa. The certain equivalent is calculated as follows:

$$\sqrt{50,000} = .5\sqrt{70,000-20,000} + .5\sqrt{20,000+30,000}.$$

Notice the implied risk premium for the new activity is negative here. The new activity insures the existing ones.

The other extreme is perfect positive correlation. If the status quo turns out well, so does the new product, and vice versa. This is dreadful:

$$\sqrt{25,000} = .5\sqrt{70,000+30,000} + .5\sqrt{20,000-20,000}.$$

Here we have the potential for two types of interactions. The risk that is present depends on how the new and old risks combine. Diversification matters. And, as before, the scale of operations may by itself affect the attitude toward risk.

Of course, the importance of either or both interactions depends on the situation at hand. (Yes, professional judgment is important.) All we can say with generality is that *if* the organization is risk averse and *if* it has constant absolute risk aversion and *if* the status quo and proposed lotteries are probabilistically independent, then it does not matter. Risk aversion means risk matters. Constant absolute risk aversion means scale of operations does not affect attitude toward risk; and probabilistic independence means the risks do not interact.[22]

interaction with taxes

Once we start looking for interactions, it seems they appear at every twist and turn. What started out as a nicely contained analysis of small decisions has served to warn us that the boundary between small and not so small is often subtle and idiosyncratic.

Just to turn this message a little deeper, we should acknowledge the importance of taxes. We often think (or claim) income taxes are important in long-run but not short-run decision settings. Suppose the marginal tax rate is some constant τ. For every incremental dollar of profit, the organization then receives $(1 - \tau)$ net of taxes.

Under risk neutrality, maximizing profit and maximizing $(1 - \tau)$ times profit lead to the same decisions. Some modest care is necessary when we move into risk aversion, as we must be careful to distinguish pre- and post-profit utility functions.

---

[22]This issue of identifying the organization's goal or goals will lead us in the following chapter to think in terms of risk and return. There, in the spirit of modern finance, we will use discounting techniques with a market determined discount rate that is appropriate for the risk at hand. Although there is a temptation to invoke this machinery here, doing so would obscure the point that with less than perfect markets the organization itself may have diversification incentives. If so, the boundary between large and small decisions becomes more obscure.

But then we also should admit a constant marginal tax rate is not guaranteed. What if a loss occurs? The immediate marginal rate might drop to zero.[23]

Taxes are not benign.

Summary

The accounting library is retrospective, while decision making is prospective. The library may contain important information that helps us analyze a particular decision problem. The library also will record the accounting interpretations of whatever decisions we make.

The link between our decision analysis and the accounting library may be close or tenuous. It all depends on the decision circumstance, decision frame, and library procedures.

Small decisions are somewhat free of interactions with other activities and do not contemplate movement outside the relevant range of the prevailing LLAs. Thus, small decisions often exhibit a close link between their portrayal in the accounting library and their analysis. Simple cost-volume-profit exercises, such as estimating the profitability of an additional customer or break-even analysis, are illustrative of this fact. (Of course, we should remember the difference between gross and contribution margin here. A short-run profitable venture may appear unprofitable if we record it using full costing procedures.)

Even so, we should not be naive. The direct material odyssey illustrates the point. There we had an accounting cost, presumably historical standard cost, of the material in question. Yet the cost of this material in our highlighted decision frame depended in intimate ways on current and future prices and plans. The inherently short-run problem had an inherently long-run connection.

The make or buy, product evaluation, customer evaluation, and work force vignettes all illustrate ways in which small decisions may take on larger dimensions. Introducing uncertainty further clouds the distinction. We stress the distinction because it highlights the important managerial art of knowing how much detail to load into a decision analysis.

On a final note, our study of accounting information in short-run decisions has been silent on who makes these decisions. This depends on the authority structure within the organization. Whether the decision is pondered at a "high" or "low" level in the organization is independent of the importance of framing. Whether the importance of the accounting library varies with location in the organization is another matter. To answer this we would have to specify the availability of other sources of information across the organization. A traveling sales agent knows costs and market conditions. A maintenance supervisor knows repair costs, subcontract-

---

[23]For example, risk neutrality and an increasing marginal tax rate imply risk aversion in pre-tax dollars.

ing alternatives, and so on. A grocery clerk knows products (e.g., kumquats versus tangerines) and prices.

Bibliographic Notes

The idea here is to frame a decision with the smallest possible package; a small decision is very accommodating in this respect. The three principles of consistent framing are clearly at work. A more pragmatic view has us use a frame that is further reduced by ignoring modest or small complications and interactions. Admitting this implies the analysis is an approximation. Howard [1971] calls this proximal decision analysis. Demski and Feltham [1976] highlight the approximation theme in terms of a simplification and tie it to costing questions.

Problems and Exercises

1. What is the distinction between (i) a large and a small decision and between (ii) a short-run and a long-run decision? Give an example where a short-run decision is small, another where a short-run decision is large. Then give two more examples, where a long-run decision is small and where a long-run decision is large.

2. Discuss the relationship between break-even analysis and our earlier study of variable costing.

3. Why are the graphs in Figure 14.1 truncated?

4. The text illustration surrounding Table 14.2 concerns the question of whether to produce an extra product. It was framed in terms of incremental revenue less incremental cost of the extra product. Provide an alternate frame, one that does not call for measurement of the extra product's cost. Carefully contrast your frame with that used in the text.

5. Suppose we have a decision that is small, with the possible exception of risk considerations. Further suppose constant, nontrivial risk aversion is present. If the randomness in the current decision is independent of any other randomness, the decision is small; otherwise, it is large. Carefully explain. Is the statement correct under risk neutrality?

6. *break-even calculations*
Ralph is planning a visit to the bank to solicit a small business loan. Ralph's business plan, in summary form, is given by the following LLAs:

revenue	$TR = 240q$;
manufacturing cost	$TMC = 125{,}000 + 100q$; and
selling and administrative	$S\&A = 85{,}000 + 20q$.

a] The bank, after studying Ralph's numbers, asks what the break-even point is. What is it, and why might the bank be interested in it?

b] Ralph then points out that the business plan calls for production of q = 2,500 units the first year. Under GAAP style income measurement, using actual, full costing, how many units must Ralph sell in the first year for accounting income to be zero?

c] Explain the difference between your two break-even calculations.

d] What would you, as the banker, say to Ralph's comment in [b] above?

7. *large break-even and output calculations*[24]
Ralph's cost curve is piece-wise linear. For output of $0 \le q \le 1,000$ units it is given by $C(q) = 1,000 + 6q$; for $1,000 \le q \le 2,000$ it is given by $C(q) = 3,000 + 4q$; and for $2,000 \le q$ it is given by $C(q) = -5,000 + 8q$.

a] Plot Ralph's cost curve.

b] Suppose the selling price is $P = 7$ per unit. Plot the implied total revenue curve on your graph in [a]; also locate Ralph's break-even point. Repeat for cases where the selling price is $P = 8$ and $P = 9$.

c] Again assume the selling price is $P = 7$. Locate Ralph's optimal output.

d] Now approximate Ralph's cost curve with an LLA of $3,000 + 4q$; notice this approximation is consistent with the optimal output chosen above as well as the original break-even calculation. Suppose the selling price unexpectedly drops to $P = 4.8$. Using the LLA of $3,000 + 4q$, calculate Ralph's best choice of output (somewhere between shutdown and a maximum of 2,000 units).

e] What mistake has Ralph made in part [d] above?

8. *cost versus expenditure*
It is often claimed that arranging a long term supplier contract for necessary direct materials will insulate you from price changes in the materials market. Coase [1968] contends this is erroneous. Carefully analyze the claim. (You may want to reflect on the example surrounding Table 14.1.)

9. *cost versus expenditure*
The material cost illustration in Table 14.2 stresses the difference between an appropriate measure of cost for some purpose and the expenditure on the factor in question. Does a similar comment apply to labor cost? Carefully explain.

---

[24]Contributed by Richard Sansing.

10. *cost versus expenditure*

Return to the two period inventory setting of Table 14.2, where we framed a new product opportunity in terms of incremental revenue less incremental cost.

a] Carefully explain the shadow prices on the initial inventory for the six cases in Table 14.1. Why is this shadow price the appropriate material cost in the incremental cost frame?

b] Give a variation on the assumed prices and quantities such that the appropriate material cost in the incremental formulation is 8.1. Do not change any of the first period prices.

c] What happens in the setting of Table 14.2 if we set $P^+ = 15$ and $P^- = 14$? What does this tell you about a formulation that uses these second period prices?

d] Is the historical cost of the material a sunk cost? Can you provide a frame of the new product decision that makes this most obvious?

e] Briefly discuss what happens in this setting if the firm faces a constant 40% marginal tax rate on accounting income.

11. *interactions in customer evaluation*

Return to the product evaluation discussion in the text, where a potential third product, with quantity q_3, was under consideration. Presuming limited market conditions for the other products (of $q_1 \leq 2,000$ and $q_2 \leq 2,000$), and a selling price of $P = 1,000$, we derived a break-even quantity of $q_3 = 15,000/[1,000 - 620] \approx 40$. We now assume there are no market constraints on the first two products (thereby dropping the $q_1 \leq 2,000$ and $q_2 \leq 2,000$ constraints). Suppose we acquire the necessary tooling, at a cost of 15,000, and produce q_3 units of this new product.

a] Without the noted market constraints, the production of the first two products is affected by production of the third. Suppose $0 \leq q_3 \leq 2,000$. Determine the best choice of q_1 and q_2, given an exogenous q_3 in the noted range. (Recall their respective selling prices are $P_1 = 600$ and $P_2 = 1,100$.)

b] Now suppose the selling price of the new product is $P = 1,000$ per unit. How many units must be produced and sold if accepting this new product is a good idea?

c] Carefully explain the difference between the original break-even calculation and that you performed in [b] above.

d] Suppose $q_3 = 800$ units. What is the minimum price for this to be an interesting product?

e] Again presuming $0 \leq q_3 \leq 2,000$, what is the incremental cost of the third product?

12. *LLAs, product choice, and income measurement*

We now find Ralph managing a two product firm, Ralph's LP, with constrained capacity. The production process consists of fabrication and assembly departments. A service group that supplies maintenance, minor engineering, material handling, and miscellaneous services to these two departments is also present. Let q_1 and q_2 denote the quantities of the two products. The fabrication department is constrained as follows: $2q_1 + q_2 \leq 300$. Think of this as expressed in hours of direct labor. The first product requires two such hours, and the second one; 300 hours in total are available. The assembly department is constrained via $q_1 + 3q_2 \leq 600$. This, too, should be thought of in terms of direct labor hours. (The data are scaled for convenience.)

For budgeting and accounting purposes, Ralph recognizes seven cost categories. Respective LLAs are detailed below. (Selling and administrative is the only period cost category.)

selling and administrative:	$S\&A = 5{,}000 + 3q_1 + 5q_2$;
direct labor in fabrication:	$DL^f = 22[2q_1 + q_2]$;
direct labor in assembly:	$DL^a = 35[q_1 + 3q_2]$;
direct material (all in fabrication):	$DM = 120q_1 + 200q_2$;
overhead in fabrication:	$OV^f = 5{,}000 + 1DL^f$;
overhead in assembly:	$OV^a = 6{,}000 + 3DL^a$; and
manufacturing service group:	$MS = 2{,}000 + DL^f + .2DL^a$.

These LLAs reflect underlying standard quantities and standard prices. Direct labor in the fabrication department, for example, is priced at 22 dollars per hour, while in the assembly department it is priced at 35 per hour. For later reference, we interpret the direct material LLA as reflecting "units" of raw material, priced at 20 per unit. Finally, the selling prices are estimated to be, respectively, 600 and 800 per unit. This implies a revenue LLA of $600q_1 + 800q_2$.

Determine an optimal production plan for Ralph. What income is implied by this profit plan? Present this income calculation in a GAAP style statement, where revenue less cost of goods sold, based on full costing, identifies the gross margin, and gross margin less all period costs identifies net income. Also present the income calculation in variable costing format, where revenue less all (period and product) variable costs identifies contribution margin, and contribution margin less all "fixed" costs identifies net income. Why are the two income figures identical here?

13. *continued analysis of LLA choice*

Return to the make or buy illustration in the text, surrounding Table 14.3, where we used the regression based LLA of $OV = 2{,}425{,}200 + 3.1DL$, along with $P_1 = 600$, $P_2 = 1{,}100$, and $P = 250$.

a] Are the error terms consistent with the assumptions of regression analysis?

b] Concentrate on the slope of 3.1. Determine the range over which this slope can vary without changing the decision of $q_1^* = 3{,}000$, $q_2^* = 3{,}000$ and $\hat{q}_2^* = 500$.

14. *choice of LLA*

Consumer, Inc. produces and distributes a variety of consumer products. For simplicity, the story is condensed to highlight two products, consumer staples (with quantity q_1) and fashion goods (with quantity q_2). The production process is simple. Prefabricated items and packaging materials are purchased from suppliers, the items are then assembled, packaged, and shipped. Assembly and packaging have limited capacities. Relevant technology and cost estimates are provided below.

sales revenue	$95q_1 + 180q_2$;
direct material costs in assembly	$12q_1 + 18q_2$;
direct material costs in packaging	$2q_1 + 9q_2$;
direct labor costs in assembly	$14q_1 + 28q_2$;
direct labor costs in packaging	$10q_1 + 10q_2$; and
distribution cost	$2q_1 + 3q_2$.

The standard wage rate is 14 per hour in assembly and 10 per hour in packaging. The capacity constraints are expressed in terms of direct labor hours, with 600,000 available in assembly and 480,000 available in packaging.

Three overhead categories are recognized: assembly (OV_A), packaging (OV_P) and general (OV_G). The third category, general, includes cost items that cannot be identified with individual products or departments. A firm-wide overhead charging rate of 27 per hour of direct labor is used.

a] The tentative production plan calls for emphasis on fashion goods (q_2), as this product is estimated to be far more profitable than the consumer staple product. Verify this claim, using the noted overhead charging rate. Also, using this charging rate, estimate the firm's income using this production plan.

b] The middle level managers find the tentative plan in [a] flawed, and confide in Ralph. They claim the firm has for too long been influenced by outdated accounting measures and scoff at the profitability measures used in part [a]. Further discussion reveals they harbor the following overhead estimates:

$OV_A = 2,000,000 + 200\%$ of assembly direct labor cost;

$OV_P = 1,000,000 + 125\%$ of packaging direct material cost; and

$OV_G = 5,000,000 + 3.5$(total direct labor hours).

Using these LLAs, determine the firm's best output schedule. What income can the firm expect if this plan is used? How much additional income does the improved plan contribute?

c] At this point the overhead LLAs are called into question. The data listed below (000 omitted) are collected from 15 recent periods. OV_A, OV_P and OV_G are the respective overhead amounts. DLH denotes total direct labor hours, $DL\$_A$ denotes direct labor dollars in assembly, and $DM\$_P$ denotes direct material dollars in packaging. Are the middle managers' conjectures consistent with the data?

d] How much would you pay to distinguish between the managers' conjectures and the statistical estimates you derived in [c] above?

e]   Those who advocated the original plan are now somewhat contrite. They acknowledge the use of a full cost charging rate in estimating the product costs but are not convinced the use of separate overhead pools is worth the extra effort. Statistically estimate the single overhead pool LLA, and use this estimate to locate an optimal production plan. Carefully explain your findings.

t	OV$_A$	OV$_P$	OV$_G$	DLH	DL$\$_A$	DM$\$_P$
1	19,603	3,235	6,189	1,085	8,652	1,991
2	20,118	3,961	5,524	1,229	9,884	2,327
3	22,832	4,003	4,452	1,331	10,668	2,489
4	23,104	4,093	6,452	1,315	10,542	2,461
5	23,064	4,286	3,906	1,316	10,640	2,540
6	23,418	3,896	4,139	1,334	10,696	2,498
7	21,821	3,932	4,818	1,228	10,038	2,464
8	24,016	4,015	4,715	1,384	11,186	2,668
9	20,525	3,782	5,565	1,201	9,506	2,143
10	22,021	3,863	6,325	1,284	10,304	2,412
11	21,460	4,187	2,979	1,234	9,912	2,326
12	20,562	3,813	5,668	1,169	9,282	2,111
13	20,484	3,976	6,509	1,225	9,716	2,203
14	22,511	4,216	5,074	1,310	10,570	2,510
15	18,180	2,665	4,601	989	7,798	1,739

15. *possible misspecification of overhead LLA*
     Ralph works for a municipality and is studying a proposal that the city subcontract with a small neighboring community to extend its municipal garbage collection service to that community. This has some appeal, as Ralph's municipality has the capacity and flexibility to do this and also has access to a regeneration facility. The overhead cost is the troublesome part of the analysis. The cost structure suggests overhead varies with direct labor hours. Statistical analysis, a regression of overhead on direct labor hours, confirms this and suggests an LLA with a slope of 44.9. The underlying regression is free of specification concerns.
     At this point the mayor's assistant claims the regression is seriously flawed because of "asset record keeping inadequacies." It turns out that no depreciation accounting is done in the municipality and the overhead has been systematically understated by a total of 3,000,000 during the sample period in question. (Capital equipment is recorded, on a cash basis, in a separate fund.)
     What will happen to Ralph's regression if the 3,000,000 is allocated across time periods, and then into the overhead account each period, using straight line depreciation? Contrast this with the case of sum-of-the-years'-digits depreciation.

16. *possible misspecification of overhead LLA*

Empire Electronics (EE) is an assembler of custom electronic components. It faces an opportunity to bid on a particular assembly. Direct material is estimated to cost 14,000 and direct labor 112,000. Variable overhead is allocated at 61.75% of direct labor cost. A special consulting fee of 18,000 will also be incurred if the assembly project is taken on. (An incremental cost of 213,160 is thus implied.) This fee reflects the standard retainer arrangement EE has with a human resources consulting firm. Labor is in short supply and EE will hire 2 temporary laborers if it successfully bids on the project. The consulting firm does the necessary search, interviewing, applicant testing, and so on, all for a price of 9,000 per employee supplied. The temporary laborers will leave after the assembly work is completed, with no additional compensation.

The 61.75% datum stems from a recent cost analysis. The overhead account contains mainly labor support activities, fringe benefits, supervision, inventory control, payroll administration and so on. The data listed in the table below were used to produce this estimate.

t	OV (000)	DL$ (000)	no. of hires
1	5,915	11,326	120
2	5,922	11,339	120
3	6,600	12,074	160
4	5,648	11,127	110
5	3,903	8,976	100
6	3,097	6,275	70
7	4,491	8,625	110
8	6,556	11,863	180
9	5,321	9,837	110
10	4,579	9,689	80

At this point a member of the management team questions the cost estimate of 213,160. Research indicates the consulting fee is always charged to manufacturing overhead. So a question of double counting arises. Is it correct to combine the regression estimate of variable overhead with the 18,000 datum?

Provide an estimate of the cost to EE of performing the assembly in question.

17. *small choices under constant risk aversion*

Return to the discussion of uncertainty, where the gamble that resulted in a gain of 30,000 or a loss of 20,000, with equal odds, was analyzed and the status quo was riskless. Now, constant risk aversion is present (so the utility measure is $-exp(-r\hat{w})$ where we interpret $\hat{w}$ as ending wealth).

a] Suppose r = .0001. Is this an interesting gamble? What is its certain equivalent?

b] Find the value of r such that you would be indifferent between accepting and rejecting this gamble.

c] Using the value of r determined in [b] above, your break-even view of risk aversion, determine the risk premium you would demand to take on a bet on a fair coin, where under "heads" you win $1,000 and under "tails" you lose $1,000.

18. *taxes and risk aversion*
    Ralph has been offered an interesting gamble. With probability .5, Ralph will gain $500 and with probability .5 Ralph will gain $100. The gain is net of the purchase price; also, the possible outcomes are independent of any other items in Ralph's portfolio.

a] Suppose Ralph is risk neutral. Determine the gamble's certain equivalent.

b] Ralph remains risk neutral, but faces a constant marginal tax rate of 40%. Determine the gamble's certain equivalent. Can Ralph safely ignore taxes in this circumstance?

c] Now suppose Ralph is risk averse, with a utility measure defined over wealth $\hat{w}$ of $-exp(-r\hat{w})$ and r = .001. (So Ralph's risk aversion is constant.) Repeat parts [a] and [b] above.

19. *LLA errors*
    Twin Products produces two products, with quantities denoted q_1 and q_2. Its cost curve is given by $C(q_1,q_2) = 100q_1 + 100q_2 + 10q_1^2 + 10q_2^2$. The firm, however, aggregates the two products together and uses a simplified specification based on an LLA of $C(\hat{q}) = 200\hat{q}$, where $\hat{q} = q_1 + q_2$. The firm has been offered a chance to supply two extra units of the first product to a special customer. The customer is willing to pay a total of 600 for these two units.

a] Suppose the current production schedule calls for $q_1 = 10$ and $q_2 = 0$. Is this a reasonable LLA to use for purposes of analyzing the special opportunity?

b] Repeat part [a], assuming the current production schedule calls for $q_1 = 0$ and $q_2 = 10$.

c] Stay with the story in [b] above. Assume the offer is accepted and total cost turns out to be precisely as estimated by the $C(q_1,q_2)$ function. Also assume the firm uses standard costing, based on the noted LLA. What will be the net "plug" to cost of goods sold, reflecting the difference between actual and standard cost of products manufactured during the period?

15

Large Versus Small Decisions: Long-Run

In this chapter we continue our exploration of decision making, but with a focus on decisions with long-run consequences. Again our concerns are with distinguishing large and small decisions and with links to the accounting library.

The large versus small concern is a recurring theme. Have we strained the credibility of our LLAs to the extent they should be modified? Should we worry about interactions with other decisions? As we have stressed, there is no readymade answer to these concerns. Short-run decisions are not necessarily small, just as long-run decisions are not necessarily large. On the other hand, it seems we should expect many long-run decisions to be large, reflecting the *local* nature of our LLAs.

Whether small or large, decisions always have links to the accounting library. Earlier events, recorded in the library, may give important clues to consequences of the contemplated choice. For example, cost experiences with earlier products may be useful in contemplating new products. Similarly, whatever choice is made and whatever consequences follow, some portrayal will eventually be catalogued in the library. Oddly, it turns out we usually use one model to analyze a long-run decision and another to reflect its consequences in the accounting library. (This was the point of annuity based depreciation schedules encountered in earlier study of introductory accounting.)

Long-run decisions, by definition, have consequences that fall over an extended time frame. This suggests a focus on present value, and for this reason we begin with a review of discounting, or present value, techniques. This provides another opportunity to study decision framing, and it also returns us to the awkwardness of an incompletely specified organization objective. In the fortuitous world of perfect and complete markets, the organization's long-run decisions would be governed by present value maximization, with market specified discount rates. In a less friendly market structure, the organization's objectives are ambiguous, and so is the use of present value analysis. Lacking guidance on this score, we adopt the traditional approach and emphasize present value techniques in the analysis of long-run decisions.[1]

With the review of discounting techniques in place, we turn to the question of estimating cash flows. Questions of LLA adequacy, taxes, and interactions with other decisions naturally arise. Finally, we return to the accounting library and contrast the decision analysis and accounting renderings of the forces that play on the organization in this setting.

---

[1]This is not capricious. We have repeatedly encountered ambiguity in specifying the organization's objective. At the same time, we know present value techniques are widely used.

Discounting Fundamentals

In Chapter 2 we reviewed the notion of present value of a sequence of cash flows. In abstract terms, we imagined a sequence of cash flows as follows.

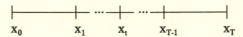

$$x_0 \qquad x_1 \quad x_t \quad x_{T-1} \qquad x_T$$

We then defined the present value as the market value, at time $t = 0$, of this sequence of cash flows.

To refine the story further, we assumed the periods were of equal length and that a constant interest or discount rate of $r > 0$ prevailed. Under these circumstances, the present value is easily rationalized and calculated. It is simply the sum of the discounted values of each cash flow datum in the sequence of cash flows, where the discount factor in period t is $(1+r)^{-t}$:

$$PV = \Sigma_t x_t (1+r)^{-t} = x_0 + x_1(1+r)^{-1} + x_2(1+r)^{-2} + \cdots + x_T(1+r)^{-T}.$$

In such a market regime, PV and the $x_0, x_1, ..., x_T$ sequence of dated cash flows are equivalent. They have the same market value. x_1 dollars at time $t = 1$ is equivalent to $x_1(1+r)^{-1}$ at time $t = 0$, just as x_t dollars at time t is equivalent to $x_t(1+r)^{-t}$ dollars at time $t = 0$.

Tables, calculators, and spreadsheets are routinely used to automate these calculations. (The latter two are so common we do not include discounting tables here.) We also might acknowledge a more or less continuous cash flow series. That is getting ahead of the story.

a prototypical question

Now suppose our organization is contemplating expansion. The choice boils down to (1) expand or (2) not expand. Analysis reveals the proposed expansion will result in the following annual *incremental* cash flow sequence (000 omitted):

Table 15.1: End-of-Period Cash Flows for Capacity Expansion						
t = 0	t = 1	t = 2	t = 3	t = 4	t = 5	t = 6
-383.000	89.500	100.300	88.780	81.868	231.868	5.184

That is, an immediate investment, or cash outflow, of 383 will be followed by cash inflows of 89.5 one year hence, 100.3 two years hence, and so on. Rejection means the opportunity is lost forever; it cannot be deferred.

Several features of this display should be noted. By convention, we record cash outflow as negative and cash inflow as positive. The cash flows are also depicted as occurring at the end of the respective periods. They are treated as annual amounts, for example. We might want to think in monthly, quarterly, or semi-annual amounts. Practice suggests that the annual reckoning is often adequate, as is the assumption cash flows occur at the end of the respective years. Finally, these are cash flow, not income, data.

present value calculations

Assume a discount rate of $r = 12\%$. The present value of this sequence of cash flows is now readily calculated:

$$PV = -383(1.12)^0 + 89.5(1.12)^{-1} + 100.3(1.12)^{-2} + 88.78(1.12)^{-3} +$$
$$81.868(1.12)^{-4} + 231.868(1.12)^{-5} + 5.184(1.12)^{-6} = 26.284$$

$$\approx -383 + 89.5(.8929) + 100.3(.7972) + 88.78(.7118) + 81.868(.6355) +$$
$$231.868(.5674) + 5.184(.5066) = 26.283.$$

Notice we show two calculations for the present value. The first is exact, up to the rounding error inherent in a typical spreadsheet. The second is based on a 4-digit approximation to $(1.12)^{-t}$, as would be found in a typical present value table. Using more than 4 significant digits is more accurate. Given that the cash flow estimates themselves are projections, concern over this degree of accuracy suggests a misunderstanding of what issues are present. Use the calculation method that is most convenient, period.

We also should be aware many refer to this calculation as *net* present value (or NPV). The adjective is carried along to remind us we are including the cash inflows and the cash outflows in the calculation. PV seems sufficient.

the present value investment criterion

The proposed expansion calls for immediate investment of 383, followed by subsequent cash inflows in future years of 89.500, 100.300, and so on. The present value of this sequence of cash flows, at $r = 12\%$, is 26.284. This consists of the present value of the future cash inflows less the present value of the necessary investment.

The present value of the investment amount or cash *outflow* is 383, as it all occurs at time $t = 0$ in our story. The present value of the subsequent cash *inflows* is $409.284 = 89.5(1.12)^{-1} + 100.3(1.12)^{-2} + 88.78(1.12)^{-3} + 81.868(1.12)^{-4} + 231.868(1.12)^{-5} + 5.184(1.12)^{-6}$.

Thus, the proposed capacity expansion calls for trading 383 time $t = 0$ dollars for 409.284 time $t = 0$ dollars. This is a good idea! The net gain is

$$PV = 409.284 - 383 = 26.284.$$

Taking the expansion proposal is equivalent to collecting a windfall gain of 26.284 current dollars.

This illustrates the present value investment criterion. In abstract terms, let $A = \{a_1, ..., a_n\}$ be a set of investment proposals. Some of these projects can be taken jointly or separately. For example, the packaging equipment can be upgraded despite whether a corporate jet is acquired. Other combinations might be undoable. For example, we might upgrade the packaging equipment with machines from one supplier or with machines from another supplier but not both as they are incompatible. It is also possible that some proposals interact. For example, some new product proposals may have different cash flows if they are developed in tandem, or if they are developed together with upgrading the packaging equipment.

Let a denote any combination of projects in A that is feasible. Also let PV_a denote its present value. We then take the feasible combination of projects with the largest present value.[2] Do the best we can, where best is defined by present value.

Mutually exclusive projects are a special case of this general rule. Here one and only one member of A is to be taken. Denote their respective present values PV_1, ..., PV_n. Project a_j is best if $PV_j \geq PV_i$ for i = 1, ..., n. Take the project with the largest present value.[3]

Did we follow this criterion in our above analysis? We had two proposals: a_1 = expand and a_2 = do not expand. One and only one was to be chosen. We framed the choice in incremental terms and calculated $PV_1 - PV_2 = 26.284 > 0$. Thus, $PV_1 > PV_2$ and a_1 = expand is the choice. Always identify the decision frame!

Another way to frame our analysis is with the notion of opportunity cost. We have two choices: a_1 (expand) and a_2 (do not expand). Suppose we explicitly consider only the proposed project, a_1. Using the terminology from Chapter 11, A_1 contains only this project. Clearly, taking the project is the best choice among those in A_1.

Of course, everything else is in A_2. In this case, everything else consists of a_2. If we are discounting at r = 12% and if this is the market price of funds, then "do not expand" implies funds cost and earn at the rate of r = 12%. In short, r = 12% is the opportunity cost of capital. Further notice any investment at r = 12% has a present value of zero. So we know the best choice in A_2 has a present value of zero. Therefore, taking the expansion project, with its present value of 26.284, is the best choice.

The present value criterion is straightforward. Do the best we can. Best is measured by present value.[4] Implementing the present value rule begs two

---

[2]In formal terms, let Ā be the set of combinations of projects in A that are feasible. The present value criterion then states that we should select the combination of projects, a, by maximizing PV_a subject to the constraint that a∈Ā. Further observe that if the status quo, doing nothing, is a feasible option, it, too, is included in the list of opportunities.

[3]Notice that if projects can be taken in various combinations, then each such combination can be described as a "super" project. If we specify the set of projects in this fashion, then they are, by definition, mutually exclusive projects. So we then take that combination of projects, that super project, with the largest present value.

[4]Suppose, due to market or organizational imperfections, that available funds are limited. The present value criterion then says pick that combination of projects that maximizes the total present

important questions: Where did the cash flow estimates come from? Where did the discount rate r come from?

If markets are complete and perfect, we know the cash flows as a function of whatever events beset the economy. We also know the market price for a dollar at every point in time, as a function of whatever events beset the economy. So if markets are complete and perfect, we have our questions answered.[5] Of course, this is by definition. Such a world only exists in textbooks. Real markets are not complete and perfect.

Modern finance emphasizes discounting the expected values of the respective cash flows at a discount rate appropriate for the project's risk.[6] Projects with the same risk are in the same risk class. Projects are thus discounted at the rate appropriate for their risk class. A risk free project, for example, would be discounted at the risk free rate. Similarly, a project in the organization's risk class would be discounted at the organization's weighted average cost of capital, which is tautologically the discount rate appropriate for the risk class. A project in another firm's risk class would be discounted at that firm's cost of capital.

---

value, subject to not exceeding the available investment funds. The rationalization does get thin. Perfect markets leads to the present value rule, and we now invoke its use when some type of friction is present.

[5]Another way to express this is to remember insurance is always available, for a price, in a regime of complete and perfect markets. Thus, in such a regime, any project we might think up is insurable. This implies an equivalent way to evaluate projects is to think of their expected cash flows as occurring for certain, while their necessary expected investment outflow increases by the market demanded insurance premium.

[6]By analogy, we have in earlier chapters distinguished the expected value of a lottery from its certain equivalent. We might think of this as "discounting" the expected value to restate it in certain equivalent terms. In a broader sense we are recycling our ever-present theme of explicating the organization's goals or preferences. Whether we are faced with a single or a multi-period exercise, analysis of decision alternatives presupposes some specification of these preferences. This is why, for example, the casually obvious notion of risk is so difficult to define. Consider two lotteries with the same expected value. Call them α and β. Let $\wp$ be a set of utility functions. Lottery α is less risky than lottery β for "preference class $\wp$" if for each utility function in $\wp$ the expected utility of α is weakly greater than the expected utility of β. The difficulty is that what we mean by risk depends on the utility function. If $\wp$ only contains well-behaved quadratic functions, then risk is measured by variance. Otherwise, it is not. Therefore, depending on $\wp$ we may be able to be highly specific about how to measure risk. Varying $\wp$ alters what we mean by risk; and the broader $\wp$ is the more difficulty we have guaranteeing that one lottery is more risky than another. Inherently, then, thinking in risk and return terms presumes we have said something about the organization's preferences.

And as if this were not enough, we also must remember the framing possibilities. Suppose mean and variance of all lotteries is what is important. In incremental terms, then, we worry about covariance. To illustrate, let x and y be two random variables. The variance of x + y is the variance of x plus the variance of y plus twice the covariance of x and y. Incrementally, then, adding y to the portfolio increases the variance by the variance of y plus twice the covariance.

In pragmatic terms, we *estimate* the cash flows and the organization makes a managerial judgment as to the appropriate discount rate to use in the calculation. The organization may have a policy that prescribes the discount rate as a function of the type of investment. For example, new product projects might be discounted at r = 14%, expansion of existing stable projects at r = 11%, and so on.

The organization's approach to identifying, selecting, and managing investment opportunities is likely to have a significant effect on its success. We typically find considerable involvement, documentation, and monitoring. The organization also may use a variety of analysis techniques, besides a present value calculation, to portray investment possibilities.

Additional Techniques

Two commonly used portrayals are internal rate of return and payback. These are discussed below. A third, the accounting rate of return, will be discussed later in the chapter.

internal rate of return

Recall our illustrative capacity expansion proposal (Table 15.1). Discounting the cash flow sequence at r = 12% gave us a present value of 26.284. It seems our project would earn more than r = 12%. Its present value, that is, would be zero for some discount rate larger than 12%.

After all, this project calls for immediate investment of 383, followed by cash inflows with a present value (at r = 12%) of 409.284. Raising the discount rate will lower the present value of these future cash inflows. At some point, their present value will be 383, and the project's present value will then be zero.

The internal rate of return for some given cash flow sequence is that discount rate r = *irr* such that the present value is zero. Fix the cash flow sequence. If we think of PV as a function of r, the internal rate of return is the value of r for which PV is zero.

For the case at hand, we solve the following expression to determine the internal rate of return:

$$PV = 0 = -383(1+irr)^0 + 89.5(1+irr)^{-1} + 100.3(1+irr)^{-2} + 88.78(1+irr)^{-3} + 81.868(1+irr)^{-4} + 231.868(1+irr)^{-5} + 5.184(1+irr)^{-6}.$$

The solution is *irr* = 14.364%.

Dwell on the intuition. The project calls for us to invest 383 immediately, in exchange for some future cash inflows. Discounting those future cash inflows at r = 12% gives a positive present value. Discounting them at a rate over 12% lowers their present value. The crossing point, between positive and negative present value, is 14.364%.

The analogy to break-even calculations should be apparent. See Figure 15.1, where we plot present value of this cash flow sequence as a function of the discount rate, r.

Figure 15.1: Present Value as a Function of r

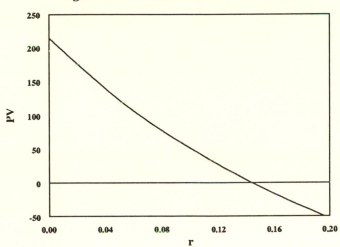

Many find this an intuitive and comfortable portrait. If we take the expansion project, funds will earn at the rate of *irr* = 14.364%. This is more than their cost, r = 12%. Beyond that, "earning 14.364%" is a more intuitive statement than "capturing a present value of 26.283." Two difficulties emerge.

multiple internal rates of return

One difficulty with internal rate of return is the ambiguity caused by multiple internal rates of return. Jump back to the above expression where we solved for *irr* using the data in Table 15.1. Instead, multiply the expression by $(1+irr)^6$. With PV = 0 (by definition of *irr*), this gives us:

$$PV = 0 = -383(1+irr)^6 + 89.5(1+irr)^5 + 100.3(1+irr)^4 + 88.78(1+irr)^3 + 81.868(1+irr)^2 + 231.868(1+irr)^1 + 5.184(1+irr)^0.$$

Notice this is a polynomial of degree T = 6. In solving for *irr*, we solved a 6th degree polynomial.

Recall from algebra that a polynomial of degree T has T roots. The roots might all be the same, in which case they are called repeated roots. They also might be different (or even imaginary). Our example has a single positive root of 14.364% (along with a negative root and two pairs of imaginary roots). With a single positive root, there is no ambiguity as to what the internal rate of return is. In fact, this is the case whenever x_0 is negative and all subsequent cash flows are positive.

More generally, though, multiple roots are possible.[7] To illustrate, consider the following cash flow sequence:

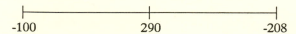

$$-100 \qquad\qquad 290 \qquad\qquad -208$$

Think of this as an environmentally sensitive project that calls for significant cleanup or restoration at the end of its useful life.

PV as a function of the discount rate r is plotted in Figure 15.2. PV is zero at $irr = 30\%$ and at $irr = 60\%$. PV is positive between these two values, and negative otherwise. We have two values for irr, 30% and 60%! What, then, is the project's irr? There simply is no unambiguous answer.

Figure 15.2: $PV = -100+290(1+r)^{-1}-280(1+r)^{-2}$

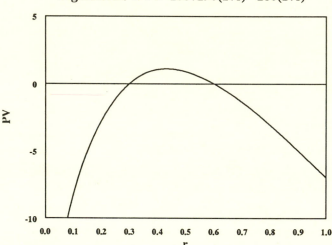

Even this observation does not exhaust the unusual nature of this illustration. Suppose the appropriate discount rate is r = 10%. We then have a present value of $-100 + 290(1.1)^{-1} - 208(1.1)^{-2} = -8.2645$. *If* we are using a present value criterion, this project is unacceptable. Yet it has an irr of 30% > 10% and of 60% > 10%. This further illustrates the fact, we should say tautological observation, that whenever present value and internal rate of return analyses differ, the latter is wrong if the former is correct.

---

[7]Descartes' rule of signs is helpful. Let k be the number of changes of sign in the coefficients of our polynomial. Then the number of positive roots of the polynomial is k or k reduced by an even integer. If x_0 is negative and all other x_t are positive, we have one change of sign and therefore one positive root. This is the case in Figure 15.1.

Parenthetically, can you identify the source of the inconsistency here? The project has a negative salvage value. If r is sufficiently large, this is not too onerous. For low r it is. Recall Figure 15.2. So we want the lower *irr* below r to make certain the negative salvage value is not too onerous. But then if r is quite large, we again lose interest in the project from a present value perspective. The reason is the intermediate inflows become less and less valuable as we increase r, and eventually are overwhelmed by necessary outflows.

mutually exclusive projects

The second potential inconsistency between present value and internal rate of return frames arises in choice among mutually exclusive projects. To illustrate, suppose we must select between project 1 and project 2, below.

Project 1:

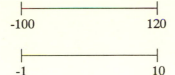

Project 2:

Project 1 calls for us to invest 100 current dollars in exchange for 120 dollars at time $t = 1$. Its internal rate of return is clearly $irr_1 = 20\%$:

$$- 100 + 120(1+.2)^{-1} = - 100 + 100 = 0.$$

Project 2 calls for us to invest 1 current dollar in exchange for 10 dollars at time $t = 1$. Its internal rate of return is $irr_2 = 900\%$:

$$- 1 + 10(1+9.0)^{-1} = -1 + 1 = 0.$$

We thus have $irr_1 = 20\% < irr_2 = 900\%$. (No multiple solution ambiguity is present.)

Now suppose the discount rate is $r = 10\%$. The two projects have respective present values of

$$PV_1 = - 100 + 120(1.1)^{-1} = 9.09; \text{ and}$$
$$PV_2 = - 1 + 10(1.1)^{-1} = 8.09.$$

Therefore, $irr_2 > irr_1$ while $PV_1 > PV_2$. Present value and internal rate of return give conflicting advice. Maximizing internal rate of return is not consistent with maximizing present value. The difficulty arises because the present value frame assumes the cash flow is reinvested at the presumed rate r, while the internal rate of return frame assumes it is reinvested at *irr*.

To dramatize, suppose we could scale the second project up, so it required an investment of 100 dollars, and returned 100(10) dollars at $t = 1$. Again, we have $irr_2 = 900\%$; but we also have $PV_2 = 809$. The present value rule now identifies the project with the higher internal rate of return. Of course, this scaled-up project was constructed on the assumption we could invest the additional amount at 900%.

What if the best we can do is invest this additional amount at r = 10%? Viewed in this fashion, the scaled up-project calls for us to invest one dollar to receive 10 dollars at t = 1 and invest 99 dollars to receive (1.10)99 = 108.9 dollars at t = 1.

Scaled-Up Project 2:

$$\begin{array}{l} \vdash\!\!\!-\!\!\!-\!\!\!-\!\!\!-\!\!\!-\!\!\!-\!\!\!-\!\!\!-\!\!\!-\!\!\!-\!\!\!-\!\!\!-\!\!\!-\dashv \\ \text{-1-99} \qquad\qquad\qquad \text{10+108.9} \end{array}$$

This calls for us to invest 1 + 99 = 100 current dollars in exchange for 10 + 108.9 = 118.9 dollars at time t = 1. Its present value is 8.09.[8] Its internal rate of return is 18.9% (which is below irr_1 = 20%):

$$- 100 + 118.9(1+.189)^{-1} = 0.$$

The message here is not deep. Present value analysis assumes reinvestment at the exogenously specified r. Internal rate of return analysis assumes reinvestment at the endogenously determined *irr*. The two may conflict when we face mutually exclusive choices that have unequal investment amounts, unequal investment lives, or even equal investment amounts and lives but at least two periods.[9]

payback

Another frequently encountered portrayal of investment opportunities is payback. This is simply the minimal length of time for the cumulative net cash flow from the investment opportunity to be positive. Again using the data in Table 15.1

---

[8]This is no surprise. We know the present value of the first component of the project is 8.09, while that of the second is zero. The second component is assumed to be a zero present value story; it earns at the assumed discount rate.

[9]Consider two mutually exclusive projects, each requiring an immediate investment of 100. The first has cash inflow at t = 1 of 0 and at t = 2 of 129.96. The second has cash inflow at t = 1 of 115 and at t = 2 of 0. The first project lives for two periods, while the second for only one period. (Draw the cash flow diagrams.) Further assume r = 10%. This gives us respective present values of PV_1 = 7.405 and PV_2 = 4.545. The internal rates of return, though, are 14% and 15%, respectively. Now consider a different pair of mutually exclusive projects. Each requires an immediate investment of 200. The first has cash inflows of 150 at t = 1 and 120 at t = 2. The second has cash inflows of 1 at t = 1 and 290 at t = 2. Using r = 10%, we find PV_1 = 35.54 < PV_2 = 40.58. We also find respective internal rates of return of 23.56% > = 20.67%.

The difficulty in each case stems from the mutually exclusive frame. In the latter example, we know the first project is acceptable, relative to not investing. Its present value is positive, and its internal rate of return exceeds 10%. If we had this project, would we then trade it for the second? This amounts to framing the choice between the first and second projects in incremental terms. In this format, the incremental cash flows (i.e., those of project 2 less project 1) are 0, -149, and 170, respectively. Would we give up 149 at t = 1 to receive 170 at t = 2? The incremental present value is strictly positive, and the internal rate of return on the incremental investment is 14.09%!

for illustrative purposes, we have the following calculation of the cumulative cash flow, as of each period:

Table 15.2: Cumulative End-of-Period Cash Flows						
$t = 0$	$t = 1$	$t = 2$	$t = 3$	$t = 4$	$t = 5$	$t = 6$
-383.000	89.500	100.300	88.780	81.868	231.868	5.184
	-383.000	-383.000	-383.000	-383.000	-383.000	-383.000
		89.500	89.500	89.500	89.500	89.500
			100.300	100.300	100.300	100.300
				88.780	88.780	88.780
					81.868	81.868
						231.868
-383.500	-293.500	-193.200	-104.420	-22.552	209.316	214.500

Notice the cumulative cash flow from the proposed investment is negative before $t = 5$, and positive after that. The project's payback is $t_{PB} = 5$. In five periods (years here), the total cash flow from the project is positive.

In abstract terms, we wrote the cash flow sequence as x_0, x_1, ..., x_T. The payback period is the minimum time, t_{PB}, such that $x_0 + x_1 + \cdots x_{PB} \geq 0$. No discounting is involved. Cash flow beyond t_{PB} is ignored.[10]

A long payback is often thought of as a risky project. We must wait quite a while before earning positive cash flows; and this gives us a long time in which to encounter bad luck. This is certainly a casual notion of risk (pun); and it is unlikely to agree with a more sophisticated notion of risk. Payback surely does not provide a reliable frame of a sophisticated investment decision.[11]

Still, we should not be too hasty to condemn the calculation. If the payback is one year, and the project lasts 10 years it sounds attractive. If the payback is 20 years, and the project lasts 21 years, we are immediately suspicious that it is not very interesting. Somewhere in between might be a pragmatic filter. A "short" payback is a signal, other things equal, that risk considerations are not of first order impor-

---

[10]A caveat should be noted. If the cash flows beyond t_{PB} are not all positive, we should call the payback period the minimum time beyond which the cumulative cash flow remains positive. With this subtlety, we then worry about cash flows beyond the identified t_{PB} to the extent they might turn the cumulative cash flow negative at a later date. Naturally, $x_0 < 0$ and all other cash flows positive (as in Table 15.1) do not cause such a concern.

[11]You might enjoy the following (thanks to Gordon [1955]). Let x_0 be negative, and $x_1 = x_2 = \cdots = x_T = z$ be positive. The payback period is now, roughly, $t_{PB} = x_0/z$. Further suppose T is large. The present value, at discount rate r, of the cash inflows is $z[1 - (1+r)^{-T}]/r$. If we now solve for the internal rate of return, we will find that it is approximated by z/x_0, or the reciprocal of the payback period. This does not imply the payback period is, more broadly, useful. It does, however, remind us to understand the economic environment we encounter and how well various decision frames stand up in that environment.

tance. A "long" payback is the opposite signal.[12] For example, does a payback period of 5 years in our running example signal we have a lot of time for things to go wrong?

framing

We dwell on the possible inconsistencies between present value and alternative analyses because they provide another lesson in the art of framing. Our first principle of consistent framing was the irrelevance of strictly increasing transformations. Figure 15.1 tells such a story. A positive PV and *irr* above r are the same thing in that picture. In fact, holding r constant, a larger PV corresponds to a larger *irr*. We have an increasing transformation. Figure 15.2 is the absence of an increasing transformation from PV to *irr*. Similarly, naive analysis of mutually exclusive projects can produce inconsistencies between the present value and internal rate of return portraits.

We suspect these inconsistencies are not of major concern in most practical cases. For example, multiple internal rates of return require multiple sign switches in the cash flow projections. This sounds like replacement problems (where we periodically replace an aging asset such as a large truck) or those with unusual salvage characteristics. Similarly, mutually exclusive projects can be framed in terms of incremental projects relative to a base case.

To illustrate, suppose projects 1 and 2 are mutually exclusive. Only one can be chosen. Denote their respective cash flows CF_{1t} and CF_{2t}. First examine an incremental project: if we had the second, would switching to the first make sense? Is $CF_{1t} - CF_{2t}$ an interesting project? If so, we know the choice is between project 1 and nothing. If not we know the choice is between project 2 and nothing. In turn, these subanalyses may be amenable to an internal rate of return analysis.[13]

In short, internal rate of return and present value frames do not always agree. We do, however, know when this is likely to happen and can guard against an ambiguous or misleading frame of the investment decision.

Use of payback presents a somewhat different framing story. If present value is the norm, we might find internal rate of return more intuitive and use it so long as

---

[12]Ruthless application of a payback filter would thereby bring longer term projects under closer scrutiny and perhaps create an organization wide bias against such projects. Might this, for example, lead to a bias against long-term projects, such as careful maintenance of customer loyalty or high risk, high expected return R&D projects?

[13]Suppose the only negative cash flow occurs at t = 0. Further suppose $x_0 + x_1 + \cdots + x_T > 0$. Then we know present value at r is strictly positive if and only if the internal rate of return is strictly greater than r. This is the story in Figure 15.1. With only one sign change, we know the associated polynomial has one positive root. The sum of the cash flows being positive means present value is positive at r = 0. Taken together, this means *irr* is also positive. (Remember the polynomial we solve is for 1 + *irr*, so a positive root does not imply a positive *irr*. But with the sum of the cash flows positive, we also know the root in our polynomial is greater than 1, or *irr* is positive.)

we are not led (too far) astray. Yet, if present value is the norm it is difficult to understand why anyone would bother to compute the payback period. We do know payback is often computed, together with other calculations, such as present value. This suggests ambiguity in the present value frame itself. Perhaps there is concern over well-specifying the cash flow uncertainties or the appropriate discount rate. Payback may then enter as one of several analytic pictures that are taken of the investment opportunities. In this case, we then acknowledge an ambiguous framing exercise coupled with a portfolio of approaches to the framing task.

Present value is an intuitive frame. It also has its roots in a world of complete and perfect markets. While tempting to advocate use of a present value frame, we should pause to remember that framing is a managerial art. It is informed by theory and practice, and it is crafted with a heavy dose of managerial judgment. The astute manager knows the frame that is being used, and is tuned to its strengths and weaknesses.

Cash Flow Estimation

Of course the frames in place rely on judicious estimation of the cash flows. As usual, we stress the importance of managerial judgment. We also emphasize the potential largeness of investment decisions. They can easily cut across boundaries within the organization, call LLAs into question, and raise issues of competitive response in the product markets.

an earlier story

Our data in Table 15.1 are illustrative. They actually reflect a capacity expansion opportunity in the two product illustration of Chapter 14. Recall, the story concerned manufacture and sale of two consumer products. Two production departments were present: subassembly and assembly. Capacity constraints were:

subassembly: $q_1 + q_2 \leq 6,000$ and
assembly: $q_1 + 2q_2 \leq 10,000,$

where q_1 and q_2 denote quantities of the two products.

The short-run cost function was estimated by aggregating direct material, direct labor, and overhead cost components. With an "S" subscript denoting subassembly and an "A" subscript denoting assembly, we assumed the following LLAs:

$DL_S = 10q_1 + 10q_2;$
$DM_S = 110q_1 + 200q_2;$
$DL_A = 40q_1 + 80q_2;$ and
$DM_A = 12q_1 + 15q_2.$

We also assumed respective selling prices of $P_1 = 600$ and $P_2 = 1,100$. This implies total revenue of $600q_1 + 1,100q_2$. Any variable selling and administrative is netted out here. We will continue this pattern, simply to keep the discussion at a reasonable length.

Overhead was estimated in several ways in the original example. Initially we used a plant-wide overhead LLA of $OV = 2,000,000 + 3.5(DL_S + DL_A)$. This plant-wide model was then estimated with a regression of $OV = 2,425,200 + 3.1DL$. Finally, departmental models were also estimated:

$$OV_S = 483,500 + 1.8DM_S; \text{ and}$$
$$OV_A = 659,700 + 2.6DL_A.$$

Using these latter expressions, we then estimated contribution margins:[14]

price	600	1,100
direct labor in subassembly	10	10
direct labor in assembly	40	80
direct material in subassembly	110	200
direct material in assembly	12	15
1.8(subassembly direct material)	198	360
2.6(assembly direct labor)	104	104
total variable cost	474	873
contribution margin	126	227

From here we solved our LP:

$$\text{maximize } \pi(q_1,q_2) = 126q_1 + 227q_2$$
$$\text{subject to: } q_1 + q_2 \leq 6,000;$$
$$q_1 + 2q_2 \leq 10,000; \text{ and}$$
$$q_1, q_2 \geq 0.$$

The solution was $q_1^* = 2,000$ and $q_2^* = 4,000$; with an optimal contribution margin of $\pi^* = 1,160,000$. In addition, the shadow prices on the constraints were 25 and 101.

the proposed project

The investment project before us is whether to increase the capacity of each department by 1,500 units. This incremental capacity can be purchased for 200,000. It will last 5 years. Estimating the cash flows (besides the purchase price of the additional equipment) requires we foretell how this additional capacity will be used. A good starting point is to redo the above LP, but with the added capacity:

$$\text{maximize } \pi(q_1,q_2) = 126q_1 + 227q_2$$

---

[14]The original example also entertained a variation on one of the products that used an out-sourced component. We drop this possibility from the current illustration. We should reflect on how the possibility of these types of opportunities further clouds our ability to make precise cash flow estimates to feed the present value or related investment model.

$$\text{subject to:} \quad q_1 + q_2 \leq 6{,}000 + 1{,}500 = 7{,}500;$$
$$q_1 + 2q_2 \leq 10{,}000 + 1{,}500 = 11{,}500; \text{ and}$$
$$q_1, q_2 \geq 0.$$

The solution is $q_1^* = 3{,}500$ and $q_2^* = 4{,}000$; with $\pi^* = 1{,}349{,}000$. In addition, the shadow prices on the constraints are 25 and 101, respectively. This implies an annual gain of $1{,}349{,}000 - 1{,}160{,}000 = 189{,}000$.[15]

Investing 200,000 to receive 189,000 per year for five years sounds fairly attractive. (The present value at 12% is more than 480,000.) Our quick and dirty analysis, though, presumes no change whatever in the original cost and revenue structures, not to mention the question of tax effects.

is this a small or a large decision?

We now document several alterations to our original analysis. This should not be taken as a checklist to be examined in each and every setting, but as a suggestive encounter with the art of estimation.

In working through these alterations, keep in mind we are estimating the cash flows. Think of the original LP solution, documented above, as being the production plan that will be in place if no expansion occurs. We then must determine what production plan will be in place if expansion occurs. The difference in cash flows between these two regimes is the cash flow picture we seek. In a broader sense, we do not mean to suggest a well-done estimation exercise rests on a series of short-run LP exercises. We do mean to suggest it rests on a thorough understanding of what is to be done with the altered set of resources.

Our overall approach consists of three steps. First, we will assume the original LP, as outlined above, accurately depicts the status quo. If the investment is not taken, the noted production plan will be in place along with the noted cost and revenue structures. Second, we will appropriately alter the cost and revenue structures in this LP to determine the production plan that will be in place if the investment proposal is accepted. Third, we will then adjust the difference in total contribution margins between the two plans to account for additional cash flow consequences.

selling prices

Selling prices depend on market forces. We have also lumped any variable selling and administrative items, for convenience, into the revenue estimates.

---

[15]Notice we have $189{,}000 = 1{,}500(25) + 1{,}500(101)$. The alteration of the right hand side parameters in the LP has left the shadow prices unchanged; and the incremental effect can be estimated by the change in parameters multiplied by their respective shadow prices. This, of course, is not guaranteed; and for that reason we stress the more pedantically appearing approach of laying out and formally solving the altered LP.

Expanding output may, or may not, call these estimates into question. The new production schedule, we shall see, entails considerable expansion of the first product's output. For this reason, we assume the selling price of the first product will drop 1.5% if capacity is expanded. The second product's selling price remains constant. Total revenue is estimated to be $591q_1 + 1,100q_2$ in any given period while the proposed investment would be in place. Implicitly, we further assume any effect on selling and administrative costs is negligible.[16]

manufacturing costs

The added capacity will result in altered work flows in the production process. The direct costs are not expected to change. Overhead costs will, however, change. If capacity is expanded, we estimate the overhead LLAs as follows:

$$OV_S = F_S + 1.9DM_S; \text{ and}$$
$$OV_A = F_A + 2.0DL_A.$$

The slope of the LLA for the subassembly department goes up slightly, reflecting added congestion. The slope of the LLA for assembly drops noticeably, reflecting new economies that are available with the expansion. In addition, the total of the two intercepts increases by 185,000.

If these cost expressions were highly accurate, the story would be one of increasing fixed cost (by 185,000), decreasing per unit variable (overhead) cost in one department (from 2.8 to 2.0) and increasing per unit variable (overhead) cost in the other (from 1.8 to 1.9). Literally, though, we have documented changes in the slopes and intercepts of our LLAs. More properly, then, we should imagine moving to another pair of LLAs. This alters the marginal cost estimates in the neighborhood in which we expect to operate, and thus has a bearing on how we anticipate using the additional capacity.

We also interpret the change in intercepts, totaling 185,000, as a cash outflow. No depreciation considerations have yet entered. Any accrual, as opposed to cash, items must be treated in their period of payment. Do not lose sight of this fact. Our decision frame calls for estimation of cash flows, as a function of time.

the new plan

From here we estimate the contribution margins that would hold under the expansion proposal.

---

[16]We should also interpret the analysis as taking place in real terms. (12% is therefore interpreted as the real discount rate appropriate for projects in this risk class.) Inflation considerations can be approached in two equivalent ways. One is to work with real dollars and discount at the real rate. The other is to work with nominal dollars and discount at the nominal rate. Notice that, absent price level adjustments, the accounting library operates in nominal terms.

price	591	1,100
direct labor in subassembly	10	10
direct labor in assembly	40	80
direct material in subassembly	110	200
direct material in assembly	12	15
1.9(subassembly direct material)	209	380
2.0(assembly direct labor)	80	160
total variable cost	461	845
contribution margin	130	255

The altered LP now comes into view; it reflects the newly estimated contribution margins and the additional capacity:

$$\text{maximize } \pi(q_1, q_2) = 130q_1 + 255q_2$$
$$\text{subject to: } q_1 + q_2 \leq 6,000 + 1,500 = 7,500;$$
$$q_1 + 2q_2 \leq 10,000 + 1,500 = 11,500; \text{ and}$$
$$q_1, q_2 \geq 0.$$

The solution is $q_1^* = 3,500$ and $q_2^* = 4,000$; with $\pi^* = 1,475,000$. In addition, the shadow prices on the constraints are 5 and 125, respectively.

We previously estimated the annual contribution margin with no capacity expansion to be 1,160,000. This provides a difference of 1,475,000 - 1,160,000 = 315,000. Recall the intercepts on the overhead LLAs have increased by 185,000. This implies a net gain of 315,000 - 185,000 = 130,000. Thus, we estimate change in total contribution margin less change in "fixed" cost (of a cash based nature) to be 130,000 per year, if capacity is expanded. This is our estimate of the incremental net cash flow from operations.

expansion costs

Next is the question of investment cost. The equipment, we noted earlier, will cost 200,000, and last 5 years. Salvage value is zero. Additional costs, of training new workers, of altering the plant to accommodate the new equipment, and so on will total 60,000. So the immediate cash outflow will be 260,000.

taxes

Taxes are also important. They are paid periodically throughout the year, though for simplicity we will assume they are paid at the year's end (as we assume all cash flows occur at year's end). There is also a significant cash flow timing wedge between acquisition and tax consequences of a long-term decision.

Tax law is complex and constantly changing. A well thought out tax strategy is equally complex. We cannot hope to introduce all of the specifics at this point, so will content ourselves with a broad brush treatment.

We assume the tax rate is a constant 45% of taxable income. Taxable income is accounting income, except we are careful to use a taxation determined depreciation schedule.[17] For tax purposes, we assume the investment will be classified as five-year property. Under the modified accelerated cost recovery system (MACRS) the tax basis of the investment will be depreciated 20% in the year of acquisition, 32% the next year, and 19.2%, 11.52%, 11.52%, and 5.76% in the remaining years.

Table 15.3: Incremental End-of-Period Cash Flows (000)							
	t = 0	**t = 1**	**t = 2**	**t = 3**	**t = 4**	**t = 5**	**t = 6**
contribution margin	0.000	315.000	315.000	315.000	315.000	315.000	0.000
less fixed (cash flow)		185.000	185.000	185.000	185.000	185.000	0.000
cash flow from operations	0.000	130.000	130.000	130.000	130.000	130.000	0.000
depreciation (tax)		40.000	64.000	38.400	23.040	23.040	11.520
other tax expenses	60.000						
taxable income	-60.000	90.000	66.000	91.600	106.960	106.960	-11.520
tax	-27.000	40.500	29.700	41.220	48.132	48.132	-5.184
cash from operations less tax	27.000	89.500	100.300	88.780	81.868	81.868	5.184
acquisition cash flows							
acquisition	-200.00						
alteration	-60.000						
working capital	-150.000					150.000	
net cash flow	-383.000	89.500	100.300	88.780	81.868	231.868	5.184

What is the basis? Here we assume the acquisition price of 200,000 is the basis, or depreciable amount. We assume the additional cost of 60,000, associated with worker training and minor plant alteration, will be immediately expensed for tax purposes.[18]

Carefully study Table 15.3. The incremental taxable income in any period is incremental contribution margin (of 315,000) less incremental fixed cost (of

---

[17]We know the spread between book and tax income is driven by more than depreciation. Some items are accrued for book but not tax purposes. Others are accrued for tax but not for book purposes.

[18]This need not be the case. Expenditures that keep the assets in an ordinarily efficient condition without adding value or extending their life would be treated as incidental repairs, as opposed to capital expenditures. We purposely identify a gray area here, to caution the reader tax treatment is complex, ever-changing, and may have a significant bearing on an investment's attractiveness.

185,000) less incremental depreciation. 45% of this amount then provides incremental cash outflow for taxes.

Notice the depreciation expense, for tax purposes, continues into period t = 6. As we assume the project lasts 5 years, the only incremental effect in period t = 6 is depreciation for tax purposes of 11,520. This reduces taxable income in period t = 6 by 11,520, and thus reduces taxes payable in that period by .45(11,520) = 5,184.

Also notice what occurs at time t = 0. The alteration expenditures of 60,000 are fully expensed at that time. The incremental effect is to reduce taxable income at that time by 60,000. This reduces taxes payable in that period by .45(60,000) = 27,000.

Both calculations, at t = 0 and at t = 6, presume the status quo taxable income is sufficiently positive these tax reductions occur at the noted times.

working capital

One other item should have caught our attention in Table 15.3: working capital. We assume additional working capital of 150,000 is required. This will be infused at the start of the project and returned at the end of the project's life, at t = 5. No tax implications are involved. A more realistic portrait might have the working capital gradually build up at the start of the project, and gradually decline in periods t = 5 and t = 6. But this reminds us to search for important cash flows that do not show up in the visible investment and more readily identified periodic amounts.

Tabulating our work, we have incremental contribution margin, less incremental (cash based) fixed cost. Subtracting incremental cash tax payments, we have incremental net cash flow from operations. From this we subtract the acquisition and alteration cash flows at t = 0. Incremental working capital is negative at t = 0 and positive at t = 5. (Notice how return of working capital takes on the appearance of salvage value.)

imponderables

This gives a deeper picture of how the cash flows we so glibly analyzed in earlier sections were derived. One way or another, managerial judgment enters at every twist and turn. Even with our best insight and patience, there is no guarantee our judgments tally to an accurate picture. We have left many possibilities out of the exercise. Recall, for example, our earlier encounter with this story where subcontracting was a possibility, as was the production of alternate products. We also might worry about new competition, technology changes, price changes (e.g., selling prices, wages, energy, and materials), income tax law changes, employment tax changes, and so on.

Investment decisions are usually "large" decisions. In this case we have altered some of our LLAs. We are also worried about interactions with other decisions. Indeterminate, imponderable facets of the choice are part and parcel of a "large" decision.

Rendering in the Accounting Library

The final question in our look at long-run, investment decisions is how these decisions are recorded in the accounting library. As we have stressed, present value analysis relies on cash flow estimates. Yet cash flow is the antithesis of accrual reporting.

illustrative entries

The easiest way to focus this question is to work through several entries that would be made in the accounting library. As we proceed, keep in mind we framed the analysis in terms of incremental cash flow. So we will now compute incremental assets and income. Also, we will deal with aggregate amounts, avoiding the many details of day-to-day record keeping.[19]

Initially the alteration and acquisition occur. The acquisition is recorded as follows:

plant and equipment	200,000	
cash		200,000

Notice the credit is to cash. One of the dictates of modern finance is a separation between investment and the source of funds for that investment. Here, cash from short-term investments might be used, debt might be issued, or whatever. We view the amount as working through the cash account and do not speculate on its original source. This is why financing questions were not raised in the earlier present value analysis.[20]

The alteration and training costs are also recorded in the library. An interesting question is whether to capitalize some or all of this amount. Our tax treatment called for immediate expensing, and we do the same here.[21]

miscellaneous expense	60,000	
cash		60,000

The increase in working capital follows a similar pattern. Here we envision a net increase in short-term assets less liabilities, mainly associated with inventories and receivables.

---

[19]For example, where do labor wage payments, employment taxes, pensions, and other benefits show up in our analysis?

[20]Notice the library recording would be different if the equipment were leased. Here nothing would pass through the cash account, and we would have a credit to a lease liability account. (Presumably capital lease provisions would prevail.)

[21]Otherwise we must deal with deferred taxes. Since this will come up shortly, we opt for the more straightforward treatment on the alteration and training costs.

| inventories and receivables | 150,000 | |
| cash | | 150,000 |

To round out the t = 0 recordings, we must acknowledge the tax effects. Recall the acquisition and training expense is also treated as an immediate tax expense. This implies an aggregate effect, as opposed to actual entry, as follows:

| cash | 27,000 | |
| tax expense | | 27,000 |

Do not take this literally. The 60,000 expense is also an expense for tax purposes. This lowers taxable income by 60,000, and the tax liability by .45(60,000) = 27,000. So tax expense is lowered, as is tax liability. We also assume the taxes are actually paid. So relative to the status quo it is as if cash increased by 27,000. (In fact, it decreased less by 27,000.)

Now consider time t = 2. The incremental cash flow from operations is summarized in the library as follows:

| cash | 130,000 | |
| revenue less expense | | 130,000 |

Notice we net incremental revenue and incremental expense to save on detail.

What about depreciation? For the sake of illustration, let's assume straight line depreciation, with a 5-year life and zero salvage value, is used for book purposes. This implies the following entry for t = 2, with 200,000/5 = 40,000:

revenue less expense	40,000	
plant and equipment,		
allowance for depreciation		40,000

We know from Table 15.3 that incremental taxable income is 66,000 this period, implying a tax liability of .45(66,000) = 29,700. Our book income differs, because of the depreciation expense. It is 130,000 - 40,000 = 90,000. This implies a book tax liability of .45(90,000) = 40,500. Deferred taxes arise.

tax expense	40,500	
deferred tax		10,800
cash		29,700

We know the actual payment is 29,700; and we know the book expense is 40,500. The difference is deferred tax.

The calculations for t = 1 are perfunctory, as tax and book depreciation happen to agree. Table 15.4 presents details for each period.

As students of accounting, we should understand the calculations in Table 15.4. Notice accrual (i.e., book) income contains no working capital effects. (This is why a statement of cash flows is important.) Also can you explain how the deferred tax expense was calculated and why the sum of these items nets to zero?[22]

	t = 0	t = 1	t = 2	t = 3	t = 4	t = 5	t = 6
Table 15.4: Incremental Accounting Income							
cash flow from operations	0.000	130.000	130.000	130.000	130.000	130.000	0.000
book depreciation		40.000	40.000	40.000	40.000	40.000	0.000
other expenses	60.000						
book pretax income	-60.000	90.000	90.000	90.000	90.000	90.000	0.000
tax expense (45%)							
payable	-27.000	40.500	29.700	41.200	48.132	48.132	-5.184
deferred		0.000	10.800	-0.720	-7.632	-7.632	5.184
	-27.000	40.500	40.500	40.500	40.500	40.500	0.000
net income	-33.000	49.500	49.500	49.500	49.500	49.500	0.000

the accounting rate of return

With these calculations before us we are now in a position to introduce the accounting rate of return. The idea is simple. Just as we used the cash flow sequence to think in terms of an internal rate of return on capital invested (where it made sense), we can use the associated accounting income sequence to think in terms of an accounting rate of return on capital invested. Naturally, we take an incremental approach.

Two procedural questions arise. First, since the accounting income varies from period to period, what income number do we want to place in the numerator? The usual answer is the average incremental accounting income over the project's life. Second, what investment base did we have in mind? The usual answer is to take the initial amount that is capitalized. Of course, we might use an average investment amount, we might add in working capital changes, and so on.

Incremental accounting income totals 214,500. With T = 6, this implies an average of 35,750. The implied accounting rate of return is 35.75/200 = 17.88%. Again, we caution, working capital is not included here (though it could be), and we have treated the investment base in a manner consistent with the initial entry in the plant and equipment account.

---

[22]Deferred tax is the assumed constant marginal tax rate multiplied by the difference between tax and book depreciation. Naturally, it nets to zero as both depreciation schedules allocate an investment cost of 200,000 to the 6 periods. As connoisseurs of accounting subtlety, we might recall it is possible to have permanent differences between book and tax income because some items never fall into the taxable income category. Interest on tax-free instruments is an example.

Calculated in this fashion, the accounting rate of return is simply a grand average of periodic income divided by investment base. It provides yet another portrayal of the investment opportunity. Equally clear is its departure from the timing considerations that are the central feature of present value analysis.

Although it may appear particularly uninteresting, its mere existence should remind us of an important point. The accounting library will record any investment activity. It will record periodic income, asset, and liability manifestations of the investment activity. This means the informed, professional manager is ready and prepared to interpret the library based reports in terms of the investment activity and the accounting conventions at work.

Ponder the task of preparing a long term planning budget for this organization. Cash flow projections would include the effects of any planned investment activity. Income and balance sheet projections also would include the effects of any planned investment activity. And there is not a simple, direct relationship between the two projections. Rather, the income and balance sheet projections reflect both the anticipated investment activity and the accounting treatment of that activity. For example, what would differ in our lengthy illustration if tax and book depreciation were the same or if annuity depreciation were used?

Summary

Decision making interacts with the accounting library in two respects: the library contains information that is useful in the decision activity; and the consequences of whatever decision is rendered will be recorded in the library. Much of the managerial art that is brought to bear in long-run decisions concerns recognizing decision opportunities, and subsequently teasing out the large and small components of those opportunities. No sure-fire guidelines can be offered. Skilled professional management transcends guidelines. This is why we concentrated on a variety of decision frames and an extended illustration that raises cash flow estimation concerns at each and every turn.

We emphasized present value techniques for framing purposes. This carries considerable weight when markets are well functioning.[23] Otherwise, we encounter ambiguity in delineating cash flows, their riskiness, and the appropriate discount rate. Other, sometimes competing and sometimes complementary, frames surface: internal rate of return, payback, and accounting rate of return are illustrative. Our list is far from exhaustive (e.g., simple urgency or ad hoc sensitivity analysis).

We also emphasized the distinction between small and large decisions for estimation purposes. The accounting library relies on LLAs; and we suspect many long-term investment projects are not that local in nature.

---

[23]In the extreme, we would have no taxes, we would have market prices to evaluate each and every project, and no project would earn a positive present value, or economic rent. Do not lose sight of the fact our lengthy illustration had all these characteristics, not to mention a fair dose of ambiguity.

Two additional considerations should be acknowledged. First, strategic considerations may be present. Will a competitor follow or be scared off by a major capacity expansion or new product development? Will capacity expansion lead to unstable market prices and the possibility of price wars? Will work force learning from increased production give us a cost advantage? Do some projects also bring options to the table? For example, development of product A might place us in a position to develop product B at a later date. The product A project then has two components, the A component and the option of accessing the B component. Astute analysis will recognize the value of this option in sorting out whether to pursue product A. (Investing in flexible manufacturing is illustrative; this lowers the marginal cost of various products but also opens the door to possible future products.)

Second, administrative considerations are present. One side to this concerns the assignment of decision rights in the organizations. Analysis and choice of minor projects are likely to be decentralized, while analysis and choice of major projects are likely to be at least partially centralized and subject to considerable review (and monitoring). Another side concerns the motivation of various actors in the organization. Advocating a major project places the manager's reputation on the line. (In this sense, the project produces cash flow and information about those who did and did not advocate it in the first place.) This suggests control considerations are important. They are, and the accounting library enters yet again in their resolution. Our study is partially complete.

Bibliographic Notes

Our treatment of long-run decisions is necessarily brief. Important questions of competitor reaction and investment timing under interest rate uncertainty, for example, have not been discussed. Nor have we broached the subject of financial structure. The starting point for further exploration is, of course, a finance text. From there, more sophisticated treatments are in order. A personal favorite is Haley and Schall [1979]. (An excellent discussion of present value versus internal rate of return is also found there.) Scholes and Wolfson [1992] focus on tax effects; and Wolfson [1985] examines leasing.

The link between accounting and economic measures surfaces, yet again, here. Horwitz [1984] is a good introduction to the subtlety of using accounting rates of return to make economic inferences. Sutton [1991] studies industrial structure, bringing together the strategic side of investment and the difficulty in using available data to make economic inference.

Problems and Exercises

1.   What is the relationship between present value analysis of investment proposals and economic income?

2. The project analyzed throughout most of the chapter, Table 15.1, leads to a strictly positive present value. Yet the accounting library is slow to recognize this value, as in Table 15.4. Do the present value and accrual accounting renderings recognize the same cash flow? Why is the accounting treatment less aggressive in reporting the good news of a project with benefits significantly above its costs?

3. *present value versus accrual accounting*
Return to Table 15.4. Suppose the alteration costs must be capitalized and amortized along with the investment for tax purposes, but will be expensed for book purposes. Determine the project's present value. Also, following Table 15.4, determine the incremental accounting income for each of the relevant periods.

4. *present value and economic income*
Return to the setting of Table 15.1. Using a discount rate of 12%, we know the project has a present value of 26.284. Investing 383, at t = 0, brings an immediate gain of 26.284, as the forthcoming cash flow has a present value of 409.284. Suppose, then, we invest and immediately write up the asset value to equal its present value of 409.284. This implies a period t = 0 income of 26.284. From this point, calculate economic depreciation and economic income for the asset, presuming an interest rate of 12%. Carefully contrast your income numbers with those reported in Table 15.4. Does each income series sum to the net cash flow?

5. *consistent framing*
Return to the illustration in Figure 15.2, where the cash flow sequence is -100, 290 and -208. Assume r = 10% is the correct discount rate. Suppose we take the initial investment of 100 and invest it at r = 10%. In two periods this will grow to $100(1.10)^2 = 121$. Alternatively, suppose we invest in this project. In one year we receive 290. Take this amount and invest it for one year. Hence, at t = 2 we have 290(1.10) = 319. Of course, we also must pay out an additional 208 at this point. So we have 319 - 208 = 111. In this way, accepting the project is equivalent to investing 100 now and receiving 111 two periods later; rejecting the project is equivalent to investing 100 now and receiving 121 two periods later. How, then, can the project have internal rates of return of 30% and 60%? What principle of consistent framing is violated here?

6. *consistent framing*
Verify the calculations in footnote 9.

7. *polynomial roots*
Return to the cash flow sequence in Table 15.1. Write out the equation for the present value, as a function of r. Multiply both sides by $(1 + r)^6$. Notice this gives you the equivalent, or future, value at the end of time t = 6. Naturally, if the future value is zero the present value is zero.

a] Determine the future value, assuming $(1 + r) = 1.143636$. Interpret the result.

b] Determine the future value, assuming $(1 + r) = -.022533$. Interpret the result.

8. *short-run and long-run coordination*

Return to Ralph's LP, problem 12 in Chapter 14. There you determined an optimal short-run production plan, given a set of LLAs. Here Ralph is contemplating expansion of the fabrication department, increasing its capacity from 300 to 450 units (scaled in direct labor hours).

a] Assume all LLAs in the original setting continue to hold and that variable costs are cash expenditures. Determine the incremental cash flow from operations that would follow from such an expansion.

b] Thinking about this some more, Ralph concludes this increased activity will reshape the cost structure in the manufacturing service group. Automation will result in an LLA of MS = 12,000, an entirely fixed cost. Assuming all of the service group costs (both with and without expansion) are cash expenditures, determine the incremental cash flow from operations associated with the proposed expansion.

c] Ralph anticipates the economic structure in [b] above will last for 3 years. For modeling purposes of this sort, Ralph treats all cash flow as occurring at the end of the respective period. Ralph's marginal tax rate is 40%, and positive taxable income from other sources will be present if any of the periods result in a negative tax income. The expansion will cost 30,000 (an immediate outlay). For tax purposes, MACRS will be used (requiring depreciation of 33.33%, 44.45%, 14.81% and 7.41% over a 4-year horizon). No salvage value or costs are anticipated.

In addition, some minor plant modification and work force training will be required. Ralph estimates this will result in an expenditure of 5,000. This will occur at the start of the project (when the investment outlay is made), and will be expensed for tax purposes at the end of the first year.

Determine whether this is an attractive expansion proposal. Assume a 9% cost of capital.

d] Finally, briefly speculate on how risk, learning, competition, and technology change might affect your analysis.

9. *present value versus accounting renderings*

This is a continuation of problem 8 above. Assume, for book purposes, that Ralph uses straight line depreciation. Also assume the 5,000 modification and training expenditure will be expensed in the first year. Prepare a series of proforma statements that detail incremental book income over the next 4 years if this expansion proposal is implemented.

10. *real versus nominal rates*

Return to problem 8 above. Suppose investment and operating cash flow projections are all in real terms. Ralph's real cost of capital is 9%. A 6% inflation rate is anticipated over the next 4 years. (This implies a nominal cost of capital of $(1.09)(1.06) - 1 = 15.54\%$.) Determine the project's present value.

11. *new product with investment and inventory*
Ralph is now trying to decide whether to accept a customer's proposal to sign a long-term supplier contract. The customer will require 1,000 or 3,000 units of a specialized assembly in each of the next 3 years. The three periods are independent, and the probability of 1,000 units being required is .5 in each period. (Thus, the expected number of units is 2,000 each period.) The customer is willing to pay an up-front retainer of 90,000 dollars, plus 100 per unit ordered and delivered. The customer, though, determines the amount required (resulting in the noted probabilities).
Ralph's per unit cost analysis breaks down as follows:

| direct material | 32 and |
| direct labor | 18. |

Labor is costed at 18 per hour. Overhead is costed at a full cost rate of 150% of material plus 50% of direct labor. Half of each rate is fixed overhead allocation. Ralph's marginal tax rate is 42% in each period. Ralph is working below capacity and has under-absorbed overhead that is being expensed for tax purposes. This situation is expected to persist for at least 4 more years. (Notice that the retainer of 90,000 will be booked as revenue, both for financial and tax purposes, during the period of production. A reasonable assumption is 1/3 is booked at the end of the 3 production periods.)
Ralph must also acquire a specialized machine in order to manufacture this assembly. The machine can be acquired in the machine market for 125,000. It will have zero salvage value at the end of the contract, and will be depreciated for tax purposes on a 3-year MACRS basis (33.33%, 44.45%, 14.81%, 7.41%). In addition, Ralph would be forced to maintain an inventory of 500 units, which would be depleted in the third year. Thus, if the customer orders 1,000 units in the first year, 1,500 will be produced in the first year. If 3,000 units are ordered in the first year, 3,500 will be produced in the first year. Production in the third year will be actual demand less 500 units. (Assume the machine depreciation will be treated as a period cost for tax purposes.)
For planning purposes, Ralph has decided to ignore estimated tax payments and intraperiod cash flow timing differences. Thus cash flow associated with production occurs at the end of the production year, tax payments occur at the end of the year in question, and so on. This is not accurate, but it is the way Ralph has decided to take an initial cut at the problem.
Suppose Ralph is risk neutral and discounts after tax cash flow at a rate of 9%. Should Ralph accept the customer's proposal?

12. *make or buy*
Ralph's Enterprise (RE) manufactures hydraulic components for the aircraft industry. One element common to a variety of products is a specialized valve that RE manufactures. The standard cost for this valve reveals the following:

| direct material | 8.20; |

direct labor	9.30;
variable overhead	3.10; and
fixed overhead	9.30.

Quality problems have surfaced and RE has decided the existing valve manufacturing equipment must be replaced. An automated machine is available, at a cost of 2,500,000. It has a 5 year life, no salvage, and would be depreciated as 5 year equipment (MACRS percentages of 20%, 32%, 19.2%, 11.52%, 11.52% and 5.76%) for tax purposes. Straight line is used for book purposes. RE expects the direct material cost to remain the same, though direct labor will be cut in half if the new equipment is acquired. Also, variable overhead will remain at 1/3 of direct labor cost, although cash outlays presently in the fixed overhead, totaling 450,000 per year, will not be incurred if the existing machine is retired. (It has zero salvage now, as well as a zero tax basis.) The marginal tax rate is a constant 40%.

RE anticipates an annual demand of 50,000 valves. Just before signing the purchase contract for the new equipment, another firm in the industry offers to supply RE all the valves needed, at a guaranteed price of 30 per valve over the next 5 years. The after tax discount rate is 9%.

a]   Which option is best, make the valve with the new equipment or buy the valve from the outside supplier? What qualitative concerns do you see here?

b]   What will happen to the first year's accounting income under each of the alternatives in [a]?

c]   What annual demand for the valve leads to indifference between the two alternatives?

13. *expansion via leasing*
Return to problem 14 of Chapter 14, Consumer, Inc. A competitor, experiencing bad times, has offered to lease Consumer, Inc., productive capacity that will increase the assembly capacity from 600,000 to 650,000 direct labor hours. This is a 4-year, noncancellable lease. The annual payment is 750,000, due at the start of each year. For accounting purposes this would be treated as a capital lease, though for tax purposes it is an operating lease. (Ralph will treat this as a deductible tax expense at the end of the year.) The marginal tax rate is 45%, and the appropriate after tax discount rate is 10%.

a]   Using the 4 estimates of product profitability (the original full costing approach, managements' subjective estimate, the regression estimates, and the firm-wide overhead pool approach), determine the value of agreeing to the lease arrangement.

b]   After the excitement settles down, those who advocated the original short-run plan based on full costing become argumentative. They claim that at this juncture the full costing approach is more valid because long-run adjustments will necessitate long-run adjustments in the overhead structure. Carefully analyze their argument.

c]   Suppose the lease is signed. Describe the treatment that the typical accounting library would apply to the arrangement.

16

Competitive Response

We conclude our study of the accounting side of decision making by introducing the possibility of competitive response, or strategic encounter. Adding a product to our product line may affect one or more competitors and may evoke a response. For example, they may decide to cede the new product's market to us or they may retaliate with vigor. Extensive investment in R&D may scare off potential competitors. Access to proprietary technology may give us a cost advantage.

The list goes on, and the anecdotes are endless: airline pricing, proprietary versus open architectures in the computer industry, financial aid to students, curriculum development, predatory pricing, shortened product development cycles in the auto industry, auction of treasury bills, community based policing, buying or selling a used car, or designing a political campaign.

The common feature in these settings is the consequences of what we do depend in part on what someone else does. One might think the way to proceed is to assign a probability to what this someone else might do and then proceed. Game theory takes a more consistent approach, by simultaneously analyzing the situation from each player's perspective and by combining these perspectives with the notion of equilibrium behavior. In this way, the analysis renders as endogenous the description of what someone else might do.

We explore this theme by looking at pricing decisions. Strategic considerations clearly are found well beyond the confines of pricing, and this should be kept in mind. We emphasize pricing because of its importance and because it is frequently encountered in everyday life.

Pricing practice is highly varied. We often see posted prices, as in grocery stores. In other settings we negotiate or haggle, as when buying a new car or a house or transacting at a flea market. Yet in other settings we see formal auctions. Bankruptcy liquidations, oil drilling rights, wine, livestock, financial securities, art objects, and bidding to provide various supplies and services to a municipality are illustrative.

Our work begins with a review of market based approaches where an endogenous demand curve governs the pricing behavior. Then we examine auctions and conclude with a brief look at haggling. Keep in mind these decisions may be large or small; and their links to the product costing art may be direct (e.g., asking whether the observed price is above marginal cost) or mysterious (e.g., using a price equals cost plus markup rule tentatively to price a variety of products).

Also keep in mind that when it comes time to describe another player's behavior, we will resort to equilibrium analysis. This has the advantage of disciplining our intuition. It has the disadvantage of calling for us to specify the setting from our perspective as well as from that of our competitor or competitors. It also has the disadvantage of requiring an understanding of the rudiments of equilibrium analysis, as presented in Chapter 4, for example.

Market Based Approaches

A market is a particular type of organized trade mechanism. The New York Stock Exchange, the college placement office, and the local want ads are examples. The market might be perfect or imperfect. Pricing might be perfunctory or it might be the organization's primary strategic variable. Restaurants tend to compete more with culinary style, location, and quality than price; software mail order houses compete more with price and delivery.

the perfect market setting

A perfect market, recall, is one in which the good or service in question is tradable without restriction and without transaction cost, under known, constant terms of trade. Though largely fictional, it provides an important benchmark.

Consider an organization that produces a single product. Let q denote the number of units it produces and places on the market. Also denote its cost curve by $C(q)$. Further suppose this product is sold in a perfectly competitive market. The market price is P per unit. So total revenue is Pq. The market price is set by the market and does not depend on how many units our organization offers for sale. Profit, as a function of quantity q, is simply Pq - $C(q)$. Our organization's choice problem is familiar:

$$\text{maximize } \pi(q) = Pq - C(q).$$

The only decision variable is quantity q. The solution is characterized by the usual marginal revenue equals marginal cost dictum:

$$P = C'(q).$$

The thing to notice here is price is a known parameter. We not only know P, but presume it is constant when we calculate marginal revenue by differentiating Pq.

In Chapter 2 we studied a particular version of this story with P = 119, and a cost curve of $C(q) = 200q - 18q^2 + q^3$. Profit maximization implies

$$P = 119 = C'(q) = 200 - 36q + 3q^2.$$

From here we concluded q = 9, along with $\pi(9) = 119(9) - C(9) = 0$.

Presumably we have many competitors, and we are free to produce and sell any number of units. The only catch is the market price is P = 119. To drive this point home, ask what we varied to maximize the above profit function, $\pi(q)$. The answer is *only* quantity. Price is given.

The perfect market fully separates us from any competitive response. No one will contact us if we ask for a price above 119. All customers but no competitors will respond to a price below 119. (This, of course, would ensure bankruptcy.) In addition, we can sell any number of units we please at the posted price of P = 119.

The perfectly competitive market offers no room for concern over prices. Prices are set by market forces and are beyond the control of all individual actors. This is an important lesson. We envision many customers and many competitors in this setting. The perfect market insulates us from all of their activities, calling on us to treat the equilibrium market price of P = 119 as a parameter.[1]

the pure monopoly setting

Now suppose our organization is the sole producer of this product. It must decide how much output to produce and at what price that output should be offered for sale. Of course, these choices are linked. The demand curve specifies the link between price and quantity.

Again returning to our Chapter 2 illustration, suppose the market clearing price per unit, as a function of the quantity produced, is given by $P(q) = 340 - 2q$.[2] This implies each additional unit placed on the market depresses the market clearing price by 2 per unit. So total revenue, as a function of quantity, is $P(q)q = (340 - 2q)q$.

With revenue expressed as a function of quantity, we again write profit solely as a function of quantity: $\pi(q) = P(q)q - C(q) = (340 - 2q)q - 200q + 18q^2 - q^3$. Differentiating this version of $\pi(q)$ produces

$$340 - 4q - C'(q) = 0; \text{ or } 340 - 4q = C'(q).$$

Again we set marginal revenue equal to marginal cost. The only difference is the selling price now depends on the quantity produced. (In Chapter 2 we pushed through to conclude the optimal output is q = 14, implying $\pi(14) = 2,352$.)[3]

---

[1]This use of the word *equilibrium* should be carefully noted. In a perfect market setting we assume atomistic, price taking behavior. In a monopoly setting, the monopolist recognizes the market price is influenced by its output, just as oligopolists recognize the market price is influenced by the sum of their output. Equilibrium in these settings refers to supply quantity equaling demand quantity, and all actors treating price as a parameter unless assumed otherwise (as with the monopoly or duopoly producers). In short order we will invoke best response equilibrium behavior, by which we mean each player's behavior is a best response to the others' behavior. Our forthcoming duopoly setting will have best response equilibrium output choices by the two producers that result in a market equilibrium price (defined by supply equals demand).

[2]$P(q) = 340 - 2q$ is called the inverse demand curve. For the record, a demand curve gives quantity as a function of price; and an inverse demand curve gives price as a function of quantity. The inverse demand curve gives a price of $P(q) = 340 - 2q$, while the demand curve gives a quantity of $D(P) = .5(340 - P)$.

[3]Further inspection of the marginal revenue equals marginal cost condition reveals we may express it as $P - 2q = C'(q)$. This is readily interpreted in terms of demand elasticity. Since price is given by $P = 340 - 2q$, the demand curve (linking quantity to price) is simply $q = D(P) = .5(340 - P)$. In turn, the elasticity of demand is given by $\varepsilon = -[dD(P)/dP][P/q]$, or $-[\Delta q/\Delta P]/[P/q]$ in discrete terms. This

price discrimination

The pure monopoly story presumes the organization selects its quantity and places that amount on the market. The market allocates this quantity by setting a price to clear the market. Implicitly we assume each purchaser pays the same price.

Price discrimination occurs when different purchasers pay different prices. Examples abound. Young and old are charged lower prices at movie theaters. Students with fewer financial resources receive financial aid. Gas, water, and electricity rates usually differ between residential and commercial customers. Products are often priced higher early in the product life cycle. Sales are common in many retail markets.

To illustrate, suppose, in our continuing example, the monopolist can perfectly price discriminate. Each customer will be charged a personalized price. Using the inverse demand function of $P(q) = 340 - 2q$, a perfectly discriminating monopolist will charge the first customer $340 - 2 = 338$, the second customer $340 - 4 = 336$, and so on. See Table 16.1, where we verify the best (integer) choice is $q = 15$ units. Notice how incremental revenue (the price charged the last customer) exceeds incremental cost for $q \leq 15$. The profit of 2,535 exceeds the monopoly profit of 2,352, because the prices are now fine tuned to each customer's willingness to pay.[4,5]

Of course, this is an extreme case, based on an assumption the monopolist can perfectly identify each customer and prevent those with a low price from reselling to those who value the product more. Other, more mild, forms take place when a market is segmented, for example, by some observable characteristic such as age or private versus commercial. Nonlinear prices (such as the multipart pricing familiar on a telephone bill) are also used to segment markets.[6]

---

reduces to $\varepsilon = P/2q$ in our case. The marginal revenue equals marginal cost condition now simplifies to $P[1 - 1/\varepsilon] = C'(q)$. In other words, price is a markup over *marginal* cost, where the markup depends on the price elasticity of demand. In our case, of course, we find $P[1 - 1/\varepsilon] = P - 2q$.

[4]Using calculus, notice total revenue of the perfectly discriminating monopolist is:

$$\int_0^q [340-2x]dx = 340q - q^2.$$

This implies total profit of $340q - q^2 - 200 + 18q^2 - q^3$. Differentiating, or equating marginal revenue and marginal cost, gives us: $340 - 2q = 200 + 36q + 3q^2$. Thus, marginal revenue equals price charged the last customer equals marginal cost. We find $q = 14.54$, along with total profit of 2,555.67.

[5]We have a lengthy, rich history of antitrust covering nearly a century of case law. U.S. federal regulations forbid collusion and individual firm attempts to obtain monopoly power (the Sherman Act of 1890). The Clayton Act (1914) forbids various practices, including price discrimination, whose effect may be to substantially lessen competition. The Robinson Patman Act (1936) allows for price discrimination due to cost differences in production and delivery, or due to "good faith" meeting of competition.

[6]Suppose the monopolist can segment the market into two markets, with respective demand

Table 16.1: Perfect Price Discrimination Example					
number of customers	price charged last customer	incremental cost	total revenue	total cost	profit
2	336	153	674	336	338
4	332	111	1,340	576	764
6	328	93	1,998	768	1230
8	324	99	2,648	960	1688
10	320	129	3,290	1,200	2090
12	316	183	3,924	1,536	2388
13	314	219	4,238	1,755	2483
14	312	261	4,550	2,016	2534
15	310	309	4,860	2,325	2535
16	308	363	5,168	2,688	2480
17	306	423	5,474	3,111	2363

Notice, in any event, how the market structures the pricing decision. In the perfectly competitive case there is no decision. In the monopoly case, the firm uses its power to control quantity (equivalently, price) to determine price and quantity simultaneously. In the perfectly discriminating monopoly case, it goes one step further and sets personal prices for each customer. The "market" closes the model in each case. Knowledge of the demand curve, together with knowledge of the cost curve, points toward the role of pricing decisions in the particular setting.

the duopoly case

As a final stop on our survey of market based analyses, suppose we add a second, identical firm to the monopoly story. Let q_1 be the quantity produced by the first firm and q_2 be the quantity produced by the second firm. This implies a total quantity of $q = q_1 + q_2$. The market price will therefore be $P(q) = 340 - 2(q_1 + q_2)$.

We noted in Chapter 2 that our friends might collude, presumably in violation of antitrust statutes. They also might play noncooperatively. Suppose they view quantity produced and sold as the strategic variable, and simultaneously place their output on the market. The market then clears, according to the noted inverse demand function of $P(q) = 340 - 2(q_1 + q_2)$. (Think of this as two producers of a perishable commodity, such as fish. Each player's catch is turned over to a whole-saler, who clears the market.)

---

elasticities of ε_1 and ε_2. Then the profit maximizing condition of setting marginal revenue in each market equal to marginal cost reduces to $P_1(1 - 1/\varepsilon_1) = P_2(1 - 1/\varepsilon_2) = C'(q_1+q_2)$, where the subscripting refers to the respective markets. We now have another markup rule, but the markup in each market depends on the demand elasticity in that market.

Examine the first firm's profit. It depends on its own output, q_1, as well as the output of its competitor, q_2. Suppose the latter is given by $q_2 = x$. We then write the first firm's profit as follows:

$$\pi^1(q_1;x) = P(q)q_1 - C(q_1) = (340 - 2q_1 - 2x)q_1 - 200q_1 + 18q_1^2 - q_1^3.$$

Holding x constant, this is once again profit as a function of quantity. Suppose this firm guesses its competitor will bring $q_2 = x$ units to market. What should it do?

To maximize its profit, it should pick the value of q_1 that maximizes $\pi^1(q_1;x)$, holding x constant. The maximum occurs when the derivative vanishes. So we have an optimality condition of:

$$\frac{d\pi^1(q_1;x)}{dq_1} = 0 = 340 - 4q_1 - 2x - 200 + 36q_1 - 3q_1^2 = 140 - 2x + 32q_1 - 3q_1^2.$$

This is a quadratic equation, and the only positive root is given by the following expression.[7]

$$q_1(x) = \frac{32 + \sqrt{32 \cdot 32 + 12(140 - 2x)}}{6}.$$

For example, x = 8 implies $q_1(x) = 13.6866$. See Figure 16.1, where we plot firm 1's output as a function of $q_2 = x$. Thus, if firm 1 conjectures firm 2 will produce $q_2 = x$ units, its best choice is to produce $q_1(x)$. We call $q_1(x)$ firm 1's *reaction function*. It slopes downward because more output by the rival lowers this firm's marginal revenue.

So what is a good conjecture to make? Well, let's place ourselves in the other firm's shoes. Suppose firm 2 guesses firm 1 will produce $q_1 = y$ units. What should it do? Not surprisingly, its profit is given by

$$\pi^2(q_2;y) = P(q)q_2 - C(q_2) = (340 - 2y - 2q_2)q_2 - 200q_2 + 18q_2^2 - q_2^3.$$

Rehashing the details, we find firm 2's best response to a conjecture of $q_1 = y$ to be the following:

$$q_2(y) = \frac{32 + \sqrt{32 \cdot 32 + 12(140 - 2y)}}{6}.$$

The last step is we want the two conjectures to be consistent. Examine Figure 16.1, where we plot $q_1(x)$ and $q_2(y)$. They intersect at x = y = 13.4656. At this point, firm 1 conjectures x = q_2 = 13.4656. Given this conjecture, it selects q_1 = 13.4656. Conversely, firm 2 conjectures q_1 = y = 13.4656 and on this basis selects q_2 =

---

[7]We must make certain the profit function is concave. The second derivative is $32 - 6q_1$, which is negative for $q_1 \geq 32/6$. This is why, in the subsequent graph, we concentrate on $q_1 \geq 32/6$.

13.4656. Conjectures and best responses are mutually consistent.[8] Now we know how we found the solution presented in Chapter 2.

Figure 16.1: Reaction Functions for Both Firms

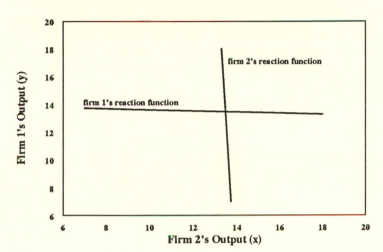

Several points are in order. First, notice how we attack the problem by simultaneously thinking through the details from our perspective and from that of our rival. Second, we rely on the market to set the price. Competition occurs in terms of quantities that are simultaneously brought to the market.

Finally, do organizations really do this? Not literally, at least to my knowledge. We would need a duopoly with known demand and cost curves, as well as an understanding that competition takes place using quantity as the strategic variable. But the principle of simultaneously thinking through one's position and that of one's rival holds. This is the essence of strategic planning.[9]

On some occasions this is done intuitively, on others with elaborate simulations (e.g., business games or war games), and still others with formal equilibrium analyses. It is important, as a professional manager, to understand strategic considerations may be present even in the face of a highly organized product market.

---

[8]The solution is symmetric because the cost curves are the same. What would happen if firm 2's marginal cost were higher than firm 1's?

[9]Historical note: this story, called Cournot competition, originates in 1838, in Cournot's *Recherches sur les Principes Mathematiques de la Theorie des Richesses*. Another story, called Bertrand competition, would have the rivals compete by announcing a price. This gets awkward when the prices differ, because we must then specify what happens following the price announcements (assuming homogeneous goods). Presumably, the entire market goes to the low cost announcer. Conversely, if the prices are the same, we must resolve how total demand is split between the rivals.

Computer software, consulting, and auto markets are illustrative. When competitive response is important, the professional manager envisions a significantly wider frame of the decision at hand.

Auction Mechanisms

The economist's notion of a market, as an organized trade mechanism, is largely a black box. Customers respond in a way portrayed by the demand curve.[10] In turn, product cost plays a passive role, emerging in the familiar marginal revenue equals marginal cost calculation. Yet we are familiar with anecdotes in which cost plays more of a role in pricing. The auto dealer advertises at cost plus 1%, the steel fabricator quotes a price only after carefully estimating its cost, and charges of unfair competition often take the form of "selling below cost." It turns out that cost plays a more visible role in pricing when we move beyond the setting of a well-functioning market.

To explore this theme, we examine an auction mechanism with a small number of bidders (actually, 2 in number). Though we concentrate on a sealed bid auction, we should be aware that various types of auctions are used. In an English auction, the auctioneer begins with a low price and solicits successively higher bids. In a Dutch auction, the auctioneer starts out high and lowers the price until someone takes the object. A second price auction is one in which the highest bid wins, but pays the second highest price.

To set the stage, suppose a potential customer has asked for bids on a special project. Think of this as a construction project, a specialized machine, a custom fabricated product, or a specialized service. It is unique and must be supplied according to the customer's specifications.

The rules are simple. We bid or not. Any bid is prepared without knowledge of any other bid. The buyer examines the bids. Among those submitting bids, the low bidder wins the contract. The low bidder is paid the winning (low) bid, and supplies the product or service, as specified. In the unlikely event of a tie, one potential winner is randomly selected.[11]

Further suppose there are two potential suppliers. Each faces the same cost structure, with *incremental* cost given by

$$\text{cost} = \alpha x + \beta y + \gamma z.$$

---

[10]In a larger model, we would search for an equilibrium price in which individual producer and consumer choices aggregate so supply equals demand. Even so, the process by which this happens is unmodeled.

[11]Life is often not so well-defined. The specifications may change, at the behest of the supplier, the customer, or both. They may even be negotiated before bids are submitted. The total number of units might be variable, as might the required completion date. Either party might breach; the parties might disagree about quality. The winning bidder might turn around and subcontract with one of the competitors.

α, β and γ are known, positive constants. x, y, and z are independent, identically distributed random variables; with uniform densities between 0 and 1.[12] Such a density has $f(t) = 1$, for $0 \le t \le 1$, and $f(t) = 0$ otherwise. Also recall this density has an expected value of

$$E(t) = \int_0^1 tf(t)dt = \int_0^1 tdt = .5t^2 \Big|_0^1 = .5.$$

Each bidder's expected incremental cost is therefore

$$E(cost) = E(\alpha x + \beta y + \gamma z) = \alpha E(x) + \beta E(y) + \gamma E(z) =$$
$$\alpha(1/2) + \beta(1/2) + \gamma(1/2) = (\alpha + \beta + \gamma)/2.$$

For example, if $\alpha = 10$, $\beta = 10$, and $\gamma = 40$, we have $E(cost) = 60/2 = 30$.

Finally, both competitors are risk neutral. This cost structure probably appears awkward and unintuitive. It is chosen to illustrate a number of points once we understand the bidding behavior. Be patient.

Now suppose firm 1 bids an amount b_1. If this bid loses, firm 1's incremental profit is precisely zero. If this bid wins, firm 1's incremental profit is b_1 - cost = b_1 - αx - βy - γz.

Would the bid ever be below the expected incremental cost? Certainly not. This would result in zero profit (if the bid loses), or a loss (if the bid wins). Suppose firm 2 bids an amount above $E(cost)$, say $b_2 = E(cost) + k$. Firm 1 might consider bidding $b_2 = E(cost) + k/2$. This is a winning bid and provides a positive expected incremental profit. Of course, if firm 1 is bidding in this fashion, firm 2 might bid $b_2 = E(cost) + k/4$. Continuing on this odyssey should convince us the *equilibrium* is for each firm to bid $b_i = E(cost)$. In particular, firm 1 can do no better than bid $b_1 = E(cost)$, if this is how firm 2 is behaving. Conversely, firm 2 can do no better than bid $b_2 = E(cost)$ if this is how firm 1 is behaving.[13]

To be less abstract, suppose $\alpha = 10$, $\beta = 10$, and $\gamma = 40$, implying $E(cost) = 30$. Identical competitors are vying for the customer's business. With the potential suppliers facing the same cost, the customer is in an advantageous position. Bidding the expected cost is equilibrium behavior. If firm 1 bids 30, firm 2's best response is to bid 30, and vice versa. The power of competitive sourcing is evident. Here, the competitors bid cost plus a markup, and the bidding competition drives the markup to zero![14]

---

[12]This example is patterned after an auction illustration in Myerson [1991, pp. 132-136], in which two competitors bid for a single object (e.g., an art object) with an unknown but common value.

[13]Think back to the work we have done on product costing. This is a delicate art, suggesting the importance of cost estimation in a pricing decision. Our auction example leaves no room for product costing debate. We know the cost is $\alpha x + \beta y + \gamma z$.

[14]What would happen if firm 1's cost were 30 while firm 2's cost were 35?

equilibrium bidding with private information

Implicitly, our story assumes both bidders know E(cost), no more and no less. Let's change the story. Before bidding, firm 1 observes x and y; and firm 2 observes x and z. Both know x; firm 1 also knows y; and firm 2 also knows z. In addition, firm 1 knows firm 2 is privately observing z, and so on. This is a story in which each bidder knows something about the cost that the other does not know.

For example, one firm might be better at engineering and the other at fabrication. Both know something about the product in question (x), the first also has insight into the engineering part of the story (y), and the second has insight into the fabrication part of the story (z). Notice how our simple model captures this intuitive idea. Firm 1 sees y, but not z and firm 2 sees z, but not y. Both see x.

So what happens when firm 1 observes x and y, while firm 2 observes x and z. Since the three random variables are independent, firm 1 now perceives an expected cost, given x and y, of

$$E(\text{cost} \mid x,y) = \alpha x + \beta y + \gamma E(z) = \alpha x + \beta y + \gamma/2.$$

Similarly, firm 2 now perceives an expected cost, given observation of x and z, of

$$E(\text{cost} \mid x,z) = \alpha x + \beta E(y) + \gamma z = \alpha x + \beta/2 + \gamma z.$$

Notice how the assumption x, y, and z are mutually independent simplifies these calculations. (Also notice our earlier story in which both firms knew the same thing can be interpreted as one in which $\beta = \gamma = 0$.)

With this preamble, we now examine firm 1's bidding strategy more closely. Suppose it submits a bid of $b_1 = b$. If $b_2 < b$, it loses the auction, and gains nothing. If $b_2 > b$, it wins the auction outright. What does it gain? It gains the customer's payment less the cost, or $b - \alpha x - \beta y - \gamma z$. From firm 1's perspective, this is a random variable, as it does not know z. Firm 1 knows x and y. It does not know z. But it knows something about z. Presumably firm 2 knew z when it bid, and bid in such a way firm 1 won the auction outright. Does this imply firm 2 perceived a higher cost, suggesting z might be "large?" This will turn out to be the case. For now just express the expected gain as

$$b - \alpha x - \beta y - \gamma E(z \mid b_2 > b).$$

That is, we allow the expected value of z to depend on the fact we bid b and we won the auction outright. Intuitively, firm 2 knowing z and bidding above b tells us something about z. Equilibrium analysis will give some meat to our intuition.

Remember we also flip a coin if the bids tie. So we calculate firm 1's profit from bidding $b_1 = b$, given x and y, as:

$$E(\pi^1 \mid b;x,y) = [0] \cdot prob\{b_2 < b\} + [b-\alpha x-\beta y-\gamma E(z \mid b_2 > b)] \cdot prob\{b_2 > b\}$$
$$+ .5[b-\alpha x-\beta y-\gamma E(z \mid b_2 = b)] \cdot prob\{b_2 = b\}.$$

This is certainly a mouthful. It is also troubling, as we must specify such things as the probability that firm 1's bid wins the auction outright, i.e., *prob*$\{b_2 > b\}$.

To specify the missing probabilities, we must think in equilibrium terms. For this purpose, tentatively suppose firm 2 uses a bidding rule of

$$b_2 = \alpha x + (\beta + \gamma)/2 + (\beta + \gamma)z/2.$$

Notice this is a linear function of what firm 2 has observed, x and z; more will be said about this later. (If we are on our toes, we will suspect this is half the equilibrium and we are about to verify the other half.)

Given firm 2 bids in this manner, firm 1's bid of b will win outright whenever

$$b < \alpha x + (\beta + \gamma)/2 + (\beta + \gamma)z/2.$$

Manipulating this expression leads to

$$\frac{b - \alpha x - (\beta + \gamma)/2}{(\beta + \gamma)/2} = g(b) < z.$$

In other words, the bid of $b_1 = b$ wins outright provided z exceeds $g(b)$.

From here we can bracket the interesting bids. Given x, the lowest bid firm 2 will submit (which occurs when $z = 0$) is $b_2 = \alpha x + (\beta + \gamma)/2$; and the highest bid it will submit is $b_2 = \alpha x + (\beta + \gamma)/2 + (\beta + \gamma)/2 = \alpha x + (\beta + \gamma)$. There is no reason for firm 1 to bid below the lowest or above the highest conceivable value of b_2. But then the interesting bids for firm 1 imply $g(b)$ ranges between 0 and 1.

Continuing, if $0 \leq z < g(b)$ we have $b > b_2$ and the bid of b loses; firm 1's incremental profit is zero. If $g(b) < z \leq 1$ we have $b < b_2$ and the bid of b wins; firm 1's incremental profit is b - cost = $b - \alpha x - \beta y - \gamma z$. Since a tie actually occurs with probability zero (as z is a continuous random variable), we have the following expression for firm 1's expected incremental profit:

$$E(\pi^1|b;x,y) = \int_0^{g(b)}[0]dz + \int_{g(b)}^1 [b-\alpha x-\beta y-\gamma z]dz =$$

$$[0]z + [(b-\alpha x-\beta y)z-.5\gamma z^2]\ \Big|_{g(b)}^1 =$$

$$(1-g(b))[b-\alpha x-\beta y-.5\gamma(1+g(b))].$$

The first integral covers the case where the bid loses, while the second covers the case where it wins the auction. Notice how the *assumed* bidding rule by firm 2 allows us to deal directly with such things as the probability firm 1's bid of b wins the auction.

Firm 1 wants $E(\pi^1 \mid b;x,y)$ as large as possible; so we focus on the point where the derivative vanishes.[15]

---

[15]$E(\pi^1 \mid b;x,y)$ is a concave (and differentiable) function of b; so we know the maximum occurs at

$$\frac{d\pi^1(b;x,y)}{db} = -g'(b)[b-\alpha x-\beta y-.5\gamma(1+g(b))] + (1-g(b))[1-.5\gamma g'(b)].$$

Two additional steps complete the torture. Substitute $g'(b) = 1/(\beta + \gamma)/2 = 2/(\beta + \gamma)$. Also substitute the earlier expression for $g(b)$. Collecting terms leads to

$$b = b_1(x,y) = \alpha x + (\beta + \gamma)/2 + (\beta + \gamma)y/2.$$

Whew! Now, if we repeat this from the other side we will discover that *if* firm 1 uses this bidding rule, firm 2's best response is to use the bidding rule that we originally conjectured. The two bidding rules form equilibrium behavior. Each is a best response to the other.

cost, profit, and the winner's curse

Let's summarize some expressions. Each firm bases its bids on what it observes; so b_1 depends on x and y while b_2 depends on x and z. Write the equilibrium pricing strategies as follows:

$$b_1(x,y) = \alpha x + (\beta + \gamma)/2 + (\beta + \gamma)y/2; \text{ and}$$
$$b_2(x,z) = \alpha x + (\beta + \gamma)/2 + (\beta + \gamma)z/2.$$

In turn, the relevant cost expressions (i.e., expected incremental cost) for each of the firms, given what they have observed *and* that they have won the bidding, are:

$$E(\text{cost} \mid x,y,b_1 \text{ wins}) = \alpha x + \beta y + \gamma(1 + y)/2; \text{ and}$$
$$E(\text{cost} \mid x,z,b_2 \text{ wins}) = \alpha x + \gamma z + \beta(1 + z)/2.$$

These expressions can be derived as follows. Using the above bidding strategies, $b_1 < b_2$ occurs only if $y < z$. To see this, notice

$$b_1(x,y) - b_2(x,z) = .5(\beta + \gamma)y - .5(\beta + \gamma)z = .5(\beta + \gamma)(y - z).$$

With $\beta + \gamma > 0$, we have $b_1 - b_2$ negative only if $y < z$.[16] Now, with a uniform density between 0 and 1, $y < z$ implies the *conditional* expected value of z is simply $y + (1 - y)/2 = (1 + y)/2$. A parallel construction applies for firm 2's case.

We belabor this because of its importance. Winning carries information. We use an equilibrium argument to specify the pricing behavior of each party. The bids turn out to be linear functions of what was observed. Firm 1 bids higher if y is

---

the point the derivative vanishes.

[16]In equilibrium, then, firm 1's bid wins if $y < z$. What is the probability that $y < z$? The uniform distribution assumption makes this an easy calculation. It is $1 - y$. For example, suppose we know $y = .3$. What is the probability that $.3 < z$? The answer is .7. It is important to understand we have used equilibrium behavior to calculate these probabilities. It is the equilibrium behavior that drives the claim firm 1 wins the auction if $y < z$.

higher, just as firm 2 bids higher if z is higher. Winning therefore tells us the other bidder's private observation was "large."

To reinforce this point, contrast the above cost calculations with those when we do not condition on winning the auction:

$$E(\text{cost} \mid x,y) = \alpha x + \text{ß}y + \gamma/2; \text{ and}$$
$$E(\text{cost} \mid x,z) = \alpha x + \text{ß}/2 + \gamma z.$$

The first is downward biased by

$$E(\text{cost} \mid x,y,b_1 \text{ wins}) - E(\text{cost} \mid x,y) = \gamma y/2$$

and the second is downward biased by

$$E(\text{cost} \mid x,z,b_2 \text{ wins}) - E(\text{cost} \mid x,z) = \text{ß}z/2,$$

given the firm in question has observed its respective information and followed its equilibrium bidding strategy.

This phenomenon is called the *winner's curse*. If we win the auction, our initial estimate is biased. Winning implies that we initially underestimated the cost. More precisely, the fact of winning should cause us to raise our perception of the cost of supplying the object in question. This stems from the fact the eventual cost will be the same regardless of producer, and each party in the auction is observing something the others are not observing. Under these circumstances our bid wins only when our "news" is better than that received by our competitor.

To avoid the winner's curse, we bid with the understanding our bid wins only if our private information is more favorable than that of our competitor. We "overbid" in recognition of the fact we win only if our cost calculation was too low.

For example, if two similar competitors bid on repairing a highway, the winning bid should tell us something about what the other competitor thought the cost of performing the repairs might be. Likewise, similar competitors bidding for oil drilling rights must deal with the fact that if they win the bid their information must have suggested a more valuable oil reserve than that of the competitors. Winning carries information!

Finally, if we take the time to substitute the equilibrium bidding strategy into each firm's expected incremental profit calculations, we will find:[17]

$$E(\pi^1 \mid \text{equilibrium bidding;}x,y) = .5\text{ß}(1 - y)^2; \text{ and}$$
$$E(\pi^2 \mid \text{equilibrium bidding;}x,z) = .5\gamma(1 - z)^2.$$

---

[17]If, upon observing x and y, firm 1's equilibrium bid wins, it will be paid the winning bid of $b_1(x,y) = \alpha x + (\text{ß} + \gamma)/2 + (\text{ß} + \gamma)y/2$ and face an expected cost of $\alpha x + \text{ß}y + \gamma(1 + y)/2$. Revenue less expected cost is $.5\text{ß}(1 - y)$. In turn, observing x and y and bidding in this fashion yields a winning bid if $y < z$. This has a probability of $1 - y$. So with probability $1 - y$ we obtain the above conditional expected profit and with probability y we lose the auction and gain nothing. Overall, then, the expected profit is $.5\text{ß}(1 - y)^2$.

Thus, if firm 1 observes x and y, the best it can do (by following the noted bidding rule) will return an expected incremental profit of $.5\beta(1 - y)^2$.

numerical illustrations of cost based pricing

It is natural to interpret these bidding strategies as cost plus pricing. The delicate issues are what we mean by cost, and where the plus comes from. Let's agree to call cost the expected cost once the firm observes the private information. For firm 1, then, we focus on the cost measure of $E(\text{cost} \mid x,y) = \alpha x + \beta y + \gamma/2$. Now indulge in some algebra and write the bidding strategy as follows:

$$b_1(x,y) = E(\text{cost} \mid x,y) + plus.$$

Here, *plus* is the amount we add to cost (as defined) to come up with the bid. Viewed in this manner, the *plus* part of the formula compensates for the fact that our estimate of cost is downward biased, if we win the auction. The *plus* term compensates for the winner's curse.

For some specific calculations, let $\alpha = 0$ and $\beta = \gamma = 10$. The common term has no effect, for simplicity, and each firm is on an "equal footing" in the sense they are each observing something of equal importance. Table 16.2 reports firm 1's equilibrium bid, cost, and profit calculations as a function of y. Study it carefully.

Table 16.2: Cost, Bid, and Profit Results for $\alpha = 0$, $\beta = \gamma = 10$				
y	$E(\text{cost}\mid x,y) =$ $10y+5$	$b_1(x,y) =$ $10+10y$	$E(\text{cost}\mid x,y,b_1$ wins) $= 15y+5$	expected profit $= 5(1-y)^2$
0.0	5	10	5.0	5.00
.1	6	11	6.5	4.05
.2	7	12	8.0	3.20
.3	8	13	9.5	2.45
.4	9	14	11.0	1.80
.5	10	15	12.5	1.25
.6	11	16	14.0	0.80
.7	12	17	15.5	0.45
.8	13	18	17.0	0.20
.9	14	19	18.5	0.05
1.0	15	20	20.0	0.00

Notice how the naive cost expression of $E(\text{cost} \mid x,y) = 10y + 5$ increases linearly as we step through various values of y. Adjusting for the winner's curse, though, we have $E(\text{cost} \mid x,y,b_1 \text{ wins}) = 10y + 5 + 5y = 15y + 5$. The bias in the naive estimate is 5y. Here, the sophisticated cost expression increases linearly as we step through values of y, but at a 50% higher rate.

Intuitively, the bias increases with y because firm 1's bid increases with y. If firm 1 perceives a high cost (i.e., high y) and still wins the auction, $z > y$ is implied and therefore z is well removed from the original mean of .5. Conversely, if firm 1 perceives a low cost (i.e., low y) and wins the auction, $z > y$ is again implied, but this is not now compelling evidence z is well removed from the original mean.

Next examine the optimal bid of $b_1(x,y) = 10 + 10y$. We can write this as

$$b_1(x,y) = E(cost \mid x,y) + 5.$$

That is, we can express the equilibrium bidding behavior in terms of taking the naive expected cost and adding a constant amount of *plus* = 5.

This being the case, ask what explains the constant amount of 5. In particular, why are we not just adding the winner's curse adjustment to our cost expression? The reason is our bid affects what we are paid if we win as well as the probability we win the auction.

Suppose $y = .1$ is observed. If we follow the equilibrium bidding strategy and bid $b_1(x,y) = 11$, we face an expected profit of 4.05. Examine this more closely. With $\alpha = 0$ and $\beta = \gamma = 10$, each player's bid varies uniformly (and independently) between 10 and 20. So a bid of 11 will win with probability .9. But if we win with such a bid we know $z \geq .1$. So the expected value of z jumps to $.1 + .45 = .55$. Therefore, $E(cost \mid x,y=1,b_1 \text{ wins}) = 10(.1) + 10(.55) = 6.5$. Check Table 16.2.

Anyway, the bid of 11, if it wins, shows an expected profit of $11 - 6.5 = 4.5$. The bid wins with probability .9, so we face an expected profit of $.9(4.5) = 4.05$.

Here we are bidding $b_1 = 11$, for a project whose expected cost will be 6.5 if the bid wins. This seems unnecessarily conservative. Try a more aggressive bid, say, $b_1 = 10$, upon observing $y = .1$. This guarantees we win the auction, as firm 2 will bid above $b = \alpha x + (\beta + \gamma)/2 = 10$ (unless $z = 0$, a zero probability event). If we win no matter what firm 2 bids, then the expected cost, conditional on winning (and $y = .1$), must be $10(.1) + 10(.5) = 6$. This delivers an expected profit of $1(10 - 6) = 4 < 4.05$. We win more often with the lower bid, but gain less in the process.

Two forces are at work, given firm 2's behavior. How firm 1 bids determines the probability that its bid wins. This, in turn, influences what the firm learns about z if its bid wins. Put differently, the value of what firm 1 wins in the auction depends on the bidding strategy it employs. To calculate the expected profit we must think in terms of probability of winning times the quantity of bid less expected cost given what we observed *and* given we won the bidding. The *plus* in our cost plus pricing formula is a direct manifestation of this fact. It is part of an equilibrium strategy. It compensates for the winner's curse, in light of the competitor's strategic behavior.[18]

---

[18]The winner's curse would become more pronounced if we had more bidders, each with their own information. This implies the *plus* in the cost plus bidding formula depends on the number of bidders.

In short, cost plus pricing can be exhibited as equilibrium behavior in an auction. The *plus* in the cost plus pricing formula is an equilibrium calculation. It reflects a delicate balancing of odds of winning against the ex post value of the object if we happen to win.

Now turn to Table 16.3, where we summarize pricing strategies and expected profits for several possible cost structures. Case 2 has $\alpha = 10$ along with $\beta = \gamma = \varepsilon$. Think of ε as small. The story here is what the competitors learn in common (namely x) overwhelms everything else. Their profits are near zero, just as we discussed earlier for the case of no private information. The winner's curse phenomenon is trivial, and competition drives the *plus* in the pricing strategies to near zero.

case	α	β	γ	$b_1(x,y)$	$b_2(x,y)$	$E(\pi^1|x,y)$	$E(\pi^2|x,z)$
				Table 16.3: Bid and Expected Profit Expressions			
1	0	10	10	$10(1+y)$	$10(1+z)$	$5(1-y)^2$	$5(1-z)^2$
2	10	ε	ε	$10x+\varepsilon(1+y)$	$10x+\varepsilon(1+z)$	$.5\varepsilon(1-y)^2$	$.5\varepsilon(1-z)^2$
3	10	$20-\varepsilon$	ε	$10x+10(1+y)$	$10x+10(1+z)$	$.5(20-\varepsilon)(1-y)^2$	$.5\varepsilon(1-z)^2$
4	10	10	40	$10x+25(1+y)$	$10x+25(1+z)$	$5(1-y)^2$	$20(1-z)^2$

Contrast this with case 3, where $\alpha = 10$ and $\gamma = \varepsilon$ again but $\beta = 20 - \varepsilon$. Here firm 1 has an advantage; it is learning the really important stuff. And this shows in the profit calculations. Firm 1's naive cost expression is downward biased by $\gamma y/2 = \varepsilon y/2$, a trivial amount. Firm 2's is downward biased by $\beta z/2 = (20 - \varepsilon)z/2$. Firm 2 is disadvantaged and bids accordingly.

Another way to interpret this is firm 1 knows a great deal about its cost, while firm 2 does not. Firm 1 bids its cost, increased by *plus* = $10 - \varepsilon/2 - y(10 - \varepsilon)$. Firm 2 bids its cost, increased by *plus* = $\varepsilon/2 + z(10 - \varepsilon)$. Firm 1, in the know, bids more aggressively for large y, while firm 2 bids less aggressively for large z. The *plus* for firm 1 decreases in y, while its counterpart for firm 2 increases in z. Knowing more about our cost allows us to bid more aggressively.

Case 3, with $\alpha = \beta = 10$ and $\gamma = 40$, is a muted version of the same phenomenon, except firm 2 is now informationally advantaged.

In each case, then, we interpret the behavior as a form of cost plus bidding. The bidding, or pricing behavior, is equilibrium behavior. The *plus* in the cost plus formula is an equilibrium concept. Its purpose is to correct a bias in the naive cost expression, in light of the competitor's behavior. It depends on the structure of private information.

Similarly, what we call cost here is an equilibrium concept. We have the expected cost in the absence of any information. We have the expected cost in the presence of private information; this is the cost expression on which our cost plus interpretation is based. We also have the expected cost in the presence of private information after winning (or losing) the auction.

postscript

It is time to step back from the details and ponder the larger picture in this setting. Focus on firm 1's decision. It sees the x and y realizations, or learns something about the cost. It must then submit a bid. At that point, there is more to learn about the cost (z in our story), and there is also the question of what firm 2 might be bidding.

Think of this in terms of a decision tree for firm 1. It knows the probabilities for x, y, and z. It also knows x and y before selecting its bid. Two subsequent events govern the outcome: z and firm 2's bid. If we had a probability specification for firm 2's bid, we would then be all set. The decision tree would be fully specified and it could be massaged in familiar fashion.

The difficulty is firm 2's bid is under the control of an adversary. It seems naive just to assign or decree some probability. Instead, we use equilibrium reasoning, formally or informally, to say something about firm 2's bid, b_2. In the particular illustration, b_2 turns out to be a (linear) function of x and z. To figure this out we had to think simultaneously through firm 1's problem and firm 2's problem. This is the essence of Figure 16.1. We use equilibrium reasoning to specify the behavior of other actors.

Several additional thoughts round out our discussion of auctions. First, notice the neutrality of the αx term. Whatever it is, both competitors see it and add it to their bids. Profit is unaffected.

Second, ask what happens if the αx term is sunk. For example, each firm might have done preliminary work and incurred a cost of αx. Following this, the auction takes place. Competition will now remove the αx term from the equilibrium bids.

Finally, the situation changes drastically if there is no competitor. For the sake of discussion, suppose the customer values this project at some amount V in excess of E(cost). What will firm 1 bid if it knows firm 2 is not bidding? Surely it will bid V. Of course the plot thickens if firm 1 does not know V; but that is yet another private information story. The plot also thickens if the buyer is not so naive and realizes there is no competitor.

Haggling

The final stop in our survey of competitive response, as manifest in pricing decisions, is the subject of haggling. We are all familiar with bargaining, negotiating, or arguing over items of interest. Buying an automobile is a classic example in our society. Real estate, divorce, labor contracts, and consulting fees provide additional examples.

Each setting evokes particular structural details. We often have a buyer, a seller, and a real estate agent in between in the real estate story. We usually have two lawyers (and perhaps a judge) in between in the divorce story. Individuals particularly adept at negotiation are often center stage in labor negotiations. And then there is the unflattering caricature of the quintessential used car salesperson.

The point is not idle. Haggling becomes interpersonal, and places a premium on the skills of the individuals involved. These skills, in turn, are often buttressed by careful design of the setting. Do we meet in a formal though neutral setting? Does the professor always sit behind the desk when a student complains about a grade? Does the auto salesperson always have to check with the boss, thereby introducing another party into the encounter? Can management hire replacement workers if the current workers go on strike?

We will streamline our earlier setting to highlight some of these issues. Most important, let's now assume there is but one possible supplier. In this way, the buyer must deal with the supplier, and not have the advantage of another potential supplier. Also set $\beta = \gamma = 0$, so the supplier's cost is given by cost = αx.

As we hinted earlier, let the value of this project to the buyer be V. The net social gain, then, is zero if no deal is struck, and it is V - cost if a deal is struck. Let's further assume V > cost, so it makes sense to close a deal. The question then becomes one of how to share the gain of V - cost between the two players.

milquetoast players

Suppose both parties are nonaggressive, cooperative types. A natural solution is to split the difference. So the price is P = cost + .5(V - cost). The buyer then gains V - P = .5(V - cost), and the seller likewise gains P - cost = .5(V - cost). In fact, this is precisely the solution predicted by the theory of bargaining. The idea, roughly, is that there are gains to cooperation (here, V - cost), and we also know what happens to each player in the absence of any agreement (here, they each get zero). Treating the parties symmetrically then calls for splitting the gain in this particular setting.[19]

This vignette was prefaced with the idea of nonaggressive, cooperative players. A cooperative, nonstrategic approach is pursued by both parties. To the contrary, what happens if some give and take occurs? For example, suppose the parties simultaneously announce a way to split the gain. If their proposals agree, they have an agreement. If not, they simultaneously announce whether to stand pat or accede to the other's proposal. If both stand pat, no trade occurs. If one holds firm and the other accedes, they have an agreement. If they both accede, they again have no agreement.

Now for the catch. Suppose the buyer proposes to keep k(V - cost) where $0 \leq k \leq 1$, with the seller keeping (1 - k)(V - cost). Further suppose the buyer will stand

---

[19]Our goal here is to suggest splitting the difference is a familiar and it turns out theoretically defensible solution. The theoretical formulation, due to John Nash, envisions the parties as cooperatively searching for a way to split the gain. They do not renege, they do not posture, they do not "game" in any sense. The substance of the axiomatic setup is then the requirement that all gains to trade be pursued (efficiency), that the parties be treated symmetrically, and that irrelevant alternatives not influence the split. With risk neutrality and zero gain nonagreement points, the solution is simply a price P such that the expression (V - P)(P - cost) is maximized.

pat if no agreement is reached in the first round. Seller's best response to such a strategy is to propose keeping at least $(1 - k)(V - cost)$ in the first round, and to accede in the second.[20] Moreover, buyer's best response to such a strategy is to propose and then stand pat, as noted. We have an equilibrium. Unfortunately, k can be anywhere between 0 and 1, so we have paid a large price (pun) for our attempt to introduce some nitty gritty details of bargaining into the exercise. Any solution, any split we had in mind, can be "defended" with an equilibrium argument. We have too much of a good thing. Of course, our friends might naturally focus on the 50-50 split of $k = .50$.[21]

Price, in the haggling story, then, depends on how and with what skill the parties haggle. Since the seller can always walk away, the substantive question is how to split the gain, of V - cost, between the two players.

private cost information

We have implicitly assumed both parties know V and cost, so they know what they are bargaining over. Suppose, to the contrary, cost is either 1 or 2, with equal probability, and is known only by the seller. Also set $V = 4$, so it makes sense to trade even under the high cost condition. The difficulty is the superior information of the seller-producer. The parties might agree to share evenly the gain, but this leaves the seller with an incentive to report high cost even when the cost is low.

Now suppose the buyer makes a take-it-or-leave-it offer to the seller. The seller then accepts or rejects the offer. If accepted, production takes place and the agreed upon price is paid. If rejected, no production takes place. Renegotiation is ruled out. The buyer's ability to commit to a take-it-or-leave-it offer gives the buyer substantial bargaining power. Nevertheless, we will find that the seller is somewhat protected by private information about cost.

If the buyer offers $P = 2$, the seller can do no better than always accept. The buyer gains $V - P = 2$. The seller gains P - cost, which is 1 in the low cost event and 0 in the high cost event. Alternatively, if the buyer offers $P = 1$, the seller can do no better than accept in the low cost event, and reject in the high cost event. The seller now gains zero, no matter what the cost. The buyer gains $V - P = 3$ in the low cost event, and nothing in the high cost event.

Remember the odds are 50-50. Would the buyer prefer to gain 2 or $.5(3) + .5(0) = 1.5$? Before jumping to any conclusions, repeat the story for the case where the

---

[20]An example of this type is analyzed in Kreps [1990, Chapter 15].

[21]The indeterminacy would disappear if the V - cost term declined the longer it took the parties to reach an agreement. Haggling, after all, takes time, and time carries an opportunity cost in the sense we have left other uses of time outside the formal analysis. Pursuing this deeper game, however, takes us into the finer, more subtle details of noncooperative game theory.

probability of low cost is .8. Here, the buyer's best choice is to forego the project when cost = 2, even though V > 2.[22]

Recall in our earlier look at auctions how privately knowing our cost gave us an advantage. The same occurs here. We set the rules so the buyer has all the bargaining power, being able to make a take-it-or-leave-it offer. If the buyer knows the seller's cost, the offer will be P = cost, no more and no less. By not knowing the seller's cost, though, the buyer is reduced to one of two possibilities. One is to offer a price equal to the high cost. Then trade always occurs, but the seller captures some surplus. The other is to offer a price equal to the low cost. Then trade only occurs under the low cost condition, but none of the surplus is shared.

The buyer cannot capture the full gain, despite the advantageous position. The gain is dissipated in one of two ways: it is shared or trade is cut short in the high cost event.

Some more subtle points are also present here. Notice how either scheme, namely offer P = 2 or offer P = 1, can be thought of in terms of a mild negotiation encounter. Buyer says, tell me your cost, and I'll pay P = 2, or tell me your cost and we'll deal (at P = 1) if the cost is low. We will learn in later chapters that this is a revelation game in which the informed party is induced to reveal what is known. The price, so to speak, is not using that revelation in aggressive fashion. The buyer cannot, under the rules of the game, subsequently renege on the take-it-or-leave-it offer.

This suggests, on the surface, renegotiation might be useful. But this is not so. What happens if buyer says, I'll pay P = 1, unless you say cost is high, in which case I'll pay P = 2? This is just a long-winded version of the initial scheme of paying P = 2, whatever the cost.[23]

At any rate, we have arrived at yet another type of strategic encounter. Here, the encounter is easier to analyze because we assume the buyer is able to make a take-it-or-leave-it offer. The seller then moves with full knowledge of what the buyer has chosen.[24]

---

[22]It is tempting to conclude haggling can be inefficient. If everyone knows everything, we know in this case trade should occur. But it is a mistake to take this "full information" answer and blindly presume we should implement it in the private information setting. We will see this theme repeatedly in subsequent chapters when we explore control problems in depth.

[23]It also turns out the buyer's optimal solution in this case is one of the two schemes portrayed. The reasoning is somewhat involved. Initially ask yourself what could buyer offer, but in such a way seller always revealed the true cost. Among all such schemes, the best is always one of the two we identified. Now take any other scheme in which buyer does not always reveal true cost. This can be replicated by a scheme in which seller honestly reveals the cost, and buyer makes any "adjustments" in the trade arrangement that would have obtained had the falsehood taken place.

[24]Now return to the earlier discussion of price discrimination. Haggling is the ultimate price discrimination story, as everything is personalized. Our focus on private information details is meant to further suggest the importance of private information in price discrimination settings. The insurance

The larger lesson remains. The key to equilibrium analysis is analyzing both sides of the encounter. This has the advantage of disciplining our intuition for speculating about what our competitors might do, given what we are contemplating. It also has the advantage of pointing out the importance of fully understanding the "rules" of the game and the motives of the other players.

To end the story, can you guess what happens when cost = αx, but is uniformly distributed as in the auction illustration? Let $\alpha = 2$, implying $0 \leq cost \leq 2$. Suppose the buyer offers to pay $P \leq 2$. The seller's profit is $P - cost = P - 2x$. This is positive for $x \leq P/2$. So the offer will be accepted with probability $P/2$. For $P \leq 2$, the buyer's expected gain is now

$$(1 - P/2)[0] + (P/2)[V - P].$$

The buyer selects P to maximize the expected gain. Simple differentiation implies $P = V/2$ (presuming $V \leq 4$). With $V = 4$, the buyer offers the highest possible cost. With $V = 3$, the buyer offers $P = 1.5$, and so on.[25]

Summary

This is a dual purpose chapter, dealing on one level with pricing decisions and more abstractly on another level with strategic or competitive concerns. The competitive response topic may seem interstitial. Yet that is hardly the case. The natural pedagogical sequence is to add more factors to the decision setting, and this eventually gets us to competitive response. In addition, we shall see the same notion of equilibrium behavior will hold the key to our forthcoming study of control problems.

Pricing decisions must be understood in context. Trade mechanisms are highly varied. They might be organized and impersonal, as in a market where standardized products are bought and sold at stated prices. Market forces then have a great deal to say about price. Less standardized items might be traded in an auction forum. Here, pricing may be perfunctory or highly subtle, depending on the nature of the setting. Haggling rounds out the picture, where we get down to the finer details of one-on-one negotiation.

Stepping back from our survey, we have used various pricing or trade vignettes to interject the topic of competitive encounter. Competitive response is a subtle and open-ended topic. The subtlety comes in two waves. One is that some details we worry about are truly chance phenomena (e.g., weather driven) while others are heavily influenced by other actors. Describing what these other actors might be

---

industry has long recognized this fact. Higher deductibles are used to motivate customers who are more careful or more healthy to reveal themselves. Personalized prices in the face of asymmetric information thereby arise.

[25]More typically, we think of bargaining in terms of a sequence of offers and counter offers. The ideas implicit in the take-it-or-leave-it example carry over to these more elaborate bargaining games.

doing calls for a more expansive analysis, one that includes their opportunities and motives as well. This is why we stressed equilibrium behavior as a device for disciplining our intuition.

The second wave of subtlety comes from the fact we must somehow draw the line, deciding what is sufficiently important to be thought of in strategic terms. For example, if we redesign our product and alter the price, what will happen to the product designs and prices charged by competitors? In turn, the demand for our product will, in principle, reflect the qualities of all the offerings and their respective (and presumably adjusted) prices. At what point do we sever the chain of interactions?

Similarly, an organization often has many opportunities to engineer important strategic encounters. Information may or may not be released. The sales force may not know what new products are under development, thereby putting them more on an equal footing with the customers. A reputation for playing hard ball may be carefully nurtured. The sales force may be given high powered incentives so they react aggressively to competitors in a pricing encounter.

Framing decisions with strategic elements requires imagination and judgment. Both are qualities of the professional manager.

Bibliographic Notes

Dixit and Nalebuff [1991] provide an excellent introduction to strategic thinking. Milgrom [1989] gives an introduction to auctions, equilibrium bidding behavior in various settings, and the design of the auction from the seller's perspective. Nash [1950] is the original source on cooperative bargaining. A superb introduction is presented in the classic Luce and Raiffa [1957]. Beyond that, Kennan and Wilson [1993] and Osborne and Rubinstein [1990] provide introductions to more modern themes of private information and alternating offers. Strategy or strategic planning considerations are explored in a variety of manners. Oster [1990] provides an economics flavor. You might also enjoy Milgrom and Roberts [1987] and Porter [1991]. Spulber [1989] provides an introduction to Robinson Patman issues. More specific information is available in the ABA Antitrust Sections' *The Robinson-Patman Act: Policy and Law* (Monograph No. 4, Volume II, 1983).

Problems and Exercises

1. A central theme of competitive analysis is equilibrium behavior. What does it mean for your strategy to be mutually consistent, in the sense of equilibrium behavior, with that of your competitor?

2. The text stresses the idea that a wider decision frame is implied by the presence of significant competitive response concerns. Illustrate this adage with the duopoly example portrayed in Figure 16.1.

3. *cost and price*

An often heard theme in pricing is that price should reflect full cost, otherwise all costs are not covered and in the long-run the enterprise is not viable. Suppose we have a perfectly competitive industry, where the supply is produced by many (perfectly competitive) single product firms. Does this alleged connection between price and full cost stand up to scrutiny in this setting? Alternatively, suppose we have an industry characterized by product differentiation and multiproduct firms. Does the alleged connection stand up to scrutiny in this setting?

4. *cost and price*

Consider a monopolist who faces a market clearing price of $P(q) = 400 - 5q$ and a cost curve of $C(q) = 400q - 20q^2 + q^3$.

a] Determine the monopolist's optimal quantity and maximal profit.

b] Suppose the monopolist can perfectly discriminate among the customers; determine the optimal quantity and maximal profit.

c] What role does the product market play in determining your answers above? What role does the monopolist's cost play?

5. *price discrimination*

Return to the setting in the text where we compared the monopolist with the perfectly discriminating monopolist. The former had an output of $q = 14$, and the latter of $q = 15$. Why does the discriminating monopolist produce more?

6. *duopoly and sequential play*

Return to the duopoly setting in the text, summarized in Figure 16.1. Suppose, instead of simultaneous play, the first firm can announce and commit to a production plan for itself before the second firm decides on a production plan. Find the first firm's best quantity choice, and the second firm's best choice upon hearing the first firm's announcement. How does this change in the "rules of the game" help the first firm? What does it do to the second firm?

7. *best response bidding*

Return to the setting of Table 16.3, case 1. The second firm is bidding according to the noted strategy. Suppose the first firm observes $y = 0.6$. Determine its expected profit if it bids (i) 15, (ii) 16 or (iii) 17.

8. *cost plus equilibrium bidding*

Return to the bidding story in Table 16.3. Suppose we define cost for the first firm as the expected value of its cost given x and y and for the second as the expected value of its cost given x and z. For case 3 in the table, determine the *plus* that is added to each firm's cost if it bids according to the noted equilibrium.

9. *winner's curse*

Table 16.2 summarizes the bidding illustration for the case of $\alpha = 0$ and $\beta = \gamma = 10$. Plot firm 1's bid as a function of y. Also plot firm 1's expected cost, given it has observed y, on the same graph. Finally, plot firm 1's expected cost, given it has observed y, bid as noted, and won the bidding.

a]   Carefully explain the relationship among the three graphs.

b]   We interpret this as an instance of cost plus pricing. Assume cost is defined as in the second graph, i.e., as firm 1's expected cost given it has observed y. What explains the amount that is added to this cost estimate to determine firm 1's bid?

10. *winner's curse*[26]

Ralph wants to purchase a family heirloom from a neighbor. The heirloom has private value to the neighbor denoted v. Neighbor knows v; Ralph only knows v is uniformly distributed between v = 0 and v = 100. Neighbor knows this about Ralph. Finally, whatever v is, the value of the heirloom to Ralph is 1.5v. Neighbor also knows this about Ralph.

a]   Who should own the heirloom, Ralph or neighbor?

b]   Suppose the trade encounter between the two individuals proceeds as follows. Ralph offers to purchase the heirloom at price P. If neighbor agrees, Ralph pays P in exchange for the heirloom. If neighbor does not agree, the game ends, and neighbor keeps the heirloom. Now, from Ralph's perspective, what is the expected value (to Ralph) of the heirloom, before any conversation with neighbor? Conversely, suppose Ralph offers price P > 0 and neighbor accepts the offer; what now is the expected value (to Ralph) of the heirloom? (As an aside, if Ralph pays P for the heirloom, at what price will Ralph's accountant value the heirloom?)

c]   What is the equilibrium in this game? Why does no trade take place, despite the fact Ralph is known to value the object higher than the neighbor?

11. *winner's curse*

Return to problem 10 above, but now assume v is uniformly distributed between v = 20 and v = 120. Repeat your earlier analysis. Why does trade take place here, for some values of v, but not in the original setting?

12. *rules of the game*

Our discussion of competitive response focused on several well-defined encounters where the "rules of the game" were well-specified and understood. A larger question addresses the "rules of the game." Return to the haggling example

---

[26]This game, though with a different story, is discussed in Bazerman [1986] and drawn from Samuelson and Bazerman [1985]. The continuation in problem 11 was contributed by Richard Sansing.

in the text where the buyer had a value of V = 4, but the seller's cost was privately known to be either 1 or 2. Let θ denote the probability the cost is 1.

a] Who should own the object, buyer or seller?

b] Suppose buyer makes a take-it-or-leave-it offer. Plot buyer's best offer as a function of θ. What is seller's best response?

c] Change the rules so seller makes a take-it-or-leave-it offer. What is seller's best offer? How does it depend on seller's cost and on θ?

d] Why does trade always occur in the second set of rules but only in some instances in the first? Which set of rules does each player prefer?

13. *sunk cost and bidding*

Return to the bidding story in Table 16.3, but assume $\alpha = 1,000$ and $\beta = \gamma = 10$. We will also now interpret the αx term as a type of design cost that must be incurred before the bidding. So at the time of bidding the αx term is a sunk cost; the firms incurred this cost before submitting their bids. Verify that the case 1 bidding strategies in Table 16.3 are equilibrium strategies here as well. What is the explanation?

Of course, the firms would not have done this initial design work, and incurred the αx cost, had they looked ahead to the bidding exercise. What might the buying firm do in this instance in order to ensure a supply of bidders?

14. *inferring competitor's cost*

Ralph is considering entering the custom keyboard market for personal computers. The keyboard is customizable and will operate across a variety of systems. Before proceeding, Ralph decides to appraise the competition. The closest is Enterprise Products (or EP). EP markets a similar product, though it lacks the versatility of Ralph's design. A consultant gathers recent data from EP's financials and reports the following regression that relates reported cost of goods sold (cgs) to sales for the EP product:

$$cgs = 938,248 + 59(\text{units sold})$$
$$(960,960) \quad (8.2)$$
$$r_a^2 = .79.$$

Specification analysis indicates no autocorrelation, heteroscedasticity or whatever. Ralph is encouraged, since the estimated variable cost of 59 per unit is well above Ralph's variable cost of 42 per unit.

The next day Ralph accidentally sees a confidential cost analysis prepared by the accounting group at EP. Their report includes the following regression of total production cost (tpc) on units produced:

tpc = 2,230,207 + 43(units produced)
      (389,545)   (3.6)

$$r_a^2 = .91.$$

Carefully explain the difference between the two regressions.

15. *confusing a competitor*

Ralph has invented and patented a new consumer recording device. The projected manufacturing cost is low, and Ralph is worried that once this fact becomes known, many competitors will enter the market, using marginally different product designs that circumvent the patent. A cousin suggests merging with an unrelated business. That way, the cousin explains, even with line-of-business reporting a well-chosen cost allocation scheme will obfuscate the low production cost. Ralph is not particularly pleased with this idea but also acknowledges that disclosure laws can be disadvantageous. (Ralph is also aware that a private firm is not subject to these disclosure requirements.)

To explore this further, Ralph puts together a sample of 9 data points from two hypothetical firms. The new recording device has a cost curve of $cost_1 = 150,000 + 10q_1 + \varepsilon_1$, where q_1 denotes units of production and ε_1 is a random error term. The target firm has a cost structure of $cost_2 = 450,000 + 90q_2 + \varepsilon_2$ (where q_2 denotes units of production and ε_2 is another random error term). The data are listed below. You should assume no finished goods inventories are present, so production and sales are perfectly aligned.

t	q_1	q_2	$cost_1$	$cost_2$
1	17,241	4,882	305,762	882,462
2	1,825	3,095	152,786	717,372
3	8,357	8,747	262,312	1,228,470
4	13,078	8,805	263,136	1,237,098
5	10,272	1,297	249,436	571,502
6	11,729	1,115	282,526	523,300
7	19,097	6,490	342,652	1,036,410
8	19,754	183	343,678	428,554
9	1,819	1,970	164,352	629,828

a] Regress $cost_1$ on q_1. Does this suggest Ralph's competitors will have an easy time identifying the cost curve?

b] Suppose the two hypothetical firms are merged. Total cost, consisting of $cost_1 + cost_2$, is allocated to the two product lines on the basis of physical units. What happens when you regress cost allocated to the first product on units of that product? Does this suggest Ralph's competitors will have a difficult time identifying the cost curve if the merger is consummated and the accountant's art is fully engaged?

c] What mistake is Ralph making? (Hint: using, say, the allocated data in [b] regress total cost on q_1 and q_2.)

16. *diagnosis of competitive position*[27]

Ralph's Packaging, Inc., (RP) designs and produces specialized packages for a variety of industrial product firms. Most jobs are won on a competitive bid. The major steps in the production process are design, printing, cutting, and assembly. Historically, RP has earned a 14% margin, but lately the margin has been declining and most recently was 7.2%.

RP fears its earlier success has led to complacency and its costs are unnecessarily high. The accounting library identifies labor, material, subcontracting, energy, and space costs. Some are broken down by design, printing, cutting and assembly. Since work in process has never been a significant problem, no formal job costing system has been used.

At this point Ralph decides to look a little more closely at the cost conjecture. A recently completed job, job 113, is randomly selected. Ralph searches through the purchase orders, stores requisitions, and subcontracting invoices and locates the following cost items that pertain to job 113:

miscellaneous materials	$ 125
standard packaging materials	1,875
subcontracted printing	425

Working through payroll records, Ralph is also able to identify direct labor time. Three labor groups are present, regular, semi-skilled and skilled. Their respective wage rates are 11, 18 and 22 dollars per hour. The time sheets record the following hours:

	unskilled	semi-skilled	skilled
design	10	11	34
printing	10	18	20
cutting	12		
assembly	10	10	24

Overhead averages 110% of labor cost. (To identify overhead cost, Ralph took the total of all manufacturing cost, subtracted the labor cost that could be identified with specific jobs and the material and subcontracting costs that could be similarly identified.)

a] What was the cost of job 113?

b] The bid sheet for job 113 shows that, at the time the job was bid, RP estimated the direct cost as follows:

materials	2,100
subcontract work	400

---

[27]Inspired by an IMEDE case titled Tipografia Stanca S.P.A.

design labor   918
printing labor   799
cutting labor   238
assembly labor   714

for a total direct cost of 5,169. In turn, the job was bid using RP's standard bidding
rule of bid = 180% of estimated direct cost. For bidding purposes, labor is costed
at 17 per hour. What was RP's bid on job 113? Did RP earn a positive profit on this
job?

c] Suppose RP's labor cost does average 17 per hour and that materials and subcontract work is, on average, equal to direct labor cost. Further suppose overhead
averages 110% of labor cost. Presuming many bidding successes using the noted
bidding rule, what should RP's margin be?

d] What advice can you give RP? Do you think they should invest in a job order
costing system?

17. *value of information*

Two competitors, Row and Column, are fighting it out as the only merchants
on a remote island. Each has two strategies, and nature will provide one of two
states (with equal probability). If state one obtains, the players' payoffs are given
below, where Row player has possible choices of *up* or *down* and Column of *left* or
right. (The payoffs are denoted x,y -- with x to Row and y to Column.)

	left	*right*
up	10, 10	0, 12
down	40, -40	2, 2

Conversely, if state two obtains, the players' payoffs are as follows.

	left	*right*
up	4, 4	10, 0
down	-40, 12	10, 10

Thus, if state one obtains, the game actually played is that in the first matrix; and if
Row has chosen *up* and Column has chosen *right*, their respective payoffs are 0 and
12. The game is played in noncooperative fashion, with simultaneous moves by
each player.

a] Suppose neither player can gather any additional information. Verify that
equilibrium payoffs are 7 for Row and 7 for Column. (Here they play the game
defined by the expected value of the two matrices.)

b] Suppose Row gets perfect information before acting. Column knows this and
Row knows that Column knows, and so on. Verify that an equilibrium has Row play

down no matter what state occurs, and Column play *right*, with expected payoffs of 6 for each. (Here Row has four strategies: *up* no matter what; *down* no matter what; *up* in state one and *down* in state two; and vice versa.) How do you explain the equilibrium? Is Row better off with the information?

c] Suppose both Row and Column get perfect information. Determine and interpret the competitor's equilibrium behavior.

17

Library Procedures for Performance Evaluation

We now turn to the subject of performance evaluation. In broadest terms, *performance evaluation occurs when we make provision (at the time of choice) to evaluate (that choice) at a later date.* It is a process of evaluation, of appraisal and assessment. It is also not happenstance. Being able to evaluate presumes we took care to lay in the requisite information in the first place. An important managerial task is planning for subsequent evaluation. For example, it is difficult to control telephone costs without knowledge of who makes what use of the telephones. Similarly, use of customer satisfaction measures in the evaluation process presumes we have found the necessary data to make a reasoned assessment of customer satisfaction.

Performance evaluation is also not without purpose. (Double negatives have a distinguished history in academic writing.) Evaluation is done for a reason. We want to learn and adapt; we also want to appraise the performance of various actors in the organization. In the broadest terms, we envision this as evaluating a choice.

Thus, the professor announces the grading policy at the start of the course, administers various evaluation instruments throughout the course, and eventually assigns grades. The professor learns, and the students' performance is appraised. The facility manager begins the period, say, a quarter, with a budget and various service expectations. At the end of the period, spending is compared to budget; and various service statistics are calculated (e.g., average response time for equipment repairs or office space reconfiguration) and compared with expectations. The manager learns, and others use these data to evaluate the manager's performance.

The fast food manager begins the period with various performance goals, detailing, say, profit, employee training, and customer service expectations. At the end of the period a formal assessment is made, focusing on each stated goal. The legislator must stand for re-election.

In each vignette we retrospectively evaluate choice. That is the idea of performance evaluation.

The typical organization relies heavily but far from exclusively on the accounting library for performance evaluation purposes. The advantages of the accounting library for this purpose are twofold. It stresses financial matters, and financial matters are important. It also stresses integrity. Performance evaluation can be consequential, as when a major product or promotion is at stake; and this places a premium on reliable appraisal. The disadvantage of the accounting library is its limited nature. It is a financial library, and integrity carries an implicit price.

The accounting library cannot simultaneously be well protected and capture all we would like to have at our fingertips for evaluation purposes.

The point is simple. We should expect to find a variety of important evaluation insights in the accounting library; and we should expect to look elsewhere for additional, important information. To say "only the bottom line matters" is to reveal a distinctly uninformed and unprofessional conception of the art of performance evaluation. Market share, customer satisfaction, order books, quality, and the subjective opinion of the supervisor are potentially important sources of evaluation insight.

As you suspect (and dread), the typical accounting library employs specialized procedures to aid the library users in the performance evaluation task. The purpose of this chapter is to introduce these procedures and tie them into our earlier work on product costing. Subsequent chapters will take up the important question of how these procedures are used in various evaluation tasks.

We begin with an overview of a decomposition trick that is the building block for these procedures. We then explore cost performance settings, applying the decomposition device to structure the evaluation task. Finally, in the Appendix we extend the procedures to a profit performance setting and link them to our earlier work on decision framing, using an ex post or hindsight reconstruction of the decision.

Overview of Decomposition

Suppose we are considering a cross country automobile trip. One of the many costs will be gasoline. We estimate the trip will require 100 gallons, at an average price of $1.50 per gallon, for a total of $150. It turns out we actually spent $154 and used 110 gallons. We paid an average of 154/110 = $1.40 per gallon. The story is folksy and the numbers are small but we want to focus on essentials.

Now recast the story in accounting language. The budgeted cost was 150, and the actual cost was 154. This implies a budget overrun of 154 - 150 = 4. What caused the budget overrun?

prices and quantities

The budget was constructed by forecasting a price ($1.50 per gallon) and a quantity (100 gallons). What if we had forecast a price of $1.50 per gallon, but a quantity of 110 gallons? The budget would have been 1.50(110) = 165, and the budget overrun would have been 154 - 165 = -11.

Now indulge in the following algebraic maneuver:

$$154 - 150 = 154 - 165 + 165 - 150$$
$$= [154 - 165] + [165 - 150] = [-11] + [15] = 4.$$

We have subtracted and added 165, and grouped the terms in suggestive fashion. Overall we are calculating 154 - 150, the actual cost less the budgeted cost.

What is [154 - 165] = -11? The first term in the expression is actual cost, or actual price times actual quantity. The second term is forecast price times actual quantity. It is what total cost would have been had the actual price equaled the forecast price of $1.50 per gallon, but the forecast quantity equaled the actual quantity of 110 gallons. As we move from 154 to 165, quantity is held constant at 110 gallons and price varies from $1.40 (i.e., actual) to $1.50 (i.e., forecast) per gallon. [154 - 165] = -11 is a *price effect*.

What is [165 - 150] = 15? The first term in the expression, of course, is forecast price times actual quantity. The second term is our budget of forecast price times forecast quantity. As we move from 165 to 150, price is held constant at $1.50 per gallon and quantity varies from 110 (i.e., actual) to 100 (i.e., budget) gallons. [165 - 150] = 15 is a *quantity effect*.

In short, the budget was overrun. This is the net effect of a price being under budget (-11) and a quantity being over budget (15). We saved on price but lost on quantity.

Interjecting the modified calculation of forecast price times actual quantity allows us to decompose the budget overrun into a price effect and a quantity effect. The following diagram is a useful mnemonic.

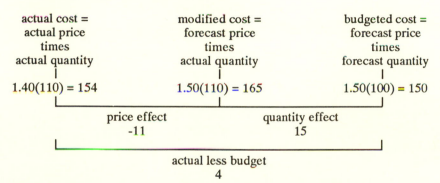

a closer look

To understand this device, let P denote the budgeted or forecast price and Q the budgeted quantity. Also let actual price be $P + \Delta P$ and actual quantity be $Q + \Delta Q$. With this notation, the calculation of actual cost less budgeted cost becomes

$$(P + \Delta P)(Q + \Delta Q) - PQ = P\Delta Q + \Delta PQ + \Delta P\Delta Q.$$

We have a pure quantity effect, $P\Delta Q$, a pure price effect, ΔPQ, and a joint effect, $\Delta P\Delta Q$.

Can you locate these three terms in our above diagram? Let's reconstruct it, using our notation:

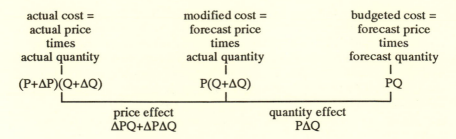

The price effect in our layout consists of a pure price effect (ΔPQ) and a joint term ($\Delta P\Delta Q$). The quantity effect is a pure quantity effect ($P\Delta Q$).

We might ask, why not separate out the joint term, or why not place it in the quantity effect calculation. The answer is that *by convention* the typical accounting library calculates the price and quantity effects in the manner shown. Generally, the price effect is calculated as change in price times actual quantity.[1]

terminology

In accounting terminology, any difference between an actual and budget is called a *variance*. In our gasoline story, the overall variance is 4. The *price variance* (notice the adjective) is -11 and the *quantity variance* is 15. Be careful to distinguish *accounting* variance from *statistical* variance.[2]

In a related vein, keeping track of algebraic signs becomes cumbersome; so additional terminology is used. If the actual cost is below the budgeted counterpart, convention refers to this as a *favorable* (F) variance. An actual above budgeted cost is called an *unfavorable* (U) variance. So our price variance is 11 (F) and our quantity variance is 15 (U).

---

[1]Practice is more varied as we allow for additional effects. Somewhat casually, suppose we produce n products, with respective quantities denoted q_j and unit costs denoted c_j. Let v be a scalar volume measure, and express q_j as $q_j = m_j v$. Then total cost is simply $\Sigma_j\ c_j q_j = \Sigma_j\ c_j m_j v$. Think of this as budgeted cost. Extending the notation in familiar fashion, we have a corresponding actual total cost of $\Sigma_j\ (c_j + \Delta c_j)(m_j + \Delta m_j)(v + \Delta v)$. Breaking the difference down into cost (Δc_j), mix (Δm_j) and volume (Δv) effects is done by interjecting two intermediate calculations. Of course, this begs the question of where to put such terms as $\Delta c_j \Delta v$, and that is why practice varies on this score. At the simple case of a price and quantity effect, though, practice is consistent on calling the joint term part of the price effect.

[2]Let x be a random variable characterized by probability mass or density $g(x)$. Denote the mean of g by $\mu = E(x)$. The (statistical) variance of g is $E(x - \mu)^2$. The mean and variance are properties of g. (Also, E denotes the expectation operator with respect to g here.) Now suppose we think of this as a budget and an actual. Let the mean μ be the budget. For any particular realization of the random variable, then, the accounting variance is $x - \mu$. The accounting variance is a property of x, while the statistical variance is a property of g.

It is also important in what follows to adopt a broad interpretation of the term budget. Suppose we combine various LLAs into a total cost budget of TC = F + vq. This is a flexible budget in that it varies with the quantity produced (q) or the work accomplished. We would then compare actual cost with budgeted cost, given the work accomplished. On other occasions we will see these techniques used with a fixed budget, a budgeted norm that is held constant. Suppose we develop a profit plan for the coming period, with a budgeted profit of 490,000. Later, we compare actual profit with planned profit. The planned profit is now a fixed budget. The context will tell whether we are dealing with a fixed or flexible budget.

Cost Performance Variances

Having identified the basic decomposition procedure, we now turn to its use in the accounting library. For this purpose, we return to the job order costing illustration studied in Chapter 6 (Tables 6.1 through 6.6) and Chapter 7 (Tables 7.1 through 7.4). Three products or jobs were worked on during the accounting period. Jobs 2 and 3 were started and completed. Job 1 was started, but remains incomplete. Five aggregate manufacturing cost categories are used by the accounting system: direct labor, specialty direct materials, stock direct materials, overhead A, and overhead B. In Chapter 7 we introduced estimated or budgeted cost expressions for each of these cost categories and set the accounting records up to report standard product costs.

Tables 17.1 and 17.2 summarize our earlier work. Table 17.1 gives the total picture, while Table 17.2 summarizes the standard cost constructions. Notice this is a flexible budget story. The underlying standards imply cost should have totaled 244,230, given the work accomplished. Table 17.3 displays the underlying data.

This may appear to be a numbing and needless amount of detail, but it is essential to our study of library procedures.

Table 17.1: Actual versus Budgeted Cost Totals			
product cost category	total actual cost	total standard cost	variance
direct labor	48,000	47,300	700 (U)
direct material			
specialty	30,000	30,000	0
stock	30,000	31,000	(1,000) (F)
overhead A	96,000	99,330	(3,330) (F)
overhead B	42,000	36,600	5,400 (U)
total	246,000	244,230	1,770 (U)

Table 17.2: Standard Product Cost Constructions				
	job 1	job 2	job 3	total
direct labor cost	11,000	18,700	17,600	47,300
direct material cost				
specialty materials	11,000	5,000	14,000	30,000
stock materials	5,000	9,000	17,000	31,000
overhead A	23,100	39,270	36,960	99,330
overhead B	9,600	8,400	18,600	36,600
standard product cost	59,700	80,370	104,160	244,230

The standard cost system begins with standard product costs. These are forecasted or projected costs for each product that are based on identified LLAs. The accounting library then captures the actual costs, converts the inventory records to standard product costs, and closes the difference to cost of goods sold. Figure 7.1 in Chapter 7, recall, summarizes account entries for the illustration.[3]

We summarize the recording of these events in the accounting library in the following fashion. First, as developed in Chapter 7, the actual costs are recorded, for each cost category. (See Table 17.1 for details.) This can be visualized in terms of a set of control accounts.

direct labor cost control	48,000	
direct material, specialty	30,000	
direct material, stock	30,000	
overhead A	96,000	
overhead B	42,000	
various accounts		246,000

Table 17.3: Data from Chapter 7 Standard Costing Illustration				
	job 1	job 2	job 3	total
direct labor cost				
estimated direct labor hours	1,000	1,700	1,600	4,300
estimated direct labor cost				
(@ 11/hour)	11,000	18,700	17,600	47,300
actual direct labor hours	900	1,800	1,300	4,000
actual direct labor cost	12,000	18,000	18,000	48,000

---

[3]Here we review the initial recordings detailed in Chapter 7. The one difference is instead of using a single "direct material cost control" account we separate the specialty and stock items. This is done so we can separate price and quantity effects for each type of material.

Table 17.3 Continued: Data from Standard Costing Illustration				
	job 1	job 2	job 3	total
direct material cost				
estimated cost of specialty materials purchased for product in question	11,000	5,000	14,000	30,000
actual cost of specialty materials purchased for product in question	10,000	5,000	15,000	30,000
estimated cost of direct materials removed from stock for product	5,000	9,000	17,000	31,000
actual cost of direct materials removed from stock for product	5,000	10,000	15,000	30,000
overhead cost				
estimated overhead A cost (@ 2.1 per *estimated* DL$)	23,100	39,270	36,960	99,330
actual overhead A cost				96,000
estimated overhead B cost (@ .6 per *estimated* DM$)	9,600	8,400	18,600	36,600
actual overhead B cost				42,000

Next, we set the work-in-process account at standard product cost. Using the standard cost calculations summarized in Table 17.2, we have the following picture, recording total standard product costs of 244,230:

work in process (job 1)	59,700	
work in process (job 2)	80,370	
work in process (job 3)	104,160	
direct labor cost control		47,300
direct material, specialty		30,000
direct material, stock		31,000
overhead A		99,330
overhead B		36,600

We have now recorded actual costs totaling 246,000 in the various control accounts, and transferred 244,230 = 59,700 + 80,370 + 104,160 to work in process. This latter total is the total standard product cost, as we assume the work-in-process inventory is recorded at standard product cost.

The control accounts, being temporary accounts, must be closed at the end of the accounting cycle. We did this, recall, by moving the balances to cost of goods sold. In summary form, the entry was as follows:

cost of goods sold	1,770	
direct material, specialty	0	
direct material, stock	1,000	
overhead A	3,330	
direct labor cost control		700
overhead B		5,400

These calculations are summarized in Table 17.1. This is where the illustration in Chapter 7 ended.

The standard cost system, in other words, gives us total product cost incurred, sets up the inventory valuations at standard product cost, and closes the difference to cost of goods sold. It also provides the fodder for a comparison of actual with budget.[4]

Think of actual manufacturing cost as reflecting work accomplished this period. Also think of the standard product cost expressions as being combined to form a budgeted total cost *for the work accomplished this period.* We started and completed jobs 2 and 3 this period. Their respective standard product costs are 80,370 and 104,160. In addition, we started and partially completed job 1. The standard cost equivalent of work on job 1 to date is 59,700. We thus have a budgeted cost of 80,370 + 104,160 + 59,700 = 244,230. The actual cost was 246,000, implying a variance of 1,770 (U).

It is no accident the details emerge in this fashion. When we use a standard cost system we base the standard costs on various LLAs and underlying price and quantity standards. The plug figure that is eventually closed to cost of goods sold is then the net budget variance, where the budget uses the underlying standards together with the work accomplished. Take another look at Table 17.1. The standard cost system gives us budget variances for each manufacturing cost category. We now decompose these budget variances into price and quantity effects.

direct labor variances

We begin with direct labor. Refer to Table 17.3, where we see the estimated direct labor hours *for the work accomplished* is 1,000 + 1,700 + 1,600 = 4,300 hours.

---

[4]An alternative sequence is to set initially the work-in-process account up at actual cost, and then convert it to standard cost. The procedure summarized in our running illustration is more timely and has the added advantage of keeping details to a minimum as we push the numbers around. Either way the variances we are about to calculate turn out to be the same. After all, we are reconciling actual cost (246,000) to budgeted cost, as implied by the standards (244,230).

The estimated price is 11 per hour. So our budget is 11(4,300) = 47,300. Further notice actual direct labor hours totaled 900 + 1,800 + 1,300 = 4,000.

Price and quantity variances are now readily calculated:

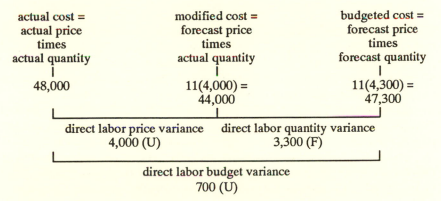

actual cost = actual price times actual quantity	modified cost = forecast price times actual quantity	budgeted cost = forecast price times forecast quantity
48,000	11(4,000) = 44,000	11(4,300) = 47,300

direct labor price variance
4,000 (U)　　　direct labor quantity variance
3,300 (F)

direct labor budget variance
700 (U)

From our earlier entries, we know actual direct labor cost exceeded the direct labor component of the standard cost of the work accomplished by 700. The variance procedure decomposes this budget overrun into an unfavorable price variance of 4,000 and a favorable quantity variance of 3,300. The price was above what was forecast, while the quantity was below. Perhaps higher skilled workers were used, commanding a higher wage but working more efficiently. This can only be ascertained by bringing more information to the exercise.[5]

Many call these variances a (direct labor) wage rate variance and a (direct) labor efficiency variance. These are synonyms for price and quantity variances. We will stick with the more generic labels.

Also notice we are in a position to break these price and quantity variances down by product. It turns out job 3 is the source of the favorable quantity variance. We duck the details in the interest of rationing our patience.[6]

Before moving on, we should reflect on the larger picture. In this (direct labor) cost category, we incurred a total cost of 48,000. Looking at the production that took place during the period, our standards suggest a total cost of 47,300 should have been incurred. We look to the actual production to determine the budgeted cost. That is, we begin with the work accomplished (jobs 2 and 3 started and completed and job 1 started and partially completed). We then take standard price times the

---

[5]The organization might, for example, have a number of units or departments, and direct labor might move on occasion from one to the other. This would explain the possibility of a direct labor group with higher than anticipated skill and wages. Particular workers on vacation provides a competing explanation.

[6]Our calculation, and the details provided in Table 17.3, assume the average wage is the same across jobs. This need not be the case.

standard quantity allowed given this work accomplished. The exercise treats actual production as the independent variable.

direct material variances

Next we examine the direct material cost categories. Consider the specialty materials. Again using data in Table 17.3, we see that specialty materials totaled $10,000 + 5,000 + 15,000 = 30,000$; and the budgeted amount, *for the work accomplished*, was $11,000 + 5,000 + 14,000 = 30,000$. We have an unusual event in which the actual and budgeted figures are the same.

Of course, we might have offsetting price and quantity variances. Let's assume each of these items is a subcomponent that was specially acquired for the respective jobs. This means there is no sense of price versus quantity, the quantity is one in each case. Under these circumstances it makes little sense to decompose the budget variance into price and quantity variances. Given our interpretation, it is all a price variance; and in this instance the price variance across the three jobs nets to zero.

raw material maintained at actual prices

Now consider the stock materials. These are materials that are routinely stocked, and removed from inventory as needed. Table 17.3 reports the actual cost of these materials was $5,000 + 10,000 + 15,000 = 30,000$; and the budgeted amount, *for the work accomplished*, was $5,000 + 9,000 + 17,000 = 31,000$. The direct material (stock) budget variance is 1,000 (F). This is what surfaced in our earlier entry. We reiterate that we are decomposing the overall plug to cost of goods sold.

To decompose this into price and quantity variances, we must supply more specific details. For this purpose, we assume this is some generic raw material with a standard price of $1 per pound. Standard and actual usages (in pounds) are given below.

	job 1	job 2	job 3	total
standard pounds of stock direct material	5,000	9,000	17,000	31,000
actual pounds of stock direct material	6,250	11,250	20,000	37,500

Further assume the actual price of the material was .8 per pound. This implies a total cost in this cost category of $37,500(.8) = 30,000$.

Price and quantity variances now follow in familiar fashion. Here we see the budget variance reflects a sizable (and favorable) price variance nearly offsetting a sizable (and unfavorable) quantity variance. Perhaps lesser quality materials were acquired (at a lower price), but resulted in excessive scrap. We also may be seeing an interaction with the earlier labor variances. For example, the labor may have been more skilled than anticipated, and held down the unfavorable direct material quantity variance.

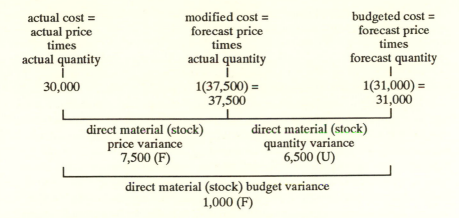

As before, though, we stress that interpretations of this sort depend on additional information. The comparison of actual with budget provides the initial step in a well-reasoned and studied evaluation.[7]

timely identification of price effects

This brings us to an important qualification. The actual direct material cost of 30,000 here was tallied with a debit to the raw material control account and a credit to raw material inventory. Since we isolated price and quantity variances, this implies the raw material inventory account is maintained at actual price. (From here one quickly descends into the depths of LIFO, FIFO, or whatever.)

An alternate procedure is to maintain the raw material inventory at standard price. If this is the case, the actual (stock) direct material cost recorded in the raw material control account would have been actual usage of 37,500 pounds valued at the standard price of 1 per pound, or a total cost of 37,500. Our handy calculation format would then show a nil price variance and a quantity variance of 6,500 (U).

Well, not quite. We're forgetting one thing. What happens when raw material is purchased, and the price is not equal to the standard price? To round out the story, suppose 20,000 pounds were purchased this period, at an average price of 1.1 per pound, implying a total of 22,000. If raw material inventory is maintained at standard price, the entry on acquisition would be as follows:

direct material, stock	20,000	
raw material price variance	2,000	
accounts payable		22,000

---

[7]This additional information may be readily in hand, or it may be acquired once the variances are examined. For example, a simple management by exception rule would suggest we concentrate on the larger variances, looking for explanations.

We must record the liability of 22,000. Similarly, maintaining the raw material inventory at standard price requires we record an inventory addition of 1(20,000) = 20,000. We need an additional 2,000 to balance the entry; and this is nothing other than our missing raw material price variance. In turn, this price variance is disposed of in the usual fashion. The standards remain as before, only the time at which the material price variance is recognized is altered.

This procedure, in other words, recognizes the raw material price variance at the time of acquisition. It has the advantage of bringing the current price information into the variance calculations as quickly as possible. It has the disadvantage of requiring a more elaborate acquisition recording procedure.[8] In contrast, the first procedure we demonstrated, the one that directly clones the direct labor procedure, recognizes the direct material price variance at the time of use. Naturally, a just-in-time inventory policy would collapse the two approaches into the former.

We will continue with the first procedure. It is less complicated, and we have additional material to cover.[9]

overhead variances

Our basic theme repeats in the overhead cost categories. Consider the overhead A category. Table 17.1 reveals an actual cost of 96,000, compared with a budgeted cost of 99,330. The latter follows from a full costing procedure based on a standard burden rate of 2.1 per direct labor dollar.

From details in Chapter 7, recall the LLA for this cost category is given by OV_A = 55,000 + 1(DL\$), where DL\$ denotes direct labor dollars. Under a full costing procedure, we average the intercept over some normal volume, or estimated amount of the LLA's explanatory variable. In this case we used a normal volume of DL\$ = 50,000. For overhead A, then, we estimated an "average overhead cost" of

$$[55,000 + 1(50,000)]/50,000 = 55/50 + 1 = 1.1 + 1 = 2.1.$$

Standard product costs accumulate overhead A cost at the rate of 2.1 per direct labor dollar.

price, quantity, and volume variances

We now have three types of explanations for a difference between actual and budgeted overhead cost. The intercept and slope of the LLA might be off; the amount of the independent variable in the LLA might vary from the amount allowed

---

[8]In turn, if for financial reporting purposes the organization wanted to report ending raw material inventory at actual price, a simple adjustment would be made in the closing process. This would be particularly easy if LIFO were used and the base had not been depleted.

[9]The Appendix rounds out our discussion of the procedure when raw material inventory is maintained at standard prices.

given the work accomplished; and the amount allowed might vary from the normal volume assumed in the "average overhead cost" construction.

Recall that actual direct labor dollars totaled 48,000, while the budgeted direct labor cost, given the work accomplished, was 47,300. We use these amounts to construct two modified budgets: the LLA evaluated at actual DL$ of 48,000: 55,000 + 1(48,000) = 103,000; and the LLA evaluated at budgeted DL$ given work accomplished, 55,000 + 1(47,300) = 102,300.

More generally, think of the overhead LLA as using variable x as its independent or explanatory variable (so the LLA is a + bx). Let x^A denote the *actual* level of the explanatory variable. The LLA evaluated at x^A is the 103,000 datum above. Also let x^S denote the level of the explanatory variable if the work accomplished this period had used exactly the amount of the explanatory variable predicted by the underlying *standards*. The LLA evaluated at x^S is the 102,300 datum above. In a full costing system, then, overhead applied to products will total $f \cdot x^S$, where f is the standard burden rate (of 2.1 per direct labor dollar in the case of overhead A).

Examine the string of comparisons listed below. The first comparison is between actual cost and the LLA evaluated at the *actual* independent variable value of x^A = 48,000. The independent variable is held constant, while the intercept and slope of the LLA are allowed to vary. This is a price effect.

$$
\begin{array}{lll}
\text{actual cost} & = & 96,000 \\
\text{LLA @ DL\$ of 48,000 } (x^A) & = & 103,000
\end{array} \Bigg\} = 7,000 \text{ (F)}
$$

$$
\begin{array}{lll}
\text{LLA @ DL\$ of 48,000 } (x^A) & = & 103,000 \\
\text{LLA @ DL\$ of 47,300 } (x^S) & = & 102,300
\end{array} \Bigg\} = 700 \text{ (U)}
$$

$$
\begin{array}{lll}
\text{LLA @ DL\$ of 47,300 } (x^S) & = & 102,300 \\
2.1(47,300) \text{ (or } f \cdot x^S) & = & 99,330
\end{array} \Bigg\} = 2,970 \text{ (U)}
$$

The second comparison is between the LLA evaluated at the actual independent variable value of x^A = 48,000 and the LLA evaluated at the budgeted amount of the independent variable given the work accomplished, x^S = 47,300. This is a quantity effect, attributable to variation in the independent variable while holding the work accomplished constant.

The final comparison is between the LLA evaluated at the budgeted amount of the independent variable given the work accomplished and 2.1 times the budgeted amount of the independent variable given the work accomplished. This reflects the fact the cost allocation procedure used a normal volume of DL$ = 50,000, while actual production should have led to a volume of DL$ = 47,300. In effect, 47,300 slices of the unitized fixed cost were assigned to product while the underlying standard was based on 50,000 such assignments. It is customary to call this a *volume* effect, but that is more a misnomer than an accurate description, as we shall see.

We summarize the calculations with a mnemonic that parallels those of the direct cost categories.

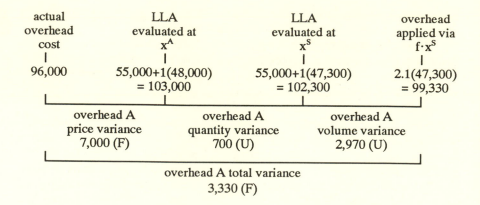

actual overhead cost	LLA evaluated at x^A	LLA evaluated at x^S	overhead applied via $f \cdot x^S$
96,000	$55,000 + 1(48,000)$ $= 103,000$	$55,000 + 1(47,300)$ $= 102,300$	$2.1(47,300)$ $= 99,330$

| | overhead A price variance 7,000 (F) | overhead A quantity variance 700 (U) | overhead A volume variance 2,970 (U) |

overhead A total variance
3,330 (F)

Notice the stringing together of decomposition tricks. We have an actual cost of 96,000 and a budgeted cost of 99,330:[10]

$$96,000 - 99,330 = 96,000 - 103,000 + 103,000 - 102,300 + 102,300 - 99,330$$
$$= [96,000 - 103,000] + [103,000 - 102,300] + [102,300 - 99,330]$$
$$= 7,000 \text{ (F)} + 700 \text{ (U)} + 2,970 \text{ (U)}$$
$$= 3,330 \text{ (F)}.$$

a closer look

An abstract display of these calculations will help understand their content. Suppose the overhead LLA is given by $OV = F + vx$, where x is some independent variable (DL\$ here). As before, let x^S be the total of this independent variable that is allowed given the work accomplished. (Remember, we key on the amount of the independent variable that is allowed by the underlying standards, given the work accomplished during the period.)

Also, as before, let x^A be the actual value of this independent variable. Think of this as $x^A = x^S + \Delta x$. Extending the notation, we then write the actual overhead cost as $F + \Delta F + (v + \Delta v)x^A$, an awkward but intuitive expression.

Finally, let x_N be the normal volume that is used to specify the standard burden rate. This implies the standard burden rate is $F/x_N + v$ per unit of the independent variable. Products will now be assigned overhead totaling

$$(F/x_N + v)x^S$$

---

[10]Suppose we interpret the intercept of the overhead LLA as a fixed cost. Then the overhead A quantity variance is a variable cost phenomenon. It is the difference between the overhead LLA evaluated at the actual and standard values of the independent variable. $1(48,000 - 47,300) = 700$ (U). Similarly, the overhead A volume variance is a fixed cost phenomenon. It is the difference between the budgeted fixed cost and that applied to product. $55,000 - (55,000/50,000)(47,300) = 2,970$ (U).

this period, as the standard burden rate is $f = F/x_N + v$ and the total of the independent variable allowed given the work accomplished is x^S.

Now redo our display, with these symbols inserted:

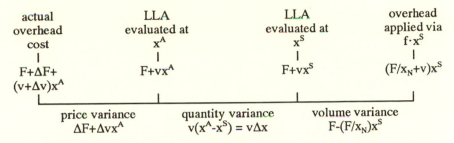

actual overhead cost	LLA evaluated at x^A	LLA evaluated at x^S	overhead applied via $f \cdot x^S$
$F + \Delta F + (v + \Delta v)x^A$	$F + vx^A$	$F + vx^S$	$(F/x_N + v)x^S$

price variance $\Delta F + \Delta vx^A$	quantity variance $v(x^A - x^S) = v\Delta x$	volume variance $F - (F/x_N)x^S$

The overhead price variance is the difference between actual overhead and the LLA estimated amount, while holding the independent variable constant at its actual amount of x^A. We should interpret this as a "price" effect, given the actual quantity of the independent variable.

The overhead quantity variance is simply the variation in the independent variable, $x^A - x^S = \Delta x$, priced at the "standard price" of v per unit. For example, here we are using DL\$. Suppose labor fringe costs are included in the overhead A cost category, and they do vary as a function of actual wages paid. Then any variation in actual wages paid, Δx, carries with it an incremental overhead A cost of $v\Delta x$.[11]

So far so good. We have a price effect and a quantity effect. They play the same role and have the same interpretations as the price and quantity variances in the direct cost settings. The volume variance remains to be interpreted.

The easiest way to understand the volume variance is to remember we are comparing actual overhead with the amount of overhead assigned to products in the standard costing system. We pull off a price effect and a quantity effect, as noted. Under a full costing system, a residual amount remains. It is equal to

$$F - (F/x_N)x^S = (F/x_N)x_N - (F/x_N)x^S = (F/x_N)(x_N - x^S).$$

This is zero if $x_N = x^S$; it is favorable if $x_N < x^S$; and it is unfavorable if $x_N > x^S$.

Remember what unfavorable and favorable mean. Unfavorable means closing the item to cost of goods sold increases (i.e., debits) cost of goods sold. Favorable means the opposite. So what does it mean to alter cost of goods sold by the amount $(F/x_N)(x_N - x^S)$? Economically, it means nothing; it is the garbage that remains after an attempt to average the fixed cost in the LLA over an estimated normal volume.

We originally estimated a normal volume of x_N. We experienced an actual volume allowed of x^S. This fact might be good news, bad news, or no news. We may have capitalized on or lost profit opportunities, but this surely has nothing to do

---

[11]Many call the overhead price variance an overhead budget variance and the overhead quantity variance an overhead efficiency variance.

with the volume variance.[12] Whatever the circumstance, we are guaranteed one thing: $(F/x_N)(x_N - x^S)$ is the amount that remains in the overhead control account once we have assigned overhead to products and closed the price and quantity variances to cost of goods sold. It is a plug figure.

To reinforce this point, what would the decomposition of the overhead variance look like under a variable product costing system? There we would assign variable overhead to the products, but treat the "fixed" overhead as a period cost. As before, the total overhead incurred would be $F + \Delta F + (v + \Delta v)x^A$. Standard fixed cost, the intercept of the LLA, would be expensed as a period cost. vx^S would be assigned to products. So the residual amount in the overhead control account would be actual cost less that expensed and assigned, or

$$F + \Delta F + (v + \Delta v)x^A - F - vx^S = \Delta F + \Delta vx^A + v(x^A - x^S).$$

Only the above computed price and quantity effects remain.

Our earlier symbolic summarization takes on the following appearance:

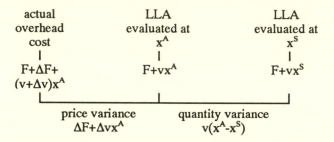

The volume variance is solely an artifact of the full costing calculation. It only appears in a full costing calculation, and there only to tidy up the difference between x^S and x_N. The overhead price and quantity variances are the same under the two costing motifs.

Examine Figure 17.1 where we graphically portray these overhead calculations. The point (x^A, A) represents the actual cost, the point (x^A, B) represents the LLA evaluated at x^A. The point (x^S, C) represents the LLA evaluated at x^S. Finally, under standard full costing, the total overhead applied to product is represented by the point (x^S, D). Also notice $(F/x_N + v)x$ goes through the origin. This particular picture assumes $x^A > x_N > x^S$, while our numerical example has $x_N > x^A > x^S$. Can you locate x_N on the graph?

Under a full costing regime, overhead cost is estimated to be $F + vx$, but is assigned to products presuming an "LLA" of $(F/x_N + v)x = fx$. The difference between these two cost expressions is the volume variance. Under a variable costing regime, overhead cost is again estimated to be $F + vx$. F is now assigned to the

---

[12]Concern for production and sales quantities is highlighted when we focus on profit as opposed to cost variances. This is explored in the Appendix.

period, and vx is assigned to products. There is no difference between the cost expression used to budget the overhead cost and the cost expression used to allocate the cost to the period and products.

Figure 17.1: Overhead Variances

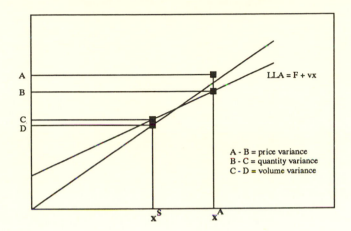

In short, a variable costing system uses the overhead LLA to allocate overhead cost to products and the period. A full costing system mutates the overhead LLA for allocation purposes. The volume variance reconciles the two, by identifying the error associated with the mutation of the LLA, given x^S.

more details

The overhead B cost category is treated in parallel fashion. Here the LLA is given by $OV_B = 32,000 + .2(DM\$)$, where DM$ denotes total direct material dollars. For full costing purposes, a normal volume of DM$ = 80,000 was assumed, implying a standard burden rate of $32/80 + .2 = .4 + .2 = .6$ per dollar of direct materials.

Actual overhead B incurred totaled 42,000. The total direct material cost allowed for the work accomplished is 30,000 for specialty materials and 31,000 for stock materials, for a total of 61,000. The standard cost system would therefore assign $.6(61,000) = 36,600$ to products. This is the budgeted cost. We have an overhead B variance of $42,000 - 36,600 = 5,400$ (U). (These details will be found in the earlier tables.)

We have the calculations displayed below for overhead B. Here we face a slight problem in isolating the price and quantity effects. Should we use actual materials at standard prices or actual materials at actual prices in defining x^A? There is no ready answer. It all depends on what the organization thinks will provide the most insight. We illustrate the first option, using actual materials at standard prices.

In particular, we know 37,500 pounds of stock materials were used, with a standard price of 1 per pound. The specialty materials used, at standard prices, totaled 30,000. The "actual" level of the LLA's independent variable, x^A, is thus 30,000 + 37,500 = 67,500. The remaining details follow in straightforward fashion.

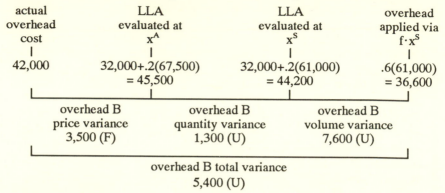

actual overhead cost	LLA evaluated at x^A	LLA evaluated at x^S	overhead applied via $f \cdot x^S$
42,000	32,000+.2(67,500) = 45,500	32,000+.2(61,000) = 44,200	.6(61,000) = 36,600

overhead B price variance 3,500 (F)   overhead B quantity variance 1,300 (U)   overhead B volume variance 7,600 (U)

overhead B total variance 5,400 (U)

recapitulation

Now step back and reexamine the larger details. Our job order costing story began with 246,000 in actual cost. Standard costing is used, in a full product cost format. Standard product costs are assigned, totaling 244,230. We interpret this as the budgeted cost, given the work accomplished. In turn, closing the various control accounts results in a net debit to cost of goods sold of 246,000 - 244,230 = 1,770. This is an overall variance of 1,770 (U).

Table 17.1 disaggregates this variance into a comparison of actual with budget for each of the five cost categories. Table 17.4, in turn, further disaggregates these variances into price and quantity components. Volume variances are also identified for the overhead cost categories, as full costing is employed by the accounting library. The next step is to break the variances down by product, a chore we defer to the reader.

Table 17.4: Cost Variances Broken Down by Category			
cost category	price variance	quantity variance	volume variance	total variance
direct labor	4,000 (U)	3,300 (F)		700 (U)
direct material				
specialty	0	0		0
stock	7,500 (F)	6,500 (U)		1,000 (F)
overhead A	7,000 (F)	700 (U)	2,970 (U)	3,330 (F)
overhead B	3,500 (F)	1,300 (U)	7,600 (U)	5,400 (U)
total	14,000 (F)	5,200 (U)	10,570 (U)	1,770 (U)

It is also important to understand the only difference between this library procedure and one based on variable costing is the presence of a volume variance for each overhead account. Table 17.5 summarizes the budget construction for the variable costing case. Table 17.6 repeats the grand summary of Table 17.4, but in variable costing format. It also presents a reconciliation to the full costing case.

Table 17.5: Standard Product Costs and Budget under Variable Costing				
	job 1	job 2	job 3	total
direct labor cost	11,000	18,700	17,600	47,300
direct material cost				
specialty materials	11,000	5,000	14,000	30,000
stock materials	5,000	9,000	17,000	31,000
"variable" overhead A				
(@ 1DL$)	11,000	18,700	17,600	47,300
"variable" overhead B				
(@ .2DM$)	3,200	2,800	6,200	12,200
standard product cost	41,200	54,200	72,400	167,800
"fixed" cost				
overhead A				55,000
overhead B				32,000
total budgeted cost				254,800

Table 17.6: Cost Variances under Variable Costing			
cost category	price variance	quantity variance	total variance
direct labor	4,000 (U)	3,300 (F)	700 (U)
direct material			
specialty	0	0	0
stock	7,500 (F)	6,500 (U)	1,000 (F)
overhead A	7,000 (F)	700 (U)	6,300 (F)
overhead B	3,500 (F)	1,300 (U)	2,200 (F)
total under variable costing	14,000 (F)	5,200 (U)	8,800 (F)
overhead A volume variance			2,970 (U)
overhead B volume variance			7,600 (U)
total under full costing			1,770 (U)

Whatever the details, the picture is one of estimating the cost, and then decomposing the difference between actual and estimated cost into price and quantity effects. In turn, the total of these effects is intimately related to the plug to cost of goods sold that tidies up the control accounts in a standard costing system.

Also notice how the library procedure accords with our earlier definition of performance evaluation. Various choices go into the planning process, culminating in product selections, methods of production, and standard costs. In turn, the comparison of actual with budget relies on the capture of various financial details, such as actual direct costs. We make provision at the time of choice for retrospective analysis of that choice.

Summary

Comparing actual with budgeted results is the quintessential example of performance evaluation. We must have in place a budget and the ability to discern actual results. Evaluation then follows by injecting other sources of information and judgment. This is particularly evident in a standard costing system where the eventual plug to cost of goods sold is the net of all production cost variances. Product costing and performance evaluation become intertwined.

More broadly, the actual versus budget comparison might be a comparison of actual with budgeted cost for some unit in the organization, it might be a comparison of actual with planned profit for some unit, or for the organization as a whole. It might cover a short period, or it might cover a longer period. Investment activities might or might not be included. Accrual measures might be emphasized, just as cash flow might be emphasized. Likewise, the budget itself might be fixed, as when we reconcile to an original profit plan, or it might be flexible, as when we reconcile to what we thought cost should have been given the work accomplished during the reporting period.

The accounting library procedures provide the basis for comparison of actual with budget, appropriately decomposed into various variances. It does not, however, provide the interpretations that are central to their use. The procedures provide the raw material for evaluation.

Appendix: Variations on the Decomposition Theme

In this Appendix we continue the exploration of the decomposition theme. The mechanical aspects of timely recognition of material price variances are briefly explored. We then turn to the comparison of actual with budgeted profit. This introduces sales quantities and prices into the story, as well as the host of period costs.

material price variances at time of acquisition

When direct material price variances are identified at the time of acquisition, we maintain raw material inventory records at standard prices. This has the dual advantage of simplifying the inventory records and identifying price variances in more timely fashion. It also causes us to alter our variance calculation format. We must reflect the fact the price variance is based on quantity *purchased* while the quantity variance is based on quantity *used*.

With this in mind, the decomposition format takes on the appearance noted below. These are, of course, the variances we computed earlier for this particular recording story. Notice how the first two columns vary price, holding quantity constant at the quantity *purchased*. Similarly, the last two columns hold price constant, but vary the quantity between quantity *used* and quantity *allowed*.

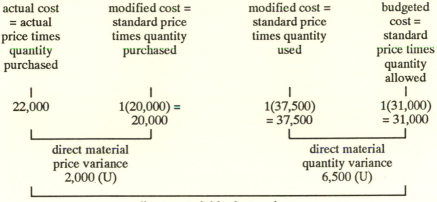

actual cost = actual price times quantity purchased	modified cost = standard price times quantity purchased	modified cost = standard price times quantity used	budgeted cost = standard price times quantity allowed
22,000	1(20,000) = 20,000	1(37,500) = 37,500	1(31,000) = 31,000

direct material price variance 2,000 (U)

direct material quantity variance 6,500 (U)

direct material budget variance 8,500 (U)

Can you now visualize the associated library entries? We already noted the entry to record acquisition of additional raw materials, resulting in the debit to raw material price variance. Removal of 37,500 pounds of raw material from inventory, for use in production, would now be recorded using the fact raw material inventory is also maintained at standard price (of 1 per pound). The summary entry to record actual costs would now be:

direct labor cost control	48,000	
direct material, specialty	30,000	
direct material, stock	37,500	
overhead A	96,000	
overhead B	42,000	
various accounts		253,500

The single difference from the earlier entry is the control account for use of stock materials is now debited for 37,500 pounds at the standard price of 1 per pound, instead of at .8 per pound.

The entry to set up the work-in-process account at standard cost is the same as before. After all, we have not changed the standard costs! The entry to close the control accounts is another matter. The direct material, stock control account now has a different balance; it is a debit balance of 37,500 - 31,000 = 6,500. We also have the earlier recorded direct material price variance that must be closed to cost of goods sold. So our summary entry to close the various temporary accounts now becomes:

cost of goods sold	11,270	
direct material, specialty	0	
overhead A	3,330	
direct labor cost control		700
overhead B		5,400
direct material, stock		6,500
direct material price variance		2,000

The direct material price and quantity variances remain subcomponents of the difference between actual direct material cost incurred and the budgeted total of 31,000. The difference between the two pictures reflects the treatment of the price variance.

profit variances

Enlarging the evaluation exercise to a focus on profit allows us to examine sales prices and quantities, period costs, and changes in the mix of products. To provide a glimpse of the possibilities, we revisit a two product LP illustration in Chapter 14. The organization's cost curve is $TC = 2,000 + 347q_1 + 620q_2$, where q_i denotes units of product i produced and sold. (We express revenue, cost, and units in thousands.) Revenue is given by $TR = 600q_1 + 1,100q_2$. Various LLAs underlie these forecasts. Combining the two aggregate expressions, we have a profit expression of $\pi(q_1,q_2)$ $= 253q_1 + 480q_2 - 2,000$.

From here we identify the following LP, by rescaling to a contribution margin format:

$$\text{maximize} \quad 253q_1 + 480q_2$$
$$\text{subject to:} \quad q_1 + q_2 \leq 6;$$
$$q_1 + 2q_2 \leq 10; \text{ and}$$
$$q_1, q_2 \geq 0.$$

The constraints reflect capacity limitations. The solution is $q_1^* = 2$ and $q_2^* = 4$; with $\pi(q_1^*,q_2^*) = \pi(2,4) = 426$. We interpret this solution as the organization's profit plan.

Now suppose it turns out actual production and sales are $q_1 = 1$ and $q_2 = 4.5$. Selling prices are as forecasted, but the cost curve turns out to be $TC = 2,000 + 500q_1 + 620q_2$. Actual profit is

$$(600 - 500)1 + (1,100 - 620)4.5 - 2,000 = 260.$$

We are confronted with a difference between planned and actual profit. (The profit of 426 is a fixed profit budget.) The simple decomposition trick is now invoked to factor this difference into underlying components. In particular, planned profit of 426 versus actual profit of 260 is broken down into price/cost and quantity effects. We do this by inserting an intermediate calculation of planned profit based on the actual quantities. The decomposition is as follows:

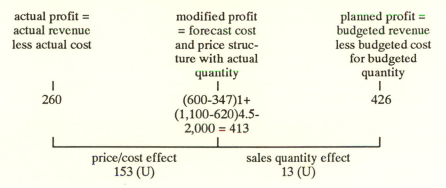

actual profit =	modified profit	planned profit =
actual revenue	= forecast cost	budgeted revenue
less actual cost	and price struc-	less budgeted cost
	ture with actual	for budgeted
	quantity	quantity
|	|	|
260	(600-347)1+	426
	(1,100-620)4.5-	
	2,000 = 413	

price/cost effect   sales quantity effect
153 (U)   13 (U)

The price/cost effect reflects actual versus forecast revenue and cost structures, evaluated at the actual output of $q_1 = 1$ and $q_2 = 4.5$. With our particularly simple story, this all occurs in the first product's domain where actual less budgeted cost for one unit is 500 - 347 = 153 (U).[13] The sales quantity effect reflects the difference between actual and planned output.

modified profit: (600 - 347)(1) + (1,100 - 620)(4.5) - 2,000 = 413
planned profit: (600 - 347)(2) + (1,100 - 620)(4) - 2,000 = 426

Notice this breaks down into (600 - 347)(-1) + (1,100 - 620)(.5) = -253 + 240 = -13. The shift away from the first product seems to have lessened the damage of the first product's cost overrun.[14]

We see, then, how the basic decomposition theme extends to a comparison of planned and actual profits. The link to the accounting library, though, is more subtle than implied by our streamlined story. Three caveats should be noted, all centering on the fact we are now comparing actual with budgeted profits. First, we should remember the distinction between period and product costs. The plug to cost of goods sold that we have been examining is a standard product cost phenomenon. The profit budget also will contain period costs, such as selling and administrative

---

[13]Actual total cost is 2,000 + 500(1) + 620(4.5), while budgeted total cost at this output is 2,000 + 347(1) + 620(4.5). The difference is 500 - 347 = 153.

[14]Reality is not this transparent. We then invoke a further decomposition based on mix and quantity notions to separate the profit difference into that due to a change in aggregate volume and that to a change in the product mix. Footnote 1 introduced this theme.

costs. So we should expect to see the product cost portion of the overall cost effect in the standard cost based accounting library. The period cost portion would be in the "extended" library, where the organization tracks actual and budgeted period costs.[15]

Second, the comparison and decomposition are based on the profit structure that is assumed in the budgeting exercise. The underlying cost structure need not be the cost curve that is assumed for product costing purposes. Suppose the organization approximates its cost curve with a set of LLAs and uses these LLAs in its planning process. This sounds like a variable costing structure. The organization, however, may use full product costing. The point is we must be careful to distinguish where the accounting library and planning process cost structures diverge. The most prominent example is where planning presumes a variable cost structure while the standard costing apparatus uses full costing. In that case, we would find the cost variances identified in our profit analysis would differ from the plug to cost of goods sold by the unrecorded variances in period costs and the recorded volume variance in product costs.

Third, the accounting library is reserved for actual events. It will record revenue and costs associated with actual production and actual sales. It will not record events associated with budgeted production and sales, just as it will not record the price of factors of production or the supposed cost of those products not used or produced. Profit performance variances take us beyond the accounting library. This is why we refer to the "extended" library. These data will be present, but in an adjunct format.[16]

planning model based variances

More insight along these lines is possible if we take advantage of the presence of a formal planning model, an LP model in our example. To whet our appetite, suppose the only deviation between the planned and actual revenue and cost structures is that direct material for the first product costs 153 more per unit of output than anticipated. Our above analysis hints at a 153 (U) direct material variance, coupled with a 13 (U) production/sales quantity variance.

---

[15]Recall that bookkeeping ease is one of the reasons for using a standard costing system. Since period costs are expensed, there is no bookkeeping ease associated with extending the standard costing apparatus to the period costs. From a budgeting perspective, though, it would be naive to exclude these costs. This is why it is important to distinguish where the conventional library procedure ends and what we call an "extended" library procedure begins.

[16]Inventory adds a complication at the profit analysis stage. If production and sales are not identical, production variances will relate to one activity (production) while sales variances will relate to another (sales). Actual profit would then include all of the manufacturing variances. Why?

Let's dig a little deeper. With the benefit of hindsight, we might now say we should have represented the cost curve as $TC = 2,000 + 500q_1 + 620\ q_2$. Using this specification, our LP would have been

$$\text{maximize} \quad (600\text{-}500)q_1 + (1,100\text{-}620)q_2$$
$$\text{subject to:} \quad q_1 + q_2 \leq 6;$$
$$q_1 + 2q_2 \leq 10; \text{ and}$$
$$q_1, q_2 \geq 0.$$

The solution is $q_1^* = 0$ and $q_2^* = 5$; with a hindsight optimal profit of 400.

Use this hindsight calculation to decompose our difference between actual and planned profit:

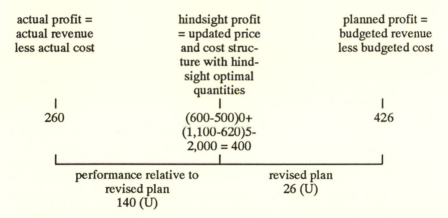

actual profit = actual revenue less actual cost	hindsight profit = updated price and cost struc- ture with hind- sight optimal quantities	planned profit = budgeted revenue less budgeted cost
260	(600-500)0+ (1,100-620)5- 2,000 = 400	426

performance relative to   revised plan
    revised plan   26 (U)
    140 (U)

The revised plan effect of 26 (U) contrasts two planning model solutions: one based on the hindsight estimates and the other on the original planning estimates. This variance reflects inadequacies in the planning process. It would be nil if the original planning estimates were without error.[17]

Performance relative to the revised plan, the 140 (U) variance, contrasts actual profit with the revised, hindsight profit. This comparison stresses actual profit versus what profit could have been with complete anticipation of the underlying events. It provides an indication of how well the organization responded to unanticipated events. In the particular story before us, the shortfall is due entirely to the inability to move more aggressively to emphasize the second product as the first became less profitable. (Though we skip the details, it should be evident how we would decompose this variance into its own price/cost and quantity effects.)

Our earlier, more conventional breakdown suggested a large price/cost effect coupled with a modest quantity effect in reconciling actual to planned profit. To the contrary, reinterpreting events in light of the revised planning decision, we see the

---

[17]In a deeper sense, it is the result of having less than perfect information at the planning stage.

quantity effect as dominant. (The 140 (U) variance is due entirely to the difference between actual and hindsight optimal quantities.)

To draw this out a little further, suppose the cost curve shifted as noted, but actual production was $q_1 = 0$ and $q_2 = 5$, implying an actual profit of 400. The conventional analysis would report a zero price/cost effect (as the second product's price and cost are right on target), and a sales quantity variance of 26 (U). Our hindsight calculation, though, would attribute 26 (U) to the revised plan and acknowledge perfect performance relative to the revised plan, giving full credit for altering the original planned quantities.

Finally, reverse the story. Suppose the original LLA is TC = 2,000 + 500q_1 + 620q_2. The original plan would then call for $q_1^* = 0$ and $q_2^* = 5$, with a profit of 400. Actual production is also $q_1^* = 0$ and $q_2^* = 5$, but actual cost is TC = 2,000 + 347q_1 + 620q_2. The conventional decomposition would report actual and planned profit of 400, with no variances whatever. The only off-budget item occurred with the first product, and that is not being produced. But the hindsight approach would pick this up. It would report a revised optimum plan of $q_1^* = 2$ and $q_2^* = 4$, with a hindsight profit of 426. A performance shortfall of 26 (U) relative to the revised plan would be noted, suggesting the lost opportunity to exploit the more attractive features of the first product.

The conventional analysis reconciles actual to planned profit but is silent on how recognition of the underlying events might influence the period's goals. If the planning process makes use of a formal planning model, we are able to add more insight to the variance analysis. The idea is to center the underlying events on a recycled, hindsight spin of the planning process. This forces us to distinguish the economic structure assumed in the planning process from that used in the profit measurement process (e.g., period versus product cost distinctions or full versus variable product costing). It also forces us to confront all of the planning assumptions, not just those associated with products produced and therefore reflected in the traditional accounting library.

Bibliographic Notes

The procedures discussed here can be extended to break out the effects of output variations in a multiproduct firm, to productivity measurement and so on. Kaplan and Atkinson [1989] is a good reference. Structuring the analysis on a planning model is developed in Demski [1967].

Problems and Exercises

1.   Suppose an organization uses standard costs. Discuss the relationship between the decomposition procedures developed in the text and the overall "plug" in the standard costing system that is closed to cost of goods sold.

2. Might a marketing organization, where most of the costs are period costs, find these variance procedures useful? Explain. How might the procedures differ from those discussed in the text?

3. Redraw Figure 17.1 for the case where the accounting library uses standard, variable costing.

4. *price and quantity effects*
Ralph purchases prefabricated containers, assembles them and sells them to local merchants. Assembly errors occur on occasion, and the affected container must be scrapped. Ralph figures this happens 5% of the time. The prefabricated containers cost 100 per unit. The material cost, then, is estimated at $100(1.05)q$, where q denotes the number of units assembled. During a recent period, 900 units were successfully assembled. 930 prefabricated containers were used, costing a total of 96,000. There is no beginning or ending work-in-process inventory. Explain Ralph's performance in terms of price and quantity effects.

5. *price, quantity, and volume effects*
An organization has an overhead LLA of $OV = 100,000 + 25DLH$, where DLH denotes direct labor hours. It is also able to identify the underlying costs and separately aggregate those associated with the LLA's intercept (or the "fixed" cost) in one account and those associated with the slope (or the "variable" cost) in another account. During a recent period the "fixed" overhead totaled 95,000 and the "variable" overhead totaled 122,000. 5,100 direct labor hours were used, but given the work accomplished the underlying standards show 4,800 hours should have been used. Full, standard costing is used, with a normal volume of 5,000 direct labor hours.
Prepare a list of variances for both accounts. Why is there no volume variance for the "variable" overhead category? Why is there no quantity variance for the "fixed" overhead category?

6. *variances under variable and full costing*
This is a continuation of the saga in Ralph's Job, problem 7 in Chapter 7 and problem 9 in Chapter 6. Suppose the average wage rate for direct labor turned out to be 20 per hour, and direct material turned out to cost 12.5 per unit. Calculate all manufacturing cost variances, assuming standard full costing is employed. Comment on any patterns in the variances.
Repeat for the case where standard variable costing is employed.

7. *exogenous events and variances*
Return to the setting of Ralph's Job above. Suppose all of Ralph's employees are covered by a health plan. The health services are provided by a local provider, and cost Ralph 3,500 per employee covered per year. Where are these employee

benefit costs likely to be recorded in the accounting system? Continuing, suppose in the middle of the year the provider raises the price to 3,900 per employee. Where and how will this show up in the standard cost variances?

Now suppose one of Ralph's employees has just won the state lottery. This causes considerable excitement and even results in an impromptu celebration (of which Ralph approves). Where and how will this show up in the standard cost variances?

8.   *variances for individual products*

Return to the setting of Table 17.6, where variable costing is used in our main illustration. Prepare a companion table that breaks the various variances down by job, to the extent possible (given the information in the example) and to the extent you feel relevant.

9.   *departmental variances*

This is a continuation of Ralph's LP, problem 12 in Chapter 14. Ralph has implemented the production and sales plan determined in the original problem. Events did not quite turn out, though. Budgets are based on the LLAs noted in the original problem. Sales and production of the first product totaled $q_1 = 145$ units. The selling price turned out to be 610 per unit. (There was no production or sale of the second product during the period.) The following actual costs were incurred:

selling and administrative	S&A = 5,500;
direct labor in fabrication	DL^f = 6,556 (298 hours);
direct labor in assembly	DL^a = 5,180 (140 hours);
direct material (all in fabrication)	DM = 19,285;
overhead in fabrication	OV^f = 11,900;
overhead in assembly	OV^a = 21,000; and
manufacturing service group	MS = 9,100.

The direct material cost is based on an average price of 19 per "unit" of direct material. Also, the accounting library uses variable costing for internal purposes.

a]   Determine (i) net income for the period; (ii) actual manufacturing cost; (iii) the standard variable cost of the work accomplished; (iv) the "plug" to cost of goods sold associated with the standard cost system; and (v) all manufacturing cost variances.

b]   Prepare a schedule of variances for the fabrication and assembly departments. Here you must decide how, or whether, to allocate the manufacturing service group costs to the fabrication and assembly departments.

10.   *recognition rules, variances and product costs*

Ralph produces two products, code named X and Y. The cost structure is estimated by the following LLAs:

direct material dollars	DM = 40X + 60Y;
direct labor hours	DLH = 2X + 1Y;

direct labor dollars $DL = 15DLH$; and
overhead $OV = 200,000 + 2DM + 0.8DL$.

For simplicity, no other cost elements are present. Also, DM consists of a single chemical compound purchased at a standard price of 10 per gallon. Ralph employs just-in-time inventory so raw material inventory is negligible.

a]   Determine the standard variable cost for each product.

b]   With multiple independent variables in the OV budget, full costing is problematic. Suppose normal production volume calls for $X = Y = 500$ units. Determine the standard full cost for each product in each of three ways: by allocating the fixed overhead on the basis of physical units, on the basis of direct labor hours, and on the basis of total variable overhead.

c]   Product X is produced for the local municipality. The contracting relationship with Ralph has been questioned by the local newspaper. Ralph contends selling X to the municipality is actually done at a loss. The negotiated price is 400 per unit. What cost datum might Ralph supply to support the contention of a loss?

d]   Now assume Ralph uses standard variable costing for internal purposes. During a recent period production totaled $X = 500$ and $Y = 600$. Sales totaled 450 units of X and 700 units of Y. Actual manufacturing costs were as follows:

> Direct Materials: 5,500 gallons purchased and used, with a purchase price of 10.5 per gallon;
> Direct Labor: 1,700 total hours, at the posted wage rate of 15 per hour; and
> Overhead: 365,000 in total, of which 210,000 is estimated to be fixed.

Calculate all relevant variances.

e]   What was the cost of goods sold during the period in part [d] above?

f]   Suppose X sells for 400 per unit (as noted) while Y sells for 350 per unit. Further suppose Ralph faces a capacity constraint such that total direct labor hours cannot exceed 2,000 hours. Determine Ralph's optimal production schedule.

g]   With this additional structure, would you care to change your answer to [c] above? If so, what answer would you give now?

h]   Suppose Ralph implements the solution you determined in part [f] above. Actual costs are precisely as predicted, except the labor required to manufacture product X is one instead of two hours. What variances will Ralph's internal accounting system report? (Remember, you explored this accounting system in part [d] above.)

i]   Suppose Ralph had known of this change in labor requirements at the time the analysis in part [f] above was done. What would the optimal production schedule have been? How much did this mistake cost Ralph? Why does Ralph's accounting system not record the cost of this mistake?

j] Finally, suppose Ralph "implements" the solution you determined in part [f] above. Actual costs are precisely as predicted, except the labor required to manufacture product Y is two hours instead of one hour. (Remember, capacity totals 2,000 direct labor hours. Under these circumstances, only 1,000 units of Y could be produced.) What variances will Ralph's internal accounting system report? What does this mistake cost Ralph? Why does Ralph's accounting system record the presence of this mistake but assign it an "incorrect" number?

11. *variances with multiple independent variables*

Ralph's Fancy Costing Company (RFCC) produces a variety of fabricated products to customer order. Product costing and budgeting at RFCC are based on the following LLAs:

direct labor: DL$ = 35DLH (where DLH denotes direct labor hours);
direct material: DM$ = priced per market; a just-in-time inventory
          policy is in place;
overhead: OV = 450,000 + 1.2(DL$) + 3(DM$) + 2,700(number of setups);
G&A: 400,000 + .1(DL$+DM$+OV).

For full costing purposes, RFCC assigns the "fixed" overhead to products at a rate of 85% of variable overhead.

During a recent period, three separate products were manufactured. Their standard costs are based on the following estimates:

	product 1	product 2	product 3
direct labor hours	1,000	4,000	3,000
direct material	$45,000	$30,000	$25,000
number of setups	5	14	20

In addition, the following costs were incurred:

direct labor (9,000 hours)	320,000
direct materials	125,000
overhead	1,200,000
G&A	520,000

a] Determine the standard variable and full product costs for each product, as they would be reported by a typical standard costing system.

b] Determine the estimated contribution margin for each product. For this purpose assume product 1 sells for P_1, product 2 for P_2 and product 3 for P_3.

c] Calculate all relevant variances.

13. *profit variances*

This is a continuation of Ralph's LP, problem 9 above. Using the original production plan (of $q_1 = 150$ and $q_2 = 0$) and the actual results noted above, provide a detailed variance analysis that breaks down the difference between planned and actual profit. Be certain to include all the manufacturing cost variances you identified in problem 9 above. Interpret your results.

14. *variances based on planning model*

This is a continuation of Ralph's LP, most recently problem 13 above. Ralph decides, upon further reflection, two significant errors were made in specifying the original LLAs. The first product's selling price should have been 610 per unit (instead of 600); and the first product's direct material standard should have allowed 6.5 (instead of 6) units of direct material per unit of output. Use the revised LLAs to construct a hindsight profit plan, and determine all relevant variances. Be certain to separate performance relative to the revised plan into price/cost and quantity effects. Interpret your results.

Now suppose we change one additional standard, the direct material standard for the second product. Suppose Ralph also decides, based on hindsight, that the second product should require 7.5 (instead of 10) units of direct material. Again construct a hindsight optimal profit plan and determine all relevant variances. Be certain to separate performance relative to the revised plan into price/cost and quantity effects. Again, interpret your results.

Contrast your variances with those that would be identified by a "traditional" profit variance analysis.

15. *raw material inventory at standard price*

Return to the manufacturing cost variances in Ralph's LP, problem 9 above. Now suppose an inventory of raw material is maintained. During the period, 1,200 units were acquired at a total cost of 23,500. (Recall the standard price is 20 per unit.) Determine (i) cost of goods sold; (ii) net income; and (iii) all manufacturing cost variances. Also reconcile your net income number with that in problem 9.

16. *variances in classical setting*

In Chapter 2 we examined a single product firm that used three factors of production. The cost of producing output q was the minimum total expenditure on the three factors that would allow for production of q units.

$$C(q) = \underset{z_1, z_2, z_3}{\text{minimum}} \hat{P}_1 z_1 + \hat{P}_2 z_2 + \hat{P}_3 z_3$$
$$\text{subject to:} \quad q = f(z_1, z_2, z_3)$$

where P_i is the price of factor i and z_i is its quantity. Suppose the firm's accounting library uses three cost accounts, one for each factor of production. Assume it produced $\hat{q}$ units, and incurred a total cost for factor i of $\hat{P}_i \hat{z}_i$. Total cost should have been $C(\hat{q})$. Factor the difference between actual and total cost into price and quantity effects for each of the three factors. Is it reasonable to assume the noted variances are interrelated?

18

Managerial Performance Evaluation

We have seen how the organization's accounting library emphasizes financial data, while keeping an eye on their integrity. We have also seen how the building blocks of *cost aggregation* and *linear approximation*, interlinked with *cost allocation*, are used to construct that library. Variance analysis procedures expand this theme to a comparison of actual with budget. What remains is the question of use. How might we use this overwhelming amount of data in some evaluation task?

We address this question by focusing on the evaluation of a manager. Alternatively, we might evaluate a product, product line, manufacturing facility, or whatever. These tasks were addressed in our earlier study of framing and large and small decisions. Our focus now shifts to the evaluation of a manager.[1]

Imagine a departmental manager in a large organization. Should we evaluate this manager based on cost incurred or profit earned? How should revenue be measured if the department's products are transferred to another department, managed by a separate manager? Might we use the department's asset base in the evaluation? If so, do we prefer historical or current cost valuation approaches?

Suppose the department consumes maintenance and personnel services produced by other departments. Should costs associated with these services be allocated to the department in question? If so, should they reflect actual or budgeted "prices?" Similarly, suppose a cost overrun occurs and is largely the result of unanticipated direct material price increases. Should this fact be recognized in the manager's evaluation?

What about nonfinancial information? Might we use measures of quality and productivity? Might a supervisor's subjective evaluation be relevant? Might the performance of a peer group be introduced, as in a sales contest or grading on the curve?

We provide the foundation for answering these questions in this chapter. In particular, we return to the economist's setting of Chapter 2 and explore the questions of why and how we might want to evaluate the performance of a manager. Two features of the setting are emphasized. The inputs supplied by the manager are not necessarily observable; and the manager and the employing organization may

---

[1] There is an important qualitative difference between evaluating a manager and evaluating a product. We evaluate the product to determine whether it should be continued, modified, or dropped. We evaluate the manager as part of the web of controls used to help insure desirable behavior, as well as to determine whether the manager should be continued, dropped, or continued with modified instructions. The prospect of evaluation and its consequences help specify the environment in which the manager labors. Putting the two together, an organization must worry whether its managerial group is well-motivated to evaluate its product line.

have conflicting tastes over how best to allocate these inputs. For example, the manager may excessively worry over personal career concerns in deciding whether to push a new product proposal, just as the professor may worry more about a current research project than an upcoming lecture. We are thus led to worry about the inputs supplied by the manager or by the professor.

This worry creates a profound juxtaposition with the story in Chapter 2. The perfect market setting portrays the manager as supplying factor inputs and being paid a market determined price per unit. Desired and actual inputs always agree, and no price ambiguity is present. Clouding this picture implies desired and actual inputs need not agree. The price per unit calculation also breaks down, since we do not see the inputs supplied. In this way a market imperfection exposes the economist's world to an interest in managerial performance evaluation.

The organization uses inputs, including managerial inputs, to produce outputs. Arranging for the inputs is a trivial task if they are available in perfect markets. If the managerial market is imperfect to the extent we do not necessarily observe inputs supplied, contracting for these inputs must be based on an inference as to what inputs were supplied. This inference is the task of performance evaluation. We make provision at the time of choice, at the time of input supply, retrospectively to evaluate that choice, that input supply.

The theme is developed as follows. Initially we streamline the setting in Chapter 2 to a focus on a single factor of production. Interpreting this factor as managerial services, we then have the essentials of acquiring managerial services in a particular short-run setting. Next we examine contracting arrangements that might surface in the absence of a perfectly functioning market, based on input observability. These contracting arrangements, it turns out, use available information to infer what inputs were supplied. This provides the key insight in our study of performance evaluation.

The material is conceptual. We used the material in Chapter 2 to anchor our study of product costing. Chapter 18 is a companion to Chapter 2. We will use this material to anchor our study of managerial performance evaluation.

A Streamlined Production Setting

Return to the Chapter 2 review of the economic theory of the firm, where we had three inputs (z_1, z_2, and z_3) and one output (q). Inputs and output are linked by the production function $q = f(z_1, z_2, z_3)$. Respective factor prices are given by $\hat{P}_i$.

With the latter two factors fixed, say, at $\bar{z}_2$ and $\bar{z}_3$, we would construct the firm's short-run cost function by solving the following optimization problem for each output $\hat{q}$:

$$C(\hat{q}; \bar{z}_2, \bar{z}_3) = \underset{z_1, z_2, z_3}{\text{minimum}} \ \hat{P}_1 z_1 + \hat{P}_2 z_2 + \hat{P}_3 z_3$$
$$\text{subject to:} \ \hat{q} = f(z_1, z_2, z_3), \ z_2 = \bar{z}_2 \text{ and } z_3 = \bar{z}_3.$$

We now add some additional simplifying assumptions. First, assume the remaining input can be one of two amounts, L ("low") or H ("high"), with L < H. Second, assume output is uncertain. It will be either x_1 or x_2, with $x_1 < x_2$. Uncertainty and factor input are linked by the following probability structure.

output

	x_1	x_2
input H	$1-\alpha$	α
input L	1	0

The idea is input L guarantees the low output of x_1. Input H, though, will result in the larger output with probability α, and the smaller output with probability $1 - \alpha$.[2]

Finally, the organization is assumed to be risk neutral. It seeks to maximize the expected value of its short-run profit.

To complete the analogy to our earlier setting, think of output x as revenue less all fixed costs. Output x can be either x_1 or x_2. Then interpret quantity q as the expected value of the output. So quantity q can be either $q_H = (1-\alpha)x_1 + \alpha x_2$, which requires input H; or it can be $q_L = x_1$, which requires input L.

The firm's expected profit, then, will be $(1-\alpha)x_1 + \alpha x_2 - C(q_H)$ if it selects quantity q_H and $x_1 - C(q_L)$ if it selects quantity q_L. $C(q)$, of course, is the cost of quantity q.

To recap, we focus on a short-run setting in which all factors of production are fixed, except the first. Output is also uncertain. We frame the firm's decision to emphasize net revenue (revenue less all fixed costs) less the cost of the remaining factor. We interpret this remaining factor as managerial labor. It also seems natural to interpret output x as the firm's cash flow exclusive of payments for labor.[3]

The next step is to highlight the transaction with the supplier of this input. In this way we extend our characterization of a firm to include the idea of arranging and managing transactions. Viewed in this more expansive manner, the firm and the market are competing institutions for arranging transactions. To illustrate, a firm may internally produce (a largely internal transaction) or externally acquire (a largely market mediated transaction) some subcomponent.

Comparative advantage and transaction technology are now important elements of the larger picture. Performance evaluation, in turn, is a major ingredient in the firm's transaction technology. It is the information glue that supports the trade arrangements.

---

[2] There is no inherent reason for input L to lead to output x_1 for certain. This is done merely to keep our story as simple as possible.

[3] Reflecting on the material in Chapter 2, we should remember the labor factor here subsumes all issues of quality, skill, talent, and so on. The story is purposely streamlined.

Resolution with a Perfect Labor Market

Our simple story has the firm acquiring managerial services in a market transaction. To provide a benchmark we initially examine the nature of this transaction in a perfect labor market.

Given the decision frame, managerial labor is the only variable input and all fixed costs are netted into the output measure. So the cost function can be interpreted as the cost of managerial labor. $C(q_L)$ is simply the cost of input L. Similarly, $C(q_H)$ is the cost of input H.

To specify this cost function, we step into the shoes of a potential supplier. Competition in the labor market then ensures a mutually advantageous match of firm and supplier.

preferences of the supplier

The potential supplier of labor is risk averse, with a utility function defined over wealth. It will best suit our purpose to assume a negative exponential function. This implies we express the utility of wealth level $\hat{w}$ as $U(\hat{w}) = -exp(-r\hat{w})$, where $r > 0$ is the risk aversion parameter.

Most important, this utility function represents constant risk aversion. Whatever the aversion to risk, it is independent of initial wealth. Since this feature will be important in what follows, we review briefly some underlying details.

Suppose we have an initial wealth of zero but hold a lottery ticket. This lottery ticket will pay 1,000 with probability .5 and 0 otherwise. So the expected value of wealth is 500. Also, the utility associated with this prospect is the expected value of $U(\hat{w})$, or

$$.5U(0) + .5U(1,000) = -.5exp(0) - .5exp(-r[1,000]).$$

Expressing this in terms of a certain equivalent is more intuitive. The lottery's certain equivalent, recall, is the guaranteed amount that is equivalent to the lottery in question. With zero initial wealth, this amount, call it k, is defined by

$$U(k) = -.5exp(0) - .5exp(-r[1,000]).$$

For example, if $r = .0001$ we find $k = 487.5052$:

$$\begin{aligned}
-exp(-.0001[487.5052]) &= -.5exp(0) - .5exp(-.0001[1,000]) \\
&= -.5exp(0) - .5exp(-.1) \\
&= -.5(1) - .5(.9048) = -.9524.
\end{aligned}$$

We are indifferent between the risky lottery, which has an expected value of 500, and a certain amount of 487.5052.

Now suppose initial wealth is some other amount, say $w = 250$. So, with probability .5 ending wealth will total $w = 250$ and with probability .5 it will total $w + 1,000 = 1,250$. The certain equivalent of this prospect, CE, is given by

$$U(CE) = .5U(250) + .5U(250+1,000) = -.5exp(-r[250]) - .5exp(-r[1,250]).$$

We find CE = 250 + 487.5052 = 250 + k. Doing this for any initial wealth w, we will find CE = w + k.[4]

Think about this. Wealth consists of the 0/1,000 gamble overlaid on a starting point of w. This is equivalent to a guaranteed wealth of CE = w + k. Clearly we would trade the 0/1,000 risky part for the guaranteed amount k. And k does not depend on initial wealth w. The attitude toward risk is independent of the starting point w.

Another way to express this attitude toward risk is with the risk premium we demand. The risk premium, recall, is the lottery's expected value less its certain equivalent. For our numerical illustration, where the lottery's expected value is 500, the risk premium is: 12.4948 = 500 - 487.5052.

The particular modeling advantage of the negative exponential utility function is the attitude toward risk is independent of the initial wealth. A lottery's risk premium and certain equivalent do not depend on the initial wealth. Stated differently, wealth induced changes in risk aversion are irrelevant.

A final note in our excursion is that the degree of risk aversion is specified by the parameter r > 0. As r approaches zero, the attitude toward risk approaches risk neutrality. Let w = 0, so CE = k. In Figure 18.1 we plot CE as a function of r. CE ranges from 500 (the gamble's expected value) to minuscule (the case of terminal risk aversion).[5]

Dealing with the negative exponential specification probably strikes you as awkward or arcane; yet it is the most direct avenue to our study of performance evaluation. We want risk aversion in the stew and elect to do this without the added nuisance of changing risk aversion. This leads, inexorably, to the negative exponential specification.[6]

---

[4] An important feature of the negative exponential is its factoring. Conveniently, we have $exp(a+b)$ = $exp(a) \cdot exp(b)$. Exploiting this in the CE expression, for arbitrary initial wealth w, we have
$$U(CE) = exp(-r[w])\{-.5exp(0) - .5exp(-r[1,000])\} = exp(-r[w]) \cdot U(k).$$
The last step follows from our earlier definition of k, via $U(k) = -.5exp(0) - .5exp(-r[1,000])$. So we have $U(CE)/exp(-r[w]) = U(k)$. But,
$$U(CE)/exp(-r[w]) = -exp(-r[CE])/exp(-r[w]) = -exp(-r[CE-w]).$$
Bringing this together, for initial wealth w we find CE = w + k.

[5] Let w = 0. CE is now defined by $U(CE) = -.5exp(0) - .5exp(-r[1,000])$. Negating, and then taking the natural logarithm of each side gives us the following expression:
$$ln\{exp(-r[CE])\} = -r[CE] = ln\{.5exp(0) + .5exp(-r[1,000])\}; \text{ or}$$
$$CE = -(ln\{.5exp(0) + .5exp(-r[1000])\})/r.$$
What happens as r approaches zero? We use L'Hospital's rule to identify the limit of the CE expression as r approaches zero. (With mild regularity, the limit of $f(r)/g(r)$ as r approaches zero, when $f(0) = g(0) = 0$, is the limit of $f'(r)$ divided by the limit of $g'(r)$.) This gives us a limiting value of CE, as r approaches zero, of 500/1 = 500. The CE converges to the lottery's expected value as risk aversion disappears.

[6] As an aside, the expected utility apparatus uses a scaling that is far from unique. $U(\hat{w})$ may be

Figure 18.1: Certain Equivalent when $U(\hat{w}) = -exp(-r\hat{w})$

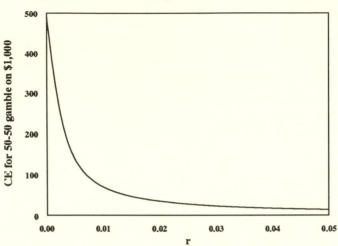

personal cost

Within this framework, we now further assume the supplier of labor incurs a personal cost in supplying labor services to our firm. The underlying idea is one of consumption at work. Bouts of enjoyment, collegial rapport, power, prestige, self-satisfaction, curiosity, drudgery, loss of leisure, pressure to perform, anxiety, and so on, are elements of the typical employment relationship. What we have in mind is something in the employment relationship that is important to the employee but not equally important to the employer. Personality and circumstance will give this more precise meaning. For now we want to acknowledge the general idea; not all aspects of the employment relationship are valued the same by both parties.[7]

With this in mind, let c_L be the personal cost to the manager of supplying input L, and c_H be the personal cost of supplying input H. We assume H is more costly, $c_H \geq c_L$. Interpreting these costs as monetary (or their monetary equivalent), the manager's wealth will increase by $I - c_a$ if input $a \in \{L,H\}$ is supplied and payment I is received from the firm.

---

multiplied by any positive number, or be increased by an arbitrary constant. So an equivalent story is to use, say, $U(\hat{w}) = 20 - 2exp(-r\hat{w})$. We stick with the uncluttered scale of $-exp(-r\hat{w})$.

[7]Another interpretation is the manager is a subcontractor. The personal cost is then readily interpreted as the cost to the subcontractor of performing the desired service. This interpretation will be used, especially when we overlay this abstraction on a make or buy decision.

market discipline

The manager is also not held captive by the firm. Suppose among all alternatives, except working for this firm, the most attractive has a certain equivalent of M (for market). This implies the manager's opportunity cost of working for our firm is $-exp\langle-rM\rangle$.

It is now a simple exercise to specify the cost function. If the firm is to secure input H from this manager, it must offer a payment of I_H such that the manager finds the package attractive. In utility terms, this requires $U(I_H-c_H) \geq U(M)$. Expressing this in certain equivalent terms, the requirement is

$$I_H - c_H \geq M.$$

So the minimum payment to the manager is $I_H = c_H + M.$[8] Similarly, the minimum payment to secure input L is $I_L = c_L + M.$[9]

To illustrate, consider the data in Table 18.1. $\alpha = .5$, $x_1 = 10,000$ and $x_2 = 20,000$. In addition, let $c_L = 2,000$, $c_H = 5,000$ and $M = 3,000$. This implies $I_H = 5,000 + 3,000 = 8,000$ while $I_L = 2,000 + 3,000 = 5,000$. The firm's choice is now apparent. Use of input L gives an expected profit to the firm of

$$1(10,000) + 0(20,000) - 5,000 = 5,000;$$

while use of input H provides

$$.5(10,000) + .5(20,000) - 8,000 = 7,000.$$

Table 18.1: Data for Labor Contracting Illustration
production function   cash flow exclusive of labor payments: $x_1 = 10,000$; $x_2 = 20,000$ possible labor inputs: L or H   probability of high output under H: $\alpha = .5$
manager characteristics   risk aversion parameter: $r = .0001$ personal cost of inputs: $c_H = 5,000$; $c_L = 2,000$ opportunity cost: $-exp\langle-r[3,000]\rangle$; $M = 3,000$

Several features of this abstract development should be noted. First, the firm is risk neutral while the manager is risk averse. The best risk sharing arrangement

---

[8]This construction holds regardless of the manager's initial wealth. We have developed the story on the presumption this initial wealth is zero. Adding an arbitrary initial wealth has no effect on our calculations.

[9]In turn, imagine a large number of identical potential suppliers. Competition then ensures the firm's cost of input a will be $c_a + M$.

is for the firm to carry all the output risk, and pay the manager a wage in exchange for supply of managerial services. This is why we developed the argument *assuming* the manager would be paid a flat wage.

Second, the incremental cost of higher output to the firm under this flat wage arrangement is $I_H - I_L = c_H - c_L$. It does not depend on the manager's opportunity cost. This is one reason for using the constant risk aversion specification of $U(\hat{w})$. It does not allow for an interaction between managerial opportunity cost and incremental cost to the firm. This keeps us focused on essentials.

Third, market discipline together with the manager's personal cost sets the wage. The market guarantees the manager a net of M; so the firm must pay $c_a + M$ for input $a \in \{L,H\}$.

Resolution in the Face of Market Frictions

We now introduce two frictions that stand in the way of the firm arranging for supply of managerial input. The first is self-interested behavior by the manager. The second is limited information, so the firm has concern for and difficulty in knowing whether the wanted services have been supplied.

self-interested behavior

To this point we have implicitly assumed the firm can arrange for supply of any feasible input from the manager. The cost to the firm is determined by the manager's personal cost and market opportunities. The labor market disciplines the trade arrangement.

Subtly tucked away here is the idea any arrangement meeting the market test will be honored. The firm will not renege in paying the manager; and the manager will not renege in supplying the agreed upon input. This is the idea of *cooperative* behavior. Agreements are honored or enforced with some unmodeled mechanism. The transaction, once agreed upon, will be implemented without a hitch.

We now introduce one sided *noncooperative* behavior into the story. The firm is able to commit to any payment arrangement with the worker, if that arrangement is conditioned on publicly observable events. The firm can commit to pay the manager a flat wage, a bonus dependent on accounting income, a bonus dependent on market share, or whatever. The only catch is the payment can depend only on variables that are publicly observed. Once agreed upon, though, the firm does not renege; the contracted payment arrangement is costlessly enforceable. The payment arrangement will be honored.[10]

---

[10]With the contracted payment depending only upon public observables, a court is in a position to confirm and enforce the contractual terms. We should not assume this is always the case. Litigation over employment contracts is not uncommon. We use the assumption of honorable behavior by the firm merely to present a streamlined story in which performance evaluation is substantively important.

The manager, on the other hand, has no such commitment power. The manager will renege if self-interest so dictates; and self-interest is defined by the manager's expected utility of wealth in our story. To see the power of this assumption, suppose we use the contractual arrangement of the perfect market setting. There the firm offers the manager a flat wage in exchange for supply of input H. Using the data in Table 18.1, the firm would offer a wage of 8,000 in exchange for input H.

Having agreed to this arrangement, the manager now faces a decision. Input H can be supplied, or input L can be supplied. If input H is chosen, the manager's expected utility will reflect the flat wage of 8,000 and the personal cost of 5,000:

$$E[U|H] = U(I_H-c_H) = U(3,000) = -exp\langle-.0001[8,000-5,000]\rangle = -exp\langle-.3\rangle = -.7408.$$

The notation should be obvious. $E[U|H]$ denotes the expected value of the manager's utility, given selection of input H. In contrast, choice of input L implies an expected utility, $E[U|L]$, of

$$E[U|L] = U(I_H-c_L) = U(6,000) = -exp\langle-.0001[8,000-2,000]\rangle = -exp\langle-.6\rangle = -.5488.$$

Choice of input L is compelling. The manager is paid for the more costly input H, but surreptitiously supplies input L and incurs the lower cost of c_L.

If we assume the manager can commit to the original terms of the agreement, the manager has no choice to exercise at this point. Input H was agreed upon, and input H will therefore be supplied. If we assume the manager cannot so commit, a choice is predestined. Without the ability to commit, when it comes time to supply the input the manager must choose between H and L. Opportunistic behavior is invited. When low output (x_1) is observed, the manager can claim H was supplied but bad luck resulted in low output.

The manager's choice is governed by self-interested behavior in this caricature. Input H will be supplied at this juncture only if it is in the manager's self-interest, as defined by the expected value of $U(\hat{w})$.

This is not a flattering view of the manager. If we think broadly about the manager's concerns, issues of family, self-satisfaction, intrinsic interest, career development, and so on are all likely to influence what the manager does. A conflict between organizational and personal goals seems inevitable. We model this conflict with the assumption of self-interested behavior in the face of personal cost.[11]

While less than flattering, conflict is far from uncommon. Auditing and internal control, for example, would not surface without conflict. Similarly, we would be hard pressed to explain such phenomena as sizable bonus payments, sales contests, supervision, and piece rates without conflict.[12] Recognizing the potential for

---

[11]Technically, we structure the encounter between the firm and the manager as a noncooperative game. The firm moves first, announcing contract terms. This move is observed before the manager moves by selecting the feasible input to supply (or by refusing to work for the firm). A best response, or Nash, equilibrium is identified.

[12]Without conflict, the manager's pay component that is at risk would be explained by risk sharing.

conflict in this most elementary fashion also, it turns out, reveals a key insight in the art of performance evaluation.

limited public information

Self-interested behavior implies the manager will supply L, against the firm's wishes. This argument, however, is based on the assumption the firm naively offers a contract paying 8,000 in exchange for an unenforceable promise to supply H. The firm has other options.

Initially, suppose the manager's supply of input will be publicly observed. This means input supplied can be used in the contracting arrangement between the firm and the manager. Consider the following contract, where the manager's pay depends on the input supplied.

$$I(\text{input}) = \begin{cases} 8,000 \text{ if input} = H \\ 0 \text{ if input} = L \end{cases}$$

The manager will be paid $I(H) = 8,000$ if input H is supplied and $I(L) = 0$ if input L is supplied.

What might a self-interested manager do at this point? Again we resort to expected utility calculations:

$$E[U|H] = U(3,000) = -exp(-.0001[8,000-5,000]) = -exp(-.3); \text{ and}$$

$$E[U|L] = U(-2,000) = -exp(-.0001[0-2,000]) = -exp(.2).$$

Choice of H is compelling.

The idea is simple. With input publicly observed, a penalty contract can be used. The manager is paid the same amount as in the perfect market case if the agreed-upon input is supplied; otherwise, a nonperformance penalty is incurred. Opportunistic behavior by the supplier disappears. Self-interest now leads to supply of input H.

With the manager's behavior publicly observed, then, a simple penalty contract renders a story that mirrors the earlier one in which the manager could commit to

---

This is an uninteresting explanation, especially in light of a well functioning capital market that exists to orchestrate risk sharing arrangements.

We reiterate that the idea is some returns to employment accrue to the employer while others accrue to the employee; and we posit a conflict stemming from these two return streams. Mark Twain was eloquent on the point of conflict in an employment relationship when he wrote that "...Work consists of whatever a body is *obliged* to do, and that Play consists of whatever a body is not obliged to do." (*The Adventures of Tom Sawyer*, Chapter 4). Though we tell the story with $c_H > c_L$ we should not interpret this as a model based on an assumption of managerial laziness or aversion to work. It is a model based on differently valued returns to employment, at the margin.

supply the promised input.[13] In equilibrium, the manager supplies H and is paid 8,000.

Now suppose the only public observable is the output. The manager's input is not observable, so our penalty contract cannot be used. We cannot specify pay as a function of input, since input is not publicly observed. But we can specify pay as a function of output. Abstractly, we envision the following payment schedule:

$$I(output) = \begin{cases} I_1 \text{ if output} = x_1 \\ I_2 \text{ if output} = x_2. \end{cases}$$

Examine Figure 18.2, where we draw the manager's decision tree at the point of deciding between input H and input L.

Figure 18.2: Manager's Induced Decision Tree at Time of Input Supply

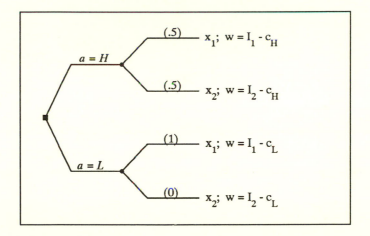

Expected utilities are readily expressed, using the noted probabilities:

$E[U|H] = .5U(I_1\text{-}c_H) + .5U(I_2\text{-}c_H);$ and

$E[U|L] = 1U(I_1\text{-}c_L) + 0U(I_2\text{-}c_L) = U(I_1\text{-}c_L).$

If the self-interested manager is to supply H, we must have

$E[U|H] \geq E[U|L].$ [IC]

This is called an *incentive compatibility* constraint. In designing the compensation arrangement, the firm faces the constraint that the desired behavior, supply of H

---

[13]This assumes a large enough penalty is feasible. If the manager's pay could not fall below 7,000, for example, this arrangement would not lead to supply of H with a wage of 8,000.

here, be incentive compatible. Goal congruence, the manager preferring to supply H, is a constraint!

Naturally, many payment arrangements are incentive compatible. Several are presented in Table 18.2. The first pays $I_1 = 2,000$ if low output, x_1, is observed and 18,000 if high output is observed. From the firm's perspective, this entails an expected payment of $E[I] = .5(2,000) + .5(18,000) = 10,000$, presuming the manager supplies input H. From the manager's perspective, we find

$$E[U|H] = -.5exp(-.0001[2,000-5,000]) - .5exp(-.0001[18,000-5,000])$$

$$= -.5exp(.3) -.5exp(-1.3) = -.8112 >$$

$$E[U|L] = -exp(-.0001[2,000-2,000]) = -exp(0) = -1.000.$$

Choice of H is incentive compatible.

Table 18.2: Selected Pay-for-Performance Schemes						
I_1	I_2	E[U|H]	E[U|L]	CE for H	CE for L	E[I]
2,000.00	18,000.00	-.8112	-1.000	2,092.46	0.00	10,000
4,000.00	14,000.00	-.7559	-.8187	2,798.85	2,000.00	9,000
2,000.00	25,266.39	-.7408	-1.0000	3,000.00	0.00	13,633
5,000.00	12,305.66	-.7408	-.7408	3,000.00	3,000.00	8,653

To make the expected utility numbers more intuitive, Table 18.2 also presents the respective certain equivalents. Thus, choice of input H here is equivalent to receiving a net payment of 2,092.46; that is, 2,092.46 is the certain equivalent of the I_i - c_H lottery (given input H is supplied).

Notice all the payment arrangements listed in Table 18.2 are incentive compatible. In each case it is in the manager's self-interest to supply input H instead of input L. Remember, however, that the manager has another employment option, one that promises a certain equivalent of M = 3,000. The first two schemes in Table 18.2 fail this test. The manager would never agree to them in the first place. Thus, another requirement for our payment arrangement is the so-called *individual rationality* condition of

$$E[U|H] \geq U(M). \tag{IR}$$

Finally, examine the last two schemes in Table 18.2 more closely. Each is incentive compatible (as supplying H is weakly in the manager's self-interest) and each is individually rational. Faced with either offer, the manager can do no better than accept the offer and then supply H. This results in a certain equivalent prospect of 3,000 = M, which precisely matches the outside opportunity. Here we assume that if indifferent the manager will honor the firm's wishes.[14]

Choice between these two schemes is thus a matter of indifference to the manager. Not so the firm; the expected payment to the manager is decidedly lower under the fourth scheme.

In fact the fourth scheme of $I_1 = 5,000$ and $I_2 = 12,305.66$ is the best such scheme. To see this, notice we want to minimize the cost to the firm while simultaneously attracting the manager from the labor market and maintaining an incentive to supply H over L. This implies we want to find the payment amounts I_1 and I_2 that solve the following optimization problem:

$$C(H) = \underset{I_1, I_2}{\text{minimum}} \; .5I_1 + .5I_2$$

$$\text{subject to:} \quad E[U|H] \geq U(M); \text{ and} \qquad \text{[IR]}$$
$$E[U|H] \geq E[U|L]. \qquad \text{[IC]}$$

The idea is the risk neutral firm wants to obtain input H at minimum cost. With risk neutrality, minimum cost means minimum expected payment to the manager, given input H is supplied. The manager's market opportunity and private supply of input provide two constraints. The payment scheme must be individually rational and incentive compatible.

Intuition guides us to the solution. Suppose we have a solution in which $E[U|H]$ is strictly greater than $U(M)$. We could then lower each payment a small amount, lowering the firm's cost and not upsetting the other constraint.[15] So anytime we have $E[U|H] > U(M)$, we can find a less costly scheme. Therefore, the best scheme must have $E[U|H] = U(M)$.

Similarly, suppose we have a scheme in which $E[U|H] > E[U|L]$. Now the incentive scheme is needlessly strong. Incentives, however, are not a free good. The manager's pay is at risk, and the manager must be compensated for carrying this risk. So if the incentives are too strong, they can be weakened in a way that lowers the cost to the firm. Hence, the best scheme must have $E[U|H] = E[U|L]$.[16]

---

[14]The alternative is to increase the incentive payment ever so slightly. This creates an annoying complication that offers no practical or intellectual insight. We thus assume when faced with indifference that the manager will follow the firm's instructions.

[15]To see the effect on the incentive compatibility constraint is neutral, write out the constraint for arbitrary I_1 and I_2. If this constraint is satisfied, payments of $I_1 - k$ and $I_2 - k$ also will satisfy the constraint, as *exp*(rk) factors out of both expected utility expressions.

[16]A more formal argument runs as follows. Delete the $E[U|H] \geq E[U|L]$ constraint and solve for the best payment scheme. This is our earlier arrangement in which $I_1 = I_2 = 8,000$. We know it is not incentive compatible. The solution must have the constraint imposed and binding, i.e., $E[U|H] = E[U|L]$. Our intuitive explanation is aided by using the negative exponential utility function and having two possible outcomes and two possible inputs. This is sufficient for our purpose. More generally, solving the design program of minimizing the firm's expected payment subject to individual rationality and incentive compatibility constraints requires additional work. Some spreadsheets contain nonlinear

We now have a constraint set of two equations in two unknowns: $E[U|H] = U(M)$ and $E[U|H] = E[U|L]$. Solving for I_1 and I_2 provides our solution.

Several features of this exercise should be noted. First, all the schemes in Table 18.2 have $I_2 > I_1$. This is no accident. Incentive compatibility requires $I_2 > I_1$. To the contrary, suppose we have $I_1 > I_2$. (We already know $I_1 = I_2$ does not work.) The manager would then face the following: at a lower cost, of c_L, the larger prize ($I_1 > I_2$) could be guaranteed. What a deal!

Second, with $I_2 > I_1$ the manager labors under an incentive arrangement. A bonus of $I_2 - I_1$ is paid if high output, i.e., x_2, is produced. Of course, this means the manager's wealth is at risk. This is contrary to efficient risk sharing, as the firm is risk neutral. In a sense, then, we trade off efficient risk sharing for incentive compatibility.

Also, by assuming $E[U|H] \geq U(M)$, we see the effect of this inefficient risk sharing in the firm's cost function. The cost to the firm is

$$C(H) = .5(5,000) + .5(12,305.66) = 8,652.83,$$

whereas the best arrangement when input is observable has a cost of 8,000. The difference of 652.83 is precisely the risk premium demanded by the manager to be saddled with the risky incentive package.[17]

Third, a popular euphemism is that the manager is now paid for results, or "only results count." This masks a subtle and important point. We want the manager to supply input H, but cannot directly observe whether input H is supplied. Output is observed, and we therefore use output to infer input. Casually, high output (i.e., x_2) is consistent with supply of input H, while low output (i.e., x_1) is more ambiguous. This is why the agent is paid more for high output.

Fourth, the overall exercise is one of engineering the manager's decision tree, at minimum cost to the firm. Figure 18.2 was designed to convey this insight. At the time of contracting, the manager has three alternatives: reject the firm's offer, accept the firm's offer and supply L (be disobedient), or accept the firm's offer and supply H (be obedient). Individual rationality requires $E[U|H] \geq U(M)$, and incentive compatibility requires $E[U|H] \geq E[U|L]$. The constraints literally ensure the manager's decision tree rolls back to the conclusion that supply of input H is desirable behavior from the manager's perspective.

---

optimization routines. We return to this theme in the Appendix to Chapter 19.

[17]8,000 is the manager's certain equivalent of a lottery that pays 5,000 with probability .5 and 12,305.66 with probability .5. Stated differently, 652.83 is the risk premium associated with this lottery. With $U(M)$ held constant throughout the exercise, the manager must be compensated to carry the risk of an incentive arrangement. Here the necessary compensation totals 652.83. Notice the story presumes the firm bears this added cost. We have structured the setting, holding the manager's opportunity cost constant, so this will be the case. More generally, we would take a broader view of equilibrium in the labor market to address the question of who bears this cost.

Finally, our story sharply distinguishes the cases of observable and unobservable input. In the former, the cost to the firm of input H is 8,000. In the latter, where only output is observed, the cost is 8,652.83 > 8,000. The cost arises because output is an imperfect indicator of input, requiring a risky payment to the manager; and we have grounded the model so the cost of the manager's risk bearing is borne by the firm. In this way we readily see that the firm would pay up to 652.83 to be able to observe the manager's input.

The Bad News

We might be growing impatient with this wedding of a simple story and tedious mathematics. So we pause for reassurance, and in the process will pull out additional insight.

trivial managerial risk aversion

What happens to the story if the manager is not risk averse? A convenient feature of the negative exponential utility function, recall, is that the parameter r measures risk aversion.

In Figure 18.3 we plot C(H) as a function of r. The plot uses the data in Table 18.1 and reflects the optimal incentive scheme when the only public observable is output. Notice how C(H) decreases as r decreases and converges to 8,000 as r goes to zero. When the manager is risk neutral, the firm can just as well contract on output as input. No substantive contracting friction is present when the manager is risk neutral. In such a case the firm would not pay to observe the manager's input.

Figure 18.3: Cost of Input H as a Function of r

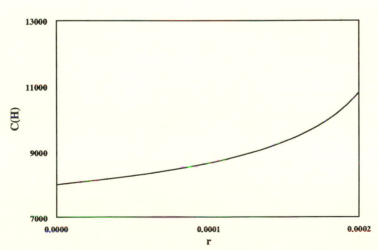

The intuition is straightforward. Efficient risk sharing and proper incentives generally are at odds. With efficient risk sharing, the manager receives a flat wage. This creates a free rider problem, as the manager incurs the personal cost of input H but receives none of the benefit. Tilting the payment package allows the manager to share in the benefit of costly input H, but at the implicit cost of inefficient risk sharing.

When the manager is close to risk neutral, tilting the payment package carries a trivial inefficiency. In the limit, the inefficiency disappears.[18] Efficient risk sharing and proper incentives have become one and the same.[19]

trivial odds of low output under input H

Now consider what happens as we allow the probability of high output under input H, parameter α, to increase. Our running example uses $\alpha = .5$. In Figure 18.4 we plot the C(H) as a function of probability α. Notice how increasing α decreases the firm's cost of input H. Stated differently, the contracting friction is lessened as α increases; and it disappears at the extreme of $\alpha = 1$.[20]

This illustrates the subtlety of the notion that we "pay-for-performance." The firm is arranging for the supply of input H but under difficult circumstances. It cannot see the input that is eventually supplied; and the supplier incurs an unobservable cost in supplying the wanted input.

The only indicator of input supply is the output. So the firm uses output to infer input. Output is used as a source of information in the contracting arrangement with the supplier. Now, as α increases, the quality of this information increases. In particular, x_2 becomes more likely given supply of H. With better information, the control problem is more easily solved, the risk sharing inefficiency decreases, and C(H) correspondingly decreases. In the limiting case of $\alpha = 1$, output becomes a perfect indicator of input. If $\alpha = 1$ and we see low output, we know without doubt the manager has not supplied H. This takes us back to the input observable case.

Output is here used to infer input for contracting purposes. Output is both a source of value to the firm and a source of information in dealing with the con-

---

[18]Conversely, increasing the manager's risk aversion increases C(H). In a more thorough analysis, then, we should allow the choice of input to vary as we indulge in comparative statics; and in the limit we should allow the firm to shut down.

[19]When the manager is risk neutral we have an entire spectrum of equivalent solutions. They all have the property that the expected payment to the manager is 8,000 and $I_2 - I_1 \geq 6,000$. Holding both the incentive compatibility and individual rationality constraints as equalities implies $I_1 = 5,000$ and $I_2 = 11,000$. Alternatively, the firm might simply sell out to the manager (a management take over) for a fixed price of 7,000. The manager then gets the entire output, so $I_1 = 10,000 - 7,000 = 3,000$; and $I_2 = 20,000 - 7,000 = 13,000$.

[20]You may wonder why the graph begins at $\alpha = .4$. The constraints are infeasible if α is too low. Examine the extreme case of $\alpha = 0$!

tracting frictions. The better output is as an indicator of input, the less costly the contracting friction.

Figure 18.4: Cost of Input H as a Function of α

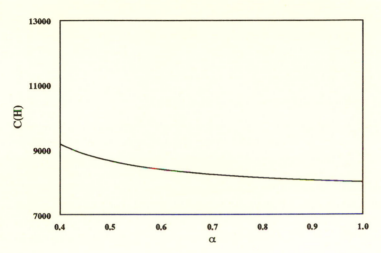

trivial incremental personal cost

A final drill focuses on c_L. The contracting friction is caused by the manager's personal cost and the lack of information. What happens when we hold the information constant but vary the personal cost? In Figure 18.5 we plot C(H) as the manager's personal cost of the low input, c_L, increases from 2,000 to 5,000. Notice that C(H) declines as c_L increases, and in the limit (where $c_L = 5,000$) we have no substantive contracting friction.

Once the manager agrees to the firm's offer, a choice between H and L must be faced. The incremental personal cost to the manager of supplying input H is $c_H - c_L$ = 5,000 - c_L. As we increase c_L toward 5,000, this incremental cost declines. In this sense, the magnitude of the control problem declines. As this happens, the inefficient risk sharing that is essential to motivate input H (using output to infer input, remember) declines. So C(H) declines. In the limit, the incremental personal cost to the manager is zero, and no control problem is present.

the unavoidable conclusion

These observations carry an important message for the study of performance evaluation. If the manager is risk neutral (r goes to zero), if the output is an unusually powerful source of information (α goes to one), or if the manager's incremental personal cost is trivial (c_L goes to c_H), the firm incurs no additional cost by not being able to observe the manager's input. In these extreme cases there is no demand for additional information to help resolve the control problem. There is no substantive control problem. There is no meaningful conflict of interest between the firm and the manager.

Figure 18.5: Cost of Input H as a Function of c_L

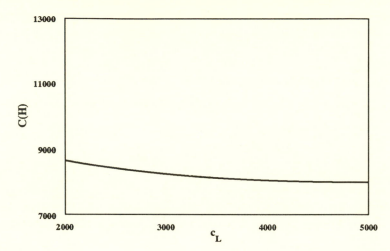

Our study requires a logically consistent story in which performance evaluation is a useful and nontrivial exercise. We therefore must avoid cases where the manager is risk neutral, where other sources of information are definitive in identifying the manager's input, and where the manager's personal cost is not an active friction. There is no reason to evaluate the manager in these cases.

Stated differently, if our stylization of contracting for managerial services is to admit an interest in nontrivial performance evaluation, we are forced to acknowledge several requirements. We must assume the manager is risk averse, $r > 0$; otherwise the manager is able to carry the risk of production and will fully internalize the potential conflict. We must assume uncertainty is nontrivially present in the production process, $\alpha < 1$; otherwise output can be used to infer the manager's input without error and performance evaluation is a trivial exercise. We must assume some inherent conflict, some personal cost of $c_H > c_L$, is present; otherwise there is nothing to control or worry about. Absent risk aversion, uncertainty, and personal cost, we base our study on a setting where there is no substantive interest in the art of performance evaluation.

The bad news is we must carry along considerable baggage if our story is to admit an economic reason for evaluating the manager's performance. The minimum baggage consists of risk aversion, uncertainty, and an inherent conflict of interest.

Professional management is not an easy task, and neither is the study of professional management.

The Firm's Choice

Somewhat masked by our focus on contracting details is the firm's primary choice of production plan. With the assumptions in Table 18.1 and output the only contracting variable, we know the firm's cost of input H is C(H) = 8,652.83.

Its cost of input L is unambiguous. With no contracting frictions, the firm would pay $I_L = c_L + M = 2,000 + 3,000 = 5,000$ for input L. Paying a constant amount in exchange for input L is also incentive compatible. Supplying H instead merely increases the manager's personal cost, with no attendant benefit to the manager.

The firm's expected profit, then, will be

$$(1-\alpha)x_1 + \alpha x_2 - C(H) = .5(10,000) + .5(20,000) - 8,652.83 = 6,347.17$$

if it selects the larger expected output and input H. Alternatively, it will be

$$x_1 - C(L) = 10,000 - 7,000 = 3,000$$

if it selects the smaller output and input L.

Larger expected output, requiring input H, is chosen. The contracting arrangement with the manager entails a bonus payment when larger output (x_2) is produced. Lack of information in the contracting arena results in a pay-for-performance arrangement.

In this sense we substitute inefficient risk sharing for lack of information. While descriptive, we should be selective in our labeling. The risk sharing is inefficient relative to the case of no contracting friction. But it is the best possible given the contracting frictions. A more precise description, then, would be the efficient *second best* arrangement distributes the risk between the firm and the manager in a way that is not efficient in the *first best* setting. First best refers to the case of no contracting frictions; second best refers to the case of contracting frictions.[21]

Pay-for-Performance When Performance Evaluation Information Is Available

The final step in our odyssey is the use of performance evaluation information. Stay with the story in Table 18.1. If the only contracting variable is the firm's output, we know the firm will select input H; and the manager will be compensated with a pay-for-performance arrangement that carries a cost to the firm of C(H) =

---

[21]Another point here concerns the choice of input. Our example in Table 18.1 is structured so the choice of input is the same in the first best and second best regimes. In general this will not be the case. Burdening the manager with risky pay increases the cost of managerial services. In addition, different production plans lead to output being more or less informative about the manager's input. Putting the two forces together, it would be unusual to have the choice of input the same in the first and second best settings.

8,652.83. As this exceeds the first best cost of 8,000, the firm would pay up to
652.83 for a performance evaluation system that revealed the manager's input.

We should hardly expect performance evaluation to be definitive. The
substantive question is, how much would the firm pay for a less than definitive
performance evaluation system? Answering this requires that we say something
about how the performance evaluation information will be used.

illustration

To illustrate, consider a performance evaluation system that will report one of
two observations: g (good news) or b (bad news). This report will be publicly
observed at the end of the game, at the same time the output is publicly observed.
The firm's contract with the manager can now depend on both the output and the
evaluative measure.

The joint probabilities are displayed in Table 18.3. Notice the consistency with
our earlier specification. The probability of high output under input H remains at α
= 0.5; and low output occurs for certain under input L. The conditions in Table 18.1
have merely been expanded to accommodate this second source of information.

Table 18.3: Joint Probabilities for Evaluation Example					
input H	x_1	x_2	input L	x_1	x_2
signal g	.35	.40	signal g	.2	0
b	.15	.10	b	.8	0

As noted, the manager's pay can now depend on output and the performance
evaluation measure:

$$I(\text{output,evaluation}) = \begin{cases} I_{1g} \text{ if output} = x_1 \text{ and evaluation} = g \\ I_{1b} \text{ if output} = x_1 \text{ and evaluation} = b \\ I_{2g} \text{ if output} = x_2 \text{ and evaluation} = g \\ I_{2b} \text{ if output} = x_2 \text{ and evaluation} = b \end{cases}$$

We now replicate our earlier analysis to find the firm's minimum cost method
of compensating the manager for supply of input H. Given some such compensation
arrangement, the manager's expected utilities are:

$$E[U|H] = .35U(I_{1g}\text{-}c_H) + .15U(I_{1b}\text{-}c_H) + .40U(I_{2g}\text{-}c_H) + .10U(I_{2b}\text{-}c_H); \text{ and}$$

$$E[U|L] = .2U(I_{1g}\text{-}c_L) + .8U(I_{1b}\text{-}c_L).$$

In turn, the firm's best choice of compensation arrangement is the solution to
the following program:

$$C(H) = \underset{I_{1g},I_{1b},I_{2g},I_{2b}}{\text{minimum}} .35I_{1g} + .15I_{1b} + .40I_{2g} + .10I_{2b}$$

$$\text{subject to: } E[U|H] \geq U(M); \text{ and}$$
$$E[U|H] \geq E[U|L].$$

The solution is displayed in Table 18.4, where we also repeat the solution for the case where the performance evaluation measure is not available. When the information is not available, the manager's payment can depend only on the output, implying $I_{1g} = I_{1b}$ and $I_{2g} = I_{2b}$.[22]

The optimal payment arrangements in the two regimes clearly differ; the firm's cost drops from $C(H) = 8,652.83$ to $C(H) = 8,148.70$ when we introduce the evaluation measure. More important is the manner in which this information is used.

Initially notice we find $I_{2g} = I_{2b}$. The evaluation measure will report good news (g) with probability .75 if the manager supplies input H. Under input L it will report good news with probability .2. Yet this information is not blindly followed in the compensation arrangement. When high output is reported (x_2), it is unmistakably clear the manager supplied input H. So the additional information in the presence of high output is superfluous. It is not used, and we find $I_{2g} = I_{2b}$.

	I_{1g}	I_{1b}	I_{2g}	I_{2b}	$C(H)$
Table 18.4: Optimal Pay-for-Performance Schemes					
evaluation measure used	8,590.23	4,272.98	9,002.35	9,002.35	8,148.70
no evaluation measure	5,000.00	5,000.00	12,305.66	12,305.66	8,652.83

Also notice we find $I_{1b} < I_{1g} < I_{2g}$. The manager's lowest payment occurs when output is low and the evaluation is bad news. We know from our earlier work that low output is an ambiguous outcome. If low output occurs, the probability of a good evaluation is .7 if input H is supplied and .2 if input L is supplied. Using obvious notation, these probabilities are verified as follows:

$$p(g|x_1,H) = p(x_1,g|H)/p(x_1|H) = .35/.50 = .7; \text{ and}$$

$$p(g|x_1,L) = p(x_1,g|L)/p(x_1|L) = .20/1.0 = .2.$$

See Table 18.3.

Given low output, then, an accompanying evaluation measure of bad news is relatively more consistent with the manager supplying L than H. When low output and a bad news evaluation occur, all indicators of the manager's input are unfavorable. The evaluation is negative. The manager's pay is therefore depressed. Conversely, low output together with a good news evaluation measure leads to an intermediate evaluation. One indicator is positive and the other is negative. The manager's evaluation and pay are therefore at an intermediate level.

---

[22]The solution is rounded to the nearest penny here. This is getting a bit far fetched, but it seems prudent not to round to the point a reader verifying the calculations would be led astray.

Overall, the contracting problem with the manager is resolved with a less risky incentive arrangement. With or without the evaluation information, the individual rationality condition ensures the manager's expected utility equals U(M). However, the risk premium necessary to maintain the arrangement's attractiveness declines when the evaluation information is used. This illustrates the insurance side of performance evaluation. Introducing the monitor allows the firm to maintain incentives with less risk placed on the manager. The monitor provides a basis for insuring, to a limited degree, the manager against the noisy relationship between output and input.

the likelihood ratio

A more mechanical explanation will reinforce these observations and prove useful later. The trick is to rewrite the expected utility notation in a more convenient format. If the manager is paid amount I while supplying input a, the utility measure is $U(I-c_a)$. In the exponential specification, this expression factors:

$$U(I-c_a) = -exp\langle -r[I-c_a]\rangle = -exp\langle -rI\rangle \cdot exp\langle rc_a\rangle.$$

From here, we express the L input case in a seemingly awkward but useful way as

$$U(I-c_L) = -exp\langle -rI\rangle \cdot exp\langle rc_L\rangle = -exp\langle -rI\rangle \cdot exp\langle r[c_L-c_H+c_H]\rangle.$$

Now reshuffle one of the c_H terms:

$$U(I-c_L) = -exp\langle -r[I-c_H]\rangle \cdot exp\langle r[c_L-c_H]\rangle$$

$$= U(I-c_H)\cdot exp\langle r[c_L-c_H]\rangle = kU(I-c_H).$$

where the constant $k = exp\langle r[c_L-c_H]\rangle$ is strictly positive.

Next, suppose there are n possible output realizations, indexed by $i = 1, ..., n$, and m possible evaluation realizations, indexed by $j = 1, ..., m$. (The story in Table 18.4 has $n = m = 2$.) Denote the probability that combination i and j will occur under input H by α_{ij}. We will assume $\alpha_{ij} > 0$. Also denote the probability that combination i and j will occur under input L by $\bar{\alpha}_{ij}$. Likewise, let I_{ij} be the payment to the manager when i and j occur. This notation allows us to express the incentive compatibility constraint as:

$$E[U|H] = \Sigma_i\Sigma_j \alpha_{ij}U(I_{ij}-c_H) \geq E[U|L] = \Sigma_i\Sigma_j \bar{\alpha}_{ij}U(I_{ij}-c_L) = \Sigma_i\Sigma_j \bar{\alpha}_{ij}kU(I_{ij}-c_H).$$

Now rearrange the terms in judicious fashion:

$$E[U|H] - E[U|L] = \Sigma_i\Sigma_j [\alpha_{ij}U(I_{ij}-c_H) - \bar{\alpha}_{ij}kU(I_{ij}-c_H)] \geq 0; \text{ or}$$

$$\Sigma_i\Sigma_j [\alpha_{ij}U(I_{ij}-c_H)][1-k\bar{\alpha}_{ij}/\alpha_{ij}] \geq 0.$$

This is revealing. The first pair of brackets in the summation encloses the expected utility term for the i and j combination, presuming supply of H. The second pair of brackets encloses an adjustment factor of one less a constant times the likelihood ratio, $\tilde{\alpha}_{ij}/\alpha_{ij}$. This ratio might be zero, large, or intermediate. (Recall we assume the denominator $\alpha_{ij} \geq 0$.) Table 18.5 displays the ratio for our running example, along with the optimal incentive payments. Notice the higher the ratio, the lower the manager's payment.

Table 18.5: Likelihood Ratios and Optimal Payments				
	x_1 and g	x_1 and b	x_2 and g	x_2 and b
probability under L	.20	.80	0	0
probability under H	.35	.15	.40	.10
ratio ($\tilde{\alpha}_{ij}/\alpha_{ij}$)	.57	5.33	0	0
optimal payment	8,590	4,273	9,002	9,002

Suppose the ratio is large for some i and j combination. If $U(I_{ij}-c_H)$ is also large, we have exacerbated our problem of satisfying the inequality. So a large ratio implies $U(I_{ij}-c_H)$ should be small, or I_{ij} should be small. Similarly, a small ratio implies I_{ij} should be larger. Intuitively, if the ratio is large, then occurrence of the i and j combination is more likely under input L than input H. This is bad news. Performance is judged not good. Low payment is in order. If the ratio is small, occurrence of the i and j combination is more likely under input H. This is good news. Performance is judged to be good; and a higher payment is in order.

The joint information content of the output (index i) and the evaluation (index j) is related to the likelihood ratio, $\tilde{\alpha}_{ij}/\alpha_{ij}$. It is akin to testing the hypothesis that the manager supplied input H. If the i and j realization is largely consistent with this hypothesis, a larger payment is delivered. Otherwise, a smaller payment is in order. Information content is the key.

Summary

This chapter focuses on managerial performance evaluation. The central theme is a firm seeking to acquire managerial inputs in a less than perfect market setting. When input is not observed, directly or indirectly, and when there is a natural conflict between the supplier and the firm, we have an interest in evaluating the performance of the manager. The purpose of the evaluation is to form a basis for inferring the input supplied by the manager.

The solution to this exercise is a pay-for-performance arrangement. Better performance is rewarded. This common euphemism, though, clouds the underlying idea that performance is an indicator of input. Literally, we use performance to infer input. The best use of the information is to pay-for-performance.

The model we have sketched will provide considerable insight in subsequent chapters; but we should also acknowledge its heavily streamlined, nearly simplistic nature. We have not addressed such confounding features as taxes, reputation, nonpecuniary rewards, culture and long-term relationships. Taxes, for example, may influence payment arrangements. Some forms of compensation are tax advantaged. Health benefits, work place ambiance, and retirement savings are ready examples.[23] The manager's reputation also may be an important factor in the employment relationship. Defined entry portals may be used so the firm can calibrate the manager's talent. In this way, some jobs are designed to provide the firm with important information about the talent of its work force. Long-term arrangements, in turn, usually take the form of implicit arrangements. The firm may have a policy of filling managerial vacancies by promotion. It may assign a management team to a particularly troubled division with the understanding that a future assignment will be in a more affable environment.

The list goes on. Our purpose is not to cover the entire spectrum of human resource management.[24] Rather, we want to proceed at this point with the basic insight that we use output, broadly interpreted, to infer input. This leads to the question of which accounting outputs are useful in inferring a particular manager's inputs.

Though sufficient for our purpose, we should keep in mind that a broader view of contracting frictions recognizes various types of frictions. So-called moral hazard problems arise when there is the possibility of post-contract opportunism. This was emphasized in our exploration, where the manager but not the firm knew the input supplied. Adverse selection refers to pre-contract opportunism. Buying a used car from its current owner is an example, where the seller but not the buyer knows whether the car is a lemon. And lack of commitment ability can further hinder contracting arrangements. Our manager could not commit to deliver an agreed upon input supply. The firm may not be able to commit to explicit long-term arrangements or to use fairly any information it privately acquires in the evaluation process.

Bibliographic Notes

The principal-agent model, developed here in highly stylized fashion, has become an important model of trade and resource allocation. Sappington [1991] provides an excellent introduction and survey. Kreps [1990], Chapter 16, provides

---

[23]Another example is provided by a startup organization. Here the firm is unlikely to have taxable income in its early years. Other things equal, then, it is likely a mutually advantageous compensation package can be designed that defers some compensation until the firm is profitable. In this case, sophisticated tax planning between the firm and its labor force takes on the appearance of pay-for-performance.

[24]As one more example, the highly stylized model does not explicitly address fairness. It treats the manager's opportunity cost as exogenous, and identifies the minimum cost solution from the firm's perspective, while recognizing this opportunity cost and whatever information limitations are present. In broader terms this can be interpreted as a focus on a second best efficient arrangement, with the question of level of compensation outside the analysis.

a comprehensive introduction to the technical details. Hart and Holmstrom [1987] provide an overview of the larger picture. Arrow [1974] is particularly eloquent on trade frictions. Our use of the model is patterned after that in Grossman and Hart [1983]. The likelihood ratio connection is developed in Holmstrom [1979] and Shavell [1979]. Additional threads of the story used here are developed in Stiglitz [1974], Demski and Feltham [1978], and Harris and Raviv [1978]. We will see in subsequent chapters how this building block is used to examine such themes as communication, decentralization, responsibility accounting, and coordination.

Problems and Exercises

1. The central idea in the chapter is that some productive inputs are not acquired in perfect markets, are not necessarily delivered in the quality and quantity intended. In turn, this creates an interest in controls of some sort, controls designed to address frictions inherent in the trade of labor for compensation. The stylized model of personally costly input highlights the use of output in the control apparatus. How, in this model, is output used to facilitate the purchase of input? Why is the supplier paid for performance?

2. Goal congruence is said to exist when members of the management team (or more broadly the work force) share the same goals; and in this perspective goal congruence is seen as an essential objective of organization design. The stylized model presented in the chapter offers a subtly different perspective. Goal congruence is a constraint, manifest in the [IC] restriction requiring the self-interested manager find it personally desirable (or incentive compatible) to behave in the organization's best interest. Carefully discuss this notion of goal congruence as a constraint.

3. The development beginning in Table 18.1 results in a cost to the organization of input H that we denoted $C(H)$. Without contracting frictions, the manager would be paid the sum of reservation price plus personal cost, or $M + c_H$. It turns out the quantity $C(H) - (M+c_H)$, is equal to the manager's risk premium for the compensation risk presuming input H is supplied. Carefully explain why this linkage between incremental cost to the organization and risk premium to the manager arises in the contracting model.

4. *certain equivalents*
Verify the certain equivalent calculations summarized in Table 18.2. Notice, in this case, the certain equivalents can be calculated in two ways. One method calculates the certain equivalent of the I_i lottery and then subtracts the c_a cost. The other method focuses directly on the certain equivalent of the lottery of net gains, $I_i - c_a$. Why are the two methods equivalent here?

5. *manager's opportunity cost*

Return to the last row in Table 18.2, where the optimal pay-for-performance arrangement is displayed. The underlying data (in Table 18.1) assume M = 3,000. Locate an optimal contract for the following cases: (i) M = 2,500; (ii) M = 2,000; (iii) M = 1,000; and (iv) M = 0. Carefully explain the emerging pattern.

6. *insurance and incentives*

The contracting model presented here is called a "hidden action" or "moral hazard" model. The latter term comes from the insurance phenomenon where an insured subject has reduced care incentives. For example, is it likely that the owner-operator of an automobile drives more diligently and less frequently when the auto's insurance has lapsed? Is the implied delicate balancing of risk sharing, or insurance, and proper incentives present in the labor input model? Explain, using the data in Table 18.2.

7. *optimal contract*

Return to the setting of Table 18.1 (and solution in Table 18.2). Now assume the probability of output x_1 under input L is .9 instead of 1.0. Determine the optimal pay-for-performance arrangement. Carefully explain the difference between this arrangement and that identified in Table 18.2. (Hint: $I_1 = 4,372.17$.)

8. *optimal contract*

Ralph owns a production function. Randomness in the environment plus labor input from a manager combine to produce output. The output can be one of two quantities: $x_1 < x_2$. The manager's input can be one of two quantities, L < H. Ralph is risk neutral. The probabilities are given below:

	x_1	x_2
input H	.1	.9
input L	.8	.2

Assume the higher output is sufficiently attractive that Ralph wants supply of input H in all that follows.

Ralph's manager is risk averse and also incurs an unobservable personal cost in supplying the labor input. We model this in the usual way. The manager's utility for wealth $\hat{w}$ is given by $U(\hat{w}) = -exp(-r\hat{w})$. If the manager supplies input $a \in \{H,L\}$, thereby incurring personal cost c_a, and is paid amount I, wealth will total $I - c_a$. We use $c_H = 5,000$ and $c_L = 0$, along with a risk aversion parameter of $r = .0001$. Also, the manager's opportunity cost of working for Ralph is U(M), with M = 10,000.

a] Suppose the manager is trustworthy and will honor any agreement (or, equivalently, serious penalties are feasible and the manager's input can be observed.) What is the cost to Ralph of acquiring input H?

b] Suppose the only observable for contracting purposes is the manager's output. Determine the optimal pay-for-performance arrangement.[25] What is the cost to Ralph of acquiring input H? Draw the manager's decision tree and verify the manager can do no better than accept Ralph's terms and then supply input H. What is the manager's certain equivalent for the payment lottery that is faced?

c] Why, in your solution to part [b] above, is the manager paid more when the largest feasible output (i.e., x_2) is observed?

9. *shape of optimal incentives*

This is a continuation of problem 8 above. Now assume there are three possible outputs, $x_1 < x_2 < x_3$. The probability structure is listed below, and input H is desired.

	x_1	x_2	x_3
input H	.1	.8	.1
input L	.7	.2	.1

Determine an optimal pay-for-performance arrangement. Why has Ralph's cost gone up, compared with the setting in the original problem? Also, why is the manager now paid more for intermediate than for the most desirable (x_3) output?

10. *smoothing behavior*

Return to the problem 9 above. Casually, we might interpret the story as one in which the manager receives a bonus when x_2 is produced, but no additional reward if even more is produced. Might the manager now be tempted to inventory or otherwise "hide" output in the short-run once enough output has been produced to qualify for the bonus? What (convenient) assumption in the simple model removes this possibility?

---

[25]You will want to use an optimization program as found in, say, a typical spreadsheet software package here. These are modest packages that, on occasion, may have difficulty locating an optimal solution. A simple, though laborious, change of variables will usually work when this happens. The trick is to frame the problem so the [IR] and [IC] constraints are linear.

Recall the manager is paid I_i when output x_i is observed. Define $V_i = -exp(-rI_i)$; also define the constants $k_1 = exp(rc_L)$ and $k_2 = exp(rc_H)$. We now have $U(I_i-c_L) = k_1V_i$ and $U(I_i-c_H) = k_2V_i$. (You should verify this.) Also, notice $ln(-V_i) = -rI_i$, or $I_i = -\{ln(-V_{ij})\}/r$.

Now use these expressions to write down the problem of minimizing the organization's expected cost subject to the [IR] and [IC] constraints. The trick is to focus on the utility rather than the cash delivered to the manager:

$$C(H) = minimum \ (-1/r)[.1ln(-V_1) + .9ln(-V_2)]$$
$$V_i$$
$$subject \ to: \ k_2[.1V_1 + .9V_2] \geq U(M); \ and$$
$$k_2[.1V_1 + .9V_2] \geq k_1[.8V_1 + .2V_2].$$

Finally, the objective function can be further streamlined by invoking the first principle of consistent framing. Maximization of $(-V_1)^1(-V_2)^9$, subject to the noted linear constraints, will identify the optimal pay-for-performance arrangement.

11. *qualitative shape of optimal incentives*

Consider a costly input setting in which output (x_i) can take one of four possible values. Input can be either L or H, with H desired by the risk neutral organizer. The input supplier is risk averse, and incurs an unobservable personal cost associated with input supply. We use the preference structure in problem 8 above, with r = .0001, $c_H = 5,000$ and $c_L = 0$. Let the supplier's next best opportunity offer a wealth of M = 7,000. The output probabilities are given below.

	x_1	x_2	x_3	x_4
input H	.1	.2	.3	.4
input L	.4	.3	.2	.1

Let I_i denote the payment to the input supplier when output x_i is observed. Without solving for an optimal arrangement, rank the four payments from lowest to highest. Carefully explain your answer.

12. *optimal contract*

Determine an optimal contract for the setting in problem 11 above.

13. *optimal production plan*

Ralph, who is risk neutral, owns a production process. Production requires input from a manager. This input can be one of three possible quantities: L < B < H. Output will be one of two possible quantities: $x_1 < x_2$. The manager is risk averse and incurs a personal cost in supplying input. The manager's utility for wealth $\hat{w}$ is given by $U(\hat{w}) = -exp(-r\hat{w})$, with r = .0001. If the manager supplies input a∈{L,B,H} and subsequently is paid amount I, wealth totals $\hat{w} = I - c_a$. We assume $c_L = 0$, $c_B = 4,000$ and $c_H = 10,000$. Also, the manager's outside opportunity guarantees a wealth of M = 40,000. The output probabilities are as follows.

	x_1	x_2
input H	0	1
input B	.1	.9
input L	.9	.1

a] Suppose the parties can contract on the output and the input supplied. Determine the best contract from Ralph's perspective that will insure supply of input (i) H, (ii) B, and (iii) L.

b] Suppose the parties can contract on the output, but not the input supplied. Determine the best contract from Ralph's perspective that will insure supply of input (i) H, (ii) B, and (iii) L.

c] Let $x_1 = 0$ and $x_2 = 55,000$. Determine Ralph's optimal plan under the contracting conditions in [a] and under the contracting conditions in [b] above.

d] Let $x_1 = 0$ and $x_2 = 59,000$. Determine Ralph's optimal plan under the contracting conditions in [a] and under the contracting conditions in [b] above. Carefully explain your conclusions.

e]   Let $x_1 = 41,000$ and $x_2 = 46,100$. Determine Ralph's optimal plan under the contracting conditions in [a] and under the contracting conditions in [b] above. Carefully explain your conclusions.

14. *taxes and incentives*

Consider a setting where the manager's input can be L or H and the output can be $x_1 = 10,000$ or $x_2 = 50,000$. The manager's preferences are described in the usual fashion, with utility for wealth $\hat{w}$ given by $U(\hat{w}) = -exp(-r\hat{w})$, where $\hat{w}$ is the net of payment I and personal cost c_a. Let $r = .0001$. Also, the manager's opportunity cost of working for this organization is $U(M)$, with $M = 0$. The owner is risk neutral. The output probabilities are:

	x_1	x_2
input H	.1	.9
input L	.8	.2

Assume $c_H = c_L = 5,000$. Input H is desired throughout the exercise.

a]   Determine and interpret an optimal contract.

b]   Suppose the owner is subject to a 20% income tax (i.e., a tax equal to 20% of the net of $x_i - I_i$), while the manager faces a zero marginal tax rate. Determine and interpret an optimal contract.

c]   Repeat [b] above for the case where the owner is subject to a 20% income tax on income in excess of 20,000.

d]   Repeat [c] above for the case $c_L = 4,000$.

e]   Repeat [c] above for the case $c_L = 0$.

15. *square root utility*

Ralph owns a production function that uses labor input to produce output. Output will be either $x_1 = 10,000$ or $x_2 = 20,000$. Labor is supplied by an agent. One of three possible supplies will be used: H > B > L. The output probabilities are displayed below:

	x_1	x_2
input H	0	1
input B	.5	.5
input L	1	0

Ralph is risk neutral. The agent has a utility function for payment z and labor supply a of $U(z,a) = \sqrt{z} - V(a)$, with $V(H) = 60$, $V(B) = 30$, and $V(L) = 5$. In addition, the agent's next best offer carries a pay, labor supply package that provides an expected utility of 40. So whatever Ralph dreams up, the expected value of $U(z,a)$ must be at least 40 if the agent is to be attracted.

a]   Ralph must decide which a∈{L,B,H} to acquire, and how to compensate the agent for this supply of labor. If the agent can be trusted to supply whatever is agreed upon, it is straightforward to figure out $C(a) = [40 + V(a)]^2$. Determine $C(a)$ for each a∈{L,B,H}. What is Ralph's best choice?

b]   Now assume output is the only contracting variable. Determine the best compensation package to motivate supply of (i) a = L, (ii) a = B, and (iii) a = H. In turn, what is Ralph's best choice and why does this differ from the best choice in the case where the agent can be trusted?

c]   In the a = B case immediately above, you should have found the agent is paid more if the high output is produced. Why is this the case?

16. *framing*
        In note 25 we reformulated the problem of locating a best pay-for-performance arrangement to focus on the manager's utility, as opposed to pay, as the choice variable. Since the manager's preferences were measured by expected utility, this allowed us to write the constraints as linear inequalities. The final step was to suggest transforming the objective to maximization of $(-V_1)^{-1}(-V_2)^9$. Justify this last step in terms of the first principle of consistent framing, as developed in Chapter 11.

17. *personal cost*
        At this point some reflection is in order. What role does personal cost play in the contracting model developed in this chapter? Does the theory require c_a to be everywhere positive? Is the model based on the idea managers find work repulsive?

19

Evaluation Based on Controllable Performance

We now extend our use of the managerial input model to examine which data in the accounting library might be used in the evaluation of a manager. The idea is to ask the model what types of data it finds useful in the evaluation exercise. Studying the model's answer will provide important clues for understanding the selective use of accounting and nonaccounting information in the managerial evaluation process.

The longstanding intuition here is a manager should be evaluated based on variables the manager can control. For example, a retail store manager is typically evaluated based on the store's income, or revenue and expense. The manager is able to influence, to a degree, the productivity of the store's labor force through work assignments, supervision, and so on. Similarly, activities of the work force indirectly affect the store's attractiveness to customers and thereby influence demand. Revenue and expense are, to a degree, controllable by the manager.

Now complicate the story. Suppose central management selects the merchandise that will be stocked. If some of this merchandise does not sell and must be put on sale, the store's revenue will be less than it otherwise would be. Should the manager then receive credit for the sales markdown?[1] For example, suppose the store's revenue totaled 430,000 dollars but would have totaled 500,000 had the same merchandise been sold but with no markdowns. Do we want to evaluate the store manager in terms of 430,000 revenue or in terms of 500,000? More broadly, the question is whether to evaluate the manager based on revenue and expense or based on revenue, expense, and markdowns.

The answer to this question depends on what we will term the information content of the markdown. The evaluation question is not as simple as whether the manager controls markdowns. Nor is it as simple as whether markdowns tell us something about the manager's performance. Properly framed, the question is whether, given that we know revenue and expense, the markdowns tell us something about the manager's performance.

An analogy may be helpful. Suppose we are told it is raining in New York City. Is the communication informative? It is if we know nothing else. What if we are

---

[1]A markdown is the difference between the original price and the actual price. Consider an item with an original retail price of 25 dollars. Suppose it is subsequently placed on sale, at a price of 19, and is sold. Revenue is 19. One way to record this transaction is to record revenue of 19. Another way is to record revenue of 25 less a markdown of 6. The markdown is simply a variance in standard cost terminology.

habitual readers of weather reports? The fact of rain is not going to be very informative, as we already know the up to date forecast. (This is not to say the fact of rain would be completely uninformative.) The key to understanding what data might be useful in evaluating a manager is to ask what a particular measure tells us, not by itself but in the presence of the other measures we are using.

We begin with some evaluation anecdotes, selected to convey the breadth of practice. Next we return to the model developed in Chapter 18 and explore the information content of an evaluation measure. This leads to a refined notion of evaluation based on controllable performance. The evaluation anecdotes are then reinterpreted. We then conclude with a brief look at management by exception, where unusual performance is examined more closely than customary or normal performance.

Performance Evaluation Vignettes

Consider a supervisor in a manufacturing department in a job shop. To give the story more content, think of the supervisor in the service department in a large auto dealership. Many customers arrive, requiring a variety of repair services. The supervisor schedules the repair tasks and oversees the work of the mechanics. Standard labor times are available for each repair task. A primary evaluation measure is the direct labor quantity variance. The evaluation process takes the repair tasks performed as a given and asks whether they were done efficiently.

The story does not end here. The dealership asks customers to mail in a service quality questionnaire; the general manager regularly visits the service facility; and the service manager is likely to receive a year-end bonus if the dealership as a whole is profitable. We see a mix of accounting data, qualitative assessment by the general manager, nonfinancial data from the customers, and firm-wide profitability used in the evaluation of the service department manager.

Next consider a sales person. This individual contacts and visits many individuals, searching for new customers and managing the implicit relationship between the firm and its customers. The primary evaluation measure is orders received. The sales group is also engaged in a contest. The sales person with the largest total sales for the period receives special recognition, a holiday trip, and a bonus. In this fashion the performance of peer sales personnel is used to evaluate the sales person in question. Performance is evaluated relative to that of a peer group.

This tactic of relative performance evaluation is quite common. Grading students "on the curve" is another illustration. Use of industry comparisons, where an executive is evaluated based on division income relative to the income of competitors, is another. The State of Connecticut uses spending and student performance measures from peer schools to evaluate each school district under its jurisdiction.

Now envision the manager of a manufacturing facility in an integrated organization. Goods manufactured in this facility are transferred to a marketing group, where warehousing, distribution and so on are handled. Standard manufacturing costs have been established for each product. These standards set the stage for using actual versus budgeted manufacturing cost, given the list of goods manufactured, as a primary evaluation measure. Other statistics are also used, including summaries of equipment downtime, employee turnover, on time delivery, and warranty claims that arise from customer use of previously manufactured and sold products.

Primarily the manufacturing manager is evaluated as a cost center. This raises the question of whether the manager would be better evaluated as a profit center. Shipments to the marketing group could be recognized at some agreed-upon standard price. The manager would then have more of a profit enhancement rather than manufacturing cost minimization orientation.[2]

Finally, ponder the plight of the local manager in a fast food chain. Cost control is important, as is revenue growth. The manager is evaluated as a profit center. A profit goal is negotiated with a regional supervisor, reflecting performance of peer outlets in the chain and local conditions. For example, a nearby construction project may temporarily increase or decrease demand at this outlet. In addition, the manager's performance is rated on a variety of nonfinancial dimensions, relating to the outlet's appearance and quality of the standardized food products offered.

Taken together, we have a variety of evaluation practices. Portions of the accounting library are brought to bear, together with qualitative and quantitative information from a variety of sources. The common theme is supply of useful information to the evaluation task.

We now return to the managerial input model to give more structure to this notion of information that is useful for evaluation purposes.

Back to the Managerial Input Model

The managerial input model explored in Chapter 18 features a risk neutral organization that contracts for the services of a manager. The manager incurs an unobservable personal cost in supplying these services, or input. Two input quantities are feasible, high (H) and low (L). High is wanted by the organization. The catch is the manager's supply is not observed, and the manager prefers, other things equal, to supply low.

The details are filled in by assuming the manager is strictly risk averse, with utility for wealth $\hat{w}$ given by $U(\hat{w}) = -exp(-r\hat{w})$. If the manager supplies input $a \in \{H,L\}$, incurring personal cost c_a, and is subsequently paid the amount I, wealth will total $I - c_a$. We continue to use $c_H = 5,000$ and $c_L = 2,000$, along with a risk

---

[2]We might continue to expand the evaluation base in this manner and also focus on the assets utilized in the manufacturing operation. We then have revenue, cost, and assets brought into the evaluation. This is called an investment center, in the sense profit relative to investment base is an important focus in the evaluation.

aversion parameter of r = .0001. Also, the manager's opportunity cost of working for this organization is U(M), with M = 3,000.[3]

In Table 19.1 we summarize several versions of this basic story. All are keyed to a base case in which observable output will be low (x_1) or high (x_2). Low input (L) results in low output for certain. High input (H) results in high output with probability .5. The organization seeks supply of input H from the manager. The control problem centers on the fact the manager incurs less personal cost with input L, and output is an ambiguous indicator of input. Low output, in particular, is consistent with low input and with high input coupled with bad luck.

The notation is carried over from Chapter 18. Output can be low or high, and is indexed by i (= 1,2). An evaluation measure can be "good" or "bad" and is indexed by j (= g,b). The joint probability of output i (i = 1,2) and evaluation j (j = g,b) when the manager supplies input H is denoted α_{ij}. The corresponding joint probability under input L is denoted $\bar{\alpha}_{ij}$. Finally, the manager's compensation, upon observing output i and evaluation j, is denoted I_{ij}.

The base case in Table 19.1 is one in which the evaluation measure is not available.[4] The pay-for-performance plan can only depend on output. The best arrangement is to pay 12,305.66 for high output and 5,000 for low output.

By way of contrast, an ideal arrangement would have the risk neutral organization bear the output risk and the risk averse manager face a guaranteed wage. (This would imply an input cost to the organization of C(H) = 8,000.) With input unobservable and the inherent conflict of interest, though, the ideal arrangement is not incentive compatible. So the organization and manager instead agree upon a mutually satisfactory pay-for-performance arrangement. In this way, output is used to infer input. The inference, though, is not perfect, and the resulting expected payment to the manager of 8,652.83 reflects the additional cost of compensating the manager for bearing nontrivial compensation risk.

Cases A through D are all variations on this theme. All are consistent with the base case. Under input H the probability of low output is $\alpha_{1g} + \alpha_{1b} = .5$. Similarly, the probability of low output under L is $\bar{\alpha}_{1g} + \bar{\alpha}_{1b} = 1$ in each case. Within these guidelines only the high input probabilities vary. They vary in such a way that the evaluation measure (of j = g or b) is useful in cases A and B, and useless in cases C and D. In particular, the optimal incentive arrangements in cases C and D have $I_{ig} = I_{ib}$. The evaluation measure is not used and the solution is identical with that in the base case where no evaluation information is available. This is in contrast to cases A and B, where the information is used.

---

[3]An initial wealth of w_0 is also present; but an advantage of the particular utility function is risk aversion is not affected by initial wealth. So we continue with the implicit assumption that initial wealth is zero. For that matter, M, too, is simply an arbitrary constant here.

[4]If the evaluation measure is not available, the story is one in which j = g,b is not observed. This is equivalent to a story in which the evaluation measure is available but always reports the same thing, say j = g. The layout in Table 19.1 relates the story in this fashion.

Table 19.1: Optimal Incentive Payments in Various Cases				
	output (i = 1,2) and evaluation (j = g,b)			
	x_1 and g	x_1 and b	x_2 and g	x_2 and b
base case				
probability under L $(\bar{\alpha}_{ij})$	1.	0	0	0
probability under H (α_{ij})	.50	0	.50	0
likelihood ratio $(\bar{\alpha}_{ij}/\alpha_{ij})$	2.00		0.00	
payment; $E[I_{ij}]$ = 8,652.83	5,000.00		12,305.66	
case A				
probability under L $(\bar{\alpha}_{ij})$	.20	.80	0	0
probability under H (α_{ij})	.35	.15	.40	.10
likelihood ratio $(\bar{\alpha}_{ij}/\alpha_{ij})$	.57	5.33	0	0
payment; $E[I_{ij}]$ = 8,148.70	8,590.23	4,272.98	9,002.35	9,002.35
case B				
probability under L $(\bar{\alpha}_{ij})$	.20	.80	0	0
probability under H (α_{ij})	.15	.35	.05	.45
likelihood ratio $(\bar{\alpha}_{ij}/\alpha_{ij})$	1.33	2.29	0	0
payment; $E[I_{ij}]$ = 8,557.56	8,053.70	4,362.86	11,645.01	11,645.01
case C				
probability under L $(\bar{\alpha}_{ij})$	.20	.80	0	0
probability under H (α_{ij})	.10	.40	.40	.10
likelihood ratio $(\bar{\alpha}_{ij}/\alpha_{ij})$	2.00	2.00	0	0
payment; $E[I_{ij}]$ = 8,652.83	5,000.00	5,000.00	12,305.66	12,305.66
case D				
probability under L $(\bar{\alpha}_{ij})$	.20	.80	0	0
probability under H (α_{ij})	.10	.40	.10	.40
likelihood ratio $(\bar{\alpha}_{ij}/\alpha_{ij})$	2.00	2.00	0	0
payment; $E[I_{ij}]$ = 8,652.83	5,000.00	5,000.00	12,305.66	12,305.66

To understand this pattern of solutions, we must explore the organization's problem of locating an optimal pay-for-performance package. In broad terms the control problem centers on motivating the manager's supply of input H, as opposed to input L, and simultaneously making the employment package sufficiently attractive. Given some pay-for-performance schedule of I_{ij}, the manager's expected utility measure under input H is

$$E[U|H] = \Sigma_i\Sigma_j\ U(I_{ij}\text{-}c_H)\alpha_{ij} = \text{-}\Sigma_i\Sigma_j\ exp\langle\text{-}r(I_{ij}\text{-}c_H)\rangle\alpha_{ij}.$$

Under input L the measure is

$$E[U|L] = \Sigma_i\Sigma_j\ U(I_{ij}\text{-}c_L)\tilde{\alpha}_{ij} = \text{-}\Sigma_i\Sigma_j\ exp\langle\text{-}r(I_{ij}\text{-}c_L)\rangle\tilde{\alpha}_{ij}.$$

An incentive compatibility constraint of $E[U|H] \geq E[U|L]$ ensures that when faced with choice between H and L the manager will select H. Similarly, an individual rationality constraint of $E[U|H] \geq U(M)$ ensures the package is attractive to the manager. Together, these constraints guarantee it is in the manager's best interest to accept the arrangement and, once accepted, to supply H rather than L.

Among all such arrangements, the organization selects the one that offers it the minimum expected cost. The incentive arrangements displayed in Table 19.1, then, are all derived by solving the following design program:

$$C(H) = \underset{I_{ij}}{\text{minimum}}\ \Sigma_i\Sigma_j\ I_{ij}\alpha_{ij}$$
$$\text{subject to:}\ \ E[U|H] \geq U(M);\ \text{and}$$
$$E[U|H] \geq E[U|L].$$

As hinted in Chapter 18, the key to understanding the pattern of the solutions in Table 19.1 is the likelihood ratio $R_{ij} = \tilde{\alpha}_{ij}/\alpha_{ij}$.

Incentive compatibility requires $E[U|H] - E[U|L] \geq 0$. The exponential utility function setup allows us to express $U(I\text{-}c_L) = exp\langle r(c_L\text{-}c_H)\rangle U(I\text{-}c_H) = kU(I\text{-}c_H)$, with constant $k = exp\langle r(c_L\text{-}c_H)\rangle$. We use this to rewrite the incentive compatibility constraint in a way that highlights the likelihood ratio:

$$E[U|H] - E[U|L] = \Sigma_i\Sigma_j\ [U(I_{ij}\text{-}c_H)\alpha_{ij} - kU(I_{ij}\text{-}c_H)\tilde{\alpha}_{ij}]$$
$$= \Sigma_i\Sigma_j\ \alpha_{ij}U(I_{ij}\text{-}c_H)[1\text{-}k\cdot R_{ij}] \geq 0.$$

The incentive compatibility constraint takes the form of each term in the manager's expected utility calculation given input H being weighted by a factor that depends on the likelihood ratio.

With this algebra behind us, we turn to economic substance. Suppose for low output (x_1) we find the likelihood ratio is the same for each evaluation outcome, $R_{1g} = R_{1b}$, as occurs in cases C and D. Then the best incentive arrangement will have $I_{1g} = I_{1b}$. With the manager risk averse, any variation in I_{ij} is costly. Yet $I_{1g} \neq I_{1b}$ does not help satisfy the incentive compatibility constraint when $R_{1g} = R_{1b}$. Thus, we maintain $I_{1g} = I_{1b}$ in such a case. Otherwise we needlessly impose risk on the manager.[5]

---

[5]This intuitive argument is verified in the Appendix, where we discuss methods for locating the

Next recall the probability of events A and B can be expressed as p(A and B) = p(A|B)p(B). Rewrite our joint probabilities along these lines: $\alpha_{1g} = p(x_1 \text{ and } g|H)$ = $p(g|x_1,H)p(x_1|H)$, and so on. $R_{1g} = R_{1b}$ now implies the following:

$$\frac{\overline{\alpha}_{1g}}{\alpha_{1g}} = \frac{p(g|x_1,L)p(x_1|L)}{p(g|x_1,H)p(x_1|H)} = \frac{\overline{\alpha}_{1b}}{\alpha_{1b}} = \frac{p(b|x_1,L)p(x_1|L)}{p(b|x_1,H)p(x_1|H)}.$$

Remove the common expression of $p(x_1|L)/p(x_1|H)$ from both sides. We have the following implication:

$$\frac{p(g|x_1,L)}{p(g|x_1,H)} = \frac{p(b|x_1,L)}{p(b|x_1,H)}.$$

But this implies $p(g|x_1,L) = p(g|x_1,H)$ and $p(b|x_1,L) = p(b|x_1,H)$.[6] In short, $R_{1g} = R_{1b}$ implies that once having observed output x_1, further observation of evaluation g or b is of no use in inferring what input the manager has supplied. Given x_1 has been observed, the evaluation conveys no *additional* information. It is simply noise, unaffected by the manager's input, given we already know x_1 has occurred.

The key feature here is the information content of the evaluation. Given we are already observing output, does the evaluation tell us anything else about the manager's behavior? If high output is observed (x_2), the answer is unequivocally no. The example is purposely structured so high output occurs only under input H. High output implies input H. Low output, on the other hand, is ambiguous. Input L may have been supplied, or input H may have been supplied and the manager simply been unlucky. Which is it?

Given we see low output, then, the evaluation might tell us something useful. This, in turn, can only be the case if the likelihood ratio for low output differs across the possible evaluations. But this occurs only when the evaluation outcome's conditional probability, $p(j|x_1,a)$, varies with the manager's input $a \in \{L,H\}$.

In cases A and B of Table 19.1 the evaluation measure is useful. It allows for supply of input H at lower cost to the organization. The manager's pay-for-performance contract depends on output and the evaluation. In cases C and D the evaluation measure is not useful. The best possible use is to ignore the evaluation and contract only on the output. R_{1j} varies with the evaluation in the first two cases, and is constant in the last two.

To recap, we are using output to infer the manager's input. This is unlikely to be an error-free process. So we seek additional information. This additional information can only be useful if it improves our inference. Given output is observed, the

---

optimal pay-for-performance arrangement.

[6]This is readily deduced from the fact $p(g|x_1,a) + p(b|x_1,a) = 1$.

inference can only be improved if $R_{1g} \neq R_{1b}$. Otherwise no new information is brought to the evaluation task.[7]

Our next task is to link this insight to controllability.

controllability

A common, intuitive evaluation norm is that a manager should be evaluated based on controllable performance. The manager's evaluation should be confined to measures that are controllable by the manager. For example, a manufacturing manager who is obliged to accept a rush order brought by the marketing group should not be held responsible for overtime costs incurred to get the order out on a timely basis. These overtime costs are not controllable by the manager. Similarly, the manager should be held responsible for the cost of manufacturing the item, once we have removed the overtime costs. The manager is responsible for, can control, the ordinary costs of production.

Turning to our stylized contracting model we have two possible variables on which to contract, output and the evaluation measure. What does it mean for the manager to control one or both variables? The manager supplies input; so we ask whether the manager's input affects the probability with which the variable occurs. If the variable's outcome is unaffected by the manager's behavior, the manager does not control the variable. If the variable's outcome is affected by the manager's behavior, the manager does control, to some degree, the variable.

More precisely, let v be some potential evaluation variable, accounting, non-accounting, or whatever. Also denote the associated probability p(v|a). *Variable v is controllable by the manager if p(v|a) depends nontrivially on the manager's supply of input a.* In each of the four cases, the manager does control output in this sense. Supply of input $a \in \{L,H\}$ affects the probability, $p(x|a)$, with which low or high output occur. For example, under input H we have $p(x_1|H) = .5$ while under input L we have $p(x_1|L) = 1$ in all four cases.

What about the evaluation measure (j = g,b)? In Table 19.2 we tabulate p(g|a) and p(b|H) for the four cases. The manager controls the evaluation in cases A and C but not in cases B and D.

Our intuition is faulty at times. In case A the evaluation is useful and controllable, while in case B it is useful and not controllable. In case C it is controllable and useless. The difficulty is we have sought the easy answer. Whether an evaluation measure is useful depends on whether it tells us something useful about the manager's behavior. If we know nothing else, it can only tell us something if it is controllable. Yet we already know output.

---

[7]More generally we want the likelihood ratios to differ for some output level. The examples are purposely constructed so high output is completely informative about the manager's behavior. This reminds us that the game is seeking to learn something we don't already know.

conditional controllability

This suggests a conditional version of the controllability argument. We will say a variable is conditionally controllable if the manager's supply of input affects the probability with which the variable occurs conditional on the other information we have. Here this takes the form of asking whether $p(g|x_1,a)$ is affected by the manager's choice of $a\in\{L,H\}$. More generally, *variable v is conditionally controllable, in the presence of information y, by the manager if $p(v|y,a)$ depends nontrivially on the manager's supply of input for some realization of y.* Controllability centers on $p(v|a)$, while conditional controllability centers on the probability conditioned by what we already know, $p(v|y,a)$.

Table 19.2: Controllability and Conditional Controllability				
	cases			
	case A	case B	case C	case D
controllability				
$p(g|H)$	.75	.20	.50	.20
$p(b|H)$	.25	.80	.50	.80
$p(g|L)$	.20	.20	.20	.20
$p(b|L)$	.80	.80	.80	.80
conditional controllability				
$p(g|x_1,H)$	.70	.30	.20	.20
$p(b|x_1,H)$	.30	.70	.80	.80
$p(g|x_1,L)$	.20	.20	.20	.20
$p(b|x_1,L)$	.80	.80	.80	.80
information valuable?	yes	yes	no	no

We tabulate $p(g|x_1,L)$, and so on. in Table 19.2 for the four examples. Conditional controllability and usefulness of the evaluation are aligned. Unconditional controllability and usefulness are not aligned. Conditional controllability does not imply controllability; and controllability does not imply conditional controllability. This is apparent in the tabulation below.

	Case A	Case B	Case C	Case D
controllable	yes	no	yes	no
conditionally controllable	yes	yes	no	no
evaluation useful	yes	yes	no	no

Stepping back, we want the evaluation to be useful in helping resolve the control problem. We use the evaluation measure to infer the manager's behavior. The evaluation measure is a source of information. What matters is the information content of the evaluation measure. Intuitively, we ask whether the manager can control the information content of the evaluation measure, as opposed to the evaluation measure per se. This is tantamount to asking whether the measure is conditionally controllable. Our information content calculus must make provision for the information conveyed by other sources.

Controllability is a compelling, intuitive notion. The distinction between controlling a measure and controlling the information content of a measure is subtle and important. Conditional controllability says it all. Saying a variable is conditionally controllable is the same as saying the information content of the variable is controllable by the manager (given that we condition on whatever other information is at hand). In our streamlined example, a differing likelihood ratio, R_{ij}, and conditional controllability are the same thing.[8]

In this way the managerial input model leads us to focus on the information content of a potential evaluation measure. We face a control problem, and the task assigned the evaluation is to bring information to the contracting arena that will help resolve that control problem. The evaluation's information content, given whatever else is known, is the central driving force in the argument. We use the evaluation measure to refine the process of inferring the manager's behavior. To be useful in this process the evaluation must bring new information to the inference task.[9]

---

[8]A word of caution is in order. Conditional controllability is necessary for a variable to be useful for contracting purposes. But we can readily construct settings where a variable is conditionally controllable but not useful. Take our four cases and change the story so the organization seeks supply of input L. The evaluation remains conditionally controllable in the first two cases but is not useful. For the logically minded, usefulness implies conditional controllability but not vice versa. The managerial insight is the first half of the connection. We should confine ourselves to variables that are conditionally controllable by the manager in question. Equivalently, we should confine ourselves to variables whose information content is controllable by the manager, controllable given whatever other information is being observed.

[9]A slightly more complicated version of the argument arises if we assume the organization is also risk averse. In this case we have two parties, the organization and the manager, who are risk averse. The organization faces a risky choice. It will then be in the interest of both parties to share in the risk. So nontrivial risk sharing will arise. Even without a control problem, then, the manager's compensation would be at risk. Now overlay a control problem. We will then generally see this ideal risk sharing arrangement distorted by a pay-for-performance arrangement that addresses incentive compatibility concerns. And conditional controllability will again surface as the inherent feature of an evaluation measure that makes it potentially useful in resolving the control problem.

To illustrate, let both parties be risk averse and also assume an evaluation measure that perfectly identifies the manager's input is available. The two parties will then share in the risk of the venture, and the evaluation measure will be used to control the input supplied by the manager. Given we are observing the manager's input, output is not informative. Yet it will be used in the compensation arrangement simply because of risk sharing. We emphasize a risk neutral organization in our stylized

Interpretation of Performance Evaluation Vignettes

Armed with this insight we return to the earlier performance evaluation stories. We begin with the service department supervisor in the auto dealership.

service department manager

The primary measure used in evaluation of the service department manager is direct labor cost. It is used in the format of direct labor cost given the work accomplished. Actual is compared to budget, where the budget reflects work accomplished. Clearly we use the standard times allowed for the jobs worked on to raise the information content of the direct labor cost measure. Without knowing which jobs were worked on the direct labor cost would be largely meaningless.

The direct labor quantity variance, then, is an important measure in the manager's evaluation. Notice how it is constructed by taking direct labor cost (at standard prices) and then using the jobs worked on to specify the budgeted direct labor cost. The two underlying variables are direct labor cost and jobs worked on. Yet jobs worked on is largely uncontrollable by the supervisor. In the short-run, it reflects a random arrival of customers. (Of course poor service will eventually affect the supply of jobs!) Together, though, direct labor cost and jobs worked on provide an insightful basis on which to evaluate the service department manager.

Continuing, a heavy focus on cost incurred given the jobs worked on does not reveal the entire story. The supervisor might rush the repairs, cutting quality in the process. Particularly difficult repair tasks may be put off. So customers are invited to mail in a questionnaire; and the general manager periodically visits the service facility. Both activities provide additional information to help infer how well the service manager is performing.

Beyond this the auto dealership relies on its general image to promote sales and service. Some service facility activities spill over into the sales domain. A reputation for good service may help the sales force close a sale, for example. Given the other information, it should come as no surprise that dealership profitability is also used to evaluate the service manager.

In short, the service manager supplies a variety of managerial inputs across a variety of tasks. The evaluation system responds with a variety of measures, including actual cost relative to standard for the work accomplished, firm-wide profit, customer satisfaction, and the general manager's qualitative impressions. The measures are used to infer the manager's behavior. This results in a mix of seemingly controllable and uncontrollable variables. But information content is linked to conditional controllability, as opposed to unconditional controllability.

---

model because information content is more readily examined in a setting where ideal risk sharing is trivial. In addition, capital markets exist for sharing risk, and it seems odd to introduce risk sharing as a primary consideration in a labor market transaction.

sales contest

Now turn to the sales person. It seems intuitive that orders booked would be an important, and controllable, evaluation measure. The attendant sales contest, though, introduces the orders booked by another sales person. The peer's sales are not controllable by the sales person in question, just as the exam performance of other students is not controllable by a particular student. Yet important evaluation information is conveyed by this use of relative performance evaluation.

Was the student's performance the result of luck or skill and effort? The test itself may have been easy or difficult. Another student's score tells us something about whether the test was difficult. Similarly, the orders booked by other sales people tells us something about the market and how the product line is faring. Important environmental information is conveyed by using peer performance in the evaluation process.

For example, suppose the output of manager i (where i = 1,2) is equal to that manager's input, a_i, plus noise. Some noise is idiosyncratic, say ε_i, while other noise is common to both environments, say, μ. So manager i's output is $a_i + \varepsilon_i + \mu$. Each manager's output is influenced by the common noise, μ. The difference in their output removes this common term. This is the intuitive idea behind relative performance evaluation.[10]

profit center

Now turn to the manufacturing manager in the integrated organization. This manager is evaluated based on cost incurred, given output produced. Additional statistics relating to equipment downtime, employee turnover, timeliness of delivery and warranty claims are also used. These speak, respectively, to issues of maintenance, employee training and morale, scheduling, and product quality. Again we see a mix of measures, designed to aid the task of inferring what the manager has done.

The novelty of the story is the suggestion we convert the division from a cost to a profit center. This would be done by introducing a measure of revenue into the milieu. We already know the quantity produced and shipped to the marketing division. So to measure revenue of the manufacturing division we must come up with a price.

Consider two extremes. On the one hand, this may be a basic commodity with sales largely driven by market forces and the activities of the marketing division. In

---

[10]Relative performance evaluation requires some commonality in the environments. It also runs the risk of sabotage. Couldn't one sales person encroach on the territory of another or couldn't one student be less than amiable in helping another understand some particular material? Similarly, if the exam is graded on the curve and the students all party the night before, their joint behavior will undermine the information provided by relative performance evaluation. This points to the fact that evaluation is an expansive task.

this story the product specifications are well established and the manufacturing division simply produces in response to a schedule largely set by the marketing division. It is unlikely actual sales revenue tells us anything substantive about the manufacturing division, given the other evaluation information already in place. This leads us to suspect the best way to measure revenue at the manufacturing division is with a standard price per unit.

Measurement is easy, and we seem to get what we pay for here. We already know the units manufactured and shipped. Let q denote this quantity. Suppose the standard price is set at 12 per unit. We already know q; 12q is hardly going to be useful at this point. Being able to measure profit at the division level simply does not imply the additional measurement of revenue is useful. Here it seems revenue is uncontrollable and conditionally uncontrollable (and therefore useless). A profit center may have more prestige, but prestige and information content are simply not the same.

The other extreme is a specialized product with sales driven by market forces, marketing activities, and the ability of the manufacturing division to help design and eventually produce the product in question. Here it is likely the sales revenue will tell us something about the manufacturing division, despite the other evaluation information in place. One possibility is also to use firm-wide profit to evaluate the manufacturing manager. This brings in sales revenue, but commingles the information with randomness associated with various activities in the marketing division. Another possibility is to establish a revenue measure at the manufacturing level. Price at this point might, for example, be negotiated by the two division managers. This runs the risk of being influenced by their relative bargaining skills; but it also offers the possibility of a revenue measure that helps infer the activities of the manufacturing manager.

overtime on rush orders

Next, think back to the case of the manufacturing manager who receives a rush order and manufacturing costs are excessive due to overtime. Here the question is whether to evaluate based on total manufacturing cost or total manufacturing cost less the overtime. This is a question of whether overtime cost is informative, given that we know total cost. One answer is yes. In this narrative the manager is instructed to run a tight schedule and deal with any rush jobs by using overtime, as necessary. A cost overrun that is due to overtime work on rush orders is then not very interesting. We remove it by tempering the total manufacturing cost with the overtime costs associated with the rush job.

A second answer is in the negative. Here the manager is instructed to keep a relatively tight schedule, but with a modest amount of slack should rush orders appear. A cost overrun that is due to rush orders is now somewhat interesting. We therefore do not remove the overtime cost from the analysis.

sales markdowns

Finally, return to the department store where central management selects the merchandise to be stocked. Sales markdowns may be used to sell some of this merchandise. If so, should this affect the store manager's evaluation? If not, the primary evaluation measures are revenue and expense. The question, then, is whether markdowns provide useful evaluation information given revenue and expense. Suppose market-wide forces heavily influence the price at which merchandise is sold. Markdowns now convey information, as they help remove market based noise from the revenue measure. In the limit, the best evaluation measures might be net revenue and expense.

Conversely, suppose the manager's sales efforts, display locations, and so on can affect revenue. This argues against using markdowns in the evaluation. Yet markdowns may still be informative. For example, if they are concentrated on a few products the manager was particularly opposed to stocking, this may suggest that sales effort is not being properly allocated. It also may suggest the original stocking decision was not well thought out.

Either way, we look for information content in the presence of whatever else is being used in the evaluation task. That is the central message.

Management by Exception

Each vignette portrays a variety of evaluation measures. Management by exception further enriches the array. The idea is simple: concentrate attention on the unusual or exceptional. Suppose we are scanning a manager's performance statistics and notice something unusual, say an unusual material quantity variance. We would likely seek an explanation. In our conceptual model of the evaluation process this amounts to a two-stage procedure. Initially we examine a set of measures. Then, with that information in hand, we decide whether to seek additional information. In this way we harbor our information resources.

To illustrate this theme, return to the running managerial input model in Table 19.1. Output, but not input, is observed just as before. The evaluation measure, though, is now perfect. It will report good news (g) only if input H is supplied and bad news (b) only if input L is supplied.

Let's further assume the manager's payment cannot be negative, so we have a constraint of $I_{ij} \geq 0$. The obvious solution here is to pay the manager ($I_{ig} = 8,000$) if input H is supplied and deliver minimal compensation otherwise ($I_{ib} = 0$). This works just fine.

$$E[U|H] = U(M) = U(3,000) > E[U|L] = U(0-c_L) = U(-2,000).$$

Further observe output is not a useful evaluation measure given we are observing the manager's input!

Now add another wrinkle. Suppose this evaluation measure costs the organization 2,000 dollars. We have two ways to acquire input H. One is to observe the manager's input by paying the necessary cost to install the measurement system. The total of compensation and information cost will then be $8,000 + 2,000 = 10,000$. The second is to forego the definitive but costly evaluation and rely on output as the evaluation measure. From Table 19.1 (base case), this has a compensation cost of 8,652.83, and of, course, zero information cost. The definitive information is simply too costly.

Next, overlay the two-stage procedure. Suppose we can first observe output and then decide whether to acquire the costly information, again at a cost of 2,000. If we observe high output, we know input H was supplied. If we observe low output, we do not know whether the story is one of high input and bad luck or low input. It is at this point we would be interested in further exploration of the manager's behavior.

Also assume the organization can commit to provide the costly information with probability ß once low output is observed. The evaluation story, then, is a two-stage procedure. Initially output is observed. If high output is observed, no additional information is gathered. If low output is observed, additional information is provided with probability ß. In equilibrium, the costly information will be acquired with probability $p(x_1|H) \cdot ß = .5ß$. In this way we have three conceivable evaluation results: $j = g$ (good news), $j = b$ (bad news), and $j = n$ (no news). More to the point, we acquire the costly information only when it is useful and further save on information cost by judiciously randomizing on its acquisition.

Consider the following scheme. Pay the manager the minimum amount if low output is observed, the information is produced, and it reveals supply of L; $I_{1b} = 0$. Otherwise pay the manager $I_{2n} = I_{1g} = I_{1n} = 8,000$. If the manager supplies H, compensation of 8,000 is guaranteed and we have $E[U|H] = U(M)$. If L is supplied, low output will be observed and the manager's supply of L will be discovered with probability ß. This gives an expected utility measure of:

$$E[U|L] = ß \cdot U(0-2,000) + (1-ß) \cdot U(8,000-2,000).$$

If ß is large enough, supply of input H will be incentive compatible (i.e., $E[U|H] \geq E[U|L]$); and the organization's total cost of input H will be $8,000 + .5ß(2,000) = 8,000 + 1,000ß$.

The critical value is $ß = .2855$.[11] Below this amount the chance of being caught is too low and the manager is invited to supply L. Above this amount, the information is being produced to excess. The cost totals $8,000 + 1,000(.2855) = 8,285.50$. Not bad. For an expected information cost of just under 286 we can resolve completely the control problem.

---

[11] ß is located by equating $E[U|H]$ and $E[U|L]$, or $-exp(-.3) = -ß exp(.2) - (1-ß) exp(-.6)$. Notice use of the assumption that the lowest possible payment to the manager is zero. If the lowest possible payment is some amount less than zero, then the critical value of ß declines. In the limit we have a minuscule probability of catching supply of L coupled with an enormous penalty paid by the manager in such an event.

managed tensions

This solution belies an important point. With $\beta = .2855$ we abandon direct use of the manager's output as an evaluation device. Instead, we rely on catching supply of L with positive probability to resolve the control problem. Output is used only to direct the subsequent information choice. Yet less than complete reliance on the costly but definitive evaluation is optimal. It turns out the best solution here is to set $\beta \approx .22 < .2855$. This is accompanied by a payment schedule of $I_{2n} = 8,680.33 = I_{1g}$, $I_{1n} = 7,020.83$, and $I_{1b} = 0$. Total cost is $E[I_{ij}] + .5\beta(2,000) = 8,253.12$.

Notice the mixing of the two evaluation devices. The manager's compensation varies with output. Naturally the maximal penalty is administered whenever input L is definitively discovered; and in equilibrium the manager supplies input H so this penalty is never administered. On the other hand, if supply of input H is definitively discovered, either by observing high output or by acquiring the costly information and observing result g, the manager receives a relatively large payment. Otherwise, when low output is observed but the costly information is not acquired, a lower payment is received. In this way both output and the costly evaluation measure are actively used in the evaluation. Output is not a definitive measure, and we wind up with the manager facing (and being compensated for) a modest amount of compensation risk.

Intuitively, if we set $\beta = .2855$ we have removed all compensation risk from the manager. At this point, a very small reduction in β can be achieved by relying somewhat on output as a measure of performance. This places risk on the manager. In the neighborhood of $\beta = .2855$, though, this risk is awfully small. So the saving on information cost is a first order effect while the cost of compensating the manager for a small risk is a second order effect. The net effect is a discernible saving if we reduce β.

This illustrates the underlying idea of managing the tension between using resources to resolve better a control problem versus using those resources in another activity. We should expect to see, to work under, and to design evaluation schemes that use a variety of instruments that are collectively less than definitive.

organization incentive compatibility

This modest extension of our example also illustrates the question of organization incentive compatibility. Notice that with $\beta = .22$ the solution has a payment structure of $I_2 = I_{1g} = 8,680.33 > I_{1n} = 7,020.83$. Suppose low output is observed. The organization is now supposed to randomize and produce the additional information with probability $\beta = .22$. If it does produce the information, it will pay information costs of 2,000 and will discover the manager has supplied H, which calls for payment to the manager of 8,680.33. If it does not produce the information, it saves the information costs and must pay the manager only 7,020.83. Why not renege?

Of course, our example assumed the organization could commit not to do this sort of thing. The underlying theme, though, should not go unnoticed. Evaluation places a burden on the organization, a burden that it may find tempting to diminish. Here we should not forget the comparative advantage of the accounting library. It is well defended and thus more difficult for either party to manipulate in the potentially high stakes game of performance evaluation.

In this way we see the subtlety of a management by exception orientation. It is tempting to think of this as a process by which we subject the pattern of outcomes to a statistical test to decide whether intervention is in order. Yet the statistical pattern we should be observing is determined in part by the manner in which we will intervene. The incentives of both parties come together to determine the statistical patterns we would expect to see. The statistical pattern of a well-behaved control problem is endogenous.

Summary

Performance evaluation is a well-practiced art. Many measures can be used, ranging from financial to nonfinancial, from quantitative to qualitative, from periodic to occasional, and so on. Practice is varied and ever changing. This is why we stress a conceptual overview, one that models an explicit control problem (of inherent conflict over supply of managerial input) and the use of information to resolve that control problem (by inferring the input supplied).

The imperative to evaluate based on controllable performance is intuitive, appealing, and unfortunately incomplete. An additional measure is useful in the evaluation task if it conveys new, additional information. The central feature is conditional controllability, not unconditional controllability. The professional manager's task here is to sort out which potential measures carry additional information (in a cost effective fashion) into the evaluation arena. This task is vastly more delicate than identifying a list of controllable performance indicators.

Again the underlying theme is the use of professional expertise. Our modeling and our intuition strongly suggest information content is the key to understanding which measures might be useful for evaluating a particular manager. Information content, in turn, is logically equivalent to conditional controllability. This points the way toward identifying useful evaluation measures, but it leaves considerable room for their identification, design, and use.

Appendix: Solving for an Optimal Incentive Function

It is time to bite the bullet and examine how to solve for an optimal incentive function. Though software packages offer this service, we should ground our intuition. The program to be solved, recall, is:

$$C(H) = \underset{I_{ij}}{\text{minimum}} \ \Sigma_i \Sigma_j \ I_{ij} \alpha_{ij}$$

subject to: $E[U|H] \geq U(M)$; and   [IR]
$$E[U|H] \geq E[U|L].$$ [IC]

The first constraint, labeled [IR], is the individual rationality requirement and the second, [IC], is the incentive compatibility requirement.

The solution technique rests on a shadow price formulation. Let λ be a shadow price attached to the individual rationality constraint; also let μ be a shadow price attached to the incentive compatibility constraint. Now construct an augmented objective function, consisting of the original expression plus the two constraints multiplied by their respective shadow prices:

$$\mathcal{L} = \Sigma_i \Sigma_j\, I_{ij}\alpha_{ij} - \lambda\{E[U|H] - U(M)\} - \mu\{E[U|H] - E[U|L]\}.$$

This is called a Lagrangian (in honor of an 18th century French mathematician). Notice the weighting of the constraints. This provides a setting where we seek, simultaneously, to locate the optimal values of the variables and the shadow prices on the constraints. At the optimum, if a constraint is not binding its shadow price will be zero. If it is binding, its shadow price will be positive, and it will be satisfied as an equality.

Assuming our objective function and constraints are well behaved (something we always assume), the necessary conditions for an optimum are that the derivatives of $\mathcal{L}$ are zero and the constraints are satisfied. We summarize these conditions with the following family of relationships:

$$\partial\mathcal{L}/\partial I_{ij} = 0, \text{ for all i and j;}$$ [FOC$_{ij}$]
$$\lambda\{E[U|H] - U(M)\} = 0; \text{ and}$$ [IR$'$]
$$\mu\{E[U|H] - E[U|L]\} = 0.$$ [IC$'$]

For the Table 19.1 cases, we have four i,j combinations. This gives us a system of six equations in six unknowns (I_{ij}, λ and μ).

The intuition is more straightforward than the notation. Condition [FOC$_{ij}$] says that payment I_{ij} should be set such that the tension between paying the manager and satisfying the constraints should be precisely balanced. [IC$'$] is a complementary slackness condition. Either the multiplier on the [IC] constraint should be zero or we should have $E[U|H] = U(M)$. (We assume there are no binding constraints on the payments here; otherwise, these constraints will have to be recognized as well.)

Working with these conditions is usually a chore. Our task will be simplified by a change in variables. (Also, this change in variables is sometimes more amenable to numerical solution.) For this purpose we focus on the manager's utility. Define $V_{ij} = -exp\langle -rI_{ij}\rangle$. Also define the constants $k_1 = exp\langle rc_L\rangle$ and $k_2 = exp\langle rc_H\rangle$. We now have $U(I_{ij}-c_L) = k_1 V_{ij}$ and $U(I_{ij}-c_H) = k_2 V_{ij}$. The manager's expected utility measures are readily delineated. For example $E[U|H] = k_2\Sigma_i\Sigma_j\, \alpha_{ij}V_{ij}$. Also, the payments are recovered via the definition of V_{ij}: $ln\langle -V_{ij}\rangle = -rI_{ij}$.

Now rewrite the original program, to focus on locating the best V_{ij}'s. You should convince yourself of the following:

$$C(H) = \text{minimum}_{V_{ij}} \ (-1/r)\Sigma_i\Sigma_j \ \alpha_{ij}ln(-V_{ij})$$
$$\text{subject to:} \ k_2\Sigma_i\Sigma_j \ \alpha_{ij}V_{ij} \geq U(M); \text{ and} \qquad [IR]$$
$$k_2\Sigma_i\Sigma_j \ \alpha_{ij}V_{ij} \geq k_1\Sigma_i\Sigma_j \ \tilde{\alpha}_{ij}V_{ij}. \qquad [IC]$$

This exhibits a nonlinear objective function and a pair of linear inequality constraints. It is in this form that the examples in Table 19.1 were solved, using a nonlinear optimization routine. Popular spreadsheets also offer nonlinear optimization options.

The above noted [FOC$_{ij}$] expression now simplifies to the following:

$$1/V_{ij} = \lambda r k_2 + \mu r[k_2 - k_1\tilde{\alpha}_{ij}/\alpha_{ij}] = \lambda r k_2 + \mu r[k_2 - k_1 R_{ij}] \qquad [FOC_{ij}]$$

where R_{ij} is the likelihood ratio we examined in Table 19.1. Notice what happens when the likelihood ratio is the same for two distinct i,j combinations. We then have the same expression on the right hand side for the two combinations. This implies we have the same V_{ij} and therefore the same I_{ij} whenever the likelihood ratio is the same for two distinct i,j combinations.[12]

Bibliographic Notes

When and how additional information is used in an efficient pay-for-performance arrangement is the central question in understanding which items in the accounting library might be used to advantage in evaluating a particular manager. Holmstrom's [1979, 1982] papers are the major references here. Shavell [1979] and Harris and Raviv [1978] are also important. The connection to the accountant's use of controllability is explored in Antle and Demski [1988].

Problems and Exercises

1.   Discuss the difference between an evaluation measure being controllability versus conditionally controllability by a manager.

2.   The chapter stresses the idea that the *information content* of a monitor must be controllable by the manager in question; otherwise, the particular monitor cannot possibly be of any use in evaluating the manager. Carefully discuss this idea and relate it to the notion of conditional controllability.

---

[12]Of course, the same picture emerges without the change in variables. Also, relating back to earlier work, what happens here if we divide through by k_2?

3. Return to the case A data in Table 19.1. The monitor is useful, yet it is not used when output x_2 is observed. Carefully explain.

4. *optimal contract with monitor*
    Consider a setting where labor input of L or H leads to uncertain output. The owner is risk neutral. Output can be x_1 or x_2. The labor supplier is modeled in the usual fashion, i.e., risk averse with constant risk aversion and with a personal cost of input supply. Let the risk aversion parameter be $r = .0001$, $c_H = 5,000$ and $c_L = 0$. Also assume the supplier's next best alternative offers a certain equivalent of M = 7,000. The output probabilities are listed below.

	x_1	x_2
input H	.3	.7
input L	.7	.3

Input H is desired throughout the exercise.

a] Determine an optimal pay-for-performance arrangement.

b] Now suppose a monitor is also available. It will report good (g) or bad (b) news, at the same time the output is observed. The joint probabilities, conditional on the supplier's labor input, are:

	$b;x_1$	$g;x_1$	$b;x_2$	$g;x_2$
input H	.1	.2	.3	.4
input L	.4	.3	.2	.1

Without solving for an optimal contract, rank the four possible evaluations from most to least favorable.

c] Determine an optimal pay-for-performance arrangement.

d] Carefully explain the connection between this exercise and that in problems 11 and 12 of Chapter 18.

5. *information content of monitor*
    Ralph, who is risk neutral, owns a production process. One of three feasible labor inputs, $L < B < H$, must be selected. H, in fact, is desired. Output probabilities are displayed below.

	x_1	x_2
input H	.1	.9
input B	.7	.3
input L	1	0

The labor supplier's preferences are given by $-exp(-r(I-c_a))$, where I denotes payment from Ralph and c_a is the usual personal cost term. The supplier's outside opportunity offers a certain equivalent of M = 10,000. Assume $r = .0001$, $c_H =$

5,000, c_B = 2,000 and c_L = 1,000. Contracting is limited to the jointly observable output.

a] Determine an optimal pay-for-performance arrangement.

b] Suppose it is possible to install a monitor. This monitor will report bad news if input L is supplied and good news otherwise. Is this monitor useful?

c] Is the monitor in [b] controllable? Is it conditionally controllable? Carefully explain this case of a serious control problem, a monitor that is both controllable and conditionally controllable, and yet is not useful.

6. *controllable versus conditionally controllable measure*

This is a continuation of problem 8 in Chapter 18. The basic story and preference specifications remain as before. Ralph owns a production function, recall; and randomness in the environment plus labor input from a manager combine to produce output. The output is now one of two quantities: $x_1 < x_2$. As before, the manager's input can be one of two quantities, L < H. The manager's preferences should be familiar. If the manager supplies input $a \in \{H,L\}$, and is paid the amount I, the resulting utility is $-exp(-r(I-c_a))$. c_H = 5,000 and c_L = 0, along with a risk aversion parameter of r = .0001. Also, the manager's opportunity cost of working for this organization is U(M), with M = 10,000. Ralph is risk neutral, and seeks supply of input H.

Here, however, the parties can contract on the observable output and on a monitor. The monitor will report what will be labeled good news (g) or bad news (b). It is observed at the time the output is observed. Suppose the probabilities are as follows:

	$g;x_1$	$b;x_1$	$g;x_2$	$b;x_2$
input H	.05	.05	.45	.45
input L	.40	.40	.10	.10

As a base case, suppose the parties cannot contract on what the monitor reports. Their contracting is confined to the output. We should recall from the earlier problem the optimal payment arrangement is I_1 = 8,934.62 and I_2 = 15,972.54 along with an expected wage of 15,268.75. (It will also become clear below that throughout we maintain the same relationship between output and input as in the original problem.)

a] Determine an optimal contract when both the monitor and output can be used. Interpret your finding. Is the monitor controllable, in the sense the probability of what the monitor reports depends on the agent's supply of input? Is it conditionally controllable?

b] Repeat for the following probability structure:

	g;x$_1$	b;x$_1$	g;x$_2$	b;x$_2$
input H	.00	.10	.90	.00
input L	.00	.80	.20	.00

c]   Repeat for the following probability structure:

	g;x$_1$	b;x$_1$	g;x$_2$	b;x$_2$
input H	.06	.04	.54	.36
input L	.32	.48	.08	.12

d]   Repeat for the following probability structure:

	g;x$_1$	b;x$_1$	g;x$_2$	b;x$_2$
input H	.01	.09	.49	.41
input L	.35	.45	.15	.05

e]   In each of the four cases carefully explain, in qualitative terms, why the pay-for-performance arrangement selects the monitor/output combinations it does for high and for low reward. What connection do you see with the idea the monitor should be used if the agent can control it?

7.   *controllable versus conditionally controllable measure*
    Construct a setting, using a risk averse manager, two possible input supplies, and so on in which a monitor is not controllable but is useful.

8.   *randomized monitoring*
    This is a continuation of problem 8 in Chapter 18. Everything remains as before, except Ralph now has an information source. For a cost of 4,000 the source will report, without error, whether the manager supplied input H or input L. If input H is reported, the manager will be paid I = 15,000. If input L is reported, the manager will be fired, with a payment of I = 0. (No negative payments are allowed.) This is certainly effective but far too costly.

a]   Suppose Ralph can commit to buying the information only when output x$_1$ is observed. Ralph will then pay (i) I = 0 whenever the information is purchased and reveals the input is L and (ii) 15,000 otherwise. Will this motivate supply of input H? Will the manager have any compensation at risk, in equilibrium? Is this a good idea?

b]   Now suppose Ralph can commit to buying the information only when output x$_1$ is observed and only then with probability ß. (Think of this as random monitoring.) Again, Ralph will pay (i) I = 0 whenever the information is purchased and reveals the input is L and (ii) I = 15,000 otherwise. Find the lowest ß that will motivate supply of input H. Is this a good idea?

c]   Finally, consider a more elaborate plan. Set $ß = .20738$. Pay $I = 0$ if the information is purchased and input L is reported. Pay $I = 15,130.97$ if x_1 is observed, the information is purchased and reports input H; pay $I = 13,909.36$ if output x_1 is observed and the information is not purchased; and pay $I = 15,098.98$ if output x_2 is observed. Is this a better idea? What is the explanation? (Hint: what has happened to the expected information cost and to the manager's risk premium?)

d]   Finally, do you perceive any incentive problems on the part of Ralph?

9.   *root utility*

This is a continuation of problem 15 in Chapter 18, where the manager's utility function is given by $U(z,a) = \sqrt{z} - V(a)$. You should review the original problem to refresh the details. Further suppose the a = H act is no longer available; so the question revolves around a = B and a = L.

A monitor can also be used. This monitor will report good (g) or bad (b) news at the end of the game. The probabilities are: $p(g|B) = p(b|L) = .75$, regardless of what output is produced. The monitor calls it correct with probability .75.

a]   Find an optimal contract that will induce the agent to supply a = B.

b]   Carefully contrast your answer in the earlier problem, where the monitor was not available and the pay-for-performance arrangement paid the agent 2,025 for low output and 9,025 for high output.

c]   Why does the optimal solution not use the monitor's report when high output is observed?

10.   *risk taking and insurance*

A major retailer, at one time, moved toward more centralized buying of merchandise that would be inventoried by its many locations. Each such location was evaluated in terms of profit earned at that location. To account for the overhead costs of centralized buying, the retailer booked the centrally purchased merchandise at each store according to the formula of invoice plus t%. With t at 10, for example, an item costing 1,000 would be "sold" by center to the retail outlet for 1,100.

The retail managers were not totally pleased with some of center's merchandising decisions, and complained that, at times, they were stuck with merchandise that could not be sold. The retailer dealt with this by allowing, upon approval, a markdown. To illustrate, suppose the above noted 1,000 item was initially listed at 1,600 retail, but marked down 400. Suppose it sells for 1,600 - 400 = 1,200. The retail manager is now credited with 1,600 in revenue and the shortfall of 400, the markdown, is debited to the above noted centralized buying overhead account.

What tensions are created by the move toward more centralized purchasing in this case? How are some of these tensions ameliorated by the markdown arrangement? What are the likely consequences? What do you suspect will happen to the percentage t as time goes on?

11. *flexible budget*

Consider a manager who produces goods or services according to customer demand. The accounting library uses an estimate of total cost based on an LLA of $TC = F + vq$, where q is some aggregate measure of output. This is, of course, a flexible budget. Is the "flex" in the flexible budget useful in evaluating the manager? If you know total cost, is it likely learning output will bring additional, useful information to the evaluation task? Carefully explain. Can the manager control output?

12. *service department cost allocation*

In Chapter 8, working with data in Table 8.2, we examined a procedure in which the cost incurred in a service department might be allocated to the consuming departments. Discuss such a procedure in terms of the usefulness of the cost allocation in evaluating the performance of the managers of the departments that consume the service department's services.

13. *spending comparisons*

The State of Connecticut monitors per pupil spending in the various local school districts. Each district is associated with peer districts, in terms of various demographics such as income distribution. Discuss this evaluation technique. What are the apparent control concerns?

14. *nonfinancial measures*

Performance evaluation has a long history. For example, Bokenkotter [1979, page 153] reports the following practice in the Medieval Church. "The tasks of the bishop were many and varied: administrative, judicial, and spiritual. One of his chief duties was to conduct visitations of the religious institutions in his Diocese. He usually held the visitation in the local church and would summon the clergy of the area and several laymen to attend. After verifying the credentials of the clergy, the bishop would interrogate the laymen about the behavior of the clergy -- whether they performed their duties properly, whether they wore the clerical dress, whether they frequented taverns or played dice. And the laity too had to answer for their conduct. Finally, the bishop would inspect the physical state of the church and the condition of its appurtenances." Carefully discuss this practice.

15. *nonfinancial measures*

A common practice in the fast food industry is to evaluate a store manager on the basis of profitability and a set of nonfinancial measures. These supplementary measures relate to such things as the outlet's cleanliness, the quality of its product and service, and so on. (A regional supervisor periodically scores the outlet on these measures.) Carefully discuss this practice.

16. *evaluation practices*

Suppose you, as manager, have just been moved to a new location. One of your initial tasks is a quick study of how the individuals whom you will now supervise have been evaluated. You are particularly interested in how the items in the accounting library are used for this purpose. The notion of controllability implies this quick study is a relatively easy task: select a particular individual and ask which of the many accounting measures might that individual control. The notion of conditional controllability is not so accommodating. How does it imply that your quick study should be organized?

17. *local and firm-wide bonus determinants*

A common practice is to define an overall bonus pool in terms of how well the organization has performed. For example, the pool might be a percentage of accounting income. A division manager's share in this pool, in turn, is heavily influenced by how well that manager has performed, for example, in terms of profitability of the division managed. Implicitly, then, the manager is evaluated in terms of local and global measures. Discuss this practice.

20

Responsibility Accounting

We now return to the accounting library and its use in performance evaluation. The idea is to cull from the library those accounting measures we find useful for evaluating some specific manager. This gives rise to what is termed *responsibility accounting*. A particular manager is held responsible for, is held accountable for, some identified array of accounting measures. In this way the organization assigns responsibility for various accounting outcomes, such as manufacturing cost, product profitability, and division return on investment. Stated differently, responsibility accounting is a scheme in which the accounting measures by which each manager's performance will be evaluated are identified. Responsibility, so to speak, is assigned. Each item in the accounting library is associated with a list of managers who bear responsibility for that item.

This is easy enough if we are talking about a small organization, or about the head of an organization. We simply use the entire array of accounting measures in evaluating the manager's performance. Otherwise, we encounter nuances of organization life. An organization is vastly more complicated than a production function that is guided through factor and product market interactions, under the skillful watch of a well-motivated management team. An organization has a life of its own, an ethos, if you will. The organization also enjoys economic success because it is more efficient than a market at arranging some types of transactions.

Parts, sales, and service are grouped together in a typical auto dealership. Large organizations maintain internal labor markets, training their work force and often promoting from within. A university offers specialized studies across a variety of disciplines. It also maintains libraries and physical plant; many administrative functions such as scheduling, record keeping, and food services are also involved. A fast food chain actively trains managers, designs and test markets new products, acquires raw materials from vendors and may even engage in limited manufacturing.

The consistent picture is a variety of transactions that occur inside an organization. The accounting library is designed to record, in aggregate form, transactions across the organization's boundaries as well as within its boundaries. This raises two related questions: which transactions properly fall within the purview of a particular sphere of managerial activity; and how should these transactions be recorded?

For example, suppose a fast food entrepreneur owns several outlets in a community. Each outlet is managed by an on-site manager. All advertising is common; no site specific advertising is used. Should the advertising cost be allocated to the individual sites? All purchasing is also common and is managed by a purchasing group. Should the cost of this purchasing group be allocated to the individual sites? Routine maintenance is also provided on a common basis. Should maintenance cost be allocated to the individual sites? An affirmative answer raises the question of what allocation base to employ. It also raises the question of whether actual or standard costs should be emphasized in the allocation.

Answering these questions presumes we have identified the purpose or use to which the information will be put. Our focus in this chapter is the task of evaluating a manager's performance. A related concern is evaluating the organization's activity, such as a product line, organization arrangement, or support activity. This type of concern has been dealt with in earlier chapters. It is important to remember the two types of evaluations use similar data and often take on a similar appearance. Yet they are fundamentally different.[1] When we refer to a department as a cost center, then, we should interpret this as code for the manager of the department being evaluated primarily on the basis of cost incurred in the department.

The accounting library provides balance sheet and income statement renderings. Revenues and expenses of various sorts are identified. Assets and liabilities of various sorts are also identified. These accounting renderings are inevitably used in evaluating the head of the organization. The head is answerable, accountable, and responsible for these renderings.

The manager at a lower level in the organization is another matter. Where, in this vast array of accounting recordings and aggregations, are we to find measures that are useful in evaluating this manager? Naturally, our earlier work on conditional controllability will serve as a guide in identifying measures that are useful in evaluating a particular manager.

We should be prepared for highly varied answers. Sometimes it will seem best to emphasize flow variables and use cost incurred or income generated during the period as a primary evaluation measure. In other cases, it will seem best to emphasize stock and flow variables. A division manager, for example, may be responsible for division income, division assets, and perhaps some liabilities. Similarly, in some cases cost allocation will be compelling while in others it will not appear reasonable. Nonfinancial measures also surface.

Initially we explore the use of standard cost variances in evaluating a manager. The story is then complicated by admitting the manager's productive activity uses inputs supplied by another managerial unit within the organization. This returns us to our earlier theme of cost allocation. We then move on to contrasting cost, profit, and investment centers. Nonfinancial information is then considered. The exploration concludes with a look at the hierarchical nature of responsibility accounting.

---

[1]Somewhat casually, evaluating a product can be thought of in terms of whether the organization is better off with or without the product. Evaluating a manager calls for preparation to report on the manager's behavior for a variety of possible activities. In equilibrium, only some will be observed but the threat of what might be reported is a central concept. This role of threat is absent in the product evaluation activity.

The unifying theme is information content. Practice is varied, as one would expect. Our survey is tied together with the idea of conditional controllability. Adding another performance measure to the stew makes sense if it brings additional information to the evaluation task.

A Classic Cost Center

We begin with an uncomplicated cost center. A manager supervises a facility that produces a single product according to customer demand.

Let q_1 denote units produced. (We will eventually have other departments and products.) The accounting library recognizes three cost categories: direct labor, direct material, and a single overhead account. LLAs for these categories, and the underlying standards, are displayed in Table 20.1.[2]

Table 20.1: Data for Cost Center Illustration	
LLAs for department	
direct labor (2 hours @25/hour)	$DL_1 = 50q_1$
direct material (3 units @10/unit)	$DM_1 = 30q_1$
overhead	$OV_1 = 300{,}000 + 1.6DL_1$
departmental budgeted cost	$cost_1 = 300{,}000 + 160q_1$
actual costs incurred under $q_1 = 900$ (actual $cost_1 = 473{,}300$)	
	$DL_1 = 51{,}300$ (1,900 hours @27/hour)
	$DM_1 = 27{,}000$ (3,000 units @9/unit)
	$OV_1 = 395{,}000$

Notice the independent variable in the overhead LLA is direct labor cost (DL_1). From here we readily determine the facility's cost budget:

$$cost_1 = DL_1 + DM_1 + OV_1$$
$$= 50q_1 + 30_1 + 300{,}000 + 1.6(50q_1)$$
$$= 300{,}000 + 160q_1.$$

This is a flexible budget, identifying total facility cost as a function of facility output.

Continuing, suppose $q_1 = 900$ units are produced, and the actual cost totals 473,300. Details are given in Table 20.1.

Simply knowing total cost is 473,300 does not tell us very much about the manager's performance. We immediately turn to the flexible budget and contrast the 473,300 with its budget counterpart of $300{,}000 + 160(900) = 444{,}000$. A cost overrun or variance of 29,300 (U) has occurred.

---

[2]The setting in Table 20.1 is a continuation of that in Table 8.2. The single difference is we now introduce actual costs for the noted production quantities.

Using a flexible budget this way is so natural we rarely bother to examine the underlying logic. Cost by itself is not very informative, just as production quantity by itself is not very informative. Together, they are quite interesting. Assume units are produced according to customer demand. If we learn 900 units were produced, we have not learned very much. Alternatively, if we learn total cost was 473,300, we have not learned very much. But if we learn 900 units were produced at a total cost of 473,300, we know cost exceeded budget by 29,300.

Dwell on this. Cost by itself is not very informative. With units produced according to customer demand, output is not controllable by the manager. Yet once we know cost incurred, units produced is a useful (and therefore conditionally controllable) variable. The flexible budget evaluation motif is useful because it brings cost incurred and work accomplished to the evaluation exercise!

Now ask whether breaking this 29,300 (U) variance down into direct labor, direct material, and overhead components might be informative. Again, the exercise is so natural that we rarely bother to examine the underlying logic. Identifying the cost category totals and their individual variances brings additional information to the evaluation task.

You know what's next. If we know the cost category totals, could it be interesting to identify price and quantity variances for each. The inevitable calculations are summarized in Table 20.2.

Table 20.2: Variances for Cost Center Illustration					
cost category	total cost	budgeted cost	price variance	quantity variance	total variance
direct labor	51,300	45,000	3,800 (U)	2,500 (U)	6,300 (U)
direct material	27,000	27,000	3,000 (F)	3,000 (U)	0
overhead	395,000	372,000	12,920 (U)	10,080 (U)	23,000 (U)
total	473,300	444,000	13,720 (U)	15,580 (U)	29,300 (U)

Notice we have offsetting direct material variances; also, the variances average about 6% of budgeted cost.

Introducing the price and quantity variances brings knowledge of actual prices and quantities to the evaluation. So we have added units produced, cost category totals, and finally the underlying price and quantity components to the evaluation.

From here we look for additional information, or explanations. (This is reminiscent of our foray into management by exception at the end of the prior chapter.) Suppose labor were scarce and the manager were forced to use some temporary employees. This resulted in a slightly higher average direct labor wage as well as slightly less direct labor productivity. In short, the direct labor quantity and price variances are both due to this short supply. Now recall the independent variable in the overhead LLA is direct labor cost. Realistically, then, we might argue the cost of this shortage is the total direct labor variance of 6,300 plus 1.6(6,300), or 16,380. Over half the cost overrun is associated with the labor shortage.

With this in mind, do we now want to exclude 16,380 of the cost overrun from the manager's evaluation? At this point the drill should be familiar. We are now proposing use of the fact there was a labor shortage in the manager's evaluation. Excluding 16,380 of the overrun uses this fact; otherwise the fact is not considered germane to the evaluation. Suppose this is a purely random phenomenon and we do not want the manager worrying about such a possibility. We want the manager to run a tight ship. This argues for exclusion. Suppose to the contrary it is random, but we want the manager to be aware these shortages may arise and to plan accordingly. This argues for inclusion of the 16,380. Excluding or including the 16,380 labor shortage cost revolves around whether it speaks to the control problem at hand.

The theme in this simple story is important. Cost incurred is the primary evaluation measure for our manager. We use units produced, or work accomplished, to place the cost figure in context. We disaggregate into cost categories and even into price and quantity variances. We then bring local conditions to bear. A cost-based evaluation is considerably more intricate than simply focusing on the cost incurred.

Interdepartmental Cost Allocation

We now complicate the setting to introduce cost allocation questions. For this purpose, we envision two products and three departments. Department 1 produces the first product and department 2 produces the second; department 1 is the facility in Table 20.1. Department 2's cost structure is exhibited in Table 20.3. Output and cost incurred data are exhibited in Table 20.4.

Table 20.3: Data for Extended Cost Center Illustration	
LLAs for department 1	
direct labor (2 hours @25/hour)	$DL_1 = 50q_1$
direct material (3 units @10/unit)	$DM_1 = 30q_1$
overhead	$OV_1 = 300,000 + 1.6DL_1$
total departmental cost incurred	$cost_1 = 300,000 + 160q_1$
LLAs for department 2	
direct labor (1 hour @20/hour)	$DL_2 = 20q_2$
direct material (2 units @50/unit)	$DM_2 = 100q_2$
overhead	$OV_2 = 200,000 + 1DM_2$
total departmental cost incurred	$cost_2 = 200,000 + 220q_2$
LLA for department 3	
total departmental cost incurred	$cost_3 = 200,000 + .5(DL_1 + DL_2)$

The third department provides essential services to the other two departments. Its cost structure is given by the following LLA:

$$cost_3 = 200,000 + .5(DL_1 + DL_2)$$

where DL_i denotes total direct labor cost in department i (= 1,2). Details are summarized in Table 20.4, where we also present actual costs and outputs. Keep in mind the details for department 1 are identical to those used in Tables 20.1 and 20.2.

Table 20.4: Extended Cost Center Illustration (under $q_1 = 900$ and $q_2 = 1,800$ with total cost = 1,316,800)	
department 1: (actual cost$_1$ = 473,300)	$DL_1 = 51,300$ (1,900 hours @27/hour) $DM_1 = 27,000$ (3,000 units @9/unit) $OV_1 = 395,000$
department 2: (actual cost$_2$ = 588,500)	$DL_2 = 38,500$ (1,750 hours @22/hour) $DM_2 = 180,000$ (4,000 units @ 45/unit) $OV_2 = 370,000$
department 3: (actual cost$_3$ = 255,000)	

Though our concern is the department 1 evaluation, we must do some preliminary work with the service department. Given the output of $q_1 = 900$ and $q_2 = 1,800$, direct labor cost should have totaled 50(900) + 20(1,800) = 81,000. The department's flexible budget gives an expected cost of 200,000 + .5(81,000) = 240,500. This implies a cost overrun of 255,000 - 240,500 = 14,500 in the service department. From here we readily calculate price and quantity variances.[3] See Table 20.5. In this breakdown we think of the quantity variance as reflecting the fact of over-budget use of direct labor by the other departments, and the price variance as reflecting the fact of a service department cost overrun given the actual direct labor cost in the other departments.

Table 20.5: Service Department Variances				
total cost	budgeted cost	price variance	quantity variance	total variance
255,000	240,500	10,100 (U)	4,400 (U)	14,500 (U)

Now turn to department 1. The service department provides essential services for this department. We know from our earlier work in product costing that the

---

[3]In particular we have actual direct labor cost in the first two departments of 51,300 + 38,500 = 89,800. At this level of the independent variable, budgeted cost would be 200,000 + .5(89,800) = 244,900. This is the intermediate calculation we use to identify the price and quantity variances.

accounting library would allocate the service department costs for product costing purposes. The question is whether any of the service department cost should be allocated to department 1 for evaluation purposes. If we answer no, we confine the evaluation to the situation summarized in Table 20.2. If we answer yes, we add the allocated cost to the list of evaluation variables.

How might we go about this? The service department's LLA uses total direct labor cost as the independent, or explanatory, variable. This suggests we use direct labor cost as the basis for allocating department 3's cost. We might use (1) actual direct labor cost; (2) actual direct labor hours at standard price; or (3) standard direct labor hours allowed at standard price. Beyond this we must deal with whether we want to pursue full or variable costing in the allocation, as well as whether to pass through actual service department costs or purge the department's price variance before allocation takes place.

Since the department's LLA uses actual direct labor cost as the explanatory variable, we will focus on actual direct labor cost as the allocation base. Let's also agree to pursue a variable costing theme.

variable costing with a standard rate

With this setup we allocate service department cost totaling $k[\text{actual } DL_1]$ to department 1. If we also base the allocation on a standard rate, we set $k = .5$, the slope of the underlying LLA. Department 1 will now be allocated $.5(51,300) = 25,650$ service department cost. Similarly, department 2 will be allocated $.5(38,500) = 19,250$.

These allocations will be anticipated in the departmental budgets. Recall department 1's direct labor LLA of $DL_1 = 50q_1$. Allocating service department cost to department 1 implies its flexible budget will now include a provision for allocated service department cost of $.5(DL_1)$. With $q_1 = 900$, the service cost budget is $.5(50)(900) = 22,500$. Reworking the cost variances gives us the variances displayed in Table 20.6.

Table 20.6: Department 1 Variances for Cost Center Illustration with Service Cost Allocated at Standard Variable Rate					
cost category	total cost	budgeted cost	price variance	quantity variance	total variance
direct labor	51,300	45,000	3,800 (U)	2,500 (U)	6,300 (U)
direct material	27,000	27,000	3,000 (F)	3,000 (U)	0
overhead	395,000	372,000	12,920 (U)	10,080 (U)	23,000 (U)
allocated service cost	25,650	22,500	N/A	3,150 (U)	3,150 (U)
total	498,950	466,500	13,720 (U)	18,730 (U)	32,450 (U)

Notice the single alteration from the story in Table 20.2 is addition of an allocated service cost variance of 3,150 (U). This is the difference between allocated service cost and what the allocated service cost should have been, given $q_1 = 900$.

If you verify these calculations, you will notice this additional variance is simply .5[direct labor variance]. This reflects the fact we are treating direct labor cost as the allocation base. This variance is also catalogued as a quantity variance, as it reflects off-budget use of the quantity (measured by direct labor dollars) at the standard rate.[4]

A parallel calculation for department 2 would identify an allocated service cost variance of 1,250 (U). Together, the two allocated service cost variances total 3,150 + 1,250 = 4,400. Check back to Table 20.5. 4,400 is the service department's quantity variance. This is no accident. If we allocate on a variable cost basis and if we use the standard rate (i.e., the slope of the $cost_3$ LLA) the allocation procedure simply apportions the service department's quantity variance to the consuming departments. In this way the consuming departments are responsible for service department quantity but not price variances.

Think about this. For evaluation purposes we already know the direct labor, direct material, and overhead variances for department 1. Does the allocated service cost variance contribute new information? Not really, as it is mechanically linked to the direct labor cost variance. The allocation does not provide additional information.

It does, however, simplify the evaluation task. In examining the allocation free variances in Table 20.2, we must remember activities in department 1 affect the service department. The allocation offers a mechanical transformation that reformats the information in a more interpretable manner. Also recall the earlier story where labor was scarce for department 1. We attributed 16,380 of the direct labor and overhead cost overrun to this shortage. At this point, we would also attribute the allocated service cost variance to the labor shortage. In this way we paint a clearer picture of the labor shortage's effects.

Casually, we may be attuned to conveying the evaluation information with variances. If so, we must be careful to put reasonable relative weights on the underlying price and quantity variables. Allocations of this sort then enter to increase the weight on selected variables. This has the advantage of formatting the information in a manner that parallels the underlying economic structure that would be exhibited for decision making purposes.

variable costing with an actual rate

Regardless, the substance of this procedure is the assumption that the variables used in calculating the service department's quantity variance are useful in

---

[4]Naturally we might go further and split the variance between that amount associated with the direct labor price variance and that with the direct labor quantity variance!

evaluating the other departmental managers. A more expansive alternative also uses the service department's price variance in evaluating the other managers. This is the case, for example, when we allocate service department cost based on an actual rate. In a variable costing format, this amounts to allocating service department cost of $k[\text{actual } DL_1]$ to department 1, but with k now reflecting the actual slope of the LLA.

Pulling this off presumes we can identify the actual slope of the LLA. This amounts to subdividing the department 3 price variance into "fixed" and "variable" components. For the sake of argument, assume the "fixed" component is zero. We now, in effect, allocate the service department's quantity and price variance to the consuming departments. Department 1's portion of the story is related in Table 20.7.

cost category	total cost	budgeted cost	price variance	quantity variance	total variance
direct labor	51,300	45,000	3,800 (U)	2,500 (U)	6,300 (U)
direct material	27,000	27,000	3,000 (F)	3,000 (U)	0
overhead	395,000	372,000	12,920 (U)	10,080 (U)	23,000 (U)
allocated service cost	31,420	22,500	5,770 (U)	3,150 (U)	8,920 (U)
total	504,720	466,500	19,490 (U)	18,730 (U)	38,220 (U)

Table 20.7: Department 1 Variances for Cost Center Illustration with Service Cost Allocated at Actual Variable Rate

The change from Table 20.6 is the addition of the price variance for allocated service cost. Compared with the earlier story, we now adjoin some of the service department's price variance to each consuming department's evaluation. From here we invoke conditional controllability to ask ourselves whether this seems sensible.

One story is the department 3 price variance reflects that manager's ability and attention to detail, and says nothing about the other managers. In this case, the additional cost allocation is not useful. Another story is one of correlated environments. It might be the case, for example, that all three managers contribute to the working environment of the service department. Clever scheduling on all their parts, for example, may lead to more efficient operations in the service department. If so, it seems sensible to use the service department's price variance in the evaluation of the consuming departments. Given that we know the other variances, the service department's price variance may be informative.

capacity costs

Continuing our odyssey, we now consider the service department's fixed costs. Think of the service department LLA intercept of 200,000 as approximating capacity costs, and the variable component of $.5(DL_1+DL_2)$, as approximating short-run variable costs.[5] Allocating the intercept, then, amounts to allocating the capacity costs to the consuming departments.

In a variable costing system, we treat the intercept, the capacity cost, as a period cost and thus do not flow it through the product cost calculations. This does not imply we would not allocate these costs to the first two departments for performance evaluation purposes. For example, we may expect the service department will, on average, be dealing with a demand that is 60% from department 1 and 40% from department 2. We might then assign $.6(200,000) = 120,000$ of the intercept to department 1.

This has the often claimed advantage of reminding the department 1 manager that a significant factor of production in the department 1 setting is provided by department 3. The total cost is represented by the $cost_3$ LLA, not just the variable component thereof. Service department capacity costs are significant. Yet, if we know the $cost_3$ LLA and if we know, on average, 60% of the activity in department 3 is caused by department 1, we hardly need a cost allocation of a constant 120,000 to remind us of this fact. It is one thing to argue, as we did above, that allocating the department 3 quantity variance aids interpretation of underlying events in department 1. It is quite another to argue allocating a constant capacity cost from department 3 to department 1 serves to remind the parties this capacity is not cost free.

Changing the story somewhat makes this more interesting. Suppose the department 1 and 2 managers have something to say about the capacity installed in department 3. They may, for example, be asked what activity level they anticipate. These forecasts then play an important part in deciding how much capacity to install in department 3. This, in turn, results in a particular $cost_3$ LLA. We now know, from our budget records, the role each manager played in the capacity decision. Yet allocating the intercept, or capacity cost, to the consuming departments now carries this into the accounting records and serves to remind the parties of the larger picture and set of events that led to the particular department 3 cost structure.[6]

full costing

Intermixing capacity and short-run variable costs in the allocation brings us to the question of whether a full costing approach to the allocation might be desirable. In such a scheme we identify price, quantity, and volume variances in the service

---

[5]Remember we are dealing with a local linear approximation, one that we regard as sufficiently accurate within a particular range of the explanatory variable.

[6]A variation on this theme has the consuming departments negotiate the share of the service department's capacity over which each will have priority. This initial agreement is then used to allocate the capacity cost. Subsequently, one consuming department may release some of the capacity over which it has priority to another department, in exchange for a reshuffling of the allocated capacity cost. This has the effect of creating a stylized market inside the firm, both for options on capacity and for subsequent trading of the options.

department. If we then allocate service cost based on a standard rate, we allocate $k[DL_i]$ to department i (=1,2). k, however, is now the standard full cost rate.

From here we paraphrase our analysis of variable costing with a standard rate. The only difference is we now display the additional, allocated term with a larger implicit price. If we thought about these variances in long-term fashion, this might make sense. Similarly, if we thought the $cost_3$ LLA was incorrectly identified and a rate in excess of the LLA's slope was in order, this might make sense. The more likely story is one in which full costing is being pursued and we want a format that tallies with the product cost calculations. No additional information is carried either way.[7]

Use of an actual rate, reflecting actual service cost per direct labor dollar here, seems to add more noise than insight. We might argue that cost incurred in the service department helps us interpret the department 1 manager's performance, as we did earlier in our discussion of variable costing with an actual rate. But in the full costing format, this also means the allocation to department 1 will depend on the activity in department 2.

To illustrate, suppose the service department experiences no price or quantity variance. Further suppose $DL_1 = 50,000$ and $DL_2 = 50,000$. Service department cost totaling $100,000 + .5(50,000) = 125,000$ will now be allocated to department 1. Conversely, with the same DL_1 but $DL_2 = 0$, department 1's allocation will total 225,000. It seems strange to increase department 1's allocation simply because DL_2 declines.[8]

Naturally, we might use the accounting records to remove this noxious possibility. Recall, under full costing, we would identify price, quantity, and volume variances. Allocating the price and quantity variances, but not the volume variance, now allows us to retain the full costing approach, but without this activity level interdependency. This returns us perilously close to the story of variable costing with an actual rate.

The larger point is one of understanding the manner in which the accounting library presents information. Allocation of service department costs will lead to an additional variance in the receiving department's accounts. Only a quantity variance surfaces if the allocation uses a standard rate; otherwise a price and a quantity variance surface. Moreover, the variances may be joined with a variable or with a full costing motif. Regardless, the information content is there, displayed in a

---

[7]If the allocation is forced to run in tandem with the product costing apparatus, it becomes more difficult to vary the allocation procedure. This has the obvious disadvantage of preventing adaptation to local circumstances. It also has the advantage of making it more difficult to manipulate the evaluation picture by changing the allocation procedure.

[8]This can also happen under variable costing. Remember the costing procedure is driven by an LLA, one that is presumably sufficiently accurate within some relevant range. Dramatic shifts in activity, then, might well drive us to a different LLA. So even under variable costing, the activity in one consuming department may affect the allocation to the other department.

particular format. The professional manager will know how to untangle the myriad events to render an appropriate performance appraisal.

additional observations

We conclude this exploration of the importance of cost allocation in performance evaluation with three additional observations. First, we focused our discussion on evaluation of the department 1 manager. Depending on the circumstances, we might use the service department's (i.e., department 3's) quantity or price variances in the evaluation of the department 1 manager. Suppose we use the quantity variance in this manner. Does this imply we use the price but not the quantity variance in the evaluation of the service department manager?

Certainly not. At this point we must work through the drill again, but now in terms of evaluating the service department manager. Simply because the service quantity variance is informative about the other managers does not imply it is not informative about the service manager. Life is not that easy. A particular measure may be useful for evaluating a variety of managers.

Second, the underlying idea in allocating cost for evaluation purposes is to introduce additional information to the evaluation task. In this sense, we want the manager's cost statistics with allocated costs to be more informative than they would be without the allocation. Otherwise the allocation has not improved the information basis for the evaluation task.[9]

Third, the central theme of bringing additional information to the evaluation, conditional controllability, speaks to information content but not to how this information might best be presented or formatted. Disaggregating department 1's cost into price and quantity variances carries additional information to the evaluation task. Cost categories are introduced, along with price and quantity descriptions of each. The precise format, though, is more a matter of convention. Similarly, allocating service department cost is a combination of convention and information content. If a standard rate is used, the procedure is akin to using the service department's quantity variance in the evaluation of the consuming departments. Yet with direct labor the explanatory variable in the LLA, this becomes a simple mechanical transformation of their direct labor variances. Presumably this is a format with which the parties are comfortable. If an actual rate is used, the service department's price variance is also brought to bear in the consuming department evaluations.

---

[9]We do not have a direct measure of the quantity of services provided each of the consuming departments. This is why we resort to cost allocation to reflect the use of these services in the consuming departments' evaluations. The same issue will arise when we do have a direct measure of quantity. Then we will search for a cost or price per unit of this service in order to reflect its use in the evaluations. This is the topic of transfer pricing.

The broader picture centers on the use of cost allocation in performance evaluation. Practice routinely holds a manager responsible for some allocated costs. Information content and formatting conventions are likely to be present in such a case. Moreover, as our continual reference to variances suggests, standard cost mechanics play an important role in the exercise.

Cost, Revenue, Profit, and Investment Centers

Our exploration to this point uses various components of cost to evaluate a manager. The accounting library is hardly confined to measures of cost. Top management releases an annual (not to mention quarterly) report, a report to the shareholders on its stewardship. This report lists assets, liabilities, revenue, expense, and so on. Quite literally, the library's temporary accounts are closed and the permanent accounts are aggregated into the picture conveyed by the annual report.

It seems reasonable that the board of directors would use this entire portrayal in its evaluation of top management. At the opposite extreme, it seems equally reasonable that supervising management would take a highly focused view in evaluating, say, the manager of the customer billing group. Here they would worry about accuracy and timeliness of customer billing, coupled with some expression of labor, materials, and computer costs. The larger set of financial measures would be superfluous. This raises the question of selecting some subset of the accounting library's data for purposes of evaluating a particular manager.

We broadly categorize the answers into cost, revenue, profit, and investment centers. A manager in a cost center is evaluated primarily on the basis of cost incurred. A manager of an investment center is evaluated primarily on the basis of income relative to the asset base. The progression should be clear. Begin with cost. Introduce a measure of revenue. If it is useful, we have a profit center. The primary evaluation variables are cost and revenue. Next introduce a measure of assets. If it is useful, we have an investment center; the primary evaluation variables are cost, revenue, and assets. In turn, if it works out that cost and investment are not useful in the presence of revenue, we have a revenue center.

investment centers

Investment center status is the consummate evaluation focus. The manager is responsible for short-term and long-term events. Revenues, inventories, expenses, and so on are identified in the evaluation. Only a manager of considerable skill and responsibility could be held accountable on such a broad scale; or at least so the story goes.

Consider a chain of hotels. Treating each specific location in the chain as an investment center presents few difficulties. The asset base at the location is considerable and readily identified. Liabilities are also easily identified, even to the point of debt secured by the facility. Revenue and expense are readily identified. The usual accrual problems of estimating depreciation, pension expense, and so on are not trivial; but the additional problem of assigning the asset base to a specific location is inconsequential. In the larger picture this is straightforward accounting; everything is localized at the individual facility level. Each facility is close to a stand alone entity.

Even so, difficulties emerge. We will likely compare this manager's performance with that of other managers in roughly comparable facilities. Should we adjust each of the asset bases to current cost? Should we use all assets, some assets, or assets less liabilities?

From here we are led to the question of how best to summarize these impressive measures. One way is to highlight return on investment or assets. The accounting rate of return, accounting income divided by accounting assets, is the accounting cousin of the internal rate of return. Another way is to highlight residual income. This is income less a capital charge equal to the asset base multiplied by an appropriate cost of capital. (The usual rate in the academic literature is 10%.) Residual income is the accounting cousin of present value.[10] This, of course, returns (pun) us to the discussion in Chapter 15 of present value versus internal rate of return.

The point is simple. An investment center is accounting nirvana. We can envision a full set of financial reports dealing with a single manager. Just beneath the surface, though, is the sea of complication we encounter in financial reporting. Our prior study of financial accounting should help us quickly picture the issues that need to be resolved at this point.

Even so, we have been putting ease of accounting ahead of usefulness of accounting. Suppose we know revenue and cost for our hotel manager.[11] Does a measure of assets add anything more? Remember, we know who the manager is and which facility is being managed. Introducing the asset base at this point is unlikely to carry any additional information. The inventory of things like supplies and linens might. Measuring the vast majority of the assets, though, is simply not germane to the evaluation task at hand.

Using the asset base here is akin to allocating a flat 60% of 200,000 capacity cost to the consuming department in our earlier cost allocation example. This reminds us of the asset base, but it taxes one's imagination to understand how such a reminder would be necessary, especially when we place the evaluation in the context of a periodic budgeting process in which revenue, cost, cash flow, and occupancy goals are established. The asset base is fundamental to the business, but

---

[10]If accounting and economic value were identical, the accounting rate of return would be the economic rate of return; and residual income would be economic rent.

[11]An awkward terminology is in use here. Properly, we should speak of revenue and expense at this point. This distinction will be explored shortly when we switch to a nonservice setting where inventories are important.

is largely static and does not tell us anything additional about the manager's performance.[12]

Now turn to the product line manager in a large, integrated organization. Consider a manager of a division that designs, manufactures, and distributes various consumer products. Suppose we know revenue and cost. Is a measure of assets likely to be informative? Inventories might be, as might the stock of manufacturing and distribution facilities. For example, the manager may be responsible for design, manufacture, and distribution of the product line. Customer requirements and competition change through time. Targeting the right level and mix of resources for market research, product development, and engineering may be an important part of the manager's assignment. Asset measurement now starts to sound like an informative variable, given that we know revenue and cost.

An important aside here will test our understanding of the variance procedures studied in Chapter 17. Suppose work-in-process and finished good inventories are important in our investment center. This implies that the evaluation addresses both product market and manufacturing performance. Product market performance is reflected in the income statement, where we highlight recognized revenue and the matched expenses. Manufacturing performance is reflected in the array of manufacturing cost variances, derived by comparing actual with budgeted manufacturing cost. These variances, however, are closed to the income statement. In this way the income statement is designed to reflect both manufacturing and market performance, even when inventories are significant. From here, asset measures, including inventory measures, are worked into the investment center evaluation.[13]

profit centers

The cut between a profit and an investment center, then, is a question of whether assets (however measured) convey useful evaluation information in the presence of revenue and expenses. This is related to asset measurement difficulties. For example, historical cost depreciation of the major assets does not sound like it would lead to a very informative asset measure. Yet it does not follow that well-measured assets imply an investment center orientation is called for. The additional information may be redundant.

---

[12]Even so, anecdotes from practice suggest an investment center approach is used in this industry, at least by some players. I interpret this as a formatting device, as opposed to introducing additional evaluation information. It also has the advantage of linking the format of the manager's and the product's evaluation.

[13]The temptation to be pithy is too great at this point. The investment center uses cost, revenue, and asset measures in the evaluation; but the accounting procedure reformats this to expense, revenue, and asset measures!

In parallel fashion, the cut between a profit and a cost center is a question of whether revenues convey useful evaluation information in the presence of cost. Here we usually think of revenue as easier to measure. In turn, this leads to the suspicion a profit center dominates a cost center orientation. After all, the financial press routinely reports earnings, and interprets a particular report as conveying good, bad, or mixed news. Projecting this orientation onto a particular manager, then, is a seemingly compelling idea. Let's focus on the manager's value added, so to speak.

Of course, we may have trouble finding a revenue measure. The service department manager in our earlier cost allocation story is illustrative. We lack a useful measure of the department's contributions to the other departments, other than cost incurred. The principal in the local public school is another example. There we take a cost center approach, supplemented with nonfinancial measures such as student achievement scores.

Other times we have a revenue measure, but the picture remains incomplete. The local parish priest is an example. Expenditures are important, as are collections. The spiritual life of the parish, though, remains an overriding consideration. Again, nonfinancial measures are used; attendance and unsolicited communication from parishioners are examples. The bishop may even formalize the process with a periodic visit in which all parish activities are examined.[14]

Yet other times we have a straightforward revenue measure and it is simply not informative. The manufacturing manager discussed in the prior chapter is illustrative. There, the product in question was standardized and turned over to a marketing group on completion. Output and cost incurred are the primary evaluation measures. Revenue would simply be output multiplied by a known price, and thus would not introduce additional information.

Continuing, we might encounter a setting where revenue is the primary evaluation variable. A telemarketing group is illustrative.

diversification

A concluding observation concerns the large variety of evaluation sources that one typically encounters. We have stressed the idea of cost, revenue, profit, or investment centers as describing the primary evaluation measurement under which the manager labors. A common arrangement for an organization with publicly traded securities is an evaluation along the lines sketched above, coupled with formal incentives and stock options. Use of stock options in this manner amounts to use of the security's market price as an evaluation measure. In this way, the information reflected in the security price is introduced as an evaluation variable.

Also, the formal bonus arrangement is often structured in two steps: a bonus pool is defined and then division of the pool among the eligible managers is addressed. The bonus pool itself is often defined as a function of firm-wide

---

[14]See problem 14 in Chapter 19.

accounting income. Notice this introduces firm-wide profit as an evaluation variable. In turn, division of the pool often reflects a variety of measures, including the primary measures as well as central management's subjective opinions. In this way, central management's qualitative information also becomes a variable in the evaluation arena.[15]

It should come as no surprise that we diversify across a variety of measures when faced with imperfect measurement. Nonfinancial measures are common in this regard.

Nonfinancial Information

Nonfinancial evaluation information is commonplace. As noted earlier, the fast food location is often scored on such things as quality and appearance. Information content is again the key to understanding such practice. Suppose the location is treated as a profit center for evaluation purposes. Attention to detail, cleverly scheduling the work force, and honoring company-wide guidelines for aesthetics and appearance are important managerial tasks. Given we know revenue and cost, it seems likely a measure of quality and location appearance would be informative. In the short-run, labor costs can be reduced by slacking on maintenance, just as material cost can be reduced by inventorying prepared food for an excessive time. Additional information, aimed at the control problem, is the rationalization for these types of supplementary performance measures.

Naturally enough, many examples of nonfinancial measures of performance arise in settings where financial measurement is particularly difficult. Student attendance, teacher absenteeism, and student scores on standardized tests are familiar measures in secondary education. Student evaluations are common in post secondary education. Citations issued are used in traffic enforcement. Peer review is used in surgery. Fielding and batting statistics are used in baseball. Supervision, itself, is a form of nonfinancial evaluation. The supervisor gathers qualitative impressions of skill, work habits, capacity for growth, and so on.

Still, nonfinancial measures are commonplace in settings where the art of financial measurement is well perfected. Consider a manufacturing manager, evaluated as a cost center. The number of employee suggestions might also be monitored, as might the percentage of output that requires rework. Customer complaints and warranty claims might be monitored.

Scrap might be an unavoidable but manageable fact of life. Metal filings, sawdust, and malformed products from an injection molding operation are illustrative. So are early drafts of a consultant's report. In this sense, we have useful products and scrap being produced as joint products. Presuming the scrap has recognizable accounting value, by product accounting is then applied to recognize

---

[15]See problem 17 in Chapter 19.

scrap in the accounting library. Even so, simple physical measures, such as percentage of defects or pounds of filings, might be used in the evaluation.

Other measures might address delivery. What is the average cycle time, say, from customer arrival to delivery? What is the on-time delivery performance?

So-called productivity measures are also popular. Here the idea is to track the ratio of output to input, however measured. Passenger miles per pilot, sales revenue per direct labor hour, units of output per unit of energy consumed, and sales revenue per dollar of labor cost are ready examples. Often times in these cases we find the underlying variables, such as energy consumption or labor input, are used in the basic financial measurement. Highlighting the particular productivity statistics maintains a particular focus, and for this reason we interpret it more as a formatting than an information content exercise.[16]

The Hierarchical Structure of Responsibility Accounting

Now return to the earlier setting of three cost centers, where we examined the use of departmental output, departmental cost, and perhaps allocated cost to evaluate a departmental manager. Now add to the story a general manager who supervises the three departmental managers. Again putting our information content argument to work, it seems intuitive that a primary evaluation basis for this general manager would be the costs and outputs of the three departments.

This simple linkage gives a hierarchical appearance to responsibility accounting. Consider direct labor cost incurred in department 1. This cost datum is used in the evaluation of the department 1 manager. Similarly, the cost incurred in department 3 is used in the evaluation of that manager, and perhaps the other two department managers depending on how we resolve the cost allocation question. For evaluation purposes, each cost category is the responsibility of at least one of the department managers. Introducing the general manager, we see each cost category is also the responsibility of the managers' supervisor.

Continuing, we might imagine a marketing group alongside this manufacturing group. A division manager might supervise the whole affair. Central management eventually surfaces in the story, as a globally responsible manager. In this way, information content often leads to the hierarchical structure of responsibility accounting.

---

[16]Another example, though one based entirely on financial variables, is the idea of categorizing costs into those that reflect value added to the product and those that do not. Production of high quality units does, while production of scrap does not. Machine breakdowns do not. Quality testing, material handling, work-in-process inventory and supervision all fail a ruthless value-added test. From here, we categorize the various costs and track the percentage (or absolute amount) of the value added. The idea is not to cast pejoratives. It is to highlight where the organization hopes it can find cost-saving innovations. The underlying data are in the typical library and are used in the primary cost evaluation. They are now being reformatted to highlight a particular interpretation and concern.

Quite simply, performance of subordinates is often informative about the performance of the subordinates' supervisor. So performance statistics of the subordinates carry over to provide a performance measure for the supervisor. Of course, aggregation is also in place. The general manager's evaluation might begin with some summary measures of the departmental performances, say, the net manufacturing cost variances. A management by exception approach would then be followed to paint a more thorough picture, as warranted.

Summary

Our survey of responsibility accounting stresses the variety of approaches to specifying the accounting basis on which a manager will be evaluated. Cost, profit, and investment center approaches are commonplace. Within any broad category, we find many accounting alternatives ranging across such issues as whether to use historical or current cost, whether to allocate selected costs, when to recognize revenue, and so on. This is no accident. Accounting practice is idiosyncratic.

We have stressed the unifying theme of information content. If an additional measure, such as revenue given that we are observing cost, is to be useful, it must say something useful about the control problem at hand. This amounts to conditional controllability.

Standard cost procedures enter the fray in two respects. First, the underlying price versus quantity separation is often based on additional information. Knowing direct labor cost is less informative than knowing the total hours and average wage rate. In this way the disaggregation into price and quantity variances carries additional information to the evaluation task. Second, the juxtaposition with a norm, or budget, is a convenient format in which to present performance statistics.

Our analysis has stressed managerial evaluation. This should not be confused with activity evaluation. Questions of whether a department or product should be dropped or expanded are different from whether the manager in place should be praised or reprimanded. One issue in activity evaluation is understanding the control problems that might be present and how they might best be attacked. More deeply, though, activity evaluation is a question of whether the organization's interests are best served by the activity while managerial evaluation is a question of whether the manager's inputs, broadly interpreted, have been in the organization's interests. Activity and managerial evaluation are different.

Our analysis has also stressed the idea of extracting the most useful data from the accounting library to aid in the managerial evaluation task. The library itself will, however, be designed with an eye toward the evaluation tasks it will be called on to support. Similarly, the organization structure will reflect anticipation of control problems. For example, a major advantage of a just-in-time production facility is it minimizes costly work-in-process inventories. A corollary advantage is the lack of work-in-process inventories means a quality problem at one manufacturing stage is more likely to become visible almost immediately. It cannot be hidden in inventory. This lessens the interest in other sources of quality information at that stage. Similarly, an advantage of a multiplant operation is the performance statistics of one facility are often useful in evaluating the performance of the other facility. Relative performance evaluation is built into the organization design.

Finally, our analysis has stressed responsibility, not authority. Responsibility accounting is a phrase used to describe the use of accounting data in managerial evaluation. If the costs accumulated in a particular account are used in evaluation of a particular manager, that manager is responsible for those costs. The manager is answerable, is held accountable, for the costs in that category. Similarly, cost and revenue measures are used in the evaluation of the manager's performance in a profit center arrangement. This does not mean the manager has the power to decide, say, products and prices or even production methods. Authority and responsibility are distinct. For example, the manager of a fast food facility is usually evaluated as a profit center. Yet the menu and prices, not to mention cooking procedures and ingredients, are determined by central management. The manager has little authority, but considerable responsibility. Information content is the key.

Bibliographic Notes

Gordon [1964] explores responsibility accounting in terms of designing internal prices to which the managers should respond. Baiman and Demski [1980] link responsibility accounting to the information content of the measures for which the manager is held responsible. The associated hierarchical structure is examined in Demski and Sappington [1989]. Gjesdal [1981] explores the subtle differences between evaluating a product and evaluating a manager. Merchant [1989] provides a vivid description of the evaluation practices in a sample of firms. Solomons [1965] is a classic reference on performance measurement at the divisional level, use of investment centers, and so on.

Problems and Exercises

1.   The idea of responsibility accounting is straightforward: we hold a manager responsible for those accounting measures that tell us something about that manager's performance. Carefully discuss this idea. What does it mean to hold the manager responsible for an accounting measure? What does it mean that an accounting measure tells us something about a manager's performance?

2.   Responsibility *accounting* focuses on the use of accounting measures in evaluating a manager. Might a manager be held responsible for nonaccounting measures? Give an example. How does the use of nonaccounting measures relate to the notion of responsibility accounting?

3. We often associate responsibility accounting with variances. What role is played by price and quantity variances in the use of responsibility accounting?

4. *cost center variances*
Ralph manages a generic production facility. For simplicity, there is no overhead, only direct labor and direct material. The LLAs are:
direct labor   DL = 15(2)q; and
direct material   DM = 40(1.1)q,
where q denotes units of output. The standard price for labor is 15 per hour, and the standard price for material is 40 per unit. During a recent period, 1,100 units were produced, labor cost totaled 36,000 (with an average price of 18 per hour), and material cost totaled 50,000 (with an average price of 40 per unit).

a] Calculate all variances.

b] Which variances do you feel should be used to evaluate Ralph's performance? Carefully explain your reasoning.

c] Ralph complains that a new firm moved in next door and hired a number of the employees. This forced Ralph to take on new and more costly workers. Where does this show up in the variances? Should Ralph be held responsible for this labor turn-over? Explain your reasoning.

5. *cost center variances*
Verify the variance calculations in Table 20.2. Suppose a raw material shortage was present and the cost center was forced to use materials of lower quality, but at a lower price. This also resulted in excessive direct labor. Assume 90% of the labor quantity variance is due to this lower quality direct material. Prepare an alternate variance presentation that isolates the difficulties caused by the raw material shortage. Should the cost center manager be held responsible for the variances you have isolated?

6. *cost center variances*
Using the data in Tables 20.3 and 20.4, prepare a table displaying price and quantity variances for each cost category in each department. (Variable costing is used.) Do not allocate any of the service department cost to the other departments. Notice that Tables 20.5 and 20.6 give you a head start.

7. *cost center variances with allocations*
This is a continuation of problem 6 above. Now assume service department cost is allocated to the other two cost centers. The firm's policy is to base these allocations on standard variable rates, applied to the actual quantity of the service department's LLA.

a]   What, now, is the presumed flexible budget for each of the consuming departments? Give the journal entries to record the allocation. Then amend your table displaying price and quantity variances for each cost category in each department to reflect this allocation.

b]   Give an explanation for why the firm might want to hold the consuming departments responsible for the service quantity but not the service price variances. Does this imply the service center manager is not responsible for the quantity variance?

c]   What happens here if the firm's policy is to allocate service department cost to the consuming departments at standard variable cost (i.e., using the standard variable rate and the standard quantity of the LLA's independent variable)?

8.   *cost center variances with allocations*
Amend your table in problem 7 above for the case where the firm allocates actual variable service cost to the consuming departments. For this exercise assume there was no price variance associated with the service department's "fixed" cost. Why might the firm hold the consuming departments responsible for price and quantity variances in the service department?

9.   *cost versus profit center and information content*
Ralph owns a production function and seeks the services of a manager. The manager's input can be L or H; Ralph desires input H. The manager will oversee a process that will incur a cost that is low or high. Denote the scaled cost possibilities as cost = 1 and cost = 2. Associated revenue, in scaled format, will be revenue = 4 or revenue = 5. The cost/revenue probabilities are displayed below:

	cost/revenue combination			
	1/4	1/5	2/4	2/5
input H	.49	.41	.01	.09
input L	.15	.15	.35	.35

Ralph is risk neutral. The manager is described in the usual fashion. The manager's utility for wealth $\hat{w}$ is given by $U(\hat{w}) = -exp(-r\hat{w})$. If the manager supplies input $a \in \{H,L\}$, thereby incurring personal cost c_a, and is paid amount I, wealth will total $I - c_a$. We use $c_H = 5,000$ and $c_L = 1,000$, along with a risk aversion parameter of r = .0001. Also, the manager's opportunity cost is U(M), with M = 4,000. Ralph cannot observe the manager's input, so contracting is confined to the observable cost and revenue.

a]   Suppose Ralph treats the manager as a cost center. Determine an optimal pay-for-performance arrangement. Why is the manager paid more when a low cost is observed?

b]   Suppose Ralph treats the manager as a revenue center. What difficulty emerges when Ralph attempts to secure input H by evaluating the manager in terms of the revenue outcome? Is revenue controllable by the manager?

c] Suppose Ralph treats the manager as a profit center. Determine an optimal pay-for-performance arrangement that uses the cost and revenue outcomes. Explain the structure of the optimal arrangement. Why is revenue a useless contracting variable when used alone, but useful when used in conjunction with the cost observation?

d] What general principle for choosing between a cost center and a profit center evaluation is illustrated here? How does this apply to choice between a profit center and an investment center?

10. *summary measure myopia in a profit center*

Return to problem 9 above and case [c] where a profit center is used. Suppose instead of contracting on cost and revenue, the parties contract on profit itself, or revenue less cost. Determine an optimal-pay-for-performance arrangement; contrast it with the one determined earlier.

What does this imply about heavy reliance on a summary measure of performance, such as profit in a profit center or return on investment in an investment center?

11. *inventory in profit center*

Ralph manages the manufacture and distribution of a consumer product. The investment base is relatively stable, and Ralph is evaluated on the basis of profitability, market share, inventory, and a changing mix of nonfinancial goals that vary with the circumstance. The profit budget is based on a revenue estimate of $TR = 50q_S$, a manufacturing cost estimate of $TMC = 300,000 + 14q_M$ and a distribution cost estimate of $TDC = 200,000 + 6q_S$. q_M refers to units manufactured and q_S to units sold. The product is manufactured at a fairly steady rate, and inventory is used to absorb random demand fluctuations. Standard, variable costing is used.

a] The current period budget also calls for production and sale of 25,000 units. What profit total is budgeted for the period? What is the break-even quantity?

b] During the period Ralph manufactured 27,000 units and sold 24,000 units. Manufacturing cost totaled 695,000 and distribution cost totaled 339,000. The selling price turned out to average 50.2 per unit. Determine the profit in Ralph's profit center. Factor the difference between actual and budgeted profit into as many variances as you can identify. What do you think of Ralph's performance? Why do you think Ralph's inventory is monitored?

12. *inventory in profit center*

This is a continuation of problem 11 above. Suppose standard full costing is used, based on a normal volume of 25,000 units. Determine the profit in Ralph's profit center; and factor the difference between actual and budgeted profit into as many variances as you can identify. Contrast your performance assessment with that in the prior problem.

13. *extenuating circumstances*

Ralph manages an in-house engineering team that provides consulting services for a variety of product design, manufacturing, and application problems. The unit requesting this service usually reaches an agreement with Ralph on the estimated hours required to deal with the request, and the requesting unit is subsequently allocated a cost of actual hours priced at 85 per hour. Unusual requests that subsequently result in significantly more or less hours are renegotiated by the parties; this renegotiation is rare, and has not been a source of friction. Ralph is evaluated on the basis of service, internal revenue (at the noted 85 per hour rate), and cost.

During a recent performance appraisal, it was noted various units in the organization are pleased with the engineering group and regard it as one of the organization's strengths. The one sensitive point in the evaluation is a cost overrun. Ralph's budget is largely fixed, as a policy of retaining the engineers has long been honored. When excess demands are placed on the group, Ralph subcontracts with one or two of the local consulting firms. During this period, Ralph's total demand did not warrant any subcontracting, yet the bulk of the 224,000 budget overrun is caused by subcontracting. Ralph, in a slightly defensive manner, explains that the industrial products group brought in two rush orders that required immediate attention. It was impossible to meet the other parts of the schedule without subcontracting some work. The industrial products group confirmed the story, to the point of acknowledging the quick turnaround in Ralph's group was essential for their landing the business.

Should Ralph be held responsible for the subcontracting cost in this instance? What about the products group that demanded the rush work?

14. *return on investment*

Ralph manages a regional home products store. A variety of hardware, lumber, and small appliance items are stocked and sold to the general public. A smaller portion of the business deals with commercial customers. The store is but one of many such outlets owned and operated by a large organization. Center, or central management, locates the various stores, makes merchandising and supply decisions, provides advertising, and so on. The store managers deal with the day-to-day operations of their store. A regional manager assists the store manager on such items as merchandising, the need for special promotions when selected products don't sell, and so on.

The major financial evaluation that Ralph labors under is the store's return on investment. The major assets are land, building, display fixtures, and inventory. The debt is centrally held. Cash is centrally managed.

Ralph's particular store has been unusually successful in recent years, and center is contemplating expansion. Ralph, in a dark moment, has begun to worry that the expansion will be disruptive in the short-run, but will also bring additional land and buildings, not to mention inventory, onto the store's balance sheet. Running the numbers suggests the accounting rate of return will drop from 18% to around 11% if the expansion goes forward and sales keep pace at their current level of dollars per square foot of display space.

Carefully appraise the organization's evaluation practices. Might residual income be a better summary measure? Also relate your observations to the examination of summary measure myopia in problem 10 above.

15. *customer satisfaction*

Ralph owns a group of auto dealerships, each a franchised sales and repair facility for a particular national brand. Ralph uses sales, inventory, and profitability measures of a specific dealership to evaluate the performance of that dealership's management team. Another important source of information is customer satisfaction. Ralph has a staff person contact each repair customer within 24 hours of their work being completed. Comment on this use of nonfinancial measurement.

16. *current cost*

Ralph manages a consumer products outlet. Inventory is important. Customers will not return if the outlet is out of stock; and inventory carrying costs are far from trivial. Changing prices are also an issue.

At present the historical cost of the outlet's inventory is 2,036,000 (based on LIFO), while the current cost of the inventory is 2,345,000. A compensation consultant has suggested Ralph be evaluated on the basis of current cost performance, where inventory would be valued at current cost and holding gains would be recognized as income. Ralph is suspicious, since this will add to the income measure's volatility.

Carefully discuss the use of current cost measures in the evaluation context. Do you see any connection with the way GAAP handles foreign currency translation?

17. *overhead LLAs*

In problem 12 of Chapter 9 you examined an activity based costing procedure in which overhead categories were allocated to products based on a diverse set of independent variables (direct labor, direct material, setups, inventory transactions, and complexity). Now suppose each product is manufactured in a separate department. For any given department, then, we would have locally incurred manufacturing costs coupled with allocated overhead costs. For managerial evaluation purposes, is the organization better off allocating overhead to these departments using the LLAs in the earlier problem or using a firm-wide allocation procedure. Explain your reasoning.

18. *information content of interdepartmental cost allocations*

Return to Chapter 17, problem 9, where departmental variances were calculated. You were asked in part [b] to decide how, or whether, to allocate the manufacturing service group costs to the fabrication and assembly departments. Allocate the manufacturing service group variable costs to the fabrication and assembly departments (i) using standard price and standard quantities; (ii) using standard price and actual quantities; and (iii) using actual price and actual quantities. For the latter case, assume all of the price variance is associated with the "variable" cost.

For each allocation method, identify the manufacturing service group price and quantity variances that now appear in the fabrication and assembly department evaluations. Carefully discuss the appropriateness of holding the fabrication and assembly department managers responsible for these additional variances; link your discussion to the notion of conditional controllability.

21

Communication and Budget Participation

Gathering and communicating information are important managerial tasks. The production manager has superior information and insight in the production sphere, just as the product line manager is in the best position to forecast demand. Product development teams often combine engineering, manufacturing, industrial design, and marketing experts. Various managers are likely to have insights into competitor strengths and weaknesses. The manager faced with a budget shortfall is likely to know better than most the major events that led to the shortfall. The same manager probably contributed important information when the budget was originally set.

These communication and budget participation activities put new stress on the relationship between the organization and its management team. Consider a familiar example: our auto fails to start and we have it towed to a garage. The mechanic quickly examines the problem. At this point the mechanic has an information advantage. We ask for a quotation. The mechanic knows a somewhat padded quotation will be advantageous. Eventually we agree to terms, and return when the repair is completed. The mechanic again has an information advantage. Did the repair take as long as noted on the bill? Was it necessary to replace the noted parts? Are the replaced parts fairly priced?

Of course, various institutional features come into play. The mechanic is required to offer us the replaced parts, so we can personally inspect them. Our permission is required if the repair bill is to exceed the original estimate. The mechanic has a reputation to uphold. The mechanic may also use a book of standards, listing standard times for various repair tasks, and quote a price based on standard time at the garage's prevailing labor rate.

Additional options surface. We might have our auto towed to a competing mechanic or to an independent diagnostic center. We also might go to the library or bookstore and read up on our particular set of troubles.

Parallel concerns and institutional arrangements surface inside an organization. The periodic planning process will solicit opinions from various managers. Budget analysts serve to diminish the information advantage of the managers whose opinions are being solicited. After the fact measurement of the managers' performance will be reconciled against their forecasts. Longer term reputation considerations are important in the budget "game." Competing forecasts may be sought. Some services or products may be acquired from another division or plant or acquired outside the organization.

Our exploration begins with a transparent setting in which an information advantage leads to budget slack, or padding. We then move on to extend our managerial input model to a hybrid case where a manager supplies important information as well as directly productive inputs. This allows us to study how various facets of a control problem interact and in particular how we extend the web of controls to address communication incentives. From here we enrich the exploration by introducing various timing and interaction wrinkles. The goal is to understand how an organization might go about providing incentives to communicate and participate productively in the management exercise. Naturally, a specialized version of the story is where we provide incentives to record entries in the accounting library in a timely and accurate fashion.

What Did You Say It Would Cost?

We begin with a folksy but revealing (pun, as we shall see) story. Suppose we seek the services of an expert, say a particular electronic or valuation expert. The services of this expert are worth 4,000 dollars to us. There is only one such expert. The cost to the expert of producing the service we want is either low (1,000) or high (3,000). We do not know whether the cost is low or high, and assign probability α that it is low. Everyone is risk neutral. For the moment let $\alpha = .5$.

If this is all there is to the story, the seller's expected cost is simply 2,000 = .5(1,000) + .5(3,000). The buyer's value is 4,000. Trade should take place, presumably by paying the seller something between 2,000 and 4,000. If the seller has all the bargaining power, the price will be 4,000. The seller simply makes a take-it-or-leave-it offer, with a price of 4,000. If the buyer has all the bargaining power, the price will be 2,000. The buyer simply makes a take-it-or-leave-it offer of 2,000. Trade always occurs; the only question is how the two parties split the gains to trade.

Alternatively, suppose both parties know whether the seller's cost is low or high. Then trade occurs at some price between the seller's cost and the buyer's value in each event. Nothing unusual surfaces when both parties are on an equal information footing.

Now complicate the story. The buyer does not know the cost, but the expert, seller, does. If the informed party, the seller, has all the bargaining power, trade again occurs at a price of 4,000. If the uninformed party, the buyer, has all the bargaining power, the story is quite different. Suppose the buyer makes a take-it-or-leave-it offer of P. If $P \geq 3,000$, the seller will accept the offer, regardless of cost. If $3,000 > P \geq 1,000$, the seller will accept if cost is low but will reject if cost is high. The obvious choices are for the buyer to offer either P = 3,000 or P = 1,000.

Dwell on this. Two approaches are possible. One is for the buyer to make certain the service is acquired. The only way to guarantee the offer is agreeable to the informed seller is to set the price at least equal to the seller's highest conceivable cost. So $P \geq 3,000$ will ensure trade occurs in all cases. The razor's edge is P = 3,000. The second approach is for the buyer to be selective in acquisition. In our simple case this means acquiring the service only when the buyer's cost is low. Offering a price of $1,000 \leq P < 3,000$ will motivate the informed seller to accept the offer only in the low-cost event. The razor's edge is 1,000.

If the buyer offers P = 3,000, trade always occurs; and the buyer's net gain is 4,000 - 3,000 = 1,000. If the buyer offers P = 1,000, trade only takes place when the seller has low cost. The buyer's gain is:

$$\alpha(4,000 - 1,000) + (1-\alpha)(0) = 3,000\alpha.$$

With α = .5, the buyer's choices boil down to taking a gain of 1,000 or of 3,000(.5) = 1,500. The buyer offers P = 1,000 and trade does not occur if the seller is high cost. The buyer finds it desirable to ration the service in response to the seller's information advantage.

slack versus rationing

What's the explanation? The buyer is trying to secure gains from trade. The seller has an information advantage. Pursuing trade under all circumstances leaves a lot of the gains from trade with the seller. Limiting trade diminishes the gains from trade the seller can capture, but at the implicit cost of foregoing the desired service. On balance, limiting trade is the better choice here. By foregoing trade when the seller has high cost, the buyer removes the seller's information advantage. The buyer then captures all the gains to trade, but must limit trade to the low-cost case to ensure these gains.

Figure 21.1: Net Gain to Buyer Trading with Informed Seller

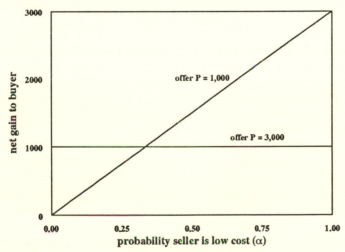

Of course, if α is small, the best choice is to set P = 3,000. The seller is likely to be high cost and there is no sense denying trade to hold down the seller's share of the gains from trade.[1] This is sketched in Figure 21.1. Which approach offers the

---

[1]The simple device of the buyer offering P cannot be improved on, given the buyer is able to

buyer the largest net gain? The buyer's best choice is to offer the seller a price of P = 3,000 for $\alpha \leq 1/3$, and P = 1,000 otherwise.

The message here is important: private information is a friction. Think of this as a case where the buyer asks the informed seller what the cost is. If the buyer then promises to pay the seller's claimed cost, the seller has an incentive to pad the cost claim. If the buyer is less aggressive in using the seller's revelation, the seller has less incentive to pad the cost forecast. The buyer is caught between the proverbial rock and hard place. One choice is not learning the cost and paying 3,000. The other choice is learning the cost, but not trading if high cost is revealed.

Stated differently, the buyer can allow the seller's budget to be padded, to have some slack, by offering 3,000. Or the buyer can remove the slack, by denying trade when the seller is a high-cost type. It is impossible for the two parties to communicate fully and faithfully and use the information as if both possessed it in the first place. The implicit cost of introducing the seller's private information is to under-utilize that information. The choices boil down to a potentially padded budget for the seller or rationing the desired service for the buyer.

a broader perspective

More generally, we have a case where two parties perceive gains to trade but at least one has an information advantage. This information advantage creates a friction in the exchange process. One possible avenue is to tolerate the friction as best we can. Here that strategy amounts to a choice between a potentially padded budget or restricted trade, as illustrated by our simple story. Another avenue is to seek additional information. For example, if the buyer could eventually see the seller's actual cost, there would be a basis for auditing the seller's original claim. (Of course this would then introduce the possibility of noise in the cost observation that is designed to reduce the buyer's ability to audit the original claim.) Alternatively, the buyer might seek an alternate source and rely on competition between the prospective suppliers to lessen the contracting friction. Or the buyer might seek the services of another, someone expert in discerning the seller's cost!

An analogy with budgeting is insightful. Suppose center and a division manager are negotiating a budget. The division manager has superior information. If times are likely to be good and the manager knows this, admitting it is tantamount to receiving a budget with increased performance requirements. Center must be more accommodating if it wants to encourage the manager to reveal the information. The implicit cost of motivating the manager to reveal private information is a commitment to less than aggressive, to flexible use of that information.

---

commit to any particular pricing strategy. For instance, suppose the buyer offers P = 1,000; if the seller rejects the offer, the buyer will then offer P = 4,000. The seller's best response to such a strategy by the buyer is always to refuse the first offer.

For example, if the manager is always treated in an abusive fashion when bad news is conveyed, bad news, when present, will not be communicated in timely fashion. If center always raises the quota every time it is met, the stage is set for underachieving the quota. The cost center manager who negotiates productivity goals with the division manager and then finds that manager more and more insistent on continued improvements will have a natural reluctance to agree to significant improvement goals.[2] If the governor offers amnesty to tax deadbeats, while the attorney general announces a policy of aggressive prosecution of all who come forward, the amnesty program will have few takers. If the manager who offers a new product idea is reminded constantly that future promotion depends on the success of the product, the organization will find a shrinking supply of new product ideas. If the partner in charge of the audit engagement downgrades the audit team manager's performance whenever the audit is over budget, the audit team is encouraged to underreport overtime or to lower the quality of its audit efforts.

The choices are to neutralize the information advantage or to foster self-revelation with a policy of less aggressive use of the information. Either way, the control problem is expanded by the manger's possession of private information.[3] More broadly, the acquisition of this information in the first place may be a plus or a minus. Accurate weather forecasting is useful across society. On the other hand, it is important that the bank manager but not the public know the combination to the vault. Similarly, research and development often lead to advantages in the product market. Equally obvious is the fact life insurance cannot be purchased retroactively.

Self-Reporting Incentives in the Managerial Input Model

The next task is to pass these ideas through our managerial input model. This will sharpen our understanding and set the stage for additional work on coordinating various managerial activities. For this purpose we work an example that is a slight variation on that in Chapter 18, where we explored controllability.

The setting features a risk neutral organization that contracts for the services of a manager. There are two possible input quantities (H and L) and two possible output quantities ($x_1 < x_2$). The manager incurs an unobservable personal cost in supplying either input.

The manager is strictly risk averse, with the usual utility for wealth $\hat{w}$ given by $U(\hat{w}) = -exp(-r\hat{w})$. The manager's personal cost of supplying input $a \in \{H,L\}$ is denoted c_a. Supply of input a followed by payment I provides the manager with a net wealth of $I - c_a$. We again use $c_H = 5,000$ and $c_L = 2,000$, along with a risk

---

[2]The organization that pursues aggressive implementation of a just-in-time inventory policy runs the risk of hidden inventories. Increasing pressure to perform, without inventory buffers, invites the holding of some reserve stock, just as a precautionary item.

[3]Another alternative is to try to remove the manager's access to the private information. Separation of duties in an internal control exercise is often designed to do this.

aversion parameter of r = .0001. Also, the manager's opportunity cost of working for this organization remains at U(M), with M = 3,000.

In addition, an information source is available. This source will report "good" news (g) or "bad" news (b). The difference now is this information is available after the parties contract but before the manager's input is supplied.

Table 21.1: Conditional Probabilities for Budget Participation Example		output x_1	output x_2
good environment (g):	$p(x_i|g,L)$	1.0	0
	$p(x_i|g,H)$	.1	.9
bad environment (b):	$p(x_i|b,L)$	.5	.5
	$p(x_i|b,H)$	.5	.5

Let $p(x_i|m,a)$ denote the probability that output x_i occurs, given environment $m \in \{g,b\}$ and input supply $a \in \{L,H\}$. These probabilities are displayed in Table 21.1. Notice that input H is productive in the good (g) environment, where it raises the odds of high output. It is not productive in the bad (b) environment. We clearly want input L in the bad environment. Input H is more costly, and produces no benefit relative to input L in that environment. Input H is productive in the good environment, and there we assume input H is desired.

The idea is we want to adapt the managerial activity to the environment, and we have the information to do just that. We also assume the two environments are equally likely: p(g) = p(b) = .5.

The way to proceed is uncomplicated when no contracting frictions are present. Pay the manager 8,000 for input H in the good environment and 5,000 for input L in the bad environment. In this way the risk averse manager's net wealth is constant, at (8,000-5,000) = (5,000-2,000) = 3,000; and the risk neutral party absorbs all the risk. The organization's expected cost is .5(8,000) + .5(5,000) = 6,500.

Inability to observe the input, though, creates a contracting friction. In the good environment we have difficulty distinguishing input H and bad luck from input L.

matching incentives to the environment

We deal with this difficulty in familiar fashion. Let I_{mi} denote the payment to the manager when environment m is observed and output i is produced. The manager's expected utility when input a is supplied in environment m is:

$$E[U|m,a] = p(x_1|m,a) \cdot U(I_{m1} - c_a) + p(x_2|m,a) \cdot U(I_{m2} - c_a).$$

Any payment scheme must be attractive to the manager, and motivate the desired behavior in each environment. This suggests the scheme must satisfy the following family of constraints if it is to (1) be attractive to the manager, (2) ensure supply of input H in the good environment, and (3) ensure supply of input L in the bad environment:

$$p(g) \cdot E[U|g,H] + p(b) \cdot E[U|b,L] \geq U(M); \qquad \text{[IR]}$$
$$E[U|g,H] \geq E[U|g,L]; \text{ and} \qquad \text{[IC}_g\text{]}$$
$$E[U|b,L] \geq E[U|b,H]. \qquad \text{[IC}_b\text{]}$$

Initially the parties do not know whether the environment will be good or bad. Overall, the manager must face personal prospects at least as attractive as those in other pursuits. This is the expected utility requirement identified in the individual rationality, or [IR], constraint. The first incentive compatibility constraint, [IC$_g$], requires that if the good environment is revealed, the manager is motivated to supply input H. The last constraint requires that, if the bad environment is revealed, the manager is motivated to supply input L.

Any payment arrangement that satisfies these constraints will be acceptable to the manager, and will ensure supply of H in the good environment and supply of L in the bad environment. The organization seeks the least costly alternative. Denote this cost by C(H,L), the cost of acquiring input H under environment g and input L under environment b. The design program is:

$$C(H,L) = \underset{I_{mi}}{\text{minimum}} \; p(g)\Sigma_i \, p(x_i|H,g) \cdot I_{gi} + p(b)\Sigma_i \, p(x_i|L,b) \cdot I_{bi}$$

subject to [IR]; [IC$_g$]; and [IC$_b$].

Table 21.2: Payment Schemes for Budget Participation Illustration					
case	payment under environment m and output i				
	g; x_1	g; x_2	b; x_1	b; x_2	E[I_{mi}]
information not used	4,252.82	7,649.31	4,252.82	7,649.31	6,630.36
public information used	5,000.00	8,396.49	5,000.00	5,000.00	6,528.42
private information used	3,130.45	8,286.91	4,633.97	6,186.06	6,590.64

Three payment arrangements are displayed in Table 21.2. All satisfy the [IR], [IC$_g$], and [IC$_b$] constraints. Consider the first case where $I_{g1} = I_{b1} = 4,252.82$ and $I_{g2} = I_{b2} = 7,649.31$. Here the manager's pay-for-performance scheme does not vary with the environment. The pay-for-performance incentives are turned on in the good environment, where they are needed, and in the bad environment, where they are not needed. As we suspect, this needlessly exposes the manager to risk.

The second case in Table 21.2 targets the incentives to the good environment, where they are needed. The payment is flat in the bad environment (at 5,000), and appropriately tilted in the good environment (with $I_{g1} < I_{g2}$). The expected payment to the manager declines (to 6,528.42), reflecting the fact that less risk is now being shouldered by the manager.

This is the optimal arrangement. C(H,L) = 6,528.42. We use the public observation of a good or bad environment to fine tune the incentive structure. This allows for the least cost method of acquiring input H in the good environment and input L otherwise, given the contracting friction.

participation incentives

With this idea before us we now change the story in one important way. Suppose the manager privately observes the environment. This means only the manager will observe the environment variable, $m \in \{g,b\}$. The contracting alternatives are less attractive. We no longer have the option of contracting on the observed environment. Instead, we now must ask the manager what was observed and contract on the reported environment.

The idea, then, is we replace the observed environment variable with the manager's claimed or self-reported environment variable. The sequence of play, following agreement on a contract, is (1) the manager observes $m \in \{g,b\}$, supplies $a \in \{L,H\}$ and reports $\hat{m} \in \{g,b\}$; (2) output is observed by both parties; and (3) payment is made according to the specified contract. Notice the manager's task has expanded to include supplying H in the good environment, supplying L in the bad environment, and revealing which environment is present.

This calls for new notation. Let $I_{\hat{m}i}$ denote payment when the manager has announced environment $\hat{m}$ and output x_i is observed. Suppose the manager observes environment m, supplies input a, and reports environment $\hat{m}$. The manager's expected utility is:

$$E[U|m,a,\hat{m}] = p(x_1|m,a) \cdot U(I_{\hat{m}1} - c_a) + p(x_2|m,a) \cdot U(I_{\hat{m}2} - c_a).$$

Carefully notice the role played by the manager's claim of $\hat{m}$. The output probabilities depend on the *observed* environment and input. The payment depends on the output and the *claimed* environment. The manager's claim of $\hat{m}$ amounts to a selection by the manager of which pay-for-performance arrangement (I_{gi} or I_{bi}) is to be used.

This provides a depiction of participation, in the sense the manager now brings significant information to the table. In a larger sense the parties would exchange information, engage in some give and take, and eventually settle on performance goals for the manager. Our depiction streamlines this in important ways.

Here the organization offers the manager a menu of pay-for-performance arrangements, one for each possible environment. The manager, once informed, selects one arrangement from the menu. The bargaining, the give and take, has been replaced by this slick "pick from the menu" story. This preserves the essential idea that the manager brings important resources to the table. The manager now actively participates in the budgeting process. Selecting a pay-for-performance arrangement

from the menu amounts to a self-report by the manager as to what private information has been acquired.[4]

This leads to the important point that the manager must now be motivated to
participate effectively. In our stylized story this point is captured by the requirement
we must make certain the manager is motivated to reveal the observed environment.
Participation incentives must be designed into the infrastructure.

To appreciate this, return to our best payment arrangement in Table 21.2 where
serious pay-for-performance was turned on only in the good environment: $I_{g1} =$
5,000 and $I_{g2} = 8,396.49$, along with $I_{b1} = I_{b2} = 5,000$. Can we import this selective
scheme into the setting where the agent self-reports the environment? Suppose the
manager sees the bad environment. Revealing $\hat{m} = b$ leads to a constant payment of
5,000 (along with $c_L = 2,000$). Claiming $\hat{m} = g$, however, leads to payment of 5,000
or of 8,396.49 with equal odds (along with $c_L = 2,000$). We have a problem.

The tack we take is again to envision the manager's decision tree and then to
engineer it so desired behavior is efficiently motivated. Suppose, for some payment
structure, the manager observes environment g. One of four options must now be
selected: (1) report g and supply H, (2) report g and supply L, (3) report b and
supply H, or (4) report b and supply L. Figure 21.2 sketches the relevant portion of
the manager's decision tree.

Figure 21.2: Manager's Decision Tree upon Observing Environment g

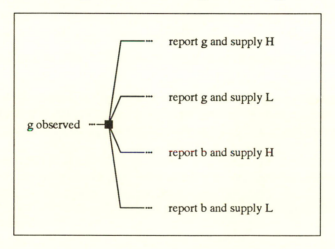

[4]In our initial story when the supplier was offered P = 1,000, acceptance of the offer was the same
as revealing the seller was a low-cost type; and rejection of the offer was the same as revealing the
seller was a high-cost type.

At this point, we want the manager to report environment g (i.e., set $\hat{m} = g$) and supply input H. The payment structure, then, must satisfy the following inequalities:

$$E[U|g,H,\hat{m}=g] \geq E[U|g,L,\hat{m}=g];$$ $[IC_{g1}]$
$$E[U|g,H,\hat{m}=g] \geq E[U|g,H,\hat{m}=b]; \text{ and}$$ $[IC_{g2}]$
$$E[U|g,H,\hat{m}=g] \geq E[U|g,L,\hat{m}=b].$$ $[IC_{g3}]$

The first inequality guarantees the manager is not inclined to report accurately but supply input L. The other two guarantee a lack of inclination to misreport and supply either H or L.

This covers the situation when the good environment is present. A parallel set of constraints ensures accurate reporting and supply of L in the bad environment:

$$E[U|b,L,\hat{m}=b] \geq E[U|b,H,\hat{m}=b];$$ $[IC_{b1}]$
$$E[U|b,L,\hat{m}=b] \geq E[U|b,L,\hat{m}=g]; \text{ and}$$ $[IC_{b2}]$
$$E[U|b,L,\hat{m}=b] \geq E[U|b,H,\hat{m}=g].$$ $[IC_{b3}]$

Finally, the overall package must remain attractive to the manager. The obvious modification of the earlier individual rationality, or [IR], constraint is:

$$p(g) \cdot E[U|g,H,\hat{m}=g] + p(b) \cdot E[U|b,L,\hat{m}=b] \geq U(M).$$ $[IR']$

With this engineering of the manager's decision tree in place, we are in a position to identify the pay-for-performance arrangement that motivates the desired behavior, at minimum expected cost to the organization:

$$C(H,L) = \underset{I_{thi}}{\text{minimum}} \ p(g)\Sigma_i \, p(x_i|H,g) \cdot I_{gi} + p(b)\Sigma_i \, p(x_i|L,b) \cdot I_{bi}$$

subject to $[IR']$; $[IC_{g1}]$; $[IC_{g2}]$; $[IC_{g3}]$; $[IC_{b1}]$; $[IC_{b2}]$; and $[IC_{b3}]$.

The first and last schemes presented in Table 21.2 satisfy these constraints. The first sidesteps reporting incentives by ignoring the manager's report altogether. Reporting concerns are irrelevant when the report is not used. The last scheme, presented in the bottom row of Table 21.2, is the optimal scheme. Notice pay-for-performance incentives are now active in the bad environment. This is necessary to maintain the participation incentives. There is a temptation here for the manager in the bad environment to claim the good environment and vice versa.[5]

---

[5]The binding constraints in the solution are [IR], $[IC_{g3}]$, and $[IC_{b2}]$. In terms of incentives, the manager's most tempting alternative in the good environment is to report bad and supply L; and the most tempting alternative in the bad environment is to report good and supply L. Intuitively, a good pay-for-performance scheme in the good environment is too attractive in the bad environment. For the record, we have

$$E[U|g,H,\hat{m}=g] = E[U|g,L,\hat{m}=b] = -.7684; \text{ and}$$
$$E[U|b,L,\hat{m}=b] = E[U|b,L,\hat{m}=g] = -.7132.$$

We should lay out the manager's decision tree and verify the claim that this pay-for-performance arrangement motivates accurate self-reporting along with supply of input H in the good environment.

the implicit cost of participation

Reflect on the progression. We want input H supplied in the good environment, and input L otherwise. If no contracting frictions are present, the cost is C(H,L) = 6,500. If the information is public but the input supply cannot be observed we resort to a pay-for-performance arrangement. The cost increases to C(H,L) = 6,528.42. In this case participation incentives are moot, since the information is public. If the information is private, participation incentives enter and the cost further increases to C(H,L) = 6,590.64.

We want the privately informed manager to participate substantively in the budget process and then to work diligently to bring the resulting plan to fruition. In our stylized managerial input model this entails accurately reporting the environment and appropriately matching input to the environment. The web of controls must be expanded to address both activities. In our specific example, we do this by using the revealed environment to fine tune the pay-for-performance incentives. Yet this fine tuning is less aggressive than if the environment were publicly observed. Maintaining incentives to bring the information forward requires a degree of delicacy in its use. Participation is not free.

In our first example, that of an informed seller, the buyer's best choice (with α = .5) was to ration the seller's service, in effect buying it only in the low-cost case. Here, the organization's best choice is to solicit and use the manager's information, but less aggressively than would be so if the information were public. In both cases we use the information less aggressively; we allow for slack or leeway compared with the public information case. The theme is scaled-back use of the information, as an implicit cost of acquiring it from the privately informed party.

For a less formal illustration, suppose two products are being produced; one is routine and the other is unusual. We know the total direct labor and direct material used, based on payroll and inventory records. The split between the two products must be self-reported, however. Aggressive use of standards invites a report that biases the cost of the unusual product upward (and the routine product downward).

more illustrations

We wrap this up with an important technical point. If the environment is publicly observed in the managerial input example, the control problem centers on motivating input H in the good case and input L otherwise. If the environment is privately observed by the manager, we have these motivation problems coupled with ensuring that the manager is motivated to reveal the environment accurately. The privately informed story is equivalent to the public observation story coupled with some additional constraints.

What happens when we optimize some function subject to constraints and then add some additional constraints? The additional constraints never help. They are either neutral or painful. Moving from public to private information in our managerial input model, by analogy, will not be efficiency enhancing. The implicit cost of getting the information out will be zero, modest, or severe.[6] In our specific example, the cost is modest. We have some performance degradation compared with the public information case, but are still able to use the self-reported information.

Now change the conditional probabilities in our example so input H in the good environment guarantees high output. See Table 21.3. This is unusual in that output is overwhelmingly informative in the good environment, where we have a potential control problem. If we know the good environment is present, low output is an unmistakable signal that low input was supplied. With public information, then, the control problem is resolved in obvious fashion. The manager is offered I = 8,000 for high output in the good environment (along with a penalty of, say, zero payment for low output in that environment) and I = 5,000 otherwise.

Precisely the same arrangement works in the private information case, where the manager is asked to self-report the environment. If the manager registers a claim of m̂ = b, payment of 5,000 is guaranteed. If a claim of m̂ = g is registered, payment of 8,000 requires high output. The manager is motivated to accurately report the environment and supply the desired input. The reason is the stronger incentives are turned on only in the good environment, but there the link between high input and high output removes any degree of freedom the manager might have to mimic the good environment when the bad environment is present. This illustrates the fact that sometimes the implicit cost of self-reporting will be trivial.

Table 21.3: Conditional Probabilities for Variation on Budget Participation Example		output x_1	output x_2
good environment (g):	$p(x_i|g,L)$	1.0	0
	$p(x_i|g,H)$	0	1.0
bad environment (b):	$p(x_i|b,L)$	.5	.5
	$p(x_i|b,H)$	.5	.5

A slightly enlarged version of our running example illustrates the opposite extreme. For this purpose we use three possible outputs, $x_1 < x_2 < x_3$. The conditional probabilities are displayed in Table 21.4. Everything else remains as before.

Here we want input H in both environments. The critical addition is the fact output x_1 can only occur in the good environment, and only then when input L is supplied. In effect, supply of input L in the good environment runs a 20% chance of detection. This is a stochastic version of the idea in the preceding example. If,

---

[6]Remember, this is information that is confined to our managerial input model. If we expand the story so that, for example, any public information or even revelation of private information is observed by a competitor, we may be harmed and thus strictly prefer the information be private and not revealed.

then, the good versus bad information is public, the payment structure is straightforward. In the good environment the manager receives a flat wage, unless output x_1 is observed. This would signal input L and lead to, say, dismissal and forfeiture of a performance bond. So the manager supplies H and receives a flat wage.[7] Of course, pay-for-performance incentives must be in place for the bad environment. As usual, the information helps match the incentive structure with the environment.

Table 21.4: Conditional Probabilities for Second Variation on Budget Participation Example				
		output x_1	output x_2	output x_3
good environment (g):	$p(x_i|g,L)$	.2	.3	.5
	$p(x_i|g,H)$	0	.1	.9
bad environment (b):	$p(x_i|b,L)$	0	.5	.5
	$p(x_i|b,H)$	0	.1	.9

In contrast, the private information story offers no room to maneuver. We would like to saddle the manager with less performance risk in the good environment, because the x_1 possibility under input L allows for the strongest of incentives. Any attempt to do this, though, is thwarted by the fact input H provides the same output lotteries in both environments. The best way to motivate the manager's self-report here is not to use it!

This may appear strange, but the idea behind the example is straightforward. Suppose we have a monitor that will perfectly reveal the manager's behavior, when it works. (In Table 21.4, input L can be detected with positive probability in the good environment, but not in the bad environment.) Now suppose the manager can learn whether the monitor is working or spewing out noise. Asking the manager whether the monitor is working is likely to be unproductive. Similarly, the manager knows the input supplied; and asking the privately informed manager what input was supplied is not going to bring any additional, useful information to the contracting exercise.

As we said, self-reporting or participation carries an implicit cost. Usually we expect this cost to be moderate. It is possible to lay out cases where the cost is nil or overwhelming, but these extremes belie the important point: if part of the manager's set of duties is to participate, then we must pay attention to the manager's incentives to participate.[8]

---

[7]Study the good environment more closely. In equilibrium the manager supplies H, output x_1 does not arise and a flat wage is delivered. This is made possible by the off-equilibrium threat of dismissal (and forfeiture of a performance bond) should x_1 be observed, which is only possible under input L. The power of a control device may lurk fairly deep behind the scene.

[8]You may be wondering why we insist on complete, honest revelation. It turns out that in these

This should not be interpreted as suggesting such a low opinion of human behavior that honesty in communication must be motivated at each and every turn. Rather, the idea is that putting too much pressure on communication is likely to cause the communication's quality to decline.[9] How do we capture this in our stylized managerial input model? The easiest way is to stay with preferences defined over wealth, and address directly the question of motivating communication. This keeps the clutter to a minimum, and allows us to address the basic point.

Variations on a Theme

This theme of designing participation incentives extends well beyond our setting of a manager who acquires private information before the production plan is finalized. The manager's superior information might be in place before the parties contract. For example, the consultant arrives with considerable industry expertise, just as the seller in our first illustration was privately informed.[10] The information might arrive after the input has been supplied, but before output is observed; or it might arrive after output is observed. The manager may be in contact with customers, soliciting product performance information based on prototypes or well after delivery of the final product.

timing

This is worth a closer look. Suppose our informed manager receives the $m \in \{g,b\}$ information as noted, but is unable to communicate this observation until after the output is observed. This delay is unimportant if the information eventually becomes public. It arrives (privately) in time to inform the manager's input choice; and is publicly observed in (the nick of) time to guide the payment of pay-for-

---

types of games, where the contract designer can commit to how a communication will be used, any equilibrium can be recast into an equivalent one in which honest and full communication is motivated. This is intuitive and makes the modeling easier.

[9]Examples are all around us. The CPA exam is proctored. Periodic financial reports are audited. Tax filings are randomly audited. Hospitals must submit quality control records to an accreditation agency. Fraudulent reporting stories have surfaced in all of these arenas. And on the other side of the fence, the Fifth Amendment to the U.S. Constitution states "...nor shall any person...be compelled in any criminal case to be a witness against himself...."

[10]The initial example, where the seller is privately informed, is illustrative. To sketch the story in more detail, suppose the buyer offers two contracts, and the seller accepts one contract from this menu. The first, designed for the low-cost seller, asks for service quantity $q_L \in \{0,1\}$ and offers payment of P_L. The second, designed for the high-cost seller, asks for service quantity $q_H \in \{0,1\}$ and offers payment of P_H. The low-cost type must find this attractive, i.e., $q_L(P_L-1,000) \geq 0$, and incentive compatible, i.e., $q_L(P_L-1,000) \geq q_H(P_H-1,000)$. The high-cost type also must see this as attractive and incentive compatible, i.e., $q_H(P_H-3,000) \geq 0$ and $q_H(P_H-3,000) \geq q_L(P_L-3,000)$. The seller maximizes $\alpha q_L(4,000-P_L) + (1-\alpha)q_H(4,000-P_H)$ subject to these constraints. This is how our solution was derived.

performance incentives. In the private information case, though, this reporting delay is fatal. The information cannot be used at that point.

To see this, suppose the good environment is present, and before declaring this fact the manager sees high output (x_2). All that is at stake at this point is the manager's pay; the personal cost is sunk. So we must have $I_{g2} \geq I_{b2}$; otherwise $\hat{m} = b$ will be declared. Conversely, suppose our friend observed the bad environment, followed by high output. Motivating accurate reporting now requires $I_{b2} \geq I_{g2}$. Together, the inequalities imply we must have $I_{g2} = I_{b2}$. A parallel argument implies $I_{g1} = I_{b1}$. The communicated information cannot be used. Our slight change in timing reversed the sequence of communication followed by public observation of output.

Remember that output plays two roles here, as a source of value and as a source of information about the manager's behavior. In the latter capacity it is informative about the manager's input supply and self-reporting activities. Reversing the sequence destroys its ability to address the self-reporting control problem. The output is no longer available to discipline the reporting behavior. This points out the importance of timing in these types of encounters. More significant is it reminds us participation incentives must be designed into any participation exercise.

two-sided opportunistic behavior

Participation incentives are not one-sided either. The private information may reside with the manager or with the other party to the contract. The manager's supervisor, for example, might privately gather impressions of the manager's skill and dedication. Can we trust the supervisor to be fair and thorough in developing and reporting this performance appraisal? It is no accident we find formal grievance procedures in place in many such circumstances. Similarly, we are in possession of considerable private information when confronted by the tax auditor; and the tax auditor knows a great deal more than we about reporting patterns that have surfaced in compliance audits.[11]

To reinforce this observation, consider what happens in our running example when the organization instead of the manager privately observes the environment. Now we must worry about the incentives of both parties to the trade arrangement. It turns out that the best pay-for-performance arrangement, in Table 21.2, when the information is public is feasible here. Yet it is routine to identify settings where the organization providing itself incentives to act honorably in the trade arrangement is

---

[11]Yet another variation on the theme concerns who moves first in the trading encounter when one of the parties is already informed. This was illustrated in our original example of a buyer and informed seller. If the informed person has the first move, they try to "signal" what they know. If the uninformed person has the first move, they try to "screen" the other person according to what they know. For example, an insurance company will use a variety of deductibles to screen its customers. The new venture, on the other hand, will try to signal to the investing community the quality of its entrepreneurial activities.

a substantive issue. The IRS, for example, is well known to offer less than candid tax advice.

counterproductive information

Our set of illustrations also offers an opportunity to explore our earlier, cryptic observation that information can be counterproductive. The seller being privately informed in our first example (with $\alpha = .5$) is a setting where trade that would otherwise occur is not engaged because of the seller's private information. Yet public information, in that case, does not hinder trade.

The Table 21.1 story, where the good or bad environment can be discerned before the manager's input is delivered, is quite another story. The information is productive, whether private or public. It allows for matching the costly input to the environment. The information is most productive when it is public, as opposed to privately, observed by the organization. Otherwise, the best contracting arrangement must saddle the manager with more pay-for-performance risk.[12]

Contrast this with the three output case in Table 21.4, where input H is desired regardless of the environment. If no information is available, the manager is readily motivated to supply input H. Having the information, whether public or in the hands of the manager, destroys this flawless contracting story. The information reveals whether the control system is working; and this possibility necessitates the use of more costly controls.

the larger picture

Regardless, the general theme remains. Self-reporting, by either party, raises the question of motivating that self-reporting. Introducing participation options into the relationship calls for an expansion of the web of controls to address incentives that are lurking in any such participation encounter.

These incentives might be influenced by the introduction of other sources of information. A consultant might provide a second opinion. Other managers might be solicited. For example, the audit committee of the board of directors may communicate directly with the internal audit staff, as well as top management. This suggests a type of reporting tournament between lower and upper management. The manager's reporting history is also likely to be important. For example, the manager whose forecasts are always confirmed, to the penny, by subsequent accounting reports will be suspected of gaming the participation exercise, as will the manager whose forecasts are always well below actual results.

---

[12]We should be careful here. The only distortion identified is the amount of risk placed on the manager as a consequence of the best pay-for-performance arrangement. In a richer setting, we would expect the production plan to be altered as well.

These incentives might also be influenced by the way the organization uses the information communicated. As a rule, we expect less aggressive use of communicated as opposed to publicly observed information. Here, organization reputation enters. The organization that has a long history and culture of encouraging participation has invested in stable self-reporting incentives.

Moving beyond our stylized model, we expect contracts to be incompletely specified. Details will be filled in later, or renegotiated, as circumstances warrant. Contracting is a costly exercise itself; and unforseen circumstances are a possibility. The proverbial "whistle blower" is a case in point. Bringing bad news forward leaves the whistle blower vulnerable to retribution.

Finally, these participation incentives may be influenced by nonpecuniary factors. Participation is a forum for recognition, a forum for exhibiting skills (or lack thereof), and a forum for building group cohesiveness. A well-maintained participation ethos may lead to commitment to and personal identification with the organization's goals, a commitment and identification that are indispensable in organization success.

From the micro details of our stylized manager reporting a good or bad environment to the sweeping picture of management style, the underlying message is consistent. Participation begets concern over incentives to play the participation game.[13]

Summary

The topic of budget participation, or communication, is a natural extension of the managerial input story. If participation, or communication, is to be engaged, the organization's control problem expands to accommodate the managers' incentives to play the enlarged budget game. Concerns of this nature are all around us. The judicial system relies on its reputation to convince the state's witness that its immunity offer will be honored. We don't ask the students to grade and self-report their final examinations. We do ask the cost center manager for a cost forecast, and then evaluate the manager based on actual cost and that forecast.

Participation incentives are provided by the organization's culture and by the way the organization manages the participation encounter and uses the self-reports. Aggressive use is not conducive to full, timely, and accurate revelation. This, of course, surfaces in our managerial input model, where we saw self-reported information used in a less aggressive fashion than would be the case were that

---

[13]Once we think in terms of resources devoted to participation and how this might affect group behavior it is unclear where the participation line should be drawn. Stated differently, how much participation is desirable? On the other hand, the answer to this question in our managerial input model is straightforward. The organization moves first in the contracting game, laying a contract on the table. This means, according to the rules of the game, the organization can always commit to how it will use any communication from the manager. One option is to commit to ignore the communication. So all participation should be encouraged in this model. After all, it is done without cost and may be useful.

information publicly observed. It is also important to understand that this is a two-way street. The organization itself may be prone to opportunistic behavior, as when it faces the temptation of selectively honoring commitments or manipulating information flows to its work force.

These concerns extend to our earlier study of library integrity in Chapter 10. The organization's internal control system uses a variety of devices, including separation of duties, to maintain the integrity of the financial records. Separation of duties introduces a reporting tournament, a type of relative performance evaluation. Similarly, auditing introduces an independent check. We are also careful not to put too much stress on the accounting numbers.

The consistent theme is that controls and managerial activity are coextensive. The organization's controls must be as expansive as the managerial activity that is contemplated. The organization provides the environment in which the work force labors. Call it the web of controls, the environment, or whatever. The theme of controls that extend to the entire array of managerial activity is the central point.[14]

Bibliographic Notes

A modeling trick used in our study of communication is to motivate honest revelation. In the type of games analyzed this is always done without loss of generality, since any other equilibrium behavior in these cases can be converted to equilibrium behavior in which candid, full communication is motivated. This motivation, in turn, is ensured by a commitment to "underutilize" the communication. Myerson [1979] is an important reference for this "revelation principle." Christensen [1982] studies participation incentives and returns to information in the contracting model. Of course, with the trick of motivating full communication it is always possible to guarantee the information is communicated simply by committing to ignore it. This raises the question of when it makes sense to listen to the informed party in the first place. Dye [1983], among others, examines this question. Non-pecuniary returns to participation are examined in a variety of places, including Becker and Green [1962]. Hofstede [1967], Hopwood [1972], Merchant [1989], and Swieringa and Moncur [1975] provide field study evidence on, among other things, communication and budget participation.

---

[14]Our theme of providing requisite incentives for participation, or self-reporting more narrowly, has been focused by our use of the managerial input model. Stepping back, we might think of the various managers as experts that are called upon to offer a prediction. Here we confront human cognition and the fact simple linear models often outperform expert predictions in cases where the outcomes (e.g., bankruptcy or pathology) can be confirmed. This adds yet another layer to the communication and budget participation story.

Problems and Exercises

1. The stylized contracting model accommodates the idea that a well-informed player might be induced to communicate what is privately known. This requires we pay attention to incentives; after all, it would be naive to expect the player to freely give away any private-information-based advantage. In turn, revelation incentives take the form of a commitment to "underutilize" the communicated information. Explain this general principle of nurturing communication incentives by less than aggressive use of what is communicated.

2. Our study of communication and budget participation stresses the theme that a control system must be coextensive with the control problem it is designed to address. If a player is called on to supply input and to communicate, for example, the control system must deal with both input supply and communication incentives. Carefully explain this theme.

3. *hidden inventory*
A familiar contention when a just-in-time inventory is implemented is the suspicion that the work force hides inventory. Why might inventory be concealed in such a circumstance? How does this relate to our general theme of motivating participation and communication?

Similarly, a familiar contention when a new management team takes over is the suspicion that various expenses associated with the outgoing team have been aggressively identified, thereby creating some hidden "reserves" for the new team. How does this relate to our general theme of motivating participation and communication?

4. *communication from subcontractor*
Ralph is trying to finish a rush job for a favored customer. The schedule is tight and Ralph can save 8,000 in overtime cost if part of the job is turned over to a local subcontractor. The subcontractor's opportunity cost is either 4,000 or 6,000. The subcontractor knows its cost, but Ralph is uninformed. Let α be Ralph's probability the subcontractor's cost is low (i.e., 4,000). Ralph is risk neutral; time is critical and Ralph must make a take-it-or-leave-it offer to the subcontractor.

a] Suppose $\alpha = 0$, so the subcontractor is a high-cost type and Ralph knows it; what should Ralph do?

b] Suppose $\alpha = 1$, so the subcontractor is a low-cost type and Ralph knows it; what should Ralph do?

c] Determine Ralph's optimal strategy for all possible values of α. Why does Ralph forego trade with the subcontractor on occasion, even though it is common knowledge such trade would be mutually beneficial?

d]   The strategy you determined in [c] above can be interpreted as one in which Ralph designs a contract in which trade will take place at known terms, depending on what the subcontractor claims the cost is; and the subcontractor is motivated to candidly reveal that cost. Provide such an interpretation. Why does Ralph commit to "underutilize" the subcontractor's revelation?

5.   *rules of the game*
    What happens in the trading encounter in the above problem if the subcontractor rather than Ralph makes a take-it-or-leave-it offer?

6.   *communication and input supply incentives*
    Return to the example in Table 21.1. For the first two cases in Table 21.2, draw the manager's decision tree. Then verify that the manager can do no better than accept the offered terms, supply H in the good environment, and supply L in the bad environment. Why is the manager's compensation independent of output in the bad environment in the case where public information is used?
    Now draw the manager's decision tree for the third case. Verify the manager can do no better than accept the offered terms, supply H and reveal the good environment if that environment is observed, and supply L and reveal the bad environment if that environment is observed. Why is the manager's compensation at risk in the bad environment?

7.   *valuable private information*
    Return, again, to the example in Table 21.1. Suppose no information is available, and the owner desires supply of input H. Determine an optimal pay-for-performance arrangement, and contrast it with the Table 21.2 case where the information is privately obtained by the manager but not communicated. How much would the risk neutral owner pay for the manager to observe the environment before acting? Does this amount depend on whether communication is feasible? Why?

8.   *private information with negative value*
    Return to the example in Table 21.4. First suppose no information is available, either publicly or privately. Determine and interpret an optimal pay-for-performance arrangement. (Assume the manager can post a large performance bond.) Second, suppose the good or bad environment is privately revealed to the agent before the agent acts; this revelation cannot be communicated to the owner. Determine and interpret an optimal pay-for-performance arrangement. How much would the owner pay to keep the manager from observing this information? Does the manager benefit from having the private information? Why?

9.   *information management*
    In problems 7 and 8 above you have encountered numerical examples where private information in the hands of a manager is or is not in the best interests of the

organization. Sketch two corresponding institutional settings, one where the organization wants the manager to be informed and one where it does not. Is it possible an organization might want to exclude some information from the accounting library for strategic or control purposes?

10. *friction free revelation*

Draw the manager's decision tree for the case in Table 21.3. Verify the claim in the text that the manager's private communication can be fully utilized here, and trade takes place without any apparent friction. Provide an intuitive explanation.

11. *information arrives after manager acts*

This is a continuation of problem 6 in Chapter 19 (and problem 8 in Chapter 18). The basic story and preferences remain. A high input is desired; the agent experiences an unobservable personal cost; the only contracting variables are output and a monitor, and so on. The single difference is the probabilities are as follows:

	g/x_1	b/x_1	g/x_2	b/x_2
input H	.05	.25	.45	.25
input L	.45	.25	.05	.25

The monitor report (g or b) is observed after the manager acts, but before the output is observed.

a] Find an optimal pay-for-performance arrangement that will implement the H input when only the output can be used for contracting purposes.

b] Repeat [a] for the case where the monitor is publicly observed and both the monitor and the output can be used for contracting purposes.

c] Repeat [b] for the case where the manager privately observes the monitor and communicates this observation, so output and the agent's *claim* as to what the monitor is reporting can be used for contracting purposes. (Hint: here you should find $I_{g1} = 7,086.02$.)

d] Carefully contrast your three solutions above.

e] What happens in part [c] above if the manager's communication is delayed until after the output is observed?

12. *information arrives before manager acts*[15]

Repeat your analyses in problem 11 above, but now under the assumption the manager privately observes the good or bad news after contracting but before acting. Assume Ralph desires input H in the good news case and input L in the bad news case.

---

[15]Suggested by Richard Sansing.

13. *useless participation*

Return to problem 6 in Chapter 19 and the probability structure in part [d]. Verify that if only the manager observes the monitor's report, then the best Ralph can do is commit in the pay-for-performance arrangement to ignore whatever the agent claims the monitor said. Give an intuitive explanation.

14. *evaluation dynamics*

An apparel manufacturer centrally plans production schedules and treats each manufacturing facility as a cost center. Well-engineered standards are in place for each facility, and the major evaluation measure is cost incurred relative to budgeted cost given the output achieved. Labor, material, and overhead variances are examined; and output quotas are closely monitored.

Depending on market conditions, the production plan will be revised on a monthly basis. It also turns out that a facility that has exceeded its output quota can expect a more ambitious quota whenever the schedule is revised.

An internal review of operations has discovered the production managers routinely hold back some output whenever they exceed their quota; this safety stock is then used to cushion the inevitable shortfall when the quota is not met. In response, the review team has recommended the manufacturing facilities be upgraded to profit centers. This would, they argue, elevate the prestige of the production managers, make them more conscious of the larger goal of profitability, and better align their local interests with those of center. Evaluate the review team's suggestion.

15. *accounting library*

The accounting library, we have stressed, is well defended; its integrity is important. In the larger picture, revenue recognition is an important policy instrument. We delay recognition of revenue, and hence income, until the earnings cycle is largely complete.

Suppose the manager has private information about the firm's customer base. The accounting library would not admit this information on a timely basis, preferring instead to honor the revenue recognition rule. Explain this, especially given the theme in the chapter of underutilizing private communication as the implicit price for ensuring its integrity.

16. *communication in root utility case*

Ralph's manager acquires information after acting, but before output is realized. As usual, Ralph, the principal, is risk neutral. The manager has preferences for cash income z and labor input a given by $\sqrt{z} - V(a)$. Two labor inputs are possible, $a = H$ and $a = L$. Ralph seeks supply of H. Conflict is present, as $V(H) = 20 > V(L) = 0$. Also, the manager demands an expected utility of 40 to sign on with Ralph.

Weather plays an important role in the production process. Suppose the weather can be dry, regular, or wet with equal probability. The output possibilities (interpreted as cash before any payments to the manager) are as follows:

	dry	regular	wet
input H	11,000	11,000	5,000
input L	11,000	5,000	5,000

Notice the ideal arrangement, where the manager's behavior is observed (or the manager is committed to cooperative behavior), is explained by risk sharing; the manager is paid a wage of 3,600 dollars in exchange for input H.

a] Suppose the manager acts in a self-interested manner and that only the output can be contracted on. Determine an optimal pay-for-performance arrangement.

b] Now suppose a monitor is available. This monitor will report good news if the weather is not wet and bad news if the weather is wet. (The monitor does not distinguish dry from regular weather.) The monitor's report will be publicly observed at the end of the game. Determine an optimal pay-for-performance arrangement.

c] Next, suppose the monitor will be privately observed by the manager, after the manager acts but before the output is observed. The manager can now tell Ralph what was observed, and the contract can depend on the claimed observation as well as the publicly observed output. Determine an optimal pay-for-performance arrangement.

d] Do you think private observation and communication are always equivalent to public observation? Why?

e] What happens in part [c] if the manager communicates after observing the output? What does this tell you about how the information conveyed by the output is used in your elaborate input supply, communication scheme in part [c]? More broadly, what roles are played by output in part [c] above?

17. *prior informed manager*

Ralph wants to hire a highly skilled manager. The venture will succeed (output x_2) or fail (output x_1). The difficulty is the manager might be a high-skill type or a low-skill type. The probabilities are listed below:

	x_1	x_2
input from high-skill type	1/3	2/3
input from low-skill type	2/3	1/3

Notice the high-skill type has a higher probability of success. For simplicity there is no concern over the quantity of input supply. There is concern, however, over the skill of the supplier. Two managers populate the labor market. Both are known to have a utility function defined over wealth of $U(\hat{w}) = -exp(-r\hat{w})$., with r = .0001. One is high skilled and one is low skilled. They know their own skill, but have no way of convincing Ralph of any such claim. The high-skilled type has a next best alternative that delivers a utility of U(M) with M = 10,000, while the low-skilled type faces M = 5,000. (In a sense, the suppliers privately know their respective costs.)

a]   Locate a pay-for-performance arrangement that will entice the high-skilled type to apply for Ralph's job, but the low-skilled type to shun Ralph's job. Provide an intuitive explanation for how this "separating" contract works.

b]   The contract in [a] above entices the high-skilled type to seek out Ralph, as desired, but at the added cost of productive risk being borne by the risk averse party. An alternative is to not separate the types, i.e., simply offer a wage of 10,000 and flip a coin to select between the applicants. What is the implicit cost of this approach?

18. *ask the manager*

Return to problem 11, part [a] above. The manager knows the input supplied; suppose Ralph asks the manager to reveal which input was supplied. Assume the game is designed so the manager's revelation is received before the output is observed. Find an optimal pay-for-performance arrangement that will motivate the manager to candidly reveal which input is supplied and to supply input H. Interpret your arrangement.

22

Coordination

We now turn to the topic of coordination. On one level this is the task of making certain that all the details of the organization's mission come together in harmonious fashion. The cross-country flight relies on a well-maintained aircraft, proper fuel and flight plan, and the services of many air traffic controllers. Arrival at the destination airport presumes a waiting gate and prepared ground personnel. By the same token, it does little good to release new product advertising when the distribution channels are empty. The assembly line would exhibit grid-lock without well-executed arrivals of component parts and skilled labor. Shopping for the dinner party is made much easier by knowing the recipes for the dishes that will be prepared and served. Traffic lights serve a useful function. Coordination is a well-practiced, vital art.

On another level, coordination also concerns the incentives to provide the variety of pieces that come together in harmonious combination. It does little good to design and advertise a product of exceptional quality, and then saddle the manufacturing arm with stringent production quotas. It is also counterproductive to stress a long-run view while emphasizing short-run incentives.

Our exploration begins with a brief look at aggregate budgeting. This provides an opportunity to remind ourselves of the importance of financial coordination. Next we introduce coordination concerns into our managerial input model, by envisioning the manager as supplying a variety of inputs. This raises the important question of allocating the overall input across a variety of tasks. Planning and control tasks, short-run and long-run tasks, old and new customer solicitations are illustrative. We then use these insights to examine the tensions between short-run and long-run incentives. Finally, we conclude with a brief look at the tensions between coordination that serves the organization's interests with coordination that serves the individuals' more than the organization's interests. The central theme is management of tensions.

Master Budgets

We have casually and intuitively used the term *budget* throughout our study. In most general terms a budget is a projected set of consequences.[1] Given the

---

[1]We speak of a projection here as though it were a single number or specific event. This is common practice. Do not assume, however, budgets are never prepared in probabilistic format. What are the odds our revenue projection will be exceeded? What product warranty statistics do we anticipate and how much risk do we face in this regard? What are the odds our competitor's diversification strategy will fail?

environment and given our plan of action, we project sales will total 14,500 units during the coming (fiscal) year; we project the pipeline will be 75% complete by the end of the quarter; we project our personal finances will be under control in four months; and so on. A master budget is an all-inclusive budget that brings all of the organization's activities into a single picture. It is the organization's most inclusive projection of the consequences of its various activities.

aggregation into a global view

One way to think of the master budget is a projection of what the organization's financial statements will look like at the end of the period in question. These are called *pro forma financial statements*. Given the various production and sales activities we anticipate, given the capital investment and financial transactions we anticipate, and so on, what will the ending balance sheet look like? What will the income statement look like? What about the cash flow statement? We could even imagine this for a group of subsidiaries and their aggregation into the parent's pro forma financials.

The financial statements are an important summarization of the organization's activities and health. It makes sense management would not blindly pursue a set of policies without bothering to ask how the forthcoming financial summarizations might appear. This forces a global look at the organization and provides a reference point for interpreting the financial statements at the end of the period. It also provides the foundation for working capital management.

Strategic considerations are likely to find expression at this point. What do we project that our quality statistics will look like at the end of the budget year? What are our market share projections? What productivity gains do we project, and how do these projections compare with those for our competitors?

disaggregation into a sea of coordinated details

The other side of the master budget is the underlying details that have been aggregated into the pro forma statements. These details are important. They speak to the coordination that is essential for the organization to move forward with minimal friction.

Details at this point are overwhelming, as they should be. Imagine a sizeable organization. Sales projections count in the millions, covering a variety of products. These projections are broken down by product type and subperiod, say, by quarter. They are meshed with tentative production schedules that reflect existing inventory, production capacity, and desired ending inventory. In turn, the production schedules are further broken down into schedules for the various factors of production. Work force schedules and adjustments are recognized. For example, hiring and training plans may be called for. Similarly, acquisition of various materials must be arranged and scheduled. New material handling devices may be called for, requiring design and testing before bids are solicited. The myriad factors we combine into an overhead pool must be thought through and coordinated with the tentative production plan. This eventually provides the overhead LLAs we have been using in product costing and performance evaluation. A parallel pattern emerges in the marketing and administrative areas. These details combine to provide an *operations budget* for the organization.

Investment activities are also part of the stew. Here tentative plans for various investments, say, equipment replacement and expansion (or divestiture) are detailed. These details combine to provide the *capital budget*.

Finally, we have the *cash budget*. These various activities call for an enormous number of transactions between the organization and external entities. Payrolls must be met, deposits covering withholding must be made with the appropriate federal agency, suppliers must be paid, customer payments must be monitored, and so on. This does not happen by accident. Short-term (or long-term) financing may be necessary. Short-term investment opportunities may be available. Detailed, micro management of the organization's working capital is an essential financial service.

The master budget, then, in highly aggregate format leads to a set of pro forma financials. In disaggregate format it leads to detailed operations, capital, and cash budgets. As you suspect, the year is not sacrosanct. Highly detailed plans are likely for the near term. The annual budget has a natural rhythm. Longer term, and more tentative, budgets are also commonplace. Coordination relies on an enormous array of carefully meshed details.

authorization and communication

The master budget enterprise also provides authorization and communication services. It is a primary vehicle for informing the various parties of what overall steps are contemplated and what individual components of those steps are involved. Just as the annual teaching schedule is an important communication to the faculty, product development and promotion plans are an important communication to the consumer product company's sales force. The discipline of the master budget has the virtue of bringing these plans into common view.[2]

Authorization is also an essential activity. Suppose a 10% increase in the work force is contemplated. The human resources group requires instruction or authorization to proceed with the search and hiring. The master budget exercise is such a vehicle. Similarly, a research and development group may operate in largely decentralized fashion, with little explicit direction. Here control is channeled through the

---

[2]This should not be interpreted as an endorsement for complete communication of all plans. Communication is not cost free; and strategic concerns are present. For example, you may want your competitors to know of your product development plans (so-called vaporware in the software industry) or you may want these plans held from public view.

authorization process. The budget process authorizes a total expenditure ceiling. Central management must be consulted if additional resources are sought.[3]

A governmental entity heavily relies on the master budget as an authorization vehicle. The typical municipal budget, for example, includes an overall spending total coupled with a detailed breakdown into line items. These line item breakdowns serve as spending authorizations. For example, the budget might include a line item totaling $2 million for central administration supplies and equipment. In effect, spending up to $2 million in this category has been authorized.[4]

ties to responsibility accounting

The master budget enterprise also has close ties to responsibility accounting. As explored in Chapter 20, we expect to see some of the data in the accounting library used in the evaluation of a particular manager. These accounting summarizations, in turn, are likely to be compared with a budget. The budget has its roots in the earlier master budget exercise. This should be obvious upon reflection.

Notice how communication and participation incentives are, hopefully, at work here. The underlying budget will be, perhaps tragically, flawed if it has been misinformed or informationally starved. The eventual performance evaluation and budget exercise for the next cycle will also be in jeopardy if the results summarized in the accounting library are inaccurate. Another part of the delicate fabric, then, is maintaining accurate source documents that feed into the accounting library.

Management by objectives (or MBO) is a popular euphemism for this activity. The manager and supervisor jointly discuss, explore, negotiate, and settle on performance goals for the manager. These might include such diverse items as overhead cost containment, employee turnover, product quality improvement, and subordinate training goals. Another round of joint discussion, exploration, and negotiation at the end of the cycle formalizes the manager's success in meeting the articulated objectives. The MBO theme highlights the importance of an interactive, largely continuous as opposed to intermittent view of the budget process.

---

[3]Many refer to costs of this sort as discretionary fixed costs. They are discretionary in the sense central management decides on the overall level of activity, and hence cost, that will be incurred. This is the primary control point. Also, they are generally constant across contemplated output variation and thus viewed as fixed costs.

[4]At this point encumbrance accounting comes into play. Tracking expenditures in such a category on a cash basis is not very timely. It's likely to be too late when the bills arrive, since commitments in excess of the authorized spending may already be in place. Encumbrance accounting takes an extremely aggressive approach to recognition. If the supplies are ordered, the overall total of $2 million is immediately written down, or "encumbered" to reflect this commitment. Contrast this with a more typical accrual system that would not record anything in the formal records until the supplies were received from the vendor. Naturally, a well-run cash management operation would take a more forward-looking approach, something that is highly formalized in encumbrance accounting.

budget administration

As becomes clear, the master budget enterprise is serious business. Formalized, rhythmic planning is essential for coordination. It is also a costly activity. Time is devoted to the task, not to mention a variety of staff. Budget planning models (and more formalized scheduling models) are often used. Product costing models may also be used, especially in a setting where product development and redesign are frequent activities occurring throughout the budget cycle.

It is also common practice to begin the budget cycle with a review of the current year. This places the exercise in an incremental format: What's next, compared with this year? This frame has the advantage of parsimony (recall our study of framing in Chapters 11 and 12). It has the disadvantage of not questioning more basic activities.

Zero base budgeting is a phrase used for a process that seriously questions various organization activities during the budget process. For example, rather than look for incremental adjustments to some particular activity, such as strategic planning for a particular product line, also look into the possibility of abandoning that activity. Sunset legislation where a particular government activity has a legislated termination point serves the same purpose. The operative is to budget from a base of zero. The art of management surfaces, yet again, to suggest when these more expansive and costly budgeting activities are likely to be productive.[5]

Intramanager Coordination

Large-scale synchronization, epitomized by the master budget, is a fairly obvious side to the coordination exercise. At the opposite extreme is intramanager synchronization. The manager faces a variety of tasks, and time and talent must be allocated appropriately across these tasks. For example, the professor devotes time to teaching, research, and administrative duties. The manager of the fast food outlet devotes time to supervision, training, maintenance, communication with central administration, customer contact, and so on. Providing incentives to deal, in an appropriate mix, with a variety of tasks turns out to be a delicate exercise.

back to the managerial input model

We explore this by returning to our managerial input model, but expanding it to include two tasks faced by the manager. As usual, we have a risk neutral organization seeking the services of a manager. The manager must deal with two tasks. For each task there are two possible input quantities (H and L), and two

---

[5]Never questioning an activity is a form of possibly costly myopia. Constant questioning is equally flawed. Imagine the two zero base budgeting devotees who are married and discuss the possibility of divorce each morning!

possible output quantities ($x_1 < x_2$). For simplicity, the possible outputs are the same for each task, so the total output will be $2x_1$, $2x_2$, or x_1+x_2. Also, with inputs of H or L applied to either task, the possible input combinations are H to each (HH), L to each (LL), H to the first and L to the second (HL), or vice versa (LH).

Further recall the risk averse manager's utility for wealth $\hat{w}$ is given by the exponential function $U(\hat{w}) = -exp(-r\hat{w})$. The manager's personal cost of supplying input a is denoted c_a. Supply of input a followed by receipt of payment I leaves the manager with net wealth of $I - c_a$. To build as closely as possible on our earlier work we use $c_{HH} = 10,000$, $c_{LL} = 4,000$, $c_{HL} = c_{LH} = 7,000$, and a risk aversion parameter of $r = .0001$. Also, the manager's opportunity cost of working for this organization is $U(M)$, with $M = 6,000$. Our earlier stories, based on a single task, used $c_H = 5,000$, $c_L = 2,000$ and $M = 3,000$. We have merely doubled the original story.

The output probabilities for two different tasks are displayed in Table 22.1. We assume that for either task the organization seeks supply of input H. With this input, both tasks provide the same output odds. Notice output x_2 is an unambiguous indicator of input H for the first task but not so for the second. The first task is easier to control.

Table 22.1: Probabilities for Task Allocation Example		output x_1	output x_2
task one:	$p(x_i|one,L)$	1.0	0
	$p(x_i|one,H)$	.4	.6
task two:	$p(x_i|two,L)$	.7	.3
	$p(x_i|two,H)$	.4	.6

Now suppose the manager is assigned two such tasks, in a setting where the total but not individual task output is observed. In this way the observed output will be a total of $2x_1$, $2x_2$ or x_1+x_2. We further assume the output events are independent and the manager supplies each input before either output is observed. With this independence assumption, the output probabilities are readily calculated. For example, the probability of $2x_1$, given a = HH, is

$$p(x_1|one,H) \cdot p(x_1|two,H) = (.4)(.4) = .16.$$

With the input decision on the second task forced before any output is observed, the supply choices are confined to HH, HL, LH, or LL.[6]

---

[6]An alternative story has the manager supply input to one of the tasks, observe the output, and then supply input to the second task. Working on advertising copy for two products illustrates the story in the text. Direct selling, where each successive customer either places an order or not, illustrates the alternative story.

Table 22.2 presents the optimal pay-for-performance arrangements for three cases: where the manager is assigned two type one tasks, two type two tasks, and one of each type.

Table 22.2: Pay-for-Performance Plans for Task Assignment Example				
tasks assigned	payment under total output (j)			
	$2x_1$	x_1+x_2	$2x_2$	$E[I_j]$
both type one	9,398.70	16,410.98	20,492.43	16,758.34
both type two	4,475.86	19,252.99	24,973.18	18,947.92
one of each type	4,475.86	19,252.99	24,973.18	18,947.92

It should come as no surprise the organization's cost is lower when a pair of type one tasks is contemplated. Absent contracting frictions, supply of a = HH in any case would cost $16,000 = c_{HH}+M$. The type one task is easier to control, and this manifests itself in the lower cost pay-for-performance arrangement. The combination case is indistinguishable from the case where a pair of type two tasks is assigned. This occurs because the problem of motivating the manager to supply input H over input L in the type two task overshadows its counterpart in the type one task. More will be said about this shortly.

Now suppose the organization wants four such tasks performed, two of each type. Two identical managers will be employed. Skill, personal cost, risk aversion and opportunity cost are the same for each manager. The only question is how to allocate the tasks between the two managers. One option is to assign the managers like tasks, so one manager is assigned a pair of type one tasks and the other a pair of type two tasks. Reading off Table 22.2, the organization's expected cost will be $16,758.34+18,947.92 = 35,706.26$. The other option is to assign each manager a pair of dissimilar tasks. The organization's expected cost will then be $2(18,947.92) = 37,895.84 > 35,706.26$.

The expected cost to the organization is less when the managers are assigned similar tasks. This merely reflects the fact that the control problems are lessened with assignment of similar rather than dissimilar tasks. The type two task is more difficult to control. It is best, here, to keep this control difficulty from polluting the control problem with a type one task.

If we look back at Table 22.2, we will see this is precisely what happens when the tasks are mixed. The pollution is so complete that the best pay-for-performance arrangement in the mixed task assignment is the one that deals with the worst control problem (a pair of type two tasks). The control problem with a mixed task assignment is best handled with the same instrument the organization would use to deal with the worst control problem.[7]

---

[7]Other subtleties can be explored here. If the two tasks lead to independent outcomes, as we

Intramanager coordination is an important issue. Here we deal with the manager's allocation of inputs to two tasks. The organization's control problem appropriately expands to deal with this allocation problem faced by the manager. Furthermore, as the example suggests, an important instrument for the organization is the ability to assign groups of tasks to particular managers. A vivid example is separation of duties for internal control purposes. Other examples include whether to subcontract maintenance, to separate initiation from approval of investment projects, or to separate checkout from bagging at the local grocery store. Task assignments are usually thought of in terms of bringing appropriate skills to bear on specific tasks. Underneath is another dimension, that of using task assignment to put together collections of tasks that ease intramanager coordination difficulties.

good measures might drive out bad measures

These coordination difficulties can lead to highly intuitive or highly nonintuitive evaluation arrangements. For example, we expect more reliable evaluation measures to be emphasized in the evaluation process. This intuition is confirmed in our stylized managerial input model.

To illustrate, suppose in our earlier story we also have a monitor that will report good (g) or bad (b) news. The monitor reports good news if the manager supplies a = HH, and bad news otherwise. The best pay-for-performance arrangement is now to pay the manager $I_{gj} = 16,000$ if the monitor reports good news, regardless of the output, and some trivial amount, say, $I_{bj} = 0$, if the monitor reports bad news. Here we have two evaluation measures, the aggregate output and the monitor. Given the monitor, the aggregate output is uninformative. The best arrangement uses only the definitive monitor. (Of course, if the monitor were nearly perfect, it would be relied on much more heavily than, but not to the total exclusion of, the output.)

Intuitively, then, we have "good" driving out the use of "bad" measures of performance in the evaluation process. Yet our story is a little too slick. It correctly uses our earlier informativeness argument, but it also exploits the task question at precisely the correct spot. We want H supplied to each task here, and the monitor discriminates this assignment from all others.

bad measures might drive out good measures

The picture may change when we contemplate better or worse measures that are focused on some but not all of the assigned tasks. The reason is we may have inter-

---

assume, is there an interest in separating the output from each? It turns out the answer is no when similar tasks are assigned, but yes when dissimilar tasks are assigned. This reflects constant risk aversion and independence; of course, with dissimilar tasks the outputs are differentially informative and it would be nice to separate them. Also, to test our intuition, what might happen if the outputs were correlated?

actions between the problem of motivating input for the task per se and the problem of coordinating supply of inputs across the array of tasks.

Suppose we have assigned a pair of type one tasks to the manager. Also suppose it is possible to observe the manager's supply of input to the first of the two assigned tasks. Think of this as a monitor that reports good news if a = HH or a = HL and bad news if a = LH or a = LL.

In principle, the presence of this monitor reduces the control problem, because it is now trivial to ensure that H is supplied in the task that is monitored. Merely administering an appropriate penalty, say, $I_{bj} = 0$ when bad news (b) is observed will do the trick. With this in mind, examine the two incentive arrangements displayed in Table 22.3. Two aggregation possibilities are displayed. In the first, only aggregate output is observed. In that case aggregate output of x_1+x_2 implies one task output was high and the other low, but we do not know which was which. So in this case, x_1+x_2 (interpreted as low output from the first task and high from the second) cannot be distinguished from x_2+x_1. In the second case, the output from each task is separately observed, so these two cases can be distinguished.

Table 22.3: Pay-for-Performance Plans for Task Assignment Example with Perfect Monitor for First Task					
aggregation	payment under output (j) when good news (g) reported ($I_{bj} = 0$)				
	x_1+x_1	x_1+x_2	x_2+x_1	x_2+x_2	$E[I_{mj}]$
total output	9,398.70	16,410.98	16,410.98	20,492.43	16,758.34
task specific output	13,000.00	18,655.80	13,000.00	18,655.80	16,393.48

The first arrangement displayed, then, relies on total but not task-specific output as the output measure in the pay-for-performance scheme. So the contracting variables are total output and the monitor's report (m = g,b) concerning the first task's input. The best such payment scheme is the one we would use if no such monitor were available. (Glance back at Table 22.2.) The problem is our fancy monitor speaks to an area where the control problem is not binding.

This is best understood by studying the pay-for-performance structure for the case where each task's output is separately observed. When the monitor reports good news (g), we know input H was supplied to the first task. Think of this as resulting in a flat wage of 8,000. If, together with good news, the second task's output is low, an additional payment of 5,000 is made (implying a total payment of 13,000). Conversely, if good news is accompanied by high output from the second task, an additional payment of 10,655.80 is made (implying a total payment of 18,655.80).

Suppose we arranged for these inputs from two separate managers. They are identical and fit the usual description. For either one, $c_H = 5,000$, $c_L = 2,000$ and M

= 3,000. (Notice these personal and opportunity costs sum to the totals we are using in our example.) The monitor is used in dealing with the first manager, who is then paid $c_H+M = 8,000$ for supply of input H. The arrangement with the second manager must rely on output to infer input, and there the best arrangement would pay $I_1 = 5,000$ for low output and $I_2 = 10,655.80$ for high output.

This separability is what shows up in the bottom row of Table 22.3, where we have the monitor working on the first of the assigned tasks and separate observation of the output from each task. The independence and constant risk aversion assumptions are clearly at work here, so we should not get excited and interpret this as a general phenomenon.

Instead, the important point is to be found in contrasting the two solutions in Table 22.3. When we move from the individual to the aggregate output stories, we have the monitor at work on the first task but aggregate the output measure. The output measure is the only source of information for controlling the input supply on the second task. Here the lowered quality of information for dealing with the second task drives out the ability to use the higher quality information on the first task. In the aggregate case, the information for dealing with the second task is so bad we do not use the monitor on the first task. We return to the payment structure displayed in Table 22.2, where no such monitor was available. Motivating supply of H to the second task here spills over into the first task's domain. The spillover is so great there is no demand for any information dealing with the first task. Bad information drives out the use of good information in this case![8]

Here's another example. Suppose we have the usual two input levels and two tasks. The manager's personal cost is $c_{HH} = 10,000$, $c_{HL} = 5,500$, and $c_{LH} = c_{LL} = 4,000$. The personal costs interact. The incremental personal cost of input H to either task depends on the input supplied to the other task.

Now suppose we have a perfect monitor for the first task, but must rely on output to infer input for the second task. If we impose input H on the first task, the manager's incremental cost of supplying H to the second task is 4,500. Yet if we impose input L on the first task, this incremental cost is zero. It might turn out we would prefer to forego the benefits of input H in the first task so as to have an easy control problem with the second task.

Alternatively, suppose we have no observable output for the second task, but do have observable output for the first. Consider use of input H in the first task. This requires steep pay-for-performance incentives on the first task (with observable output). In turn, this guarantees supply of L for the second task. The reason is $c_{HL} < c_{HH}$ and there is no way whatever to infer the supply of input to the second task.

---

[8] The incentive compatibility constraints require HH be chosen over HL, LH, and LL. When the manager is assigned a pair of type one tasks and only aggregate output is observed, symmetry ensures indifference between HL and LH on the part of the manager. Also, the only binding incentive compatibility constraint is choice of HH over either HL or LH. Introducing the perfect monitor on the first task still leaves us with the problem of HH versus HL.

Yet if we turn the pay-for-performance incentives off on the first task, supply of H to the second task can be accomplished. This is possible because $c_{LH} = c_{LL}$. Overall, the feasible choices are HL or LH. The only way to ensure supply of H to the second task is to foster supply of L to the first; and this is done by turning off the incentives on the first task. Bad performance measures drive out good performance measures.

The example is contrived to illustrate how control problems interact in a multitask setting. Yet the phenomenon is widespread. For example, it is routinely claimed that the traffic officer does not work under a quota system, emphasizing number of citations issued. To do so would motivate too much attention to citations, away from other more difficult-to-assess duties. A similar concern for explicit pay-for-performance incentives arises in secondary education. There the debate over use of bonus payments based on student test scores raises the question of whether this would motivate too much attention to "teaching the test" and away from a variety of other more difficult-to-assess activities.

two-sided opportunistic behavior

Publish or perish is another example. It also returns us to the theme of two-sided opportunistic behavior briefly touched on in the last chapter. To begin, suppose the professor's performance is measured by research output. This is, after all, tangible and can be evaluated by peers. This practice also raises the concern of whether it drives out teaching activities. In turn, student evaluations are introduced. This helps address the control problem of balancing the professor's attention to various tasks, but at the cost of creating other control problems.

These additional control problems come from two directions. First, teaching covers a variety of tasks, including course design, development, and delivery. Today's curriculum must be delivered, and preparations must be laid for tomorrow's. Introduction of student evaluations raises the question of whether this invites too much attention to the task of delivering the current course, another version of the task allocation idea.

Naturally, student evaluations, course reading lists, examinations, assignments, and personal observation all provide insight into the professor's teaching activities and skills. This leads to the second control problem. The more comprehensive evaluation examines all these sources. Yet the student evaluations are numerically scored and readily tabulated. This invites concern over whether those responsible for preparing the evaluation have been comprehensive and thorough. The readily available evidence, that is, may drive out the production of other evidence.

These two-sided (or double moral hazard) concerns, in which important control considerations arise on both sides of a relationship, are commonplace. The insurance company worries whether the fact we are insured reduces our diligence; and we worry whether the insurance company is sufficiently frugal in its investment activities so that it can pay should a major claim occur. Is the manufacturer of the consumer durable sufficiently attentive to quality and are we sufficiently attentive to maintenance requirements in use of the product? Is the manager sufficiently attentive to the variety of assigned tasks, and is the manager's supervisor sufficiently attentive to the task of evaluating the manager's performance? Coordination concerns interact.

It is no accident we often find grievance procedures in place. The concerned professor might turn to the university ombudsman. The annoyed new automobile owner might invoke the apparatus surrounding the state's "lemon law." The mistreated arrest victim might turn to the citizen review board. The grieved taxpayer might turn to the IRS problem resolution officer following an abusive, aggressive audit.

Intramanager coordination is a fascinating subject. The full array of managerial art is pressed into play. For which tasks should high-powered incentives be used? Which task combinations properly balance comparative advantage of the individuals and control difficulties? What is the best way to deal with multisided control difficulties, as between a manager and supervisor?

Short-Run Versus Long-Run Incentives

Balancing short-run and long-run incentives is a particularly vexing coordination problem. Should we skimp on maintenance or R&D during a period of reduced demand? Should we forego worker training in order to increase output, at lower quality, during a period of unusually high demand? Should we go on the ski trip or continue to study this text? We are concluding an unusually good year. Should we salt some earnings away in a "reserve" to be called upon when times are not so good? Just underneath is the question of whether our control apparatus motivates some such behavior that we consider dysfunctional.

A common caricature here is the hot-shot manager whose division is an investment center. Times have been good, and the accounting rate of return hovers around 30%, with a projected asset base of 100 and income of 30 for the coming year. An unusually attractive investment opportunity surfaces. It will cost 100 but will earn well beyond the organization's hurdle rate for investments in this risk class. The difficulty is most of the returns come in years three and beyond. In the short-run, income stays at 30 and the asset base doubles. The hot-shot's short-run performance measure will be cut in half if the investment opportunity is taken. Why damage a stellar reputation?

Balancing short-run and long-run incentives is an important and continuing issue, but not for the reasons implied by this caricature. Think about it. If the investment is made, in the short-run assets will double and income will be unaffected. For budget purposes we know what to expect. Merely confining the evaluation to the income and old assets or using a budget of $30/(100+100) = 15\%$ accounting rate of return seems to neutralize the short-run depression of the performance measure that is caused by the introduction of the attractive investment. Surely there is more to the problem than this.

a sequence of performance measures

Let's begin to sort this out by thinking in long-run terms. We seek inputs, say, managerial and capital (to name a couple) that will have consequences for a number of periods into the future. Take the easy case where capital is fixed, and we are trying to orchestrate the manager's input. The significant difference from our stylized managerial input model is we have output that occurs in a number of periods. So evaluation, and compensation, in the first period depend on the first period's results; in the second period they depend on the first and second periods' results; in the third period they depend on the three periods' results, and so on. In this way, the evaluation at any point in time reflects current (yes, short-run) results and the recent history of results. The evaluation process cannot see into the future, but it is not prevented from seeing into the past and using the pattern of history in the evaluation.[9]

Viewed in this manner, nothing of conceptual substance is added to our earlier cut on the problem. We seek inputs but cannot observe them. Output, broadly construed, is used as an informational base on which to infer input. Pay-for-performance surfaces. Here, then, we would expect to see a mixture of short-run and long-run evaluations.

Think of this as a profit center. We have cash flow and accrual income reported each period. The accounting library uses restrictive recognition rules and we would not expect it to reflect fully all available information; but we would expect both cash flow and accounting income to be useful in the evaluation. For example, production versus sales would be attenuated by use of a revenue recognition rule. Expected warranty costs would be accrued. R&D would be budgeted. We would also likely delve into other aspects of performance, say, some indicators of quality, of work force training, or whatever, depending on the circumstances.

The incentive problem stretches out over time. We worry about intramanager task allocation through time, but nothing else has been added. Input supply occurs over time, and evaluation takes place over time.

additional frictions

As comforting as this sounds, we have judiciously ignored a variety of additional frictions. Commitment powers are lessened when the time horizon

---

[9] Do not discount the importance of history here. Accrual procedures, in a sense, accumulate history. Also, it is the historical pattern that would help in distinguishing the case of proper attention to short-run and long-run concerns from mortgaging the long-run prospects to improve the current evaluation statistics.

expands. For example, we may have an unusually harmonious working relationship with our supervisor, and then find our supervisor has switched jobs or been promoted. We, too, may switch jobs or be promoted. In addition, the sheer complexity of designing a lasting, long-term contract is overwhelming. We therefore expect incomplete contracts and renegotiation to occur. In addition, we do not condone absolute hands tying labor supply commitments. The manager can quit. Performance bonds and noncompetition clauses are possible, but the fact remains that the manager can reenter the labor market through time.

Reliance on less than complete contracts brings up the possibility of implicit contracts. It is "understood" the manager's pay is keyed to labor market conditions; it is "understood" whenever possible promotion will be from within; it is "understood" the accounting library and its array of responsibility accounting subtleties will not be changed with any frequency, resulting in the proverbial moving target.

Career concerns also enter. The manager's human capital and reputation can be affected by current period activities. Working in the new product arena may, as a by-product, put the manager in a position to learn the ins and outs of emerging technology in some area. Similarly, working with an established product may diminish the manager's possibilities of staying up with this emerging technology. In addition, each set of results provides additional evidence as to the manager's skill and talents.

For example, the understanding may be the manager is compensated at a level comparable to that of comparable managers in roughly comparable organizations. Compensation consultants are used periodically to calibrate this arrangement. Further suppose our manager has been highly successful and is generally regarded as a top performer. Will this induce unusual risk aversion, as the manager seeks to protect this reputation? Conversely, suppose our manager has been floundering and is generally regarded as a middling performer. Will this induce unusual risk seeking, as the manager seeks the big hit that will raise this reputation?

These control concerns are also not one-sided. The organization may be less than attentive to its promise to evaluate performance. Promised rotation through a variety of assignments may not be forthcoming. Good performance may be met by ever increasing demands for better performance.[10]

Short-run versus long-run balancing is important for the organization; and it is important for the individual. The picture is one of intramanager coordination that takes place through time. The tensions and pitfalls are enormous.

balancing devices

This should not suggest that balancing short-run and long-run considerations is insoluble. Rather, it is a dimension to organization life that requires nurturing with professional skill. One avenue is additional information (surprise). Places where

---

[10]This phenomenon is called ratcheting. Good performance ratchets the performance standard.

concern for short-run versus long-run tensions is particularly strong invite additional monitoring. If we don't want maintenance cut back in difficult times, we may want to monitor maintenance activity. If we are worried the present management team in the division is not devoting sufficient resources to new product development or manufacturing improvement, we may want to engage an external consultant to perform a strategic audit of their activities compared with those of our competitors.

Performance statistics can also be pointed toward a longer horizon. Change in net worth over a 10-year period, for example, places an emphasis on growth and downplays the importance of short-run variations in income. The organization's equity price, presuming common shares are traded in an organized market, is a significant source of information. Think of this share market as taking a long-run view and as being informationally efficient. It then can be viewed as processing a vast array of information into the price statistic. In this way we interpret managerial stock ownership or stock options as an evaluation-compensation arrangement that uses the security price as a performance statistic.

Organization arrangements also surface. The organization can nurture a particular view of short-run versus long-run tensions. More direct orchestration is also used. To illustrate, we often find a committee used to pass judgment on major investment proposals. One reason is to assemble a variety of experts to explore the desirability of major proposals. A second reason is to ensure communication among the managers. A third reason is to ensure, given managerial mobility within and between organizations, that someone is still in the organization when the fruits of this investment decision take shape.

We also should not forget the manager's reputation. The trick is to recognize when the manager's reputation concerns work for the organization.

Coordinated Sabotage

The final stop in our look at coordination raises the question of whether there might be too much coordination. Certainly the "over-centralized" organization is too controlled, too coordinated from the top. Likewise, the officious, bureaucratic procedure suggests too much coordination.

A deeper side to this question also exists. Large-scale fraud and bribery require coordination across individuals. Here the coordination is done with the intent of bypassing the organization's internal controls.[11]

More subtle forms of dysfunctional coordination also occur. Suppose the students in one class have a midterm in another class. Study time for the first class will be diminished while the students study for the midterm in the other class. No explicit coordination has occurred. Self-interest leads to the seemingly coordinated

---

[11]The Foreign Corrupt Practices Act explicitly prohibits a variety of corrupt practices; it also requires that adequate accounting records and internal controls be maintained.

behavior in which no one is prepared for the first class. A work slowdown occurs when the labor force complies with each facet and nuance of the labor contract.

The classroom and slowdown illustrations arise in the context of relative performance evaluation. The idea, recall, is to use the performance of one individual as a gauge for the other, presuming that they labor in related environments.[12] For example, grading on the curve implies a relative as opposed to absolute standard. Using an absolute standard exposes the students to the risk of an unusually difficult examination instrument. Grading on the curve removes most of this risk.

uninvited coordination

The link to coordination is easily spotted when we recast this in the setting of our managerial input model. Suppose we want a pair of the type one tasks in Table 22.1 performed. Now, however, a pair of managers will be used, each supplying input to one of the tasks. Our managers are as specified in the single task setting: $c_H = 5,000$, $c_L = 2,000$, $r = .0001$ and $M = 3,000$. Without contracting frictions, each manager would be paid $c_H + M = 8,000$ for supply of input H. In contrast, if output is the only performance measure, the best pay-for-performance measure for either manager is $I_1 = 5,000$ (for low output) and $I_2 = 10,655.80$ (for high output). The expected payment to each manager is 8,393.48.

This incentive structure presumes the two managers labor in independent environments. Then the performance of one offers no insight into the performance of the other.

Now suppose the two environments are perfectly correlated. If both supply input H, both outputs will be low, with probability .4; and both outputs will be high, with probability .6. The only way a mixture of low and high output can occur is if one supplies H and the other supplies L. We're on to something.

Examine the following payment scheme: pay each manager $I = 8,000$ if their outputs are the same and pay each $I = 0$ if they differ. Suppose one manager supplies input H. Given this, if the other supplies input H, their outputs always agree and each winds up with a net of $8,000 - c_H = 3,000$. On the other hand, if the first supplies input H and the second supplies input L, they chance fate. Recall that low input guarantees low output, while high input leads to low output with probability .4. High input by one and low input by the other implies both produce low output with probability .4, and their outputs differ with probability .6. So supply of H by the first and L by the second gives the second a personal cost of $c_L = 2,000$ along with a 40% chance at picking up $I = 8,000$. This prospect has a certain equivalent of 488.06:

$$U(488.06) = .4U(8,000-2,000) + .6U(0-2,000).$$

---

[12]In Chapter 19 we explored the idea of a sales contest as a performance device and linked it to conditional controllability. Here we explore an associated coordination angle.

Pulling this together, our little scheme defines a relative performance evaluation game between the two managers. An equilibrium in the game is for each manager to supply input H. In particular, if one manager supplies H, the other's best response is to also supply H. This provides a certain equivalent of 3,000, as opposed to 488.06.

We summarize this in terms of a bimatrix game. Each player has two pure strategies, H or L. To keep the display as intuitive as possible, we express the players' payoffs in terms of certain equivalents. These are noted below, where we have rounded and omitted 000. Remember in this type of display that, for any pair of strategies, expected utilities or payoffs are displayed with an ordered pair (α,β); α denotes the row player's and β the column player's payoff.

	H	L
H	3.0, 3.0	-2.5, 0.5
L	0.5, -2.5	6.0, 6.0

Suppose Column plays H. Then Row receives a certain equivalent of 3.0 if H is played and 0.5 if L is played. H is best. On the other side, suppose Row plays H. Column might play H, with a payoff of 3.0, or L, with a payoff of 0.5. Each supplying H is an equilibrium.

Unfortunately, each playing L is also an equilibrium. If Row plays L, Column's best response is to play L and vice versa. Moreover, this second equilibrium is decidedly better for the two players. We have inadvertently designed a game with multiple equilibria. One of the equilibria results in a higher payoff for each player. It doesn't take much thought to suspect each will supply input L.

In the end, our clever relative performance evaluation is unraveled by implicit coordination. It is in the best interest of each manager to play the (L,L) equilibrium. The organization winds up paying each 8,000, and each player in turn nets 8,000 - $c_L = 6,000$.[13]

lessened coordination incentives

Let's try again. If the two outputs disagree, the manager with the higher output has surely supplied input H, and just as surely the other has supplied input L. Leave the second (Column) player's compensation structure as before, payment of 8,000 if the outputs agree and zero otherwise. The first manager (Row), though, we now put in a somewhat different position: payment of 8,000 if the outputs agree, payment of 14,500 if they disagree *and* the first manager's output is higher, and zero otherwise.

---

[13]The -2.5 payoff occurs when the player in question supplies H while the other player supplies L. The resulting certain equivalent is: $U(-2,511.94) = .4U(8,000-5,000) + .6U(0-5,000)$.

Now suppose the second manager supplies input L. With this whistle blower style arrangement, the first manager faces the following if input H is supplied:

$$U(6,379.55) = .4U(8,000-5,000) + .6U(14,500-5,000) > U(8,000-2,000).$$

The first manager's best response to the other manager's supply of L is now to supply H. The personal cost goes up, but the 14,500 prize is too tempting to turn down.

With this change, our bimatrix display becomes (recall the 000 scaling):

	H	L
H	3.0, 3.0	6.4, 0.5
L	0.5, -2.5	6.0, 6.0

The first manager finds supply of H a dominating choice. The game has a unique equilibrium. Each manager supplies input H. In equilibrium, their outputs always agree, and each receives a payment of 8,000. Given equilibrium play, the prize of 14,500 is never received; yet its possibility is what holds the arrangement together.

If, then, the managers approach their relative performance evaluation game as a noncooperative exercise, the equilibrium calculus is compelling. Each supplies input H. What if, on the other hand, they decide to cooperate? Here they might agree to have the first manager supply H and the second L. If their outputs agree, they have a total of 2(8,000) - 5,000 - 2,000 = 9,000 to split between themselves. If their outputs disagree, they have a total of 14,500 - 5,000 - 2,000 = 7,500 to split between themselves. This beats what they gain by playing noncooperatively. Better still, they might agree to simply play the L,L combination after all.

Our little yarn is acquiring a life of its own. We began with a setting where relative performance evaluation is called for. With perfectly correlated environments it provides a way to shield each manager from risky production, while maintaining input supply incentives. Coordination temptations then enter. The orchestrated competition between the agents can be turned off by playing a second and more advantageous equilibrium. The retort is then to drive a wedge between the managers, giving an unusually high prize for stellar performance compared with the other.[14] This removes the earlier coordination temptation, but at the cost of introducing another. Now the managers have even more of a reason to collude.

We don't design control systems to make every collusion or circumvention possibility unrewarding. A balance is struck, defending against some and taking our chances against others. If the *maitre d'*, waiters, and bartender all conspire, the restaurant owner is surely at risk. If the real estate developer is a crook, the silent partners are surely at risk. If the division management team decides to take an

---

[14]Here we keep the penalty payment at zero, presuming payments cannot be negative.

enormously risky strategy and under-inform central management, the organization is at risk.

The trick is to understand the limits of coordination. There can be too much, and there can be too little. The well-run organization knows when and where to take advantage of cooperative tendencies, and when to worry about them.

Summary

Coordination activities are a center piece of organization life. The organization exists because it is better able to manage various types of transactions. This leads, naturally, to the study of coordination. Here we encounter the seemingly mundane issues of making certain the details fit together. Also included are incentives to foster the coordination process.

We also recognize intramanager coordination concerns. Managers face a variety of tasks, through time. Orchestrating these tasks is another dimension of the coordination exercise. Attention to a variety of short-run tasks or to a proper balance between short-run and long-run considerations are illustrative. This, in turn, places more burden on the performance evaluation exercise.

Finally, we recognize that the organization can have too much of a good thing. Coordination is not cost free, so we expect less than complete coordination to be the rule. Moreover, coordination can subtly shift from being advantageous to being dysfunctional. Carefully coordinated behavior can sabotage the organization's control system, just as surely as it can pave the way for efficiency gains that provide an advantage in the product market.

Bibliographic Notes

Coordination has been studied extensively. Anthony [1965; 1988] stresses a managerial perspective. Marschak and Radner [1972] focus on information differences at different locations in an organization, and coordination of the local decision behavior, in the absence of control problems. Balancing an agent's allocation across tasks in a contracting model is examined in numerous settings. A good introduction is provided by Antle and Fellingham [1990], Demski and Sappington [1987], Holmstrom and Ricart I Costa [1986], Lewis and Sappington [1989], and especially Holmstrom and Milgrom [1987, 1990, 1991]. Coordination among agents becomes more subtle when they work in correlated environments. There it is natural to use relative performance evaluation, as in a sales contest. This invites coordination among agents, excessive to the point it creates difficulties for the control system (as in our example of uninvited coordination). This has led to elaborate whistle blower games as in Ma, Moore, and Turnbull [1988] and Rajan [1992]. In the limit, the agents may collude. This is studied by Tirole [1986] and Suh [1987].

Problems and Exercises

1. In Chapter 21 the tasks of input supply and communication were combined, and we stressed the idea a control system should be coextensive with the tasks that are assigned the manager. Here we examine a larger variety of tasks. Does the same idea hold? Carefully discuss.

2. Separation of duties is a time-honored control technique. Access to the cash register is limited, the inventory clerk does not count the inventory at year's end, and the warden does not grant paroles. Relate separation of duties to the idea that some combinations of tasks are easier to control than others.

3. If a manager is assigned a single task, we expect high-quality evaluation information to drive out lesser quality evaluation information. For example, a monitor that identified the precise input supplied to the task would render any noisy indicator of input superfluous. Yet when multiple tasks are assigned a single manager, difficulty assessing performance on one of the tasks may overshadow the ability or desire to use high-quality evaluation information on the other task. Carefully explain how this might occur.

3.   *accrual accounting*
Accrual accounting attempts to match accomplishments (e.g., revenue) and effort (e.g., expenses) on a period-by-period basis. Cash basis accounting is less consistent in this regard. In balancing short-run and long-run incentives, then, it would seem accrual accounting has an advantage. Is this correct? Provide an illustration of a setting in which the proper balance between short-run and long-run incentives is best maintained by examining cash flow, accrual income, and other events (e.g., order books, market share, and labor turnover) not explicitly identified by the accounting library.

4.   *source documents*
Ralph's agent delivers confidential and valuable documents among a number of buildings in a metropolitan area. Rapid delivery is essential, and the agent's average delivery time between locations is an important productivity measure. Ralph is also expected to maintain detailed records: a log of the delivery requests and completions, release and acceptance signatures, and so on. What difficulties do you see with this arrangement, especially the concern for accurate records? What might Ralph do to help ensure accurate records and in such a way that delivery productivity is not compromised?

5.   *cash flow budget*
Return to problem 12, Chapter 14, where a linear program was used to locate an optimal production schedule. To avoid overwhelming detail, now assume the

data relate to a quarter; so the optimal plan calls for production of $q_1 = 50$ (and $q_2 = 0$) in each of the next three months. Also assume, for convenience, that direct labor is paid at the end of the current month, while direct material suppliers are paid with a one month lag. 70% of the customers pay with a one month lag, while the others pay immediately. 40% of the "fixed" costs, the intercepts of the various LLAs, are accounting accruals; the remainder as well as the "variable" portions are cash expenditures that are paid at the end of the respective months. Prepare a statement of month-by-month cash flows for this production plan. Notice in the fourth month you will record some cash items but none associated with production in the fourth month, just as in the first month you will record cash flows associated with the current plan but none associated with existing payables or receivables.

6. *interacting control problems*
Return to the setting of Table 22.2, and concentrate on the first case where two of the type one tasks are assigned to a single manager.

a] Draw the manager's decision tree and verify the manager can do no better than accept the contract terms and supply input H to both tasks (i.e., supply HH).

b] Suppose the manager can delay choice between H and L for the second task until the output from the first task is observed. Using the noted pay-for-performance arrangement, can the manager be counted on to supply input H to the second task?

c] Find an optimal pay-for-performance arrangement for the situation in [b] above where the manager observes the first task's output before supplying input to the second task. Explain the difference between your arrangement and that given in Table 22.2.

7. *interacting control problems*
Return to the setting of Table 22.1 and concentrate on the first task. If this is the only task assigned to the manager, how much would the organization pay to be able to observe the manager's input? Conversely, if two of the type one tasks are assigned to the same manager, under the conditions in Table 22.2, how much would the organization pay to be able to observe the manager's input to the first of the two tasks? Give an intuitive explanation for your answers.

8. *aggregation*
Table 22.2 deals with a case where two tasks are assigned a manager, input to each task must be supplied immediately and only aggregate output is observed.

a] Determine optimal pay-for-performance arrangements for the three cases under the assumption the output from each task is separately observed.

b] Give an intuitive explanation for the reason aggregation is not harmful in some instances but is in others.

c] Relate your intuition above to the accounting library's use of aggregation.

9. *multiple tasks*

Ralph owns a production function. Output can be either x_1 or x_2, with $x_1 < x_2$. The manager's input can be one of two quantities, L or H. Ralph is risk neutral. The probabilities are:

	x_1	x_2
input H	.1	.9
input L	.8	.2

Ralph wants supply of input H in all that follows.

The manager is risk averse and incurs an unobservable, personal cost in supplying the labor input. We model this in the usual way. The manager's utility for wealth $\hat{w}$ is given by $U(\hat{w}) = -exp(-r\hat{w})$ and wealth is the net of payment I and personal cost c_a. Set $c_H = 5,000$, $c_L = 0$, and $r = .0001$. Also, the manager's opportunity cost of working for this organization is $U(M)$, with $M = 10,000$. The only observable for contracting purposes is the manager's output.

a] What is the best way to motivate supply of input H by the manager? What is the cost (i.e., the expected payment from Ralph to the manager)? How much would Ralph pay to be able to observe the manager's input?

b] Call the above task *one*. A second task, task *two*, requires the same personal cost, and so on. The only difference is the probability structure:

	x_1	x_2
input H	.1	.9
input L	.7	.3

Suppose only this task is present. What is the best way to motivate supply of input H? What is the cost (i.e., the expected payment from Ralph to the manager)? How much would Ralph pay to be able to observe the manager's input?

c] Now suppose both tasks are present, and Ralph wants supply of input H to both. To keep things closely aligned to the above two stories, change the manager's outside opportunity to $M = 20,000$. The output of each task is separately observed. Also, the manager does not see the outcome of the first task before providing input to the second; so the input supply options are H to both, L to both, L and H or H and L. Will the above two incentive schemes motivate supply of input H to both tasks? Verify your claim, and give the intuition.

d] What is the best way to motivate supply of input H to both tasks?

e] How much would Ralph pay to observe the input supplied to task *one*? Why does this differ from your original answer when task *one* is the only task?

10. *aggregation*

Return to problem 9 above. Both tasks are present as above, but now only the total output is observable. This implies low output from task *one* and high output from task *two* cannot be distinguished from high output from *one* and low output from *two*. How much would Ralph now pay to observe the input to task *one*? Give an intuitive explanation.

11. *multiple tasks and delayed evaluation*

The manager of a facility that manufactures automobile components is evaluated on the basis of output (relative to an output budget) and cost (relative to a cost budget). Product quality is also important, and it is well recognized short-run performance measures can be favorably influenced by degrading quality. In turn, quality is monitored by inspection, scrap, and rework statistics. Warranty claims that are filed by customers are also important, though they can arise up to four years after the component was manufactured. The organization tracks warranty claims by component, facility and manager at the time of manufacture. Thus, if the manager is promoted, the warranty statistics will continue to be compiled, thereby stretching out the evaluation period. Comment on this evaluation practice.

Financial reporting requires the firm provide an accrual to estimate the warranty expense and liability at the time of sale. Why does the firm not find this accrual sufficient for the evaluation exercise?

12. *encouraging profitable investment*[15]

Ralph's firm is always looking for new, innovative products. A manager in Ralph's firm every now and then discovers a new product. Any such discovery is privately known, and it is up to the manager to reveal to Ralph the new product idea. Any new product will eventually result in success (S) or failure (F). The odds of success, however, are higher if the manager is of higher talent. This is because higher talented managers are better at identifying high-quality projects and are also better at implementing them.

People inside and outside the firm observe whether a new product proposal is brought forward, and whether it succeeds or fails. In this way, the labor market learns when a particular manager brings forward a new product and whether that product turns out to be successful. (Gossip can be quite powerful.) The manager's reputation, in other words, improves if a product proposal is brought forward and if the product turns out to be successful. A failed product lowers the manager's reputation. No product proposal is a somewhat intermediate story, because we have to worry about whether the reputation is influenced by a lack of proposal. Let's forget about this latter possibility.

---

[15]Inspired by Holmstrom and Ricart I Costa [1986].

Any new product is risky to Ralph's firm; it is also risky for the proposing manager as an investment proposal places that manager's reputation at risk. What does this do to product development incentives in Ralph's firm, and what might Ralph do to address the situation best?

13. *discouraging end of year games*

A software development firm is funded by a venture capital group and a large pension fund. These investors closely monitor the firm and expect it to meet its sales and income projections.

Nearing the end of a recent year, it has become apparent the announced income goal is in jeopardy. The firm is contemplating (i) laying off market research personnel; (ii) requesting that an important subcontractor delay a progress billing until after the close of the year; (iii) delaying some scheduled maintenance and capitalizing the cost of other maintenance; and (iv) asking several large customers to accept early shipment on orders they have placed.

a] How could each of these actions affect the end-of-year financial statements?

b] Conversely, suppose near the end of the year it becomes apparent that the announced income goal has already been met. The firm might now engage in various acts that will provide a cushion for the following year. Describe several such acts that the firm might contemplate.

c] What might the outside investors do to reduce the temptation to pursue these types of actions?

14. *relative performance evaluation*

Ralph is at it again. Output from the production process owned by Ralph can be x_1 or x_2. The manager's input can be L or H. Ralph is risk neutral. The probabilities are:

	x_1	x_2
input H	.1	.9
input L	1	0

Ralph wants supply of input H.

The manager is risk averse, and is described by the usual personal cost and constant risk aversion story. The manager's utility is $U(\hat{w}) = -exp(-r\hat{w})$. Wealth $\hat{w}$ is the net of payment I and personal cost c_a. Let $c_H = 5,000$ and $c_L = 1,000$, and $r = .0001$. Also, the manager's opportunity cost is $U(M)$, with $M = 4,000$. The only observable for contracting purposes is the manager's output.

a] Determine an optimal pay-for-performance arrangement.

b] Suppose Ralph owns two such production processes and employs an identical manager on each. Further suppose the two environments are perfectly correlated. So if both managers supply input H, their outputs will always agree (both x_1 or both

x_2). Suppose Ralph offers to pay each 9,000 if their outputs agree and zero otherwise. Verify that if one manager supplies input H the best the other can do is supply input H.

c]   What happens in the arrangement in [b] above if one manager supplies input L? Is the other's best response also to supply input L? How do you think the managers will play the game?

d]   Amend Ralph's scheme in [b] so that, in the game played between the two managers, both supplying input H is a unique equilibrium. Give an intuitive explanation for why your modification leads to a unique equilibrium. What difficulty is associated with your scheme?

15. *interactive controls*

Whistle blower type arrangements are designed to encourage revelation of substandard performance. The most simple example is where an employee is legally protected when disclosing fraud. Ralph also knows these games. Suppose an absentee owner wants to hire Ralph to supply some service. The difficulty is Ralph's cost is privately known to Ralph and this places the owner at a contracting disadvantage. So the owner also hires a boss whose job it is to control Ralph.

If the boss works hard, all there is to know about the productive setting will be learned and this will allow for perfunctory control of Ralph. If the boss shirks, nothing will be learned. Working hard carries an incremental personal cost of 10 units, and the boss requires an expected utility of at least 30. So paying the boss 40 is part of an efficient arrangement (where we want the boss to work).

Continuing, we assume Ralph's cost is either 30 or 80. In addition, Ralph's cost is correlated with the productive environment. Output will be 45 or 50 units. The probability of 50 units is .8 if Ralph's cost is 30 and .6 if Ralph's cost is 80. Ralph is also risk averse.

The following scheme materializes. The owner hires the boss. Ralph and the boss simultaneously announce whether Ralph is high or low cost. If their announcements agree, the boss is paid 40 and Ralph is paid the announced cost. If their announcements disagree, each is paid the minimum amount of zero.

a]   Verify this scheme works: an equilibrium is for the boss to work and Ralph's cost to be identified. If the boss works hard and plays fair, the best Ralph can do is be honest; and if Ralph is being honest, the best the boss can do is work hard and play fair.

b]   Suppose the boss shirks and always says 80. What is the best Ralph can do? Is this an equilibrium? Are boss and Ralph better off? Is the owner pleased?

c]   Try the following elaborate scheme. Boss announces Ralph's pay of 30 or 80. If 30 is announced, Ralph may produce and be paid 30 or quit and work elsewhere. If Ralph quits, the boss is paid zero. If Ralph works, the boss is paid 40. Also, if 80 is announced, Ralph may produce and be paid 80 or may claim the cost really is 30.

If Ralph produces, the boss is paid 40 and Ralph is paid 80. If Ralph claims 30, the boss is paid zero and Ralph is paid 79 plus a modest bonus if the output is 50 units. Verify that the equilibrium in this game between Ralph and the boss is for the boss to work and tell the truth, and for Ralph always to acquiesce and be paid according to the boss' claim.

d] The scheme in [c] above relies on Ralph's ability to blow the whistle on the boss. Of course, in equilibrium this does not happen. What control problems would be apparent from watching the game be played? What would a case writer observe in such a setting?

16. *two-sided control problem*

Ralph wants to hire a manager. The manager's output can be either x_1 or x_2. The manager's input can be L or H. Ralph is risk neutral. The probabilities are:

	x_1	x_2
input H	.2	.8
input L	.6	.4

Ralph wants supply of input H in all that follows.

The manager is modeled in the usual way, with utility for wealth $\hat{w}$ given by $U(\hat{w}) = -exp(-r\hat{w})$ and wealth measured as the net of payment I and personal cost c_a. The manager's next best opportunity offers a certain equivalent of M = 8,000. Assume $c_H = 5,000$, $c_L = 0$ and r = .0001.

a] Determine an optimal pay-for-performance arrangement, assuming the only observable for contracting purposes is the manager's output.

b] Now suppose a monitor is available. Independent of the output this monitor will report good news with probability .90 if input H is supplied, and bad news otherwise. Also it will report bad news with probability .90 if input L is supplied, and good news otherwise. Determine an optimal pay-for-performance arrangement. Explain the ranking of the performance payments.

c] Now suppose Ralph (not the manager) privately sees the monitor report in [b] above. This observation is made before the output is known. Is it incentive compatible for Ralph to use the pay-for-performance schedule in [b] and honestly announce to the manager what the monitor has reported?

d] Consider the following payment structure for the story in [c] above: $I_{1g} = 13,059.77$, $I_{1b} = 4,505.37$, $I_{2g} = 13,132.04$ and $I_{2b} = 15,270.64$. (I_{ij} is the manager's payment when Ralph claims to have received report j and output i is subsequently observed.) Verify that the best the manager can do is accept this contract and supply H; and the best Ralph can do is honestly convey whatever report is delivered by the monitor. Carefully explain how and why this scheme differs from that in [c].

17. *reversed roles*

Repeat problem 17 above for the case where the manager rather than Ralph privately observes and then communicates the monitor's report. Why does it matter who privately observes the performance evaluation information?

23

Interdivision Coordination

The final stop in our study of coordination concerns interdivision coordination. In this setting the organization contains various divisions, based on, say, location (e.g., East Coast, West Coast, and Northern Europe) or function (e.g., manufacturing and marketing); and the divisions trade with one another. The critical feature is trade between responsibility centers. We stylize this to a story of interdivision trade.

Examples are numerous. The branch bank writes loans funded by center. Goods manufactured in a foreign subsidiary are marketed by the domestic division. R&D in one division leads to a patented pharmaceutical that is manufactured in a second division and marketed by a third division. Component parts are manufactured in one division and assembled in another. The large audit firm loans audit personnel to another office. Coal is mined in one division and used to generate electricity in another. The political science professor teaches a course in the business school.

The common theme is trade between divisions. This raises the issue of motivating desirable trades or coordinating the divisions' activities. The unusual feature is these trades occur within the umbrella of the parent organization. From the parent organization's point of view, this amounts to asking how it should regulate trade between the divisions.

We begin by expanding on this theme of regulating trade between divisions and the associated problem of how to record these trades in the accounting library. *Transfer pricing* is the name given these recording procedures. We then review the classical solution to this regulation question. Here, the idea is to mimic a price system so that prices governing trade between divisions lead to the efficient solution. Control problems enter, and we are led back to our managerial input model. In this way we identify a decentralized arrangement in which division profit measurement is an important control instrument.

We then expand this theme to examine a variety of transfer pricing and sourcing policies center might employ. Finally, the links to taxation and our earlier study of cost allocation are briefly explored.

Regulating Trade Between Divisions

Consider a setting where the organization consists of three subentities: central management (from now on, simply *center*), division A, and division B. Division A produces a good or service that is essential for division B. For the moment, division B has no alternative source for this essential good or service. Let q_A denote units of output from division A that are transferred to division B; also let q_B denote units of output from division B that are sold in the product market.

For the sake of discussion, we interpret division A's output as an essential subcomponent for division B. This implies the output decisions should be coordinated, so $q_A = q_B = q$. We expect market conditions and cost will inform the coordinated output decision.

Here it is reasonable to assume each division knows something the other does not know. Division A likely knows more about its cost, and division B likely knows more about its cost and the product market. Division A, for example, might produce a variety of products. Its cost of producing this subcomponent for division B depends on the production levels of its other products. Division A's market opportunities for these other products are constantly changing, which in turn implies its cost of producing subcomponents for division B is constantly changing. Division A, itself, has the best insight into these important, changing economic forces. A parallel story is told for division B.

This raises the question of how best to bring this dispersed information to bear on the underlying coordination decision. One extreme is to centralize the decision; the other is to decentralize it to the two divisions.

centralized coordination

In a centralized regime the common quantity decision, $q_A = q_B = q$, is set by central administration. Center makes the output decision; and the various units receive instruction from center. Of course, center does not do this in a vacuum. Preceding the decision by center is a solicitation of information. The story, then, is the divisions pass information to center. In turn, center collects the information, generates its own information and folds this into a centralized decision that is subsequently communicated to the individual units.

The advantage of centralization is the ability to apply a global perspective to the coordination activity. Center, presumably, is in the best position to assimilate the various bits and pieces, and to apply an overall perspective in balancing the various tensions. The disadvantage is the possibility the coordination activity can become cumbersome to the point of slowing and straining communication paths.

Also notice the possible control frictions. Although center can apply directly its perspective, it is not free from the divisions' perspectives. We know from earlier chapters that the divisions' motives in communicating with center and in following center's instructions are important ingredients in the organization stew. (We also know the reverse perspective is important, that of center's motives in dealing with the divisions.)

decentralized coordination

In a decentralized regime the common quantity decision is set by the two divisions. Here the communication flow between the divisions and center is replaced by communication flow between the divisions. Naturally, the divisions do not do this in a vacuum. Center oversees their activities, and designs and manages the environment in which they operate.

The advantage of decentralization is the ability to keep the decisions close to the information sources. It also offers important decision making opportunities for the division managers and frees center from the distraction of routine involvement with the divisions' activities. In this way center has more time for other responsibilities, and the organization indirectly benefits by the added decision making experience its division management team acquires.

The disadvantages are the weakening in overall perspective that is applied to the coordination task and the possibility of conflict between the division managers. From a control perspective, decentralization leads center to worry about the communication between the divisions and the decision perspective they bring to their coordination task.

Trade between the divisions, then, might be directly regulated by center, or it might be indirectly regulated by center. Each approach carries its own advantages and drawbacks.[1]

common sense

A small dose of common sense brings the extreme cases into view. At one end, we have something like an airline. Suppose we have two sets of flights, one set from A to B (q_A) and the other from B to A (q_B). Each time a flight is made from A to B, the aircraft can be returned to A to prepare for the next flight, or it can be used to move passengers from B to A. We want these flights coordinated so the aircraft are used as efficiently as possible. Sorting this out might be left to the managers at each location, or to center. Expand the story to many destinations. Surely the answer for a large airline is centralized determination of the flight schedule. The interrelationships of moving equipment around, assigning flight crews, and coordinating hub activities cry for a centralized perspective.

At the other end we have something like parking at the university. Think of q_A as the parking space supplied by building and grounds to individuals in division B. Surely central administration would not concern itself with parking assignments. It might oversee the work of a parking committee, but detailed management of the parking resources is not what central administration is about!

---

[1]It is important to understand control problems are present in both regimes. To dramatize this, suppose we have a setting where the quantity traded, q, is observed by center. Applying the techniques used in our stylized managerial input model, it then turns out the centralized and decentralized regimes are equivalent in performance. Neither offers a control advantage over the other. This is intuitive, in that informing and then living with center's decision carries the same control weight as locally making the decision. The caveat is center must see the quantity traded and the information that was passed between the divisions. This way, any control apparatus in the one regime can be converted to its counterpart in the other. Of course, this presumes that communication and contracting are costless.

The interesting and challenging cases are in between. Suppose division B assembles and distributes automobiles while division A manufactures engines. The production schedule (for autos and engines) might be set relatively high in the organization, or by the divisions themselves. Either way, the accounting library will be engaged.

library procedures

Stay with the auto manufacturing example. Suppose each division is a profit center. Further suppose division A uses a standard variable cost system, with the standard cost of the engine type in question set at 700. Completion of each engine, then, creates an accounting library image of a 700 increase in finished goods inventory. Further suppose q such engines are transported to division B during the accounting period. (We ignore transportation cost.)

This implies A's inventory has declined a total of 700q, while B's has increased. The physical tally is easy: A's engine inventory has declined q units, while B's has increased. The accounting valuation image of this event is more involved.

Consider division B. Assume the transfers from A are recorded at an average of T_B per unit. So B's inventory goes up a total of T_Bq. Further suppose the q autos are eventually assembled and sold. Revenue less all (standard variable) product cost except the engine cost averages 1,900 per unit. The organization books an incremental profit of $(1,900-700)q = 1,200q$.[2] Division B, on the other hand, books an incremental profit of $\Delta\pi_B = (1,900-T_B)q$.

Now look at division A. Suppose the transfers to B are recorded at an average of T_A per unit. The incremental revenue to division A, then, is T_Aq; and its incremental profit is $\Delta\pi_A = (T_A-700)q$.

Several points are in order. First, this recording procedure is called a transfer pricing arrangement. The transfer of q units from A to B results in a credit on division A's books of T_Aq, and a charge on division B's books of T_Bq. T_A is the average accounting credit, or transfer price, received by division A per unit transferred to B. T_B is the average accounting charge, or transfer price, incurred by division B per unit transferred from A.[3] In contrast, the net effect of any such transfer on the organization's books is nil. Manufacture of q units by A carries an incremental cost to the organization of 700q. Manufacture and sale of q autos carries

---

[2] This is the noted 1,900 per unit less the 700 per unit incurred in division A. Our calculations presume the firm's LLAs are reasonably accurate. Also notice we are relying on a variable costing system to link directly (pun) the product cost and incremental income calculations.

[3] In this way the respective divisions are credited or charged as a function of the quantity transferred. A transfer pricing arrangement orchestrates credits and charges in this fashion on the basis of the quantity transferred. Cost allocation attempts the same thing (e.g., when we allocate the cost of some central service to the divisions) but without benefit of an explicit measure of quantity.

an incremental profit to the organization of 1,200q. But transfer of q engines from A to B per se has no immediate net effect on the organization's records. Inventory is merely moving from one location to another inside the organization.[4]

Second, we have articulated this recording scheme in terms of an average credit or charge per unit. There is no reason whatever for the transfer price to be constant. Nonlinear pricing may be used; quantity discounts are illustrative. Similarly, a two-part price may be used, in which the buying division is charged a flat fee plus so much per unit transferred. Also, the credit or charge takes place in the accounting library; no cash changes hands. Transfer pricing is a procedure for calculating the entries in the accounting library that recognize trade between divisions. Goods are traded for accounting numbers.

Third, the transfer pricing procedure has the (intended) effect of assigning overall profit to the two divisions. Setting $T_A = T_B = T$ in our running example implies an incremental profit for Division A of $\Delta\pi_A = (T-700)q$, and an incremental profit for division B of $\Delta\pi_B = (1,900-T)q$. The internal record keeping is now tidy:

$$\Delta\pi_A + \Delta\pi_B = (T-700)q + (1,900-T)q = 1,200q.$$

The organization's incremental profit of 1,200q is equal to the sum of the incremental profits of division A and division B. Make no mistake. The transfer pricing arrangement allocates or assigns the overall profit to the trading divisions. So to speak it "parks" the jointly produced profit in the two divisions.

Setting $T_A = T_B = T$ with a low T favors division B while a high T favors division A. Suppose center decrees the use of a single price scheme and negotiation between the managers to set the quantity and the price. Further suppose A has the advantage in the negotiation; then we would expect to see a relatively high T, as this would assign most of the profit to A. Alternatively, center may set the quantity itself or may leave it up to division B. Either way, suppose center also decrees the transfer price should approximate marginal cost. Then T = 700.

Alternatively, we might have a case where the transfers are modest in size, and go in both directions. Sometimes they move from A to B and other times from B to A. On balance the transfers are expected to average out. Center may then leave the ongoing coordination problem to the managers and also keep it outside the formal records, implying T = 0.

In broadest terms, transfer pricing has the effect of assigning the profit associated with interdivision trade to the two divisions. The assignment is exact when the two transfer prices are equated; otherwise, it is not.[5] When the transfer

---

[4]Physical movement of the inventory may itself be a fiction. Divisions A and B may share the same location, and A's output assigned to B might reside at the same location as A's other output, prior to shipment.

[5]This should not bother us. Suppose T = 1,300; so A's share of the profit is 600 per unit. Suppose q units are transferred to B, but B does not make any sales this accounting period. Then for financial accounting purposes the profit of (1,300-700)q assigned to division A must be removed in tallying the

prices are not the same, the system is called a dual-price arrangement. The vast majority of organizations use a single-pricing arrangement.

Transfer pricing, then, is a procedure for recording trade between divisions. It takes place within an atmosphere of regulated trade that is designed and managed by center, perhaps emphasizing centralization or decentralization. Transfer pricing has the overall effect of assigning the trade derived profits to the two divisions. The purpose is interdivision coordination.

The Classical Approach

One possible fix on this coordination problem is provided by a direct overlay of the classical economist's price system. For this purpose we return to the example of a single product firm used in Chapter 2. For output q, the short-run cost curve[6] was given by $C(q) = 162 + 204.5q - 25q^2 + 1.5q^3$. We now assume the short-run price at which the output sells is $P = 199$ per unit. The firm's profit, or income, as a function of q, is $\pi(q) = 199q - C(q)$.

The profit maximizing output is located by differentiating the profit function, or equating marginal revenue with marginal cost:

$$\pi'(q) = 0 = 199 - C'(q) = 199 - 204.5 + 50q - 4.5q^2.$$

The implied solution is $q^* = 11$, with a maximum short-run profit of $\pi(11) = 806$.

We now embellish this story to provide an interdivision coordination setting. Let the firm consist of center, division A, and division B. Division A manufactures the product and transfers it to division B. In turn, division B performs marketing and distribution tasks. Cost curves for the two divisions are as follows:

$$C_A(q_A) = 100 + 150q_A - 20q_A^2 + q_A^3; \text{ and}$$

$$C_B(q_B) = 62 + 54.5q_B - 5q_B^2 + .5q_B^3.$$

Further suppose no cost is incurred at center. Assuming coordinated production, $q_A = q_B = q$, the firm's total cost is the sum of the divisions' components: $C(q) = C_A(q) + C_B(q)$. Portions of the original cost curve, that is, are associated with each division. This gives us a divisionalized structure and raises the question of coordinating the divisions' activities.

---

periodic income, as it is premature to recognize revenue. From here it is a simple step to admit we might use different prices for each division. Then, if all units are sold during the period in question, the difference between the sum of the two division profits and organization profit would be removed in tallying the periodic income.

[6]The example uses three factors of production, z_1, z_2, and z_3. The particular short-run story examined has the third factor fixed at $\bar{z}_3$. We then denoted the cost curve $C(q;\bar{z}_3)$. Here that notation is simplified to $C(q)$ merely to avoid clutter.

coordination with a tatonnement procedure

The question, then, is how might the firm go about coordinating the divisions' activities and, simultaneously, give at least lip service to the divisional structure? The price system comes to mind.

Suppose we use a common transfer price of $T = T_A = T_B$. Further suppose division A produces and transfers q_A units. Then its profit will be revenue from the transfer of Tq_A less its cost:

$$\pi_A(q_A;T) = Tq_A - C_A(q_A) = Tq_A - 100 - 150q_A + 20q_A^2 - q_A^3. \qquad [a]$$

Similarly, suppose division B distributes q_B units. Then it receives revenue of $199q_B$ and incurs costs totaling $C_B(q_B) + Tq_B$. So division B's profit measure is:

$$\begin{aligned}\pi_B(q_B;T) &= 199q_B - C_B(q_B) - Tq_B \\ &= 199q_B - 62 - 54.5q_B + 5q_B^2 - .5q_B^3 - Tq_B. \qquad [b]\end{aligned}$$

Of course these nifty calculations presume the two quantities are coordinated. Otherwise, A makes more than B wants or B wants more than A makes.

Now assume the firm is so decentralized each division goes its own way, given T. Division A, with knowledge of T, selects the quantity that maximizes its profit, $\pi_A(q_A;T)$. Division B behaves in similar fashion, and with knowledge of T selects the quantity that maximizes its profit, $\pi_B(q_B;T)$. Each division is guided by its divisional profit measure.

Next apply a little intuition. Suppose T is "large." Then A wants to supply many units and B wants only a few. Supply exceeds demand. Conversely, suppose T is "small." Then A wants to supply only a few units, and B wants more than a few. Demand exceeds supply. The magic T is the one that equates demand and supply.

Examine Figure 23.1. There we vary T from 50 to 100. Division A's supply, $q_A(T)$, increases with T. Division B's demand, $q_B(T)$, decreases with T. Supply equals demand at $T = 73$, where $q_A(73) = q_B(73) = 11$. Bingo. This is the solution center itself would select, maximizing firm-wide profit.[7] At $T = 73$, the two sets of maximizing decisions implied by [a] and [b] above are consistent. Supply and demand are equal (at 11 units). Also, $\pi_A(11;73) = 142$ and $\pi_B(11;73) = 664$.

The idea, then, is to treat the transfer pricing apparatus as a price system that functions inside the firm. Each division acts as a price taker and selects quantity to maximize its own profit, or income. The price is correct, is in equilibrium, when the induced quantity choices agree, when supply equals demand. We might even imagine a formal adjustment or tatonnement procedure, in which a sequence of T's

---

[7] To verify this claim, take division A's profit as defined in [a] and solve for the optimal quantity as a function of T. This is the $q_A(T)$ graph in Figure 23.1. Do the same for B's profit as defined in [b]. The quantities agree when the two graphs intersect: $q_A(T) = q_B(T)$. This occurs at $T = 73$, which implies a common quantity of 11 units.

is called out (raising T if demand exceeds supply and vice versa) until the magic T is located.

Figure 23.1: Division Quantity Choices

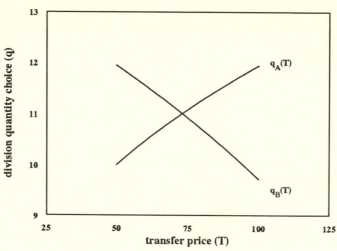

In this way the market price system is mimicked inside the organization. The equilibrium price, so to speak, guides each division to the fully coordinated solution.

a streamlined procedure

Calling out a sequence of transfer prices until coordination is achieved is a bit far fetched. Yet it serves the purpose of highlighting the importance of the transfer price as a guide to action. Given the coordinating T, each division is led inexorably to the solution. A streamlined procedure would have one division set the transfer quantity, based on what it knows and the information supplied by the other division. To illustrate such a scheme we will assume division B sets the quantity.

We know from our earlier work that the profit maximizing solution has $q = 11$, and a transfer price of $T = 73$ will guide the two divisions to this solution. Also recall the firm's cost is $C(q) = C_A(q) + C_B(q)$, presuming coordinated output. So the firm's profit can be expressed as $\pi(q) = 199q - C_A(q) - C_B(q)$. The marginal revenue equals marginal cost condition can be displayed using the division cost expressions as

$$\pi'(q) = 199 - C_A'(q) - C_B'(q).$$

Restate this in suggestive format:

$$199 - C_B'(q) = C_A'(q).$$

The net marginal benefit to division B should equal the marginal cost to division A. At the profit maximizing output of q = 11 we have:[8]

$$199 - C_B'(q) = C_A'(q) = 199 - 126 = 73.$$

Our magic T from the tatonnement procedure is division A's marginal cost at the optimal coordinated output.

Dwell on the intuition. When division B focuses on its divisional profit, of $199q - C_B(q) - Tq$, it is led to the division profit maximizing condition of

$$199 - C_B'(q) = T.$$

If this grand scheme is going to work, we must have T = 73. T must equal division A's marginal cost at the optimal output quantity.

The streamlined procedure exploits this fact. Let the transfer price depend on the quantity transferred and set it equal to division A's marginal cost. So the transfer price as a function of the quantity transferred is simply $T(q) = C_A'(q)$. A's marginal cost depends on q, and going into the exercise we do not know the quantity that will be selected. Division B, therefore, is presented with a price schedule, T(q). Its profit remains as depicted in expression [b], except the transfer price is defined by the posted price schedule. Division B, the buying division, is then instructed to locate the quantity by the condition

$$199 - C_B'(q) = T(q) = C_A'(q).$$

This amounts to instructing B to maximize its divisional profit, subject to price taking behavior.

In effect, we presume that division A knows best its cost curve and that division B knows best the market price and its cost curve. To assemble all the information at the point of decision, A is instructed to reveal its marginal cost as a function of q. Division B then treats this as a parametric price schedule and makes the overall decision. That is, division A reveals its marginal cost curve, $C_A'(q)$, and division B selects the quantity using the requirement $199 - C_B'(q) = T(q) = C_A'(q)$.[9]

---

[8]We should verify the calculations, beginning with $C_A'(q) = 150 - 40q + 3q^2$; and $C_B'(q) = 54.5 - 10q + 1.5q^2$.

[9]A caveat is in order. Division B is instructed to maximize $\pi_B(q;T(q)) = 199q - C_B(q) - T(q)q$, subject to the proviso of price taking behavior. Differentiating $\pi_B(q;T(q))$ produces $199 - C_B'(q) - T(q) - qT'(q)$. The last term surfaces because the transfer price varies with the quantity. If B ignores this last term, as instructed, q = 11 will be selected and B's profit will be 664. If B behaves in opportunistic fashion and recognizes this last term, q ≈ 8.5 will be selected and B's profit will be 993. While making B look good, this opportunistic behavior lowers the firm's profit from 806 to 676. A similar assumption of price taking behavior is imbedded in Figure 23.1.

If division B is not reliable in this matter, an equivalent procedure (thanks to Ronen and McKinney [1970]) uses the trick of structuring each division profit measure so it is the same as firm-wide profit. To impart some of the flavor, suppose we set the transfer price schedule for B at A's

This tortuous development has a point. Division A knows its cost curve while B does not. A and B must be coordinated, as B has no other source for the essential input produced by A (and A has no other market for its output). A simple way to coordinate their behavior is to instruct A to announce a price schedule of $T(q) = C_A'(q)$ and B to then find the joint quantity by maximizing its profit, subject to price taking behavior. A policy of pricing the transfers at marginal cost is thereby implied.

lingering doubts

It seems, then, an internal price system, properly managed, can be used to achieve interdivision coordination. The trick is to structure each division's profit measure so that maximization of their respective profits identifies the same marginal revenue versus marginal cost conditions that would be identified if we framed the problem directly in terms of firm-wide maximization. A well-functioning decentralized organization would certainly have local decisions reflect an organization-wide perspective; but there is the lingering doubt we have been too casual in our identification of division-level behavior. After all, the organization exists because it is a preferred organizer of transactions; so it seems unusual to conclude then that the way it should organize transactions is to establish a market structure.

Our overlay of the price system also seems to be an unusual combination of make work and naivete. Why not abandon division profit measures and instruct both managers to do their best to maximize overall profit? Then further instruct A simply to tell B what its cost curve is, and instruct B to pick the best quantity. Further notice we have been assuming both managers will maximize whatever division profit measure is specified (though conveniently with a side constraint of price taking behavior). Should we worry that center and the division management teams see the world somewhat differently?

Survey data reveal a variety of transfer pricing schemes are used in practice, both within and across organizations. (Examples are variable cost, full cost, full cost plus a markup, market based in various forms and negotiated prices.) Field study data are consistent with this impression of variety in practice and also suggest that transfer pricing is often a contentious issue. It is a source of friction in the organization. It matters to the managers how the overall profit is parked in their respective divisions. More broadly, this seems to suggest larger control frictions than the classical analysis admits.

---

average cost (presuming $q > 0$). Notice this implies $qT(q) = q[C_A(q)/q] = C_A(q)$; and differentiation leads division B to look at $C_A'(q)$. Incentive compatibility is established for both divisions by having each reveal their local conditions to center, and center then announce transfer price schedules of $C_A(q)/q$ for B and $199 - C_B(q)/q$ for A. Of course, we continue to assume the manager will faithfully maximize whatever division profit measure center invents; and a single product setting allows us the luxury of working with average cost.

This should not come as a major surprise. We have grounded our study of accounting on the classical theory of the firm, but have consistently found we must append a variety of frictions to accommodate the substance and art of professional management. Interdivision coordination is no different in this regard.

Transfer pricing invites confusion on this point. Replicating the price system inside the organization sounds like a clever idea, at first blush. Yet the interdivision relationship is hardly a market-based relationship in the first place; and the organization exists because it has comparative advantage at organizing transactions within its borders. The point to understand is that transfer pricing uses prices calibrated in accounting numbers, not in hard currency. Division income, in the accounting library, is being calculated in a price times quantity format. Why, then, does the organization find division profit measurement useful?

Return to the stylized managerial input model. Recall we had no substantive control problem without uncertainty, risk aversion, and some private returns to employment. Without these ingredients the labor market is too slick, too well-functioning, to exhibit any control concerns. The classical analysis of interdivision coordination rests on an equally generous view of the labor market. It presumes the division managers will be happy to maximize their division profit measures. Risk and personal returns are absent, so we should not be surprised that coordination is emphasized without major concern for control frictions.

Regulating Interdivision Trade in the Face of Control Frictions

Our next step is to combine the divisional structure and managerial input themes. This leads to a richer view of interdivision coordination, one where division profit measurement provides an important performance evaluation measure together with firm-wide profit and a variety of other measures. Transfer pricing, in turn, is used to make the profit measure more informative in this milieu and thereby to help structure the environment in which the divisions engage in trade.

vertically integrated, tightly managed settings

We begin with the case of a vertically integrated organization. Division A is a dedicated supplier to division B. A's only customer is division B. A might be a coal mine and B an adjacent electrical generating facility. A might be the manufacturing facility for an integrated clothing firm and B the marketing group.

The essential feature here is a dedicated relationship between the divisions. Coordination is likely to be of paramount concern in such a setting. This implies the coordination mechanism will be carefully managed and well informed. It will likely receive detailed cost and productivity reports from the divisions, market reports, and a variety of supplementary pieces of information. Coordination will be a thoroughly informed and carefully managed activity.

This suggests a heavy reliance on a combination of firm-wide profit and division specific results, as opposed to nearly exclusive reliance on division profit measures. The divisions are too interlinked to treat in somewhat separate fashion; and the coordination task is too important to cloud with profit allocations.

Control frictions are present. Information is dispersed, different managers prefer different agendas for the organization, and so on. The tight linking of the divisions, though, invites an approach that uses a variety of information sources without stressing division specific profit allocations. Transfer pricing issues crop up, but mainly for inventory valuation purposes. Division profit and transfer pricing do not play a serious coordination role here. Trade between the divisions is so important it is tightly managed.

decentralized, less integrated settings

The other end of the spectrum is a setting where the divisions have a life of their own, though they do encounter trading opportunities. Here division A produces a variety of products, some of which are destined for division B. In turn, division B deals with a variety of products and suppliers, one of which is division A. This suggests regulating trade between A and B is less important than in the vertically integrated case.[10]

With a variety of activities taking place in the divisions we expect to see more decentralization. Center concerns itself more with policies and maintaining the organization environment. Center also relies on more aggregate information for this purpose. In turn, division profit becomes a more important source of information as center goes about its evaluation and planning activities.

Think this through a little more closely. Suppose a trading opportunity arises. Center will not actively manage at this point. The divisions are on their own. They will communicate, argue, cajole, or whatever. If they agree to trade, their respective division profit measures will be affected. Yet their respective decisions are more complicated than maximizing division profit. Uncertainty is present. For example, what additional risk does A take on and how does A value the option on its productive capacity that will be devoted to supplying B? Division profit is also an accounting measure, an imperfect measure at best. It is likely that the organization's incentives gently nudge the managers to look at and beyond their profit measures. Trade dynamics and personality differences may also enter the calculus.

The image, then, is not one in which a trading opportunity surfaces and the transfer price fully informs each manager. Instead, the managers communicate and decide; the transfer price apparatus then kicks in to allocate the gains to trade, as measured by accounting profit, between them. Transfer pricing is used to record interdivision trades in the accounting library. The recording system is designed so

---

[10]Survey data by Vancil [1979] suggest that, on average, internal transfers account for a small percentage of the typical division's sales.

that, when trade occurs, the transfer price adjusted division profit measures are more informative than they otherwise would be.[11]

back to the managerial input model

This more subtle view of transfer pricing can be illustrated by returning to our managerial input model. Suppose each division in our two-division firm is managed by a separate manager. Division B may, with probability .5, encounter a customer whose product requires a coordinated transfer from A to B. Each division is treated as a profit center. The idea is an opportunity for trade may arise.

The manager of division A is described in familiar fashion. Managerial input may be high (H) or low (L). The manager is risk averse, with utility for wealth $\hat{w}$ given by $U(\hat{w}) = -exp(-r\hat{w})$, and incurs a personal cost in supplying input a. As usual, denote this cost by c_a; so the manager's net wealth, given payment I and input a is $I - c_a$. We assume $c_H = 5,000$, $c_L = 2,000$ and a risk aversion parameter of $r = .0001$. Also, the manager's opportunity cost of working for the organization is $U(M)$, with $M = 3,000$. The story is structured so input H is always desired, and if the special customer arrives at division B, it is profitable to produce the additional output.

Table 23.1: Probabilities for Division A Profits		division A profit (π_A)		
		100	**200**	**300**
no transfer:	$p(x_A|$no transfer,L$)$	0	1	0
	$p(x_A|$no transfer,H$)$	0	.4	.6
transfer:	$p(x_A|$transfer,L$)$	1	0	0
	$p(x_A|$transfer,H$)$	.4	.6	0

Division A's profit possibilities are displayed in Table 23.1. (We scale the profit for clarity.) If A is not called on to transfer any output to B, its profit will be 200 or 300, depending on the manager's input and luck. If called on to transfer some output to B, its profit will be 100 or 200, again depending on the manager's input and luck.

---

[11]This is why we were careful to distinguish this case from the tightly managed, vertically integrated divisions. If we routinely observe volumes of cost data, transfer quantities, and external sales, we have all of the data before us with which to adjust the respective division measures. Making such an adjustment would likely help us interpret the period's events; but no new information would be conveyed by the adjusted profit figures. In the present story we envision center as relying on more aggregate data in its routine monitoring of the divisions. This is why explicitly adjusting the profit measures to reflect the interdivisional transfers has the potential to bring new or better information to the evaluation task.

The pattern should be familiar. Suppose no transfer occurs. If the risk neutral center knows this, then it knows division A's profit will be low (200) or high (300). Assuming no other information, the best pay-for-performance arrangement is to pay the manager 5,000 for low output and 10,655.8 otherwise. This implies a cost to center of C(H) = 8,393.48. Similarly, suppose a transfer occurs. The pattern repeats exactly, with low output now being 100 and high output 200.

To keep the discussion uncluttered we assume no control problems are present in division B. Profit possibilities for division B are detailed in Table 23.2 below.[12] We also assume conditional independence. For example, if no transfer occurs, and input H is supplied in division A, the probability that respective profits are 200 and 400 is $(.4)(.1) = .04$.

Table 23.2: Probabilities for Division B Profits		division B profit (π_B)		
		200	**300**	**400**
no transfer:	$p(x_B|\text{no transfer})$	.3	.6	.1
transfer:	$p(x_B|\text{transfer})$	0	0	1

The idea, then, is only division B knows whether a transfer opportunity arises. (This event has probability .5.) Division A's profit prospects are lowered if it is called on to divert some of its output to division B. Division A profit of $\pi_A = 200$, then, is ambiguous. This is bad news if no transfer took place and good news if a transfer did take place.

The key to evaluating division A's performance is to know whether a transfer took place. The example is structured to reveal a familiar pattern in such a case. If the division A manager's performance evaluation can depend on π_A, π_B and whether a transfer took place, it is best to pay 5,000 for bad news and 10,655.80 for good news.[13] Our noted independence assumption guarantees the profit of division B is not used in the evaluation of the A manager here. Also, our example is about to expand so we will round the payments to the nearest dollar from this point on.

An important point is buried here. Do we have any interest in transfer pricing at this point? The answer is a resounding "no." We know the unadjusted division profits and whether a transfer occurred. Introducing transfer pricing merely

---

[12]The manager's personal cost might be constant across the inputs; or division profit might be unusually informative. For example, suppose the division B manager is a clone of the A manager, and center wants input H here as well. Also suppose division B's profit will be 100 whenever input L is supplied. We're then home free. The point is to develop insight into transfer pricing with a minimum of distracting details.

[13]That is, if no transfer takes place, pay 5,000 when $\pi_A = 200$; if a transfer takes place, pay 5,000 when $\pi_A = 100$, and so on.

recalculates the division profits, based on what we already know. No additional information is conveyed. Transfer pricing becomes interesting here only when we assign it an information conveyance role. It simply does not follow that interdivision trade demands serious transfer pricing.

Now suppose manager A's evaluation can only depend on the two divisions' profit measures. Knowledge of whether a transfer took place is now suppressed. Think of this as a case where center evaluates the managers using aggregate information. One way to proceed is to evaluate the managers on the basis of unadjusted division profits. Since $\pi_A \in \{100,200,300\}$ and $\pi_B \in \{200,300,400\}$ we have nine possible profit profiles. The best pay-for-performance arrangement is displayed in Table 23.3, for the case T = 0.[14]

Table 23.3: Incentive Payments in Transfer Pricing Example				
	T = 0		**T = 100**	
profit profile $(\pi_A;\pi_B)$	equilibrium probability	payment	equilibrium probability	payment
100;200	0	N/A	0	N/A
100;300	0	N/A	0	N/A
100;400	.20	4,827	0	N/A
200;200	.06	4,729	.06	5,000
200;300	.12	4,729	.32	5,000
200;400	.32	10,482	.02	5,000
300;200	.09	10,832	.09	10,656
300;300	.18	10,832	.48	10,656
300;400	.03	10,832	.03	10,656
expected payment		8,420		8,394

Notice it is best to evaluate manager A on the basis of π_A and π_B. For example, if $\pi_B = 400$ we know it is likely that a transfer occurred. $\pi_A = 200$ in such an event then has more of a good news than bad news flavor. On the other hand, $\pi_A = 200$ in conjunction with $\pi_B = 300$ is a bad news combination. The division B profit is conditionally controllable by the A manager. This stems from the fact π_B carries

---

[14]The pay-for-performance arrangements in Table 23.3 are located by minimizing the expected payment to manager A subject to three constraints: (1) if a transfer is called for, input H is preferred to input L; (2) if a transfer is not called for, input H is preferred to input L; and (3) the overall package is attractive relative to M = 3,000. The T = 0 case is more costly if we also assume this manager, rather than manager B, must reveal whether a transfer opportunity has arisen.

information about whether a transfer occurred; and this helps interpret the ambiguous case of $\pi_A = 200$. In turn, this displays the underlying rationale for evaluating a division manager on the basis of both division and firm-wide performance.

Another way to proceed is to use a nontrivial transfer price to adjust the division profits. Using $T = 100$ works wonders in our highly special setting. Under this regime, the transfer and no transfer cases result in the same π_A profit odds. That is, with $T = 100$, π_A will be 200 if a transfer takes place and input L is supplied, and so on. Look back at Table 23.1. More important, the transfer price adjusted π_A measure is now carrying all the essential information for evaluating the performance of the A manager. We have replicated the earlier case where the manager is paid 5,000 for bad news and 10,656 for good news.

Though absurd in its many convenient details, this example teaches us a great deal about transfer pricing. Essential information, whether a transfer opportunity exists, is available at the division level. The managers are motivated to use this information to coordinate their activities. The accounting measures are designed to be useful in evaluating these activities. The transfer pricing arrangement is used to make the division profit measures more informative; it is not used to carry information from one manager to another. The managers directly speak to each other. Transfer pricing is engaged to provide a superior aggregate set of performance statistics.

the importance of control frictions

The importance of transfer pricing depends on our view of control frictions faced by the organization. If interdivision trade can be regulated without significant friction, we are in the classical setting. There it is possible to establish a pricing policy and instructions for the managers such that faithful application of the instructions will result in well-coordinated behavior. It is equally efficient to abandon division performance measurement and concentrate on maximization of firm-wide results in such a setting.

If control frictions are important in the regulation exercise, a different picture emerges. If center regulates trade in a tightly managed fashion, relying on enormous detail and communication, there is nothing left for transfer pricing to accomplish. The pricing exercise merely recalculates what is already known. If center regulates trade with aggregate information, though, we become interested in transfer pricing. In such a case the pricing procedure can process underlying information to make the division profit measures more informative. This is the case of a decentralized, less integrated setting.

In the managerial input illustration, everyone knows a transfer will lower A's expected profit by 100 (presuming supply of input H). Transfer pricing is not required to carry information between the divisions. It is used there to make the resulting division profit measures more informative.

Variations on a Theme

Transfer pricing is used to help center regulate trade between divisions. On the surface, the division managers trade output for accounting numbers. While literal, this depiction masks the subtlety of the arrangement. The managers coordinate their activities, and transfer pricing is used to reflect these activities in the division profit measures. The accounting profit from their coordination is parked in the two division measures, according to the transfer pricing arrangement. The purpose is to make the division profit measures a more useful performance evaluation measure. The transfer prices do not coordinate the divisions' activities. The managers do this. The prices assign the combined profit from the coordinated activities to the two divisions.

This theme is consistent with our stylized managerial input model. There, unobserved behavior, personal returns, and local insight into transfer opportunities produce just such a story. Realistically, we want to think in terms of the divisions producing a variety of products, some of which entail transfer opportunities. At any given moment, the various division managers are best informed about local conditions and therefore about the organization's opportunity cost of any such transfer. The specific nature of the local information and control frictions will vary, but the underlying idea of designing the division profit measurement apparatus to convey more information remains.

make or buy

An important variation on this theme is the case where division B can obtain this essential input from division A or from some external source. From center's perspective this is a make (source with division A) or buy (source with the external supplier) type of question.[15]

The coordination exercise now expands to include internal and external sources. Quality and delivery may be better assured if the internal source is used. Diversification argues for split sourcing, though this may be more costly. For example, specialized tools or training may have to be replicated in each source. The capacity to produce this product has option value, and this value may be better managed with the internal source. For instance, in times of unusual demand variability it may be desirable to hold some capacity in reserve; and this may be more easily monitored in the internal source. On the other hand, the external source may be experiencing unusually low demand and be willing to supply the product on unusually favorable terms. Heavy reliance on the external source, though, may diminish valuable training opportunities for the organization's work force.

---

[15]A deeper plot has B able to make the component itself, acquire it from A, or acquire it from an external source.

The external source also may offer additional opportunities to address the underlying control frictions. The external source's bid may provide information about the internal source's cost. Judicious selection between the two sources may also help discipline the parties.

To illustrate the latter possibility, consider a streamlined story in which the sources have superior cost information. Also, if the internal source is used and its transfer price exceeds its cost, this incremental gain is consumed by the division in question. (This is a bit extreme, but allows us to get to the end of the chapter with fewer pages.)

Assume the internal source's cost is either 10 or 40 while the external source's cost is either 30 or 50. In each case the possibilities are equally likely. Also let's look at the easy case where they are independent. So each cost combination has a .25 probability. The rub is that, at the time of sourcing, the sources know their respective costs while center only knows the underlying probability specification.

If no control frictions are present, center would source with the lowest cost source. This is the "no friction" benchmark displayed in Table 23.4. The low-cost source is always used and paid its cost. For example, in the 40;30 event, the external source's cost of 30 is the lowest. There the external source is used, and paid its cost of 30.

As a second benchmark, consider the case where center's policy is always to source inside. The internal division now has an advantage. It will claim a cost of 40. If its cost is 10, it merely consumes the resulting slack. This is the "always make" policy in Table 23.4. Notice that the cost to center is 40, regardless of the sources' costs. (Always sourcing with the external source implies a cost to center of 50.)

Table 23.4: Center's Cost under Various Make or Buy Policies					
sourcing policy	(internal;external) cost event				E(cost) to center
	10;30	10;50	40;30	40;50	
no friction	10	10	30	40	22.5
always make	40	40	40	40	40
make or buy	10	10	50	50	30

Now assume center announces a policy of internal sourcing if the internal cost is low (i.e., 10), and external sourcing otherwise. The external source's best response to such a policy is always to bid its high cost, of 50. The internal source can do no better than bid its cost. The internal source is used when its cost is 10, and paid accordingly. Otherwise, the external source is used, and paid 50. This is the "make or buy" policy in Table 23.4. Notice what occurs in the 40;30 event. The low-cost source is used, and earns a profit. In the 40;50 event, the high-cost source is used. The threat of switching to the external source, even when it is high cost, is what disciplines the internal source.[16]

Stepping back, this reminds us that the interdivision coordination problem is concerned with trade between divisions and trade between a division and an outside or external supplier. The preferred trades are readily identified in the absence of control frictions. Yet an absence of control frictions seems inconsistent with the underlying story of a divisionalized organization. Introducing control frictions, the preferred trades become responsive to the nature and substance of the control frictions. It is here that transfer pricing carries the largest burden of providing informative division profit measures in the light of decentralized, regulated trade.

dynamics

Our convenient stories and numerical examples do not portray the dynamic side of coordination. Trade opportunities are likely to arise time and again. Absent active management by center, sourcing and reporting policies are invoked. Center addresses this with a sourcing policy. It might decree internal sourcing, split sourcing, preference for the internal source, or leave the decision to the buying division.

Center will also set a transfer pricing policy. It may leave the per unit price to be negotiated by the managers involved. It may decree that transfers are priced at standard or actual variable cost, or at standard or actual full cost. It may decree that transfers are priced at full cost plus a percentage markup. If an active market is present, it might decree use of the market price or use of the market price less a discount. Center may also establish a grievance procedure, so that it becomes actively involved in regulating trade at the discretion of the division managers.

The variety of policies noted above, all of which are used in practice, may appear unwieldy or disconcerting. The underlying idea, though, is to provide a division profit measurement procedure that helps implement a decentralized structure. With various sources of information and a variety of control frictions, we should expect a variety of ways to bring additional information into the division profit measurement apparatus.

This, of course, flies in the face of a general rule for pricing interdivision transfers. If control frictions are absent, a straightforward opportunity cost construction is insightful. To see this, recall the notion of opportunity cost developed in Chapter 11, where we were trying to select the best from a set of possible choices, using the evaluation measure $f(z)$. We divided that set into A_1 (with provisional best choice z_1^*) and A_2 (with provisional best choice z_2^*). $f(z_2^*)$ is the

---

[16]Other policies are possible. Center might ask for bids and go with the low bid, it might use the external source only if it reports a low cost (of 30), or whatever. The make or buy policy illustrated in Table 23.4 is center's best policy, given strategic behavior by both sources.

opportunity cost of confining our search to A_1. z_1^* is best overall if $f(z_1^*)$ is larger or equal to its opportunity cost.

Now interpret A_1 as all production plans that entail transfer of some item from A to B, and A_2 as all plans that entail no transfer. Transfer is called for if $f(z_1^*)$ exceeds its opportunity cost. In incremental terms, then, the transfer is called for if $f(z_1^*) - f(z_2^*) \geq 0$. Now think of this in terms of profit to the two divisions. Transfer is called for if the net gain to B less the profit A can earn elsewhere is weakly positive. This implies pricing the transfer in terms of what A can earn elsewhere. If A has no other use for its capacity, then incremental cost to A is the appropriate measure. If some other product is displaced, then the profit associated with this displaced product is part of the calculation. If tentatively idle capacity that has positive option value is used, the decline in the option value of the capacity is part of the calculation.

The larger picture, though, encompasses a decentralized attack on this question, in the face of control frictions and with important pieces of information in various hands. The organization seeks to motivate appropriate decisions in the divisions, by announcing sourcing and pricing policies and then using its various sources of information to evaluate the performance of these policies and the managers. Once we recognize that division profits are used, together with other information, including firm-wide profit, to evaluate the managers, we lose the direct connection between the opportunity cost calculus and design of the most informative aggregate performance measures.

Center wants the decision making governed by the opportunity cost calculus. But this does not imply transfer pricing should be a clone of that calculus. Control frictions distort the calculus at the margin; the divisions have important information and center has other sources of information.

Loose Ends

Two additional features of measuring division profit in the face of interdivision trade should be noted. First, a set of related issues arises in taxation. Suppose division A is in a low-tax environment while B finds itself in a high-tax environment. For tax purposes, center prefers to park as much profit as possible in division A, thereby taking advantage of its tax environment. It is not surprising, then, that state, national, and foreign tax authorities have a great deal to say about transfer pricing practice in the measurement of taxable income. The Interval Revenue Code (IRC §482), for example, states:

> In any case of two or more organizations...controlled directly or indirectly by the same interests, the Secretary may... allocate gross income, deductions, credits, or allowances between or among such...organizations...if he determines that such...allocation is necessary in order to prevent evasion of taxes or clearly to reflect the income of any such organizations....

This extends to anticompetitive concerns as well. A foreign competitor can be charged with unfair competition if the U.S. price is low in relation to the producer's product cost. Judicious transfer pricing practice, it has been alleged, is a vehicle for deflating the apparent product cost in such cases.

Second, there is a close connection between transfer pricing and cost allocation. Our earlier model of the accountant's product costing art emphasized the building blocks of aggregation and LLAs interlinked by cost allocation. Transfer pricing is simply a variation on the cost allocation theme, one in which we have an explicit measure of the quantity of the good or service involved. The various transfer pricing policies center might invoke are policies for calculating division profit in the face of interdivision trade. These calculations will be based upon the underlying product costing apparatus, making use of aggregate statistics and LLAs. This suggests a strong parallel between cost allocation and transfer pricing.

Summary

Regulating interdivision trade is a difficult subject. Absent control frictions, the task is so simple it hardly warrants our attention. We want the division managers to think in terms of firm-wide consequences. This might be done by structuring the way division profits are measured and instructing the managers accordingly, or it might be done by abandoning the divisional schism altogether.

The story is quite different when control frictions are introduced. Here we are reminded of the fact that, at the margin, control frictions alter what the organization seeks to accomplish. We don't look for a control system that will enforce the first best or friction-free solution. We are also reminded that, when faced with control frictions, the organization has a variety of instruments at its disposal. Assignment of decision responsibility and various sources of information combine to suggest a variety of solutions to the interdivision trade regulation problem.

Viewed in this light, transfer pricing is a method by which interdivision trades are recorded for profit measurement purposes. This is done to assign or park profits at the division level to make the division profit measures, in light of other sources of information, more informative. We use an accounting price system to carry information into the accounting domain. The mechanics of the calculation parallel those of a well-functioning market with arms length transactions. But the analogy is strained. We began our study documenting the sharp contrast between classical economics (Chapter 2) and accounting measurement (Chapter 3). The contrast remains in the interdivision coordination setting.

Bibliographic Notes

Divisionalized management and transfer pricing have been the subject of considerable study. To provide some entry to this literature, Hirshleifer [1956] is a classic transfer pricing reference. Solomons [1965] provides a book-length study of this theme and links it to accounting subtleties in division performance measurement. Ronen and McKinney [1970] and Groves and Loeb [1979] highlight the strategic side. Harris, Kriebel, and Raviv [1982] introduce control considerations explicitly tied to input supply. Antle and Eppen [1985] link the attendant control problems to capital rationing. Dye [1988] emphasizes information content of the division performance measure. Swieringa and Waterhouse [1982] stress behavioral connections. Holmstrom and Tirole [1991] study the interaction between transfer pricing and organization form. Eccles [1985] provides a connection to the organization's strategy and provides field study data. Interactive control problems with second sourcing are highlighted in Anton and Yao [1987] and Demski, Sappington, and Spiller [1987]. Comparative advantage at organizing trade is stressed by Williamson [1985].

Problems and Exercises

1. The chapter stresses the theme that interdivision coordination amounts to regulating trade between divisions. Explain why regulating trade between divisions might be an issue and what role transfer pricing plays in the exercise.

2. Transfer pricing uses prices and quantities to record trade between divisions. In general terms this is often thought of as using a price mechanism to guide such trade. To what extent is this analogy correct? Discuss the similarities and differences when trade passes (i) between two divisions in the same organization or (ii) between two independent entities in an organized market.

3. We used the managerial input model to highlight the importance of allocating the gains to interdivision trade between the two divisions. In that setting, how do the managers learn of possible gains to trade and what role is played by the allocation of any gains to trade?

4. *control difficulties in classical approach*
     In Chapter 18 we used the managerial input model to stress the point that a serious control problem can only be present if we have uncertainty, risk aversion, and varying personal cost in that model. The classical approach to interdivision coordination stresses the use of an internal pricing mechanism, as illustrated in Figure 23.1. Does this setting admit to a serious control problem? Explain your reasoning.

5. *trade of output for accounting currency*
     United Management has a divisionalized structure. Various divisions enjoy considerable autonomy. Central management provides oversight, financial management, and strategic planning. Cash is centrally managed.
     Division B has encountered an opportunity to provide specialized manufacturing for an established customer. The customer will pay 100. The catch is divisions

A and B will both have to contribute manufacturing resources. A will do the preliminary work and then transfer the semifinished product to B, and B will then complete the manufacturing and deliver the item to the customer. The cost will total 60, with 50 incurred in division A and 10 in division B. The transfer price, from B to A, is set at the amount T.

a] Assume the opportunity is taken. Determine the incremental profit (i) to the firm; (ii) to division A; and (iii) to division B.

b] Provide journal entries on division A's books to record all activity associated with this opportunity. Include entries for work in process, cost of goods sold, revenue, and so on. (Do not close any temporary accounts.) For convenience, assume all cost incurred by A is associated with cash expenditures. Make certain the incremental profit implied by your entries agrees with your answer in [a] above.

c] Do the same for division B's books.

d] When United Management prepares consolidated financial statements, will the consolidation process, working from your above entries, result in a firm-wide incremental profit that agrees with your answer in [a]? Explain.

e] Carefully document what happens to your answers in [b], [c], and [d] above as T is varied between 30 and 120. What is the minimum T that would not lower A's divisional income? What is the maximum T that would not lower B's divisional income?

f] As T varies between 30 and 120, how much cash is paid by division B to division A? Explain your answer.

g] What purpose is served by transfer price T in this setting? Do you think the two managers are using the transfer price to inform each other about local costs and benefits? Explain your reasoning.

6. *trade of output for fungible currency*
Return to problem 5 above. Now assume division A is unable to accommodate division B, and B must, as a result, go to an outside source. This source is paid the amount P. Everything else remains as before.

a] Assume the opportunity is taken. Determine the incremental profit (i) to the firm and (ii) to division B.

b] Provide journal entries on division B's books to record all activity associated with this opportunity. Include entries for work in process, cost of goods sold, revenue, and so on. (Do not close any temporary accounts.) For convenience, assume all cost incurred by B is associated with cash expenditures.

c] When United Management prepares consolidated financial statements, will the consolidation process, working from your above entries, result in a firm-wide incremental profit that agrees with your answer in [a]? Explain.

d] Carefully document what happens to your answers in [b] and [c] above as P is varied between 30 and 120. What is the maximum P that would not lower B's divisional income?

e] As P varies between 30 and 120, how much cash is paid by division B to the outside source?

7. classical analysis

Ralph's firm consists of divisions A and B. The output of division A is transferred to division B, where it is processed further and then sold. No costs are incurred at center. The division's cost structures are as follows:

$$C_A(q_A) = 200 + 450q_A - 10q_A^2 + (1/6)q_A^3; \text{ and}$$

$$C_B(q_B) = 300 + 250q_B - 10q_B^2 + (1/6)q_B^3.$$

The outputs are coordinated, implying $q_A = q_B$. The market price for the finished product is presently 450 per unit.

a] Determine the firm's optimal output and corresponding profit.

b] Suppose division B can order any quantity from A, and will be charged a transfer price of T per unit. A is obliged to produce as instructed. Find a T such that maximizing its division income will lead division B to prefer the output quantity you determined in [a] above.

c] Suppose division A can manufacture any quantity it desires and will be credited with an internal revenue of T per unit for each unit. Find a T such that maximizing its division income will lead division A to prefer the output quantity you determined in [a] above.

8. internal supply and demand schedules

Return to problem 7. Suppose division A can manufacture any quantity it desires and will be credited with an internal revenue of T per unit manufactured. Conversely, division B can process and sell any quantity it desires and will be charged an internal price of T per unit for the items supplied by division A.

a] Determine the output quantity for division A that maximizes its profit, as a function of T. Plot this quantity as T varies between 300 and 400. (Place T on the horizontal axis.)

b] Determine the output quantity for division B that maximizes its profit, as a function of T. Plot this quantity on the same graph.

c]   Where do the two graphs intersect? What connection do you see between the point of intersection and your work in the earlier problem?

9. *private cost information*
Return to problems 7 and 8 above. Now explicitly assume that each division manager knows its respective cost structure, though is less informed about the other's cost structure. Center is less informed. The coordination procedure calls for the two managers to negotiate a mutually satisfactory coordinated production plan (and transfer price).

Suppose each manager is evaluated on the basis of division income. Is it likely a profit maximizing solution will prevail? Explain your reasoning.

Conversely, suppose each manager is evaluated on the basis of firm-wide income. Do you think it likely a profit maximizing solution will prevail? Explain your reasoning.

10. *revelation incentives*
Verify the claim in footnote 9. What happens here if the managers are evaluated on the basis of firm-wide rather than division profit?

11. *transfer prices and responsibility accounting*
Return to the setting of Table 23.3. When $T = 0$, the optimal pay-for-performance arrangement bases the division A manager's evaluation on the income of both divisions. Carefully explain, linking this phenomenon to responsibility accounting.

Continuing, notice that when $T = 100$, the optimal pay-for-performance arrangement confines the division A manager's evaluation to the income of division A. Carefully explain.

12. *informative division profit measures*
Return to the setting of Table 23.3. Reconstruct the table for the cases where the probability that a transfer occurs is (i) .2 and (ii) .8. Contrast your findings with those in the table.

13. *informative division profit measures in presence of other information*
Transfer pricing allocates the gains from trade between the trading divisions in the sense the accounting profit associated with the trade is allocated to the divisions. In this way the division income measures are made more informative, more descriptive of the managers' performance. Return to the setting of Table 23.3. Suppose the manager's evaluation (and therefore compensation) can depend on the divisions' profit measures and whether a transfer took place. Determine an optimal pay-for-performance arrangement for division A's manager. Give an intuitive explanation for your arrangement.

With unadjusted division profit (i.e., division profit based on $T = 0$) and transfers observed, there is no interest in transfer pricing in this setting. Carefully explain why this claim is correct.

14. *product costs and transfer prices*

We now find Ralph exploring accounting questions in a vertically integrated organization. The firm has two divisions, Upstream and Downstream. Upstream manufactures a single product. The sole customer for this product is Downstream. In turn, Downstream uses this product in its own manufacturing operation, and sells the completed product to various external customers.

The question of concern is how to account for the product that is transferred from Upstream to Downstream. One unit from Upstream is required for each unit of final output by Downstream. A just-in-time inventory policy is in force, and the production schedules are therefore coordinated so that inventory is negligible. The firm accounts for this internal transfer by "charging" Downstream the actual, full cost for each unit.

a]   Ralph has recently returned from a management seminar where the possibility of misleading accounting technique was discussed. This has led to some concern on Ralph's part. Ralph estimates the two divisions' cost structures with the following LLAs:

Upstream: $C_A = 150,000 + 50q$, and
Downstream: $C_B = 500,000 + 100q$,

where q denotes the coordinated output level across the two divisions. C_B in this setting is the cost in Downstream exclusive of the cost incurred by Upstream in manufacturing the essential component. Now suppose an actual volume of $q = 5,000$ obtains. What is the cost per unit to the Downstream division for each unit of the Upstream product?

b]   Continuing, suppose an extra customer arrives at Downstream's door. This customer will purchase one unit for 160. What is the incremental profit from this extra transaction? Compute this amount from the standpoint of the firm as a whole and from the standpoint of only Downstream's books. For the latter, use the existing actual cost per unit in Upstream as the relevant transfer price.

c]   Repeat your analysis in [b] above, but for the case where the units from Upstream are transferred to Downstream using a variable cost system.

d]   Ralph is quite disturbed by the above demonstration. As a final check the output and cost data listed on the following page are assembled. Regress (i) C_A on output; (ii) C_B on output; and (iii) $C_A + C_B$ on output. Notice the latter regression uses the total of local cost plus transferred-in cost in Downstream as a dependent variable. (Why?)

t	q (000)	C$_A$ (000)	C$_B$ (000)
1	14.2	817	2,560
2	12.2	732	1,879
3	9.1	617	1,466
4	12.8	723	1,654
5	3.4	382	778
6	7.0	339	953
7	8.7	576	1,433
8	11.5	276	2,575
9	8.5	920	1,234
10	17.8	913	2,018
11	11.5	1,054	1,806
12	10.0	680	1,022

e] Now Ralph is really puzzled. The demonstration in [a] and [b] above is conclusive. The full costing technique causes Downstream to upward bias its estimate of the marginal cost. But the regression results are not consistent with this claim. Carefully explain the inconsistency between Ralph's theoretical demonstration and data analysis.

15. *product costs and transfer prices*

Return to problem 14 above. Now suppose the accounting system uses standard, full costing to transfer the product from Upstream to Downstream. The full cost datum used to record the transfer is based on the noted LLA and a normal volume of 10,000 units. Regress C$_B$ plus the transferred-in cost on output. Explain your regression's result?

Repeat the exercise for the case in which standard, variable costing is used to record the transfer from Upstream to Downstream.

16. *sourcing dispute*[17]

Ralph's Firm is a large, decentralized organization. Each major product group is manufactured and marketed by a separate division. Various coordination and financing services are provided by central management. The divisions are free to trade among themselves as opportunities arise. Each division is treated as an investment center. The managers' compensation depends on the performance of their divisions, relative to expectations, and the performance of the firm as a whole.

Division A has developed a new consumer product and is lining up final production plans. A critical subcomponent can be manufactured by division B or acquired from an outside supplier. Division A asked for formal bids. Three were

---

[17]Inspired by Harvard Business School case 158-001, titled "Birch Paper Company."

received: division B bid 1,350 per hundred, Western Industries bid 950 per hundred, and Calzig bid 957 per hundred. Western is a well-known, reliable subcontractor. Calzig is a competitor of division B.

The division A manager is ready to accept the Western bid but decided to check with division B one final time. The B manager insisted the bid of 1,350 was solid and would not be lowered. Business is picking up, the B manager explains, and the announced policy of pricing all products at full cost plus the usual 11% markup would be followed. B's variable cost appears to be about 850 per hundred. The B manager also pointed out that they helped in the product engineering work and "understood" that they would be the favored supplier if the product ever went into production. It was also pointed out that A's projected profit margin was 420 per hundred, and this was based on an estimated price of 1,400 per hundred for the sub-component in question.

Before A has time to contact Western, an urgent message from central management arrives. Division B has complained to center that A is about to source with an outside supplier. Center is forced to respond and has called a teleconference for the following morning. What should center do?

17. *insurance arrangements*

A large bank evaluates commercial lending officers in terms of the profitability and quality of their loan portfolios. When a loan is consummated, the loan officer "borrows" the principal from center at an internally posted rate. The internal rate depends on the maturity of loan. If the loan is a fixed rate loan, the loan officer is charged the posted rate on the outstanding balance each period. The rate used is fixed at the internal rate at the time the loan was booked. In this way the lending officer is insured against interest rate movements, but not against default risk (to the extent default is not related to interest rate movements). Carefully analyze this transfer pricing arrangement.

How would a variable rate loan be treated?

18. *internal cost of funds and rationing*[18]

Ralph manages a decentralized firm where division managers have significant authority to make production and investment decisions. All capital expenditures must be approved by center. Divisions must submit detailed capital budgets prior to approval by center. This is one area where Ralph is somewhat disappointed with decentralization, as divisions show a marked tendency to pad their budgets. Slack in the budgets makes life more pleasant at the divisions. If a division's budget is successfully padded, division personnel have an easier time meeting the budget. Think of this as the division personnel consuming the slack in the budget.

---

[18]Contributed by John Fellingham.

Ralph is aware one of the divisions has a capital project that will yield a cash flow of 100 at the end of one year. Ralph believes this project will cost 75 or 65, with equal probability. The division, though, knows with certainty what the cost will be. This leads to a concern the division might pad its budget on this project. To prevent this, a project auditing program, which will discover the actual project cost and report directly to center, is being considered. How much would Ralph be willing to pay for the project auditing of this capital project?

Ralph's opportunity cost of capital is 20%, and Ralph is risk neutral. For simplicity, assume the budget is submitted and funds are provided to division at the beginning of the year. The benefits of the project (100) will be available to Ralph at the end of the year.

19. *sourcing*

Ralph is Chief Procurement Officer for a large metropolitan area in the North East. This is a political appointment. Ralph is presently working on a water purification project. The quality of the area's water supply has declined, and Ralph must provide additional purification facilities. It is politically unacceptable to shut down the present water supply.

Ralph is trying to decide whether to work with the region's present purification contractor or bring in a well known, reputable West Coast contractor. To try and give some structure to this problem, Ralph decides to play with a hypothetical model. In this setting, the in-place firm will have a cost of meeting the additional purification requirements of 100 or 200 (million) dollars, while the replacement firm will have a cost of 190 or 210 (million). Each firm knows its own cost but not its competitor's. And Ralph knows only that the four cost events of 100/190, 100/210, 200/190, and 200/210 are equally likely. Either firm will provide the necessary purification for cost and will refuse any offer that places them in a loss position.

Ralph cannot ex post observe either firm's actual cost. (In reality an accounting report would be available, but each firm has numerous projects and can use various allocation techniques to obfuscate any serious enquiry into its cost structure.) Were it not for the second firm, Ralph would have to offer the in-place firm 200 (which would provide slack if cost is low) or 100 (which would lead to shutdown if cost is high). The political aspects become important here, because the water must be purified. Thus, the second option is unavailable and Ralph must simply pay 200 under these circumstances.

Consider the following mechanism. First offer the in-place firm 100. If this is accepted, the game is over. If it is rejected, offer the competitor firm 210. (You should verify that this mechanism is superior to either of the interesting options for contracting with only the in-place firm.)

Ralph is delighted and shows the analysis to the region's Board of Supervisors. One of the supervisors makes the following observation. With probability 1/4 we wind up in the 200/190 event and contract with the low-cost producer but pay an excessive amount of 210 - 190; and if that's not bad enough, with probability 1/4 we wind up in the 200/210 event and actually contract with the inefficient producer. This is wonderful for the press. How would we explain overpayment or engagement of the high-cost producer?

What should Ralph say?

24

A Dynamic Perspective

The concluding step in our odyssey is a look back, with the intention of combining the themes of product costing, decision making, and performance evaluation. For pedagogical purposes we approached these topics in stages, moving from product costing to decision making to performance evaluation. It behooves us to devote some resources to integrating these themes. We do this by emphasizing a more dynamic perspective.

Our synthesis begins by examining concurrent use of the accounting library for decision making and performance evaluation purposes. We continue the dynamic theme by next discussing the topic of governance, with special concern for the accounting library. The issue is how to adjust or change the accounting system as time and events mandate. The integrity of the accounting library turns out to be important. We then give a brief review of a canonical make or buy decision, as it passes from a classical economic formulation through decentralized choice in the face of control frictions and less than perfect recording by the accounting library. This is designed as a final reminder of the importance of professional judgment. Finally, we revisit the opening theme in Chapter 1 of a well-prepared and responsible manager.

Decision and Performance Control

Consider a division manager who has responsibility for manufacturing and marketing a line of consumer products. The manager deals with a wide array of tasks. Included are evaluating the performance of the division's management team and focusing the product line strategy in light of changing consumer tastes, technology, and competitor behavior. The manager also deals with a wide array of information sources. Product market statistics, product development trends, trade association publications, consultants, subordinates, output, sales and productivity measures, and so on, all play a part. The image, if anything, is one of being overwhelmed by information sources.

Accounting, of course, enters at this point as well. It is a well-protected source of financial summarization. Division income is disaggregated into sales and, to the extent possible, expenses by product group. A similar categorization is likely for important assets, such as inventories. Responsibility accounting refocuses these data on individual members of the management team. These summarizations are drawn from the library, and rest on the recognition rules, LLAs, aggregation, and cost allocation policies in place. Special studies will also supplement these periodic summarizations, as appropriate.

At this point the manager straddles the past and the future. Looking backward, one task is to sort out how well the management team has performed. Another is to sort out how well the division's strategy has performed. In this sense, there is a recurring theme of "learning by doing." Experience is accumulating and being interpreted. The management team may be performing admirably, though product market woes have depressed financial performance; or the team may be riding the crest of an unusually healthy product market. The quality improvement program may be paying dividends; the product design team may be breathing new vigor into the product line, or providing a forum for revisiting old and, it was hoped, long buried political frictions. The new manufacturing technology may be turning out as planned; the technology adopted by a competitor may be providing them a troublesome edge, or a helpful annoyance.

Looking forward, the manager faces the task of identifying the next steps in the division's unfolding history. These steps are informed by a variety of information sources, including the many nuances that can be discerned from recent events and what strategy the division was following as these events unfolded. They are also informed by the emerging assessment of the organization's capacity and abilities, including those of the management team.

Change and surprise are present. Some events are more endogenous than others. Transition considerations are also at work. For example, adoption of a new manufacturing policy may set off an extended adjustment of inventories throughout the manufacturing and marketing network (as excess inventories are depleted and others repositioned). This, too, will cloud the immediate picture. More broadly, the management team continues to struggle with the best balance of short-run and long-run considerations, both in its direction of the division's activities and its interpretation of recent results.

The accounting library is one among many information sources at the manager's disposal. It provides a well-defended, comprehensive financial summarization of the division's health and progress. This is part of the information fabric that is used to evaluate both the underlying decisions, or strategy, and the personnel involved.

Product costing, decision making, and performance evaluation are concurrent activities. For example, one of the division's products may be lagging. What does it cost to manufacture and distribute this product? What is the best estimate of the competitors' costs? Could out-sourcing some components lower the product cost? Is managerial replacement suggested? Have incentives been inappropriately weighted, for example stressing short-run performance to the extent investment in product updating has lagged?

The decision and performance control theme is one of working in the middle of the entity's history. The future holds sufficient promise to worry about careful decision making, and the past holds sufficient relevance to be able to inform the next round of decision making. This raises the question of how plans, policies, strategy, and even the accounting system might be changed to reflect the entity's changing circumstance.

Governance in the Dynamic Environment

Here we excessively stretch the idea of economic rationality. The consistent, fully anticipating expected utility individual would understand the events that might shape things to come, even to the point of assigning probabilities to these events. In turn, it would be a short (theoretical) step to envision an optimal decision rule that would identify events as they transpired and issue programmed directives accordingly. Surprise would be present, but unanticipated surprises would never arise. Realistically, we must admit unanticipated surprises are part of life, just as is the impossibility of thinking through all the subtle details that might best be part of a well-crafted strategy or contract.

incomplete contracts with anticipated events

This suggests we anticipate the inevitability of having to deal with the unanticipated. To anchor the development we return yet again to the stylized managerial input model. We have a risk neutral organization that contracts for the services of a manager. Two input quantities are feasible, high (H) and low (L). High is wanted but the manager's supply is not observed; and the manager prefers, other things equal, to supply low.

The manager's utility is given by $-exp(-r(I-c_a))$, where I denotes payment from the organization and c_a a personal cost of input supply. As usual, $c_H = 5,000$ and $c_L = 2,000$; also $r = .0001$. The manager's opportunity cost of working for this organization is U(M), with M = 3,000.

With input unobserved, we use output to infer the manager's input. The hopefully familiar story is detailed in Table 24.1. Low input guarantees low output, while high input results in 50-50 odds on low versus high input. (This is detailed in the table under the x_1 and y and x_2 and y columns.) With performance evaluation confined to the manager's output, a pay-for-performance arrangement is invoked.

Now suppose the organization also observes the manager's input, but the parties cannot contract on this observation. Such contracting is too costly, or the input observation is unverifiable in the sense that an enforcement authority could not verify either party's claim if a dispute should arise. It seems we are confined to the noted pay-for-performance arrangement. But are we? Further suppose the parties can renegotiate the initial contract, after input is supplied but before output is realized. Here we structure the renegotiation in a particularly forceful way. The organization offers a new contract, and the manager accepts the offer or rejects the offer. Rejection implies the initial contract remains in force.

Let the original contract be the noted pay-for-performance plan. If input H is subsequently observed, the manager faces a nontrivial lottery, thanks to the pay-for-performance schedule. The most favorable renegotiation the organization can offer, while making it acceptable to the manager, is to offer a guaranteed payment equal to the lottery's certain equivalent, $\hat{I}$ = 8,000. In particular, with H known to have been supplied, the manager's certain equivalent calculation provides U(8,000) = .5U(5,000) + .5U(12,305.66).[1] Filling in the remaining details, it is easy to verify the equilibrium in this encounter with renegotiation is for the manager to supply H and to be subsequently paid 8,000.[2]

Notice how renegotiation has improved the situation. Useful information is available but cannot for whatever reason be brought into the contract. The parties can, however, structure the possibility of renegotiation. This opens the door to using the information. Renegotiation is valuable here because it allows for more efficient contracting. It allows the eventual trade arrangement to reflect this additional information. The parties fully expect to renegotiate the initial contract. The initial contract nevertheless remains a vital link in the arrangement. It sets the status quo for the subsequent renegotiation.[3]

Table 24.1: Data for Negotiation Example				
	output (i = 1,2) and evaluation (j = y,n) combinations			
	x_1 and y	x_2 and y	x_1 and n	x_2 and n
original story				
probability under L	1	0	0	0
probability under H	.50	.50	0	0
payment; $E[I_{ij}]$ = 8,653	5,000.00	12,305.66		
problematic output story				
probability under L	.50	0	.25	.25
probability under H	.25	.25	.25	.25
payment; $E[I_{ij}]$ = 9,243	1,564.95	14,857.66	10,274.30	10,274.30

[1]Constant risk aversion assists us here. The personal cost of c_H is irrelevant in determining the certain equivalent, given our use of the exponential function.

[2]If the organization sees H, it offers the noted constant payment and the manager accepts. If it sees L, no new contract is offered. Facing these prospects, the manager can do no better than accept the original pay-for-performance contract, supply H, and anticipate renegotiation.

[3]For example, what might happen here if the initial contract called for payment of 8,000 to the manager? The contracting game has expanded to include effort supply by the manager followed by renegotiation activities by both players.

Here's another example. Suppose output could tell us something about input. The odds are 50-50. Also, both parties will learn whether this is the case. This implies four possibilities: low or high output combined with output being informative or not. This is the problematic output story in Table 24.1. Here, y (yes) denotes output is informative while n (no) denotes it is not. The optimal pay-for-performance arrangement is also listed, assuming this yes/no information can be designed into the contract. Notice the incentives are steep when output is informative, and flat otherwise.

From here we muddy the waters even further. Suppose the parties cannot contract on whether output is informative, though they can foresee the possibility it might not be informative. Also, contrary to the above story, the organization does not observe the manager's input. One possibility is to admit defeat and merely contract on output. The best such arrangement pays $I_1 = 2,695$ for low output and $I_2 = 20,030$ for high output (with an implied expected cost to the organization of 11,363).

Yet a better arrangement may be possible. The trick is again to anticipate what the parties might observe, though they cannot explicitly contract on this observation, and lay in plans for a possible renegotiation. Suppose both observe whether output is informative before the output itself is observed. Further suppose they can commit at the start to possibly renegotiate the contract, according to a specified set of options. Renegotiation will take place after the parties observe whether output is informative but before the output is observed.

Now examine the menu of possible contracts in Table 24.2. The status quo contract is what the parties agree to at the start. If no renegotiation takes place, it remains in force. Renegotiation, in turn, may replace this contract with one that is low powered.

Table 24.2: Menu of Contracts		
payment scheme	low output, x_1	high output, x_2
status quo	2,000.00	16,611.32
low powered	9,305.66	9,305.66

Again, the organization makes the renegotiation offer and the manager then accepts or rejects it. There are two keys to understanding the renegotiation here. First, the organization does not know what input was supplied and is at an information disadvantage in the renegotiation. Second, if input H was supplied, the output odds remain at 50-50, regardless of whether output is informative. The two payment schemes are structured so $.5(2,000) + .5(16,611.32) = 9,305.66$; the organization is indifferent (though the manager is not).

An equilibrium in the resulting game is: (1) the manager supplies input H; (2) if the output turns out to be informative, the organization does not offer to renegotiate and the status quo contract remains in force; and (3) if the output is uninformative, the organization offers to switch to the low powered contract, and the manager readily accepts. The expected cost to the organization is 9,305.66 (surprise). Here, the parties can use the information, but less aggressively than if they could contract up front for its use.[4]

Again we see the idea of contemplating the occurrence of events that are not covered by the contract. The contracts are incomplete, and a well-crafted renegotiation option allows for the trading arrangement to make use of this information. The keys are the ability to anticipate, to structure the renegotiation encounter, and to devise an appropriate status quo arrangement.[5]

more general incomplete contracts

The next step is to admit foreseeing and planning for all these possibilities, though they cannot be explicitly contracted, is itself a fiction. Here we turn to more institutional arrangements. Property rights and governance bodies are examples.

Suppose one task an organization wants performed is a delivery or messenger service in which a driver uses an automobile to transport various items to various destinations. In a perfect market setting it would not matter who owned the auto. Capital markets would supply the requisite capital, and the driver's use of the auto would be independent of ownership. With imperfect markets, the story is quite different.

On the labor market side, the parties will have considerable difficulty foreseeing and contracting around all the things the driver might do with the auto. What they do know is the auto is likely to be heavily used (some would say abused) if the organization owns the auto. After all, the driver's use of the auto cannot be moni-

---

[4]This particular set of contracts was located by searching for the scheme that met the manager's opportunity cost requirement and was incentive compatible, while having the additional feature of equal expected payment, presuming input H, for the two information events. Other arrangements are possible, depending on infrastructure details. For example, the parties might have access to an arbitrator who can collect a performance bond from each. The parties then simultaneously announce whether output is informative. If the announcements agree, the arbitrator implements the appropriate part of the optimal contract displayed in Table 24.1 and returns the performance bonds. If they disagree, the arbitrator keeps the performance bonds and the manager is not paid. In equilibrium, the information will be reported and used.

[5]This does not imply renegotiation is always desirable. The pay-for-performance arrangements we have studied with the stylized managerial input model rely on the ability not to renegotiate. To see this, notice that after the input is supplied it is in the players' interests to renegotiate. The risk averse manager sits on a risky payment stream, which the risk neutral organization is quite willing to insure. Of course, if they did this, the original arrangement would unravel and input H would not be incentive compatible. The manager's best response to the anticipated renegotiation (leading to I = 8,000) is to supply L. This is why we stress the point of renegotiation offering the possibility of bringing additional information into a contracting arrangement, when that information for whatever reason could not originally be designed into the arrangement and when a well-crafted renegotiation encounter can be designed.

tored, and the driver will not be around later to be confronted with the real depreciation. Therefore, it matters who owns the auto. Property rights are important. The driver who owns the auto will internalize the effects of real depreciation, while the driver who does not will be in a free rider (pun) position. The tools, here the auto, have value beyond the specific employment encounter and are subject to real depreciation. (Conversely, if specialized maintenance is important to ensuring the driver's safety, we would worry about the organization's incentives to supply proper maintenance if it rather than the driver owned the auto.)

The capital market likely cuts in the other direction. The organization may be more financially sound, and thus better able to invest in the equipment. It also is likely to be better at carrying the risks of ownership. In addition, the organization may be in a better position to capitalize on tax benefits associated with equipment ownership. Some taxi drivers own their cabs while others do not. Some employees use a company auto while others do not. These are not accidental arrangements.

The underlying story is one of trading frictions, or transaction cost. Property rights for capital equipment that lasts beyond the trading encounter confer a type of residual claim on the owner of the equipment. This matters when contracts are incom-plete or, for that matter, informationally starved. A well-crafted trading arrangement exploits this aspect of asset ownership.

Governance bodies are familiar institutional arrangements for dealing with events as they unfold. Major sports leagues have their oversight arrangements, the typical union contract contains a well-specified grievance structure and the family firm has the still active first generation family member. The U.S. Constitution carefully specifies executive, legislative, and judicial powers. The university has an ombudsman. These bodies deal with unforseen events. In a sense, they complete trade arrangements or alter the trading environment as circumstances dictate. The role of the judiciary when an unforseen product liability is encountered is illustrative. Other examples are dealing with the impact of television on the structure and conduct of major league baseball, resolution of interdivision conflict in a global banking institution, and curriculum design at your favorite university.[6]

Going a bit further, we should expect an organization's activities and its governance abilities to be well matched. For example, it may be more efficient to house a high risk product development venture in a separate organization. A larger, more stable organization likely has a variety of activities. The key players in the new product venture will be worried about their future if the product flops. If this is a stand-alone organization, the worry takes the form of what the labor market sees and might offer. If this is part of a larger organization, the worry takes the form of what the internal labor market sees and might offer. Do we want the key players worrying about their future in the one arena or the other?

---

[6]Who governs the governance body is the next question. Here oversight (deepening the chain of governance) and reputation enter. For example, a manager may have a reputation for taking a long-run or a short-run point of view when confronted with a governance issue.

Ideally, we would like their efforts focused on the new product. At the margin, career interests will creep into the setting. Are these best controlled by the organization or the labor market? If the large organization's governance arrangement is adept at this game, it might be best to house the new product venture in the organization. Otherwise, a stand alone arrangement is preferable. For example, the large organization may be able to provide reasonably adequate career insurance for the key players; after all, everyone understands the venture is high risk. On the other hand, the large organization may provide too many opportunities for the key players to worry about ingratiating themselves with other key players, as a precaution against failure of the venture.[7]

Accounting Governance

Not every event is anticipated or is the catalyst for a programmed response. An important organization function is governance, providing structure and direction as circumstances warrant. This governance function extends to the accounting library. We don't see elaborate plans to alter the organization's accounting policies in response to technology and market changes. Instead we see restrained (some would say glacial) behavior, often tied (some would say too closely) to financial reporting requirements and the opinions and advice of the external auditor. GAAP itself is defined by an elaborate governance arrangement.

In the larger picture this has merit. Accounting provides one among many sources of information. It is designed to be comprehensive yet well defended. One version of being well defended is being difficult to change. Imagine a divisionalized firm in which the division managers could routinely alter the split between expensing and capitalizing various expenditures, could routinely vary revenue recognition policies, and could routinely switch among various product costing models. The periodic accounting rendering of divisional events would likely become a game of "catch if catch can." It is claimed the U. S. federal government is particularly adept at this game.

This is why we see such things as attention to GAAP in a debt covenant (don't change the rules in the middle of the game) and frequent use of consultants when a major change in accounting policy is contemplated (let a third party, so to speak, play an important governance role). This is also why we often see cost estimating exercises that are not fully based on the prevailing accounting system. These exercises are readily adapted to the particular circumstance, without placing the accounting library at risk. Here, a good dose of professional judgment integrates the relationship between the library and cost estimation exercise. As we have stressed,

---

[7]An intermediate approach is to bring in a consultant to audit the research and analysis of the product development team.

a professional manager understands the workings of the accounting library, knows where to extract insight, and knows how current events will be recorded.[8]

Accounting governance is part of the larger, dynamic picture of organization life. Once we recognize multiple sources of information and the demands for library integrity, we recognize accounting governance is likely to be slow moving. This is not because accountants are wedded to stable procedures, but because the accounting library offers a well-defended, consistent approach to summarizing the organization's financial history. Don't assume accounting policies are frozen in time; but do recognize that a steady, cautious approach to change is one of the prices of library integrity. The organization's activities change faster than its accounting policies, for a reason.

Make or Buy

This dynamic theme also offers an opportunity to bring together the various threads of managerial activity. The often referred to make or buy decision is a case in point. Should the subcomponent, part, or service be produced in house or acquired from an outside supplier? For example, should routine maintenance be performed in house or subcontracted?

The classical theory of the firm has no difficulty with this question. Control problems are absent and market prices provide unassailable guides to action. In house provision is readily costed, as is subcontracting. No quality and timing concerns are present. Choice here is akin to finding two identical items on a supermarket shelf, but with different prices. Given prices and technology, we readily identify the least cost alternative and pursue it. Of course, knowing prices and technology, in a setting of perfect markets, is more than a modest assumption.

Removing the assumption of known prices and technology, in a setting of perfect markets, greatly clouds the issue. The choice will now be driven by production and transaction costs. Control problems of differing sorts are likely to be present in both the make and buy arenas. The relationship is likely to repeat, thus raising the issue of managing a relationship through time.

Cost may be easily discerned, but quality problematic. Can we rely on the subcontractor to provide the necessary maintenance on a timely basis? Will integration with other activities prove difficult? Will emergency service be handled efficiently? Is the subcontractor's work force adequately skilled? Conversely, the subcontractor's work force might be more skilled than the in-house group.

---

[8]The other side is management's familiarity with the library. Frequent change in the library puts it at risk, and it also depreciates the fabric of mutual understanding. The management team, for example, has a good shared view of how product costing is accomplished in the library. It is accustomed to working with and, when appropriate, seeing through these procedures. Frequent change in the library places this shared view at risk. Of course, if the change is too infrequent we run the opposite risk of a needlessly outdated, error-prone shared view. As usual, managed tensions constitute the theme.

Cost may be difficult to assess. A distressed supplier may offer an unusually favorable short-run price. Responding has the advantage of perhaps keeping this supplier in business; and it has the disadvantage of disrupting arrangements on a short-term basis. Quality might be even more difficult to discern under these circumstances. Subcontracting in these circumstances raises the issue of what happens when the supplier's distress eases. It also may run counter to a policy of protecting the organization's work force. The work force may possess important human capital that the organization seeks to protect, for example; or the implicit contract may be one of steady employment.

Control problems may be an important component of the calculus. Subjecting the in-house supplier to periodic competition may provide important sources of information and discipline for managing the organization. Here we should remember that part of such a policy may entail sourcing with what ostensibly appears to be a high-cost source, because we are balancing various frictions in the arrangement. Split sourcing may be used for the same reason, or to provide a more stable supply of quality components.

Specialized assets may make one or the other control problem more difficult to manage. For example, if production cost is lower with dedicated assets and if an external source is used, will the organization be vulnerable to opportunistic behavior by the supplier?

Governance enters at this point. Keeping the activities inside the organization may strain governance activities. For example, surly personnel may be more easily rotated by the subcontractor who has a larger variety of possible assignments for the personnel. Similarly, the larger variety of assignments may make it easier for the subcontractor to expand or contract services as needed. Alternatively, out-sourcing may advantageously place some capital in the supplier's hands. Tax considerations may cut in one or the other direction.

Similarly, the organization may be interested in maintaining both its inside activities and a cadre of loyal suppliers. The mix is driven by control and tax considerations. The larger arrangement provides useful control avenues for all concerned, for example, the ability to compare costs and delivery schedules. It also offers a variety of governance structures that can be judiciously used by placing particular activities in particular organizations.

This suggests an expanded view of the organization, one in which it manages inside its formal boundaries as well as the relationship with its suppliers (and customers). In this sense the organization is larger than the reporting entity. It has expanded to include a network of suppliers. The make or buy decision is vastly more involved than the issue of comparing two short-run cost estimates.

The Well-Prepared, Responsible Manager

This returns us to the theme in Chapter 1 of a well-prepared and responsible manager. The professional manager is well prepared. The difference between art and theory is understood, just as the subtleties of the particular economic climate are understood. Informed professional judgment and action are daily tasks. This is why we have carefully avoided rules, recipes, and guidelines for the use of accounting information. This is also why we have stressed an expanded, nearly boundless view of a make or buy decision. Professional management entails much more than a series of make or buy decisions, yet the myriad features of such a choice serve to remind us of the importance of professional vision and judgment in successful management. The professional manager is a well-prepared artisan.

The professional manager is also responsible. Fiduciary responsibilities are present, but this only scratches the surface. Ethical and moral responsibilities are also present. Trade arrangements, indeed most modern era economic interactions, become impossible without the rudiments of trust and honor. But this, too, only scratches the surface. The professional manager has a responsibility that runs deeper than efficiently administering trade arrangements. The professional manager is both well prepared and responsible. These are constant, ever present traits; they are not to be invoked opportunistically.

Having completed our study of the accounting side of professional management, it seems appropriate to end with some type of ceremonial message. Here I quote the commencement speaker: "Do well, but do good."[9] Professional management is an essential service; it presumes a well-prepared and responsible supplier.

Summary

Product costing, decision making, and performance evaluation themes are simultaneously engaged in the managerial task. In turn, managing the accounting library surfaces as an additional managerial task. This raises issues of governance and a broad conception of the professional manager's task. It also reminds us the professional manager is an astute supplier of professional skill and judgment; and this is impossible without being well prepared and responsible.

Bibliographic Notes

The dynamic theme merges into work on organizations. Perrow [1986] offers an expansive critique. Arrow [1974], Holmstrom and Tirole [1989], Milgrom and Roberts [1992], and Williamson [1985] emphasize economic foundations and trading frictions. Sappington and Stiglitz [1987] stress information based trading frictions in identifying whether production of a particular good or service is best located in the public or private sector. The ability of renegotiation to incorporate uncontractable information into trading arrangements is explored in Demski and Sappington [1991] and Hermalin and Katz [1991]. Breach, dissolution, and ownership changes are explored, respectively, in Stole [1992], Cramton, Gibbons, and

---

[9]Delivered by journalist Mike Wallace at the University of Pennsylvania, spring 1990.

Klemperer [1987], and Meyer, Milgrom, and Roberts [1992]. Ijiri [1975] emphasizes what he labels "hardness" as an essential feature of accounting measurement.
Hart [1989] and Baiman [1990] offer focused reviews of many of the themes that we
have covered in our study.

Problems and Exercises

1. The dynamic theme of decision and performance control emphasizes simultaneous use of the accounting library for decision making and performance evaluation purposes. Here the basic library building blocks of aggregation, LLAs, and
allocation enter. This suggests a managed tension, a tension between using these
building blocks to better serve decision making and to better serve performance
evaluation interests. Is this a correct view of the accounting library?

2. Accounting governance is visible (and contentious) in the world of financial
reporting, as evidenced by FASB and GASB activities. Yet accounting governance
is important inside an organization and hardly independent of the attendant external
reporting environment. Carefully discuss this theme.

3. *renegotiation and status quo*
    Return to the original story setting in Table 24.1. Carefully describe the role
played by the initial pay-for-performance arrangement. It will, in equilibrium, be
replaced by a guaranteed payment of 8,000. Why not simply begin with an arrangement that calls for payment of 8,000?

4. *renegotiation equilibrium*
    Verify the renegotiation game in Table 24.2 results in use of the status quo
contract when output is informative and use of the low powered contract when it is
not informative.

5. *an old friend*
    Return to the setting of problem 8 in Chapter 18, where the following
probability structure was assumed:

	x_1	x_2
input H	.1	.9
input L	.8	.2

Recall the best pay-for-performance arrangement used I_1 = 8,934.62 and I_2 =
15,972.54.

a]   Draw the manager's decision tree, using the noted pay-for-performance
arrangement. Determine the manager's certain equivalent for (i) going elsewhere
(i.e., rejecting Ralph's offer); (ii) accepting the offer and supplying input H; and (iii)
accepting the offer and supplying input L.

b] Now suppose both parties observe the manager's input. Ralph acquires this information before the output is observed. The catch is the parties cannot contract on their joint observation of the manager's input. This might be due to "contracting costs" (though hardly believable in this simple story) or the impossibility of a third party ever verifying the manager's input. Consider the following arrangement: initially set the above pay-for-performance arrangement in place; then, if Ralph sees input H, offer to exchange the manager's risky compensation for its certain equivalent of 15,000. Is this scheme incentive compatible for both the manager and Ralph? Does it, in equilibrium, allow for use of the input observation by Ralph? What is the explanation?[10]

c] Ralph learned this renegotiation "trick" at a management conference. The following idea comes to mind. In general, Ralph does not observe the manager's input, but knows, under equilibrium behavior, that the control system motivates supply of input H. So after the input has been supplied, Ralph will simply offer to renegotiate the manager's contract and exchange the risky pay for its certain equivalent. Will this scheme work? Explain.

6. *labor market conditions*

We usually have difficulty writing long term contracts. Suppose a manager is known to the labor market and has a reputation (good or bad). The employer cannot write an iron-clad long-term contract, and instead the parties periodically renegotiate, with knowledge of the manager's then current market value. How do the market forces help and how do they impede the structuring of a well-functioning employment relationship?

7. *factors of production*

Ralph's firm is expanding. It tentatively plans to add a sales force. The sales force will require the usual trappings of an automobile, personal computer, state-of-the-art communication equipment, and so on. Since no precedents have been set, the firm has an open mind on the question of who should own this equipment. Discuss the ownership issue. Would ownership matter in the world of Chapter 2?

8. *internal governance*

The typical fast food empire uses an array of financial and nonfinancial measures to evaluate the manager at each location. (Recall problem 15 in Chapter 19.) Improvement goals are established for each location, goals that reflect

---

[10]The best way to do this is to lay out a game tree. Let the manager's choice of reject or agree to the contract be the first choice. This is followed by the manager's choice of input L or H, given agreement on the contract. Now Ralph faces a choice: leave the pay-for-performance arrangement in place or offer to replace it with a guaranteed pay of 15,000. The manager will always accept a renegotiation offer; your earlier work on the certain equivalents should make this clear. From here you can readily identify the expected cost to Ralph at each stage.

circumstances and opportunities at that location. It is also common practice to have an established grievance structure, open to the manager if the evaluation or performance goals should appear inappropriate. Carefully discuss the role of this grievance structure.

9. *accounting governance*

Accounting, we have argued, provides a financial library; its comparative advantage is integrity. The accounting library is consciously designed to be difficult to manipulate. This means, among other things, it will have less than aggressive recognition rules and be slow to change its recognition rules. Discuss the reason for slowness to change recognition rules. Is it a surprise financial reporting is subject to an elaborate, external governance structure? Critics often contend this external governance structure unduly influences the organization's internal accounting. Carefully analyze this contention.

References

Amershi, A., J. Demski, and J. Fellingham, "Sequential Bayesian Analysis in Accounting," *Contemporary Accounting Research* (Spring, 1985).

Anthony, R., *Planning and Control Systems: A Framework for Analysis* (Division of Research, Graduate School of Business Administration, Harvard University, 1965).

Anthony, R., *The Management Control Function* (Harvard Business School Press, 1988).

Antle, R., "The Auditor as an Economic Agent," *Journal of Accounting Research* (Autumn, 1982).

Antle, R., and J. Demski, "The Controllability Principle in Responsibility Accounting," *Accounting Review* (October, 1988).

Antle, R., and G. Eppen, "Capital Rationing and Organizational Slack in Capital Budgeting," *Management Science* (February, 1985).

Antle, R., and J. Fellingham, "Resource Rationing and Organizational Slack in a Two-Period Model," *Journal of Accounting Research* (Spring, 1990).

Anton, J., and D. Yao, "Second Sourcing and the Experience Curve: Price Competition in Defense Procurement," *Rand Journal of Economics* (Spring, 1987).

Arrow, K., *The Limits of Organization* (Norton, 1974).

APB, Statement of Accounting Principles Board No. 4, *Basic Concepts and Accounting Principles Underlying Financial Statements of Business Enterprises* (AICPA, October, 1970).

Baiman, S., "Agency Research in Managerial Accounting: A Second Look," *Accounting, Organizations and Society* (No. 4, 1990).

Baiman, S., and J. Demski, "Economically Optimal Performance Evaluation and Control Systems," *Journal of Accounting Research Supplement* (1980).

Baker, K., and R. Taylor, "A Linear Programming Framework for Cost Allocation and External Acquisition when Reciprocal Services Exist," *Accounting Review* (October, 1979).

Banker, R., S. Datar, and S. Kekre, "Relevant Costs, Congestion and Stochasticity in Production Environments," *Journal of Accounting & Economics* (July, 1988).

Bazerman, M., *Judgment in Managerial Decision Making* (Wiley, 1990).

Beaver, W., *Financial Reporting: An Accounting Revolution* (Prentice Hall, 1989).

Becker, S., and D. Green Jr., "Budgeting and Employee Behavior," *Journal of Business* (October, 1962).

Bell, D., H. Raiffa, and A. Tversky, *Decision Making* (Cambridge University Press, 1988).

Bokenkotter, T., *A Concise History of the Catholic Church* (Image Books, 1979).

Buchanan, J., *Cost and Choice: An Inquiry in Economic Theory* (Markham, 1969).

Chambers, R., *Applied Production Analysis* (Cambridge University Press, 1988).

Christensen, J., "The Determination of Performance Standards and Participation," *Journal of Accounting Research* (Autumn, 1982).

Clark, J., *Studies in the Economics of Overhead Costs* (University of Chicago Press, 1923).

Coase. R., "The Nature of Costs," in *Studies in Cost Analysis*, D. Solomons, ed. (Irwin, 1968).

Cooper, R., and R. Kaplan, *The Design of Cost Management Systems* (Prentice Hall, 1991).

Cramton, P., R. Gibbons, and P. Klemperer, "Dissolving a Partnership Efficiently," *Econometrica* (May, 1987).

Dawes, R., *Rational Choice in an Uncertain World* (Harcourt Brace Jovanovich, 1988).

Demski, J., "An Accounting System Structured on a Linear Programming Model," *Accounting Review* (October, 1967).

Demski, J., *Information Analysis* (Addison-Wesley, 1980).

Demski, J., "Cost Allocation Games," in *Joint Cost Allocations*, S. Moriarity, ed. (University of Oklahoma Center for Economic and Management Research, 1981)

Demski, J., and G. Feltham, *Cost Determination: A Conceptual Approach* (Iowa State University Press, 1976).

Demski, J., and G. Feltham, "Economic Incentives in Budgetary Control Systems," *Accounting Review* (April, 1978).

Demski, J., and D. Sappington, "Delegated Expertise," *Journal of Accounting Research* (Spring, 1987).

Demski, J., and D. Sappington, "Hierarchical Structure and Responsibility Accounting," *Journal of Accounting Research* (Spring, 1989).

Demski, J., and D. Sappington, "Resolving Double Moral Hazard Problems with Buyout Agreements," *Rand Journal of Economics* (Summer, 1991).

Demski, J., D. Sappington, and P. Spiller, "Managing Supplier Switching," *Rand Journal of Economics* (Spring, 1987).

Dixit, A., and B. Nalebuff, *Thinking Strategically* (Norton & Company, 1991).

Dye, R., "Communication and Post-Decision Information," *Journal of Accounting Research* (Autumn, 1983).

Dye, R., "Intrafirm Resource Allocation and Discretionary Actions," in *Economic Analysis of Information and Contracts*, G. Feltham, A. Amershi, and W. Ziemba, eds. (Kluwer, 1988).

Eccles, R., *The Transfer Pricing Problem: A Theory for Practice* (Lexington Books, 1985).

Fama, G., and M. Jensen, "Separation of Ownership and Control," *Journal of Law and Economics* (June, 1983).

Fellingham, J., and M. Wolfson, "Taxes and Risk Sharing," *Accounting Review* (January, 1985).

Fremgren, J., "The Direct Costing Controversy--An Identification of Issues," *Accounting Review* (January, 1964).

Gjesdal, F., "Accounting for Stewardship," *Journal of Accounting Research* (Spring, 1981).

Gordon, M., "The Payoff Period and the Rate of Profit," *Journal of Business* (October, 1955).

Gordon, M., "The Use of Administered Price Systems to Control Large Organizations," in *Management Controls: New Directions in Basic Research*, C. Bonini, R. Jaedicke, and H Wagner, eds. (McGraw-Hill, 1964).

Green, D., Jr., "A Moral to the Direct Costing Controversy?" *Journal of Business* (July, 1960).

Grossman, S., and O. Hart, "An Analysis of the Principal-Agent Problem," *Econometrica* (January, 1983).

Groves, T., and M. Loeb, "Incentives in a Divisionalized Firm," *Management Science* (March, 1979).

Haley, C., and L. Schall, *The Theory of Financial Decisions* (McGraw-Hill, 1979).

Hanushek, E., and J. Jackson, *Statistical Methods for Social Scientists* (Academic Press, 1977).

Harris, M., C. Kriebel, and A. Raviv, "Asymmetric Information, Incentives and Intrafirm Resource Allocation," *Management Science* (June, 1982).

Harris, M., and A. Raviv, "Some Results on Incentive Contracts with Applications to Education and Employment, Health Insurance, and Law Enforcement," *American Economic Review* (March, 1978).

Hart, O., "An Economist's Perspective on the Theory of the Firm," *Columbia Law Review* (November, 1989).

Hart, O., and B. Holmstrom, "The Theory of Contracts," in *Advances in Economic Theory, Fifth World Congress*, T. Bewley, ed. (Cambridge University Press, 1987).

Hermalin, B., and M. Katz, "Moral Hazard and Verifiability: The Effects of Renegotiation in Agency," *Econometrica* (November, 1991).

Hermanson, R., J. Strawser, and R. Strawser, *Auditing Theory and Practice* (Irwin, 1989).

Hirshleifer, J., "On the Economics of Transfer Pricing," *Journal of Business* (July, 1956).

Hofstede, G., *The Game of Budget Control* (Van Nostrand Reinhold, 1967).

Holmstrom, B., "Moral Hazard and Observability," *Bell Journal of Economics* (Spring, 1979).

Holmstrom, B., "Moral Hazard in Teams, "*Bell Journal of Economics* (Autumn, 1982).

Holmstrom, B., and P. Milgrom, "Aggregation and Linearity in the Provision of Intertemporal Incentives," *Econometrica* (March, 1987).

Holmstrom, B., and P. Milgrom, "Regulating Trade Among Agents," *Journal of Institutional and Theoretical Economics* (March, 1990).

Holmstrom, B., and P. Milgrom, "Multitask Principal-Agent Analyses: Incentive Contracts, Asset Ownership, and Job Design," *Journal of Law, Economics, & Organization* (Special Issue, 1991).

Holmstrom, B., and J. Ricart I Costa, "Managerial Incentives and Capital Management," *Quarterly Journal of Economics* (November, 1986)

Holmstrom, B., and J. Tirole, "The Theory of the Firm," in *Handbook of Industrial Organization*, R. Schmalensee and R. Willig, eds. (Elsevier, 1989).

Holmstrom, B., and J. Tirole, "Transfer Pricing and Organizational Form," *Journal of Law, Economics, & Organization* (Fall, 1991).

Hopwood, A., "An Empirical Study of the Role of Accounting Data in Performance Evaluation," *Journal of Accounting Research Supplement* (1972).

Horwitz, I., "Misuse of Accounting Rates of Return: Comment," *American Economic Review* (June, 1984).

Howard, R., "Proximal Decision Analysis," *Management Science* (May, 1971).

Ijiri, Y., *Theory of Accounting Measurement* (American Accounting Association, 1975).

Johnson, H., and R. Kaplan, *Relevance Lost: The Rise and Fall of Management Accounting* (Harvard Business School Press, 1987).

Kanodia, C., R. Bushman, and J. Dickhaut, "Escalation Errors and the Sunk Cost Effect: An Explanation Based on Reputation and Information Asymmetries," *Journal of Accounting Research* (Spring, 1989).

Kaplan, R., "Variable and Self-Service Costs in Reciprocal Allocation Models," *Accounting Review* (October, 1973).

Kaplan, R., and A. Atkinson, *Advanced Management Accounting* (Prentice Hall, 1989).

Kennan, J., and R. Wilson, "Bargaining with Private Information," *Journal of Economic Literature* (March, 1993).

Krantz, D., R. Luce, P. Suppes, and A. Tversky, *Foundations of Measurement* (Academic Press, 1971).

Kreps, D., *Notes on the Theory of Choice* (Westview Press, 1988).

Kreps, D., *A Course in Microeconomic Theory* (Princeton University Press, 1990).

Lewis, T., and D. Sappington, "Inflexible Rules in Incentive Problems," *American Economic Review* (March, 1989).

Libby, R., *Accounting and Human Information Processing: Theory and Applications* (Prentice Hall, 1981).

Luce, D., and H. Raiffa, *Games and Decisions* (Wiley, 1957).

Ma., C., J. Moore, and S. Turnbull, "Stopping Agents from Cheating," *Journal of Economic Theory* (December, 1988).

Machina, M., "Choice Under Uncertainty: Problems Solved and Unsolved," *Journal of Economic Perspectives* (Summer, 1987).

Marschak, J., and R. Radner, *Economic Theory of Teams* (Yale University Press, 1972).

Merchant, K., *Rewarding Results: Motivating Profit Center Managers* (Harvard Business School Press, 1989).

Meyer, M., P. Milgrom, and J. Roberts, "Organizational Prospects, Influence Costs, and Ownership Changes," *Journal of Economics & Management Strategy* (Spring, 1992).

Milgrom, P., "Auctions and Bidding: A Primer," *Journal of Economic Perspectives* (Summer, 1989).

Milgrom, P., and J. Roberts, "Informational Asymmetries, Strategic Behavior, and Industrial Organization," *American Economic Review* (May, 1987).

Milgrom, P., and J. Roberts, *Economics, Organization & Management* (Prentice Hall, 1992).

Miller, B., and G. Buckman, "Cost Allocation and Opportunity Costs," *Management Science* (May, 1987).

Miller, R., Jr., *Beyond ANOVA, Basics of Applied Statistics* (Wiley, 1986).

Myerson, R., "Incentive Compatibility and the Bargaining Problem," *Econometrica* (January, 1979).

Myerson, R., *Game Theory: Analysis of Conflict* (Harvard University Press, 1991).

Nash, J., "The Bargaining Problem," *Econometrica* (January, 1950).

Nisbett, R., and L. Ross, *Human Inference: Strategies and Shortcomings of Social Judgment* (Prentice Hall, 1990).

Osborne, M., and A. Rubinstein, *Bargaining and Markets* (Academic Press, 1990).

Oster, S., *Modern Competitive Analysis* (Oxford University Press, 1990).

Parker, R., *Struggle for Survival: The History of the Second World War* (Oxford University Press, 1990).

Parker, R., G. Harcourt, and G. Whittington, *Readings in the Concept and Measurement of Income* (Philip Allan, 1986).

Paton, W., *Accounting Theory* (1922; reissued in 1962 by Accounting Studies Press).

Perrow, C., *Complex Organizations: A Critical Essay* (Random House, 1986).

Porter, R., "A Review Essay on Handbook of Industrial Organization," *Journal of Economic Literature* (June, 1991).

Rajan, M., "Cost Allocation in Multiagent Settings," *Accounting Review* (July, 1992).

Reiter, S., "Surrogates for Uncertain Decision Problems: Minimal Information for Decision Making," *Econometrica* (1957).

Ronen, J., and G. McKinney, III, "Transfer Pricing for Divisional Autonomy," *Journal of Accounting Research* (Spring, 1970).

Samuelson, W., and M. Bazerman, "Negotiating Under the Winner's Curse," in *Research in Experimental Economics, Vol. 3*, V. Smith, ed. (JAI Press, 1985).

Sappington, D., "Incentives in Principal-Agent Relationships," *Journal of Economic Perspectives* (Spring, 1991).

Sappington, D., and J. Stiglitz, "Privatization, Information and Incentives," *Journal of Policy Analysis and Management* (Summer, 1987).

Scholes, M., and M. Wolfson, *Taxes and Business Strategy: A Planning Approach* (Prentice Hall, 1992).

Shavell, S., "Risk Sharing and Incentives in the Principal and Agent Relationship," *Bell Journal of Economics* (Spring, 1979).

Shillinglaw, G., "The Concept of Attributable Cost," *Journal of Accounting Research* (Spring, 1963).

Solomons, D., *Divisional Performance: Measurement and Control* (Financial Executives Research Foundation, 1965; also published by Irwin in 1968).

Solomons, D., "The Historical Development of Costing," in *Studies in Cost Analysis*, D. Solomons, ed. (Irwin, 1968).

Sorter, G., and C. Horngren, "Asset Recognition and Economic Attributes--A Relevant Costing Approach," *Accounting Review* (July, 1962).

Spulbur, D., *Regulation and Markets* (MIT Press, 1989).

Stigler, G., *The Theory of Price* (Macmillan, 1987).

Stiglitz, J., "Risk Sharing and Incentives in Sharecropping," *Review of Economic Studies* (April, 1974).

Stole, L., "The Economics of Liquidated Damage Clauses in Contractual Environments with Private Information," *Journal of Law, Economics, & Organization* (October, 1992).

Suh, Y., "Collusion and Noncontrollable Cost Allocation," *Journal of Accounting Research Supplement* (1987).

Sunder, S., "Simpson's Reversal Paradox and Cost Allocation," *Journal of Accounting Research* (Spring, 1983).

Sutton, J., *Sunk Costs and Market Structure: Price Competition, Advertising, and the Evolution of Concentration* (MIT Press, 1991)

Swieringa, R., and R. Moncur, *Some Effects of Participative Budgeting on Managerial Behavior* (National Association of Accountants, 1975).

Swieringa, R., and J. Waterhouse, "Organizational Views of Transfer Pricing," *Accounting, Organizations and Society* (1982).

Tirole, J., "Hierarchies and Bureaucracies: On the Role of Collusion in Organizations," *Journal of Law, Economics, & Organization* (Fall, 1986).

Tirole, J., *The Theory of Industrial Organization* (MIT Press, 1988).

Vancil, R., *Decentralization: Managerial Ambiguity by Design* (Dow Jones-Irwin, 1979).

Vatter, W., *The Fund Theory of Accounting and Its Implications for Financial Reports* (University of Chicago Press, 1947).

Verrecchia, R., "An Analysis of Two Cost Allocation Cases," *Accounting Review* (July, 1982).

Weil, R., "Allocating Joint Costs," *The American Economic Review* (December, 1968).

Whittington, G., *The Elements of Accounting: An Introduction* (Cambridge University Press, 1992).

Williamson, O., *The Economic Institutions of Capitalism.* (Free Press, 1985).

Wolfson, M., "Tax, Incentive, and Risk-Sharing Issues in the Allocation of Property Rights: The Generalized Lease-or-Buy Problem," *Journal of Business* (April, 1985).

Yelle, L., "The Learning Curve: Historical Review and Comprehensive Survey," *Decision Sciences* (April, 1979).

Zimmerman, J., "The Costs and Benefits of Cost Allocation," *Accounting Review* (July, 1979).

Author Index

Subject Index